250 Best-Paying Jobs

Part of JIST's Best Jobs® Series

Second Edition

Michael Farr and Laurence Shatkin, Ph.D.

Also in JIST's *Best Jobs* Series

- *Best Jobs for the 21st Century*
- *50 Best Jobs for Your Personality*
- *200 Best Jobs for College Graduates*
- *300 Best Jobs Without a Four-Year Degree*
- *200 Best Jobs Through Apprenticeships*
- *40 Best Fields for Your Career*
- *225 Best Jobs for Baby Boomers*
- *150 Best Jobs for Your Skills*
- *150 Best Jobs Through Military Training*

- *175 Best Jobs Not Behind a Desk*
- *150 Best Jobs for a Better World*
- *50 Best College Majors for a Secure Future*
- *10 Best College Majors for Your Personality*
- *200 Best Jobs for Introverts*
- *150 Best Low-Stress Jobs*
- *200 Best Jobs for Renewing America*
- *150 Best Recession-Proof Jobs*

JIST *Works*
America's Career Publisher®

250 Best-Paying Jobs, Second Edition

© 2010 by JIST Publishing

Published by JIST Works, an imprint of JIST Publishing
7321 Shadeland Station, Suite 200
Indianapolis, IN 46256-3923

Phone: 800-648-JIST   Fax: 877-454-7839
E-mail: info@jist.com   Web site: www.jist.com

Some Other Books by the Authors

Michael Farr

The Quick Resume & Cover Letter Book

Getting the Job You Really Want

The Very Quick Job Search

Overnight Career Choice

Laurence Shatkin

Great Jobs in the President's Stimulus Plan

Quick Guide to College Majors and Careers

90-Minute College Major Matcher

Your $100,000 Career Plan

New Guide for Occupational Exploration

150 Best Recession-Proof Jobs

Quantity discounts are available for JIST products. Please call 800-648-JIST or visit www.jist.com for a free catalog and more information.

Visit www.jist.com for information on JIST, free job search information, tables of contents and sample pages, and ordering information on our many products.

Acquisitions Editor: Susan Pines   Interior Layout: Aleata Halbig
Development Editor: Stephanie Koutek   Proofreader: Jeanne Clark
Cover and Interior Designer: Aleata Halbig   Indexer: Jeanne Clark
Cover Illustration: Comstock, Fotosearch Stock Photography

Printed in the United States of America

15 14 13 12 11 10   9 8 7 6 5 4 3 2

  Library of Congress Cataloging-in-Publication Data
Farr, J. Michael
    250 best-paying jobs / Michael Farr and Laurence Shatkin. -- 2nd ed.
        p. cm. -- (JIST's best jobs series)
    Includes index.
    ISBN 978-1-59357-770-4 (alk. paper)
    1. Vocational guidance--United States. 2. Occupations--United States.
I. Shatkin, Laurence. II. Title. III. Title: Two hundred fifty
best-paying jobs.
  HF5382.5.U5F366 2010
  331.7020973--dc22

                        2009049819

We have been careful to provide accurate information throughout this book, but it is possible that errors and omissions have been introduced. Please consider this in making any career plans or other important decisions. Trust your own judgment above all else and in all things.

ISBN 978-1-59357-770-4

This Is a Big Book, But It Is Very Easy to Use

This book is designed for people who place a lot of emphasis on high income when they make a career decision.

It helps you explore high-paying career options in a variety of interesting ways. The nice thing about this book is that you don't have to read it all. Instead, we designed it to allow you to browse and find information that most interests you.

The table of contents will give you a good idea of what's inside and how to use the book, so we suggest you start there. The first part is made up of interesting lists that will help you explore 250 high-paying jobs based on earnings, career cluster, education or training level, personality type, and many other criteria. The second part provides descriptions for the jobs that met our criterion for this book (average earnings more than $48,000). Just find a job that interests you in one of the lists in Part I and look up its description in Part II. Simple.

Some Things You Can Do with This Book

❋ Identify better-paying jobs that don't require you to get additional training or education.

❋ Develop long-term career plans that may require additional training, education, or experience.

❋ Explore and select a training or educational program that relates to a high-paying career objective.

❋ Find reliable earnings information to negotiate pay.

❋ Prepare for interviews.

These are a few of the many ways you can use this book. We hope you find it as interesting to browse as we did to put together. We have tried to make it easy to use and as interesting as occupational information can be.

When you are done with this book, pass it along or tell someone else about it. We wish you well in your career and in your life.

Credits and Acknowledgments: While the authors created this book, it is based on the work of many others. The occupational information is based on data obtained from the U.S. Department of Labor and the U.S. Census Bureau. These sources provide the most authoritative occupational information available. The job titles and their related descriptions are from the O*NET database, which was developed by researchers and developers under the direction of the U.S. Department of Labor. They, in turn, were assisted by thousands of employers who provided details on the nature of work in the many thousands of job samplings used in the database's development. We used the most recent version of the O*NET database, release 14. We appreciate and thank the staff of the U.S. Department of Labor for their efforts and expertise in providing such a rich source of data.

Table of Contents

Summary of Major Sections

Introduction. A short overview to help you better understand and use the book. *Starts on page 1.*

Part I. The Best Jobs Lists. Very useful for exploring career options! Lists are arranged into easy-to-use groups. The first group of lists presents the 250 best-paying jobs, ranking them first by earnings and then showing the 100 fastest-growing jobs and the 100 with the largest projected number of job openings. More-specialized lists follow, presenting the best jobs by age, gender, level of education or training, personality type, and career cluster. The column starting at right presents all the list titles. *Starts on page 19.*

Part II. Descriptions of the Best-Paying Jobs. Provides complete descriptions of the jobs that met our criteria for high pay. Each description contains information on earnings, projected growth, job duties, skills, related job titles, education and training required, related knowledge and courses, and many other details. *Starts on page 128.*

Appendix A. Definitions of Skills and Knowledge/Courses Referenced in This Book. Defines all the skills and knowledge/courses listed in the descriptions in Part II. *Starts on page 490.*

Appendix B. The Skill-Income Connection. Identifies the skills most closely associated with high earnings and lists the jobs in Part II that demand a high level of each of these skills. *Starts on page 495.*

Detailed Table of Contents

Introduction

We kept this introduction short to encourage you to actually read it. For this reason, we don't provide many details on the technical issues involved in creating the job lists or descriptions. Instead, we give you short explanations to help you understand and use the information the book provides for career exploration or planning. We think this brief and user-oriented approach makes sense for most people who will use this book.

Who This Book Is For and What It Covers

We created this book to help students and adults learn about high-paying careers and the educational and training pathways that lead to them. Employers, educators, program planners, career counselors, and others will also find this book to be of value.

If you are a young career planner and high income is important to you, this book can be especially useful. Are you impatient with the idea of starting at the bottom and working your way up the corporate ladder toward a better-paying job? The research of labor economists shows that you are right to set your sights high for your first job. Economists compared the earnings of people who started out in lower- and higher-paying jobs and found that those who began at a lower level generally had not caught up to the others even 10 or 20 years later. So you are wise to use this book to identify a high-paying job as your initial career goal.

People who are considering a career change later in life will also find this book useful. Do you feel stuck in a low-paying job? This book can point you toward high-paying jobs that are a good fit with your interests and, perhaps best of all, do not require a great amount of additional education or training. You will be particularly interested in the lists of high-paying jobs organized by level of required education or training.

To create this book, we started with approximately 850 major jobs at all levels of training and education. From these, we selected those with earnings of at least $48,000 per year. That figure represents an income level higher than what approximately three-quarters of Americans earn as wages. Part I contains lists that rank these high-paying jobs according to many criteria, including earnings, growth, openings, education level, and interest area. Part II contains job descriptions for all of the jobs.

We think you will find many of the job lists in Part I interesting and useful for identifying high-paying career options to consider. The job descriptions are also packed with useful information.

Cautions About Choosing a Career Based on the Earnings

One of the most important reasons people work is to earn money, and many people aspire toward the best-paying job they can obtain. On the other hand, it is often said that money cannot buy happiness. This book is not the appropriate place for a philosophical discussion of the comparative merits of wealth versus poverty, but some cautionary statements are warranted nevertheless if you are basing your career choice largely on the criterion of earnings.

Working at a job means a lot more than just collecting the pay. It means putting in the required hours, doing the required tasks, being exposed to a particular work setting and to certain co-workers, and experiencing all the many other aspects of work. Therefore, when you choose a career goal, you need to consider *all* its potential rewards, as well as its possible drawbacks. Will you find the work interesting? Is the work setting an environment where you will feel comfortable? Will you work with people who don't get on your nerves? Does the work impose stress, travel, long hours, or physical demands that you would not be able to tolerate? This book can help answer some of these questions. For example, one set of lists in Part I breaks down the high-paying jobs by career clusters and another set breaks them down by personality types so you can identify jobs that are more likely to suit you. The job descriptions in Part II can also help you get some insights into the work, such as the typical tasks. Finally, Appendix B shows which skills are most closely associated with high-paying jobs. Nevertheless, any job choice you make using this book should be tentative, and before you make a commitment you should investigate the work in greater depth, ideally from seeing and talking to people on the job and maybe even taking on a related work role temporarily.

To qualify for entry to a high-paying job, you'll probably need to get some additional education or training. If you turn to the lists in Part I that group jobs by the amount of required education or training, you'll see that most of the high-paying jobs require a commitment of several years of preparation. You can learn the name of the specific educational or training program that you'll need to complete by looking at the job description in Part II. But the name of the program by itself does not tell you all you need to know about it. Can you meet the program's demands for time, money, and motivation, which may be considerable? Is it offered in a location near you or where you are willing to relocate? What sorts of academic skills does it require? Do you feel comfortable in the setting where the learning will take place (such as a library, classroom, lab, or clinic)? To answer these questions, you need to look at brochures and catalogs from providers of education and training and speak to people who are currently in the program, as well as people who have completed it and are now in the workforce.

After you talk to people in the career or preparatory program, you might start to question the assumption that more income is always better. You might find that earning a very high income will reduce some other satisfactions. For example, qualifying for a high-paying career might require you to complete years of study or an arduous training program. It might mean working under the stress of making decisions with high financial risks or with life-or-death consequences. And it might demand long work hours and travel that interfere with family life and leisure-time activities.

To gain more insights into the nature of high-paying jobs, we investigated whether certain aspects of *work context* are more closely associated with high income than others. Using data from the U.S. Department of Labor and a statistical procedure called correlation (which shows how well one variable can predict another), we found that various aspects of work context are better than others for predicting high income. Here are the factors that are most closely associated with high income:

Exposure to Radiation

Exposure to Disease or Infections

Impact of Decisions on Co-workers or Company Results

Freedom to Make Decisions

Letters and Memos

Structured versus Unstructured Work

Coordinating or Leading Others

Responsibility for Outcomes and Results

Frequency of Decision Making

Consequence of Error

Face-to-Face Discussions

Importance of Being Exact or Accurate

Telephone

Indoors, Environmentally Controlled

Electronic Mail

Working with Work Group or Team

Working Close to Others

Level of Competition

Contact with Others

Dealing with External Customers

Frequency of Conflict Situations

Spending Time Sitting

Public Speaking

Some of these factors may sound pretty good to you—for example, "Freedom to Make Decisions." But consider the responsibilities that accompany this freedom: "Impact of Decisions on Co-workers or Company Results," "Responsibility for Outcomes and Results," "Consequence of Error," and "Importance of Being Exact or Accurate."

Are some of the factors listed here unappealing or even distasteful to you? Be aware that not every high-paying job has all of these characteristics. For example, people who find indoor work confining may find satisfaction as Foresters or Insurance Appraisers, Auto Damage. People with an aversion to public speaking may work as Credit Analysts, Electrical and Electronic Engineering Technicians, or Dental Hygienists. But the highest-paying jobs are likely to have the largest number of these characteristics, so you need to decide how you feel about each of these factors (among others) and determine how much they characterize the kind of work you are considering. If a job on a list in Part I appeals to you because of its income, read its description in Part II thoroughly and don't stop there—explore it in depth using some of the resources listed at the end of this introduction under the heading "Sources of Additional Information."

Note that "Level of Competition" is one of the factors listed above. A lot of other people may be pursuing the same high-paying career goal that appeals to you, so you need to get a realistic sense of your chances of entering and succeeding in the job. One clue may be found in this book's information about how fast the job is growing and how many job openings are expected, figures you can find both in the lists in Part I and in the job descriptions in Part II. But this tells you only the demand for the occupation, not the supply of job seekers, so you need to do more research to find out the amount of competition you may expect. The *Occupational Outlook Handbook* is a good place to start, and people who do the hiring or have recently been employed can also supply useful insights. If you talk to someone who works for an educational or training institution, especially a for-profit venture, remember that what they tell you may be partly a sales pitch, and be sure to ask about their recent job-placement track record. Get a variety of opinions to balance out possible biases.

Finally, you might want to consider how secure your high-paying career goal is. If you lose your job, you also lose the paycheck. The recent recession has shown that job loss can strike even the most highly educated and experienced workers. So, when you read a job description in Part II, you might want to look at how the job is rated for Job Security.

After reading all these cautions and learning more about the highest-paying jobs, you might decide to lower your salary expectations and aim for a job that falls somewhere in the middle or lower range of the high-paying jobs in this book. This does not mean choosing a life of poverty! Remember that every job in this book pays, on average, better than what approximately three-quarters of Americans earn from their work. Furthermore, the jobs in this book are ranked by their *average* earnings. Why not aspire to be an above-average earner in your occupation? One of the lists in Part I identifies 26 jobs with a few "star" earners, but every occupation has at least a few workers whose pay greatly exceeds the average. Here are some factors that can increase your chances of becoming one of those high-end earners:

- ❋ You have outstanding natural abilities.
- ❋ You become highly skilled.
- ❋ You move into a specialization, geographic location, or industry where demand is high but you have little competition.
- ❋ You have a flair for self-promotion.
- ❋ You take on managerial duties.
- ❋ You work out a business arrangement to direct your work output to a very large market.

For example, you won't find Chefs and Head Cooks included in this book because the average earnings are $38,770. But those employed by the government earn an average of $54,990, and some pastry chefs working at casino hotels earn six figures. Chefs who author best-selling cookbooks and who get television shows earn even more. So it is possible to be a high earner even in an occupation that, on average, does not offer outstanding pay. But to achieve that exceptional income, you will have to beat the odds. You might have to expend exceptional effort, such as working long hours, to establish yourself in the occupation, perfect your skills, and demonstrate your abilities. Reaching peak earning power in your occupation also can take many years and put strains on your home life.

So, as you explore the jobs in this book, keep in mind that every career choice involves trade-offs; you will have to give up some things to get other things. But if you follow up on the research that you are beginning by using this book, you can identify the job that will require you to give up the least in order to get a comfortable income and other satisfactions.

Where the Information Comes From

The information we used in creating this book comes from three major government sources:

- ❋ **The U.S. Department of Labor:** We used a variety of data sources to construct the information we used in this book. We started with the jobs included in the U.S. Department of Labor's O*NET database. The O*NET includes information on more than 1,100 occupations and is now the primary source of detailed information on occupations. The Labor Department updates the O*NET on a regular basis, and we used the most recent version available, release 14.
- ❋ **The U.S. Census Bureau:** Because we wanted to include earnings, growth, number of openings, and other data not included in the O*NET, we used information on earnings from the U.S. Department of Labor's Bureau of Labor Statistics (BLS). Some of this data

came from the Current Population Survey (CPS) or the American Community Survey (ACS), conducted by the U.S. Census Bureau, and other data came from the BLS's own Occupational Employment Statistics (OES) survey. The information on earnings is the most reliable information we could obtain. The OES, CPS, and ACS use a slightly different system of job titles than the O*NET does, but we were able to link the OES, CPS, and ACS data to the O*NET job titles we used to develop this book. The ACS also provided information about the proportion of workers in each job who are self-employed, work part time, or are in various age brackets, plus the relative earnings of men and women.

❋ **The U.S. Department of Education:** We used the Classification of Instructional Programs, a system developed by the U.S. Department of Education, to cross-reference the education or training programs related to each job.

Of course, information in a database format can be boring and even confusing, so we did many things to help make the data useful and present it to you in a form that is easy to understand.

Data Complexities

For those of you who like details, we present some of the complexities inherent in our sources of information and what we did to make sense of them here. You don't need to know this to use the book, so jump to the next section of the introduction if you are bored with details.

Earnings, Growth, and Number of Openings

We include information on earnings, projected growth, and number of job openings for each job throughout this book. We think this information is important to most people, but getting it for each job is not a simple task.

Earnings

Because so much of the emphasis of this book is on earnings, we want you to understand exactly what our earnings statements represent and where the information comes from.

The employment security agency of each state gathers information on earnings for various jobs and forwards it to the U.S. Bureau of Labor Statistics. This information is organized in standardized ways by a BLS program called Occupational Employment Statistics, or OES. To keep the earnings for the various jobs and regions comparable, the OES screens out certain types of earnings and includes others, so the OES earnings we use in this book represent straight-time gross pay, exclusive of premium pay. More specifically, the OES earnings include the job's base rate; cost-of-living allowances; guaranteed pay; hazardous-duty pay; incentive pay, including commissions and production bonuses; on-call pay; and tips, but they do not include back pay, jury duty pay, overtime pay, severance pay, shift differentials, nonproduction bonuses, tuition reimbursements, or stock options. Also, self-employed workers are not included in the earnings estimates, and they can be a significant segment in certain occupations. The most recent earnings figures available apply to May 2008, so if the mild rate of wage inflation continues until you read this book, you can expect current earnings to have risen only slightly above the figures reported here.

The OES earnings data is reported under a system of job titles called the Standard Occupational Classification system, or SOC. These jobs can be cross-referenced to the O*NET job titles we use in this book, so we can attach earnings information to the job titles and descriptions. But several SOC titles cross-reference to more than one O*NET job title. For example, the O*NET has separate information for Accountants and for Auditors, but the OES reports earnings for a single SOC occupation called Accountants and Auditors. Therefore you may notice that the salary we report for Accountants ($59,430) is identical to the salary we report for Auditors. In reality there probably is a difference, but this is the best information that is available.

OES does not collect data on the comparative earnings of men and women, but we wanted to create a list of the best-paying jobs in which women's earnings are not greatly lower than men's. For this information we relied on data from the American Community Survey of 2005–2007, a poll conducted by the Census Bureau. This survey provided the most recent data available, but for 69 of the 250 jobs included in this book, the female workforce was so small that this survey was unable to provide reliable estimates of the ratio between female and male earnings.

For each job in Part II, we report three facts related to earnings among the bulleted items at the top of the job description:

⊛ The Annual Earnings figure shows the median earnings (half earn more, half earn less).

⊛ The Beginning Wage figure shows the 10th percentile earnings (the figure that exceeds the earnings of the lowest 10 percent of the workers). This is a rough approximation of what a beginning worker may be offered.

⊛ The Earnings Growth Potential statement represents the gap between the 10th percentile and the median. This information answers the question, "If I started at the beginning wage and then got a raise that took me up to the median, how much of a pay boost (in percentage terms) would that be?" If this would be a big boost, the job has great potential for increasing your earnings as you gain experience and skills. If the boost would be small, you probably will need to move on to another occupation to improve your earnings substantially. Because a percentage figure, by itself, might be hard to interpret, we put the figure in parentheses and precede it with an easy-to-understand verbal tag that expresses the Earnings Growth Potential: "very low" when the percentage is less than 25 percent, "low" for 25–35 percent, "medium" for 35–40 percent, "high" for 40–50 percent, and "very high" for any figure higher than 50 percent. For the 19 highest-paying jobs, those for which BLS reports the median earnings as "more than $166,400," we are unable to calculate a figure for Earnings Growth Potential. About 15 percent of the jobs in this book have very high earnings growth potential, about 40 percent have high potential, about 30 percent have medium potential, and about 10 percent have low potential.

Following the bulleted facts at the top of each job description, we present two tables that are also based on OES earnings data:

* Industries in Which Income Is Highest is based on figures for the median earnings in industries. We chose a level of industrial classification that we thought would be most useful for career exploration. For example, you'll find the category "Computer and Electronic Product Manufacturing" listed, rather than the very broad category "Manufacturing" or the very narrow category "Computer Storage Device Manufacturing." The table includes the five highest-paying industries, ordered by their median income for the occupation; where income figures are tied, industries are ordered by the size of their workforce. The table is limited to industries where 1,000 or more workers in the occupation are employed, unless total U.S. employment in the occupation is less than 10,000.

* Metropolitan Areas Where Income Is Highest is based on figures for median earnings in the standard metropolitan statistical areas defined by the Census Bureau. This table includes the five highest-paying metro areas, ordered by their median income for the occupation; where income figures are tied, metros are ordered by the size of their workforce. The table is limited to metropolitan areas where 50 or more workers in the occupation are employed, unless total U.S. employment in the occupation is less than 10,000.

Projected Growth and Number of Job Openings

This information comes from the Office of Occupational Statistics and Employment Projections, a program within the Bureau of Labor Statistics that develops information about projected trends in the nation's labor market for the next 10 years. The most recent projections available cover the years 2006 to 2016. The projections are based on information about people moving into and out of occupations. The BLS uses data from various sources in projecting the growth and number of openings for each job title; some data comes from the Census Bureau's Current Population Survey and some comes from an OES survey. In making the projections, the BLS economists assume that there will be no major war, depression, or other economic upheaval. They do assume that recessions may occur, in keeping with the business cycles we have experienced for several decades, but because the projections cover 10 years, they are intended to provide an average of both the good times and the bad times.

Like the earnings figures, the figures on projected growth and job openings are reported according to the SOC classification, so again you will find that some of the SOC jobs that we use in Part I are linked to more than one O*NET job in Part II. To continue the example we used earlier, the BLS reports growth (17.7 percent) and openings (134,463) for one SOC occupation called Accountants and Auditors, but in Part II of this book we report these figures separately for the O*NET occupation Accountants and for the O*NET occupation Auditors. In Part II, when you see that both of these occupations have the same 17.7 percent projected growth and the same 134,463 projected job openings, you should realize that the 17.7 percent rate of projected growth represents the *average* of these two occupations—one may actually experience higher growth than the other—and that these two occupations will *share* the 134,463 projected openings.

While salary figures are fairly straightforward, you might not know what to make of job-growth figures. For example, is a projected growth of 15 percent good or bad? Keep in mind that the average (mean) growth projected for all occupations by the Bureau of Labor Statistics is 10.4 percent. One-quarter of the SOC occupations have a growth projection of 3.2 percent or lower. Growth of 11.6 percent is the median, meaning that half of the occupations have more, half less. Only one-quarter of the occupations have growth projected at more than 17.4 percent.

Because the jobs in this book were selected as "best" partly on the basis of job growth, their mean growth is 13.2 percent, which compares favorably to the mean for all jobs. Among these 250 jobs, the job ranked 63rd by projected growth has a figure of 22.5 percent, the job ranked 125th (the median) has a projected growth of 11.8 percent, and the job ranked 188th has a projected growth of 7.3 percent.

The average number of annual job openings for the 250 best-paying jobs is considerably lower than the average for all occupations. The BLS projects an average of about 35,000 job openings per year for the 750 occupations that it studies, but for the 250 occupations included in this book, the average is about 14,300 openings. The job ranked 63rd for job openings has a figure of about 14,000 annual openings, the job ranked 125th (the median) has about 5,000 openings projected, and the job ranked 188th has about 1,600 openings projected.

However, keep in mind that figures for job openings depend on how the BLS defines an occupation. Consider the occupation Clinical, Counseling, and School Psychologists, which employs a workforce of more than 150,000 people and is expected to provide more than 8,000 job openings each year. The BLS regards this as one (SOC) occupation when it reports figures for earnings and job projections, but O*NET divides it into three separate occupations: School Psychologists, Clinical Psychologists, and Counseling Psychologists. If the BLS employment-projection tables were to list these as three separate occupations and divide the 8,000 openings among them, the average number of openings for all occupations would be smaller. So it follows that because the way the BLS defines occupations is somewhat arbitrary, any "average" figure for job openings is also somewhat arbitrary.

The Department of Labor provides a single figure (22.9 percent) for the projected growth of 38 postsecondary teaching jobs and also provides a single figure (237,478) for the projected annual job openings for these 38 jobs. Because these college-teaching jobs are related to very different interests—from engineering to art to forestry to social work—and because separate *earnings* figures are available for each of the 38 jobs, we thought you'd appreciate having these jobs appear separately in the lists in this book. If the trends of the last several years continue, none of these jobs can be expected to grow or take on workers at a much faster rate than the other 37. Therefore, in preparing the Part I lists and the Part II descriptions, we assumed that all of these college-teaching jobs share the same rate of projected job growth, 22.9 percent, and we computed a figure for their projected job openings by dividing the total (237,478) into 38 parts, each of which is proportional in size to the current workforce of the job.

We had to take a different approach with the occupations Locomotive Engineers and Locomotive Firers. Although the Department of Labor provides only a single figure (2.9 percent) for the growth of these two occupations and a single figure (3,548) for the number of expected job openings, the trends of the past 10 years show that Locomotive Engineers is growing in size, while Locomotive Firers is actually shrinking, and advances in railroad technology are likely to continue these trends. We did not try to estimate separate job-openings figures for these two occupations, but neither did we want to collapse them as we did with Physicians and Surgeons, because that would have driven the income level of our 250th job below the round figure of $48,000. Therefore, we allowed these jobs to appear as separate titles on lists in Part I and added a footnote to remind readers that they share their 3,548 job openings with each other and with another occupation (Rail Yard Engineers, Dinkey Operators, and Hostlers).

Perhaps you're wondering why we present figures on both job growth *and* number of openings. Aren't these two ways of saying the same thing? Actually, you need to know both. Consider the occupation Hydrologists, which is projected to grow at the outstanding rate of 24.3 percent. There should be lots of opportunities in such a fast-growing job, right? Not exactly. This is a tiny occupation, with only about 8,000 people currently employed, so although it is growing rapidly, it will not create many new jobs (about 900 per year). Now consider Team Assemblers. Because many low-tech manufacturing jobs are being offshored, this occupation is almost standing still, with a growth rate of 0.1 percent. Nevertheless, this is a huge occupation that employs more than one million workers, so although its growth rate is insignificant, it is expected to take on more than 264,000 new workers each year as existing workers retire, die, or move on to other jobs. That's why we base our selection of the best jobs on both of these economic indicators and why you should pay attention to both when you scan our lists of best jobs.

Job Security

The recession that began in 2008 has caused an unusual amount of job loss. (As this book goes to press, job growth has not yet recovered.) In response, many career decision makers now are particularly concerned about their job security in future recessions. It's true that some occupations are more sensitive to downturns in the economy than others, and if job security is important to you, you might want to focus on job choices that tend to be less sensitive. To help you do this, each job described in Part II has a Job Security rating on a scale that ranges from Most Secure to Least Secure.

These ratings are based on an article in the *Occupational Outlook Quarterly (OOQ)*, a BLS publication. It rates jobs on a four-point scale, from 0 to 3, for "economic sensitivity," which indicates how closely the jobs have, in the past, prospered or suffered along with the economy. For an additional check, we consulted the 2008–2009 edition of the *Occupational Outlook Handbook,* another BLS publication, focusing on the outlook statements given for the occupations. When necessary, we adjusted the sensitivity ratings for some jobs. Because many of the job titles are very diverse collections of jobs—for example, Designers, which includes those who work with flowers, interiors, graphics, and industrial products—we did not automatically assume that all the related specific titles deserve to share the same numerical rating for economic sensitivity. To determine separate ratings in these cases, we performed a statistical analysis comparing the historical ups and downs in the workforce size of occupations with the ups and downs in the national economy. For each job in these cases, we also considered the economic outlook projected between 2006 and 2016. In addition, we considered the likelihood that an occupation can be easily offshored. For a more detailed discussion of our methods, see the introduction to *150 Best Recession-Proof Jobs* (JIST).

Other Information in the Job Descriptions

We used a variety of government and other sources to compile the job descriptions we provide in Part II. Details on these various sources are mentioned later in this introduction in the section "Part II: The Job Descriptions."

How the 250 Best-Paying Jobs Were Selected

If you have read up to this point, you know that the jobs in this book were selected because they pay at least $48,000 per year. Here are a few more details about how we created the list of 250 jobs:

1. We began with the 800 specific SOC occupations for which the OES program collects earnings data. Four of these occupations were eliminated because OES does not provide estimates of annual earnings. We also collapsed 8 physician titles in the SOC because BLS does not provide separate job-outlook information for them and many of them share the same earnings figure, "more than $166,400." These are the physician titles: Anesthesiologists; Family and General Practitioners; Internists, General; Obstetricians and Gynecologists; Pediatricians, General; Physicians and Surgeons, All Other; Psychiatrists; and Surgeons. That left us with 789 jobs.

2. Next we eliminated 67 jobs for which we lacked useful information, such as work tasks. We also removed another 14 jobs that are expected to employ fewer than 500

workers per year and to shrink rather than grow in workforce size: Bridge and Lock Tenders; Camera and Photographic Equipment Repairers; Fabric Menders, Except Garment; Hoist and Winch Operators; Log Graders and Scalers; Model Makers, Wood; Patternmakers, Wood; Power Distributors and Dispatchers; Radio Mechanics; Radio Operators; Refractory Materials Repairers, Except Brickmasons; Shuttle Car Operators; Signal and Track Switch Repairers; and Watch Repairers.

3. From the remaining 708 jobs, we removed all jobs paying less than $48,000. This is a useful cutoff point; it is fairly close to the lowest figure for the highest-paid 25 percent of Americans ($51,540), and it allowed us to keep exactly 250 occupations on our list of high-paying jobs.

Why This Book Has More Than 250 Jobs

We didn't think you would mind that this book actually provides information on more than 250 jobs. The lists in Part I are based on the SOC taxonomy of job titles, but the job descriptions in Part II are based on information in the O*NET database. In many cases, one SOC job is linked to two or more O*NET jobs. In addition, in the Part I lists we combined several specialized medical jobs into one job called Physicians and Surgeons, but these jobs are described separately in Part II.

This means that although we used 250 job titles to construct the lists of high-paying jobs, we have a total of 365 job descriptions in Part II.

The Data in This Book Can Be Misleading

We use the most reliable data we can obtain for the earnings, projected growth, number of openings, and other information to create this book, but keep in mind that this information may or may not be accurate for your situation. This is because the information is true on the average. But just as there is no precisely average person, there is no such thing as a statistically average example of a particular job. We say this because data, while helpful, can also be misleading.

Take, for example, the yearly earnings information in this book. This is highly reliable data obtained from a very large U.S. working population sample by the Bureau of Labor Statistics. It tells us the median annual pay received by people in various job titles. This sounds very useful until you consider that half of all people in that occupation earn less than that amount and half earn more. (We often use "average" instead of "median" elsewhere in this book for ease of explanation.)

For example, people just entering the occupation or people with few years of work experience will often earn much less than the average. People who live in rural areas or who work for smaller employers typically earn less than those who do similar work in cities, where the cost of living is higher, for larger employers, or in high-growth industries. To help you focus on the most lucrative opportunities, for every occupation described in Part II we list the industries and metropolitan areas where income is highest. But remember that just as these instances exceed the average, other industries and geographical locations offer earnings that are considerably below the average.

So, in reviewing the information in this book, please understand the limitations of the data it presents. You need to use common sense in career decision-making as in most other things in life. Even so, we hope that you find the information helpful and interesting.

Part I: The Best Jobs Lists

There are 65 separate lists in Part I of this book—look in the table of contents for a complete list of them. The lists are not difficult to understand because they have clear titles and are organized into groupings of related lists.

Depending on your situation, some of the job lists in Part I will interest you more than others. For example, if you are young, you may be interested to learn the best-paying jobs that employ high percentages of workers age 16–24. Other lists show best-paying jobs within career clusters, by personality type, by level of education, and in other ways that you might find helpful in exploring your career options.

Whatever your situation, we suggest that you use the lists that make sense for you in beginning your exploration of best-paying career options. Following are the names of each group of lists along with short comments on each group. You will find additional information in a brief introduction provided at the beginning of each group of lists in Part I.

The Best-Paying Jobs

The first three lists in this group are the ones that most people want to see first. The first list presents all 250 job titles in order of their average earnings. The second and third lists are subsets of the first list: the 100 jobs projected to grow most rapidly and the 100 jobs with the most openings.

Best-Paying Jobs by Demographic

This group of lists presents interesting information for a variety of types of people based on data from the U.S. Census Bureau. The lists are arranged into groups for workers age 16–24, workers age 55 and older, part-time workers, self-employed workers, women, men, urban workers, and rural workers. Each group of lists includes jobs in which the concentration of the specific type of people is significantly above the average for all jobs. We created three lists for each group, basing the last two on the information in the first list:

- The jobs with the highest earnings (the number of jobs varies)
- The 25 jobs with the highest growth rates
- The 25 jobs with the largest number of openings

Best-Paying Jobs Lists Based on Levels of Education and Training

We created separate lists for each level of education and training as defined by the U.S. Department of Labor and put each of the 250 best-paying jobs into the list that indicates the education and training required for entry. Jobs within these lists are presented in order of their earnings. The lists include jobs in these groupings:

- Short-term on-the-job training
- Moderate-term on-the-job training
- Long-term on-the-job training
- Work experience in a related job
- Postsecondary vocational training
- Associate degree
- Bachelor's degree
- Work experience plus degree
- Master's degree
- Doctoral degree
- First professional degree

Best-Paying Jobs Lists Based on Career Clusters

These lists organize the 250 best-paying jobs into groups based on the career cluster scheme developed by the U.S. Department of Education's Office of Vocational and Adult Education around 1999 and used in many states. Within each list, jobs are presented in order of their earnings. Here are the 16 career clusters used in these lists: Agriculture, Food, and Natural Resources; Architecture and Construction; Arts, Audio/Video Technology, and Communications; Business, Management, and Administration; Education and Training; Finance; Government and Public Administration; Health Science; Hospitality and Tourism; Human Services; Information Technology; Law, Public Safety, Corrections, and Security; Manufacturing; Marketing, Sales, and Service; Science, Technology, Engineering, and Mathematics; and Transportation, Distribution, and Logistics.

Best-Paying Jobs Lists Based on Personality Types

These lists organize the 250 best-paying jobs into six personality types, which are described in the introduction to the lists: Realistic, Investigative, Artistic, Social, Enterprising, and Conventional. The jobs within each list are presented in order of their earnings.

Bonus Lists

Two bonus lists highlight jobs where the opportunities for earnings are particularly high: 26 jobs with a few "star" earners and 28 jobs in which even beginners are well-paid.

The next two bonus lists look at how jobs combine with industries and metropolitan areas to offer you high pay. The first list shows 35 occupations and the industries in which those workers earn median pay of $100,000 or more. The second list shows 61 occupations and the metropolitan areas where those workers earn a median of $100,000 or more.

The last bonus list identifies 73 occupations in which female workers earn at least 70 percent of what male workers earn.

Part II: The Job Descriptions

This part of the book provides a brief but information-packed description for each of the 365 best-paying jobs that appear on lists in this book. The descriptions in Part II are presented in alphabetical order. This makes it easy to look up any job you identify in a list from Part I that you want to learn more about.

We used the most current information from a variety of government sources to create the descriptions. We designed the descriptions to be easy to understand, and the sample that follows—with an explanation of each of its component parts—will help you better understand and use the descriptions.

⁜ **Job Title:** This is the job title for the job as defined by the U.S. Department of Labor and used in its O*NET database.

⁜ **Data Elements:** The information on earnings, growth, annual openings, percentage of self-employed workers, percentage of part-time workers, job security, and education comes from various government databases, as we explain earlier in this introduction.

⁜ **Industries in Which Income Is Highest:** When you are applying for jobs, or even while you are planning your education or training, you can use this information to aim for industries where workers are paid best. Of course, you also need to consider whether the industry interests you.

⁜ **Metropolitan Areas Where Income Is Highest:** If you are willing to relocate, this information may help you find where the pay is best. However, certain metro areas (such as Washington, San Jose, Boston, and New York) tend to appear very often in these lists because almost *all* wages there are inflated—and so are the local living costs.

- ❋ **Summary Description and Tasks:** The first part of each job description provides a summary of the occupation in bold type. It is followed by a listing of tasks that are generally performed by people who work in the job. This information comes from the O*NET database.

- ❋ **Other Considerations for Income:** This information, mostly derived from the *Occupational Outlook Handbook,* goes beyond the income figures in the first part of the job description. For some occupations, you can see income figures based on data from sources other than the OES—often more detailed but less up to date. For other occupations, there is information about unionization, moonlighting opportunities, or fringe benefits.

- ❋ **Personality Type:** The O*NET database assigns each job to its most closely related personality type, plus one or two secondary personality types. You can find definitions of the personality types in the introduction to the lists of jobs based on personality types in Part I.

- ❋ **Career Clusters and Pathways:** This information cross-references the scheme of career clusters and pathways that was created by the U.S. Department of Education's Office of Vocational and Adult Education around 1999 and is now used by many states to organize career-oriented programs and career information. In identifying a career cluster and pathway for the job (sometimes more than one), we followed the assignments of the online O*NET database. Your state might assign this job to a different career pathway or even a different cluster.

- ❋ **Skills:** For each job, we included the skills whose level-of-performance scores exceeded the average for all jobs by the greatest amount and whose ratings on the importance scale were higher than very low. We included as many as six such skills for each job, and we ranked them by the extent to which their rating exceeds the average. All skills are defined in Appendix A.

- ❋ **Education and Training Program(s):** This part of the job description provides the name of the educational or training program or programs for the job. It will help you identify sources of formal or informal training for a job that interests you. To get this information, we used a crosswalk created by the National Crosswalk Service Center to connect information in the Classification of Instructional Programs (CIP) to the O*NET job titles we use in this book. We made various changes to connect the O*NET job titles to the education or training programs related to them and also modified the names of some education and training programs so they would be more easily understood.

- ❋ **Related Knowledge/Courses:** This entry in the job description will help you understand the most important knowledge areas that are required for the job and the types of courses or programs you will likely need to take to prepare for it. We used information in the Department of Labor's O*NET database for this entry. We went through a process similar to the one described for the skills (noted earlier) to end up with entries that are most important for each job. All knowledge/courses are defined in Appendix A.

Job Title →

Avionics Technicians

Data Elements →

- ❀ Annual Earnings: $49,310
- ❀ Beginning Wage: $34,220
- ❀ Earnings Growth Potential: Low (30.6%)
- ❀ Growth: 8.1%
- ❀ Annual Job Openings: 1,193
- ❀ Self-Employed: 0.0%
- ❀ Part-Time: 0.0%
- ❀ Job Security: Less secure than most
- ❀ Education/Training Required: Postsecondary vocational training

Industries in Which Income Is Highest →

Industries in Which Income Is Highest

Industry	Average Annual Earnings	Number Employed
Air Transportation	$57,580	1,950
Transportation Equipment Manufacturing	$49,640	6,520
Federal, State, and Local Government	$49,490	2,030
Support Activities for Transportation	$45,490	4,140

Metropolitan Areas Where Income Is Highest →

Metropolitan Areas Where Income Is Highest

Metropolitan Area	Average Annual Earnings	Number Employed
Riverside–San Bernardino–Ontario, CA	$63,000	60
Omaha–Council Bluffs, NE-IA	$60,450	260
Denver-Aurora, CO	$59,230	130
Bridgeport-Stamford-Norwalk, CT	$58,710	390
Indianapolis-Carmel, IN	$58,510	110

Summary Description and Tasks →

Install, inspect, test, adjust, or repair avionics equipment, such as radar, radio, navigation, and missile control systems in aircraft or space vehicles. Set up and operate ground support and test equipment to perform functional flight tests of electrical and electronic systems. Test and troubleshoot instruments, components, and assemblies, using circuit testers, oscilloscopes, and voltmeters. Keep records of maintenance and repair work. Coordinate work with that of engineers, technicians, and other aircraft maintenance personnel. Interpret flight test data to diagnose malfunctions and systemic performance problems. Install electrical and electronic components, assemblies, and systems in aircraft, using hand tools, power tools, and soldering irons. Adjust, repair, or replace malfunctioning components or assemblies, using hand tools and soldering irons. Connect components to assemblies such as radio systems, instruments, magnetos, inverters, and in-flight refueling systems, using hand tools and soldering irons. Assemble components such as switches, electrical controls, and junction boxes, using hand tools and soldering irons. Fabricate parts and test aids as required. Lay out installation of aircraft assemblies and systems, following documentation such as blueprints, manuals, and wiring diagrams. Assemble prototypes or models of circuits, instruments, and systems so that they can be used for testing. Operate computer-aided drafting and design applications to design avionics system modifications.

Other Considerations for Income: Technicians who graduate from an aviation maintenance technician school often earn higher starting salaries than individuals who receive training in the Armed Forces or on the job. Airline mechanics and their immediate families receive reduced-fare transportation on their own and most other airlines. About 3 in 10 aircraft and avionics equipment mechanics and service technicians are members of unions or covered by union agreements. The principal unions are the International Association of Machinists and Aerospace Workers, and the Transport Workers Union of America. Some mechanics are represented by the International Brotherhood of Teamsters.

Personality Type: Realistic-Investigative-Conventional. **Career Clusters:** 13 Manufacturing; 16 Transportation, Distribution, and Logistics. **Career Pathways:** 13.1 Production; 13.3 Maintenance, Installation, and Repair; 16.4 Facility and Mobile Equipment Maintenance. **Skills:** Installation; Repairing; Equipment Maintenance; Troubleshooting; Operation and Control; Operation Monitoring; Quality Control Analysis; Systems Evaluation.

Education and Training Programs: Airframe Mechanics and Aircraft Maintenance Technology/Technician; Avionics Maintenance Technology/Technician. **Related Knowledge/Courses:** Engineering and Technology; Mechanical; Computers and Electronics; Telecommunications; Production and Processing; Design.

Other Considerations for Income ←

Personality Type ←

Career Clusters and Pathways ←

Skills ←

Education and Training Program(s) ←

Related Knowledge/Courses

Getting all the information we used in the job descriptions was not a simple process, and it is not always perfect. Even so, we used the best and most recent sources of data we could find, and we think that our efforts will be helpful to many people.

Sources of Additional Information

Hundreds of sources of career information exist, so here are a few we consider most helpful in getting additional information on the jobs listed in this book.

Print References

* *O*NET Dictionary of Occupational Titles:* Revised on a regular basis, this book provides good descriptions for all jobs listed in the U.S. Department of Labor's O*NET database. There are 950 job descriptions at all levels of education and training, plus lists of related job titles in other major career information sources, educational programs, and other information. Published by JIST.

* *Enhanced Occupational Outlook Handbook:* Updated regularly, this book provides thorough descriptions for 270 major jobs in the current *Occupational Outlook Handbook,* brief descriptions for the O*NET jobs that are related to each, brief definitions of thousands of more-specialized jobs from the *Dictionary of Occupational Titles,* and other information. Published by JIST.

Internet Resources

* **The U.S. Department of Labor Bureau of Labor Statistics Web site:** The Department of Labor Bureau of Labor Statistics Web site (http://www.bls.gov) provides a lot of career information, including links to other Web pages that provide information on the jobs covered in this book. This Web site is a bit formal and, well, confusing, but it will take you to the major sources of government career information if you explore its options.

* **O*NET site:** Go to http://www.onetcenter.org for access to the O*NET database, including links to sites that provide detailed local information on the O*NET job titles presented in Part II of this book.

Thanks

Thanks for reading this introduction. You are surely a more thorough person than those who jumped into the book without reading it, and you will probably get more out of the book as a result.

We wish you a satisfying career and, more importantly, a good life.

PART I

The Best
Jobs Lists

This part contains a lot of interesting lists, and it's a good place for you to start using the book. Here are some suggestions for using the lists to explore career options:

* The table of contents at the beginning of this book presents a complete listing of the list titles in this section. You can browse the lists or use the table of contents to find those that interest you most.

* We gave the lists clear titles, so most require little explanation. We provide comments for each group of lists.

* As you review the lists, one or more of the jobs may appeal to you enough that you want to seek additional information. As this happens, mark that job (or, if someone else will be using this book, write it on a separate sheet of paper) so that you can look up the description of the job in Part II.

* All data used to create these lists comes from the U.S. Department of Labor and the Census Bureau. The earnings figures are based on the average annual pay received by full-time workers. Some occupations have high percentages of part-time workers, and those workers would receive, of course, proportionately less pay on a weekly or annual basis. Because the earnings represent the national averages, actual pay rates can vary greatly by location, amount of previous work experience, and other factors.

Some Details on the Lists

The sources of the information we used in constructing these lists are presented in this book's introduction. Here are some additional details on how we created the lists:

* **We excluded some jobs for which very little information is available.** In the full list of 796 jobs for which the U.S. Department of Labor collects annual earnings information, 67 have no information beyond a definition and some Census Bureau data, so we dropped them from consideration.

* **We collapsed several physician jobs into one title.** The government database we used for the job titles and descriptions included eight job titles for physicians, yet the data

source we used for growth and number of openings provided data only for the more general job of Physicians and Surgeons. To make our lists more useful, we included only one job title—Physicians and Surgeons—rather than a separate tile for each specialized physician job. In Part II, however, you will find descriptions of a large number of specific physician jobs that are included in the Department of Labor's O*NET database.

❇ **We excluded some jobs that are shrinking or that offer very few opportunities.** Among the jobs for which we have both O*NET and wage information, several are expected to employ fewer than 500 workers per year and to shrink rather than grow in workforce size. These jobs can't be considered "best jobs," so we excluded them from consideration for this book.

❇ **Some jobs have the same scores for one or more data elements.** For example, in the list of occupations ordered by rate of job growth, two occupations (Actuaries and Surveyors) are growing at the same rate, 23.7%. Therefore we ordered these two jobs alphabetically, and their order has no other significance. There was no way to avoid these ties, so simply understand that the difference of several positions on a list may not mean as much as it seems.

We hope you find these lists both interesting and helpful. They can help you explore your career options in a variety of interesting ways. We suggest you find the ones that are most helpful to you and focus your attention on them. Enjoy!

The Best-Paying Jobs

The first three lists in this section are the most important of all. First is the list of the 250 best-paying jobs, listed in order of their annual earnings. These jobs are the basis for all of the other lists in this section of the book (except some of the bonus lists). For each job, you'll find figures for the average annual earnings, the projected growth through 2016, and the expected annual job openings during that time period.

Of course, a high-paying job does you no good if you can't get hired for it. Some of the occupations on the list of 250 are growing much faster than others and producing many more job openings than others, so the next two lists present the 100 jobs with the best figures for projected percentage growth and number of annual openings.

Descriptions for all of the jobs in these lists are included in Part II.

The 250 Best-Paying Jobs

This is the list that most people want to see first. It includes the 250 jobs that pay on average better than what 75 percent of American wage earners make. (The section in the introduction called "How the 250 Best-Paying Jobs Were Selected" explains in detail how we compiled this list.)

Although health-care jobs dominate the top 20, you'll also find jobs in management, transportation, science, and the law. Not far behind you'll see jobs in engineering, finance, and technology. If you're interested in seeing the 250 jobs broken down by career clusters or personality types, turn to some of the lists later in this part of the book. If you're wondering how much education, training, or experience you'll need to qualify for these jobs, we also have lists that break down the 250 jobs by these requirements.

Consider this first list a starting place, not the final word. Your career decision should not be based solely on expected income, so look at the other lists, read the job descriptions in Part II for any job that interests you, and do a lot of additional career exploration before committing to a career goal.

The 250 Best-Paying Jobs

Job	Annual Earnings	Percent Growth	Annual Openings
1. Oral and Maxillofacial Surgeons	$166,400+	9.1%	400
2. Orthodontists	$166,400+	9.2%	479
3. Physicians and Surgeons	$166,400+	14.2%	38,027
4. Prosthodontists	$166,400+	10.7%	54
5. Chief Executives	$158,560	2.0%	21,209
6. Dentists, General	$142,870	9.2%	7,106
7. Engineering Managers	$115,270	7.3%	7,404
8. Podiatrists	$113,560	9.5%	648
9. Natural Sciences Managers	$112,800	11.4%	3,661
10. Computer and Information Systems Managers	$112,210	16.4%	30,887
11. Air Traffic Controllers	$111,870	10.2%	1,213
12. Airline Pilots, Copilots, and Flight Engineers	$111,680	12.9%	4,073
13. Lawyers	$110,590	11.0%	49,445
14. Judges, Magistrate Judges, and Magistrates	$110,220	5.1%	1,567
15. Marketing Managers	$108,580	14.4%	20,189
16. Petroleum Engineers	$108,020	5.2%	1,016
17. Pharmacists	$106,410	21.7%	16,358
18. Political Scientists	$104,130	5.3%	318
19. Physicists	$102,890	6.8%	1,302
20. Astronomers	$101,300	5.6%	128
21. Financial Managers	$99,330	12.6%	57,589
22. Computer and Information Scientists, Research	$97,970	21.5%	2,901
23. Computer Hardware Engineers	$97,400	4.6%	3,572
24. Sales Managers	$97,260	10.2%	36,392
25. Nuclear Engineers	$97,080	7.2%	1,046

(continued)

(continued)

The 250 Best-Paying Jobs

Job	Annual Earnings	Percent Growth	Annual Openings
26. Optometrists	$96,320	11.3%	1,789
27. Mathematicians	$95,150	10.2%	473
28. Law Teachers, Postsecondary	$93,210	22.9%	2,169
29. Aerospace Engineers	$92,520	10.2%	6,498
30. Computer Software Engineers, Systems Software	$92,430	28.2%	33,139
31. General and Operations Managers	$91,570	1.5%	112,072
32. Public Relations Managers	$89,430	16.9%	5,781
33. Purchasing Managers	$89,160	3.4%	7,243
34. Training and Development Managers	$87,700	15.6%	3,759
35. Compensation and Benefits Managers	$86,500	12.0%	6,121
36. Electronics Engineers, Except Computer	$86,370	3.7%	5,699
37. Computer Software Engineers, Applications	$85,430	44.6%	58,690
38. Actuaries	$84,810	23.7%	3,245
39. Chemical Engineers	$84,680	7.9%	2,111
40. Health Specialties Teachers, Postsecondary	$84,390	22.9%	19,617
41. Education Administrators, Elementary and Secondary School	$83,880	7.6%	27,143
42. Economists	$83,590	7.5%	1,555
43. Industrial Production Managers	$83,290	–5.9%	14,889
44. Sales Engineers	$83,100	8.5%	7,371
45. Biochemists and Biophysicists	$82,840	15.9%	1,637
46. Engineering Teachers, Postsecondary	$82,810	22.9%	5,565
47. Electrical Engineers	$82,160	6.3%	6,806
48. Materials Engineers	$81,820	4.0%	1,390
49. Atmospheric and Space Scientists	$81,290	10.6%	735
50. Physician Assistants	$81,230	27.0%	7,147
51. Education Administrators, Postsecondary	$80,670	14.2%	17,121
52. Medical and Health Services Managers	$80,240	16.4%	31,877
53. Materials Scientists	$80,230	8.7%	1,039
54. Advertising and Promotions Managers	$80,220	6.2%	2,955
55. Economics Teachers, Postsecondary	$80,130	22.9%	2,208
56. Construction Managers	$79,860	15.7%	44,158
57. Geoscientists, Except Hydrologists and Geographers	$79,160	21.9%	2,471
58. Veterinarians	$79,050	35.0%	5,301
59. Transportation, Storage, and Distribution Managers	$79,000	8.3%	6,994
60. Biomedical Engineers	$77,400	21.1%	1,804
61. Industrial-Organizational Psychologists	$77,010	21.3%	118

The 250 Best-Paying Jobs

Job	Annual Earnings	Percent Growth	Annual Openings
62. Art Directors	$76,980	9.0%	9,719
63. Administrative Law Judges, Adjudicators, and Hearing Officers	$76,940	0.1%	794
64. Atmospheric, Earth, Marine, and Space Sciences Teachers, Postsecondary	$76,050	22.9%	1,553
65. Mining and Geological Engineers, Including Mining Safety Engineers	$75,960	10.0%	456
66. Computer Systems Analysts	$75,500	29.0%	63,166
67. First-Line Supervisors/Managers of Police and Detectives	$75,490	9.2%	9,373
68. Computer Specialists, All Other	$75,150	15.1%	14,374
69. Mechanical Engineers	$74,920	4.2%	12,394
70. Civil Engineers	$74,600	18.0%	15,979
71. Agricultural Sciences Teachers, Postsecondary	$74,390	22.9%	1,840
72. Physics Teachers, Postsecondary	$74,390	22.9%	2,155
73. Marine Engineers and Naval Architects	$74,140	10.9%	495
74. Environmental Engineers	$74,020	25.4%	5,003
75. Industrial Engineers	$73,820	20.3%	11,272
76. Management Analysts	$73,570	21.9%	125,669
77. Administrative Services Managers	$73,520	11.7%	19,513
78. Nuclear Power Reactor Operators	$73,320	10.6%	233
79. Financial Analysts	$73,150	33.8%	29,317
80. Radiation Therapists	$72,910	24.8%	1,461
81. Physical Therapists	$72,790	27.1%	12,072
82. Statisticians	$72,610	8.5%	3,433
83. Medical Scientists, Except Epidemiologists	$72,590	20.2%	10,596
84. Health and Safety Engineers, Except Mining Safety Engineers and Inspectors	$72,490	9.6%	1,105
85. Architecture Teachers, Postsecondary	$71,710	22.9%	1,044
86. Hydrologists	$71,450	24.3%	687
87. Network Systems and Data Communications Analysts	$71,100	53.4%	35,086
88. Financial Examiners	$70,930	10.7%	2,449
89. Biological Science Teachers, Postsecondary	$70,650	22.9%	9,039
90. Architects, Except Landscape and Naval	$70,320	17.7%	11,324
91. Sales Representatives, Wholesale and Manufacturing, Technical and Scientific Products	$70,200	12.4%	43,469
92. Database Administrators	$69,740	28.6%	8,258
93. Computer Programmers	$69,620	–4.1%	27,937

(continued)

(continued)

The 250 Best-Paying Jobs

Job	Annual Earnings	Percent Growth	Annual Openings
94. Elevator Installers and Repairers	$69,380	8.8%	2,850
95. Personal Financial Advisors	$69,050	41.0%	17,114
96. Operations Research Analysts	$69,000	10.6%	5,727
97. Agricultural Engineers	$68,730	8.6%	225
98. Securities, Commodities, and Financial Services Sales Agents	$68,680	24.8%	47,750
99. Sociologists	$68,570	10.0%	403
100. Gaming Managers	$68,290	24.4%	549
101. First-Line Supervisors/Managers of Non-Retail Sales Workers	$68,100	3.7%	48,883
102. Business Teachers, Postsecondary	$68,000	22.9%	11,643
103. Nuclear Technicians	$67,890	6.7%	1,021
104. Anthropology and Archeology Teachers, Postsecondary	$67,750	22.9%	910
105. First-Line Supervisors/Managers of Fire Fighting and Prevention Workers	$67,440	11.5%	3,771
106. Chemistry Teachers, Postsecondary	$67,240	22.9%	3,405
107. Political Science Teachers, Postsecondary	$67,200	22.9%	2,435
108. Occupational Therapists	$66,780	23.1%	8,338
109. Nuclear Medicine Technologists	$66,660	14.8%	1,290
110. Geographers	$66,600	6.1%	75
111. Dental Hygienists	$66,570	30.1%	10,433
112. Chiropractors	$66,490	14.4%	3,179
113. Logisticians	$66,480	17.3%	9,671
114. Computer Science Teachers, Postsecondary	$66,440	22.9%	5,820
115. Network and Computer Systems Administrators	$66,310	27.0%	37,010
116. Chemists	$66,230	9.1%	9,024
117. Commercial Pilots	$65,340	13.2%	1,425
118. Budget Analysts	$65,320	7.1%	6,423
119. Environmental Science Teachers, Postsecondary	$65,130	22.9%	769
120. Producers and Directors	$64,430	11.1%	8,992
121. Microbiologists	$64,350	11.2%	1,306
122. Home Economics Teachers, Postsecondary	$64,210	22.9%	820
123. Clinical, Counseling, and School Psychologists	$64,140	15.8%	8,309
124. Psychology Teachers, Postsecondary	$63,630	22.9%	5,261
125. Agents and Business Managers of Artists, Performers, and Athletes	$62,940	9.6%	3,940
126. Speech-Language Pathologists	$62,930	10.6%	11,160
127. Geography Teachers, Postsecondary	$62,880	22.9%	697
128. Orthotists and Prosthetists	$62,590	11.8%	295

The 250 Best-Paying Jobs

Job	Annual Earnings	Percent Growth	Annual Openings
129. Registered Nurses	$62,450	23.5%	233,499
130. Occupational Health and Safety Specialists	$62,250	8.1%	3,440
131. Forestry and Conservation Science Teachers, Postsecondary	$62,140	22.9%	454
132. Audiologists	$62,030	9.8%	980
133. History Teachers, Postsecondary	$62,000	22.9%	3,570
134. Diagnostic Medical Sonographers	$61,980	19.1%	3,211
135. Captains, Mates, and Pilots of Water Vessels	$61,960	17.9%	2,665
136. Technical Writers	$61,620	19.5%	7,498
137. Area, Ethnic, and Cultural Studies Teachers, Postsecondary	$61,490	22.9%	1,252
138. Epidemiologists	$61,360	13.6%	503
139. Sociology Teachers, Postsecondary	$61,280	22.9%	2,774
140. Fashion Designers	$61,160	5.0%	1,968
141. Mathematical Science Teachers, Postsecondary	$61,120	22.9%	7,663
142. Market Research Analysts	$61,070	20.1%	45,015
143. Electrical and Electronics Repairers, Powerhouse, Substation, and Relay	$61,040	–4.7%	1,591
144. Detectives and Criminal Investigators	$60,910	17.3%	14,746
145. Ship Engineers	$60,690	14.1%	1,102
146. Urban and Regional Planners	$59,810	14.5%	1,967
147. Environmental Scientists and Specialists, Including Health	$59,750	25.1%	6,961
148. Philosophy and Religion Teachers, Postsecondary	$59,540	22.9%	3,120
149. Food Scientists and Technologists	$59,520	10.3%	663
150. Accountants and Auditors	$59,430	17.7%	134,463
151. Postmasters and Mail Superintendents	$59,310	–0.8%	1,627
152. Nursing Instructors and Teachers, Postsecondary	$59,210	22.9%	7,337
153. Social Work Teachers, Postsecondary	$59,140	22.9%	1,292
154. Landscape Architects	$58,960	16.4%	2,342
155. Conservation Scientists	$58,720	5.3%	1,161
156. Library Science Teachers, Postsecondary	$58,570	22.9%	702
157. Power Plant Operators	$58,470	2.7%	1,796
158. Soil and Plant Scientists	$58,390	8.4%	850
159. First-Line Supervisors/Managers of Construction Trades and Extraction Workers	$58,140	9.1%	82,923
160. Art, Drama, and Music Teachers, Postsecondary	$57,820	22.9%	12,707
161. Communications Teachers, Postsecondary	$57,760	22.9%	4,074
162. Real Estate Brokers	$57,500	11.1%	18,689
163. First-Line Supervisors/Managers of Correctional Officers	$57,380	12.5%	4,180

(continued)

(continued)

The 250 Best-Paying Jobs

Job	Annual Earnings	Percent Growth	Annual Openings
164. Commercial and Industrial Designers	$57,350	7.2%	4,777
165. First-Line Supervisors/Managers of Mechanics, Installers, and Repairers	$57,300	7.3%	24,361
166. Instructional Coordinators	$56,880	22.5%	21,294
167. Insurance Underwriters	$56,790	6.3%	6,880
168. Cost Estimators	$56,510	18.5%	38,379
169. Education Teachers, Postsecondary	$56,400	22.9%	9,359
170. English Language and Literature Teachers, Postsecondary	$56,380	22.9%	10,475
171. Multi-Media Artists and Animators	$56,330	25.8%	13,182
172. Farm, Ranch, and Other Agricultural Managers	$56,230	1.1%	18,101
173. Animal Scientists	$56,030	9.8%	299
174. Social and Community Service Managers	$55,980	24.7%	23,788
175. Postal Service Clerks	$55,920	1.2%	3,703
176. Claims Adjusters, Examiners, and Investigators	$55,760	8.9%	22,024
177. Gas Plant Operators	$55,760	–9.9%	1,332
178. Telecommunications Equipment Installers and Repairers, Except Line Installers	$55,600	2.5%	13,541
179. Foreign Language and Literature Teachers, Postsecondary	$55,570	22.9%	4,317
180. Zoologists and Wildlife Biologists	$55,290	8.7%	1,444
181. Credit Analysts	$55,250	1.9%	3,180
182. Transportation Inspectors	$55,250	16.4%	2,122
183. Recreation and Fitness Studies Teachers, Postsecondary	$55,140	22.9%	3,010
184. Electrical Power-Line Installers and Repairers	$55,100	7.2%	6,401
185. Aerospace Engineering and Operations Technicians	$55,040	10.4%	707
186. Petroleum Pump System Operators, Refinery Operators, and Gaugers	$55,010	–13.4%	4,477
187. Loan Officers	$54,700	11.5%	54,237
188. Historians	$54,530	7.8%	245
189. Purchasing Agents, Except Wholesale, Retail, and Farm Products	$53,940	0.1%	22,349
190. Anthropologists and Archeologists	$53,910	15.0%	446
191. Compensation, Benefits, and Job Analysis Specialists	$53,860	18.4%	18,761
192. Foresters	$53,750	5.1%	772
193. Criminal Justice and Law Enforcement Teachers, Postsecondary	$53,640	22.9%	1,911
194. Medical and Clinical Laboratory Technologists	$53,500	12.4%	11,457
195. Insurance Appraisers, Auto Damage	$53,440	12.5%	1,030

The 250 Best-Paying Jobs

Job	Annual Earnings	Percent Growth	Annual Openings
196. Geological and Petroleum Technicians	$53,360	8.6%	1,895
197. Electrical and Electronic Engineering Technicians	$53,240	3.6%	12,583
198. Subway and Streetcar Operators	$53,220	12.1%	587
199. Writers and Authors	$53,070	12.8%	24,023
200. Fire Inspectors and Investigators	$53,030	11.0%	644
201. Surveyors	$52,980	23.7%	14,305
202. Railroad Conductors and Yardmasters	$52,830	9.1%	3,235
203. Librarians	$52,530	3.6%	18,945
204. Chemical Plant and System Operators	$52,480	–15.3%	5,620
205. Boilermakers	$52,260	14.0%	2,333
206. Funeral Directors	$52,210	12.5%	3,939
207. Radiologic Technologists and Technicians	$52,210	15.1%	12,836
208. Respiratory Therapists	$52,200	22.6%	5,563
209. Vocational Education Teachers, Secondary School	$51,580	–4.6%	7,639
210. Training and Development Specialists	$51,450	18.3%	35,862
211. Police and Sheriff's Patrol Officers	$51,410	10.8%	37,842
212. Aircraft Mechanics and Service Technicians	$51,390	10.6%	9,708
213. Special Education Teachers, Secondary School	$51,340	8.5%	10,601
214. Sales Representatives, Wholesale and Manufacturing, Except Technical and Scientific Products	$51,330	8.4%	156,215
215. Electrical and Electronics Drafters	$51,320	4.1%	4,786
216. First-Line Supervisors/Managers of Transportation and Material-Moving Machine and Vehicle Operators	$51,320	10.2%	16,580
217. Public Relations Specialists	$51,280	17.6%	51,216
218. Broadcast News Analysts	$51,260	6.0%	1,444
219. Cartographers and Photogrammetrists	$51,180	20.3%	2,823
220. Secondary School Teachers, Except Special and Vocational Education	$51,180	5.6%	93,166
221. Educational, Vocational, and School Counselors	$51,050	12.6%	54,025
222. Special Education Teachers, Middle School	$50,810	15.8%	8,846
223. Arbitrators, Mediators, and Conciliators	$50,660	10.6%	546
224. Postal Service Mail Sorters, Processors, and Processing Machine Operators	$50,600	–8.4%	6,855
225. Dietitians and Nutritionists	$50,590	8.6%	4,996
226. Film and Video Editors	$50,560	12.7%	2,707
227. Emergency Management Specialists	$50,460	12.3%	1,538
228. First-Line Supervisors/Managers of Production and Operating Workers	$50,440	–4.8%	46,144

(continued)

(continued)

The 250 Best-Paying Jobs			
Job	Annual Earnings	Percent Growth	Annual Openings
229. Postal Service Mail Carriers	$50,290	1.0%	16,710
230. Construction and Building Inspectors	$50,180	18.2%	12,606
231. Special Education Teachers, Preschool, Kindergarten, and Elementary School	$50,020	19.6%	20,049
232. Editors	$49,990	2.3%	20,193
233. Forensic Science Technicians	$49,860	30.7%	3,074
234. Rotary Drill Operators, Oil and Gas	$49,800	–5.4%	2,145
235. Stationary Engineers and Boiler Operators	$49,790	3.4%	1,892
236. Court Reporters	$49,710	24.5%	2,620
237. Middle School Teachers, Except Special and Vocational Education	$49,700	11.2%	75,270
238. Purchasing Agents and Buyers, Farm Products	$49,670	–8.6%	1,618
239. Elementary School Teachers, Except Special Education	$49,330	13.6%	181,612
240. Avionics Technicians	$49,310	8.1%	1,193
241. Fish and Game Wardens	$48,930	–0.2%	576
242. Compliance Officers, Except Agriculture, Construction, Health and Safety, and Transportation	$48,890	4.9%	15,841
243. Wholesale and Retail Buyers, Except Farm Products	$48,710	–0.1%	19,847
244. Locomotive Engineers	$48,440	2.9%	3,548
245. Electrical and Electronics Repairers, Commercial and Industrial Equipment	$48,430	6.8%	6,607
246. Occupational Therapist Assistants	$48,230	25.4%	2,634
247. Locomotive Firers	$48,190	2.9%	3,548
248. Mechanical Engineering Technicians	$48,130	6.4%	3,710
249. Tax Examiners, Collectors, and Revenue Agents	$48,100	2.1%	4,465
250. Telecommunications Line Installers and Repairers	$48,090	4.6%	14,719

Jobs 244 and 247 share 3,548 openings with each other and with another job not in this book.

The 100 Best-Paying Jobs with the Fastest Growth

Of the 250 jobs that met our criteria for this book, this list shows the 100 that are projected to have the highest percentage increase in the number of people employed through 2016. (The average growth rate for all occupations in the workforce is 10.4 percent.)

Jobs in the computer and health-care fields dominate the 20 fastest-growing jobs. Network Systems and Data Communications Analysts is the job with the highest growth rate—the number employed is projected to increase by better than half during this time. You can find a wide range of rapidly growing jobs in a variety of fields and at different levels of training and education among the jobs in this list.

The 100 Best-Paying Jobs with the Fastest Growth

Job	Annual Earnings	Percent Growth	Annual Openings
1. Network Systems and Data Communications Analysts	$71,100	53.4%	35,086
2. Computer Software Engineers, Applications	$85,430	44.6%	58,690
3. Personal Financial Advisors	$69,050	41.0%	17,114
4. Veterinarians	$79,050	35.0%	5,301
5. Financial Analysts	$73,150	33.8%	29,317
6. Forensic Science Technicians	$49,860	30.7%	3,074
7. Dental Hygienists	$66,570	30.1%	10,433
8. Computer Systems Analysts	$75,500	29.0%	63,166
9. Database Administrators	$69,740	28.6%	8,258
10. Computer Software Engineers, Systems Software	$92,430	28.2%	33,139
11. Physical Therapists	$72,790	27.1%	12,072
12. Network and Computer Systems Administrators	$66,310	27.0%	37,010
13. Physician Assistants	$81,230	27.0%	7,147
14. Multi-Media Artists and Animators	$56,330	25.8%	13,182
15. Environmental Engineers	$74,020	25.4%	5,003
16. Occupational Therapist Assistants	$48,230	25.4%	2,634
17. Environmental Scientists and Specialists, Including Health	$59,750	25.1%	6,961
18. Radiation Therapists	$72,910	24.8%	1,461
19. Securities, Commodities, and Financial Services Sales Agents	$68,680	24.8%	47,750
20. Social and Community Service Managers	$55,980	24.7%	23,788
21. Court Reporters	$49,710	24.5%	2,620
22. Gaming Managers	$68,290	24.4%	549
23. Hydrologists	$71,450	24.3%	687
24. Actuaries	$84,810	23.7%	3,245
25. Surveyors	$52,980	23.7%	14,305
26. Registered Nurses	$62,450	23.5%	233,499
27. Occupational Therapists	$66,780	23.1%	8,338
28. Agricultural Sciences Teachers, Postsecondary	$74,390	22.9%	1,840
29. Anthropology and Archeology Teachers, Postsecondary	$67,750	22.9%	910
30. Architecture Teachers, Postsecondary	$71,710	22.9%	1,044
31. Area, Ethnic, and Cultural Studies Teachers, Postsecondary	$61,490	22.9%	1,252

(continued)

(continued)

The 100 Best-Paying Jobs with the Fastest Growth

Job	Annual Earnings	Percent Growth	Annual Openings
32. Art, Drama, and Music Teachers, Postsecondary	$57,820	22.9%	12,707
33. Atmospheric, Earth, Marine, and Space Sciences Teachers, Postsecondary	$76,050	22.9%	1,553
34. Biological Science Teachers, Postsecondary	$70,650	22.9%	9,039
35. Business Teachers, Postsecondary	$68,000	22.9%	11,643
36. Chemistry Teachers, Postsecondary	$67,240	22.9%	3,405
37. Communications Teachers, Postsecondary	$57,760	22.9%	4,074
38. Computer Science Teachers, Postsecondary	$66,440	22.9%	5,820
39. Criminal Justice and Law Enforcement Teachers, Postsecondary	$53,640	22.9%	1,911
40. Economics Teachers, Postsecondary	$80,130	22.9%	2,208
41. Education Teachers, Postsecondary	$56,400	22.9%	9,359
42. Engineering Teachers, Postsecondary	$82,810	22.9%	5,565
43. English Language and Literature Teachers, Postsecondary	$56,380	22.9%	10,475
44. Environmental Science Teachers, Postsecondary	$65,130	22.9%	769
45. Foreign Language and Literature Teachers, Postsecondary	$55,570	22.9%	4,317
46. Forestry and Conservation Science Teachers, Postsecondary	$62,140	22.9%	454
47. Geography Teachers, Postsecondary	$62,880	22.9%	697
48. Health Specialties Teachers, Postsecondary	$84,390	22.9%	19,617
49. History Teachers, Postsecondary	$62,000	22.9%	3,570
50. Home Economics Teachers, Postsecondary	$64,210	22.9%	820
51. Law Teachers, Postsecondary	$93,210	22.9%	2,169
52. Library Science Teachers, Postsecondary	$58,570	22.9%	702
53. Mathematical Science Teachers, Postsecondary	$61,120	22.9%	7,663
54. Nursing Instructors and Teachers, Postsecondary	$59,210	22.9%	7,337
55. Philosophy and Religion Teachers, Postsecondary	$59,540	22.9%	3,120
56. Physics Teachers, Postsecondary	$74,390	22.9%	2,155
57. Political Science Teachers, Postsecondary	$67,200	22.9%	2,435
58. Psychology Teachers, Postsecondary	$63,630	22.9%	5,261
59. Recreation and Fitness Studies Teachers, Postsecondary	$55,140	22.9%	3,010
60. Social Work Teachers, Postsecondary	$59,140	22.9%	1,292
61. Sociology Teachers, Postsecondary	$61,280	22.9%	2,774
62. Respiratory Therapists	$52,200	22.6%	5,563
63. Instructional Coordinators	$56,880	22.5%	21,294
64. Geoscientists, Except Hydrologists and Geographers	$79,160	21.9%	2,471
65. Management Analysts	$73,570	21.9%	125,669

The 100 Best-Paying Jobs with the Fastest Growth

Job	Annual Earnings	Percent Growth	Annual Openings
66. Pharmacists	$106,410	21.7%	16,358
67. Computer and Information Scientists, Research	$97,970	21.5%	2,901
68. Industrial-Organizational Psychologists	$77,010	21.3%	118
69. Biomedical Engineers	$77,400	21.1%	1,804
70. Cartographers and Photogrammetrists	$51,180	20.3%	2,823
71. Industrial Engineers	$73,820	20.3%	11,272
72. Medical Scientists, Except Epidemiologists	$72,590	20.2%	10,596
73. Market Research Analysts	$61,070	20.1%	45,015
74. Special Education Teachers, Preschool, Kindergarten, and Elementary School	$50,020	19.6%	20,049
75. Technical Writers	$61,620	19.5%	7,498
76. Diagnostic Medical Sonographers	$61,980	19.1%	3,211
77. Cost Estimators	$56,510	18.5%	38,379
78. Compensation, Benefits, and Job Analysis Specialists	$53,860	18.4%	18,761
79. Training and Development Specialists	$51,450	18.3%	35,862
80. Construction and Building Inspectors	$50,180	18.2%	12,606
81. Civil Engineers	$74,600	18.0%	15,979
82. Captains, Mates, and Pilots of Water Vessels	$61,960	17.9%	2,665
83. Accountants and Auditors	$59,430	17.7%	134,463
84. Architects, Except Landscape and Naval	$70,320	17.7%	11,324
85. Public Relations Specialists	$51,280	17.6%	51,216
86. Detectives and Criminal Investigators	$60,910	17.3%	14,746
87. Logisticians	$66,480	17.3%	9,671
88. Public Relations Managers	$89,430	16.9%	5,781
89. Computer and Information Systems Managers	$112,210	16.4%	30,887
90. Landscape Architects	$58,960	16.4%	2,342
91. Medical and Health Services Managers	$80,240	16.4%	31,877
92. Transportation Inspectors	$55,250	16.4%	2,122
93. Biochemists and Biophysicists	$82,840	15.9%	1,637
94. Clinical, Counseling, and School Psychologists	$64,140	15.8%	8,309
95. Special Education Teachers, Middle School	$50,810	15.8%	8,846
96. Construction Managers	$79,860	15.7%	44,158
97. Training and Development Managers	$87,700	15.6%	3,759
98. Computer Specialists, All Other	$75,150	15.1%	14,374
99. Radiologic Technologists and Technicians	$52,210	15.1%	12,836
100. Anthropologists and Archeologists	$53,910	15.0%	446

The 100 Best-Paying Jobs with the Most Openings

Of the 250 jobs that met our criteria for this book, this list shows the 100 jobs that are projected to have the largest number of job openings per year. They are ordered by the number of openings, so look to the top of the list for the occupations that will have the most job openings. Occupations that have equal figures for job openings are ordered alphabetically.

Jobs with many openings present several advantages. Because there are many openings, these jobs can be easier to obtain. If part-time work is your goal, the odds of achieving that work arrangement are better when there are more openings. Although some occupations with many openings have low pay, all the jobs listed below met the criteria for this book and therefore have average earnings of at least $48,000.

Most of the jobs in the top 20 require hands-on or in-person work, so workers cannot be replaced by technology or by overseas workers.

The 100 Best-Paying Jobs with the Most Openings

Job	Annual Earnings	Percent Growth	Annual Openings
1. Registered Nurses	$62,450	23.5%	233,499
2. Elementary School Teachers, Except Special Education	$49,330	13.6%	181,612
3. Sales Representatives, Wholesale and Manufacturing, Except Technical and Scientific Products	$51,330	8.4%	156,215
4. Accountants and Auditors	$59,430	17.7%	134,463
5. Management Analysts	$73,570	21.9%	125,669
6. General and Operations Managers	$91,570	1.5%	112,072
7. Secondary School Teachers, Except Special and Vocational Education	$51,180	5.6%	93,166
8. First-Line Supervisors/Managers of Construction Trades and Extraction Workers	$58,140	9.1%	82,923
9. Middle School Teachers, Except Special and Vocational Education	$49,700	11.2%	75,270
10. Computer Systems Analysts	$75,500	29.0%	63,166
11. Computer Software Engineers, Applications	$85,430	44.6%	58,690
12. Financial Managers	$99,330	12.6%	57,589
13. Loan Officers	$54,700	11.5%	54,237
14. Educational, Vocational, and School Counselors	$51,050	12.6%	54,025
15. Public Relations Specialists	$51,280	17.6%	51,216
16. Lawyers	$110,590	11.0%	49,445
17. First-Line Supervisors/Managers of Non-Retail Sales Workers	$68,100	3.7%	48,883
18. Securities, Commodities, and Financial Services Sales Agents	$68,680	24.8%	47,750

The 100 Best-Paying Jobs with the Most Openings

Job	Annual Earnings	Percent Growth	Annual Openings
19. First-Line Supervisors/Managers of Production and Operating Workers	$50,440	–4.8%	46,144
20. Market Research Analysts	$61,070	20.1%	45,015
21. Construction Managers	$79,860	15.7%	44,158
22. Sales Representatives, Wholesale and Manufacturing, Technical and Scientific Products	$70,200	12.4%	43,469
23. Cost Estimators	$56,510	18.5%	38,379
24. Physicians and Surgeons	$166,400+	14.2%	38,027
25. Police and Sheriff's Patrol Officers	$51,410	10.8%	37,842
26. Network and Computer Systems Administrators	$66,310	27.0%	37,010
27. Sales Managers	$97,260	10.2%	36,392
28. Training and Development Specialists	$51,450	18.3%	35,862
29. Network Systems and Data Communications Analysts	$71,100	53.4%	35,086
30. Computer Software Engineers, Systems Software	$92,430	28.2%	33,139
31. Medical and Health Services Managers	$80,240	16.4%	31,877
32. Computer and Information Systems Managers	$112,210	16.4%	30,887
33. Financial Analysts	$73,150	33.8%	29,317
34. Computer Programmers	$69,620	–4.1%	27,937
35. Education Administrators, Elementary and Secondary School	$83,880	7.6%	27,143
36. First-Line Supervisors/Managers of Mechanics, Installers, and Repairers	$57,300	7.3%	24,361
37. Writers and Authors	$53,070	12.8%	24,023
38. Social and Community Service Managers	$55,980	24.7%	23,788
39. Purchasing Agents, Except Wholesale, Retail, and Farm Products	$53,940	0.1%	22,349
40. Claims Adjusters, Examiners, and Investigators	$55,760	8.9%	22,024
41. Instructional Coordinators	$56,880	22.5%	21,294
42. Chief Executives	$158,560	2.0%	21,209
43. Editors	$49,990	2.3%	20,193
44. Marketing Managers	$108,580	14.4%	20,189
45. Special Education Teachers, Preschool, Kindergarten, and Elementary School	$50,020	19.6%	20,049
46. Wholesale and Retail Buyers, Except Farm Products	$48,710	–0.1%	19,847
47. Health Specialties Teachers, Postsecondary	$84,390	22.9%	19,617
48. Administrative Services Managers	$73,520	11.7%	19,513
49. Librarians	$52,530	3.6%	18,945
50. Compensation, Benefits, and Job Analysis Specialists	$53,860	18.4%	18,761

(continued)

(continued)

The 100 Best-Paying Jobs with the Most Openings

Job	Annual Earnings	Percent Growth	Annual Openings
51. Real Estate Brokers	$57,500	11.1%	18,689
52. Farm, Ranch, and Other Agricultural Managers	$56,230	1.1%	18,101
53. Education Administrators, Postsecondary	$80,670	14.2%	17,121
54. Personal Financial Advisors	$69,050	41.0%	17,114
55. Postal Service Mail Carriers	$50,290	1.0%	16,710
56. First-Line Supervisors/Managers of Transportation and Material-Moving Machine and Vehicle Operators	$51,320	10.2%	16,580
57. Pharmacists	$106,410	21.7%	16,358
58. Civil Engineers	$74,600	18.0%	15,979
59. Compliance Officers, Except Agriculture, Construction, Health and Safety, and Transportation	$48,890	4.9%	15,841
60. Industrial Production Managers	$83,290	–5.9%	14,889
61. Detectives and Criminal Investigators	$60,910	17.3%	14,746
62. Telecommunications Line Installers and Repairers	$48,090	4.6%	14,719
63. Computer Specialists, All Other	$75,150	15.1%	14,374
64. Surveyors	$52,980	23.7%	14,305
65. Telecommunications Equipment Installers and Repairers, Except Line Installers	$55,600	2.5%	13,541
66. Multi-Media Artists and Animators	$56,330	25.8%	13,182
67. Radiologic Technologists and Technicians	$52,210	15.1%	12,836
68. Art, Drama, and Music Teachers, Postsecondary	$57,820	22.9%	12,707
69. Construction and Building Inspectors	$50,180	18.2%	12,606
70. Electrical and Electronic Engineering Technicians	$53,240	3.6%	12,583
71. Mechanical Engineers	$74,920	4.2%	12,394
72. Physical Therapists	$72,790	27.1%	12,072
73. Business Teachers, Postsecondary	$68,000	22.9%	11,643
74. Medical and Clinical Laboratory Technologists	$53,500	12.4%	11,457
75. Architects, Except Landscape and Naval	$70,320	17.7%	11,324
76. Industrial Engineers	$73,820	20.3%	11,272
77. Speech-Language Pathologists	$62,930	10.6%	11,160
78. Special Education Teachers, Secondary School	$51,340	8.5%	10,601
79. Medical Scientists, Except Epidemiologists	$72,590	20.2%	10,596
80. English Language and Literature Teachers, Postsecondary	$56,380	22.9%	10,475
81. Dental Hygienists	$66,570	30.1%	10,433
82. Art Directors	$76,980	9.0%	9,719
83. Aircraft Mechanics and Service Technicians	$51,390	10.6%	9,708

The 100 Best-Paying Jobs with the Most Openings

Job	Annual Earnings	Percent Growth	Annual Openings
84. Logisticians	$66,480	17.3%	9,671
85. First-Line Supervisors/Managers of Police and Detectives	$75,490	9.2%	9,373
86. Education Teachers, Postsecondary	$56,400	22.9%	9,359
87. Biological Science Teachers, Postsecondary	$70,650	22.9%	9,039
88. Chemists	$66,230	9.1%	9,024
89. Producers and Directors	$64,430	11.1%	8,992
90. Special Education Teachers, Middle School	$50,810	15.8%	8,846
91. Occupational Therapists	$66,780	23.1%	8,338
92. Clinical, Counseling, and School Psychologists	$64,140	15.8%	8,309
93. Database Administrators	$69,740	28.6%	8,258
94. Mathematical Science Teachers, Postsecondary	$61,120	22.9%	7,663
95. Vocational Education Teachers, Secondary School	$51,580	–4.6%	7,639
96. Technical Writers	$61,620	19.5%	7,498
97. Engineering Managers	$115,270	7.3%	7,404
98. Sales Engineers	$83,100	8.5%	7,371
99. Nursing Instructors and Teachers, Postsecondary	$59,210	22.9%	7,337
100. Purchasing Managers	$89,160	3.4%	7,243

Best-Paying Jobs by Demographic

The data we used to create this book included information about the demographic characteristics of workers in the 250 best-paying jobs. Based on this information, we were able to compile more-specialized sets of lists of jobs with high percentages of younger workers, older workers, part-time workers, self-employed workers, women, men, urban workers, and rural workers.

For each group, we set a minimum figure that defines when a job has a high percentage of workers in that group. Then for each group we created three lists that consist only of best-paying jobs that exceed that cutoff figure. For example, the best jobs lists for younger workers include

❀ Best-Paying Jobs for Workers Age 16–24 (this list is ordered by level of earnings and includes all jobs that exceeded the cutoff figure)

❀ Best-Paying Jobs with the Fastest Growth for Workers Age 16–24 (this list is ordered by growth rate and includes the top 25)

❀ Best-Paying Jobs with the Most Openings for Workers Age 16–24 (this list is ordered by the number of openings and includes the top 25)

We hope you find these lists interesting and useful. Do note that we are not suggesting that you should use the lists to limit your choices. For example, many jobs with a high percentage of women would provide excellent opportunities for, and should be considered by, men who find them interesting.

Best-Paying Jobs with a High Percentage of Workers Age 16–24

Workers age 16–24 are employed in virtually all major occupations, but they are concentrated in entry-level, part-time, seasonal, or service jobs. This makes sense in that many young workers have not yet settled into careers or are working while going to school. The jobs they get tend to be relatively easy to obtain but have relatively low wages.

For that reason, although workers age 16–24 make up about 16 percent of the total workforce, in the 250 *high-paying* jobs they make up only 4.4 percent of the workforce. We decided that a job with 8 percent of young workers has a comparatively high concentration and used that figure as the cutoff point in assembling the following list. A total of 33 occupations met or exceeded this cutoff. (We did not have age-bracket information for four of the 250 jobs.)

The jobs on this list are a very diverse set because there are several different reasons why young people would have a relatively large presence in a high-paying occupation. In some cases, the occupation is small and growing very rapidly—almost as if the occupation were just invented—and therefore it has a large contingent of young workers. Two examples are Forensic Science Technicians and Gaming Managers. In the business jobs listed here, workers who have gained experience tend to get promoted out of the job and into management.

If you're a young person, the important point to glean from this list is that there are a good number of high-paying jobs where your age is not a barrier to entry.

Best-Paying Jobs with a High Percentage of Workers Age 16–24

Job	Percent Workers Age 16–24	Annual Earnings	Percent Growth	Annual Openings
1. Computer Hardware Engineers	8.0%	$97,400	4.6%	3,572
2. Actuaries	10.5%	$84,810	23.7%	3,245
3. Chemical Engineers	9.8%	$84,680	7.9%	2,111
4. Network Systems and Data Communications Analysts	9.1%	$71,100	53.4%	35,086
5. Securities, Commodities, and Financial Services Sales Agents	8.4%	$68,680	24.8%	47,750
6. Sociologists	13.5%	$68,570	10.0%	403

Best-Paying Jobs with a High Percentage of Workers Age 16–24

Job	Percent Workers Age 16–24	Annual Earnings	Percent Growth	Annual Openings
7. Gaming Managers	13.4%	$68,290	24.4%	549
8. Agents and Business Managers of Artists, Performers, and Athletes	17.6%	$62,940	9.6%	3,940
9. Fashion Designers	10.3%	$61,160	5.0%	1,968
10. Market Research Analysts	9.7%	$61,070	20.1%	45,015
11. Electrical and Electronics Repairers, Powerhouse, Substation, and Relay	8.2%	$61,040	–4.7%	1,591
12. Commercial and Industrial Designers	10.3%	$57,350	7.2%	4,777
13. Cost Estimators	9.0%	$56,510	18.5%	38,379
14. Gas Plant Operators	8.7%	$55,760	–9.9%	1,332
15. Telecommunications Equipment Installers and Repairers, Except Line Installers	8.4%	$55,600	2.5%	13,541
16. Credit Analysts	11.6%	$55,250	1.9%	3,180
17. Aerospace Engineering and Operations Technicians	8.9%	$55,040	10.4%	707
18. Petroleum Pump System Operators, Refinery Operators, and Gaugers	8.7%	$55,010	–13.4%	4,477
19. Electrical and Electronic Engineering Technicians	8.9%	$53,240	3.6%	12,583
20. Chemical Plant and System Operators	8.7%	$52,480	–15.3%	5,620
21. Boilermakers	10.7%	$52,260	14.0%	2,333
22. Electrical and Electronics Drafters	10.0%	$51,320	4.1%	4,786
23. Public Relations Specialists	10.1%	$51,280	17.6%	51,216
24. Broadcast News Analysts	11.8%	$51,260	6.0%	1,444
25. Educational, Vocational, and School Counselors	8.0%	$51,050	12.6%	54,025
26. Film and Video Editors	14.1%	$50,560	12.7%	2,707
27. Editors	9.0%	$49,990	2.3%	20,193
28. Forensic Science Technicians	28.0%	$49,860	30.7%	3,074
29. Rotary Drill Operators, Oil and Gas	17.3%	$49,800	–5.4%	2,145
30. Court Reporters	11.3%	$49,710	24.5%	2,620
31. Wholesale and Retail Buyers, Except Farm Products	8.0%	$48,710	–0.1%	19,847
32. Electrical and Electronics Repairers, Commercial and Industrial Equipment	8.2%	$48,430	6.8%	6,607
33. Mechanical Engineering Technicians	8.9%	$48,130	6.4%	3,710

Best-Paying Jobs with the Fastest Growth with a High Percentage of Workers Age 16–24

Job	Percent Workers Age 16–24	Annual Earnings	Percent Growth	Annual Openings
1. Network Systems and Data Communications Analysts	9.1%	$71,100	53.4%	35,086
2. Forensic Science Technicians	28.0%	$49,860	30.7%	3,074
3. Securities, Commodities, and Financial Services Sales Agents	8.4%	$68,680	24.8%	47,750
4. Court Reporters	11.3%	$49,710	24.5%	2,620
5. Gaming Managers	13.4%	$68,290	24.4%	549
6. Actuaries	10.5%	$84,810	23.7%	3,245
7. Market Research Analysts	9.7%	$61,070	20.1%	45,015
8. Cost Estimators	9.0%	$56,510	18.5%	38,379
9. Public Relations Specialists	10.1%	$51,280	17.6%	51,216
10. Boilermakers	10.7%	$52,260	14.0%	2,333
11. Film and Video Editors	14.1%	$50,560	12.7%	2,707
12. Educational, Vocational, and School Counselors	8.0%	$51,050	12.6%	54,025
13. Aerospace Engineering and Operations Technicians	8.9%	$55,040	10.4%	707
14. Sociologists	13.5%	$68,570	10.0%	403
15. Agents and Business Managers of Artists, Performers, and Athletes	17.6%	$62,940	9.6%	3,940
16. Chemical Engineers	9.8%	$84,680	7.9%	2,111
17. Commercial and Industrial Designers	10.3%	$57,350	7.2%	4,777
18. Electrical and Electronics Repairers, Commercial and Industrial Equipment	8.2%	$48,430	6.8%	6,607
19. Mechanical Engineering Technicians	8.9%	$48,130	6.4%	3,710
20. Broadcast News Analysts	11.8%	$51,260	6.0%	1,444
21. Fashion Designers	10.3%	$61,160	5.0%	1,968
22. Computer Hardware Engineers	8.0%	$97,400	4.6%	3,572
23. Electrical and Electronics Drafters	10.0%	$51,320	4.1%	4,786
24. Electrical and Electronic Engineering Technicians	8.9%	$53,240	3.6%	12,583
25. Telecommunications Equipment Installers and Repairers, Except Line Installers	8.4%	$55,600	2.5%	13,541

Best-Paying Jobs with the Most Openings with a High Percentage of Workers Age 16–24

Job	Percent Workers Age 16–24	Annual Earnings	Percent Growth	Annual Openings
1. Educational, Vocational, and School Counselors	8.0%	$51,050	12.6%	54,025
2. Public Relations Specialists	10.1%	$51,280	17.6%	51,216
3. Securities, Commodities, and Financial Services Sales Agents	8.4%	$68,680	24.8%	47,750
4. Market Research Analysts	9.7%	$61,070	20.1%	45,015
5. Cost Estimators	9.0%	$56,510	18.5%	38,379
6. Network Systems and Data Communications Analysts	9.1%	$71,100	53.4%	35,086
7. Editors	9.0%	$49,990	2.3%	20,193
8. Wholesale and Retail Buyers, Except Farm Products	8.0%	$48,710	–0.1%	19,847
9. Telecommunications Equipment Installers and Repairers, Except Line Installers	8.4%	$55,600	2.5%	13,541
10. Electrical and Electronic Engineering Technicians	8.9%	$53,240	3.6%	12,583
11. Electrical and Electronics Repairers, Commercial and Industrial Equipment	8.2%	$48,430	6.8%	6,607
12. Chemical Plant and System Operators	8.7%	$52,480	–15.3%	5,620
13. Electrical and Electronics Drafters	10.0%	$51,320	4.1%	4,786
14. Commercial and Industrial Designers	10.3%	$57,350	7.2%	4,777
15. Petroleum Pump System Operators, Refinery Operators, and Gaugers	8.7%	$55,010	–13.4%	4,477
16. Agents and Business Managers of Artists, Performers, and Athletes	17.6%	$62,940	9.6%	3,940
17. Mechanical Engineering Technicians	8.9%	$48,130	6.4%	3,710
18. Computer Hardware Engineers	8.0%	$97,400	4.6%	3,572
19. Actuaries	10.5%	$84,810	23.7%	3,245
20. Credit Analysts	11.6%	$55,250	1.9%	3,180
21. Forensic Science Technicians	28.0%	$49,860	30.7%	3,074
22. Film and Video Editors	14.1%	$50,560	12.7%	2,707
23. Court Reporters	11.3%	$49,710	24.5%	2,620
24. Boilermakers	10.7%	$52,260	14.0%	2,333
25. Rotary Drill Operators, Oil and Gas	17.3%	$49,800	–5.4%	2,145

Best-Paying Jobs with a High Percentage of Workers Age 55 and Over

Older workers have had more years to gain experience and education and thus more often qualify for better-paying jobs. As a result, although workers age 55 and over make up about 18 percent of the labor market, they are more heavily represented among the 250 best-paying jobs. Therefore, we included occupations in this list if the percentage of workers 55 and over was 25 percent or higher. A total of 46 jobs met this criterion and form the basis of this group of lists.

One use for these lists is to help you identify careers that might be interesting as you decide to change careers or approach retirement. Some occupations on the lists may be attractive to older workers wanting part-time work to supplement their retirement income. For example, we think that the job of Art Directors is appealing because the job pays well, can be done less than full time and on a flexible schedule, and lends itself to self-employment. Other occupations on the lists (such as Judges, Magistrate Judges, and Magistrates) take many years of training and experience. After a person is established in that career, the person often works in that occupation until retirement. This low job turnover rate may be reflected in the small number of job openings expected for several of the occupations near the top of the list. Another factor that many of the jobs have in common is low physical demands.

Best-Paying Jobs with a High Percentage of Workers Age 55 and Over

Job	Percent Workers Age 55 and Over	Annual Earnings	Percent Growth	Annual Openings
1. Oral and Maxillofacial Surgeons	27.4%	$166,400+	9.1%	400
2. Orthodontists	27.4%	$166,400+	9.2%	479
3. Physicians and Surgeons	27.2%	$166,400+	14.2%	38,027
4. Prosthodontists	27.4%	$166,400+	10.7%	54
5. Chief Executives	31.5%	$158,560	2.0%	21,209
6. Dentists, General	27.4%	$142,870	9.2%	7,106
7. Engineering Managers	25.5%	$115,270	7.3%	7,404
8. Natural Sciences Managers	30.9%	$112,800	11.4%	3,661
9. Lawyers	27.8%	$110,590	11.0%	49,445
10. Judges, Magistrate Judges, and Magistrates	27.8%	$110,220	5.1%	1,567
11. Petroleum Engineers	25.8%	$108,020	5.2%	1,016
12. Physicists	33.3%	$102,890	6.8%	1,302
13. Astronomers	33.3%	$101,300	5.6%	128
14. Nuclear Engineers	25.5%	$97,080	7.2%	1,046
15. Education Administrators, Elementary and Secondary School	28.7%	$83,880	7.6%	27,143
16. Education Administrators, Postsecondary	28.7%	$80,670	14.2%	17,121

Best-Paying Jobs with a High Percentage of Workers Age 55 and Over

Job	Percent Workers Age 55 and Over	Annual Earnings	Percent Growth	Annual Openings
17. Veterinarians	28.4%	$79,050	35.0%	5,301
18. Industrial-Organizational Psychologists	35.0%	$77,010	21.3%	118
19. Art Directors	33.9%	$76,980	9.0%	9,719
20. Administrative Law Judges, Adjudicators, and Hearing Officers	27.8%	$76,940	0.1%	794
21. Marine Engineers and Naval Architects	44.3%	$74,140	10.9%	495
22. Management Analysts	30.1%	$73,570	21.9%	125,669
23. Administrative Services Managers	27.1%	$73,520	11.7%	19,513
24. Sociologists	37.8%	$68,570	10.0%	403
25. Clinical, Counseling, and School Psychologists	35.0%	$64,140	15.8%	8,309
26. Audiologists	25.6%	$62,030	9.8%	980
27. Electrical and Electronics Repairers, Powerhouse, Substation, and Relay	26.0%	$61,040	–4.7%	1,591
28. Ship Engineers	25.0%	$60,690	14.1%	1,102
29. Conservation Scientists	25.6%	$58,720	5.3%	1,161
30. Real Estate Brokers	34.5%	$57,500	11.1%	18,689
31. Instructional Coordinators	30.4%	$56,880	22.5%	21,294
32. Cost Estimators	29.9%	$56,510	18.5%	38,379
33. Multi-Media Artists and Animators	33.9%	$56,330	25.8%	13,182
34. Farm, Ranch, and Other Agricultural Managers	33.9%	$56,230	1.1%	18,101
35. Social and Community Service Managers	25.3%	$55,980	24.7%	23,788
36. Postal Service Clerks	29.8%	$55,920	1.2%	3,703
37. Transportation Inspectors	28.1%	$55,250	16.4%	2,122
38. Foresters	25.6%	$53,750	5.1%	772
39. Writers and Authors	33.3%	$53,070	12.8%	24,023
40. Librarians	39.0%	$52,530	3.6%	18,945
41. Funeral Directors	31.0%	$52,210	12.5%	3,939
42. Educational, Vocational, and School Counselors	25.3%	$51,050	12.6%	54,025
43. Arbitrators, Mediators, and Conciliators	27.8%	$50,660	10.6%	546
44. Construction and Building Inspectors	26.8%	$50,180	18.2%	12,606
45. Compliance Officers, Except Agriculture, Construction, Health and Safety, and Transportation	27.0%	$48,890	4.9%	15,841
46. Electrical and Electronics Repairers, Commercial and Industrial Equipment	26.0%	$48,430	6.8%	6,607

Best-Paying Jobs with the Fastest Growth with a High Percentage of Workers Age 55 and Over

Job	Percent Workers Age 55 and Over	Annual Earnings	Percent Growth	Annual Openings
1. Veterinarians	28.4%	$79,050	35.0%	5,301
2. Multi-Media Artists and Animators	33.9%	$56,330	25.8%	13,182
3. Social and Community Service Managers	25.3%	$55,980	24.7%	23,788
4. Instructional Coordinators	30.4%	$56,880	22.5%	21,294
5. Management Analysts	30.1%	$73,570	21.9%	125,669
6. Industrial-Organizational Psychologists	35.0%	$77,010	21.3%	118
7. Cost Estimators	29.9%	$56,510	18.5%	38,379
8. Construction and Building Inspectors	26.8%	$50,180	18.2%	12,606
9. Transportation Inspectors	28.1%	$55,250	16.4%	2,122
10. Clinical, Counseling, and School Psychologists	35.0%	$64,140	15.8%	8,309
11. Education Administrators, Postsecondary	28.7%	$80,670	14.2%	17,121
12. Physicians and Surgeons	27.2%	$166,400+	14.2%	38,027
13. Ship Engineers	25.0%	$60,690	14.1%	1,102
14. Writers and Authors	33.3%	$53,070	12.8%	24,023
15. Educational, Vocational, and School Counselors	25.3%	$51,050	12.6%	54,025
16. Funeral Directors	31.0%	$52,210	12.5%	3,939
17. Administrative Services Managers	27.1%	$73,520	11.7%	19,513
18. Natural Sciences Managers	30.9%	$112,800	11.4%	3,661
19. Real Estate Brokers	34.5%	$57,500	11.1%	18,689
20. Lawyers	27.8%	$110,590	11.0%	49,445
21. Marine Engineers and Naval Architects	44.3%	$74,140	10.9%	495
22. Prosthodontists	27.4%	$166,400+	10.7%	54
23. Arbitrators, Mediators, and Conciliators	27.8%	$50,660	10.6%	546
24. Sociologists	37.8%	$68,570	10.0%	403
25. Audiologists	25.6%	$62,030	9.8%	980

Best-Paying Jobs with the Most Openings with a High Percentage of Workers Age 55 and Over

Job	Percent Workers Age 55 and Over	Annual Earnings	Percent Growth	Annual Openings
1. Management Analysts	30.1%	$73,570	21.9%	125,669
2. Educational, Vocational, and School Counselors	25.3%	$51,050	12.6%	54,025

Best-Paying Jobs with the Most Openings with a High Percentage of Workers Age 55 and Over

Job	Percent Workers Age 55 and Over	Annual Earnings	Percent Growth	Annual Openings
3. Lawyers	27.8%	$110,590	11.0%	49,445
4. Cost Estimators	29.9%	$56,510	18.5%	38,379
5. Physicians and Surgeons	27.2%	$166,400+	14.2%	38,027
6. Education Administrators, Elementary and Secondary School	28.7%	$83,880	7.6%	27,143
7. Writers and Authors	33.3%	$53,070	12.8%	24,023
8. Social and Community Service Managers	25.3%	$55,980	24.7%	23,788
9. Instructional Coordinators	30.4%	$56,880	22.5%	21,294
10. Chief Executives	31.5%	$158,560	2.0%	21,209
11. Administrative Services Managers	27.1%	$73,520	11.7%	19,513
12. Librarians	39.0%	$52,530	3.6%	18,945
13. Real Estate Brokers	34.5%	$57,500	11.1%	18,689
14. Farm, Ranch, and Other Agricultural Managers	33.9%	$56,230	1.1%	18,101
15. Education Administrators, Postsecondary	28.7%	$80,670	14.2%	17,121
16. Compliance Officers, Except Agriculture, Construction, Health and Safety, and Transportation	27.0%	$48,890	4.9%	15,841
17. Multi-Media Artists and Animators	33.9%	$56,330	25.8%	13,182
18. Construction and Building Inspectors	26.8%	$50,180	18.2%	12,606
19. Art Directors	33.9%	$76,980	9.0%	9,719
20. Clinical, Counseling, and School Psychologists	35.0%	$64,140	15.8%	8,309
21. Engineering Managers	25.5%	$115,270	7.3%	7,404
22. Dentists, General	27.4%	$142,870	9.2%	7,106
23. Electrical and Electronics Repairers, Commercial and Industrial Equipment	26.0%	$48,430	6.8%	6,607
24. Veterinarians	28.4%	$79,050	35.0%	5,301
25. Funeral Directors	31.0%	$52,210	12.5%	3,939

Best-Paying Jobs with a High Percentage of Part-Time Workers

About 18 percent of workers are employed part time, but many of them are in low-wage jobs. High-wage jobs are notorious for requiring full-time commitment and sometimes long hours in the office. For that reason, part-time workers are not heavily employed in the 250 best-paying jobs, and for the following lists we defined a "high" percentage of part-time workers as 15 percent or more. A total of 77 jobs met this criterion and are the basis for this group of lists.

The good news is that despite the general trend, there are many opportunities for part-time work within high-paying jobs. The opportunities tend to be best in fields where workers have some kind of professional credential—an advanced degree, a certification, or a license that entitles the holder to premium pay. Often it is necessary to establish yourself as a full-time worker before you can shift to a part-time work arrangement.

Note that the earnings estimates in the following lists are based on a survey of both part-time and full-time workers. On average, part-time workers earn about 10 percent less per hour than full-time workers.

Best-Paying Jobs with a High Percentage of Part-Time Workers

Job	Percent Part-Time Workers	Annual Earnings	Percent Growth	Annual Openings
1. Oral and Maxillofacial Surgeons	25.9%	$166,400+	9.1%	400
2. Orthodontists	25.9%	$166,400+	9.2%	479
3. Prosthodontists	25.9%	$166,400+	10.7%	54
4. Dentists, General	25.9%	$142,870	9.2%	7,106
5. Podiatrists	23.6%	$113,560	9.5%	648
6. Pharmacists	18.1%	$106,410	21.7%	16,358
7. Political Scientists	20.1%	$104,130	5.3%	318
8. Optometrists	20.8%	$96,320	11.3%	1,789
9. Law Teachers, Postsecondary	27.8%	$93,210	22.9%	2,169
10. Health Specialties Teachers, Postsecondary	27.8%	$84,390	22.9%	19,617
11. Engineering Teachers, Postsecondary	27.8%	$82,810	22.9%	5,565
12. Physician Assistants	15.6%	$81,230	27.0%	7,147
13. Economics Teachers, Postsecondary	27.8%	$80,130	22.9%	2,208
14. Industrial-Organizational Psychologists	24.0%	$77,010	21.3%	118
15. Art Directors	22.5%	$76,980	9.0%	9,719
16. Atmospheric, Earth, Marine, and Space Sciences Teachers, Postsecondary	27.8%	$76,050	22.9%	1,553
17. Agricultural Sciences Teachers, Postsecondary	27.8%	$74,390	22.9%	1,840
18. Physics Teachers, Postsecondary	27.8%	$74,390	22.9%	2,155
19. Physical Therapists	22.7%	$72,790	27.1%	12,072
20. Architecture Teachers, Postsecondary	27.8%	$71,710	22.9%	1,044
21. Biological Science Teachers, Postsecondary	27.8%	$70,650	22.9%	9,039
22. Sociologists	24.0%	$68,570	10.0%	403

Best-Paying Jobs with a High Percentage of Part-Time Workers

Job	Percent Part-Time Workers	Annual Earnings	Percent Growth	Annual Openings
23. Business Teachers, Postsecondary	27.8%	$68,000	22.9%	11,643
24. Anthropology and Archeology Teachers, Postsecondary	27.8%	$67,750	22.9%	910
25. Chemistry Teachers, Postsecondary	27.8%	$67,240	22.9%	3,405
26. Political Science Teachers, Postsecondary	27.8%	$67,200	22.9%	2,435
27. Occupational Therapists	29.8%	$66,780	23.1%	8,338
28. Nuclear Medicine Technologists	17.3%	$66,660	14.8%	1,290
29. Geographers	20.1%	$66,600	6.1%	75
30. Dental Hygienists	58.7%	$66,570	30.1%	10,433
31. Chiropractors	23.6%	$66,490	14.4%	3,179
32. Computer Science Teachers, Postsecondary	27.8%	$66,440	22.9%	5,820
33. Environmental Science Teachers, Postsecondary	27.8%	$65,130	22.9%	769
34. Home Economics Teachers, Postsecondary	27.8%	$64,210	22.9%	820
35. Clinical, Counseling, and School Psychologists	24.0%	$64,140	15.8%	8,309
36. Psychology Teachers, Postsecondary	27.8%	$63,630	22.9%	5,261
37. Agents and Business Managers of Artists, Performers, and Athletes	18.6%	$62,940	9.6%	3,940
38. Speech-Language Pathologists	24.6%	$62,930	10.6%	11,160
39. Geography Teachers, Postsecondary	27.8%	$62,880	22.9%	697
40. Orthotists and Prosthetists	15.4%	$62,590	11.8%	295
41. Registered Nurses	21.8%	$62,450	23.5%	233,499
42. Forestry and Conservation Science Teachers, Postsecondary	27.8%	$62,140	22.9%	454
43. Audiologists	28.3%	$62,030	9.8%	980
44. History Teachers, Postsecondary	27.8%	$62,000	22.9%	3,570
45. Diagnostic Medical Sonographers	17.3%	$61,980	19.1%	3,211
46. Area, Ethnic, and Cultural Studies Teachers, Postsecondary	27.8%	$61,490	22.9%	1,252
47. Sociology Teachers, Postsecondary	27.8%	$61,280	22.9%	2,774
48. Fashion Designers	16.7%	$61,160	5.0%	1,968
49. Mathematical Science Teachers, Postsecondary	27.8%	$61,120	22.9%	7,663
50. Philosophy and Religion Teachers, Postsecondary	27.8%	$59,540	22.9%	3,120
51. Nursing Instructors and Teachers, Postsecondary	27.8%	$59,210	22.9%	7,337
52. Social Work Teachers, Postsecondary	27.8%	$59,140	22.9%	1,292
53. Library Science Teachers, Postsecondary	27.8%	$58,570	22.9%	702
54. Art, Drama, and Music Teachers, Postsecondary	27.8%	$57,820	22.9%	12,707

(continued)

(continued)

Best-Paying Jobs with a High Percentage of Part-Time Workers

Job	Percent Part-Time Workers	Annual Earnings	Percent Growth	Annual Openings
55. Communications Teachers, Postsecondary	27.8%	$57,760	22.9%	4,074
56. Real Estate Brokers	15.5%	$57,500	11.1%	18,689
57. Commercial and Industrial Designers	16.7%	$57,350	7.2%	4,777
58. Instructional Coordinators	19.7%	$56,880	22.5%	21,294
59. Education Teachers, Postsecondary	27.8%	$56,400	22.9%	9,359
60. English Language and Literature Teachers, Postsecondary	27.8%	$56,380	22.9%	10,475
61. Multi-Media Artists and Animators	22.5%	$56,330	25.8%	13,182
62. Foreign Language and Literature Teachers, Postsecondary	27.8%	$55,570	22.9%	4,317
63. Recreation and Fitness Studies Teachers, Postsecondary	27.8%	$55,140	22.9%	3,010
64. Historians	20.1%	$54,530	7.8%	245
65. Anthropologists and Archeologists	20.1%	$53,910	15.0%	446
66. Criminal Justice and Law Enforcement Teachers, Postsecondary	27.8%	$53,640	22.9%	1,911
67. Writers and Authors	21.8%	$53,070	12.8%	24,023
68. Librarians	21.2%	$52,530	3.6%	18,945
69. Radiologic Technologists and Technicians	17.3%	$52,210	15.1%	12,836
70. Respiratory Therapists	15.0%	$52,200	22.6%	5,563
71. Broadcast News Analysts	17.3%	$51,260	6.0%	1,444
72. Educational, Vocational, and School Counselors	15.4%	$51,050	12.6%	54,025
73. Dietitians and Nutritionists	27.0%	$50,590	8.6%	4,996
74. Film and Video Editors	18.9%	$50,560	12.7%	2,707
75. Forensic Science Technicians	19.4%	$49,860	30.7%	3,074
76. Wholesale and Retail Buyers, Except Farm Products	15.6%	$48,710	–0.1%	19,847
77. Occupational Therapist Assistants	17.8%	$48,230	25.4%	2,634

Best-Paying Jobs with the Fastest Growth with a High Percentage of Part-Time Workers

Job	Percent Part-Time Workers	Annual Earnings	Percent Growth	Annual Openings
1. Forensic Science Technicians	19.4%	$49,860	30.7%	3,074
2. Dental Hygienists	58.7%	$66,570	30.1%	10,433
3. Physical Therapists	22.7%	$72,790	27.1%	12,072
4. Physician Assistants	15.6%	$81,230	27.0%	7,147
5. Multi-Media Artists and Animators	22.5%	$56,330	25.8%	13,182
6. Occupational Therapist Assistants	17.8%	$48,230	25.4%	2,634
7. Registered Nurses	21.8%	$62,450	23.5%	233,499
8. Occupational Therapists	29.8%	$66,780	23.1%	8,338
9. Agricultural Sciences Teachers, Postsecondary	27.8%	$74,390	22.9%	1,840
10. Anthropology and Archeology Teachers, Postsecondary	27.8%	$67,750	22.9%	910
11. Architecture Teachers, Postsecondary	27.8%	$71,710	22.9%	1,044
12. Area, Ethnic, and Cultural Studies Teachers, Postsecondary	27.8%	$61,490	22.9%	1,252
13. Art, Drama, and Music Teachers, Postsecondary	27.8%	$57,820	22.9%	12,707
14. Atmospheric, Earth, Marine, and Space Sciences Teachers, Postsecondary	27.8%	$76,050	22.9%	1,553
15. Biological Science Teachers, Postsecondary	27.8%	$70,650	22.9%	9,039
16. Business Teachers, Postsecondary	27.8%	$68,000	22.9%	11,643
17. Chemistry Teachers, Postsecondary	27.8%	$67,240	22.9%	3,405
18. Communications Teachers, Postsecondary	27.8%	$57,760	22.9%	4,074
19. Computer Science Teachers, Postsecondary	27.8%	$66,440	22.9%	5,820
20. Criminal Justice and Law Enforcement Teachers, Postsecondary	27.8%	$53,640	22.9%	1,911
21. Economics Teachers, Postsecondary	27.8%	$80,130	22.9%	2,208
22. Education Teachers, Postsecondary	27.8%	$56,400	22.9%	9,359
23. Engineering Teachers, Postsecondary	27.8%	$82,810	22.9%	5,565
24. English Language and Literature Teachers, Postsecondary	27.8%	$56,380	22.9%	10,475
25. Environmental Science Teachers, Postsecondary	27.8%	$65,130	22.9%	769

Best-Paying Jobs with the Most Openings with a High Percentage of Part-Time Workers

Job	Percent Part-Time Workers	Annual Earnings	Percent Growth	Annual Openings
1. Registered Nurses	21.8%	$62,450	23.5%	233,499
2. Educational, Vocational, and School Counselors	15.4%	$51,050	12.6%	54,025
3. Writers and Authors	21.8%	$53,070	12.8%	24,023
4. Instructional Coordinators	19.7%	$56,880	22.5%	21,294
5. Wholesale and Retail Buyers, Except Farm Products	15.6%	$48,710	–0.1%	19,847
6. Health Specialties Teachers, Postsecondary	27.8%	$84,390	22.9%	19,617
7. Librarians	21.2%	$52,530	3.6%	18,945
8. Real Estate Brokers	15.5%	$57,500	11.1%	18,689
9. Pharmacists	18.1%	$106,410	21.7%	16,358
10. Multi-Media Artists and Animators	22.5%	$56,330	25.8%	13,182
11. Radiologic Technologists and Technicians	17.3%	$52,210	15.1%	12,836
12. Art, Drama, and Music Teachers, Postsecondary	27.8%	$57,820	22.9%	12,707
13. Physical Therapists	22.7%	$72,790	27.1%	12,072
14. Business Teachers, Postsecondary	27.8%	$68,000	22.9%	11,643
15. Speech-Language Pathologists	24.6%	$62,930	10.6%	11,160
16. English Language and Literature Teachers, Postsecondary	27.8%	$56,380	22.9%	10,475
17. Dental Hygienists	58.7%	$66,570	30.1%	10,433
18. Art Directors	22.5%	$76,980	9.0%	9,719
19. Education Teachers, Postsecondary	27.8%	$56,400	22.9%	9,359
20. Biological Science Teachers, Postsecondary	27.8%	$70,650	22.9%	9,039
21. Occupational Therapists	29.8%	$66,780	23.1%	8,338
22. Clinical, Counseling, and School Psychologists	24.0%	$64,140	15.8%	8,309
23. Mathematical Science Teachers, Postsecondary	27.8%	$61,120	22.9%	7,663
24. Nursing Instructors and Teachers, Postsecondary	27.8%	$59,210	22.9%	7,337
25. Physician Assistants	15.6%	$81,230	27.0%	7,147

Best-Paying Jobs with a High Percentage of Self-Employed Workers

About 8 percent of all working people are self-employed or own their own unincorporated business, and this is a common work arrangement among high-paying occupations. For example, many health-care professionals own their own practices, and many artists and designers own their own studios.

The jobs in the lists in this section all have 10 percent or more self-employed workers. Forty-one jobs met this requirement. In these lists you will find many of the same jobs that appear in the lists of jobs with a lot of part-time workers—jobs that require professional status or certification. But there are also several jobs in other fields, such as the arts, business, and construction. While these lists do not include data on age and gender, older workers and women make up a rapidly growing part of the self-employed population. For example, some highly experienced older workers set up consulting and other small businesses following a layoff or as an alternative to full retirement. Large numbers of women are forming small businesses or creating self-employment opportunities as an alternative to traditional employment.

Note that the earnings figures in the following lists are based on a survey that *does not include* self-employed workers. The actual earnings of self-employed workers may be higher or lower.

Best-Paying Jobs with a High Percentage of Self-Employed Workers

Job	Percent Self-Employed Workers	Annual Earnings	Percent Growth	Annual Openings
1. Oral and Maxillofacial Surgeons	30.6%	$166,400+	9.1%	400
2. Orthodontists	43.3%	$166,400+	9.2%	479
3. Physicians and Surgeons	14.7%	$166,400+	14.2%	38,027
4. Prosthodontists	51.3%	$166,400+	10.7%	54
5. Chief Executives	22.0%	$158,560	2.0%	21,209
6. Dentists, General	36.6%	$142,870	9.2%	7,106
7. Podiatrists	23.9%	$113,560	9.5%	648
8. Lawyers	26.7%	$110,590	11.0%	49,445
9. Optometrists	25.5%	$96,320	11.3%	1,789
10. Advertising and Promotions Managers	13.4%	$80,220	6.2%	2,955
11. Construction Managers	56.3%	$79,860	15.7%	44,158
12. Veterinarians	17.1%	$79,050	35.0%	5,301
13. Industrial-Organizational Psychologists	39.3%	$77,010	21.3%	118
14. Art Directors	59.0%	$76,980	9.0%	9,719
15. Marine Engineers and Naval Architects	12.4%	$74,140	10.9%	495
16. Management Analysts	27.0%	$73,570	21.9%	125,669
17. Network Systems and Data Communications Analysts	17.5%	$71,100	53.4%	35,086
18. Architects, Except Landscape and Naval	20.3%	$70,320	17.7%	11,324
19. Personal Financial Advisors	30.9%	$69,050	41.0%	17,114
20. Securities, Commodities, and Financial Services Sales Agents	17.7%	$68,680	24.8%	47,750

(continued)

(continued)

Best-Paying Jobs with a High Percentage of Self-Employed Workers

Job	Percent Self-Employed Workers	Annual Earnings	Percent Growth	Annual Openings
21. Gaming Managers	16.3%	$68,290	24.4%	549
22. First-Line Supervisors/Managers of Non-Retail Sales Workers	45.4%	$68,100	3.7%	48,883
23. Chiropractors	51.7%	$66,490	14.4%	3,179
24. Producers and Directors	29.5%	$64,430	11.1%	8,992
25. Clinical, Counseling, and School Psychologists	34.2%	$64,140	15.8%	8,309
26. Agents and Business Managers of Artists, Performers, and Athletes	55.8%	$62,940	9.6%	3,940
27. Audiologists	10.2%	$62,030	9.8%	980
28. Fashion Designers	23.6%	$61,160	5.0%	1,968
29. Food Scientists and Technologists	16.3%	$59,520	10.3%	663
30. Landscape Architects	18.5%	$58,960	16.4%	2,342
31. Soil and Plant Scientists	19.5%	$58,390	8.4%	850
32. First-Line Supervisors/Managers of Construction Trades and Extraction Workers	24.4%	$58,140	9.1%	82,923
33. Real Estate Brokers	63.5%	$57,500	11.1%	18,689
34. Commercial and Industrial Designers	29.8%	$57,350	7.2%	4,777
35. Multi-Media Artists and Animators	69.7%	$56,330	25.8%	13,182
36. Writers and Authors	65.9%	$53,070	12.8%	24,023
37. Funeral Directors	19.7%	$52,210	12.5%	3,939
38. Broadcast News Analysts	11.1%	$51,260	6.0%	1,444
39. Film and Video Editors	15.9%	$50,560	12.7%	2,707
40. Editors	13.4%	$49,990	2.3%	20,193
41. Wholesale and Retail Buyers, Except Farm Products	12.0%	$48,710	–0.1%	19,847

Best-Paying Jobs with the Fastest Growth with a High Percentage of Self-Employed Workers

Job	Percent Self-Employed Workers	Annual Earnings	Percent Growth	Annual Openings
1. Network Systems and Data Communications Analysts	17.5%	$71,100	53.4%	35,086
2. Personal Financial Advisors	30.9%	$69,050	41.0%	17,114

Best-Paying Jobs with the Fastest Growth with a High Percentage of Self-Employed Workers

Job	Percent Self-Employed Workers	Annual Earnings	Percent Growth	Annual Openings
3. Veterinarians	17.1%	$79,050	35.0%	5,301
4. Multi-Media Artists and Animators	69.7%	$56,330	25.8%	13,182
5. Securities, Commodities, and Financial Services Sales Agents	17.7%	$68,680	24.8%	47,750
6. Gaming Managers	16.3%	$68,290	24.4%	549
7. Management Analysts	27.0%	$73,570	21.9%	125,669
8. Industrial-Organizational Psychologists	39.3%	$77,010	21.3%	118
9. Architects, Except Landscape and Naval	20.3%	$70,320	17.7%	11,324
10. Landscape Architects	18.5%	$58,960	16.4%	2,342
11. Clinical, Counseling, and School Psychologists	34.2%	$64,140	15.8%	8,309
12. Construction Managers	56.3%	$79,860	15.7%	44,158
13. Chiropractors	51.7%	$66,490	14.4%	3,179
14. Physicians and Surgeons	14.7%	$166,400+	14.2%	38,027
15. Writers and Authors	65.9%	$53,070	12.8%	24,023
16. Film and Video Editors	15.9%	$50,560	12.7%	2,707
17. Funeral Directors	19.7%	$52,210	12.5%	3,939
18. Optometrists	25.5%	$96,320	11.3%	1,789
19. Producers and Directors	29.5%	$64,430	11.1%	8,992
20. Real Estate Brokers	63.5%	$57,500	11.1%	18,689
21. Lawyers	26.7%	$110,590	11.0%	49,445
22. Marine Engineers and Naval Architects	12.4%	$74,140	10.9%	495
23. Prosthodontists	51.3%	$166,400+	10.7%	54
24. Food Scientists and Technologists	16.3%	$59,520	10.3%	663
25. Audiologists	10.2%	$62,030	9.8%	980

Best-Paying Jobs with the Most Openings with a High Percentage of Self-Employed Workers

Job	Percent Self-Employed Workers	Annual Earnings	Percent Growth	Annual Openings
1. Management Analysts	27.0%	$73,570	21.9%	125,669
2. First-Line Supervisors/Managers of Construction Trades and Extraction Workers	24.4%	$58,140	9.1%	82,923

(continued)

(continued)

Best-Paying Jobs with the Most Openings with a High Percentage of Self-Employed Workers

Job	Percent Self-Employed Workers	Annual Earnings	Percent Growth	Annual Openings
3. Lawyers	26.7%	$110,590	11.0%	49,445
4. First-Line Supervisors/Managers of Non-Retail Sales Workers	45.4%	$68,100	3.7%	48,883
5. Securities, Commodities, and Financial Services Sales Agents	17.7%	$68,680	24.8%	47,750
6. Construction Managers	56.3%	$79,860	15.7%	44,158
7. Physicians and Surgeons	14.7%	$166,400+	14.2%	38,027
8. Network Systems and Data Communications Analysts	17.5%	$71,100	53.4%	35,086
9. Writers and Authors	65.9%	$53,070	12.8%	24,023
10. Chief Executives	22.0%	$158,560	2.0%	21,209
11. Editors	13.4%	$49,990	2.3%	20,193
12. Wholesale and Retail Buyers, Except Farm Products	12.0%	$48,710	–0.1%	19,847
13. Real Estate Brokers	63.5%	$57,500	11.1%	18,689
14. Personal Financial Advisors	30.9%	$69,050	41.0%	17,114
15. Multi-Media Artists and Animators	69.7%	$56,330	25.8%	13,182
16. Architects, Except Landscape and Naval	20.3%	$70,320	17.7%	11,324
17. Art Directors	59.0%	$76,980	9.0%	9,719
18. Producers and Directors	29.5%	$64,430	11.1%	8,992
19. Clinical, Counseling, and School Psychologists	34.2%	$64,140	15.8%	8,309
20. Dentists, General	36.6%	$142,870	9.2%	7,106
21. Veterinarians	17.1%	$79,050	35.0%	5,301
22. Commercial and Industrial Designers	29.8%	$57,350	7.2%	4,777
23. Agents and Business Managers of Artists, Performers, and Athletes	55.8%	$62,940	9.6%	3,940
24. Funeral Directors	19.7%	$52,210	12.5%	3,939
25. Chiropractors	51.7%	$66,490	14.4%	3,179

Best-Paying Jobs with a High Percentage of Women

To create the three lists that follow, we sorted the 250 best-paying jobs according to the percentages of women and men in the workforce. (We actually sorted 181 of the jobs because we lacked data about the percentages of men and women in 69 of the best-paying jobs.) We knew we would create some controversy when we first included the best jobs lists with high percentages (70 percent or higher) of men and women. But these lists are not meant to restrict women or men from considering job options; one reason for including these lists is exactly the opposite. We hope the lists will help people see possibilities that they might not otherwise have considered.

The fact is that jobs with high percentages of women or high percentages of men offer good opportunities for both men and women if they want to do one of these jobs. So we suggest that women browse the lists of jobs that employ high percentages of men and that men browse the lists of jobs with high percentages of women. All of the jobs pay well, and women or men who are interested in them and who have or can obtain the necessary education and training should consider them.

An interesting and unfortunate tidbit to bring up at your next party is that the average earnings for the jobs with the highest percentage of women is $56,683, compared to average earnings of $78,178 for the jobs with the highest percentage of men. (The calculations assumed that the four male-dominated jobs paying "more than $166,400" had earnings of exactly $166,400, which means that the actual average is probably higher than $78,178.) But earnings don't tell the whole story. We computed the average growth and job openings of the jobs with the highest percentage of women and found statistics of 17.7% growth and 33,833 openings, compared to 10.9% growth and 20,281 openings for the jobs with the highest percentage of men. This discrepancy reinforces the idea that men have had more problems than women in adapting to an economy dominated by service and information-based jobs. Many women may simply be better prepared, possessing more appropriate skills for the jobs that are now growing rapidly and have more job openings.

Best-Paying Jobs with a High Percentage of Women

Job	Percent Women	Annual Earnings	Percent Growth	Annual Openings
1. Training and Development Managers	70.3%	$87,700	15.6%	3,759
2. Compensation and Benefits Managers	70.3%	$86,500	12.0%	6,121
3. Physician Assistants	70.1%	$81,230	27.0%	7,147
4. Occupational Therapists	85.6%	$66,780	23.1%	8,338
5. Dental Hygienists	99.2%	$66,570	30.1%	10,433
6. Speech-Language Pathologists	98.0%	$62,930	10.6%	11,160
7. Orthotists and Prosthetists	72.1%	$62,590	11.8%	295
8. Registered Nurses	91.7%	$62,450	23.5%	233,499
9. Insurance Underwriters	71.2%	$56,790	6.3%	6,880
10. Compensation, Benefits, and Job Analysis Specialists	71.1%	$53,860	18.4%	18,761

(continued)

(continued)

Best-Paying Jobs with a High Percentage of Women

Job	Percent Women	Annual Earnings	Percent Growth	Annual Openings
11. Medical and Clinical Laboratory Technologists	75.9%	$53,500	12.4%	11,457
12. Librarians	83.2%	$52,530	3.6%	18,945
13. Training and Development Specialists	71.1%	$51,450	18.3%	35,862
14. Special Education Teachers, Secondary School	81.5%	$51,340	8.5%	10,601
15. Special Education Teachers, Middle School	81.5%	$50,810	15.8%	8,846
16. Dietitians and Nutritionists	87.6%	$50,590	8.6%	4,996
17. Special Education Teachers, Preschool, Kindergarten, and Elementary School	81.5%	$50,020	19.6%	20,049
18. Court Reporters	77.5%	$49,710	24.5%	2,620
19. Middle School Teachers, Except Special and Vocational Education	80.9%	$49,700	11.2%	75,270
20. Elementary School Teachers, Except Special Education	80.9%	$49,330	13.6%	181,612

Best-Paying Jobs with the Fastest Growth with a High Percentage of Women

Job	Percent Women	Annual Earnings	Percent Growth	Annual Openings
1. Dental Hygienists	99.2%	$66,570	30.1%	10,433
2. Physician Assistants	70.1%	$81,230	27.0%	7,147
3. Court Reporters	77.5%	$49,710	24.5%	2,620
4. Registered Nurses	91.7%	$62,450	23.5%	233,499
5. Occupational Therapists	85.6%	$66,780	23.1%	8,338
6. Special Education Teachers, Preschool, Kindergarten, and Elementary School	81.5%	$50,020	19.6%	20,049
7. Compensation, Benefits, and Job Analysis Specialists	71.1%	$53,860	18.4%	18,761
8. Training and Development Specialists	71.1%	$51,450	18.3%	35,862
9. Special Education Teachers, Middle School	81.5%	$50,810	15.8%	8,846
10. Training and Development Managers	70.3%	$87,700	15.6%	3,759
11. Elementary School Teachers, Except Special Education	80.9%	$49,330	13.6%	181,612
12. Medical and Clinical Laboratory Technologists	75.9%	$53,500	12.4%	11,457
13. Compensation and Benefits Managers	70.3%	$86,500	12.0%	6,121
14. Orthotists and Prosthetists	72.1%	$62,590	11.8%	295

Best-Paying Jobs with the Fastest Growth with a High Percentage of Women

Job	Percent Women	Annual Earnings	Percent Growth	Annual Openings
15. Middle School Teachers, Except Special and Vocational Education	80.9%	$49,700	11.2%	75,270
16. Speech-Language Pathologists	98.0%	$62,930	10.6%	11,160
17. Dietitians and Nutritionists	87.6%	$50,590	8.6%	4,996
18. Special Education Teachers, Secondary School	81.5%	$51,340	8.5%	10,601
19. Insurance Underwriters	71.2%	$56,790	6.3%	6,880
20. Librarians	83.2%	$52,530	3.6%	18,945

Best-Paying Jobs with the Most Openings with a High Percentage of Women

Job	Percent Women	Annual Earnings	Percent Growth	Annual Openings
1. Registered Nurses	91.7%	$62,450	23.5%	233,499
2. Elementary School Teachers, Except Special Education	80.9%	$49,330	13.6%	181,612
3. Middle School Teachers, Except Special and Vocational Education	80.9%	$49,700	11.2%	75,270
4. Training and Development Specialists	71.1%	$51,450	18.3%	35,862
5. Special Education Teachers, Preschool, Kindergarten, and Elementary School	81.5%	$50,020	19.6%	20,049
6. Librarians	83.2%	$52,530	3.6%	18,945
7. Compensation, Benefits, and Job Analysis Specialists	71.1%	$53,860	18.4%	18,761
8. Medical and Clinical Laboratory Technologists	75.9%	$53,500	12.4%	11,457
9. Speech-Language Pathologists	98.0%	$62,930	10.6%	11,160
10. Special Education Teachers, Secondary School	81.5%	$51,340	8.5%	10,601
11. Dental Hygienists	99.2%	$66,570	30.1%	10,433
12. Special Education Teachers, Middle School	81.5%	$50,810	15.8%	8,846
13. Occupational Therapists	85.6%	$66,780	23.1%	8,338
14. Physician Assistants	70.1%	$81,230	27.0%	7,147
15. Insurance Underwriters	71.2%	$56,790	6.3%	6,880
16. Compensation and Benefits Managers	70.3%	$86,500	12.0%	6,121
17. Dietitians and Nutritionists	87.6%	$50,590	8.6%	4,996

(continued)

(continued)

Best-Paying Jobs with the Most Openings with a High Percentage of Women				
Job	Percent Women	Annual Earnings	Percent Growth	Annual Openings
18. Training and Development Managers	70.3%	$87,700	15.6%	3,759
19. Court Reporters	77.5%	$49,710	24.5%	2,620
20. Orthotists and Prosthetists	72.1%	$62,590	11.8%	295

Best-Paying Jobs with a High Percentage of Men

We suggest you read the introductory material in the "Best-Paying Jobs with a High Percentage of Women" section to better understand the purpose of publishing the following lists. As we state in that section, we are not suggesting that the best jobs lists for men include the only jobs that men should consider.

For example, there is a strong demand for Registered Nurses, a job that employs a high percentage of women, so the few workers available are recruited aggressively and often find jobs quickly. Just as women should consider careers typically held by men, many men should consider career opportunities usually associated with women. This is particularly true now because occupations with high percentages of women workers are growing more rapidly than occupations in our similar lists for men.

In the best-paying jobs list for men, note that many of the top jobs—once you look below the professional-level health-care jobs—are in the business and technology fields and many are at the managerial level, whereas almost all of the primarily female jobs are in the health-care field and none are at the managerial level. This difference confirms the concerns of many educators, counselors, and social advocates about sexual stereotyping of occupations. In many cases, both men and women would be well advised to consider occupations typically held by the opposite sex.

Best-Paying Jobs with a High Percentage of Men				
Job	Percent Men	Annual Earnings	Percent Growth	Annual Openings
1. Oral and Maxillofacial Surgeons	71.8%	$166,400+	9.1%	400
2. Orthodontists	71.8%	$166,400+	9.2%	479
3. Physicians and Surgeons	70.0%	$166,400+	14.2%	38,027
4. Prosthodontists	71.8%	$166,400+	10.7%	54
5. Chief Executives	74.4%	$158,560	2.0%	21,209

Best-Paying Jobs with a High Percentage of Men

Job	Percent Men	Annual Earnings	Percent Growth	Annual Openings
6. Dentists, General	71.8%	$142,870	9.2%	7,106
7. Engineering Managers	92.0%	$115,270	7.3%	7,404
8. Computer and Information Systems Managers	72.2%	$112,210	16.4%	30,887
9. Airline Pilots, Copilots, and Flight Engineers	95.8%	$111,680	12.9%	4,073
10. Computer and Information Scientists, Research	72.9%	$97,970	21.5%	2,901
11. Computer Hardware Engineers	90.4%	$97,400	4.6%	3,572
12. Aerospace Engineers	89.5%	$92,520	10.2%	6,498
13. Computer Software Engineers, Systems Software	79.2%	$92,430	28.2%	33,139
14. General and Operations Managers	72.5%	$91,570	1.5%	112,072
15. Electronics Engineers, Except Computer	91.4%	$86,370	3.7%	5,699
16. Computer Software Engineers, Applications	79.2%	$85,430	44.6%	58,690
17. Chemical Engineers	78.8%	$84,680	7.9%	2,111
18. Industrial Production Managers	83.3%	$83,290	–5.9%	14,889
19. Electrical Engineers	91.4%	$82,160	6.3%	6,806
20. Construction Managers	91.9%	$79,860	15.7%	44,158
21. Geoscientists, Except Hydrologists and Geographers	70.1%	$79,160	21.9%	2,471
22. Transportation, Storage, and Distribution Managers	82.8%	$79,000	8.3%	6,994
23. Computer Systems Analysts	72.9%	$75,500	29.0%	63,166
24. First-Line Supervisors/Managers of Police and Detectives	85.5%	$75,490	9.2%	9,373
25. Mechanical Engineers	92.7%	$74,920	4.2%	12,394
26. Civil Engineers	88.5%	$74,600	18.0%	15,979
27. Industrial Engineers	82.5%	$73,820	20.3%	11,272
28. Health and Safety Engineers, Except Mining Safety Engineers and Inspectors	82.5%	$72,490	9.6%	1,105
29. Hydrologists	70.1%	$71,450	24.3%	687
30. Network Systems and Data Communications Analysts	73.7%	$71,100	53.4%	35,086
31. Architects, Except Landscape and Naval	75.3%	$70,320	17.7%	11,324
32. Sales Representatives, Wholesale and Manufacturing, Technical and Scientific Products	72.9%	$70,200	12.4%	43,469
33. Computer Programmers	75.3%	$69,620	–4.1%	27,937
34. First-Line Supervisors/Managers of Non-Retail Sales Workers	71.8%	$68,100	3.7%	48,883

(continued)

(continued)

Best-Paying Jobs with a High Percentage of Men

Job	Percent Men	Annual Earnings	Percent Growth	Annual Openings
35. First-Line Supervisors/Managers of Fire Fighting and Prevention Workers	90.8%	$67,440	11.5%	3,771
36. Chiropractors	83.2%	$66,490	14.4%	3,179
37. Network and Computer Systems Administrators	85.3%	$66,310	27.0%	37,010
38. Commercial Pilots	95.8%	$65,340	13.2%	1,425
39. Detectives and Criminal Investigators	76.8%	$60,910	17.3%	14,746
40. Environmental Scientists and Specialists, Including Health	70.1%	$59,750	25.1%	6,961
41. Landscape Architects	75.3%	$58,960	16.4%	2,342
42. First-Line Supervisors/Managers of Construction Trades and Extraction Workers	96.8%	$58,140	9.1%	82,923
43. First-Line Supervisors/Managers of Mechanics, Installers, and Repairers	94.6%	$57,300	7.3%	24,361
44. Cost Estimators	84.6%	$56,510	18.5%	38,379
45. Farm, Ranch, and Other Agricultural Managers	77.5%	$56,230	1.1%	18,101
46. Telecommunications Equipment Installers and Repairers, Except Line Installers	85.2%	$55,600	2.5%	13,541
47. Electrical Power-Line Installers and Repairers	98.6%	$55,100	7.2%	6,401
48. Aerospace Engineering and Operations Technicians	77.6%	$55,040	10.4%	707
49. Electrical and Electronic Engineering Technicians	77.6%	$53,240	3.6%	12,583
50. Railroad Conductors and Yardmasters	94.1%	$52,830	9.1%	3,235
51. Aircraft Mechanics and Service Technicians	97.9%	$51,390	10.6%	9,708
52. Sales Representatives, Wholesale and Manufacturing, Except Technical and Scientific Products	72.9%	$51,330	8.4%	156,215
53. Electrical and Electronics Drafters	79.4%	$51,320	4.1%	4,786
54. First-Line Supervisors/Managers of Production and Operating Workers	80.6%	$50,440	–4.8%	46,144
55. Construction and Building Inspectors	90.0%	$50,180	18.2%	12,606
56. Stationary Engineers and Boiler Operators	98.7%	$49,790	3.4%	1,892
57. Locomotive Engineers	94.5%	$48,440	2.9%	3,548
58. Locomotive Firers	94.5%	$48,190	2.9%	3,548
59. Mechanical Engineering Technicians	77.6%	$48,130	6.4%	3,710
60. Telecommunications Line Installers and Repairers	92.5%	$48,090	4.6%	14,719

Jobs 57 and 58 share 3,548 openings with each other and with another job not in this book.

Best-Paying Jobs with the Fastest Growth with a High Percentage of Men

Job	Percent Men	Annual Earnings	Percent Growth	Annual Openings
1. Network Systems and Data Communications Analysts	73.7%	$71,100	53.4%	35,086
2. Computer Software Engineers, Applications	79.2%	$85,430	44.6%	58,690
3. Computer Systems Analysts	72.9%	$75,500	29.0%	63,166
4. Computer Software Engineers, Systems Software	79.2%	$92,430	28.2%	33,139
5. Network and Computer Systems Administrators	85.3%	$66,310	27.0%	37,010
6. Environmental Scientists and Specialists, Including Health	70.1%	$59,750	25.1%	6,961
7. Hydrologists	70.1%	$71,450	24.3%	687
8. Geoscientists, Except Hydrologists and Geographers	70.1%	$79,160	21.9%	2,471
9. Computer and Information Scientists, Research	72.9%	$97,970	21.5%	2,901
10. Industrial Engineers	82.5%	$73,820	20.3%	11,272
11. Cost Estimators	84.6%	$56,510	18.5%	38,379
12. Construction and Building Inspectors	90.0%	$50,180	18.2%	12,606
13. Civil Engineers	88.5%	$74,600	18.0%	15,979
14. Architects, Except Landscape and Naval	75.3%	$70,320	17.7%	11,324
15. Detectives and Criminal Investigators	76.8%	$60,910	17.3%	14,746
16. Computer and Information Systems Managers	72.2%	$112,210	16.4%	30,887
17. Landscape Architects	75.3%	$58,960	16.4%	2,342
18. Construction Managers	91.9%	$79,860	15.7%	44,158
19. Chiropractors	83.2%	$66,490	14.4%	3,179
20. Physicians and Surgeons	70.0%	$166,400+	14.2%	38,027
21. Commercial Pilots	95.8%	$65,340	13.2%	1,425
22. Airline Pilots, Copilots, and Flight Engineers	95.8%	$111,680	12.9%	4,073
23. Sales Representatives, Wholesale and Manufacturing, Technical and Scientific Products	72.9%	$70,200	12.4%	43,469
24. First-Line Supervisors/Managers of Fire Fighting and Prevention Workers	90.8%	$67,440	11.5%	3,771
25. Prosthodontists	71.8%	$166,400+	10.7%	54

Best-Paying Jobs with the Most Openings with a High Percentage of Men

Job	Percent Men	Annual Earnings	Percent Growth	Annual Openings
1. Sales Representatives, Wholesale and Manufacturing, Except Technical and Scientific Products	72.9%	$51,330	8.4%	156,215
2. General and Operations Managers	72.5%	$91,570	1.5%	112,072
3. First-Line Supervisors/Managers of Construction Trades and Extraction Workers	96.8%	$58,140	9.1%	82,923
4. Computer Systems Analysts	72.9%	$75,500	29.0%	63,166
5. Computer Software Engineers, Applications	79.2%	$85,430	44.6%	58,690
6. First-Line Supervisors/Managers of Non-Retail Sales Workers	71.8%	$68,100	3.7%	48,883
7. First-Line Supervisors/Managers of Production and Operating Workers	80.6%	$50,440	−4.8%	46,144
8. Construction Managers	91.9%	$79,860	15.7%	44,158
9. Sales Representatives, Wholesale and Manufacturing, Technical and Scientific Products	72.9%	$70,200	12.4%	43,469
10. Cost Estimators	84.6%	$56,510	18.5%	38,379
11. Physicians and Surgeons	70.0%	$166,400+	14.2%	38,027
12. Network and Computer Systems Administrators	85.3%	$66,310	27.0%	37,010
13. Network Systems and Data Communications Analysts	73.7%	$71,100	53.4%	35,086
14. Computer Software Engineers, Systems Software	79.2%	$92,430	28.2%	33,139
15. Computer and Information Systems Managers	72.2%	$112,210	16.4%	30,887
16. Computer Programmers	75.3%	$69,620	−4.1%	27,937
17. First-Line Supervisors/Managers of Mechanics, Installers, and Repairers	94.6%	$57,300	7.3%	24,361
18. Chief Executives	74.4%	$158,560	2.0%	21,209
19. Farm, Ranch, and Other Agricultural Managers	77.5%	$56,230	1.1%	18,101
20. Civil Engineers	88.5%	$74,600	18.0%	15,979
21. Industrial Production Managers	83.3%	$83,290	−5.9%	14,889
22. Detectives and Criminal Investigators	76.8%	$60,910	17.3%	14,746
23. Telecommunications Line Installers and Repairers	92.5%	$48,090	4.6%	14,719
24. Telecommunications Equipment Installers and Repairers, Except Line Installers	85.2%	$55,600	2.5%	13,541
25. Construction and Building Inspectors	90.0%	$50,180	18.2%	12,606

Best-Paying Jobs with a High Percentage of Urban or Rural Workers

Some people have a strong preference for an urban setting. They want to live and work where they can find more energy and excitement, more access to the arts, more diversity, more really good restaurants, and better public transportation. On the other hand, some prefer the open spaces, closeness to nature, quiet, and inexpensive housing of rural locations. If you are strongly attracted to either setting, you'll be interested in the following lists, which are extracted from the list of 250 best-paying jobs.

We identified urban jobs as those for which 60 percent or more of the workforce is located in the 38 most populous metropolitan areas of the United States. These 38 metro areas—the most populous 10 percent of all U.S. metro areas, according to the Census Bureau—consist primarily of built-up communities, unlike smaller metro areas, which consist of a core city surrounded by a lot of countryside. In the following lists of urban jobs, you'll see a figure called the "urban ratio" for each job. This represents the percentage of the total U.S. workforce for the job that is located in those 38 huge metro areas. (We were unable to determine the urban ratio for one of the 250 best-paying jobs, Locomotive Firers.)

The Census Bureau also identifies 173 nonmetropolitan areas—areas that have no city of 50,000 people and a total population of less than 100,000. We identified rural jobs as those for which 10 percent or more of the total U.S. workforce is located in these nonmetropolitan areas. In the following lists of rural jobs, you'll see a figure called the "rural ratio" for each job. This represents the percentage of the total U.S. workforce for the job that is located in nonmetropolitan areas. (We were unable to determine the rural ratio for 25 of the 250 best-paying jobs; they probably are poorly represented in rural communities.)

After identifying the urban and rural jobs, we created three lists for each set, based on the usual three economic measures: best-paying, fastest-growing, and having the most job openings.

Best-Paying Jobs with a High Percentage of Urban Workers

Job	Urban Ratio	Annual Earnings	Percent Growth	Annual Openings
1. Engineering Managers	63.5%	$115,270	7.3%	7,404
2. Natural Sciences Managers	65.6%	$112,800	11.4%	3,661
3. Computer and Information Systems Managers	71.5%	$112,210	16.4%	30,887
4. Airline Pilots, Copilots, and Flight Engineers	60.9%	$111,680	12.9%	4,073
5. Lawyers	71.3%	$110,590	11.0%	49,445
6. Marketing Managers	71.7%	$108,580	14.4%	20,189
7. Political Scientists	83.6%	$104,130	5.3%	318

(continued)

(continued)

Best-Paying Jobs with a High Percentage of Urban Workers

Job	Urban Ratio	Annual Earnings	Percent Growth	Annual Openings
8. Financial Managers	63.8%	$99,330	12.6%	57,589
9. Computer and Information Scientists, Research	67.4%	$97,970	21.5%	2,901
10. Computer Hardware Engineers	61.2%	$97,400	4.6%	3,572
11. Sales Managers	63.7%	$97,260	10.2%	36,392
12. Computer Software Engineers, Systems Software	74.8%	$92,430	28.2%	33,139
13. Public Relations Managers	66.7%	$89,430	16.9%	5,781
14. Training and Development Managers	61.1%	$87,700	15.6%	3,759
15. Compensation and Benefits Managers	61.1%	$86,500	12.0%	6,121
16. Electronics Engineers, Except Computer	65.5%	$86,370	3.7%	5,699
17. Computer Software Engineers, Applications	75.4%	$85,430	44.6%	58,690
18. Actuaries	67.1%	$84,810	23.7%	3,245
19. Economists	73.2%	$83,590	7.5%	1,555
20. Sales Engineers	72.4%	$83,100	8.5%	7,371
21. Biochemists and Biophysicists	76.8%	$82,840	15.9%	1,637
22. Advertising and Promotions Managers	65.7%	$80,220	6.2%	2,955
23. Art Directors	75.6%	$76,980	9.0%	9,719
24. Computer Systems Analysts	70.2%	$75,500	29.0%	63,166
25. Computer Specialists, All Other	68.9%	$75,150	15.1%	14,374
26. Civil Engineers	61.6%	$74,600	18.0%	15,979
27. Management Analysts	72.1%	$73,570	21.9%	125,669
28. Financial Analysts	76.6%	$73,150	33.8%	29,317
29. Statisticians	63.9%	$72,610	8.5%	3,433
30. Medical Scientists, Except Epidemiologists	62.0%	$72,590	20.2%	10,596
31. Network Systems and Data Communications Analysts	67.3%	$71,100	53.4%	35,086
32. Financial Examiners	67.1%	$70,930	10.7%	2,449
33. Architects, Except Landscape and Naval	72.1%	$70,320	17.7%	11,324
34. Sales Representatives, Wholesale and Manufacturing, Technical and Scientific Products	66.6%	$70,200	12.4%	43,469
35. Database Administrators	66.4%	$69,740	28.6%	8,258
36. Computer Programmers	66.4%	$69,620	–4.1%	27,937
37. Elevator Installers and Repairers	60.3%	$69,380	8.8%	2,850
38. Personal Financial Advisors	72.2%	$69,050	41.0%	17,114
39. Operations Research Analysts	70.7%	$69,000	10.6%	5,727
40. Securities, Commodities, and Financial Services Sales Agents	71.0%	$68,680	24.8%	47,750

Best-Paying Jobs with a High Percentage of Urban Workers

Job	Urban Ratio	Annual Earnings	Percent Growth	Annual Openings
41. First-Line Supervisors/Managers of Non-Retail Sales Workers	61.3%	$68,100	3.7%	48,883
42. Network and Computer Systems Administrators	66.5%	$66,310	27.0%	37,010
43. Chemists	64.3%	$66,230	9.1%	9,024
44. Budget Analysts	62.5%	$65,320	7.1%	6,423
45. Producers and Directors	73.1%	$64,430	11.1%	8,992
46. Microbiologists	68.5%	$64,350	11.2%	1,306
47. Agents and Business Managers of Artists, Performers, and Athletes	70.2%	$62,940	9.6%	3,940
48. Technical Writers	67.3%	$61,620	19.5%	7,498
49. Fashion Designers	75.8%	$61,160	5.0%	1,968
50. Market Research Analysts	74.6%	$61,070	20.1%	45,015
51. Accountants and Auditors	63.9%	$59,430	17.7%	134,463
52. Landscape Architects	62.6%	$58,960	16.4%	2,342
53. Insurance Underwriters	61.5%	$56,790	6.3%	6,880
54. Multi-Media Artists and Animators	79.1%	$56,330	25.8%	13,182
55. Claims Adjusters, Examiners, and Investigators	60.9%	$55,760	8.9%	22,024
56. Telecommunications Equipment Installers and Repairers, Except Line Installers	60.9%	$55,600	2.5%	13,541
57. Credit Analysts	65.2%	$55,250	1.9%	3,180
58. Compensation, Benefits, and Job Analysis Specialists	63.8%	$53,860	18.4%	18,761
59. Writers and Authors	68.9%	$53,070	12.8%	24,023
60. Public Relations Specialists	65.5%	$51,280	17.6%	51,216
61. Postal Service Mail Sorters, Processors, and Processing Machine Operators	60.5%	$50,600	–8.4%	6,855
62. Film and Video Editors	77.6%	$50,560	12.7%	2,707
63. Editors	68.5%	$49,990	2.3%	20,193
64. Wholesale and Retail Buyers, Except Farm Products	62.2%	$48,710	–0.1%	19,847

Best-Paying Jobs with the Fastest Growth with a High Percentage of Urban Workers

Job	Urban Ratio	Annual Earnings	Percent Growth	Annual Openings
1. Network Systems and Data Communications Analysts	67.3%	$71,100	53.4%	35,086
2. Computer Software Engineers, Applications	75.4%	$85,430	44.6%	58,690
3. Personal Financial Advisors	72.2%	$69,050	41.0%	17,114
4. Financial Analysts	76.6%	$73,150	33.8%	29,317
5. Computer Systems Analysts	70.2%	$75,500	29.0%	63,166
6. Database Administrators	66.4%	$69,740	28.6%	8,258
7. Computer Software Engineers, Systems Software	74.8%	$92,430	28.2%	33,139
8. Network and Computer Systems Administrators	66.5%	$66,310	27.0%	37,010
9. Multi-Media Artists and Animators	79.1%	$56,330	25.8%	13,182
10. Securities, Commodities, and Financial Services Sales Agents	71.0%	$68,680	24.8%	47,750
11. Actuaries	67.1%	$84,810	23.7%	3,245
12. Management Analysts	72.1%	$73,570	21.9%	125,669
13. Computer and Information Scientists, Research	67.4%	$97,970	21.5%	2,901
14. Medical Scientists, Except Epidemiologists	62.0%	$72,590	20.2%	10,596
15. Market Research Analysts	74.6%	$61,070	20.1%	45,015
16. Technical Writers	67.3%	$61,620	19.5%	7,498
17. Compensation, Benefits, and Job Analysis Specialists	63.8%	$53,860	18.4%	18,761
18. Civil Engineers	61.6%	$74,600	18.0%	15,979
19. Accountants and Auditors	63.9%	$59,430	17.7%	134,463
20. Architects, Except Landscape and Naval	72.1%	$70,320	17.7%	11,324
21. Public Relations Specialists	65.5%	$51,280	17.6%	51,216
22. Public Relations Managers	66.7%	$89,430	16.9%	5,781
23. Computer and Information Systems Managers	71.5%	$112,210	16.4%	30,887
24. Landscape Architects	62.6%	$58,960	16.4%	2,342
25. Biochemists and Biophysicists	76.8%	$82,840	15.9%	1,637

Best-Paying Jobs with the Most Openings with a High Percentage of Urban Workers

Job	Urban Ratio	Annual Earnings	Percent Growth	Annual Openings
1. Accountants and Auditors	63.9%	$59,430	17.7%	134,463
2. Management Analysts	72.1%	$73,570	21.9%	125,669
3. Computer Systems Analysts	70.2%	$75,500	29.0%	63,166
4. Computer Software Engineers, Applications	75.4%	$85,430	44.6%	58,690
5. Financial Managers	63.8%	$99,330	12.6%	57,589
6. Public Relations Specialists	65.5%	$51,280	17.6%	51,216
7. Lawyers	71.3%	$110,590	11.0%	49,445
8. First-Line Supervisors/Managers of Non-Retail Sales Workers	61.3%	$68,100	3.7%	48,883
9. Securities, Commodities, and Financial Services Sales Agents	71.0%	$68,680	24.8%	47,750
10. Market Research Analysts	74.6%	$61,070	20.1%	45,015
11. Sales Representatives, Wholesale and Manufacturing, Technical and Scientific Products	66.6%	$70,200	12.4%	43,469
12. Network and Computer Systems Administrators	66.5%	$66,310	27.0%	37,010
13. Sales Managers	63.7%	$97,260	10.2%	36,392
14. Network Systems and Data Communications Analysts	67.3%	$71,100	53.4%	35,086
15. Computer Software Engineers, Systems Software	74.8%	$92,430	28.2%	33,139
16. Computer and Information Systems Managers	71.5%	$112,210	16.4%	30,887
17. Financial Analysts	76.6%	$73,150	33.8%	29,317
18. Computer Programmers	66.4%	$69,620	–4.1%	27,937
19. Writers and Authors	68.9%	$53,070	12.8%	24,023
20. Claims Adjusters, Examiners, and Investigators	60.9%	$55,760	8.9%	22,024
21. Editors	68.5%	$49,990	2.3%	20,193
22. Marketing Managers	71.7%	$108,580	14.4%	20,189
23. Wholesale and Retail Buyers, Except Farm Products	62.2%	$48,710	–0.1%	19,847
24. Compensation, Benefits, and Job Analysis Specialists	63.8%	$53,860	18.4%	18,761
25. Personal Financial Advisors	72.2%	$69,050	41.0%	17,114

Best-Paying Jobs with a High Percentage of Rural Workers

Job	Rural Ratio	Annual Earnings	Percent Growth	Annual Openings
1. Chief Executives	13.0%	$158,560	2.0%	21,209
2. Judges, Magistrate Judges, and Magistrates	17.1%	$110,220	5.1%	1,567
3. Pharmacists	13.5%	$106,410	21.7%	16,358
4. General and Operations Managers	11.5%	$91,570	1.5%	112,072
5. Education Administrators, Elementary and Secondary School	18.5%	$83,880	7.6%	27,143
6. Industrial Production Managers	16.1%	$83,290	–5.9%	14,889
7. Physician Assistants	10.4%	$81,230	27.0%	7,147
8. Education Administrators, Postsecondary	10.7%	$80,670	14.2%	17,121
9. Medical and Health Services Managers	13.0%	$80,240	16.4%	31,877
10. Veterinarians	12.6%	$79,050	35.0%	5,301
11. Mining and Geological Engineers, Including Mining Safety Engineers	15.4%	$75,960	10.0%	456
12. First-Line Supervisors/Managers of Police and Detectives	14.9%	$75,490	9.2%	9,373
13. Industrial Engineers	11.1%	$73,820	20.3%	11,272
14. Physical Therapists	12.0%	$72,790	27.1%	12,072
15. Occupational Therapists	10.1%	$66,780	23.1%	8,338
16. Dental Hygienists	12.2%	$66,570	30.1%	10,433
17. Clinical, Counseling, and School Psychologists	10.5%	$64,140	15.8%	8,309
18. Speech-Language Pathologists	12.3%	$62,930	10.6%	11,160
19. Registered Nurses	12.0%	$62,450	23.5%	233,499
20. Occupational Health and Safety Specialists	12.4%	$62,250	8.1%	3,440
21. Captains, Mates, and Pilots of Water Vessels	12.6%	$61,960	17.9%	2,665
22. Mathematical Science Teachers, Postsecondary	10.0%	$61,120	22.9%	7,663
23. Detectives and Criminal Investigators	11.8%	$60,910	17.3%	14,746
24. Postmasters and Mail Superintendents	54.6%	$59,310	–0.8%	1,627
25. Conservation Scientists	23.4%	$58,720	5.3%	1,161
26. Power Plant Operators	12.1%	$58,470	2.7%	1,796
27. First-Line Supervisors/Managers of Construction Trades and Extraction Workers	14.5%	$58,140	9.1%	82,923
28. First-Line Supervisors/Managers of Correctional Officers	22.5%	$57,380	12.5%	4,180
29. First-Line Supervisors/Managers of Mechanics, Installers, and Repairers	15.5%	$57,300	7.3%	24,361
30. Instructional Coordinators	10.6%	$56,880	22.5%	21,294
31. English Language and Literature Teachers, Postsecondary	10.7%	$56,380	22.9%	10,475

Best-Paying Jobs with a High Percentage of Rural Workers

Job	Rural Ratio	Annual Earnings	Percent Growth	Annual Openings
32. Social and Community Service Managers	14.4%	$55,980	24.7%	23,788
33. Postal Service Clerks	18.9%	$55,920	1.2%	3,703
34. Gas Plant Operators	12.3%	$55,760	–9.9%	1,332
35. Zoologists and Wildlife Biologists	17.8%	$55,290	8.7%	1,444
36. Electrical Power-Line Installers and Repairers	23.2%	$55,100	7.2%	6,401
37. Loan Officers	12.0%	$54,700	11.5%	54,237
38. Purchasing Agents, Except Wholesale, Retail, and Farm Products	10.1%	$53,940	0.1%	22,349
39. Foresters	27.5%	$53,750	5.1%	772
40. Surveyors	12.5%	$52,980	23.7%	14,305
41. Librarians	16.1%	$52,530	3.6%	18,945
42. Funeral Directors	18.3%	$52,210	12.5%	3,939
43. Radiologic Technologists and Technicians	13.3%	$52,210	15.1%	12,836
44. Respiratory Therapists	10.3%	$52,200	22.6%	5,563
45. Vocational Education Teachers, Secondary School	24.1%	$51,580	–4.6%	7,639
46. Police and Sheriff's Patrol Officers	14.6%	$51,410	10.8%	37,842
47. Special Education Teachers, Secondary School	17.0%	$51,340	8.5%	10,601
48. First-Line Supervisors/Managers of Transportation and Material-Moving Machine and Vehicle Operators	14.9%	$51,320	10.2%	16,580
49. Secondary School Teachers, Except Special and Vocational Education	17.3%	$51,180	5.6%	93,166
50. Educational, Vocational, and School Counselors	15.0%	$51,050	12.6%	54,025
51. Special Education Teachers, Middle School	15.1%	$50,810	15.8%	8,846
52. First-Line Supervisors/Managers of Production and Operating Workers	20.1%	$50,440	–4.8%	46,144
53. Postal Service Mail Carriers	16.7%	$50,290	1.0%	16,710
54. Special Education Teachers, Preschool, Kindergarten, and Elementary School	16.6%	$50,020	19.6%	20,049
55. Rotary Drill Operators, Oil and Gas	26.2%	$49,800	–5.4%	2,145
56. Stationary Engineers and Boiler Operators	12.3%	$49,790	3.4%	1,892
57. Middle School Teachers, Except Special and Vocational Education	16.3%	$49,700	11.2%	75,270
58. Elementary School Teachers, Except Special Education	16.9%	$49,330	13.6%	181,612
59. Electrical and Electronics Repairers, Commercial and Industrial Equipment	10.9%	$48,430	6.8%	6,607
60. Telecommunications Line Installers and Repairers	10.0%	$48,090	4.6%	14,719

Best-Paying Jobs with the Fastest Growth with a High Percentage of Rural Workers

Job	Rural Ratio	Annual Earnings	Percent Growth	Annual Openings
1. Veterinarians	12.6%	$79,050	35.0%	5,301
2. Dental Hygienists	12.2%	$66,570	30.1%	10,433
3. Physical Therapists	12.0%	$72,790	27.1%	12,072
4. Physician Assistants	10.4%	$81,230	27.0%	7,147
5. Social and Community Service Managers	14.4%	$55,980	24.7%	23,788
6. Surveyors	12.5%	$52,980	23.7%	14,305
7. Registered Nurses	12.0%	$62,450	23.5%	233,499
8. Occupational Therapists	10.1%	$66,780	23.1%	8,338
9. English Language and Literature Teachers, Postsecondary	10.7%	$56,380	22.9%	10,475
10. Mathematical Science Teachers, Postsecondary	10.0%	$61,120	22.9%	7,663
11. Respiratory Therapists	10.3%	$52,200	22.6%	5,563
12. Instructional Coordinators	10.6%	$56,880	22.5%	21,294
13. Pharmacists	13.5%	$106,410	21.7%	16,358
14. Industrial Engineers	11.1%	$73,820	20.3%	11,272
15. Special Education Teachers, Preschool, Kindergarten, and Elementary School	16.6%	$50,020	19.6%	20,049
16. Captains, Mates, and Pilots of Water Vessels	12.6%	$61,960	17.9%	2,665
17. Detectives and Criminal Investigators	11.8%	$60,910	17.3%	14,746
18. Medical and Health Services Managers	13.0%	$80,240	16.4%	31,877
19. Clinical, Counseling, and School Psychologists	10.5%	$64,140	15.8%	8,309
20. Special Education Teachers, Middle School	15.1%	$50,810	15.8%	8,846
21. Radiologic Technologists and Technicians	13.3%	$52,210	15.1%	12,836
22. Education Administrators, Postsecondary	10.7%	$80,670	14.2%	17,121
23. Elementary School Teachers, Except Special Education	16.9%	$49,330	13.6%	181,612
24. Educational, Vocational, and School Counselors	15.0%	$51,050	12.6%	54,025
25. First-Line Supervisors/Managers of Correctional Officers	22.5%	$57,380	12.5%	4,180

Best-Paying Jobs with the Most Openings with a High Percentage of Rural Workers

Job	Rural Ratio	Annual Earnings	Percent Growth	Annual Openings
1. Registered Nurses	12.0%	$62,450	23.5%	233,499
2. Elementary School Teachers, Except Special Education	16.9%	$49,330	13.6%	181,612
3. General and Operations Managers	11.5%	$91,570	1.5%	112,072
4. Secondary School Teachers, Except Special and Vocational Education	17.3%	$51,180	5.6%	93,166
5. First-Line Supervisors/Managers of Construction Trades and Extraction Workers	14.5%	$58,140	9.1%	82,923
6. Middle School Teachers, Except Special and Vocational Education	16.3%	$49,700	11.2%	75,270
7. Loan Officers	12.0%	$54,700	11.5%	54,237
8. Educational, Vocational, and School Counselors	15.0%	$51,050	12.6%	54,025
9. First-Line Supervisors/Managers of Production and Operating Workers	20.1%	$50,440	–4.8%	46,144
10. Police and Sheriff's Patrol Officers	14.6%	$51,410	10.8%	37,842
11. Medical and Health Services Managers	13.0%	$80,240	16.4%	31,877
12. Education Administrators, Elementary and Secondary School	18.5%	$83,880	7.6%	27,143
13. First-Line Supervisors/Managers of Mechanics, Installers, and Repairers	15.5%	$57,300	7.3%	24,361
14. Social and Community Service Managers	14.4%	$55,980	24.7%	23,788
15. Purchasing Agents, Except Wholesale, Retail, and Farm Products	10.1%	$53,940	0.1%	22,349
16. Instructional Coordinators	10.6%	$56,880	22.5%	21,294
17. Chief Executives	13.0%	$158,560	2.0%	21,209
18. Special Education Teachers, Preschool, Kindergarten, and Elementary School	16.6%	$50,020	19.6%	20,049
19. Librarians	16.1%	$52,530	3.6%	18,945
20. Education Administrators, Postsecondary	10.7%	$80,670	14.2%	17,121
21. Postal Service Mail Carriers	16.7%	$50,290	1.0%	16,710
22. First-Line Supervisors/Managers of Transportation and Material-Moving Machine and Vehicle Operators	14.9%	$51,320	10.2%	16,580
23. Pharmacists	13.5%	$106,410	21.7%	16,358
24. Industrial Production Managers	16.1%	$83,290	–5.9%	14,889
25. Detectives and Criminal Investigators	11.8%	$60,910	17.3%	14,746

Best-Paying Jobs Lists Based on Levels of Education and Training

The lists in this section separate the 250 jobs that met our criteria for this book into lists based on the education or training typically required for entry. Unlike many of the other lists, these lists are not broken down into separate lists for highest pay, fastest growth, or most openings. Instead, we provided one list that includes all the best-paying occupations in our database that fit into each of the education levels and ranked the occupations by their earnings. Where jobs have equal earnings, we ordered them alphabetically.

You can use these lists in a variety of ways. For example, they can help you identify a high-paying job with higher potential but with a similar level of education to the job you now hold.

You can also use these lists to figure out additional job possibilities that would open up if you were to get additional training, education, or work experience. For example, maybe you are a high school graduate working in the transportation field and want to advance to a high-paying job. There are many jobs in this field at all levels of education. You can identify the job you're interested in and the related training you need so you can move ahead in your field.

The lists of jobs by education should also help you when you're planning your education. For example, you might be thinking about a job in the business field, but you aren't sure what kind of work you want to do. The lists show that a job as a Purchasing Agent, Except Wholesale, Retail, and Farm Products, requires long-term on-the-job training and pays $53,940, while a job as a Public Relations Specialist requires a bachelor's degree but pays less—$51,280. If you want high earnings without many years of expensive college education, this information might make a difference in your choice.

As you review these lists, doubtless you will notice that the lists grow more crowded and feature higher-paying jobs as the amount of training or education increases. It is a basic fact of the labor market that the highest-paying jobs tend to require considerable preparation. Nevertheless, if you want to minimize the time, expense, and commitment of preparing for a career, you will find several high-paying jobs with lots of openings in the first few lists.

The Education Levels

Here are brief descriptions used by the U.S. Department of Labor for the training and education levels used in the lists that follow:

- ❋ **Short-term on-the-job training:** It is possible to work in these occupations and achieve an average level of performance within a few days or weeks through on-the-job training.
- ❋ **Moderate-term on-the-job training:** Occupations that require this type of training can be performed adequately after a 1- to 12-month period of combined on-the-job and

informal training. Typically, untrained workers observe experienced workers performing tasks and are gradually moved into progressively more difficult assignments.

❋ **Long-term on-the-job training:** This type of job requires more than 12 months of on-the-job training or combined work experience and formal classroom instruction. This includes occupations that use formal apprenticeships for training workers that may take up to four years. It also includes intensive occupation-specific, employer-sponsored training such as police academies. Furthermore, it includes occupations that require natural talent that must be developed over many years.

❋ **Work experience in a related occupation:** This type of job requires a worker to have experience—usually several years of experience—in a related occupation (such as Police Detectives, who are selected based on their experience as Police Patrol Officers).

❋ **Postsecondary vocational training:** This requirement involves training that lasts at least a few months but usually less than one year. In a few instances, there may be as many as four years of training.

❋ **Associate degree:** This degree typically requires two years of full-time academic work beyond high school.

❋ **Bachelor's degree:** A bachelor's degree usually requires 120 to 130 semester hours to complete. A full-time student usually takes four to five years to complete a bachelor's degree, depending on the complexity of courses. Traditionally, people have thought of the bachelor's degree as a four-year degree, but there are some bachelor's degrees—such as the Bachelor of Architecture—that are considered a first professional degree and take five or more years to complete.

❋ **Work experience plus degree:** Some jobs require work experience in a related job in addition to a degree. For example, almost all managers have worked in a related job before being promoted into a management position. Most of the jobs in this group require a four-year bachelor's degree, although some require an associate degree or a master's degree.

❋ **Master's degree:** This degree usually requires 33 to 60 semester hours beyond the bachelor's degree. The academic master's degrees—such as a Master of Arts in Political Science—usually require 33 to 36 hours. A first professional degree at the master's level—such as a Master of Social Work—requires almost two years of full-time work.

❋ **Doctoral degree:** The doctoral degree prepares students for careers that consist primarily of theory development, research, and/or college teaching. This type of degree is typically the Doctor of Philosophy (Ph.D.) or Doctor of Education (Ed.D.). Normally, a requirement for a doctoral degree is the completion of a master's degree plus an additional two to three years of full-time coursework and a one- to two-semester research project and paper called the dissertation. It usually takes four to five years beyond the bachelor's degree to complete a doctoral degree.

❋ **First professional degree:** Some professional degrees require three or more years of full-time academic study beyond the bachelor's degree. A professional degree prepares students for a specific profession. It uses theory and research to teach practical applications in a professional occupation. Examples of this type of degree are Doctor of Medicine (M.D.) for physicians, Doctor of Ministry (D.Min.) for clergy, and Juris Doctor (J.D.) for attorneys.

Another Warning About the Data

We warned you in the introduction to use caution in interpreting the data we use, and we want to do it again here. The occupational data we use is the most accurate available anywhere, but it has its limitations. For example, the education or training requirements for entry into a job are those typically required as a minimum—but some people working in those jobs may have considerably more or different credentials. For example, most Registered Nurses now have a four-year bachelor's degree, although the two-year associate degree is the minimum level of training this job requires (and therefore we list it here with jobs requiring the associate degree).

When you turn to Part II, you might notice that some O*NET job titles have different levels of required education even though they are linked to the same SOC occupation in the Part I lists. Perhaps the most striking example is (again) Registered Nurses. Some of the O*NET job titles linked to it, such as Acute Care Nurses and Advanced Practice Psychiatric Nurses, usually require a *master's* degree.

In addition, many people are working in jobs for which they don't have the formal educational requirements. For example, Insurance Underwriters are usually expected to have a bachelor's degree, but almost one-third of them have less college than that, and one-eighth of them have no college education at all. Some of these are workers who entered the occupation some time ago, when entry requirements were lower. Others are highly skilled workers who are able to convince employers of their ability to do the job despite their lack of the usual credentials.

So as you browse the lists that follow, please use them as a way to be encouraged rather than discouraged. Education and training are very important for success in the labor market of the future, but so are ability, drive, initiative, and, yes, luck.

Having said this, we encourage you to get as much education and training as you can. It used to be that you got your schooling and never went back, but this is not a good attitude to have now. You will probably need to continue learning new things throughout your working life. You can do so by going to school, and this is a good thing for many people to do. But there are also many other ways to learn, such as workshops, certification programs, employer training, professional conferences, Internet training, related books and magazines, and many others. Upgrading your computer and other technical skills is particularly important in our rapidly changing workplace, and you avoid doing so at your peril.

As one of our grandfathers used to say, "The harder you work, the luckier you get." It is just as true now as it was then.

Best-Paying Jobs Requiring Short-Term On-the-Job Training

Job	Annual Earnings	Percent Growth	Annual Openings
1. Postal Service Clerks	$55,920	1.2%	3,703
2. Postal Service Mail Sorters, Processors, and Processing Machine Operators	$50,600	–8.4%	6,855
3. Postal Service Mail Carriers	$50,290	1.0%	16,710

Best-Paying Jobs Requiring Moderate-Term On-the-Job Training

Job	Annual Earnings	Percent Growth	Annual Openings
1. Subway and Streetcar Operators	$53,220	12.1%	587
2. Railroad Conductors and Yardmasters	$52,830	9.1%	3,235
3. Rotary Drill Operators, Oil and Gas	$49,800	–5.4%	2,145
4. Locomotive Engineers	$48,440	2.9%	3,548
5. Locomotive Firers	$48,190	2.9%	3,548

Jobs 4 and 5 share 3,548 openings with each other and with another job not in this book.

Best-Paying Jobs Requiring Long-Term On-the-Job Training

Job	Annual Earnings	Percent Growth	Annual Openings
1. Air Traffic Controllers	$111,870	10.2%	1,213
2. Nuclear Power Reactor Operators	$73,320	10.6%	233
3. Elevator Installers and Repairers	$69,380	8.8%	2,850
4. Power Plant Operators	$58,470	2.7%	1,796
5. Claims Adjusters, Examiners, and Investigators	$55,760	8.9%	22,024
6. Gas Plant Operators	$55,760	–9.9%	1,332
7. Electrical Power-Line Installers and Repairers	$55,100	7.2%	6,401
8. Petroleum Pump System Operators, Refinery Operators, and Gaugers	$55,010	–13.4%	4,477
9. Purchasing Agents, Except Wholesale, Retail, and Farm Products	$53,940	0.1%	22,349
10. Chemical Plant and System Operators	$52,480	–15.3%	5,620
11. Boilermakers	$52,260	14.0%	2,333
12. Police and Sheriff's Patrol Officers	$51,410	10.8%	37,842

(continued)

(continued)

Best-Paying Jobs Requiring Long-Term On-the-Job Training

Job	Annual Earnings	Percent Growth	Annual Openings
13. Stationary Engineers and Boiler Operators	$49,790	3.4%	1,892
14. Purchasing Agents and Buyers, Farm Products	$49,670	–8.6%	1,618
15. Compliance Officers, Except Agriculture, Construction, Health and Safety, and Transportation	$48,890	4.9%	15,841
16. Wholesale and Retail Buyers, Except Farm Products	$48,710	–0.1%	19,847
17. Telecommunications Line Installers and Repairers	$48,090	4.6%	14,719

Best-Paying Jobs Requiring Work Experience in a Related Occupation

Job	Annual Earnings	Percent Growth	Annual Openings
1. Industrial Production Managers	$83,290	–5.9%	14,889
2. Transportation, Storage, and Distribution Managers	$79,000	8.3%	6,994
3. First-Line Supervisors/Managers of Police and Detectives	$75,490	9.2%	9,373
4. Sales Representatives, Wholesale and Manufacturing, Technical and Scientific Products	$70,200	12.4%	43,469
5. Gaming Managers	$68,290	24.4%	549
6. First-Line Supervisors/Managers of Non-Retail Sales Workers	$68,100	3.7%	48,883
7. First-Line Supervisors/Managers of Fire Fighting and Prevention Workers	$67,440	11.5%	3,771
8. Captains, Mates, and Pilots of Water Vessels	$61,960	17.9%	2,665
9. Detectives and Criminal Investigators	$60,910	17.3%	14,746
10. Ship Engineers	$60,690	14.1%	1,102
11. Postmasters and Mail Superintendents	$59,310	–0.8%	1,627
12. First-Line Supervisors/Managers of Construction Trades and Extraction Workers	$58,140	9.1%	82,923
13. Real Estate Brokers	$57,500	11.1%	18,689
14. First-Line Supervisors/Managers of Correctional Officers	$57,380	12.5%	4,180
15. First-Line Supervisors/Managers of Mechanics, Installers, and Repairers	$57,300	7.3%	24,361
16. Transportation Inspectors	$55,250	16.4%	2,122
17. Fire Inspectors and Investigators	$53,030	11.0%	644
18. Sales Representatives, Wholesale and Manufacturing, Except Technical and Scientific Products	$51,330	8.4%	156,215
19. First-Line Supervisors/Managers of Transportation and Material-Moving Machine and Vehicle Operators	$51,320	10.2%	16,580
20. Emergency Management Specialists	$50,460	12.3%	1,538

Best-Paying Jobs Requiring Work Experience in a Related Occupation

Job	Annual Earnings	Percent Growth	Annual Openings
21. First-Line Supervisors/Managers of Production and Operating Workers	$50,440	–4.8%	46,144
22. Construction and Building Inspectors	$50,180	18.2%	12,606

Best-Paying Jobs Requiring Postsecondary Vocational Training

Job	Annual Earnings	Percent Growth	Annual Openings
1. Commercial Pilots	$65,340	13.2%	1,425
2. Electrical and Electronics Repairers, Powerhouse, Substation, and Relay	$61,040	–4.7%	1,591
3. Telecommunications Equipment Installers and Repairers, Except Line Installers	$55,600	2.5%	13,541
4. Insurance Appraisers, Auto Damage	$53,440	12.5%	1,030
5. Aircraft Mechanics and Service Technicians	$51,390	10.6%	9,708
6. Electrical and Electronics Drafters	$51,320	4.1%	4,786
7. Court Reporters	$49,710	24.5%	2,620
8. Avionics Technicians	$49,310	8.1%	1,193
9. Electrical and Electronics Repairers, Commercial and Industrial Equipment	$48,430	6.8%	6,607

Best-Paying Jobs Requiring an Associate Degree

Job	Annual Earnings	Percent Growth	Annual Openings
1. Computer Specialists, All Other	$75,150	15.1%	14,374
2. Radiation Therapists	$72,910	24.8%	1,461
3. Nuclear Technicians	$67,890	6.7%	1,021
4. Nuclear Medicine Technologists	$66,660	14.8%	1,290
5. Dental Hygienists	$66,570	30.1%	10,433
6. Registered Nurses	$62,450	23.5%	233,499
7. Diagnostic Medical Sonographers	$61,980	19.1%	3,211
8. Fashion Designers	$61,160	5.0%	1,968
9. Aerospace Engineering and Operations Technicians	$55,040	10.4%	707
10. Geological and Petroleum Technicians	$53,360	8.6%	1,895

(continued)

(continued)

Best-Paying Jobs Requiring an Associate Degree

Job	Annual Earnings	Percent Growth	Annual Openings
11. Electrical and Electronic Engineering Technicians	$53,240	3.6%	12,583
12. Funeral Directors	$52,210	12.5%	3,939
13. Radiologic Technologists and Technicians	$52,210	15.1%	12,836
14. Respiratory Therapists	$52,200	22.6%	5,563
15. Fish and Game Wardens	$48,930	–0.2%	576
16. Occupational Therapist Assistants	$48,230	25.4%	2,634
17. Mechanical Engineering Technicians	$48,130	6.4%	3,710

Best-Paying Jobs Requiring a Bachelor's Degree

Job	Annual Earnings	Percent Growth	Annual Openings
1. Airline Pilots, Copilots, and Flight Engineers	$111,680	12.9%	4,073
2. Petroleum Engineers	$108,020	5.2%	1,016
3. Computer Hardware Engineers	$97,400	4.6%	3,572
4. Nuclear Engineers	$97,080	7.2%	1,046
5. Aerospace Engineers	$92,520	10.2%	6,498
6. Computer Software Engineers, Systems Software	$92,430	28.2%	33,139
7. Electronics Engineers, Except Computer	$86,370	3.7%	5,699
8. Computer Software Engineers, Applications	$85,430	44.6%	58,690
9. Chemical Engineers	$84,680	7.9%	2,111
10. Sales Engineers	$83,100	8.5%	7,371
11. Electrical Engineers	$82,160	6.3%	6,806
12. Materials Engineers	$81,820	4.0%	1,390
13. Atmospheric and Space Scientists	$81,290	10.6%	735
14. Materials Scientists	$80,230	8.7%	1,039
15. Construction Managers	$79,860	15.7%	44,158
16. Biomedical Engineers	$77,400	21.1%	1,804
17. Mining and Geological Engineers, Including Mining Safety Engineers	$75,960	10.0%	456
18. Computer Systems Analysts	$75,500	29.0%	63,166
19. Mechanical Engineers	$74,920	4.2%	12,394
20. Civil Engineers	$74,600	18.0%	15,979
21. Marine Engineers and Naval Architects	$74,140	10.9%	495
22. Environmental Engineers	$74,020	25.4%	5,003

Best-Paying Jobs Requiring a Bachelor's Degree

Job	Annual Earnings	Percent Growth	Annual Openings
23. Industrial Engineers	$73,820	20.3%	11,272
24. Financial Analysts	$73,150	33.8%	29,317
25. Health and Safety Engineers, Except Mining Safety Engineers and Inspectors	$72,490	9.6%	1,105
26. Network Systems and Data Communications Analysts	$71,100	53.4%	35,086
27. Financial Examiners	$70,930	10.7%	2,449
28. Architects, Except Landscape and Naval	$70,320	17.7%	11,324
29. Database Administrators	$69,740	28.6%	8,258
30. Computer Programmers	$69,620	–4.1%	27,937
31. Personal Financial Advisors	$69,050	41.0%	17,114
32. Agricultural Engineers	$68,730	8.6%	225
33. Securities, Commodities, and Financial Services Sales Agents	$68,680	24.8%	47,750
34. Logisticians	$66,480	17.3%	9,671
35. Network and Computer Systems Administrators	$66,310	27.0%	37,010
36. Chemists	$66,230	9.1%	9,024
37. Budget Analysts	$65,320	7.1%	6,423
38. Orthotists and Prosthetists	$62,590	11.8%	295
39. Occupational Health and Safety Specialists	$62,250	8.1%	3,440
40. Technical Writers	$61,620	19.5%	7,498
41. Market Research Analysts	$61,070	20.1%	45,015
42. Food Scientists and Technologists	$59,520	10.3%	663
43. Accountants and Auditors	$59,430	17.7%	134,463
44. Landscape Architects	$58,960	16.4%	2,342
45. Conservation Scientists	$58,720	5.3%	1,161
46. Soil and Plant Scientists	$58,390	8.4%	850
47. Commercial and Industrial Designers	$57,350	7.2%	4,777
48. Insurance Underwriters	$56,790	6.3%	6,880
49. Cost Estimators	$56,510	18.5%	38,379
50. Multi-Media Artists and Animators	$56,330	25.8%	13,182
51. Animal Scientists	$56,030	9.8%	299
52. Social and Community Service Managers	$55,980	24.7%	23,788
53. Zoologists and Wildlife Biologists	$55,290	8.7%	1,444
54. Credit Analysts	$55,250	1.9%	3,180
55. Loan Officers	$54,700	11.5%	54,237
56. Compensation, Benefits, and Job Analysis Specialists	$53,860	18.4%	18,761
57. Foresters	$53,750	5.1%	772

(continued)

(continued)

Best-Paying Jobs Requiring a Bachelor's Degree

Job	Annual Earnings	Percent Growth	Annual Openings
58. Medical and Clinical Laboratory Technologists	$53,500	12.4%	11,457
59. Writers and Authors	$53,070	12.8%	24,023
60. Surveyors	$52,980	23.7%	14,305
61. Special Education Teachers, Secondary School	$51,340	8.5%	10,601
62. Public Relations Specialists	$51,280	17.6%	51,216
63. Cartographers and Photogrammetrists	$51,180	20.3%	2,823
64. Secondary School Teachers, Except Special and Vocational Education	$51,180	5.6%	93,166
65. Special Education Teachers, Middle School	$50,810	15.8%	8,846
66. Dietitians and Nutritionists	$50,590	8.6%	4,996
67. Film and Video Editors	$50,560	12.7%	2,707
68. Special Education Teachers, Preschool, Kindergarten, and Elementary School	$50,020	19.6%	20,049
69. Editors	$49,990	2.3%	20,193
70. Forensic Science Technicians	$49,860	30.7%	3,074
71. Middle School Teachers, Except Special and Vocational Education	$49,700	11.2%	75,270
72. Elementary School Teachers, Except Special Education	$49,330	13.6%	181,612
73. Tax Examiners, Collectors, and Revenue Agents	$48,100	2.1%	4,465

Best-Paying Jobs Requiring Work Experience Plus Degree

Job	Annual Earnings	Percent Growth	Annual Openings
1. Chief Executives	$158,560	2.0%	21,209
2. Engineering Managers	$115,270	7.3%	7,404
3. Natural Sciences Managers	$112,800	11.4%	3,661
4. Computer and Information Systems Managers	$112,210	16.4%	30,887
5. Judges, Magistrate Judges, and Magistrates	$110,220	5.1%	1,567
6. Marketing Managers	$108,580	14.4%	20,189
7. Financial Managers	$99,330	12.6%	57,589
8. Sales Managers	$97,260	10.2%	36,392
9. General and Operations Managers	$91,570	1.5%	112,072
10. Public Relations Managers	$89,430	16.9%	5,781
11. Purchasing Managers	$89,160	3.4%	7,243
12. Training and Development Managers	$87,700	15.6%	3,759

Best-Paying Jobs Requiring Work Experience Plus Degree

Job	Annual Earnings	Percent Growth	Annual Openings
13. Compensation and Benefits Managers	$86,500	12.0%	6,121
14. Actuaries	$84,810	23.7%	3,245
15. Education Administrators, Elementary and Secondary School	$83,880	7.6%	27,143
16. Education Administrators, Postsecondary	$80,670	14.2%	17,121
17. Medical and Health Services Managers	$80,240	16.4%	31,877
18. Advertising and Promotions Managers	$80,220	6.2%	2,955
19. Art Directors	$76,980	9.0%	9,719
20. Administrative Law Judges, Adjudicators, and Hearing Officers	$76,940	0.1%	794
21. Management Analysts	$73,570	21.9%	125,669
22. Administrative Services Managers	$73,520	11.7%	19,513
23. Producers and Directors	$64,430	11.1%	8,992
24. Agents and Business Managers of Artists, Performers, and Athletes	$62,940	9.6%	3,940
25. Farm, Ranch, and Other Agricultural Managers	$56,230	1.1%	18,101
26. Vocational Education Teachers, Secondary School	$51,580	–4.6%	7,639
27. Training and Development Specialists	$51,450	18.3%	35,862
28. Broadcast News Analysts	$51,260	6.0%	1,444
29. Arbitrators, Mediators, and Conciliators	$50,660	10.6%	546

Best-Paying Jobs Requiring a Master's Degree

Job	Annual Earnings	Percent Growth	Annual Openings
1. Political Scientists	$104,130	5.3%	318
2. Economists	$83,590	7.5%	1,555
3. Physician Assistants	$81,230	27.0%	7,147
4. Geoscientists, Except Hydrologists and Geographers	$79,160	21.9%	2,471
5. Industrial-Organizational Psychologists	$77,010	21.3%	118
6. Physical Therapists	$72,790	27.1%	12,072
7. Statisticians	$72,610	8.5%	3,433
8. Hydrologists	$71,450	24.3%	687
9. Operations Research Analysts	$69,000	10.6%	5,727
10. Sociologists	$68,570	10.0%	403
11. Occupational Therapists	$66,780	23.1%	8,338
12. Geographers	$66,600	6.1%	75

(continued)

(continued)

Best-Paying Jobs Requiring a Master's Degree

Job	Annual Earnings	Percent Growth	Annual Openings
13. Speech-Language Pathologists	$62,930	10.6%	11,160
14. Epidemiologists	$61,360	13.6%	503
15. Urban and Regional Planners	$59,810	14.5%	1,967
16. Environmental Scientists and Specialists, Including Health	$59,750	25.1%	6,961
17. Instructional Coordinators	$56,880	22.5%	21,294
18. Historians	$54,530	7.8%	245
19. Anthropologists and Archeologists	$53,910	15.0%	446
20. Librarians	$52,530	3.6%	18,945
21. Educational, Vocational, and School Counselors	$51,050	12.6%	54,025

Best-Paying Jobs Requiring a Doctoral Degree

Job	Annual Earnings	Percent Growth	Annual Openings
1. Physicists	$102,890	6.8%	1,302
2. Astronomers	$101,300	5.6%	128
3. Computer and Information Scientists, Research	$97,970	21.5%	2,901
4. Mathematicians	$95,150	10.2%	473
5. Health Specialties Teachers, Postsecondary	$84,390	22.9%	19,617
6. Biochemists and Biophysicists	$82,840	15.9%	1,637
7. Engineering Teachers, Postsecondary	$82,810	22.9%	5,565
8. Economics Teachers, Postsecondary	$80,130	22.9%	2,208
9. Atmospheric, Earth, Marine, and Space Sciences Teachers, Postsecondary	$76,050	22.9%	1,553
10. Agricultural Sciences Teachers, Postsecondary	$74,390	22.9%	1,840
11. Physics Teachers, Postsecondary	$74,390	22.9%	2,155
12. Medical Scientists, Except Epidemiologists	$72,590	20.2%	10,596
13. Architecture Teachers, Postsecondary	$71,710	22.9%	1,044
14. Biological Science Teachers, Postsecondary	$70,650	22.9%	9,039
15. Business Teachers, Postsecondary	$68,000	22.9%	11,643
16. Anthropology and Archeology Teachers, Postsecondary	$67,750	22.9%	910
17. Chemistry Teachers, Postsecondary	$67,240	22.9%	3,405
18. Political Science Teachers, Postsecondary	$67,200	22.9%	2,435
19. Computer Science Teachers, Postsecondary	$66,440	22.9%	5,820

Best-Paying Jobs Requiring a Doctoral Degree

Job	Annual Earnings	Percent Growth	Annual Openings
20. Environmental Science Teachers, Postsecondary	$65,130	22.9%	769
21. Microbiologists	$64,350	11.2%	1,306
22. Home Economics Teachers, Postsecondary	$64,210	22.9%	820
23. Clinical, Counseling, and School Psychologists	$64,140	15.8%	8,309
24. Psychology Teachers, Postsecondary	$63,630	22.9%	5,261
25. Geography Teachers, Postsecondary	$62,880	22.9%	697
26. Forestry and Conservation Science Teachers, Postsecondary	$62,140	22.9%	454
27. History Teachers, Postsecondary	$62,000	22.9%	3,570
28. Area, Ethnic, and Cultural Studies Teachers, Postsecondary	$61,490	22.9%	1,252
29. Sociology Teachers, Postsecondary	$61,280	22.9%	2,774
30. Mathematical Science Teachers, Postsecondary	$61,120	22.9%	7,663
31. Philosophy and Religion Teachers, Postsecondary	$59,540	22.9%	3,120
32. Nursing Instructors and Teachers, Postsecondary	$59,210	22.9%	7,337
33. Social Work Teachers, Postsecondary	$59,140	22.9%	1,292
34. Library Science Teachers, Postsecondary	$58,570	22.9%	702
35. Art, Drama, and Music Teachers, Postsecondary	$57,820	22.9%	12,707
36. Communications Teachers, Postsecondary	$57,760	22.9%	4,074
37. Education Teachers, Postsecondary	$56,400	22.9%	9,359
38. English Language and Literature Teachers, Postsecondary	$56,380	22.9%	10,475
39. Foreign Language and Literature Teachers, Postsecondary	$55,570	22.9%	4,317
40. Recreation and Fitness Studies Teachers, Postsecondary	$55,140	22.9%	3,010
41. Criminal Justice and Law Enforcement Teachers, Postsecondary	$53,640	22.9%	1,911

Best-Paying Jobs Requiring a First Professional Degree

Job	Annual Earnings	Percent Growth	Annual Openings
1. Oral and Maxillofacial Surgeons	$166,400+	9.1%	400
2. Orthodontists	$166,400+	9.2%	479
3. Physicians and Surgeons	$166,400+	14.2%	38,027
4. Prosthodontists	$166,400+	10.7%	54
5. Dentists, General	$142,870	9.2%	7,106
6. Podiatrists	$113,560	9.5%	648
7. Lawyers	$110,590	11.0%	49,445

(continued)

(continued)

Best-Paying Jobs Requiring a First Professional Degree

Job	Annual Earnings	Percent Growth	Annual Openings
8. Pharmacists	$106,410	21.7%	16,358
9. Optometrists	$96,320	11.3%	1,789
10. Law Teachers, Postsecondary	$93,210	22.9%	2,169
11. Veterinarians	$79,050	35.0%	5,301
12. Chiropractors	$66,490	14.4%	3,179
13. Audiologists	$62,030	9.8%	980

Best-Paying Jobs Lists Based on Career Clusters

This group of lists organizes the 250 best-paying jobs into 16 career clusters. You can use these lists to identify jobs quickly based on your interests and on the industries that appeal to you.

Find the career cluster or clusters that interest you most. Then review the jobs in those areas to identify jobs you want to explore in more detail and look up their descriptions in Part II. You can also review career clusters where you have had past experience, education, or training to see if other jobs in those clusters would meet your current requirements.

You might notice that occasionally one occupation is listed in more than one cluster. For example, Accountants and Auditors appears in the list for Business, Management, and Administration and also in the list for Government and Public Administration. In fact, Accountants and Auditors are employed in *all* industries, but the work tasks of the job cause it to fit best in these two clusters. Consider reviewing several career clusters to find jobs that you might otherwise overlook.

Within each career cluster, jobs are listed in order of their earnings, from highest to lowest. As in the previous lists, jobs that have equal earnings are ordered alphabetically.

Note: The 16 career clusters used in these lists are those that were developed by the U.S. Department of Education's Office of Vocational and Adult Education around 1999 and that presently are being used by many states to organize their career-oriented programs and career information. They also form the structure of the *New Guide for Occupational Exploration*, Fourth Edition, published by JIST.

Descriptions of the 16 Career Clusters

Brief descriptions of the 16 career clusters we use in the lists follow. The descriptions are derived from the *New Guide for Occupational Exploration,* Fourth Edition. Some of them refer to jobs (as examples) that aren't included in this book.

❋ Agriculture, Food, and Natural Resources. *Work with plants, animals, forests, or mineral resources for agriculture, horticulture, conservation, extraction, and other purposes.* In this cluster you can work in farming, landscaping, forestry, fishing, mining, and related fields. You might like doing physical work outdoors, such as on a farm or ranch, in a forest, or on a drilling rig. If you have a scientific curiosity, you could study plants and animals or analyze biological or rock samples in a lab. If you have management ability, you could own, operate, or manage a fish hatchery, a landscaping business, or a greenhouse.

❋ Architecture and Construction. *Work designing, assembling, and maintaining components of buildings and other structures.* You might want to be part of the team of architects, drafters, and others who design buildings and render plans. If construction interests you, you might find fulfillment in the many building projects that are being undertaken at all times. If you like to organize and plan, you can find careers in managing these projects. Or you can play a more direct role in putting up and finishing buildings by doing jobs such as plumbing, carpentry, masonry, painting, or roofing, either as a skilled craftsworker or as a helper. You can prepare the building site by operating heavy equipment or installing, maintaining, and repairing vital building equipment and systems such as electricity and heating.

❋ Arts, Audio/Video Technology, and Communications. *Work in creatively expressing feelings or ideas, in communicating news or information, or in performing.* This cluster involves creative, verbal, or performing activities. For example, if you enjoy literature, perhaps writing or editing would appeal to you. Journalism and public relations are other fields for people who like to use their writing or speaking skills. Do you prefer to work in the performing arts? If so, you could direct or perform in drama, music, or dance. If you especially enjoy the visual arts, you could create paintings, sculpture, or ceramics or design products or visual displays. A flair for technology might lead you to specialize in photography, broadcast production, or dispatching.

❋ Business, Management, and Administration. *Work that makes a business organization or function run smoothly.* In this cluster, you can work in a position of leadership or specialize in a function that contributes to the overall effort in a business, a nonprofit organization, or a government agency. If you especially enjoy working with people, you might find fulfillment from working in human resources. An interest in numbers might lead you to consider accounting, finance, budgeting, billing, or financial record-keeping. A job as an administrative assistant might interest you if you like a variety of tasks in a busy environment. If you are good with details and word processing, you might enjoy a job as an administrative assistant or data-entry clerk. Or perhaps you would do well as the manager of a business.

❋ **Education and Training.** *Work that helps people learn.* In this cluster, your students might be preschoolers, retirees, or any age in between. You might specialize in a particular academic field or work with learners of a particular age, with a particular interest, or with a particular learning problem. Working in a library or museum might give you an opportunity to expand people's understanding of the world.

❋ **Finance.** *Work that helps businesses and people be assured of a financially secure future.* This cluster involves work in a financial or insurance business in a leadership or support role. If you like gathering and analyzing information, you might find fulfillment as an insurance adjuster or financial analyst. Or you might deal with information at the clerical level as a banking or insurance clerk or in person-to-person situations providing customer service. Another way to interact with people is to sell financial or insurance services that will meet their needs.

❋ **Government and Public Administration.** *Work that helps a government agency serve the needs of the public.* In this cluster you can work in a position of leadership or specialize in a function that contributes to the role of government. You might help protect the public by working as an inspector or examiner to enforce standards. If you enjoy using clerical skills, you could work as a clerk in a law court or government office. Or perhaps you prefer the top-down perspective of a government executive or urban planner.

❋ **Health Science.** *Work that helps people and animals be healthy.* This cluster involves working on a health-care team as a professional, therapist, or nurse. You might specialize in one of the many different parts of the body (such as the teeth or eyes) or in one of the many different types of care. Or you might want to be a generalist who deals with the whole patient. If you like technology, you might find satisfaction working with X-rays or new diagnostic methods. You might work with relatively healthy people, helping them to eat better. If you enjoy working with animals, you might care for them and keep them healthy.

❋ **Hospitality and Tourism.** *Work that caters to the personal wishes and needs of others so that they can enjoy a clean environment, good food and drink, comfortable lodging away from home, and recreation.* You can work in this cluster by providing services for the convenience, care, and pampering of others in hotels, restaurants, airplanes, beauty salons, and so on. You might want to use your love of cooking as a chef. If you like working with people, you might want to provide personal services by being a travel guide, a flight attendant, a concierge, a hairstylist, or a waiter. You might want to work in cleaning and building services if you like a clean environment. If you enjoy sports or games, you could work for an athletic team or casino.

❋ **Human Service.** *Work that improves people's social, mental, emotional, or spiritual well-being.* Workers in this cluster include counselors, social workers, or religious workers who help people sort out their complicated lives or solve personal problems. You might work as a caretaker for very young people or the elderly. Or you might interview people to help identify the social services they need.

❋ **Information Technology.** *Work that designs, develops, manages, and supports information systems.* This cluster involves working with hardware, software, multimedia, or integrated systems. If you like to use your organizational skills, you might work as a systems, database, or Web administrator. Or you can solve complex problems as a software engineer or systems analyst. If you enjoy getting your hands on hardware, you might find work servicing computers, peripherals, and information-intense machines such as cash registers and ATMs.

❀ Law, Public Safety, Corrections, and Security. *Work that upholds people's rights or protects people and property by using authority, inspecting, or investigating.* In this cluster, you can work in law, law enforcement, fire fighting, the military, and related fields. For example, if you enjoy mental challenge and intrigue, you could investigate crimes or fires for a living. If you enjoy working with verbal skills and research skills, you might want to defend citizens in court or research deeds, wills, and other legal documents. If you want to help people in critical situations, you might want to fight fires, work as a police officer, or become a paramedic. Or, if you want more routine work in public safety, perhaps a job in guarding, patrolling, or inspecting would appeal to you. If you have management ability, you could seek a leadership position in law enforcement and the protective services. Work in the military gives you a chance to use technical and leadership skills while serving your country.

❀ Manufacturing. *Work that processes materials into intermediate or final products or that maintains and repairs products by using machines or hand tools.* In this cluster, you can work in one of many industries that mass-produce goods or work for a utility that distributes electrical power or other resources. You might enjoy manual work, using your hands or hand tools in highly skilled jobs such as assembling engines or electronic equipment. If you enjoy making machines run efficiently or fixing them when they break down, you could seek a job installing or repairing such devices as copiers, aircraft engines, cars, or watches. Perhaps you prefer to set up or operate machines that are used to manufacture products made of food, glass, or paper. You could enjoy cutting and grinding metal and plastic parts to desired shapes and measurements. Or you might want to operate equipment in systems that provide water and process wastewater. You might like inspecting, sorting, counting, or weighing products. Another option is to work with your hands and machinery to move boxes and freight in a warehouse. If leadership appeals to you, you could manage people engaged in production and repair.

❀ Marketing, Sales, and Service. *Work that anticipates the needs of people and organizations and communicates the benefits of products and services.* The jobs in this cluster involve understanding customer demand, using persuasion, and selling. If you like using knowledge of science, you might enjoy selling pharmaceutical, medical, or electronic products or services. Real estate offers several kinds of sales jobs as well. If you like speaking on the phone, you could work as a telemarketer. Or you might enjoy selling apparel and other merchandise in a retail setting. If you prefer to help people, you might want a job in customer service.

❀ Science, Technology, Engineering, and Mathematics. *Work that discovers, collects, and analyzes information about the natural world; applies scientific research findings to problems in medicine, the life sciences, human behavior, and the natural sciences; imagines and manipulates quantitative data; and applies technology to manufacturing, transportation, and other economic activities.* In this cluster, you can work with the knowledge and processes of the sciences. You might enjoy researching and developing new knowledge in mathematics, or perhaps solving problems in the physical, life, or social sciences would appeal to you. You might want to study engineering and help create new machines, processes, and structures. If you want to work with scientific equipment and procedures, you could seek a job in a research or testing laboratory.

❋ Transportation, Distribution, and Logistics. *Work in operations that move people or materials.* In this cluster, you can manage a transportation service, help vehicles keep on their assigned schedules and routes, or drive or pilot a vehicle. If you enjoy taking responsibility, perhaps managing a rail line would appeal to you. If you work well with details and can take pressure on the job, you might consider being an air traffic controller. Or would you rather get out on the highway, on the water, or up in the air? If so, you could drive a truck from state to state, be employed on a ship, or fly a crop duster over a cornfield. If you prefer to stay closer to home, you could drive a delivery van, taxi, or school bus. You could use your physical strength to load freight and arrange it so that it gets to its destination in one piece.

Best-Paying Jobs for People Interested in Agriculture, Food, and Natural Resources

Job	Annual Earnings	Percent Growth	Annual Openings
1. Economists	$83,590	7.5%	1,555
2. Biochemists and Biophysicists	$82,840	15.9%	1,637
3. Veterinarians	$79,050	35.0%	5,301
4. Agricultural Sciences Teachers, Postsecondary	$74,390	22.9%	1,840
5. Biological Science Teachers, Postsecondary	$70,650	22.9%	9,039
6. Environmental Science Teachers, Postsecondary	$65,130	22.9%	769
7. Environmental Scientists and Specialists, Including Health	$59,750	25.1%	6,961
8. Food Scientists and Technologists	$59,520	10.3%	663
9. Conservation Scientists	$58,720	5.3%	1,161
10. Soil and Plant Scientists	$58,390	8.4%	850
11. Farm, Ranch, and Other Agricultural Managers	$56,230	1.1%	18,101
12. Animal Scientists	$56,030	9.8%	299
13. Zoologists and Wildlife Biologists	$55,290	8.7%	1,444
14. Recreation and Fitness Studies Teachers, Postsecondary	$55,140	22.9%	3,010
15. Foresters	$53,750	5.1%	772
16. Geological and Petroleum Technicians	$53,360	8.6%	1,895
17. Rotary Drill Operators, Oil and Gas	$49,800	–5.4%	2,145

Best-Paying Jobs for People Interested in Agriculture, Food, and Natural Resources

Job	Annual Earnings	Percent Growth	Annual Openings
18. Purchasing Agents and Buyers, Farm Products	$49,670	–8.6%	1,618
19. Fish and Game Wardens	$48,930	–0.2%	576
20. Mechanical Engineering Technicians	$48,130	6.4%	3,710

Best-Paying Jobs for People Interested in Architecture and Construction

Job	Annual Earnings	Percent Growth	Annual Openings
1. Engineering Managers	$115,270	7.3%	7,404
2. Engineering Teachers, Postsecondary	$82,810	22.9%	5,565
3. Construction Managers	$79,860	15.7%	44,158
4. Architecture Teachers, Postsecondary	$71,710	22.9%	1,044
5. Architects, Except Landscape and Naval	$70,320	17.7%	11,324
6. Landscape Architects	$58,960	16.4%	2,342
7. First-Line Supervisors/Managers of Construction Trades and Extraction Workers	$58,140	9.1%	82,923
8. Cost Estimators	$56,510	18.5%	38,379
9. Electrical Power-Line Installers and Repairers	$55,100	7.2%	6,401
10. Surveyors	$52,980	23.7%	14,305
11. Boilermakers	$52,260	14.0%	2,333
12. Electrical and Electronics Drafters	$51,320	4.1%	4,786
13. Cartographers and Photogrammetrists	$51,180	20.3%	2,823
14. Construction and Building Inspectors	$50,180	18.2%	12,606

Best-Paying Jobs for People Interested in Arts, Audio/Video Technology, and Communications

Job	Annual Earnings	Percent Growth	Annual Openings
1. Art Directors	$76,980	9.0%	9,719
2. Producers and Directors	$64,430	11.1%	8,992
3. Agents and Business Managers of Artists, Performers, and Athletes	$62,940	9.6%	3,940

(continued)

(continued)

Best-Paying Jobs for People Interested in Arts, Audio/Video Technology, and Communications

Job	Annual Earnings	Percent Growth	Annual Openings
4. Technical Writers	$61,620	19.5%	7,498
5. Fashion Designers	$61,160	5.0%	1,968
6. Art, Drama, and Music Teachers, Postsecondary	$57,820	22.9%	12,707
7. Communications Teachers, Postsecondary	$57,760	22.9%	4,074
8. Commercial and Industrial Designers	$57,350	7.2%	4,777
9. English Language and Literature Teachers, Postsecondary	$56,380	22.9%	10,475
10. Multi-Media Artists and Animators	$56,330	25.8%	13,182
11. Telecommunications Equipment Installers and Repairers, Except Line Installers	$55,600	2.5%	13,541
12. Historians	$54,530	7.8%	245
13. Writers and Authors	$53,070	12.8%	24,023
14. Public Relations Specialists	$51,280	17.6%	51,216
15. Broadcast News Analysts	$51,260	6.0%	1,444
16. Film and Video Editors	$50,560	12.7%	2,707
17. Editors	$49,990	2.3%	20,193

Best-Paying Jobs for People Interested in Business, Management, and Administration

Job	Annual Earnings	Percent Growth	Annual Openings
1. Chief Executives	$158,560	2.0%	21,209
2. Natural Sciences Managers	$112,800	11.4%	3,661
3. Computer and Information Systems Managers	$112,210	16.4%	30,887
4. Financial Managers	$99,330	12.6%	57,589
5. Sales Managers	$97,260	10.2%	36,392
6. General and Operations Managers	$91,570	1.5%	112,072
7. Public Relations Managers	$89,430	16.9%	5,781
8. Purchasing Managers	$89,160	3.4%	7,243
9. Training and Development Managers	$87,700	15.6%	3,759
10. Compensation and Benefits Managers	$86,500	12.0%	6,121
11. Economists	$83,590	7.5%	1,555
12. Industrial Production Managers	$83,290	–5.9%	14,889

Best-Paying Jobs for People Interested in Business, Management, and Administration

Job	Annual Earnings	Percent Growth	Annual Openings
13. Advertising and Promotions Managers	$80,220	6.2%	2,955
14. Economics Teachers, Postsecondary	$80,130	22.9%	2,208
15. Construction Managers	$79,860	15.7%	44,158
16. Transportation, Storage, and Distribution Managers	$79,000	8.3%	6,994
17. Management Analysts	$73,570	21.9%	125,669
18. Administrative Services Managers	$73,520	11.7%	19,513
19. Financial Analysts	$73,150	33.8%	29,317
20. Statisticians	$72,610	8.5%	3,433
21. Financial Examiners	$70,930	10.7%	2,449
22. Database Administrators	$69,740	28.6%	8,258
23. Operations Research Analysts	$69,000	10.6%	5,727
24. Business Teachers, Postsecondary	$68,000	22.9%	11,643
25. Logisticians	$66,480	17.3%	9,671
26. Budget Analysts	$65,320	7.1%	6,423
27. Agents and Business Managers of Artists, Performers, and Athletes	$62,940	9.6%	3,940
28. Technical Writers	$61,620	19.5%	7,498
29. Market Research Analysts	$61,070	20.1%	45,015
30. Accountants and Auditors	$59,430	17.7%	134,463
31. Communications Teachers, Postsecondary	$57,760	22.9%	4,074
32. First-Line Supervisors/Managers of Mechanics, Installers, and Repairers	$57,300	7.3%	24,361
33. Cost Estimators	$56,510	18.5%	38,379
34. Social and Community Service Managers	$55,980	24.7%	23,788
35. Postal Service Clerks	$55,920	1.2%	3,703
36. Credit Analysts	$55,250	1.9%	3,180
37. Compensation, Benefits, and Job Analysis Specialists	$53,860	18.4%	18,761
38. Training and Development Specialists	$51,450	18.3%	35,862
39. Public Relations Specialists	$51,280	17.6%	51,216
40. Postal Service Mail Sorters, Processors, and Processing Machine Operators	$50,600	–8.4%	6,855
41. First-Line Supervisors/Managers of Production and Operating Workers	$50,440	–4.8%	46,144
42. Postal Service Mail Carriers	$50,290	1.0%	16,710

Best-Paying Jobs for People Interested in Education and Training

Job	Annual Earnings	Percent Growth	Annual Openings
1. Health Specialties Teachers, Postsecondary	$84,390	22.9%	19,617
2. Education Administrators, Elementary and Secondary School	$83,880	7.6%	27,143
3. Engineering Teachers, Postsecondary	$82,810	22.9%	5,565
4. Education Administrators, Postsecondary	$80,670	14.2%	17,121
5. Atmospheric, Earth, Marine, and Space Sciences Teachers, Postsecondary	$76,050	22.9%	1,553
6. Agricultural Sciences Teachers, Postsecondary	$74,390	22.9%	1,840
7. Architecture Teachers, Postsecondary	$71,710	22.9%	1,044
8. Business Teachers, Postsecondary	$68,000	22.9%	11,643
9. Environmental Science Teachers, Postsecondary	$65,130	22.9%	769
10. Psychology Teachers, Postsecondary	$63,630	22.9%	5,261
11. Geography Teachers, Postsecondary	$62,880	22.9%	697
12. Forestry and Conservation Science Teachers, Postsecondary	$62,140	22.9%	454
13. Social Work Teachers, Postsecondary	$59,140	22.9%	1,292
14. Library Science Teachers, Postsecondary	$58,570	22.9%	702
15. Instructional Coordinators	$56,880	22.5%	21,294
16. Education Teachers, Postsecondary	$56,400	22.9%	9,359
17. English Language and Literature Teachers, Postsecondary	$56,380	22.9%	10,475
18. Foreign Language and Literature Teachers, Postsecondary	$55,570	22.9%	4,317
19. Recreation and Fitness Studies Teachers, Postsecondary	$55,140	22.9%	3,010
20. Historians	$54,530	7.8%	245
21. Criminal Justice and Law Enforcement Teachers, Postsecondary	$53,640	22.9%	1,911
22. Librarians	$52,530	3.6%	18,945
23. Vocational Education Teachers, Secondary School	$51,580	–4.6%	7,639
24. Special Education Teachers, Secondary School	$51,340	8.5%	10,601
25. Secondary School Teachers, Except Special and Vocational Education	$51,180	5.6%	93,166
26. Educational, Vocational, and School Counselors	$51,050	12.6%	54,025
27. Special Education Teachers, Middle School	$50,810	15.8%	8,846
28. Dietitians and Nutritionists	$50,590	8.6%	4,996
29. Special Education Teachers, Preschool, Kindergarten, and Elementary School	$50,020	19.6%	20,049
30. Middle School Teachers, Except Special and Vocational Education	$49,700	11.2%	75,270
31. Elementary School Teachers, Except Special Education	$49,330	13.6%	181,612

Best-Paying Jobs for People Interested in Finance

Job	Annual Earnings	Percent Growth	Annual Openings
1. Financial Managers	$99,330	12.6%	57,589
2. Actuaries	$84,810	23.7%	3,245
3. Financial Analysts	$73,150	33.8%	29,317
4. Personal Financial Advisors	$69,050	41.0%	17,114
5. Securities, Commodities, and Financial Services Sales Agents	$68,680	24.8%	47,750
6. Business Teachers, Postsecondary	$68,000	22.9%	11,643
7. Budget Analysts	$65,320	7.1%	6,423
8. Insurance Underwriters	$56,790	6.3%	6,880
9. Claims Adjusters, Examiners, and Investigators	$55,760	8.9%	22,024
10. Credit Analysts	$55,250	1.9%	3,180
11. Loan Officers	$54,700	11.5%	54,237
12. Insurance Appraisers, Auto Damage	$53,440	12.5%	1,030

Best-Paying Jobs for People Interested in Government and Public Administration

Job	Annual Earnings	Percent Growth	Annual Openings
1. Chief Executives	$158,560	2.0%	21,209
2. Political Scientists	$104,130	5.3%	318
3. General and Operations Managers	$91,570	1.5%	112,072
4. Transportation, Storage, and Distribution Managers	$79,000	8.3%	6,994
5. Administrative Services Managers	$73,520	11.7%	19,513
6. Financial Examiners	$70,930	10.7%	2,449
7. Political Science Teachers, Postsecondary	$67,200	22.9%	2,435
8. Urban and Regional Planners	$59,810	14.5%	1,967
9. Accountants and Auditors	$59,430	17.7%	134,463
10. Postmasters and Mail Superintendents	$59,310	–0.8%	1,627
11. Social and Community Service Managers	$55,980	24.7%	23,788
12. Emergency Management Specialists	$50,460	12.3%	1,538
13. Tax Examiners, Collectors, and Revenue Agents	$48,100	2.1%	4,465

Best-Paying Jobs for People Interested in Health Science

Job	Annual Earnings	Percent Growth	Annual Openings
1. Oral and Maxillofacial Surgeons	$166,400+	9.1%	400
2. Orthodontists	$166,400+	9.2%	479
3. Prosthodontists	$166,400+	10.7%	54
4. Dentists, General	$142,870	9.2%	7,106
5. Podiatrists	$113,560	9.5%	648
6. Pharmacists	$106,410	21.7%	16,358
7. Optometrists	$96,320	11.3%	1,789
8. Health Specialties Teachers, Postsecondary	$84,390	22.9%	19,617
9. Physician Assistants	$81,230	27.0%	7,147
10. Medical and Health Services Managers	$80,240	16.4%	31,877
11. Veterinarians	$79,050	35.0%	5,301
12. Industrial-Organizational Psychologists	$77,010	21.3%	118
13. Radiation Therapists	$72,910	24.8%	1,461
14. Physical Therapists	$72,790	27.1%	12,072
15. Medical Scientists, Except Epidemiologists	$72,590	20.2%	10,596
16. Nuclear Technicians	$67,890	6.7%	1,021
17. Occupational Therapists	$66,780	23.1%	8,338
18. Nuclear Medicine Technologists	$66,660	14.8%	1,290
19. Dental Hygienists	$66,570	30.1%	10,433
20. Chiropractors	$66,490	14.4%	3,179
21. Home Economics Teachers, Postsecondary	$64,210	22.9%	820
22. Clinical, Counseling, and School Psychologists	$64,140	15.8%	8,309
23. Psychology Teachers, Postsecondary	$63,630	22.9%	5,261
24. Speech-Language Pathologists	$62,930	10.6%	11,160
25. Orthotists and Prosthetists	$62,590	11.8%	295
26. Registered Nurses	$62,450	23.5%	233,499
27. Occupational Health and Safety Specialists	$62,250	8.1%	3,440
28. Audiologists	$62,030	9.8%	980
29. Diagnostic Medical Sonographers	$61,980	19.1%	3,211
30. Nursing Instructors and Teachers, Postsecondary	$59,210	22.9%	7,337
31. Medical and Clinical Laboratory Technologists	$53,500	12.4%	11,457
32. Radiologic Technologists and Technicians	$52,210	15.1%	12,836
33. Respiratory Therapists	$52,200	22.6%	5,563
34. Dietitians and Nutritionists	$50,590	8.6%	4,996
35. Occupational Therapist Assistants	$48,230	25.4%	2,634

Best-Paying Jobs for People Interested in Hospitality and Tourism

Job	Annual Earnings	Percent Growth	Annual Openings
1. Gaming Managers	$68,290	24.4%	549

Best-Paying Jobs for People Interested in Human Service

Job	Annual Earnings	Percent Growth	Annual Openings
1. Sociologists	$68,570	10.0%	403
2. Home Economics Teachers, Postsecondary	$64,210	22.9%	820
3. Clinical, Counseling, and School Psychologists	$64,140	15.8%	8,309
4. Psychology Teachers, Postsecondary	$63,630	22.9%	5,261
5. Area, Ethnic, and Cultural Studies Teachers, Postsecondary	$61,490	22.9%	1,252
6. Epidemiologists	$61,360	13.6%	503
7. Philosophy and Religion Teachers, Postsecondary	$59,540	22.9%	3,120
8. Social Work Teachers, Postsecondary	$59,140	22.9%	1,292
9. Social and Community Service Managers	$55,980	24.7%	23,788
10. Funeral Directors	$52,210	12.5%	3,939
11. Emergency Management Specialists	$50,460	12.3%	1,538

Best-Paying Jobs for People Interested in Information Technology

Job	Annual Earnings	Percent Growth	Annual Openings
1. Engineering Managers	$115,270	7.3%	7,404
2. Computer and Information Systems Managers	$112,210	16.4%	30,887
3. Computer and Information Scientists, Research	$97,970	21.5%	2,901
4. Computer Hardware Engineers	$97,400	4.6%	3,572
5. Computer Software Engineers, Systems Software	$92,430	28.2%	33,139
6. Computer Software Engineers, Applications	$85,430	44.6%	58,690
7. Engineering Teachers, Postsecondary	$82,810	22.9%	5,565
8. Computer Systems Analysts	$75,500	29.0%	63,166
9. Computer Specialists, All Other	$75,150	15.1%	14,374
10. Network Systems and Data Communications Analysts	$71,100	53.4%	35,086
11. Database Administrators	$69,740	28.6%	8,258
12. Computer Programmers	$69,620	–4.1%	27,937

(continued)

(continued)

Best-Paying Jobs for People Interested in Information Technology

Job	Annual Earnings	Percent Growth	Annual Openings
13. Computer Science Teachers, Postsecondary	$66,440	22.9%	5,820
14. Network and Computer Systems Administrators	$66,310	27.0%	37,010
15. Multi-Media Artists and Animators	$56,330	25.8%	13,182

Best-Paying Jobs for People Interested in Law, Public Safety, Corrections, and Security

Job	Annual Earnings	Percent Growth	Annual Openings
1. Lawyers	$110,590	11.0%	49,445
2. Judges, Magistrate Judges, and Magistrates	$110,220	5.1%	1,567
3. Law Teachers, Postsecondary	$93,210	22.9%	2,169
4. Administrative Law Judges, Adjudicators, and Hearing Officers	$76,940	0.1%	794
5. First-Line Supervisors/Managers of Police and Detectives	$75,490	9.2%	9,373
6. First-Line Supervisors/Managers of Fire Fighting and Prevention Workers	$67,440	11.5%	3,771
7. Detectives and Criminal Investigators	$60,910	17.3%	14,746
8. First-Line Supervisors/Managers of Correctional Officers	$57,380	12.5%	4,180
9. Criminal Justice and Law Enforcement Teachers, Postsecondary	$53,640	22.9%	1,911
10. Fire Inspectors and Investigators	$53,030	11.0%	644
11. Police and Sheriff's Patrol Officers	$51,410	10.8%	37,842
12. Arbitrators, Mediators, and Conciliators	$50,660	10.6%	546
13. Forensic Science Technicians	$49,860	30.7%	3,074
14. Court Reporters	$49,710	24.5%	2,620
15. Compliance Officers, Except Agriculture, Construction, Health and Safety, and Transportation	$48,890	4.9%	15,841

Best-Paying Jobs for People Interested in Manufacturing

Job	Annual Earnings	Percent Growth	Annual Openings
1. Nuclear Power Reactor Operators	$73,320	10.6%	233
2. Elevator Installers and Repairers	$69,380	8.8%	2,850

Best-Paying Jobs for People Interested in Manufacturing

Job	Annual Earnings	Percent Growth	Annual Openings
3. Nuclear Technicians	$67,890	6.7%	1,021
4. Occupational Health and Safety Specialists	$62,250	8.1%	3,440
5. Fashion Designers	$61,160	5.0%	1,968
6. Electrical and Electronics Repairers, Powerhouse, Substation, and Relay	$61,040	–4.7%	1,591
7. Power Plant Operators	$58,470	2.7%	1,796
8. First-Line Supervisors/Managers of Mechanics, Installers, and Repairers	$57,300	7.3%	24,361
9. Cost Estimators	$56,510	18.5%	38,379
10. Gas Plant Operators	$55,760	–9.9%	1,332
11. Petroleum Pump System Operators, Refinery Operators, and Gaugers	$55,010	–13.4%	4,477
12. Electrical and Electronic Engineering Technicians	$53,240	3.6%	12,583
13. Chemical Plant and System Operators	$52,480	–15.3%	5,620
14. First-Line Supervisors/Managers of Production and Operating Workers	$50,440	–4.8%	46,144
15. Stationary Engineers and Boiler Operators	$49,790	3.4%	1,892
16. Avionics Technicians	$49,310	8.1%	1,193
17. Electrical and Electronics Repairers, Commercial and Industrial Equipment	$48,430	6.8%	6,607
18. Mechanical Engineering Technicians	$48,130	6.4%	3,710
19. Telecommunications Line Installers and Repairers	$48,090	4.6%	14,719

Best-Paying Jobs for People Interested in Marketing, Sales, and Service

Job	Annual Earnings	Percent Growth	Annual Openings
1. Marketing Managers	$108,580	14.4%	20,189
2. Sales Managers	$97,260	10.2%	36,392
3. Sales Engineers	$83,100	8.5%	7,371
4. Advertising and Promotions Managers	$80,220	6.2%	2,955
5. Sales Representatives, Wholesale and Manufacturing, Technical and Scientific Products	$70,200	12.4%	43,469
6. First-Line Supervisors/Managers of Non-Retail Sales Workers	$68,100	3.7%	48,883
7. Business Teachers, Postsecondary	$68,000	22.9%	11,643
8. Market Research Analysts	$61,070	20.1%	45,015

(continued)

(continued)

Best-Paying Jobs for People Interested in Marketing, Sales, and Service

Job	Annual Earnings	Percent Growth	Annual Openings
9. Real Estate Brokers	$57,500	11.1%	18,689
10. Purchasing Agents, Except Wholesale, Retail, and Farm Products	$53,940	0.1%	22,349
11. Sales Representatives, Wholesale and Manufacturing, Except Technical and Scientific Products	$51,330	8.4%	156,215
12. Wholesale and Retail Buyers, Except Farm Products	$48,710	–0.1%	19,847

Best-Paying Jobs for People Interested in Science, Technology, Engineering, and Mathematics

Job	Annual Earnings	Percent Growth	Annual Openings
1. Engineering Managers	$115,270	7.3%	7,404
2. Natural Sciences Managers	$112,800	11.4%	3,661
3. Petroleum Engineers	$108,020	5.2%	1,016
4. Political Scientists	$104,130	5.3%	318
5. Physicists	$102,890	6.8%	1,302
6. Astronomers	$101,300	5.6%	128
7. Computer Hardware Engineers	$97,400	4.6%	3,572
8. Nuclear Engineers	$97,080	7.2%	1,046
9. Mathematicians	$95,150	10.2%	473
10. Aerospace Engineers	$92,520	10.2%	6,498
11. Electronics Engineers, Except Computer	$86,370	3.7%	5,699
12. Computer Software Engineers, Applications	$85,430	44.6%	58,690
13. Chemical Engineers	$84,680	7.9%	2,111
14. Health Specialties Teachers, Postsecondary	$84,390	22.9%	19,617
15. Economists	$83,590	7.5%	1,555
16. Biochemists and Biophysicists	$82,840	15.9%	1,637
17. Engineering Teachers, Postsecondary	$82,810	22.9%	5,565
18. Electrical Engineers	$82,160	6.3%	6,806
19. Materials Engineers	$81,820	4.0%	1,390
20. Atmospheric and Space Scientists	$81,290	10.6%	735
21. Materials Scientists	$80,230	8.7%	1,039
22. Economics Teachers, Postsecondary	$80,130	22.9%	2,208
23. Geoscientists, Except Hydrologists and Geographers	$79,160	21.9%	2,471

Best-Paying Jobs for People Interested in Science, Technology, Engineering, and Mathematics

Job	Annual Earnings	Percent Growth	Annual Openings
24. Biomedical Engineers	$77,400	21.1%	1,804
25. Atmospheric, Earth, Marine, and Space Sciences Teachers, Postsecondary	$76,050	22.9%	1,553
26. Mining and Geological Engineers, Including Mining Safety Engineers	$75,960	10.0%	456
27. Mechanical Engineers	$74,920	4.2%	12,394
28. Civil Engineers	$74,600	18.0%	15,979
29. Physics Teachers, Postsecondary	$74,390	22.9%	2,155
30. Marine Engineers and Naval Architects	$74,140	10.9%	495
31. Environmental Engineers	$74,020	25.4%	5,003
32. Industrial Engineers	$73,820	20.3%	11,272
33. Statisticians	$72,610	8.5%	3,433
34. Medical Scientists, Except Epidemiologists	$72,590	20.2%	10,596
35. Health and Safety Engineers, Except Mining Safety Engineers and Inspectors	$72,490	9.6%	1,105
36. Architecture Teachers, Postsecondary	$71,710	22.9%	1,044
37. Hydrologists	$71,450	24.3%	687
38. Biological Science Teachers, Postsecondary	$70,650	22.9%	9,039
39. Operations Research Analysts	$69,000	10.6%	5,727
40. Agricultural Engineers	$68,730	8.6%	225
41. Sociologists	$68,570	10.0%	403
42. Nuclear Technicians	$67,890	6.7%	1,021
43. Anthropology and Archeology Teachers, Postsecondary	$67,750	22.9%	910
44. Chemistry Teachers, Postsecondary	$67,240	22.9%	3,405
45. Political Science Teachers, Postsecondary	$67,200	22.9%	2,435
46. Geographers	$66,600	6.1%	75
47. Chemists	$66,230	9.1%	9,024
48. Microbiologists	$64,350	11.2%	1,306
49. Geography Teachers, Postsecondary	$62,880	22.9%	697
50. History Teachers, Postsecondary	$62,000	22.9%	3,570
51. Area, Ethnic, and Cultural Studies Teachers, Postsecondary	$61,490	22.9%	1,252
52. Epidemiologists	$61,360	13.6%	503
53. Mathematical Science Teachers, Postsecondary	$61,120	22.9%	7,663
54. Market Research Analysts	$61,070	20.1%	45,015
55. Cost Estimators	$56,510	18.5%	38,379

(continued)

(continued)

Best-Paying Jobs for People Interested in Science, Technology, Engineering, and Mathematics

Job	Annual Earnings	Percent Growth	Annual Openings
56. Zoologists and Wildlife Biologists	$55,290	8.7%	1,444
57. Historians	$54,530	7.8%	245
58. Anthropologists and Archeologists	$53,910	15.0%	446
59. Cartographers and Photogrammetrists	$51,180	20.3%	2,823
60. Dietitians and Nutritionists	$50,590	8.6%	4,996

Best-Paying Jobs for People Interested in Transportation, Distribution, and Logistics

Job	Annual Earnings	Percent Growth	Annual Openings
1. Air Traffic Controllers	$111,870	10.2%	1,213
2. Airline Pilots, Copilots, and Flight Engineers	$111,680	12.9%	4,073
3. Transportation, Storage, and Distribution Managers	$79,000	8.3%	6,994
4. Logisticians	$66,480	17.3%	9,671
5. Commercial Pilots	$65,340	13.2%	1,425
6. Captains, Mates, and Pilots of Water Vessels	$61,960	17.9%	2,665
7. Ship Engineers	$60,690	14.1%	1,102
8. Transportation Inspectors	$55,250	16.4%	2,122
9. Aerospace Engineering and Operations Technicians	$55,040	10.4%	707
10. Subway and Streetcar Operators	$53,220	12.1%	587
11. Railroad Conductors and Yardmasters	$52,830	9.1%	3,235
12. Aircraft Mechanics and Service Technicians	$51,390	10.6%	9,708
13. First-Line Supervisors/Managers of Transportation and Material-Moving Machine and Vehicle Operators	$51,320	10.2%	16,580
14. Avionics Technicians	$49,310	8.1%	1,193
15. Locomotive Engineers	$48,440	2.9%	3,548
16. Locomotive Firers	$48,190	2.9%	3,548

Jobs 15 and 16 share 3,548 openings with each other and with another job not in this book.

Best-Paying Jobs Lists Based on Personality Types

These lists organize the 250 best-paying jobs into groups matching six personality types. The personality types are Realistic, Investigative, Artistic, Social, Enterprising, and Conventional. This system was developed by John L. Holland and is used in the *Self-Directed Search (SDS)* and other career assessment inventories and information systems.

If you have used one of these career inventories or systems, the lists will help you identify jobs that most closely match these personality types. Even if you have not used one of these systems, the concept of personality types and the jobs that are related to them can help you identify jobs that most closely match the type of person you are.

We've ranked the best-paying jobs within each personality type based on their earnings, following alphabetical order when earnings of jobs are equal. As in the section with job lists for education levels, there is only one list for each personality type. Note that each job is listed in the one personality type it most closely matches, even though most jobs also have one or two secondary personality types. (The job descriptions in Part II identify any secondary personality types for each job.) Consider reviewing the jobs for more than one personality type so you don't overlook possible jobs that would interest you.

Following are brief descriptions for each of the six personality types used in the lists. Select the two or three descriptions that most closely resemble you and then use the lists to identify jobs that best fit these personality types.

Descriptions of the Six Personality Types

❋ **Realistic:** These occupations frequently involve work activities that include practical, hands-on problems and solutions. They often deal with plants; animals; and real-world materials such as wood, tools, and machinery. Many of the occupations require working outside and do not involve a lot of paperwork or working closely with others.

❋ **Investigative:** These occupations frequently involve working with ideas and require an extensive amount of thinking. These occupations can involve searching for facts and figuring out problems mentally.

❋ **Artistic:** These occupations frequently involve working with forms, designs, and patterns. They often require self-expression, and the work can be done without following a clear set of rules.

❋ **Social:** These occupations frequently involve working with, communicating with, and teaching people. These occupations often involve helping or providing service to others.

❋ **Enterprising:** These occupations frequently involve starting up and carrying out projects. These occupations can involve leading people and making many decisions. They sometimes require risk taking and often deal with business.

* **Conventional:** These occupations frequently involve following set procedures and routines. These occupations can include working with data and details more than with ideas. Usually there is a clear line of authority to follow.

Best-Paying Jobs for People with a Realistic Personality Type

Job	Annual Earnings	Percent Growth	Annual Openings
1. Oral and Maxillofacial Surgeons	$166,400+	9.1%	400
2. Airline Pilots, Copilots, and Flight Engineers	$111,680	12.9%	4,073
3. Civil Engineers	$74,600	18.0%	15,979
4. Nuclear Power Reactor Operators	$73,320	10.6%	233
5. Elevator Installers and Repairers	$69,380	8.8%	2,850
6. Nuclear Technicians	$67,890	6.7%	1,021
7. Commercial Pilots	$65,340	13.2%	1,425
8. Captains, Mates, and Pilots of Water Vessels	$61,960	17.9%	2,665
9. Electrical and Electronics Repairers, Powerhouse, Substation, and Relay	$61,040	–4.7%	1,591
10. Ship Engineers	$60,690	14.1%	1,102
11. Conservation Scientists	$58,720	5.3%	1,161
12. Power Plant Operators	$58,470	2.7%	1,796
13. Telecommunications Equipment Installers and Repairers, Except Line Installers	$55,600	2.5%	13,541
14. Transportation Inspectors	$55,250	16.4%	2,122
15. Electrical Power-Line Installers and Repairers	$55,100	7.2%	6,401
16. Aerospace Engineering and Operations Technicians	$55,040	10.4%	707
17. Petroleum Pump System Operators, Refinery Operators, and Gaugers	$55,010	–13.4%	4,477
18. Foresters	$53,750	5.1%	772
19. Geological and Petroleum Technicians	$53,360	8.6%	1,895
20. Electrical and Electronic Engineering Technicians	$53,240	3.6%	12,583
21. Subway and Streetcar Operators	$53,220	12.1%	587
22. Fire Inspectors and Investigators	$53,030	11.0%	644
23. Surveyors	$52,980	23.7%	14,305
24. Chemical Plant and System Operators	$52,480	–15.3%	5,620
25. Boilermakers	$52,260	14.0%	2,333
26. Radiologic Technologists and Technicians	$52,210	15.1%	12,836
27. Aircraft Mechanics and Service Technicians	$51,390	10.6%	9,708
28. Electrical and Electronics Drafters	$51,320	4.1%	4,786
29. Cartographers and Photogrammetrists	$51,180	20.3%	2,823
30. Construction and Building Inspectors	$50,180	18.2%	12,606

Best-Paying Jobs for People with a Realistic Personality Type

Job	Annual Earnings	Percent Growth	Annual Openings
31. Rotary Drill Operators, Oil and Gas	$49,800	–5.4%	2,145
32. Stationary Engineers and Boiler Operators	$49,790	3.4%	1,892
33. Avionics Technicians	$49,310	8.1%	1,193
34. Fish and Game Wardens	$48,930	–0.2%	576
35. Locomotive Engineers	$48,440	2.9%	3,548
36. Electrical and Electronics Repairers, Commercial and Industrial Equipment	$48,430	6.8%	6,607
37. Locomotive Firers	$48,190	2.9%	3,548
38. Telecommunications Line Installers and Repairers	$48,090	4.6%	14,719

Jobs 35 and 37 share 3,548 openings with each other and with another job not in this book.

Best-Paying Jobs for People with an Investigative Personality Type

Job	Annual Earnings	Percent Growth	Annual Openings
1. Orthodontists	$166,400+	9.2%	479
2. Physicians and Surgeons	$166,400+	14.2%	38,027
3. Prosthodontists	$166,400+	10.7%	54
4. Dentists, General	$142,870	9.2%	7,106
5. Podiatrists	$113,560	9.5%	648
6. Petroleum Engineers	$108,020	5.2%	1,016
7. Pharmacists	$106,410	21.7%	16,358
8. Political Scientists	$104,130	5.3%	318
9. Physicists	$102,890	6.8%	1,302
10. Astronomers	$101,300	5.6%	128
11. Computer and Information Scientists, Research	$97,970	21.5%	2,901
12. Computer Hardware Engineers	$97,400	4.6%	3,572
13. Nuclear Engineers	$97,080	7.2%	1,046
14. Optometrists	$96,320	11.3%	1,789
15. Mathematicians	$95,150	10.2%	473
16. Aerospace Engineers	$92,520	10.2%	6,498
17. Computer Software Engineers, Systems Software	$92,430	28.2%	33,139
18. Electronics Engineers, Except Computer	$86,370	3.7%	5,699
19. Computer Software Engineers, Applications	$85,430	44.6%	58,690

(continued)

(continued)

Best-Paying Jobs for People with an Investigative Personality Type

Job	Annual Earnings	Percent Growth	Annual Openings
20. Chemical Engineers	$84,680	7.9%	2,111
21. Economists	$83,590	7.5%	1,555
22. Biochemists and Biophysicists	$82,840	15.9%	1,637
23. Electrical Engineers	$82,160	6.3%	6,806
24. Materials Engineers	$81,820	4.0%	1,390
25. Atmospheric and Space Scientists	$81,290	10.6%	735
26. Materials Scientists	$80,230	8.7%	1,039
27. Geoscientists, Except Hydrologists and Geographers	$79,160	21.9%	2,471
28. Veterinarians	$79,050	35.0%	5,301
29. Biomedical Engineers	$77,400	21.1%	1,804
30. Industrial-Organizational Psychologists	$77,010	21.3%	118
31. Mining and Geological Engineers, Including Mining Safety Engineers	$75,960	10.0%	456
32. Mechanical Engineers	$74,920	4.2%	12,394
33. Marine Engineers and Naval Architects	$74,140	10.9%	495
34. Environmental Engineers	$74,020	25.4%	5,003
35. Industrial Engineers	$73,820	20.3%	11,272
36. Management Analysts	$73,570	21.9%	125,669
37. Medical Scientists, Except Epidemiologists	$72,590	20.2%	10,596
38. Health and Safety Engineers, Except Mining Safety Engineers and Inspectors	$72,490	9.6%	1,105
39. Hydrologists	$71,450	24.3%	687
40. Network Systems and Data Communications Analysts	$71,100	53.4%	35,086
41. Computer Programmers	$69,620	–4.1%	27,937
42. Operations Research Analysts	$69,000	10.6%	5,727
43. Agricultural Engineers	$68,730	8.6%	225
44. Sociologists	$68,570	10.0%	403
45. Nuclear Medicine Technologists	$66,660	14.8%	1,290
46. Geographers	$66,600	6.1%	75
47. Network and Computer Systems Administrators	$66,310	27.0%	37,010
48. Chemists	$66,230	9.1%	9,024
49. Microbiologists	$64,350	11.2%	1,306
50. Clinical, Counseling, and School Psychologists	$64,140	15.8%	8,309
51. Occupational Health and Safety Specialists	$62,250	8.1%	3,440
52. Audiologists	$62,030	9.8%	980
53. Diagnostic Medical Sonographers	$61,980	19.1%	3,211

Best-Paying Jobs for People with an Investigative Personality Type

Job	Annual Earnings	Percent Growth	Annual Openings
54. Epidemiologists	$61,360	13.6%	503
55. Market Research Analysts	$61,070	20.1%	45,015
56. Urban and Regional Planners	$59,810	14.5%	1,967
57. Environmental Scientists and Specialists, Including Health	$59,750	25.1%	6,961
58. Food Scientists and Technologists	$59,520	10.3%	663
59. Soil and Plant Scientists	$58,390	8.4%	850
60. Animal Scientists	$56,030	9.8%	299
61. Zoologists and Wildlife Biologists	$55,290	8.7%	1,444
62. Historians	$54,530	7.8%	245
63. Anthropologists and Archeologists	$53,910	15.0%	446
64. Medical and Clinical Laboratory Technologists	$53,500	12.4%	11,457
65. Dietitians and Nutritionists	$50,590	8.6%	4,996
66. Forensic Science Technicians	$49,860	30.7%	3,074
67. Mechanical Engineering Technicians	$48,130	6.4%	3,710

Best-Paying Jobs for People with an Artistic Personality Type

Job	Annual Earnings	Percent Growth	Annual Openings
1. Art Directors	$76,980	9.0%	9,719
2. Architects, Except Landscape and Naval	$70,320	17.7%	11,324
3. Technical Writers	$61,620	19.5%	7,498
4. Fashion Designers	$61,160	5.0%	1,968
5. Landscape Architects	$58,960	16.4%	2,342
6. Commercial and Industrial Designers	$57,350	7.2%	4,777
7. Multi-Media Artists and Animators	$56,330	25.8%	13,182
8. Writers and Authors	$53,070	12.8%	24,023
9. Broadcast News Analysts	$51,260	6.0%	1,444
10. Film and Video Editors	$50,560	12.7%	2,707
11. Editors	$49,990	2.3%	20,193

Best-Paying Jobs for People with a Social Personality Type

Job	Annual Earnings	Percent Growth	Annual Openings
1. Law Teachers, Postsecondary	$93,210	22.9%	2,169
2. Health Specialties Teachers, Postsecondary	$84,390	22.9%	19,617
3. Engineering Teachers, Postsecondary	$82,810	22.9%	5,565
4. Physician Assistants	$81,230	27.0%	7,147
5. Economics Teachers, Postsecondary	$80,130	22.9%	2,208
6. Atmospheric, Earth, Marine, and Space Sciences Teachers, Postsecondary	$76,050	22.9%	1,553
7. Agricultural Sciences Teachers, Postsecondary	$74,390	22.9%	1,840
8. Physics Teachers, Postsecondary	$74,390	22.9%	2,155
9. Radiation Therapists	$72,910	24.8%	1,461
10. Physical Therapists	$72,790	27.1%	12,072
11. Architecture Teachers, Postsecondary	$71,710	22.9%	1,044
12. Biological Science Teachers, Postsecondary	$70,650	22.9%	9,039
13. Business Teachers, Postsecondary	$68,000	22.9%	11,643
14. Anthropology and Archeology Teachers, Postsecondary	$67,750	22.9%	910
15. Chemistry Teachers, Postsecondary	$67,240	22.9%	3,405
16. Political Science Teachers, Postsecondary	$67,200	22.9%	2,435
17. Occupational Therapists	$66,780	23.1%	8,338
18. Dental Hygienists	$66,570	30.1%	10,433
19. Chiropractors	$66,490	14.4%	3,179
20. Computer Science Teachers, Postsecondary	$66,440	22.9%	5,820
21. Environmental Science Teachers, Postsecondary	$65,130	22.9%	769
22. Home Economics Teachers, Postsecondary	$64,210	22.9%	820
23. Psychology Teachers, Postsecondary	$63,630	22.9%	5,261
24. Speech-Language Pathologists	$62,930	10.6%	11,160
25. Geography Teachers, Postsecondary	$62,880	22.9%	697
26. Orthotists and Prosthetists	$62,590	11.8%	295
27. Registered Nurses	$62,450	23.5%	233,499
28. Forestry and Conservation Science Teachers, Postsecondary	$62,140	22.9%	454
29. History Teachers, Postsecondary	$62,000	22.9%	3,570
30. Area, Ethnic, and Cultural Studies Teachers, Postsecondary	$61,490	22.9%	1,252
31. Sociology Teachers, Postsecondary	$61,280	22.9%	2,774
32. Mathematical Science Teachers, Postsecondary	$61,120	22.9%	7,663
33. Philosophy and Religion Teachers, Postsecondary	$59,540	22.9%	3,120
34. Nursing Instructors and Teachers, Postsecondary	$59,210	22.9%	7,337
35. Social Work Teachers, Postsecondary	$59,140	22.9%	1,292
36. Library Science Teachers, Postsecondary	$58,570	22.9%	702

Best-Paying Jobs for People with a Social Personality Type

Job	Annual Earnings	Percent Growth	Annual Openings
37. Art, Drama, and Music Teachers, Postsecondary	$57,820	22.9%	12,707
38. Communications Teachers, Postsecondary	$57,760	22.9%	4,074
39. Instructional Coordinators	$56,880	22.5%	21,294
40. Education Teachers, Postsecondary	$56,400	22.9%	9,359
41. English Language and Literature Teachers, Postsecondary	$56,380	22.9%	10,475
42. Foreign Language and Literature Teachers, Postsecondary	$55,570	22.9%	4,317
43. Recreation and Fitness Studies Teachers, Postsecondary	$55,140	22.9%	3,010
44. Criminal Justice and Law Enforcement Teachers, Postsecondary	$53,640	22.9%	1,911
45. Respiratory Therapists	$52,200	22.6%	5,563
46. Vocational Education Teachers, Secondary School	$51,580	–4.6%	7,639
47. Training and Development Specialists	$51,450	18.3%	35,862
48. Special Education Teachers, Secondary School	$51,340	8.5%	10,601
49. Secondary School Teachers, Except Special and Vocational Education	$51,180	5.6%	93,166
50. Educational, Vocational, and School Counselors	$51,050	12.6%	54,025
51. Special Education Teachers, Middle School	$50,810	15.8%	8,846
52. Arbitrators, Mediators, and Conciliators	$50,660	10.6%	546
53. Emergency Management Specialists	$50,460	12.3%	1,538
54. Special Education Teachers, Preschool, Kindergarten, and Elementary School	$50,020	19.6%	20,049
55. Middle School Teachers, Except Special and Vocational Education	$49,700	11.2%	75,270
56. Elementary School Teachers, Except Special Education	$49,330	13.6%	181,612
57. Occupational Therapist Assistants	$48,230	25.4%	2,634

Best-Paying Jobs for People with an Enterprising Personality Type

Job	Annual Earnings	Percent Growth	Annual Openings
1. Chief Executives	$158,560	2.0%	21,209
2. Engineering Managers	$115,270	7.3%	7,404
3. Natural Sciences Managers	$112,800	11.4%	3,661
4. Computer and Information Systems Managers	$112,210	16.4%	30,887
5. Air Traffic Controllers	$111,870	10.2%	1,213
6. Lawyers	$110,590	11.0%	49,445

(continued)

(continued)

Best-Paying Jobs for People with an Enterprising Personality Type

Job	Annual Earnings	Percent Growth	Annual Openings
7. Judges, Magistrate Judges, and Magistrates	$110,220	5.1%	1,567
8. Marketing Managers	$108,580	14.4%	20,189
9. Financial Managers	$99,330	12.6%	57,589
10. Sales Managers	$97,260	10.2%	36,392
11. General and Operations Managers	$91,570	1.5%	112,072
12. Public Relations Managers	$89,430	16.9%	5,781
13. Purchasing Managers	$89,160	3.4%	7,243
14. Training and Development Managers	$87,700	15.6%	3,759
15. Compensation and Benefits Managers	$86,500	12.0%	6,121
16. Education Administrators, Elementary and Secondary School	$83,880	7.6%	27,143
17. Industrial Production Managers	$83,290	–5.9%	14,889
18. Sales Engineers	$83,100	8.5%	7,371
19. Education Administrators, Postsecondary	$80,670	14.2%	17,121
20. Medical and Health Services Managers	$80,240	16.4%	31,877
21. Advertising and Promotions Managers	$80,220	6.2%	2,955
22. Construction Managers	$79,860	15.7%	44,158
23. Transportation, Storage, and Distribution Managers	$79,000	8.3%	6,994
24. Administrative Law Judges, Adjudicators, and Hearing Officers	$76,940	0.1%	794
25. First-Line Supervisors/Managers of Police and Detectives	$75,490	9.2%	9,373
26. Administrative Services Managers	$73,520	11.7%	19,513
27. Financial Examiners	$70,930	10.7%	2,449
28. Sales Representatives, Wholesale and Manufacturing, Technical and Scientific Products	$70,200	12.4%	43,469
29. Personal Financial Advisors	$69,050	41.0%	17,114
30. Securities, Commodities, and Financial Services Sales Agents	$68,680	24.8%	47,750
31. Gaming Managers	$68,290	24.4%	549
32. First-Line Supervisors/Managers of Non-Retail Sales Workers	$68,100	3.7%	48,883
33. First-Line Supervisors/Managers of Fire Fighting and Prevention Workers	$67,440	11.5%	3,771
34. Logisticians	$66,480	17.3%	9,671
35. Producers and Directors	$64,430	11.1%	8,992
36. Agents and Business Managers of Artists, Performers, and Athletes	$62,940	9.6%	3,940
37. Detectives and Criminal Investigators	$60,910	17.3%	14,746
38. Postmasters and Mail Superintendents	$59,310	–0.8%	1,627

Best-Paying Jobs for People with an Enterprising Personality Type

Job	Annual Earnings	Percent Growth	Annual Openings
39. First-Line Supervisors/Managers of Construction Trades and Extraction Workers	$58,140	9.1%	82,923
40. Real Estate Brokers	$57,500	11.1%	18,689
41. First-Line Supervisors/Managers of Correctional Officers	$57,380	12.5%	4,180
42. First-Line Supervisors/Managers of Mechanics, Installers, and Repairers	$57,300	7.3%	24,361
43. Farm, Ranch, and Other Agricultural Managers	$56,230	1.1%	18,101
44. Social and Community Service Managers	$55,980	24.7%	23,788
45. Railroad Conductors and Yardmasters	$52,830	9.1%	3,235
46. Funeral Directors	$52,210	12.5%	3,939
47. Police and Sheriff's Patrol Officers	$51,410	10.8%	37,842
48. First-Line Supervisors/Managers of Transportation and Material-Moving Machine and Vehicle Operators	$51,320	10.2%	16,580
49. Public Relations Specialists	$51,280	17.6%	51,216
50. First-Line Supervisors/Managers of Production and Operating Workers	$50,440	–4.8%	46,144
51. Purchasing Agents and Buyers, Farm Products	$49,670	–8.6%	1,618
52. Wholesale and Retail Buyers, Except Farm Products	$48,710	–0.1%	19,847

Best-Paying Jobs for People with a Conventional Personality Type

Job	Annual Earnings	Percent Growth	Annual Openings
1. Actuaries	$84,810	23.7%	3,245
2. Computer Systems Analysts	$75,500	29.0%	63,166
3. Computer Specialists, All Other	$75,150	15.1%	14,374
4. Financial Analysts	$73,150	33.8%	29,317
5. Statisticians	$72,610	8.5%	3,433
6. Database Administrators	$69,740	28.6%	8,258
7. Budget Analysts	$65,320	7.1%	6,423
8. Accountants and Auditors	$59,430	17.7%	134,463
9. Insurance Underwriters	$56,790	6.3%	6,880
10. Cost Estimators	$56,510	18.5%	38,379
11. Postal Service Clerks	$55,920	1.2%	3,703
12. Claims Adjusters, Examiners, and Investigators	$55,760	8.9%	22,024
13. Gas Plant Operators	$55,760	–9.9%	1,332

(continued)

(continued)

Best-Paying Jobs for People with a Conventional Personality Type

Job	Annual Earnings	Percent Growth	Annual Openings
14. Credit Analysts	$55,250	1.9%	3,180
15. Loan Officers	$54,700	11.5%	54,237
16. Purchasing Agents, Except Wholesale, Retail, and Farm Products	$53,940	0.1%	22,349
17. Compensation, Benefits, and Job Analysis Specialists	$53,860	18.4%	18,761
18. Insurance Appraisers, Auto Damage	$53,440	12.5%	1,030
19. Librarians	$52,530	3.6%	18,945
20. Sales Representatives, Wholesale and Manufacturing, Except Technical and Scientific Products	$51,330	8.4%	156,215
21. Postal Service Mail Sorters, Processors, and Processing Machine Operators	$50,600	–8.4%	6,855
22. Postal Service Mail Carriers	$50,290	1.0%	16,710
23. Court Reporters	$49,710	24.5%	2,620
24. Compliance Officers, Except Agriculture, Construction, Health and Safety, and Transportation	$48,890	4.9%	15,841
25. Tax Examiners, Collectors, and Revenue Agents	$48,100	2.1%	4,465

Bonus Lists

All of the previous lists in this section are based on the average (median) income of the jobs. However, you should stop to consider that *almost nobody* in the occupation gets paid *exactly* the median wage. Half of the workers earn more than that; half earn less. People in some industries or locations earn more or less than that. Men and women often have different earnings.

So we thought it would be interesting to set aside the national medians and create a few bonus lists based on some other earnings figures:

❋ The *algebraic mean* of the earnings can tell us which jobs have a few "star" earners.

❋ The *10th percentile* earnings figure (which is exceeded by 90 percent of workers) can tell us which jobs have high pay even for beginners.

❋ The earnings figures for specific *industries* and *metropolitan areas* can tell us what you might specialize in or where you might move to if you want to earn six figures.

❋ The median earnings figures for *women and men* can tell us which jobs have the most female-friendly paychecks.

Bonus List: 26 Jobs with a Few "Star" Earners

Some occupations have a very unequal distribution of pay, with a few "star" earners and a lot of low earners. For example, for every Shakira or Will Smith, there are thousands of other singers and actors who don't earn even minimum wage from performing. If you think you might have the potential to star in the career field that interests you, consider the jobs in the following list, which all offer a big payoff for a small number of workers.

This list is different from the previous lists. Our focus here is not on the *middle* of the wage distribution; instead, we're looking at the *high* end for a few extremely high earners. The way we identify those occupations is to look instead at the *mean* earnings figure and how this differs from the median. The mean is the algebraic average, so if the mean is a lot higher than the median, it means that a few "star" earners are pulling up the average. (They are doing the same thing that high-achieving students do to grades when they "ruin the curve" for average students.)

Here is an example that explains what we're doing. Let's say we're looking at an occupation with only seven workers, and this is how their earnings are distributed:

Worker	Annual Earnings
A	$10,000
B	$20,000
C	$30,000
D	$40,000 (median: half earn more than D, half less)
E	$50,000
F	$60,000
G	$70,000

The median wage is $40,000, and if you do the math you'll find that $40,000 is also the mean (average) wage. That makes sense because the wages are distributed very evenly here. But let's say that worker G suddenly becomes a star and earns $400,000. The median does not change, but the mean now soars to $87,143. Having a star earner in the mix of workers creates a big gap between the median and the mean.

So to compile the following list, we identified all the jobs among the 250 best for which the mean wage figure was at least 15 percent higher than the median and we ordered them by the size of the difference, expressed as a percentage of the mean wage. It might not surprise you to find a number of entertainment-related jobs near the top of the list. (Musicians, Singers, Actors, and Dancers would probably be in this list as well if annual wage figures were available.) But did you realize that some business jobs also have star earners? Some medical specialties might also have outstanding earners (think of Hollywood plastic surgeons), but because we were unable to obtain a median wage figure for these occupations (other than "more than $166,400"), we could not do the math to determine whether they belong here.

26 Jobs with a Few "Star" Earners

Job	Percent by Which Mean Annual Earnings Exceed Median Earnings	Median Earnings	Percent Growth	Annual Openings
1. Broadcast News Analysts	38.0%	$51,260	6.0%	1,444
2. Personal Financial Advisors	34.6%	$69,050	41.0%	17,114
3. Real Estate Brokers	34.3%	$57,500	11.1%	18,689
4. Securities, Commodities, and Financial Services Sales Agents	34.0%	$68,680	24.8%	47,750
5. Agents and Business Managers of Artists, Performers, and Athletes	29.6%	$62,940	9.6%	3,940
6. Producers and Directors	28.9%	$64,430	11.1%	8,992
7. Film and Video Editors	23.6%	$50,560	12.7%	2,707
8. Chiropractors	22.3%	$66,490	14.4%	3,179
9. Writers and Authors	21.7%	$53,070	12.8%	24,023
10. Health Specialties Teachers, Postsecondary	20.9%	$84,390	22.9%	19,617
11. Sales Representatives, Wholesale and Manufacturing, Except Technical and Scientific Products	19.8%	$51,330	8.4%	156,215
12. Purchasing Agents and Buyers, Farm Products	18.3%	$49,670	–8.6%	1,618
13. Advertising and Promotions Managers	18.1%	$80,220	6.2%	2,955
14. General and Operations Managers	17.9%	$91,570	1.5%	112,072
15. Biological Science Teachers, Postsecondary	17.9%	$70,650	22.9%	9,039
16. Arbitrators, Mediators, and Conciliators	17.7%	$50,660	10.6%	546
17. Foreign Language and Literature Teachers, Postsecondary	17.5%	$55,570	22.9%	4,317
18. First-Line Supervisors/Managers of Non-Retail Sales Workers	17.3%	$68,100	3.7%	48,883
19. Credit Analysts	16.9%	$55,250	1.9%	3,180
20. Fashion Designers	16.7%	$61,160	5.0%	1,968
21. Loan Officers	16.2%	$54,700	11.5%	54,237
22. Financial Analysts	15.9%	$73,150	33.8%	29,317
23. Commercial Pilots	15.5%	$65,340	13.2%	1,425
24. Education Administrators, Postsecondary	15.2%	$80,670	14.2%	17,121
25. Art Directors	15.0%	$76,980	9.0%	9,719
26. Public Relations Specialists	15.0%	$51,280	17.6%	51,216

Bonus List: 28 Jobs in Which Even Beginners Are Well-Paid

Maybe you're a person who doesn't like to take chances, and you're not confident you have the star power needed to soar above the other earners in your career. This list features occupations in which even the beginners are doing fine. Specifically, the workers who earn at the 10th percentile (meaning that 90 percent of the workers in the occupation earn more than they do) *still* earn at least $51,540, which means they earn more than 75 percent of all American wage-earners. They are ordered by the earnings of the workers at the 10th percentile.

28 Jobs in Which Even Beginners Are Well-Paid

Job	Beginning Wage	Median Earnings	Percent Growth	Annual Openings
1. Orthodontists	$100,980	$166,400+	9.2%	479
2. Oral and Maxillofacial Surgeons	$94,650	$166,400+	9.1%	400
3. Pharmacists	$77,390	$106,410	21.7%	16,358
4. Engineering Managers	$73,420	$115,270	7.3%	7,404
5. Prosthodontists	$72,710	$166,400+	10.7%	54
6. Dentists, General	$71,870	$142,870	9.2%	7,106
7. Physicians and Surgeons	$70,370	$166,400+	14.2%	38,027
8. Computer and Information Systems Managers	$68,750	$112,210	16.4%	30,887
9. Chief Executives	$68,680	$158,560	2.0%	21,209
10. Nuclear Engineers	$68,300	$97,080	7.2%	1,046
11. Natural Sciences Managers	$65,960	$112,800	11.4%	3,661
12. Computer Hardware Engineers	$59,170	$97,400	4.6%	3,572
13. Aerospace Engineers	$58,130	$92,520	10.2%	6,498
14. Petroleum Engineers	$57,820	$108,020	5.2%	1,016
15. Computer Software Engineers, Systems Software	$57,810	$92,430	28.2%	33,139
16. Computer and Information Scientists, Research	$57,480	$97,970	21.5%	2,901
17. Physicists	$57,160	$102,890	6.8%	1,302
18. Nuclear Power Reactor Operators	$55,730	$73,320	10.6%	233
19. Education Administrators, Elementary and Secondary School	$55,580	$83,880	7.6%	27,143
20. Airline Pilots, Copilots, and Flight Engineers	$55,330	$111,680	12.9%	4,073
21. Electronics Engineers, Except Computer	$55,330	$86,370	3.7%	5,699
22. Marketing Managers	$55,270	$108,580	14.4%	20,189

(continued)

(continued)

28 Jobs in Which Even Beginners Are Well-Paid

Job	Beginning Wage	Median Earnings	Percent Growth	Annual Openings
23. Lawyers	$54,460	$110,590	11.0%	49,445
24. Financial Managers	$53,860	$99,330	12.6%	57,589
25. Chemical Engineers	$53,730	$84,680	7.9%	2,111
26. Computer Software Engineers, Applications	$53,720	$85,430	44.6%	58,690
27. Mathematicians	$53,570	$95,150	10.2%	473
28. Electrical Engineers	$52,990	$82,160	6.3%	6,806

Bonus List: Jobs and Industries in Which Earnings Average More than $100,000

Earning a good income is not just a question of getting into the right occupation; it also helps to get into the right industry. In some industries, the balance of supply and demand works out to produce higher salaries, particularly when an industry is growing so fast that skilled workers are in short supply. Fortunately, the Department of Labor's Occupational Earnings Survey (OES) reports wages not just by occupation, but also by industry, so we were able to compile industry-specific earnings figures for the 250 jobs in this book. Having done so, we found more than 200 combinations of job and industry where workers earn an average of more than $100,000 per year.

We didn't want any items on this list to reflect a handful of freakishly high earners. For example, Lawyers who are working in the Beverage and Tobacco Product Manufacturing industry earn an average of over $166,400, compared to the average of $110,590 that Lawyers earn in *all* industries. But there are only about 50 of these superstar Lawyers fighting off lawsuits directed at tobacco companies and brewers. Therefore, we limited the list to instances of industries that employ more than 1,000 workers in the occupation. (We made one exception to this rule by including Astronomers, a tiny occupation with a total workforce of fewer than 10,000.) The jobs and the industries employing the high earners for each job are ordered alphabetically.

(For a complete list of *all* job-industry combinations that earn six figures—not just those selected from the 250 jobs covered by this book—see *Your $100,000 Career Plan* by Laurence Shatkin, Ph.D., published by JIST. For more information about industries, see *40 Best Fields for Your Career* by Mike Farr and Laurence Shatkin, Ph.D., published by JIST.)

Jobs and Industries in Which Earnings Average More than $100,000

Job	Industries in Which Average Earnings Are More than $100,000 per Year
Administrative Services Managers	Motion Picture and Sound Recording Industries
Advertising and Promotions Managers	Professional, Scientific, and Technical Services
Aerospace Engineers	Administrative and Support Services; Government
Air Traffic Controllers	Government
Airline Pilots, Copilots, and Flight Engineers	Air Transportation; Couriers and Messengers
Astronomers	Government
Chief Executives	Accommodation; Administrative and Support Services; Ambulatory Health Care Services; Amusement, Gambling, and Recreation Industries; Building Material and Garden Equipment and Supplies Dealers; Chemical Manufacturing; Computer and Electronic Product Manufacturing; Construction of Buildings; Credit Intermediation and Related Activities; Data Processing, Hosting and Related Services; Educational Services; Electrical Equipment, Appliance, and Component Manufacturing; Fabricated Metal Product Manufacturing; Food and Beverage Stores; Food Manufacturing; Food Services and Drinking Places; Furniture and Related Product Manufacturing; Heavy and Civil Engineering Construction; Hospitals; Insurance Carriers and Related Activities; Machinery Manufacturing; Management of Companies and Enterprises; Merchant Wholesalers, Durable Goods; Merchant Wholesalers, Nondurable Goods; Miscellaneous Manufacturing; Motor Vehicle and Parts Dealers; Nonmetallic Mineral Product Manufacturing; Nonstore Retailers; Nursing and Residential Care Facilities; Performing Arts, Spectator Sports, and Related Industries; Personal and Laundry Services; Plastics and Rubber Products Manufacturing; Primary Metal Manufacturing; Printing and Related Support Activities; Professional, Scientific, and Technical Services; Publishing Industries (Except Internet); Real Estate; Religious, Grantmaking, Civic, Professional, and Similar Organizations; Repair and Maintenance; Securities, Commodity Contracts, and Other Financial Investments and Related Activities; Specialty Trade Contractors; Support Activities for Transportation; Telecommunications; Transportation Equipment Manufacturing; Truck Transportation; Utilities; Wholesale Electronic Markets and Agents and Brokers; Wood Product Manufacturing
Computer and Information Scientists, Research	Merchant Wholesalers, Durable Goods; Publishing Industries (Except Internet)
Computer and Information Systems Managers	Ambulatory Health Care Services; Chemical Manufacturing; Computer and Electronic Product Manufacturing; Credit Intermediation and Related Activities; Data Processing, Hosting and Related Services; Electronics and Appliance Stores; Insurance Carriers and Related Activities; Machinery Manufacturing; Management of Companies and Enterprises; Merchant Wholesalers,

(continued)

(continued)

Jobs and Industries in Which Earnings Average More than $100,000

Job	Industries in Which Average Earnings Are More than $100,000 per Year
	Durable Goods; Miscellaneous Manufacturing; Nonstore Retailers; Other Information Services; Professional, Scientific, and Technical Services; Publishing Industries (Except Internet); Real Estate; Securities, Commodity Contracts, and Other Financial Investments and Related Activities; Telecommunications; Transportation Equipment Manufacturing; Utilities; Wholesale Electronic Markets and Agents and Brokers
Computer Software Engineers, Systems Software	Other Information Services
Dentists, General	Ambulatory Health Care Services; Government
Engineering Managers	Administrative and Support Services; Chemical Manufacturing; Computer and Electronic Product Manufacturing; Construction of Buildings; Electrical Equipment, Appliance, and Component Manufacturing; Government; Heavy and Civil Engineering Construction; Management of Companies and Enterprises; Merchant Wholesalers, Durable Goods; Miscellaneous Manufacturing; Professional, Scientific, and Technical Services; Telecommunications; Transportation Equipment Manufacturing; Utilities
Financial Managers	Broadcasting (Except Internet); Chemical Manufacturing; Computer and Electronic Product Manufacturing; Data Processing, Hosting and Related Services; Funds, Trusts, and Other Financial Vehicles; Insurance Carriers and Related Activities; Management of Companies and Enterprises; Merchant Wholesalers, Durable Goods; Merchant Wholesalers, Nondurable Goods; Miscellaneous Manufacturing; Motion Picture and Sound Recording Industries; Nonstore Retailers; Oil and Gas Extraction; Professional, Scientific, and Technical Services; Publishing Industries (Except Internet); Real Estate; Securities, Commodity Contracts, and Other Financial Investments and Related Activities; Telecommunications; Transportation Equipment Manufacturing; Utilities; Wholesale Electronic Markets and Agents and Brokers
General and Operations Managers	Apparel Manufacturing; Beverage and Tobacco Product Manufacturing; Chemical Manufacturing; Computer and Electronic Product Manufacturing; Construction of Buildings; Data Processing, Hosting and Related Services; Electrical Equipment, Appliance, and Component Manufacturing; Funds, Trusts, and Other Financial Vehicles; Heavy and Civil Engineering Construction; Insurance Carriers and Related Activities; Machinery Manufacturing; Management of Companies and Enterprises; Merchant Wholesalers, Durable Goods; Miscellaneous Manufacturing; Motion Picture and Sound Recording Industries; Oil and Gas Extraction; Other Information Services; Paper Manufacturing; Petroleum and Coal Products Manufacturing; Plastics and Rubber Products Manufacturing; Primary Metal Manufacturing; Professional,

Jobs and Industries in Which Earnings Average More than $100,000

Job	Industries in Which Average Earnings Are More than $100,000 per Year
	Scientific, and Technical Services; Publishing Industries (Except Internet); Rail Transportation; Real Estate; Securities, Commodity Contracts, and Other Financial Investments and Related Activities; Telecommunications; Textile Mills; Transportation Equipment Manufacturing; Utilities; Water Transportation; Wholesale Electronic Markets and Agents and Brokers
Geoscientists, Except Hydrologists and Geographers	Oil and Gas Extraction
Industrial Production Managers	Oil and Gas Extraction; Petroleum and Coal Products Manufacturing; Professional, Scientific, and Technical Services; Utilities
Judges, Magistrate Judges, and Magistrates	Government
Lawyers	Computer and Electronic Product Manufacturing; Credit Intermediation and Related Activities; Educational Services; Insurance Carriers and Related Activities; Management of Companies and Enterprises; Professional, Scientific, and Technical Services; Publishing Industries (Except Internet); Real Estate; Securities, Commodity Contracts, and Other Financial Investments and Related Activities; Telecommunications; Utilities
Marketing Managers	Broadcasting (Except Internet); Chemical Manufacturing; Computer and Electronic Product Manufacturing; Credit Intermediation and Related Activities; Data Processing, Hosting and Related Services; Electrical Equipment, Appliance, and Component Manufacturing; Insurance Carriers and Related Activities; Machinery Manufacturing; Management of Companies and Enterprises; Merchant Wholesalers, Durable Goods; Merchant Wholesalers, Nondurable Goods; Miscellaneous Manufacturing; Motion Picture and Sound Recording Industries; Other Information Services; Professional, Scientific, and Technical Services; Publishing Industries (Except Internet); Securities, Commodity Contracts, and Other Financial Investments and Related Activities; Telecommunications; Transportation Equipment Manufacturing; Utilities; Wholesale Electronic Markets and Agents and Brokers
Mathematicians	Professional, Scientific, and Technical Services
Medical and Health Services Managers	Professional, Scientific, and Technical Services
Natural Sciences Managers	Chemical Manufacturing; Management of Companies and Enterprises; Professional, Scientific, and Technical Services
Nuclear Engineers	Professional, Scientific, and Technical Services
Optometrists	Health and Personal Care Stores
Oral and Maxillofacial Surgeons	Ambulatory Health Care Services

(continued)

(continued)

| Jobs and Industries in Which Earnings Average More than $100,000 ||
Job	Industries in Which Average Earnings Are More than $100,000 per Year
Orthodontists	Ambulatory Health Care Services
Petroleum Engineers	Management of Companies and Enterprises; Oil and Gas Extraction; Petroleum and Coal Products Manufacturing; Professional, Scientific, and Technical Services
Pharmacists	Administrative and Support Services; Ambulatory Health Care Services; Food and Beverage Stores; General Merchandise Stores; Hospitals; Insurance Carriers and Related Activities; Management of Companies and Enterprises; Merchant Wholesalers, Nondurable Goods; Nonstore Retailers
Physicists	Government; Professional, Scientific, and Technical Services
Podiatrists	Ambulatory Health Care Services
Political Scientists	Government
Public Relations Managers	Management of Companies and Enterprises; Professional, Scientific, and Technical Services; Securities, Commodity Contracts, and Other Financial Investments and Related Activities
Purchasing Managers	Management of Companies and Enterprises; Professional, Scientific, and Technical Services
Sales Engineers	Publishing Industries (Except Internet)
Sales Managers	Broadcasting (Except Internet); Chemical Manufacturing; Computer and Electronic Product Manufacturing; Construction of Buildings; Credit Intermediation and Related Activities; Data Processing, Hosting and Related Services; Electrical Equipment, Appliance, and Component Manufacturing; Insurance Carriers and Related Activities; Management of Companies and Enterprises; Merchant Wholesalers, Durable Goods; Merchant Wholesalers, Nondurable Goods; Miscellaneous Manufacturing; Motion Picture and Sound Recording Industries; Motor Vehicle and Parts Dealers; Other Information Services; Paper Manufacturing; Plastics and Rubber Products Manufacturing; Printing and Related Support Activities; Professional, Scientific, and Technical Services; Publishing Industries (Except Internet); Securities, Commodity Contracts, and Other Financial Investments and Related Activities; Telecommunications; Transportation Equipment Manufacturing; Wholesale Electronic Markets and Agents and Brokers

Bonus List: Jobs and Metropolitan Areas Where Earnings Average More than $100,000

Sometimes the best way to boost your pay is to pull up stakes and move to a region of the country where wages are higher. To be sure, sometimes high-wage localities also have a high cost of living, meaning that your improved earnings will put you into a higher tax bracket without buying you a more comfortable lifestyle.

But in other cases you can genuinely improve your circumstances by relocating. For example, for industries that involve a lot of collaborative work, businesses tend to cluster in certain geographical areas (think of Hollywood for movies, Nashville for music, or the Silicon Valley for high tech). Workers who live in such hubs of collaborative activity often can be more productive and thus more able to achieve an affluent standard of living than workers who are located elsewhere. On the other hand, for jobs where people tend to work solo (think of Dentists or Massage Therapists), the reverse is often true—workers can earn more if they move to a region where there are few colleagues and therefore little competition.

If you are thinking of relocating to improve your earnings, some other factors you should consider are the amount and cost of the commuting you may have to do. The time and expense of commuting can effectively erode your earning power. For example, let's say you're earning $1,200 per week for 40 hours of work, which equals $30 per hour. If your daily commute to and from work takes an hour each way, you're actually devoting 50 hours per week to your work, which means you are effectively earning $24 per hour. After you also subtract your costs for gasoline, tolls, and the wear and tear on your vehicle, your job in your new location actually may not be paying you more than your old job in your old location. So the relationship between the location of your job and your earnings can be a complex matter.

To create the following list, we analyzed the OES figures for the earnings of the 250 best-paying jobs in various metropolitan areas and identified those combinations where workers are earning an average of above $100,000. We did not include instances where fewer than 1,000 workers are employed in a metropolitan area unless the workers in this area represent more than three percent of the national workforce for the occupation. The jobs are ordered alphabetically.

(For a complete list of *all* job-metro combinations that earn six figures—not just those selected from the 250 jobs covered by this book—see *Your $100,000 Career Plan* by Laurence Shatkin, Ph.D., published by JIST.)

Jobs and Metropolitan Areas Where Earnings Average More than $100,000

Occupation	Metropolitan Area(s) Where Average Earnings Are More than $100,000 per Year
Actuaries	Philadelphia-Camden-Wilmington, PA-NJ-DE-MD
Advertising and Promotions Managers	New York–Northern New Jersey–Long Island, NY-NJ-PA
Aerospace Engineers	Los Angeles–Long Beach–Santa Ana, CA

(continued)

(continued)

Jobs and Metropolitan Areas Where Earnings Average More than $100,000

Occupation	Metropolitan Area(s) Where Average Earnings Are More than $100,000 per Year
Air Traffic Controllers	Atlanta–Sandy Springs–Marietta, GA; Chicago-Naperville-Joliet, IL-IN-WI; Dallas–Fort Worth–Arlington, TX; Houston–Sugar Land–Baytown, TX; Washington-Arlington-Alexandria, DC-VA-MD-WV
Airline Pilots, Copilots, and Flight Engineers	Atlanta–Sandy Springs–Marietta, GA; Charlotte-Gastonia-Concord, NC-SC; Chicago-Naperville-Joliet, IL-IN-WI; Los Angeles–Long Beach–Santa Ana, CA; Miami–Fort Lauderdale–Miami Beach, FL; Minneapolis–St. Paul–Bloomington, MN-WI; New York–Northern New Jersey–Long Island, NY-NJ-PA; San Francisco–Oakland–Fremont, CA; Washington-Arlington-Alexandria, DC-VA-MD-WV
Astronomers	Washington-Arlington-Alexandria, DC-VA-MD-WV
Biological Science Teachers, Postsecondary	San Antonio, TX
Chemists	Washington-Arlington-Alexandria, DC-VA-MD-WV
Chief Executives	Albany-Schenectady-Troy, NY; Allentown-Bethlehem-Easton, PA-NJ; Austin–Round Rock, TX; Baltimore-Towson, MD; Birmingham-Hoover, AL; Boise City–Nampa, ID; Boston-Cambridge-Quincy, MA-NH; Bridgeport-Stamford-Norwalk, CT; Charleston–North Charleston, SC; Charlotte-Gastonia-Concord, NC-SC; Chicago-Naperville-Joliet, IL-IN-WI; Cincinnati-Middletown, OH-KY-IN; Cleveland-Elyria-Mentor, OH; Columbia, SC; Columbus, OH; Dallas–Fort Worth–Arlington, TX; Denver-Aurora, CO; Detroit-Warren-Livonia, MI; Grand Rapids–Wyoming, MI; Greenville, SC; Hartford–West Hartford–East Hartford, CT; Honolulu, HI; Houston–Sugar Land–Baytown, TX; Indianapolis-Carmel, IN; Jacksonville, FL; Kansas City, MO-KS; Knoxville, TN; Los Angeles–Long Beach–Santa Ana, CA; Louisville–Jefferson County, KY-IN; Memphis, TN-MS-AR; Miami–Fort Lauderdale–Miami Beach, FL; Milwaukee–Waukesha–West Allis, WI; Minneapolis–St. Paul–Bloomington, MN-WI; Nashville-Davidson–Murfreesboro, TN; New York–Northern New Jersey–Long Island, NY-NJ-PA; Oklahoma City, OK; Orlando-Kissimmee, FL; Philadelphia-Camden-Wilmington, PA-NJ-DE-MD; Phoenix-Mesa-Scottsdale, AZ; Pittsburgh, PA; Portland-Vancouver-Beaverton, OR-WA; Providence–Fall River–Warwick, RI-MA; Riverside–San Bernardino–Ontario, CA; Sacramento–Arden-Arcade–Roseville, CA; Salt Lake City, UT; San Diego–Carlsbad–San Marcos, CA; San Francisco–Oakland–Fremont, CA; San Jose–Sunnyvale–Santa Clara, CA; Seattle-Tacoma-Bellevue, WA; Springfield, MA-CT; St. Louis, MO-IL; Tampa–St. Petersburg–Clearwater, FL; Tulsa, OK; Virginia Beach–Norfolk–Newport News, VA-NC; Washington-Arlington-Alexandria, DC-VA-MD-WV; Wichita, KS; Worcester, MA-CT
Commercial Pilots	Atlanta–Sandy Springs–Marietta, GA

Jobs and Metropolitan Areas Where
Earnings Average More than $100,000

Occupation	Metropolitan Area(s) Where Average Earnings Are More than $100,000 per Year
Compensation and Benefits Managers	Boston-Cambridge-Quincy, MA-NH; Dallas–Fort Worth–Arlington, TX; New York–Northern New Jersey–Long Island, NY-NJ-PA
Computer and Information Scientists, Research	Austin–Round Rock, TX; Boston-Cambridge-Quincy, MA-NH; Los Angeles–Long Beach–Santa Ana, CA; San Diego–Carlsbad–San Marcos, CA; San Francisco–Oakland–Fremont, CA; San Jose–Sunnyvale–Santa Clara, CA; Seattle-Tacoma-Bellevue, WA; Washington-Arlington-Alexandria, DC-VA-MD-WV
Computer and Information Systems Managers	Atlanta–Sandy Springs–Marietta, GA; Austin–Round Rock, TX; Baltimore-Towson, MD; Boston-Cambridge-Quincy, MA-NH; Bridgeport-Stamford-Norwalk, CT; Charlotte-Gastonia-Concord, NC-SC; Chicago-Naperville-Joliet, IL-IN-WI; Cincinnati-Middletown, OH-KY-IN; Cleveland-Elyria-Mentor, OH; Columbus, OH; Dallas–Fort Worth–Arlington, TX; Denver-Aurora, CO; Detroit-Warren-Livonia, MI; Durham, NC; Hartford–West Hartford–East Hartford, CT; Houston–Sugar Land–Baytown, TX; Kansas City, MO-KS; Los Angeles–Long Beach–Santa Ana, CA; Miami–Fort Lauderdale–Miami Beach, FL; Minneapolis–St. Paul–Bloomington, MN-WI; New York–Northern New Jersey–Long Island, NY-NJ-PA; Philadelphia-Camden-Wilmington, PA-NJ-DE-MD; Phoenix-Mesa-Scottsdale, AZ; Portland-Vancouver-Beaverton, OR-WA; Providence–Fall River–Warwick, RI-MA; Raleigh-Cary, NC; Richmond, VA; Rochester, NY; San Antonio, TX; San Diego–Carlsbad–San Marcos, CA; San Francisco–Oakland–Fremont, CA; San Jose–Sunnyvale–Santa Clara, CA; Seattle-Tacoma-Bellevue, WA; St. Louis, MO-IL; Tampa–St. Petersburg–Clearwater, FL; Washington-Arlington-Alexandria, DC-VA-MD-WV
Computer Hardware Engineers	Boston-Cambridge-Quincy, MA-NH; Boulder, CO; New York–Northern New Jersey–Long Island, NY-NJ-PA; San Francisco–Oakland–Fremont, CA; San Jose–Sunnyvale–Santa Clara, CA; Washington-Arlington-Alexandria, DC-VA-MD-WV
Computer Software Engineers, Applications	San Francisco–Oakland–Fremont, CA; San Jose–Sunnyvale–Santa Clara, CA
Computer Software Engineers, Systems Software	Albuquerque, NM; Boulder, CO; San Francisco–Oakland–Fremont, CA; San Jose–Sunnyvale–Santa Clara, CA; Washington-Arlington-Alexandria, DC-VA-MD-WV
Construction Managers	Jacksonville, FL; Los Angeles–Long Beach–Santa Ana, CA; New York–Northern New Jersey–Long Island, NY-NJ-PA; Sacramento–Arden-Arcade–Roseville, CA; San Diego–Carlsbad–San Marcos, CA; San Francisco–Oakland–Fremont, CA; San Jose–Sunnyvale–Santa Clara, CA; Seattle-Tacoma-Bellevue, WA
Dental Hygienists	San Francisco–Oakland–Fremont, CA

(continued)

(continued)

Jobs and Metropolitan Areas Where Earnings Average More than $100,000

Occupation	Metropolitan Area(s) Where Average Earnings Are More than $100,000 per Year
Dentists, General	Atlanta–Sandy Springs–Marietta, GA; Boston-Cambridge-Quincy, MA-NH; Chicago-Naperville-Joliet, IL-IN-WI; Dallas–Fort Worth–Arlington, TX; Denver-Aurora, CO; Detroit-Warren-Livonia, MI; Houston–Sugar Land–Baytown, TX; Los Angeles–Long Beach–Santa Ana, CA; Miami–Fort Lauderdale–Miami Beach, FL; Minneapolis–St. Paul–Bloomington, MN-WI; New York–Northern New Jersey–Long Island, NY-NJ-PA; Philadelphia-Camden-Wilmington, PA-NJ-DE-MD; Phoenix-Mesa-Scottsdale, AZ; San Francisco–Oakland–Fremont, CA; Seattle-Tacoma-Bellevue, WA; Washington-Arlington-Alexandria, DC-VA-MD-WV
Economists	Washington-Arlington-Alexandria, DC-VA-MD-WV
Education Administrators, Elementary and Secondary School	Chicago-Naperville-Joliet, IL-IN-WI; Hartford–West Hartford–East Hartford, CT; Los Angeles–Long Beach–Santa Ana, CA; New York–Northern New Jersey–Long Island, NY-NJ-PA; Philadelphia-Camden-Wilmington, PA-NJ-DE-MD; Riverside–San Bernardino–Ontario, CA; San Diego–Carlsbad–San Marcos, CA; San Francisco–Oakland–Fremont, CA; San Jose–Sunnyvale–Santa Clara, CA
Electrical Engineers	San Jose–Sunnyvale–Santa Clara, CA
Electronics Engineers, Except Computer	Oxnard–Thousand Oaks–Ventura, CA; Providence–Fall River–Warwick, RI-MA; San Jose–Sunnyvale–Santa Clara, CA; Washington-Arlington-Alexandria, DC-VA-MD-WV
Engineering Managers	Atlanta–Sandy Springs–Marietta, GA; Austin–Round Rock, TX; Baltimore-Towson, MD; Boston-Cambridge-Quincy, MA-NH; Charlotte-Gastonia-Concord, NC-SC; Chicago-Naperville-Joliet, IL-IN-WI; Cincinnati-Middletown, OH-KY-IN; Cleveland-Elyria-Mentor, OH; Dallas–Fort Worth–Arlington, TX; Denver-Aurora, CO; Detroit-Warren-Livonia, MI; Hartford–West Hartford–East Hartford, CT; Houston–Sugar Land–Baytown, TX; Huntsville, AL; Kansas City, MO-KS; Los Angeles–Long Beach–Santa Ana, CA; Minneapolis–St. Paul–Bloomington, MN-WI; New York–Northern New Jersey–Long Island, NY-NJ-PA; Philadelphia-Camden-Wilmington, PA-NJ-DE-MD; Phoenix-Mesa-Scottsdale, AZ; Pittsburgh, PA; Portland-Vancouver-Beaverton, OR-WA; Raleigh-Cary, NC; Riverside–San Bernardino–Ontario, CA; Rochester, NY; Sacramento–Arden-Arcade–Roseville, CA; Salt Lake City, UT; San Diego–Carlsbad–San Marcos, CA; San Francisco–Oakland–Fremont, CA; San Jose–Sunnyvale–Santa Clara, CA; Seattle-Tacoma-Bellevue, WA; St. Louis, MO-IL; Washington-Arlington-Alexandria, DC-VA-MD-WV
Financial Managers	Austin–Round Rock, TX; Boston-Cambridge-Quincy, MA-NH; Bridgeport-Stamford-Norwalk, CT; Charlotte-Gastonia-Concord, NC-SC; Chicago-Naperville-Joliet, IL-IN-WI; Cleveland-Elyria-Mentor, OH; Columbus, OH; Dallas–Fort Worth–Arlington, TX; Denver-Aurora, CO;

Jobs and Metropolitan Areas Where Earnings Average More than $100,000

Occupation	Metropolitan Area(s) Where Average Earnings Are More than $100,000 per Year
	Durham, NC; Hartford–West Hartford–East Hartford, CT; Houston–Sugar Land–Baytown, TX; Jacksonville, FL; Los Angeles–Long Beach–Santa Ana, CA; Miami–Fort Lauderdale–Miami Beach, FL; Minneapolis–St. Paul–Bloomington, MN-WI; New York–Northern New Jersey–Long Island, NY-NJ-PA; Oxnard–Thousand Oaks–Ventura, CA; Philadelphia-Camden-Wilmington, PA-NJ-DE-MD; Portland-Vancouver-Beaverton, OR-WA; Providence–Fall River–Warwick, RI-MA; Richmond, VA; San Diego–Carlsbad–San Marcos, CA; San Francisco–Oakland–Fremont, CA; San Jose–Sunnyvale–Santa Clara, CA; Seattle-Tacoma-Bellevue, WA; St. Louis, MO-IL; Trenton-Ewing, NJ; Washington-Arlington-Alexandria, DC-VA-MD-WV
First-Line Supervisors/Managers of Fire Fighting and Prevention Workers	Chicago-Naperville-Joliet, IL-IN-WI
First-Line Supervisors/Managers of Police and Detectives	Los Angeles–Long Beach–Santa Ana, CA; Washington-Arlington-Alexandria, DC-VA-MD-WV
General and Operations Managers	Boston-Cambridge-Quincy, MA-NH; Boulder, CO; Bridgeport-Stamford-Norwalk, CT; Charlotte-Gastonia-Concord, NC-SC; Chicago-Naperville-Joliet, IL-IN-WI; Danbury, CT; Dayton, OH; Durham, NC; Greensboro–High Point, NC; Los Angeles–Long Beach–Santa Ana, CA; Milwaukee–Waukesha–West Allis, WI; Napa, CA; New Haven, CT; New York–Northern New Jersey–Long Island, NY-NJ-PA; Oxnard–Thousand Oaks–Ventura, CA; Philadelphia-Camden-Wilmington, PA-NJ-DE-MD; Raleigh-Cary, NC; San Diego–Carlsbad–San Marcos, CA; San Francisco–Oakland–Fremont, CA; San Jose–Sunnyvale–Santa Clara, CA; Santa Rosa–Petaluma, CA; Seattle-Tacoma-Bellevue, WA; Sioux Falls, SD; Spokane, WA; Trenton-Ewing, NJ
Geoscientists, Except Hydrologists and Geographers	Denver-Aurora, CO; Houston–Sugar Land–Baytown, TX
Health Specialties Teachers, Postsecondary	Baltimore-Towson, MD; Boston-Cambridge-Quincy, MA-NH; Houston–Sugar Land–Baytown, TX; New York–Northern New Jersey–Long Island, NY-NJ-PA
Industrial Production Managers	Boston-Cambridge-Quincy, MA-NH; Houston–Sugar Land–Baytown, TX; San Francisco–Oakland–Fremont, CA; San Jose–Sunnyvale–Santa Clara, CA
Judges, Magistrate Judges, and Magistrates	New York–Northern New Jersey–Long Island, NY-NJ-PA
Law Teachers, Postsecondary	Washington-Arlington-Alexandria, DC-VA-MD-WV

(continued)

(continued)

Jobs and Metropolitan Areas Where Earnings Average More than $100,000

Occupation	Metropolitan Area(s) Where Average Earnings Are More than $100,000 per Year
Lawyers	Atlanta–Sandy Springs–Marietta, GA; Austin–Round Rock, TX; Baltimore-Towson, MD; Birmingham-Hoover, AL; Boston-Cambridge-Quincy, MA-NH; Bridgeport-Stamford-Norwalk, CT; Charlotte-Gastonia-Concord, NC-SC; Chicago-Naperville-Joliet, IL-IN-WI; Cincinnati-Middletown, OH-KY-IN; Dallas–Fort Worth–Arlington, TX; Denver-Aurora, CO; Detroit-Warren-Livonia, MI; Fresno, CA; Hartford–West Hartford–East Hartford, CT; Houston–Sugar Land–Baytown, TX; Las Vegas–Paradise, NV; Los Angeles–Long Beach–Santa Ana, CA; Madison, WI; Memphis, TN-MS-AR; Miami–Fort Lauderdale–Miami Beach, FL; Milwaukee–Waukesha–West Allis, WI; Minneapolis–St. Paul–Bloomington, MN-WI; Nashville-Davidson–Murfreesboro, TN; New Haven, CT; New York–Northern New Jersey–Long Island, NY-NJ-PA; Orlando-Kissimmee, FL; Philadelphia-Camden-Wilmington, PA-NJ-DE-MD; Phoenix-Mesa-Scottsdale, AZ; Portland-Vancouver-Beaverton, OR-WA; Providence–Fall River–Warwick, RI-MA; Raleigh-Cary, NC; Richmond, VA; Riverside–San Bernardino–Ontario, CA; Sacramento–Arden-Arcade–Roseville, CA; Salt Lake City, UT; San Diego–Carlsbad–San Marcos, CA; San Francisco–Oakland–Fremont, CA; San Jose–Sunnyvale–Santa Clara, CA; Seattle-Tacoma-Bellevue, WA; Toledo, OH; Virginia Beach–Norfolk–Newport News, VA-NC; Washington-Arlington-Alexandria, DC-VA-MD-WV
Marine Engineers and Naval Architects	Washington-Arlington-Alexandria, DC-VA-MD-WV
Market Research Analysts	San Jose–Sunnyvale–Santa Clara, CA
Marketing Managers	Atlanta–Sandy Springs–Marietta, GA; Austin–Round Rock, TX; Baltimore-Towson, MD; Boston-Cambridge-Quincy, MA-NH; Bridgeport-Stamford-Norwalk, CT; Charlotte-Gastonia-Concord, NC-SC; Chicago-Naperville-Joliet, IL-IN-WI; Dallas–Fort Worth–Arlington, TX; Denver-Aurora, CO; Houston–Sugar Land–Baytown, TX; Kansas City, MO-KS; Los Angeles–Long Beach–Santa Ana, CA; Minneapolis–St. Paul–Bloomington, MN-WI; New York–Northern New Jersey–Long Island, NY-NJ-PA; Philadelphia-Camden-Wilmington, PA-NJ-DE-MD; Pittsburgh, PA; Portland-Vancouver-Beaverton, OR-WA; San Diego–Carlsbad–San Marcos, CA; San Francisco–Oakland–Fremont, CA; San Jose–Sunnyvale–Santa Clara, CA; Seattle-Tacoma-Bellevue, WA; St. Louis, MO-IL; Tampa–St. Petersburg–Clearwater, FL; Washington-Arlington-Alexandria, DC-VA-MD-WV
Materials Engineers	San Jose–Sunnyvale–Santa Clara, CA
Mathematicians	Washington-Arlington-Alexandria, DC-VA-MD-WV

Jobs and Metropolitan Areas Where Earnings Average More than $100,000

Occupation	Metropolitan Area(s) Where Average Earnings Are More than $100,000 per Year
Medical and Health Services Managers	New York–Northern New Jersey–Long Island, NY-NJ-PA; San Jose–Sunnyvale–Santa Clara, CA; Seattle-Tacoma-Bellevue, WA
Natural Sciences Managers	Boston-Cambridge-Quincy, MA-NH; Durham, NC; Los Angeles–Long Beach–Santa Ana, CA; Minneapolis–St. Paul–Bloomington, MN-WI; New York–Northern New Jersey–Long Island, NY-NJ-PA; Philadelphia-Camden-Wilmington, PA-NJ-DE-MD; San Diego–Carlsbad–San Marcos, CA; San Francisco–Oakland–Fremont, CA; Washington-Arlington-Alexandria, DC-VA-MD-WV
Nuclear Engineers	Richmond, VA; Washington-Arlington-Alexandria, DC-VA-MD-WV
Optometrists	New York–Northern New Jersey–Long Island, NY-NJ-PA
Oral and Maxillofacial Surgeons	New York–Northern New Jersey–Long Island, NY-NJ-PA
Orthodontists	New York–Northern New Jersey–Long Island, NY-NJ-PA
Personal Financial Advisors	Boston-Cambridge-Quincy, MA-NH; Bridgeport-Stamford-Norwalk, CT; New York–Northern New Jersey–Long Island, NY-NJ-PA
Petroleum Engineers	Anchorage, AK; Dallas–Fort Worth–Arlington, TX; Denver-Aurora, CO; Houston–Sugar Land–Baytown, TX
Pharmacists	Atlanta–Sandy Springs–Marietta, GA; Austin–Round Rock, TX; Baltimore-Towson, MD; Birmingham-Hoover, AL; Buffalo–Niagara Falls, NY; Charlotte-Gastonia-Concord, NC-SC; Chicago-Naperville-Joliet, IL-IN-WI; Cincinnati-Middletown, OH-KY-IN; Cleveland-Elyria-Mentor, OH; Dallas–Fort Worth–Arlington, TX; Denver-Aurora, CO; Detroit-Warren-Livonia, MI; Hartford–West Hartford–East Hartford, CT; Houston–Sugar Land–Baytown, TX; Jacksonville, FL; Kansas City, MO-KS; Las Vegas–Paradise, NV; Los Angeles–Long Beach–Santa Ana, CA; Louisville–Jefferson County, KY-IN; Memphis, TN-MS-AR; Miami–Fort Lauderdale–Miami Beach, FL; Milwaukee–Waukesha–West Allis, WI; Minneapolis–St. Paul–Bloomington, MN-WI; Nashville-Davidson–Murfreesboro, TN; New York–Northern New Jersey–Long Island, NY-NJ-PA; Orlando-Kissimmee, FL; Phoenix-Mesa-Scottsdale, AZ; Portland-Vancouver-Beaverton, OR-WA; Riverside–San Bernardino–Ontario, CA; Sacramento–Arden-Arcade–Roseville, CA; Salt Lake City, UT; San Antonio, TX; San Diego–Carlsbad–San Marcos, CA; San Francisco–Oakland–Fremont, CA; San Jose–Sunnyvale–Santa Clara, CA; Seattle-Tacoma-Bellevue, WA; St. Louis, MO-IL; Tampa–St. Petersburg–Clearwater, FL; Virginia Beach–Norfolk–Newport News, VA-NC; Washington-Arlington-Alexandria, DC-VA-MD-WV
Physicists	Chicago-Naperville-Joliet, IL-IN-WI; San Francisco–Oakland–Fremont, CA; Washington-Arlington-Alexandria, DC-VA-MD-WV
Podiatrists	New York–Northern New Jersey–Long Island, NY-NJ-PA

(continued)

(continued)

Jobs and Metropolitan Areas Where Earnings Average More than $100,000

Occupation	Metropolitan Area(s) Where Average Earnings Are More than $100,000 per Year
Political Scientists	Washington-Arlington-Alexandria, DC-VA-MD-WV
Producers and Directors	Los Angeles–Long Beach–Santa Ana, CA
Prosthodontists	New York–Northern New Jersey–Long Island, NY-NJ-PA
Public Relations Managers	Boston-Cambridge-Quincy, MA-NH; Los Angeles–Long Beach–Santa Ana, CA; New York–Northern New Jersey–Long Island, NY-NJ-PA; San Francisco–Oakland–Fremont, CA; Washington-Arlington-Alexandria, DC-VA-MD-WV
Purchasing Managers	Boston-Cambridge-Quincy, MA-NH; Houston–Sugar Land–Baytown, TX; Minneapolis–St. Paul–Bloomington, MN-WI; New York–Northern New Jersey–Long Island, NY-NJ-PA; Philadelphia-Camden-Wilmington, PA-NJ-DE-MD; San Francisco–Oakland–Fremont, CA; San Jose–Sunnyvale–Santa Clara, CA; Washington-Arlington-Alexandria, DC-VA-MD-WV
Registered Nurses	San Jose–Sunnyvale–Santa Clara, CA
Sales Engineers	San Jose–Sunnyvale–Santa Clara, CA
Sales Managers	Austin–Round Rock, TX; Boston-Cambridge-Quincy, MA-NH; Bridgeport-Stamford-Norwalk, CT; Cincinnati-Middletown, OH-KY-IN; Cleveland-Elyria-Mentor, OH; Columbus, OH; Dallas–Fort Worth–Arlington, TX; Denver-Aurora, CO; Detroit-Warren-Livonia, MI; Houston–Sugar Land–Baytown, TX; Jacksonville, FL; Los Angeles–Long Beach–Santa Ana, CA; Miami–Fort Lauderdale–Miami Beach, FL; Milwaukee–Waukesha–West Allis, WI; Minneapolis–St. Paul–Bloomington, MN-WI; New York–Northern New Jersey–Long Island, NY-NJ-PA; Orlando-Kissimmee, FL; Philadelphia-Camden-Wilmington, PA-NJ-DE-MD; Portland-Vancouver-Beaverton, OR-WA; Richmond, VA; San Francisco–Oakland–Fremont, CA; San Jose–Sunnyvale–Santa Clara, CA; Seattle-Tacoma-Bellevue, WA; St. Louis, MO-IL; Tampa–St. Petersburg–Clearwater, FL; Washington-Arlington-Alexandria, DC-VA-MD-WV
Securities, Commodities, and Financial Services Sales Agents	Bridgeport-Stamford-Norwalk, CT; Memphis, TN-MS-AR; New York–Northern New Jersey–Long Island, NY-NJ-PA; San Francisco–Oakland–Fremont, CA
Training and Development Managers	New York–Northern New Jersey–Long Island, NY-NJ-PA
Veterinarians	New York–Northern New Jersey–Long Island, NY-NJ-PA

Bonus List: Jobs in Which Women's Average Earnings Are Not Greatly Lower than Men's

You probably have read about how female workers tend to earn less than men in the same occupation. The reason for this wage difference is the subject of a lot of controversy—is it discrimination, the "mommy track" lifestyle choices of some women (which might include part-time work or periods of absence from the workforce), or some combination of factors? Some researchers have identified jobs where women actually earn more than men, and others have pointed to benefits (most notably maternity leave) that help offset women's lower pay. But in plain dollar terms, the decennial Census and the Current Population Survey seem to show that in most occupations women can expect to earn less than men.

If you're looking for a high-paying job and you are a woman—or a man who feels more comfortable in an environment where pay is equitable—you might want to know which jobs have the smallest gap between the dollar earnings of men and women. With that goal in mind, we used figures from the American Community Survey of 2005–2007 (a survey conducted by the Census Bureau) to identify the subset of the 250 best-paying jobs in which women's earnings were at least 70 percent of men's. (Sad to say, 70 percent is a "good" ratio.) Earnings figures for women were available for only 116 of the 250 best-paying jobs, so some jobs that do not appear here might actually have a good female-to-male wage ratio. Don't assume that a job has a bad ratio just because it doesn't appear on this list.

Jobs in Which Women's Average Earnings Are Not Greatly Lower than Men's

Job	Ratio of Female to Male Earnings	Annual Earnings, Both Sexes
1. First-Line Supervisors/Managers of Fire Fighting and Prevention Workers	90.2%	$67,440
2. Agricultural Engineers	89.8%	$68,730
3. Biomedical Engineers	89.8%	$77,400
4. First-Line Supervisors/Managers of Mechanics, Installers, and Repairers	89.4%	$57,300
5. Police and Sheriff's Patrol Officers	88.8%	$51,410
6. Dental Hygienists	88.4%	$66,570
7. Engineering Managers	88.4%	$115,270
8. Computer Programmers	87.7%	$69,620
9. First-Line Supervisors/Managers of Correctional Officers	87.4%	$57,380
10. Railroad Conductors and Yardmasters	87.1%	$52,830
11. Avionics Technicians	86.9%	$49,310
12. Mechanical Engineers	86.9%	$74,920

(continued)

(continued)

Jobs in Which Women's Average Earnings Are Not Greatly Lower than Men's

Job	Ratio of Female to Male Earnings	Annual Earnings, Both Sexes
13. Telecommunications Line Installers and Repairers	86.8%	$48,090
14. Transportation, Storage, and Distribution Managers	86.8%	$79,000
15. Network and Computer Systems Administrators	86.6%	$66,310
16. Sales Engineers	86.4%	$83,100
17. Technical Writers	86.3%	$61,620
18. Electrical Power-Line Installers and Repairers	86.0%	$55,100
19. Materials Engineers	86.0%	$81,820
20. Instructional Coordinators	84.5%	$56,880
21. Budget Analysts	84.4%	$65,320
22. Computer and Information Scientists, Research	84.2%	$97,970
23. Computer Specialists, All Other	84.2%	$75,150
24. Computer Systems Analysts	84.2%	$75,500
25. Postal Service Mail Sorters, Processors, and Processing Machine Operators	83.8%	$50,600
26. Compliance Officers, Except Agriculture, Construction, Health and Safety, and Transportation	83.7%	$48,890
27. Urban and Regional Planners	83.7%	$59,810
28. First-Line Supervisors/Managers of Police and Detectives	83.6%	$75,490
29. Construction and Building Inspectors	83.4%	$50,180
30. Nuclear Engineers	83.4%	$97,080
31. Environmental Engineers	83.3%	$74,020
32. Detectives and Criminal Investigators	83.1%	$60,910
33. Postal Service Clerks	83.0%	$55,920
34. Aircraft Mechanics and Service Technicians	82.5%	$51,390
35. Radiation Therapists	82.3%	$72,910
36. Industrial Production Managers	82.2%	$83,290
37. Librarians	82.1%	$52,530
38. Speech-Language Pathologists	82.0%	$62,930
39. Aerospace Engineers	81.8%	$92,520
40. Computer and Information Systems Managers	81.3%	$112,210
41. Administrative Services Managers	80.9%	$73,520
42. Operations Research Analysts	80.6%	$69,000
43. Logisticians	79.8%	$66,480
44. Mathematicians	79.5%	$95,150

Jobs in Which Women's Average Earnings Are Not Greatly Lower than Men's

Job	Ratio of Female to Male Earnings	Annual Earnings, Both Sexes
45. Statisticians	79.5%	$72,610
46. Electrical and Electronics Repairers, Commercial and Industrial Equipment	79.4%	$48,430
47. Electrical and Electronics Repairers, Powerhouse, Substation, and Relay	79.4%	$61,040
48. First-Line Supervisors/Managers of Construction Trades and Extraction Workers	78.8%	$58,140
49. Network Systems and Data Communications Analysts	78.5%	$71,100
50. Dietitians and Nutritionists	78.3%	$50,590
51. Respiratory Therapists	78.3%	$52,200
52. Postal Service Mail Carriers	78.2%	$50,290
53. Purchasing Agents, Except Wholesale, Retail, and Farm Products	78.2%	$53,940
54. Geological and Petroleum Technicians	77.9%	$53,360
55. Gaming Managers	77.7%	$68,290
56. Economists	77.3%	$83,590
57. Stationary Engineers and Boiler Operators	77.2%	$49,790
58. Chemical Engineers	76.7%	$84,680
59. Civil Engineers	76.7%	$74,600
60. Occupational Therapists	76.3%	$66,780
61. Pharmacists	76.1%	$106,410
62. Purchasing Managers	75.7%	$89,160
63. Registered Nurses	75.4%	$62,450
64. Fish and Game Wardens	75.2%	$48,930
65. Database Administrators	74.7%	$69,740
66. Construction Managers	74.2%	$79,860
67. Producers and Directors	74.2%	$64,430
68. Editors	74.1%	$49,990
69. Sociologists	74.0%	$68,570
70. Public Relations Managers	72.5%	$89,430
71. Computer Hardware Engineers	72.2%	$97,400
72. First-Line Supervisors/Managers of Production and Operating Workers	71.9%	$50,440
73. Tax Examiners, Collectors, and Revenue Agents	70.5%	$48,100

PART II

Descriptions of the Best-Paying Jobs

This part provides descriptions for all the jobs included in one or more of the lists in Part I. The Introduction gives more details on how to use and interpret the job descriptions, but here is some additional information:

- Job descriptions are arranged in alphabetical order by job title. This approach allows you to find a description quickly if you know its correct title from one of the lists in Part I.

- If you are using this section to browse for interesting options, we suggest you begin with the Table of Contents. Part I features many interesting lists that will help you identify job titles to explore in more detail. If you have not browsed the lists in Part I, consider spending some time there. The lists are interesting and will help you identify job titles you can find described in the material that follows. The job titles in Part II are also listed in the Table of Contents.

- Each description lists the most important skills and knowledge/courses required by the job. If the name of any skill or knowledge/course is not meaningful to you, turn to Appendix A for a complete definition. Appendix B discusses which skills are most closely associated with high-paying jobs.

- Many job descriptions cover occupations that are specializations within a larger occupation listed in Part I. In such cases, you will find a note indicating that the Department of Labor reports the information for an occupation with a different job title. This job title is the one used in the Part I lists. (Exception: If the occupation is a medical doctor of some kind, the related job in Part I is Physicians and Surgeons.)

Accountants

- ❋ Annual Earnings: $59,430
- ❋ Beginning Wage: $36,720
- ❋ Earnings Growth Potential: Medium (38.2%)
- ❋ Growth: 17.7%
- ❋ Annual Job Openings: 134,463
- ❋ Self-Employed: 9.5%
- ❋ Part-Time: 9.3%
- ❋ Job Security: More secure than most
- ❋ Education/Training Required: Bachelor's degree

The Department of Labor reports this information for the occupation Accountants and Auditors. The job openings listed here are shared with other specializations within that occupation, including Auditors.

Industries in Which Income Is Highest

Industry	Average Annual Earnings	Number Employed
Motion Picture and Sound Recording Industries	$67,080	3,530
Other Information Services	$66,360	1,720
Computer and Electronic Product Manufacturing	$64,390	13,550
Utilities	$63,880	7,510
Telecommunications	$63,710	7,950

Metropolitan Areas Where Income Is Highest

Metropolitan Area	Average Annual Earnings	Number Employed
San Jose–Sunnyvale–Santa Clara, CA	$74,950	10,600
New York–Northern New Jersey–Long Island, NY-NJ-PA	$73,910	104,320
Napa, CA	$72,670	340
Bridgeport-Stamford-Norwalk, CT	$72,310	7,240
San Francisco–Oakland–Fremont, CA	$71,320	23,190

Analyze financial information and prepare financial reports to determine or maintain record of assets, liabilities, profit and loss, tax liability, or other financial activities within an organization. Prepare, examine, or analyze accounting records, financial statements, or other financial reports to assess accuracy, completeness, and conformance to reporting and procedural standards. Compute taxes owed and prepare tax returns, ensuring compliance with payment, reporting, or other tax requirements. Analyze business operations, trends, costs, revenues, financial commitments, and obligations to project future revenues and expenses or to provide advice. Report to management regarding the finances of establishment. Establish tables of accounts and assign entries to proper accounts. Develop, maintain, and analyze budgets, preparing periodic reports that compare budgeted costs to actual costs. Develop, implement, modify, and document recordkeeping and accounting systems, making use of current computer technology. Prepare forms and manuals for accounting and bookkeeping personnel and direct their work activities. Survey operations to ascertain accounting needs and to recommend, develop, or maintain solutions to business and financial problems. Work as Internal Revenue Service (IRS) agents. Advise management about issues such as resource utilization, tax strategies, and the assumptions underlying budget forecasts. Provide internal and external auditing services for businesses or individuals. Advise clients in areas such as compensation, employee healthcare benefits, the design of accounting or data processing systems, or long-range tax or estate plans. Investigate bankruptcies and other complex financial transactions and prepare reports summarizing the findings. Represent clients before taxing authorities and provide support during litigation involving financial issues. Appraise, evaluate, and inventory real property and equipment, recording information such as the description, value, and location of property. Maintain or examine the records of government agencies. Serve as bankruptcy trustees or business valuators.

Other Considerations for Income: Salaries vary because of differences in size of firm, location, level of education, and professional credentials. Wage and salary accountants and auditors usually receive standard benefits, including health and medical insurance, life insurance, a 401(k) plan, and paid annual leave. High-level senior accountants may receive additional benefits, such as the use of a company car and an expense account.

Personality Type: Conventional-Enterprising. **Career Cluster:** 04 Business, Management, and Administration. **Career Pathway:** 04.2 Business, Financial Management, and Accounting. **Skills:** Management of Financial Resources; Systems Analysis; Systems Evaluation; Operations Analysis; Judgment and Decision Making; Programming; Mathematics; Time Management.

Education and Training Programs: Accounting; Accounting and Business/Management; Accounting and Computer Science; Accounting and Finance; Auditing; Taxation. **Related Knowledge/Courses:** Economics and Accounting; Clerical; Mathematics; Computers and Electronics; Personnel and Human Resources; Administration and Management.

Accountants and Auditors

See *Accountants* and *Auditors,* described separately.

Actuaries

- ✹ Annual Earnings: $84,810
- ✹ Beginning Wage: $49,150
- ✹ Earnings Growth Potential: High (42.0%)
- ✹ Growth: 23.7%
- ✹ Annual Job Openings: 3,245
- ✹ Self-Employed: 0.0%
- ✹ Part-Time: 5.9%
- ✹ Job Security: Most secure
- ✹ Education/Training Required: Work experience plus degree

Industries in Which Income Is Highest

Industry	Average Annual Earnings	Number Employed
Professional, Scientific, and Technical Services	$96,160	3,140
Insurance Carriers and Related Activities	$83,940	11,490
Management of Companies and Enterprises	$83,860	1,650

Metropolitan Areas Where Income Is Highest

Metropolitan Area	Average Annual Earnings	Number Employed
San Diego–Carlsbad–San Marcos, CA	$114,160	70
Philadelphia-Camden-Wilmington, PA-NJ-DE-MD	$110,930	890
Buffalo–Niagara Falls, NY	$102,290	100
Fort Wayne, IN	$102,100	90
Charlotte-Gastonia-Concord, NC-SC	$98,880	120

Analyze statistical data, such as mortality, accident, sickness, disability, and retirement rates, and construct probability tables to forecast risk and liability for payment of future benefits. May ascertain premium rates required and cash reserves necessary to ensure payment of future benefits. Ascertain premium rates required and cash reserves and liabilities necessary to ensure payment of future benefits. Analyze statistical information to estimate mortality, accident, sickness, disability, and retirement rates. Design, review, and help administer insurance, annuity, and pension plans, determining financial soundness and calculating premiums. Collaborate with programmers, underwriters, accountants, claims experts, and senior management to help companies develop plans for new lines of business or for improving existing business. Determine or help determine company policy and explain complex technical matters to company executives, government officials, shareholders, policyholders, or the public. Testify before public agencies on proposed legislation affecting businesses. Provide advice to clients on a contract basis, working as a consultant. Testify in court as expert witness or to provide legal evidence on matters such as the value of potential lifetime earnings of a person who is disabled or killed in an accident. Construct probability tables for events such as fires, natural disasters, and unemployment, based on analysis of statistical data and other pertinent information. Determine policy contract provisions for each type of insurance. Manage credit and help price corporate security offerings. Provide expertise to help financial institutions manage risks and maximize returns associated with investment products or credit offerings. Determine equitable basis for distributing surplus earnings under participating insurance and annuity contracts in mutual companies. Explain changes in contract provisions to customers.

Other Considerations for Income: Insurance companies and consulting firms give merit increases to actuaries as they gain experience and pass examinations. Some companies also offer cash bonuses for each professional designation achieved.

Personality Type: Conventional-Investigative-Enterprising. **Career Cluster:** 06 Finance. **Career Pathway:** 06.4 Insurance Services. **Skills:** Programming; Mathematics; Operations Analysis; Complex Problem Solving; Active Learning; Quality Control Analysis; Troubleshooting; Critical Thinking.

Education and Training Program: Actuarial Science. **Related Knowledge/Courses:** Economics and Accounting; Mathematics; Computers and Electronics; Administration and Management; Personnel and Human Resources; Sales and Marketing.

Acute Care Nurses

- ❀ Annual Earnings: $62,450
- ❀ Beginning Wage: $43,410
- ❀ Earnings Growth Potential: Low (30.5%)
- ❀ Growth: 23.5%
- ❀ Annual Job Openings: 233,499
- ❀ Self-Employed: 0.8%
- ❀ Part-Time: 21.8%
- ❀ Job Security: No data available
- ❀ Education/Training Required: Master's degree

The Department of Labor reports this information for the occupation Registered Nurses. The job openings listed here are shared with other specializations within that occupation, including Advanced Practice Psychiatric Nurses; and Critical Care Nurses.

Industries in Which Income Is Highest

Industry	Average Annual Earnings	Number Employed
Administrative and Support Services	$67,720	98,770
Religious, Grantmaking, Civic, Professional, and Similar Organizations	$64,540	2,030
Federal, State, and Local Government	$64,340	144,990
Merchant Wholesalers, Nondurable Goods	$64,150	1,010
Hospitals	$63,890	1,535,440

Metropolitan Areas Where Income Is Highest

Metropolitan Area	Average Annual Earnings	Number Employed
San Jose–Sunnyvale–Santa Clara, CA	$109,110	14,590
San Francisco–Oakland–Fremont, CA	$97,590	32,780
Modesto, CA	$91,910	3,040
Vallejo-Fairfield, CA	$88,500	3,010
Napa, CA	$88,030	1,430

Provide advanced nursing care for patients with acute conditions such as heart attacks, respiratory distress syndrome, or shock. May care for pre- and post-operative patients or perform advanced, invasive diagnostic or therapeutic procedures. No task data available.

Other Considerations for Income: Many employers offer flexible work schedules, child care, educational benefits, and bonuses.

Personality Type: Social-Investigative-Realistic. **Career Cluster:** 08 Health Science. **Career Pathway:** 08.1 Therapeutic Services. **Skills:** No data available.

Education and Training Program: Critical Care Nursing. **Related Knowledge/Courses:** Medicine and Dentistry; Therapy and Counseling; Psychology; Biology; Sociology and Anthropology; Philosophy and Theology.

Administrative Law Judges, Adjudicators, and Hearing Officers

* Annual Earnings: $76,940
* Beginning Wage: $37,040
* Earnings Growth Potential: Very high (51.9%)
* Growth: 0.1%
* Annual Job Openings: 794
* Self-Employed: 0.0%
* Part-Time: 5.9%
* Job Security: Most secure
* Education/Training Required: Work experience plus degree

Industries in Which Income Is Highest

Industry	Average Annual Earnings	Number Employed
Federal, State, and Local Government	$76,930	13,370

Metropolitan Areas Where Income Is Highest

Metropolitan Area	Average Annual Earnings	Number Employed
Washington-Arlington-Alexandria, DC-VA-MD-WV	$110,710	430
Dallas–Fort Worth–Arlington, TX	$108,300	120
New Orleans–Metairie–Kenner, LA	$107,810	60
Minneapolis–St. Paul–Bloomington, MN-WI	$105,340	130
Baltimore-Towson, MD	$99,730	130

Conduct hearings to decide or recommend decisions on claims concerning government programs or other government-related matters and prepare decisions. Determine penalties or the existence and the amount of liability or recommend the acceptance or rejection of claims or compromise settlements. Prepare written opinions and decisions. Review and evaluate data on documents such as claim applications, birth or death certificates, and physician or employer records. Research and analyze laws, regulations, policies, and precedent decisions to prepare for hearings and to determine conclusions.

Confer with individuals or organizations involved in cases to obtain relevant information. Recommend the acceptance or rejection of claims or compromise settlements according to laws, regulations, policies, and precedent decisions. Explain to claimants how they can appeal rulings that go against them. Monitor and direct the activities of trials and hearings to ensure that they are conducted fairly and that courts administer justice while safeguarding the legal rights of all involved parties. Authorize payment of valid claims and determine method of payment. Conduct hearings to review and decide claims regarding issues such as social program eligibility, environmental protection, and enforcement of health and safety regulations. Rule on exceptions, motions, and admissibility of evidence. Determine existence and amount of liability according to current laws, administrative and judicial precedents, and available evidence. Issue subpoenas and administer oaths in preparation for formal hearings. Conduct studies of appeals procedures in field agencies to ensure adherence to legal requirements and to facilitate determination of cases.

Other Considerations for Income: Most salaried judges are provided health, life, and dental insurance; pension plans; judicial immunity protection; expense accounts; vacation, holiday, and sick leave; and contributions to retirement plans made on their behalf. In many states, judicial compensation committees, which make recommendations on the amount of salary increases, determine judicial salaries. States without commissions have statutes that regulate judicial salaries, link judicial salaries to the increases in pay for federal judges, or adjust annual pay according to the change in the Consumer Price Index, calculated by the U.S. Bureau of Labor Statistics.

Personality Type: Enterprising-Investigative-Social. **Career Cluster:** 12 Law, Public Safety, Corrections, and Security. **Career Pathway:** 12.5 Legal Services. **Skills:** Judgment and Decision Making; Reading Comprehension; Active Listening; Social Perceptiveness; Time Management; Writing; Critical Thinking; Speaking.

Education and Training Programs: Law (LL.B., J.D.); Legal Professions and Studies, Other; Legal Studies, General. **Related Knowledge/Courses:** Law and Government; Medicine and Dentistry; Psychology; Therapy and Counseling; Biology; Customer and Personal Service.

Administrative Services Managers

- ❀ Annual Earnings: $73,520
- ❀ Beginning Wage: $37,430
- ❀ Earnings Growth Potential: High (49.1%)
- ❀ Growth: 11.7%
- ❀ Annual Job Openings: 19,513
- ❀ Self-Employed: 0.6%
- ❀ Part-Time: 4.7%
- ❀ Job Security: More secure than most
- ❀ Education/Training Required: Work experience plus degree

Industries in Which Income Is Highest

Industry	Average Annual Earnings	Number Employed
Motion Picture and Sound Recording Industries	$111,990	1,420
Securities, Commodity Contracts, and Other Financial Investments and Related Activities	$92,930	3,890
Telecommunications	$92,630	2,180
Chemical Manufacturing	$91,910	1,570
Utilities	$90,590	2,070

Metropolitan Areas Where Income Is Highest

Metropolitan Area	Average Annual Earnings	Number Employed
Kennewick-Richland-Pasco, WA	$105,520	140
Poughkeepsie-Newburgh-Middletown, NY	$101,820	490
New York–Northern New Jersey–Long Island, NY-NJ-PA	$97,020	21,300
Deltona–Daytona Beach–Ormond Beach, FL	$96,040	140
Boulder, CO	$94,300	130

Plan, direct, or coordinate supportive services of an organization, such as recordkeeping, mail distribution, telephone operator/receptionist, and other office support services. May oversee facilities planning and maintenance and custodial operations. Monitor the facility to ensure that it remains safe, secure, and well-maintained. Direct or coordinate the supportive services department of a business, agency, or organization. Set goals and deadlines for the department. Prepare and review operational reports and schedules to ensure accuracy and efficiency. Analyze internal processes and recommend and implement procedural or policy changes to improve operations such as supply changes or the disposal of records. Acquire, distribute, and store supplies. Plan, administer, and control budgets for contracts, equipment, and supplies. Oversee construction and renovation projects to improve efficiency and to ensure that facilities meet environmental, health, and security standards and comply with government regulations. Hire and terminate clerical and administrative personnel. Oversee the maintenance and repair of machinery, equipment, and electrical and mechanical systems. Manage leasing of facility space. Participate in architectural and engineering planning and design, including space and installation management. Conduct classes to teach procedures to staff. Dispose of, or oversee the disposal of, surplus or unclaimed property.

Other Considerations for Income: Earnings of administrative services managers vary greatly depending on the employer, the specialty, and the geographic area.

Personality Type: Enterprising-Conventional. **Career Clusters:** 04 Business, Management, and Administration; 07 Government and Public Administration; 08 Health Science; 16 Transportation, Distribution, and Logistics. **Career Pathways:** 04.1 Management; 07.1 Governance. **Skills:** Management of Financial Resources; Management of Personnel Resources; Programming; Service Orientation; Coordination; Monitoring; Writing; Speaking.

Education and Training Programs: Business Administration and Management, General; Business/Commerce, General; Medical Staff Services Technology/Technician; Medical/Health Management and Clinical Assistant/Specialist Training; Public Administration; Purchasing, Procurement/Acquisitions and Contracts Management; Transportation/Mobility Management. **Related Knowledge/Courses:** Clerical; Economics and Accounting; Personnel and Human Resources; Customer and Personal Service; Sales and Marketing; Administration and Management.

Advanced Practice Psychiatric Nurses

❀ Annual Earnings: $62,450
❀ Beginning Wage: $43,410
❀ Earnings Growth Potential: Low (30.5%)
❀ Growth: 23.5%
❀ Annual Job Openings: 233,499
❀ Self-Employed: 0.8%
❀ Part-Time: 21.8%
❀ Job Security: No data available
❀ Education/Training Required: Master's degree

The Department of Labor reports this information for the occupation Registered Nurses. The job openings listed here are shared with other specializations within that occupation, including Acute Care Nurses; and Critical Care Nurses.

Industries in Which Income Is Highest

Industry	Average Annual Earnings	Number Employed
Administrative and Support Services	$67,720	98,770
Religious, Grantmaking, Civic, Professional, and Similar Organizations	$64,540	2,030
Federal, State, and Local Government	$64,340	144,990
Merchant Wholesalers, Nondurable Goods	$64,150	1,010
Hospitals	$63,890	1,535,440

Metropolitan Areas Where Income Is Highest

Metropolitan Area	Average Annual Earnings	Number Employed
San Jose–Sunnyvale–Santa Clara, CA	$109,110	14,590
San Francisco–Oakland–Fremont, CA	$97,590	32,780
Modesto, CA	$91,910	3,040
Vallejo-Fairfield, CA	$88,500	3,010
Napa, CA	$88,030	1,430

Provide advanced nursing care for patients with psychiatric disorders. May provide psychotherapy under the direction of a psychiatrist. No task data available.

Other Considerations for Income: Many employers offer flexible work schedules, child care, educational benefits, and bonuses.

Personality Type: Social-Investigative. **Career Cluster:** 08 Health Science. **Career Pathway:** 08.1 Therapeutic Services. **Skills:** No data available.

Education and Training Program: Psychiatric/Mental Health Nurse/Nursing. **Related Knowledge/Courses:** No data available.

Advertising and Promotions Managers

❀ Annual Earnings: $80,220
❀ Beginning Wage: $40,090
❀ Earnings Growth Potential: High (50.0%)
❀ Growth: 6.2%
❀ Annual Job Openings: 2,955
❀ Self-Employed: 13.4%
❀ Part-Time: 4.8%
❀ Job Security: Least secure
❀ Education/Training Required: Work experience plus degree

Industries in Which Income Is Highest

Industry	Average Annual Earnings	Number Employed
Professional, Scientific, and Technical Services	$102,310	9,300
Management of Companies and Enterprises	$85,950	3,470
Publishing Industries (Except Internet)	$80,770	3,320
Broadcasting (Except Internet)	$79,060	1,810
Merchant Wholesalers, Nondurable Goods	$78,610	2,330

Metropolitan Areas Where Income Is Highest

Metropolitan Area	Average Annual Earnings	Number Employed
New York–Northern New Jersey–Long Island, NY-NJ-PA	$127,920	5,670
Minneapolis–St. Paul–Bloomington, MN-WI	$107,790	300
Jacksonville, FL	$107,600	110
Trenton-Ewing, NJ	$103,360	60
Cleveland-Elyria-Mentor, OH	$103,040	170

Plan and direct advertising policies and programs or produce collateral materials, such as posters, contests, coupons, or giveaways, to create extra interest in the purchase of a product or service for a department, for an entire organization, or on an account basis. Prepare budgets and submit estimates for program costs as part of campaign plan development. Plan and prepare advertising and promotional material to increase sales of products or services, working with customers, company officials, sales departments, and advertising agencies. Assist with annual budget development. Inspect layouts and advertising copy and edit scripts, audiotapes and videotapes, and other promotional material for adherence to specifications. Coordinate activities of departments, such as sales, graphic arts, media, finance, and research. Prepare and negotiate advertising and sales contracts. Identify and develop contacts for promotional campaigns and industry programs that meet identified buyer targets, such as dealers, distributors, or consumers. Gather and organize information to plan advertising campaigns. Confer with department heads or staff to discuss topics such as contracts, selection of advertising media, or product to be advertised. Confer with clients to provide marketing or technical advice. Monitor and analyze sales promotion results to determine cost-effectiveness of promotion campaigns. Read trade journals and professional literature to stay informed on trends, innovations, and changes that affect media planning. Formulate plans to extend business with established accounts and to transact business as agent for advertising accounts. Provide presentation and product demonstration support during the introduction of new products and services to field staff and customers. Direct, motivate, and monitor the mobilization of a campaign team to advance campaign goals. Plan and execute advertising policies and strategies for organizations. Track program budgets and expenses and campaign response rates to evaluate each campaign based on program objectives and industry norms. Assemble and communicate with a strong, diverse coalition of organizations or public figures, securing their cooperation, support, and action to further campaign goals.

Other Considerations for Income: Salary levels vary substantially, depending upon the level of managerial responsibility, length of service, education, size of firm, location, and industry. For example, manufacturing firms usually pay these managers higher salaries than nonmanufacturing firms. For sales managers, the size of their sales territory is another important determinant of salary. Many managers earn bonuses equal to 10 percent or more of their salaries.

Personality Type: Enterprising-Artistic-Conventional. **Career Clusters:** 04 Business, Management, and Administration; 14 Marketing, Sales, and Service. **Career Pathways:** 04.1 Management; 04.5 Marketing; 14.1 Management and Entrepreneurship. **Skills:** Management of Financial Resources; Service Orientation; Persuasion; Negotiation; Time Management; Coordination; Management of Personnel Resources; Judgment and Decision Making.

Education and Training Programs: Advertising; Marketing/Marketing Management, General; Public Relations/Image Management. **Related Knowledge/Courses:** Sales and Marketing; Fine Arts; Design; Production and Processing; Communications and Media; Clerical.

Aerospace Engineering and Operations Technicians

❈ Annual Earnings: $55,040
❈ Beginning Wage: $34,380
❈ Earnings Growth Potential: Medium (37.5%)
❈ Growth: 10.4%
❈ Annual Job Openings: 707
❈ Self-Employed: 0.9%
❈ Part-Time: 5.9%
❈ Job Security: More secure than most
❈ Education/Training Required: Associate degree

Industries in Which Income Is Highest

Industry	Average Annual Earnings	Number Employed
Air Transportation	$69,190	580
Computer and Electronic Product Manufacturing	$55,950	1,610
Professional, Scientific, and Technical Services	$55,800	1,840
Administrative and Support Services	$55,690	100
Transportation Equipment Manufacturing	$52,050	3,850

Metropolitan Areas Where Income Is Highest

Metropolitan Area	Average Annual Earnings	Number Employed
Dallas–Fort Worth–Arlington, TX	$71,350	590
Bridgeport-Stamford-Norwalk, CT	$63,240	120
Cincinnati-Middletown, OH-KY-IN	$62,680	290
Phoenix-Mesa-Scottsdale, AZ	$61,070	50
Denver-Aurora, CO	$60,630	220

Operate, install, calibrate, and maintain integrated computer/communications systems consoles; simulators; and other data acquisition, test, and measurement instruments and equipment to launch, track, position, and evaluate air and space vehicles. May record and interpret test data. Inspect, diagnose, maintain, and operate test setups and equipment to detect malfunctions. Record and interpret test data on parts, assemblies, and mechanisms. Confer with engineering personnel regarding details and implications of test procedures and results. Adjust, repair, or replace faulty components of test setups and equipment. Identify required data, data acquisition plans, and test parameters, setting up equipment to conform to these specifications. Construct and maintain test facilities for aircraft parts and systems according to specifications. Operate and calibrate computer systems and devices to comply with test requirements and to perform data acquisition and analysis. Test aircraft systems under simulated operational conditions, performing systems readiness tests and pre- and post-operational checkouts, to establish design or fabrication parameters. Fabricate and install parts and systems to be tested in test equipment, using hand tools, power tools, and test instruments. Finish vehicle instrumentation and deinstrumentation. Exchange cooling system components in various vehicles.

Other Considerations for Income: Aerospace Engineering and Operations Technicians are among the best-paid of the various kinds of engineering technicians.

Personality Type: Realistic-Investigative-Conventional. **Career Cluster:** 16 Transportation, Distribution, and Logistics. **Career Pathway:** 16.1 Transportation Operations. **Skills:** Installation; Technology Design; Operation Monitoring; Science; Repairing; Troubleshooting; Operations Analysis; Operation and Control.

Education and Training Program: Aeronautical/Aerospace Engineering Technology/Technician. **Related Knowledge/Courses:** Engineering and Technology; Mechanical; Computers and Electronics; Production and Processing; Public Safety and Security; Design.

Aerospace Engineers

❋ Annual Earnings: $92,520
❋ Beginning Wage: $58,130
❋ Earnings Growth Potential: Medium (37.2%)
❋ Growth: 10.2%
❋ Annual Job Openings: 6,498
❋ Self-Employed: 1.4%
❋ Part-Time: 2.6%
❋ Job Security: Less secure than most
❋ Education/Training Required: Bachelor's degree

Industries in Which Income Is Highest

Industry	Average Annual Earnings	Number Employed
Administrative and Support Services	$105,760	1,630
Federal, State, and Local Government	$105,050	8,710
Professional, Scientific, and Technical Services	$95,290	17,750

Metropolitan Areas Where Income Is Highest

Metropolitan Area	Average Annual Earnings	Number Employed
Baltimore-Towson, MD	$122,540	990
Riverside–San Bernardino–Ontario, CA	$120,560	190
Cleveland-Elyria-Mentor, OH	$112,380	470
Los Angeles–Long Beach–Santa Ana, CA	$107,150	8,130
Chicago-Naperville-Joliet, IL-IN-WI	$106,060	80

Perform a variety of engineering work in designing, constructing, and testing aircraft, missiles, and spacecraft. May conduct basic and applied research to evaluate adaptability of materials and equipment to aircraft design and manufacture. May recommend improvements in testing equipment and techniques. Formulate conceptual design of aeronautical or aerospace products or systems to meet customer requirements. Direct and coordinate activities of engineering or technical personnel designing, fabricating, modifying, or testing aircraft or aerospace products. Develop design criteria for aeronautical or aerospace products or systems, including testing methods, production costs, quality standards, and completion dates. Plan and conduct experimental, environmental, operational, and stress tests on models and prototypes of aircraft and aerospace systems and equipment. Evaluate product data and design from inspections and reports for conformance to engineering principles, customer requirements, and quality standards. Formulate mathematical models or other methods of computer analysis to develop, evaluate, or modify design according to customer engineering requirements. Write technical reports and other documentation, such as handbooks and bulletins, for use by engineering staff, management, and customers. Analyze project requests and proposals and engineering data to determine feasibility, productibility, cost, and production time of aerospace or aeronautical product. Review performance reports and documentation from customers and field engineers and inspect malfunctioning or damaged products to determine problem. Direct research and development programs. Evaluate and approve selection of vendors by study of past performance and new advertisements. Plan and coordinate activities concerned with investigating and resolving customers' reports of technical problems with aircraft or aerospace vehicles. Maintain records of performance reports for future reference.

Other Considerations for Income: As a group, engineers earn some of the highest average starting salaries among those holding bachelor's degrees. Aerospace Engineers are among the better paid of the various kinds of engineers. According to a 2007 survey by the National Association of Colleges and Employers, average starting salaries for Aerospace Engineers were $53,408 with a bachelor's, $62,459 with a master's, and $73,814 with a Ph.D.

Personality Type: Investigative-Realistic. **Career Cluster:** 15 Science, Technology, Engineering, and Mathematics. **Career Pathway:** 15.1 Engineering and Technology. **Skills:** Systems Evaluation; Science; Systems Analysis; Judgment and Decision Making; Technology Design; Persuasion; Operations Analysis; Management of Personnel Resources.

Education and Training Program: Aerospace, Aeronautical, and Astronautical/Space Engineering. **Related Knowledge/Courses:** Engineering and Technology; Physics; Design; Mechanical; Mathematics; Production and Processing.

Agents and Business Managers of Artists, Performers, and Athletes

- ❀ Annual Earnings: $62,940
- ❀ Beginning Wage: $27,810
- ❀ Earnings Growth Potential: Very high (55.8%)
- ❀ Growth: 9.6%
- ❀ Annual Job Openings: 3,940
- ❀ Self-Employed: 55.8%
- ❀ Part-Time: 18.6%
- ❀ Job Security: Less secure than most
- ❀ Education/Training Required: Work experience plus degree

Industries in Which Income Is Highest

Industry	Average Annual Earnings	Number Employed
Performing Arts, Spectator Sports, and Related Industries	$62,320	10,360

Metropolitan Areas Where Income Is Highest

Metropolitan Area	Average Annual Earnings	Number Employed
Boston-Cambridge-Quincy, MA-NH	$80,550	240
New York–Northern New Jersey–Long Island, NY-NJ-PA	$79,170	1,670
Las Vegas–Paradise, NV	$77,850	120
Chicago-Naperville-Joliet, IL-IN-WI	$75,230	730
Los Angeles–Long Beach–Santa Ana, CA	$70,350	3,010

Represent and promote artists, performers, and athletes to prospective employers. May handle contract negotiation and other business matters for clients. Manage business and financial affairs for clients, such as arranging travel and lodging, selling tickets, and directing marketing and advertising activities. Obtain information about and/or inspect performance facilities, equipment, and accommodations to ensure that they meet specifications. Negotiate with managers, promoters, union officials, and other persons regarding clients' contractual rights and obligations. Advise clients on financial and legal matters such as investments and taxes. Hire trainers or coaches to advise clients on performance matters such as training techniques or performance presentations. Prepare periodic accounting statements for clients. Keep informed of industry trends and deals. Develop contacts with individuals and organizations and apply effective strategies and techniques to ensure their clients' success. Confer with clients to develop strategies for their careers and to explain actions taken on their behalf. Conduct auditions or interviews in order to evaluate potential clients. Schedule promotional or performance engagements for clients. Arrange meetings concerning issues involving their clients. Collect fees, commissions, or other payments according to contract terms.

Other Considerations for Income: No additional information.

Personality Type: Enterprising-Social. **Career Clusters:** 03 Arts, Audio/Video Technology, and Communications; 04 Business, Management, and Administration. **Career Pathways:** 03.1 Audio and Video Technology and Film; 04.1 Management. **Skills:** Management of Financial Resources; Negotiation; Persuasion; Social Perceptiveness; Speaking; Coordination; Judgment and Decision Making; Management of Personnel Resources.

Education and Training Program: Purchasing, Procurement/Acquisitions and Contracts Management. **Related Knowledge/Courses:** Fine Arts; Sales and Marketing; Communications and Media; Clerical; Customer and Personal Service; Economics and Accounting.

Agricultural Engineers

❋ Annual Earnings: $68,730
❋ Beginning Wage: $43,150
❋ Earnings Growth Potential: Medium (37.2%)
❋ Growth: 8.6%
❋ Annual Job Openings: 225
❋ Self-Employed: 0.0%
❋ Part-Time: 7.3%
❋ Job Security: More secure than most
❋ Education/Training Required: Bachelor's degree

Industries in Which Income Is Highest

Industry	Average Annual Earnings	Number Employed
Beverage and Tobacco Product Manufacturing	$78,370	180
Professional, Scientific, and Technical Services	$76,780	580
Food Manufacturing	$70,840	470
Federal, State, and Local Government	$65,580	600
Machinery Manufacturing	$61,850	370

Metropolitan Areas Where Income Is Highest

Metropolitan Area	Average Annual Earnings	Number Employed
Fort Collins–Loveland, CO	$103,820	40
Philadelphia-Camden-Wilmington, PA-NJ-DE-MD	$99,000	30
Chicago-Naperville-Joliet, IL-IN-WI	$78,410	40
Santa Rosa–Petaluma, CA	$74,260	40
New York–Northern New Jersey–Long Island, NY-NJ-PA	$68,180	40

Apply knowledge of engineering technology and biological science to agricultural problems concerned with power and machinery, electrification, structures, soil and water conservation, and processing of agricultural products. Visit sites to observe environmental problems, to consult with contractors, or to monitor construction activities. Design agricultural machinery components and equipment, using computer-aided design (CAD) technology. Test agricultural machinery and equipment to ensure adequate performance. Design structures for crop storage, animal shelter and loading, and animal and crop processing and supervise their construction. Provide advice on water quality and issues related to pollution management, river control, and ground and surface water resources. Conduct educational programs that provide farmers or farm cooperative members with information that can help them improve agricultural productivity. Discuss plans with clients, contractors, consultants, and other engineers so that they can be evaluated and necessary changes made. Supervise food processing or manufacturing plant operations. Design and supervise environmental and land reclamation projects in agriculture and related industries. Design food processing plants and related mechanical systems. Plan and direct construction of rural electric-power distribution systems and irrigation, drainage, and flood control systems for soil and water conservation. Prepare reports, sketches, working drawings, specifications, proposals, and budgets for proposed sites or systems. Meet with clients, such as district or regional councils, farmers, and developers, to discuss their needs. Design sensing, measuring, and recording devices and other instrumentation used to study plant or animal life.

Other Considerations for Income: As a group, engineers earn some of the highest average starting salaries among those holding bachelor's degrees. Agricultural Engineers are among the lowest-paid of the various kinds of engineers. According to a 2007 survey by the National Association of Colleges and Employers, the average starting salary for Agricultural Engineers with a bachelor's were $49,764.

Personality Type: Investigative-Realistic-Enterprising. **Career Cluster:** 15 Science, Technology, Engineering, and Mathematics. **Career Pathway:** 15.1 Engineering and Technology. **Skills:** Science; Programming; Technology Design; Operations Analysis; Management of Material Resources; Mathematics; Management of Financial Resources; Systems Analysis.

Education and Training Program: Agricultural Engineering. **Related Knowledge/Courses:** Food Production; Physics; Engineering and Technology; Design; Biology; Building and Construction.

Agricultural Sciences Teachers, Postsecondary

- ❀ Annual Earnings: $74,390
- ❀ Beginning Wage: $38,460
- ❀ Earnings Growth Potential: High (48.3%)
- ❀ Growth: 22.9%
- ❀ Annual Job Openings: 1,840
- ❀ Self-Employed: 0.4%
- ❀ Part-Time: 27.8%
- ❀ Job Security: Most secure
- ❀ Education/Training Required: Doctoral degree

Industries in Which Income Is Highest

Industry	Average Annual Earnings	Number Employed
Educational Services	$74,390	9,980

Metropolitan Areas Where Income Is Highest

Metropolitan Area	Average Annual Earnings	Number Employed
Washington-Arlington-Alexandria, DC-VA-MD-WV	$76,110	230
Minneapolis–St. Paul–Bloomington, MN-WI	$66,630	80
Chicago-Naperville-Joliet, IL-IN-WI	$54,040	70
Miami–Fort Lauderdale–Miami Beach, FL	$49,620	160

Teach courses in the agricultural sciences, including agronomy, dairy sciences, fisheries management, horticultural sciences, poultry sciences, range management, and agricultural soil conservation. Prepare course materials such as syllabi, homework assignments, and handouts. Evaluate and grade students' classwork, laboratory work, assignments, and papers. Keep abreast of developments in agriculture by reading current literature, talking with colleagues, and participating in professional conferences. Prepare and deliver lectures to undergraduate and/or graduate students on topics such as crop production, plant genetics, and soil chemistry. Initiate, facilitate, and moderate classroom discussions. Conduct research in a particular field of knowledge and publish findings in professional journals, books, and/or electronic media. Supervise laboratory sessions and fieldwork and coordinate laboratory operations. Supervise undergraduate and/or graduate teaching, internship, and research work. Compile, administer, and grade examinations or assign this work to others. Advise students on academic and vocational curricula and on career issues. Plan, evaluate, and revise curricula, course content, and course materials and methods of instruction. Maintain student attendance records, grades, and other required records. Write grant proposals to procure external research funding. Collaborate with colleagues to address teaching and research issues. Maintain regularly scheduled office hours in order to advise and assist students. Participate in student recruitment, registration, and placement activities. Select and obtain materials and supplies such as textbooks and laboratory equipment. Act as advisers to student organizations. Participate in campus and community events. Serve on academic or administrative committees that deal with institutional policies, departmental matters, and academic issues. Provide professional consulting services to government and/or industry. Perform administrative duties such as serving as department head. Compile bibliographies of specialized materials for outside reading assignments.

Other Considerations for Income: Earnings for college faculty vary according to rank and type of institution, geographic area, and field. According to a 2006–2007 survey by the American Association of University Professors, salaries for full-time faculty averaged $73,207. By rank, the average was $98,974 for professors, $69,911 for associate professors, $58,662 for assistant professors, $42,609 for instructors, and $48,289 for lecturers. Faculty in 4-year institutions earn higher salaries, on average, than do those in 2-year schools. Many faculty members have significant earnings in addition to their base salary from consulting, teaching additional courses, research, writing for publication, or other employment. In addition, many college and university faculty enjoy unique benefits, including access to campus facilities, tuition waivers for dependents, housing and travel allowances, and paid leave for sabbaticals. Part-time faculty and instructors usually have fewer benefits than full-time faculty.

Personality Type: Social-Investigative-Realistic. **Career Clusters:** 01 Agriculture, Food and Natural Resource; 05 Education and Training. **Career Pathways:** 01.1 Food Products and Processing Systems; 01.2 Plant Systems; 01.3 Animal Systems; 01.4 Power Structure and Technical Systems; 01.7 Agribusiness Systems; 05.3 Teaching/Training. **Skills:** Science; Management of Financial Resources; Writing; Reading Comprehension; Instructing; Complex Problem Solving; Active Learning; Management of Material Resources.

Education and Training Programs: Agribusiness/Agricultural Business Operations; Agricultural and Domestic Animal Services, Other; Agricultural and Food Products Processing; Agricultural and Horticultural Plant Breeding; Agricultural Animal Breeding; Agricultural Business and Management, General; Agricultural Business and Management, Other; Agricultural Economics; Agricultural Mechanization, General; Agricultural Mechanization, Other; Agricultural Power Machinery Operation; Agricultural Production Operations, General; others. **Related Knowledge/Courses:** Biology; Food Production; Education and Training; Geography; Chemistry; Communications and Media.

Air Traffic Controllers

- ❋ Annual Earnings: $111,870
- ❋ Beginning Wage: $45,020
- ❋ Earnings Growth Potential: Very high (59.8%)
- ❋ Growth: 10.2%
- ❋ Annual Job Openings: 1,213
- ❋ Self-Employed: 0.0%
- ❋ Part-Time: 2.1%
- ❋ Job Security: Most secure
- ❋ Education/Training Required: Long-term on-the-job training

Industries in Which Income Is Highest

Industry	Average Annual Earnings	Number Employed
Federal, State, and Local Government	$115,140	21,510
Support Activities for Transportation	$63,060	1,380

Metropolitan Areas Where Income Is Highest

Metropolitan Area	Average Annual Earnings	Number Employed
Chicago-Naperville-Joliet, IL-IN-WI	$144,240	870
Washington-Arlington-Alexandria, DC-VA-MD-WV	$141,590	1,190
San Francisco–Oakland–Fremont, CA	$139,500	470
Boston-Cambridge-Quincy, MA-NH	$138,520	560
Cleveland-Elyria-Mentor, OH	$136,170	620

Control air traffic on and within vicinity of airport and movement of air traffic between altitude sectors and control centers according to established procedures and policies. Authorize, regulate, and control commercial airline flights according to government or company regulations to expedite and ensure flight safety. Issue landing and take-off authorizations and instructions. Monitor and direct the movement of aircraft within an assigned airspace and on the ground at airports to minimize delays and maximize safety. Monitor aircraft within a specific airspace, using radar, computer equipment, and visual references. Inform pilots about nearby planes as well as potentially hazardous conditions such as weather, speed and direction of wind, and visibility problems. Provide flight path changes or directions to emergency landing fields for pilots traveling in bad weather or in emergency situations. Alert airport emergency services in cases of emergency and when aircraft experience difficulties. Direct pilots to runways when space is available or direct them to maintain a traffic pattern until there is space for them to land. Transfer control of departing flights to traffic control centers and accept control of arriving flights. Direct ground traffic, including taxiing aircraft, maintenance and baggage vehicles, and airport workers. Determine the timing and procedures for flight vector changes. Maintain radio and telephone contact with adjacent control towers, terminal control units, and other area control centers in order to coordinate aircraft movement. Contact pilots by radio to provide meteorological, navigational, and other information. Initiate and coordinate searches for missing aircraft. Check conditions and traffic at different altitudes in response to pilots' requests for altitude changes. Relay to control centers air traffic information such as courses, altitudes, and expected arrival times. Compile information about flights from flight plans, pilot reports, radar, and observations. Inspect, adjust, and control radio equipment and airport lights. Conduct preflight briefings on weather conditions, suggested routes, altitudes, indications of turbulence, and other flight safety information.

Other Considerations for Income: The Air Traffic Control pay system classifies each air traffic facility into one of eight levels with corresponding pay bands. Under this pay system, controllers' salaries are determined by the rating of the facility. Higher ratings usually mean higher controller salaries and greater demands on the controller's judgment, skill, and decision-making ability. Depending on length of service, air traffic controllers receive 13 to 26 days of paid vacation and 13 days of paid sick leave each year, in addition to life insurance and health benefits. Controllers also can retire at an earlier age and with fewer years of service than other federal employees.

Personality Type: Enterprising-Conventional. **Career Cluster:** 16 Transportation, Distribution, and Logistics. **Career Pathway:** 16.1 Transportation Operations. **Skills:** Operation and Control; Operation Monitoring; Coordination; Complex Problem Solving; Active Listening; Instructing; Judgment and Decision Making; Monitoring.

Education and Training Program: Air Traffic Controller. **Related Knowledge/Courses:** Transportation; Geography; Telecommunications; Public Safety and Security; Physics; Education and Training.

Aircraft Mechanics and Service Technicians

- ❋ Annual Earnings: $51,390
- ❋ Beginning Wage: $32,960
- ❋ Earnings Growth Potential: Medium (35.9%)
- ❋ Growth: 10.6%
- ❋ Annual Job Openings: 9,708
- ❋ Self-Employed: 0.4%
- ❋ Part-Time: 2.1%
- ❋ Job Security: Less secure than most
- ❋ Education/Training Required: Postsecondary vocational training

Industries in Which Income Is Highest

Industry	Average Annual Earnings	Number Employed
Couriers and Messengers	$83,730	4,540
Air Transportation	$57,470	32,600
Federal, State, and Local Government	$51,850	17,380
Transportation Equipment Manufacturing	$50,890	23,010
Professional, Scientific, and Technical Services	$47,440	2,120

Metropolitan Areas Where Income Is Highest

Metropolitan Area	Average Annual Earnings	Number Employed
Louisville–Jefferson County, KY-IN	$92,200	630
Indianapolis-Carmel, IN	$61,020	1,000
Los Angeles–Long Beach–Santa Ana, CA	$59,580	4,050
Chicago-Naperville-Joliet, IL-IN-WI	$58,610	2,180
Detroit-Warren-Livonia, MI	$58,520	1,120

Diagnose, adjust, repair, or overhaul aircraft engines and assemblies, such as hydraulic and pneumatic systems. Read and interpret maintenance manuals, service bulletins, and other specifications to determine the feasibility and method of repairing or replacing malfunctioning or damaged components. Inspect completed work to certify that maintenance meets standards and that aircraft are ready for operation. Maintain repair logs, documenting all preventive and corrective aircraft maintenance. Conduct routine and special inspections as required by regulations. Examine and inspect aircraft components, including landing gear, hydraulic systems, and de-icers, to locate cracks, breaks, leaks, or other problem. Inspect airframes for wear or other defects. Maintain, repair, and rebuild aircraft structures; functional components; and parts such as wings and fuselage, rigging, hydraulic units, oxygen systems, fuel systems, electrical systems, gaskets, and seals. Measure the tension of control cables. Replace or repair worn, defective, or damaged components, using hand tools, gauges, and testing equipment. Measure parts for wear, using precision instruments. Assemble and install electrical, plumbing, mechanical, hydraulic, and structural components and accessories, using hand tools and power tools. Test operation of engines and other systems, using test equipment such as ignition analyzers, compression checkers, distributor timers, and ammeters. Obtain fuel and oil samples and check them for contamination. Reassemble engines following repair or inspection and re-install engines in aircraft. Read and interpret pilots' descriptions of problems to diagnose causes. Modify aircraft structures, space vehicles, systems, or components, following drawings, schematics, charts, engineering orders, and technical publications. Install and align repaired or replacement parts for subsequent riveting or welding, using clamps and wrenches. Locate and mark dimensions and reference lines on defective or replacement parts, using templates, scribes, compasses, and steel rules.

Other Considerations for Income: Technicians who graduate from an aviation maintenance technician school often earn higher starting salaries than individuals who receive training in the Armed Forces or on the job. Airline mechanics and their immediate families receive reduced-fare transportation on their own and most other airlines. About 3 in 10 aircraft and avionics equipment mechanics and service technicians are members of unions or covered by union agreements.

Personality Type: Realistic-Conventional-Investigative. **Career Clusters:** 13 Manufacturing; 16 Transportation, Distribution, and Logistics. **Career Pathways:** 13.3 Maintenance, Installation, and Repair; 16.4 Facility and Mobile Equipment Maintenance. **Skills:** Repairing; Equipment Maintenance; Installation; Operation Monitoring; Troubleshooting; Operation and Control; Quality Control Analysis; Complex Problem Solving.

Education and Training Programs: Agricultural Mechanics and Equipment/Machine Technology; Aircraft Powerplant Technology/Technician; Airframe Mechanics and Aircraft Maintenance Technology/Technician. **Related Knowledge/Courses:** Mechanical; Design; Physics; Engineering and Technology; Chemistry; Transportation.

Airline Pilots, Copilots, and Flight Engineers

❀ Annual Earnings: $111,680
❀ Beginning Wage: $55,330
❀ Earnings Growth Potential: Very high (50.5%)
❀ Growth: 12.9%
❀ Annual Job Openings: 4,073
❀ Self-Employed: 2.5%
❀ Part-Time: 14.2%
❀ Job Security: Least secure
❀ Education/Training Required: Bachelor's degree

Industries in Which Income Is Highest

Industry	Average Annual Earnings	Number Employed
Couriers and Messengers	$142,490	4,090
Air Transportation	$114,400	67,450
Federal, State, and Local Government	$93,470	2,990
Support Activities for Transportation	$76,230	1,420

Metropolitan Areas Where Income Is Highest

Metropolitan Area	Average Annual Earnings	Number Employed
Charlotte-Gastonia-Concord, NC-SC	$129,320	1,260
New York–Northern New Jersey–Long Island, NY-NJ-PA	$124,080	7,350
San Francisco–Oakland–Fremont, CA	$123,250	2,480
Chicago-Naperville-Joliet, IL-IN-WI	$119,680	6,120
Miami–Fort Lauderdale–Miami Beach, FL	$118,900	2,080

Pilot and navigate the flight of multi-engine aircraft in regularly scheduled service for the transport of passengers and cargo. Requires Federal Air Transport rating and certification in specific aircraft type used. Use instrumentation to guide flights when visibility is poor. Respond to and report in-flight emergencies and malfunctions. Work as part of a flight team with other crew members, especially during takeoffs and landings. Contact control towers for takeoff clearances, arrival instructions, and other information, using radio equipment. Steer aircraft along planned routes with the assistance of autopilot and flight management computers. Monitor gauges, warning devices, and control panels to verify aircraft performance and to regulate engine speed. Start engines, operate controls, and pilot airplanes to transport passengers, mail, or freight while adhering to flight plans, regulations, and procedures. Inspect aircraft for defects and malfunctions according to pre-flight checklists. Check passenger and cargo distributions and fuel amounts to ensure that weight and balance specifications are met. Monitor engine operation, fuel consumption, and functioning of aircraft systems during flights. Confer with flight dispatchers and weather forecasters to keep abreast of flight conditions. Coordinate flight activities with ground crews and air-traffic control and inform crew members of flight and test procedures. Order changes in fuel supplies, loads, routes, or schedules to ensure safety of flights. Choose routes, altitudes, and speeds that will provide the fastest, safest, and smoothest flights. Direct activities of aircraft crews during flights. Brief crews about flight details such as destinations, duties, and responsibilities. Record in logbooks information such as flight times, distances flown, and fuel consumption. Make announcements regarding flights, using public address systems. File instrument flight plans with air traffic control to ensure that flights are coordinated with other air traffic. Perform minor maintenance work or arrange for major maintenance. Instruct other pilots and student pilots in aircraft operations and the principles of flight.

Other Considerations for Income: Earnings of aircraft pilots and flight engineers vary greatly depending whether they work as airline or commercial pilots. Earnings of airline pilots are among the highest in the nation, and depend on factors such as the type, size, and maximum speed of the plane and the number of hours and miles flown. For example, pilots who fly jet aircraft usually earn higher salaries than pilots who fly turboprops. Airline pilots and flight engineers may earn extra pay for night and international flights. Airline pilots usually are eligible for life and health insurance plans. They also receive retirement benefits and, if they fail the FAA physical examination at some point in their careers, they get disability payments. In addition, pilots receive an expense allowance, or per diem, for every hour they are away from home. Some airlines also provide allowances to pilots for purchasing and cleaning their uniforms. As an additional benefit, pilots and their immediate families usually are entitled to free or reduced-fare transportation on their own and other airlines. More than half of all aircraft pilots are members of unions.

Personality Type: Realistic-Conventional-Investigative. **Career Cluster:** 16 Transportation, Distribution, and Logistics. **Career Pathway:** 16.1 Transportation Operations. **Skills:** Operation Monitoring; Operation and Control; Systems Analysis; Judgment and Decision Making; Troubleshooting; Science; Systems Evaluation; Monitoring.

Education and Training Programs: Airline/Commercial/Professional Pilot and Flight Crew; Flight Instructor. **Related Knowledge/Courses:** Transportation; Geography; Physics; Public Safety and Security; Psychology; Law and Government.

Allergists and Immunologists

❋ Annual Earnings: $166,400+
❋ Beginning Wage: $49,710
❋ Earnings Growth Potential: Cannot be calculated
❋ Growth: 14.2%
❋ Annual Job Openings: 38,027
❋ Self-Employed: 14.7%
❋ Part-Time: 8.1%
❋ Job Security: No data available
❋ Education/Training Required: First professional degree

The Department of Labor reports this information for the occupation Physicians and Surgeons. The job openings listed here are shared with other specializations within that occupation, including Anesthesiologists; Dermatologists; Family and General Practitioners; Hospitalists; Internists, General; Neurologists; Nuclear Medicine Physicians; Obstetricians and Gynecologists; Ophthalmologists; Pathologists; Pediatricians, General; Physical Medicine and Rehabilitation Physicians; Preventive Medicine Physicians; Psychiatrists; Radiologists; Sports Medicine Physicians; Surgeons; and Urologists.

Industries in Which Income Is Highest

Industry	Average Annual Earnings	Number Employed
Ambulatory Health Care Services	$166,400+	147,400
Administrative and Support Services	$166,400+	1,310
Federal, State, and Local Government	$162,300	28,180
Professional, Scientific, and Technical Services	$107,470	1,210
Hospitals	$72,130	72,490

Metropolitan Areas Where Income Is Highest

Metropolitan Area	Average Annual Earnings	Number Employed
Los Angeles–Long Beach–Santa Ana, CA	$166,400+	8,810
Boston-Cambridge-Quincy, MA-NH	$166,400+	6,380
Dallas–Fort Worth–Arlington, TX	$166,400+	4,950
Tampa–St. Petersburg–Clearwater, FL	$166,400+	3,810
Portland-Vancouver-Beaverton, OR-WA	$166,400+	3,180

Diagnose, treat, and help prevent allergic diseases and disease processes affecting the immune system. No task data available.

Other Considerations for Income: Earnings of physicians and surgeons are among the highest of any occupation. Separate earnings figures for Allergists and Immunologists are not available.

Personality Type: Investigative-Social-Realistic. **Career Cluster:** 08 Health Science. **Career Pathway:** 08.1 Therapeutic Services. **Skills:** No data available.

Education and Training Program: Allergy and Immunology Residency Program. **Related Knowledge/Courses:** No data available.

Anesthesiologist Assistants

❋ Annual Earnings: $81,230
❋ Beginning Wage: $51,360
❋ Earnings Growth Potential: Medium (36.8%)
❋ Growth: 27.0%
❋ Annual Job Openings: 7,147
❋ Self-Employed: 1.8%
❋ Part-Time: 15.6%
❋ Job Security: No data available
❋ Education/Training Required: Master's degree

The Department of Labor reports this information for the occupation Physician Assistants. The job openings listed here are shared with other specializations within that occupation.

Industries in Which Income Is Highest

Industry	Average Annual Earnings	Number Employed
Hospitals	$84,850	17,660
Ambulatory Health Care Services	$80,400	47,450
Federal, State, and Local Government	$78,660	3,060
Educational Services	$74,220	1,970

Metropolitan Areas Where Income Is Highest

Metropolitan Area	Average Annual Earnings	Number Employed
Sacramento–Arden-Arcade–Roseville, CA	$109,300	640
Anchorage, AK	$107,380	120
San Jose–Sunnyvale–Santa Clara, CA	$102,890	240
Chattanooga, TN-GA	$102,550	120
Bremerton-Silverdale, WA	$96,690	60

Assist anesthesiologists in the administration of anesthesia for surgical and non-surgical procedures. Monitor patient status and provide patient care during surgical treatment. No task data available.

Other Considerations for Income: Income varies by specialty, practice setting, geographical location, and years of experience. Employers often pay for their employees' liability insurance, registration fees with the Drug Enforcement Administration, state licensing fees, and credentialing fees.

Personality Type: Realistic-Social-Investigative. **Career Cluster:** 08 Health Science. **Career Pathway:** 08.2 Diagnostics Services. **Skills:** No data available.

Education and Training Program: Physician Assistant Training. **Related Knowledge/Courses:** No data available.

Anesthesiologists

❋ Annual Earnings: $166,400+
❋ Beginning Wage: $109,970
❋ Earnings Growth Potential: Cannot be calculated
❋ Growth: 14.2%
❋ Annual Job Openings: 38,027
❋ Self-Employed: 14.7%
❋ Part-Time: 8.1%
❋ Job Security: Most secure
❋ Education/Training Required: First professional degree

The Department of Labor reports this information for the occupation Physicians and Surgeons. The job openings listed here are shared with other specializations within that occupation, including Allergists and Immunologists; Dermatologists; Family and General Practitioners; Hospitalists; Internists, General; Neurologists; Nuclear Medicine Physicians; Obstetricians and Gynecologists; Ophthalmologists; Pathologists; Pediatricians, General; Physical Medicine and Rehabilitation Physicians; Preventive Medicine Physicians; Psychiatrists; Radiologists; Sports Medicine Physicians; Surgeons; and Urologists.

Industries in Which Income Is Highest

Industry	Average Annual Earnings	Number Employed
Ambulatory Health Care Services	$166,400+	28,540
Hospitals	$160,730	5,010

Metropolitan Areas Where Income Is Highest

Metropolitan Area	Average Annual Earnings	Number Employed
New York–Northern New Jersey–Long Island, NY-NJ-PA	$166,400+	2,030
Chicago-Naperville-Joliet, IL-IN-WI	$166,400+	1,540
Minneapolis–St. Paul–Bloomington, MN-WI	$166,400+	720
Washington-Arlington-Alexandria, DC-VA-MD-WV	$166,400+	710
Baltimore-Towson, MD	$166,400+	700

Administer anesthetics during surgery or other medical procedures. Administer anesthetic or sedation during medical procedures, using local, intravenous, spinal, or caudal methods. Monitor patient before, during, and after anesthesia and counteract adverse reactions or complications. Provide and maintain life support and airway management and help prepare patients for emergency surgery. Record type and amount of anesthesia and patient condition throughout procedure. Examine patient; obtain medical history; and use diagnostic tests to determine risk during surgical, obstetrical, and other medical procedures. Position patient on operating table to maximize patient comfort and surgical accessibility. Decide when patients have recovered or stabilized enough to be sent to another room or ward or to be sent home following outpatient surgery. Coordinate administration of anesthetics with surgeons during operation. Confer with other medical professionals to determine type and method of anesthetic or sedation to render patient insensible to pain. Coordinate and direct work of nurses, medical technicians, and other health-care providers. Order laboratory tests, X-rays, and other diagnostic procedures. Diagnose illnesses, using examinations, tests, and reports. Manage anesthesiological services, coordinating them with other medical activities and formulating plans and procedures. Provide medical care and consultation in many settings, prescribing medication and treatment and referring patients for surgery. Inform students and staff of types and methods of anesthe-

sia administration, signs of complications, and emergency methods to counteract reactions. Schedule and maintain use of surgical suite, including operating, wash-up, and waiting rooms and anesthetic and sterilizing equipment. Instruct individuals and groups on ways to preserve health and prevent disease. Conduct medical research to aid in controlling and curing disease, to investigate new medications, and to develop and test new medical techniques.

Other Considerations for Income: Earnings of physicians and surgeons are among the highest of any occupation, and Anesthesiologists are among the best-paid medical specialists. The Medical Group Management Association's Physician Compensation and Production Survey of 2005 reported earnings of $259,948 for Anesthesiologists with less than two years in their specialty and $321,686 for those with more than one year in their specialty. These figures cover salary, bonus and incentive payments, research stipends, honoraria, and distribution of profits. Self-employed physicians—those who own or are part owners of their medical practice—generally have higher median incomes than salaried physicians, but their must provide for their own health insurance and retirement.

Personality Type: Investigative-Realistic-Social. **Career Cluster:** 08 Health Science. **Career Pathway:** 08.1 Therapeutic Services. **Skills:** Operation Monitoring; Science; Operation and Control; Judgment and Decision Making; Equipment Selection; Monitoring; Equipment Maintenance; Complex Problem Solving.

Education and Training Program: Medicine (MD). **Related Knowledge/Courses:** Medicine and Dentistry; Biology; Chemistry; Psychology; Physics; Therapy and Counseling.

Animal Scientists

❋ Annual Earnings: $56,030
❋ Beginning Wage: $33,060
❋ Earnings Growth Potential: High (41.0%)
❋ Growth: 9.8%
❋ Annual Job Openings: 299
❋ Self-Employed: 9.0%
❋ Part-Time: 11.4%
❋ Job Security: Most secure
❋ Education/Training Required: Bachelor's degree

Industries in Which Income Is Highest

Industry	Average Annual Earnings	Number Employed
Management of Companies and Enterprises	$70,060	40
Federal, State, and Local Government	$68,490	600
Professional, Scientific, and Technical Services	$64,190	370
Chemical Manufacturing	$60,210	40
Beverage and Tobacco Product Manufacturing	$56,990	30

Metropolitan Areas Where Income Is Highest

Metropolitan Area	Average Annual Earnings	Number Employed
New York–Northern New Jersey–Long Island, NY-NJ-PA	$73,670	60
Minneapolis–St. Paul–Bloomington, MN-WI	$52,610	90
College Station–Bryan, TX	$49,880	110
Madison, WI	$43,190	120

Conduct research in the genetics, nutrition, reproduction, growth, and development of domestic farm animals. Conduct research concerning animal nutrition, breeding, or management to improve products or processes. Advise producers about improved products and techniques that could enhance their animal production efforts. Study nutritional requirements of animals and nutritive values of animal feed materials. Study effects of management practices, processing methods, feed, or environmental conditions on quality and quantity of animal products, such as eggs and milk. Develop improved practices in feeding, housing, sanitation, or parasite and disease control of animals. Research and control animal selection and breeding practices to increase production efficiency and improve animal quality. Determine genetic composition of animal populations and heritability of traits, utilizing principles of genetics. Crossbreed animals with existing strains or cross strains to obtain new combinations of desirable characteristics.

Other Considerations for Income: No additional information.

Personality Type: Investigative-Realistic. **Career Cluster:** 01 Agriculture, Food and Natural Resource. **Career Pathways:** 01.2 Plant Systems; 01.3 Animal Systems. **Skills:** Science; Systems Evaluation; Systems Analysis; Judgment and Decision Making; Operation Monitoring; Writing; Complex Problem Solving; Management of Personnel Resources.

Education and Training Programs: Agricultural Animal Breeding; Agriculture, General; Animal Health; Animal Nutrition; Animal Sciences, Other; Dairy Science; Poultry Science; Range Science and Management. **Related Knowledge/Courses:** Biology; Food Production; Chemistry; Mathematics; Economics and Accounting; Sales and Marketing.

Anthropologists

- ❋ Annual Earnings: $53,910
- ❋ Beginning Wage: $32,150
- ❋ Earnings Growth Potential: High (40.4%)
- ❋ Growth: 15.0%
- ❋ Annual Job Openings: 446
- ❋ Self-Employed: 6.1%
- ❋ Part-Time: 20.1%
- ❋ Job Security: Most secure
- ❋ Education/Training Required: Master's degree

The Department of Labor reports this information for the occupation Anthropologists and Archeologists. The job openings listed here are shared with other specializations within that occupation, including Archeologists.

Industries in Which Income Is Highest

Industry	Average Annual Earnings	Number Employed
Federal, State, and Local Government	$63,970	1,600
Museums, Historical Sites, and Similar Institutions	$56,900	160
Professional, Scientific, and Technical Services	$48,350	2,940
Administrative and Support Services	$48,020	100
Educational Services	$44,350	300

Metropolitan Areas Where Income Is Highest

Metropolitan Area	Average Annual Earnings	Number Employed
Anchorage, AK	$67,090	50
Madison, WI	$65,880	30
Los Angeles–Long Beach–Santa Ana, CA	$65,580	130
Honolulu, HI	$62,410	220
Sacramento–Arden-Arcade–Roseville, CA	$60,400	90

Research, evaluate, and establish public policy concerning the origins of humans; their physical, social, linguistic, and cultural development; and their behavior, as well as the cultures, organizations, and institutions they have created. Collect information and make judgments through observation, interviews, and the review of documents. Plan and direct research to characterize and compare the economic, demographic, health-care, social, political, linguistic, and religious institutions of distinct cultural groups, communities, and organizations. Write about and present research findings for a variety of specialized and general audiences. Advise government agencies, private organizations, and communities regarding proposed programs, plans, and policies and their potential impacts on cultural institutions, organizations, and communities. Identify culturally-specific beliefs and practices affecting health status and access to services for distinct populations and communities in collaboration with medical and public health officials. Build and use text-based database management systems to support the analysis of detailed first-hand observational records, or "field notes." Develop intervention procedures, utilizing techniques such as individual and focus group interviews, consultations, and participant observation of social interaction. Construct and test data collection methods. Explain the origins and physical, social, or cultural development of humans, including physical attributes, cultural traditions, beliefs, languages, resource management practices, and settlement patterns. Conduct participatory action research in communities and organizations to assess how work is done and to design work systems, technologies, and environments. Train others in the application of ethnographic research methods to solve problems in organizational effectiveness, communications, technology development, policy-making, and program planning. Formulate general rules that describe and predict the development and behavior of cultures and social institutions.

Other Considerations for Income: In the federal government, social scientists with a bachelor's degree and no experience often started at a yearly salary of $28,862 or $35,572 in 2007, depending on their college records. Those with a master's degree could start at $43,731, and those with a Ph.D. degree could begin at $52,912, while some individuals with experience and an advanced degree could start at $63,417. Beginning salaries were higher in selected areas of the country where the prevailing local pay level was higher.

Personality Type: Investigative-Artistic. **Career Cluster:** 15 Science, Technology, Engineering, and Mathematics. **Career Pathway:** 15.3 Science and Mathematics. **Skills:** Writing; Science; Social Perceptiveness; Complex Problem Solving; Systems Evaluation; Reading Comprehension; Systems Analysis; Active Listening.

Education and Training Programs: Anthropology; Archeology; Classics and Classical Languages, Literatures, and Linguistics, General; Physical and Biological Anthropology. **Related Knowledge/Courses:** Sociology and Anthropology; History and Archeology; Foreign Language; Philosophy and Theology; Geography; Biology.

Anthropologists and Archeologists

See *Anthropologists* and *Archeologists,* described separately.

Anthropology and Archeology Teachers, Postsecondary

- ❊ Annual Earnings: $67,750
- ❊ Beginning Wage: $39,290
- ❊ Earnings Growth Potential: High (42.0%)
- ❊ Growth: 22.9%
- ❊ Annual Job Openings: 910
- ❊ Self-Employed: 0.4%
- ❊ Part-Time: 27.8%
- ❊ Job Security: Most secure
- ❊ Education/Training Required: Doctoral degree

Industries in Which Income Is Highest

Industry	Average Annual Earnings	Number Employed
Educational Services	$67,780	5,490

Metropolitan Areas Where Income Is Highest

Metropolitan Area	Average Annual Earnings	Number Employed
San Francisco–Oakland–Fremont, CA	$89,860	90
Providence–Fall River–Warwick, RI-MA	$82,140	50
Philadelphia-Camden-Wilmington, PA-NJ-DE-MD	$81,570	130
San Diego–Carlsbad–San Marcos, CA	$81,240	90
Riverside–San Bernardino–Ontario, CA	$81,070	50

Teach courses in anthropology or archeology. Conduct research in a particular field of knowledge and publish findings in professional journals, books, and electronic media. Keep abreast of developments in their field by reading current literature, talking with colleagues, and participating in professional conferences. Prepare and deliver lectures to undergraduate and graduate students on topics such as research methods, urban anthropology, and language and culture. Evaluate and grade students' classwork, assignments, and papers. Initiate, facilitate, and moderate classroom discussions. Write grant proposals to procure external research funding. Supervise undergraduate and/or graduate teaching, internship, and research work. Prepare course materials such as syllabi, homework assignments, and handouts. Compile, administer, and grade examinations or assign this work to others. Supervise students' laboratory work or fieldwork. Plan, evaluate, and revise curricula, course content, and course materials and methods of instruction. Advise students on academic and vocational curricula, career issues, and laboratory and field research. Maintain student attendance records, grades, and other required records. Maintain regularly scheduled office hours in order to advise and assist students. Collaborate with colleagues to address teaching and research issues. Compile bibliographies of specialized materials for outside reading assignments. Perform administrative duties such as serving as department head. Select and obtain materials and supplies such as textbooks and laboratory equipment. Serve on academic or administrative committees that deal with institutional policies, departmental matters, and academic issues. Participate in student recruitment, registration, and placement activities. Participate in campus and community events. Provide professional consulting services to government and industry. Act as advisers to student organizations.

Other Considerations for Income: Earnings for college faculty vary according to rank and type of institution, geographic area, and field. According to a 2006–2007 survey by the American Association of University Professors, salaries for full-time faculty averaged $73,207. By rank, the average was $98,974 for professors, $69,911 for associate professors, $58,662 for assistant professors, $42,609 for instructors, and $48,289 for lecturers. Faculty in 4-year institutions earn higher salaries, on average, than do those in 2-year schools. Many faculty members have significant earnings in addition to their base salary from consulting, teaching additional courses, research, writing for publication, or other employment. In addition, many college and university faculty enjoy unique benefits, including access to campus facilities, tuition waivers for dependents, housing and travel allowances, and paid leave for sabbaticals. Part-time faculty and instructors usually have fewer benefits than full-time faculty.

Personality Type: Social-Investigative. **Career Clusters:** 12 Law, Public Safety, Corrections, and Security; 15 Science, Technology, Engineering, and Mathematics. **Career Pathways:** 12.4 Law Enforcement Services; 15.3 Science and Mathematics. **Skills:** Science; Writing; Critical Thinking; Reading Comprehension; Active Learning; Instructing; Management of Financial Resources; Active Listening.

Education and Training Programs: Anthropology; Archeology; Humanities/Humanistic Studies; Physical and Biological Anthropology; Social Science Teacher Education. **Related Knowledge/Courses:** Sociology and Anthropology; History and Archeology; Geography; Foreign Language; Philosophy and Theology; English Language.

Aquacultural Managers

❋ Annual Earnings: $56,230
❋ Beginning Wage: $31,350
❋ Earnings Growth Potential: High (44.2%)
❋ Growth: 1.1%
❋ Annual Job Openings: 18,101
❋ Self-Employed: 0.0%
❋ Part-Time: 9.3%
❋ Job Security: More secure than most
❋ Education/Training Required: Work experience plus degree

The Department of Labor reports this information for the occupation Farm, Ranch, and Other Agricultural Managers. The job openings listed here are shared with other specializations within that occupation, including Crop and Livestock Managers; and Nursery and Greenhouse Managers.

Industries in Which Income Is Highest

Industry	Average Annual Earnings	Number Employed
Management of Companies and Enterprises	$79,060	160
Merchant Wholesalers, Nondurable Goods	$63,250	180
Forestry and Logging	$62,970	40
Federal, State, and Local Government	$62,360	350
Food Manufacturing	$60,360	60

Metropolitan Areas Where Income Is Highest

Metropolitan Area	Average Annual Earnings	Number Employed
Yuma, AZ	$84,050	70
Port St. Lucie–Fort Pierce, FL	$73,340	40
Salinas, CA	$72,050	140
Santa Barbara–Santa Maria, CA	$69,170	40
Visalia-Porterville, CA	$68,110	80

Direct and coordinate, through subordinate supervisory personnel, activities of workers engaged in fish hatchery production for corporations, cooperatives, or other owners. Grow fish and shellfish as cash crops or for release into fresh water or salt water. Supervise and train aquaculture and fish hatchery support workers. Collect and record growth, production, and environmental data. Conduct and supervise stock examinations in order to identify diseases or parasites. Account for and disburse funds. Devise and participate in activities to improve fish hatching and growth rates and to prevent disease in hatcheries. Monitor environments to ensure maintenance of optimum conditions for aquatic life. Coordinate the selection and maintenance of brood stock. Direct and monitor trapping and spawning of fish, egg incubation, and fry rearing, applying knowledge of management and fish culturing techniques. Direct and monitor the transfer of mature fish to lakes, ponds, streams, or commercial tanks. Determine, administer, and execute policies relating to operations administration and standards and facility maintenance. Collect information regarding techniques for fish collection and fertilization, spawn incubation, and treatment of spawn and fry. Determine how to allocate resources and how to respond to unanticipated problems such as insect infestation, drought, and fire. Operate and maintain cultivating and harvesting equipment. Confer with biologists, fish pathologists, and other fishery personnel to obtain data concerning fish habits, diseases, food, and environmental requirements. Prepare reports required by state and federal laws. Identify environmental requirements of a particular species and select and oversee the preparation of sites for species cultivation. Scuba dive in order to inspect sea farm operations. Design and construct pens, floating stations, and collector strings or fences for sea farms.

Other Considerations for Income: No additional information.

Personality Type: Enterprising-Realistic-Conventional. **Career Cluster:** 01 Agriculture, Food and Natural Resource. **Career Pathways:** 01.1 Food Products and Processing Systems; 01.2 Plant Systems; 01.3 Animal Systems. **Skills:** Management of Financial Resources; Science; Management of Material Resources; Technology Design; Operations Analysis; Systems Evaluation; Management of Personnel Resources; Equipment Selection.

Education and Training Programs: Agribusiness/Agricultural Business Operations; Agricultural Animal Breeding; Agricultural Business and Management, General; Agricultural Business and Management, Other; Agricultural Production Operations, General; Agricultural Production Operations, Other; Animal Nutrition; Animal/Livestock Husbandry and Production; Crop Production; Dairy Husbandry and Production; Dairy Science; Farm/

Farm and Ranch Management; Greenhouse Operations and Management; Horse Husbandry/Equine Science and Management; others. **Related Knowledge/Courses:** Food Production; Biology; Engineering and Technology; Building and Construction; Chemistry; Mechanical.

Arbitrators, Mediators, and Conciliators

- ❈ Annual Earnings: $50,660
- ❈ Beginning Wage: $30,530
- ❈ Earnings Growth Potential: Medium (39.7%)
- ❈ Growth: 10.6%
- ❈ Annual Job Openings: 546
- ❈ Self-Employed: 0.0%
- ❈ Part-Time: 5.9%
- ❈ Job Security: Most secure
- ❈ Education/Training Required: Work experience plus degree

Industries in Which Income Is Highest

Industry	Average Annual Earnings	Number Employed
Management of Companies and Enterprises	$86,380	210
Educational Services	$66,450	90
Hospitals	$66,170	60
Administrative and Support Services	$65,190	130
Federal, State, and Local Government	$60,110	2,620

Metropolitan Areas Where Income Is Highest

Metropolitan Area	Average Annual Earnings	Number Employed
Wichita, KS	$100,250	30
San Francisco–Oakland–Fremont, CA	$90,930	80
Albany-Schenectady-Troy, NY	$89,680	190
Detroit-Warren-Livonia, MI	$88,810	270
Memphis, TN-MS-AR	$81,800	40

Facilitate negotiation and conflict resolution through dialogue. Resolve conflicts outside of the court system by mutual consent of parties involved. Conduct studies of appeals procedures in order to ensure adherence to legal requirements and to facilitate disposition of cases. Rule on exceptions, motions, and admissibility of evidence. Review and evaluate information from documents such as claim applications, birth or death certificates, and physician or employer records. Organize and deliver public presentations about mediation to organizations such as community agencies and schools. Prepare written opinions and decisions regarding cases. Prepare settlement agreements for disputants to sign. Use mediation techniques to facilitate communication between disputants, to further parties' understanding of different perspectives, and to guide parties toward mutual agreement. Notify claimants of denied claims and appeal rights. Analyze evidence and apply relevant laws, regulations, policies, and precedents in order to reach conclusions. Conduct initial meetings with disputants to outline the arbitration process, settle procedural matters such as fees, and determine details such as witness numbers and time requirements. Confer with disputants to clarify issues, identify underlying concerns, and develop an understanding of their respective needs and interests. Participate in court proceedings. Arrange and conduct hearings to obtain information and evidence relative to disposition of claims. Recommend acceptance or rejection of compromise settlement offers. Research laws, regulations, policies, and precedent decisions to prepare for hearings. Set up appointments for parties to meet for mediation. Authorize payment of valid claims. Determine existence and amount of liability according to evidence, laws, and administrative and judicial precedents. Issue subpoenas and administer oaths to prepare for formal hearings. Interview claimants, agents, or witnesses to obtain information about disputed issues.

Other Considerations for Income: Most salaried judges are provided health, life, and dental insurance; pension plans; judicial immunity protection; expense accounts; vacation, holiday, and sick leave; and contributions to retirement plans made on their behalf. In many states, judicial compensation committees, which make recommendations on the amount of salary increases, determine judicial salaries. States without commissions have statutes that regulate judicial salaries, link judicial salaries to the increases in pay for federal judges, or adjust annual pay according to the change in the Consumer Price Index, calculated by the U.S. Bureau of Labor Statistics.

Personality Type: Social-Enterprising. **Career Cluster:** 12 Law, Public Safety, Corrections, and Security. **Career Pathway:** 12.5 Legal Services. **Skills:** Negotiation; Active

Listening; Persuasion; Judgment and Decision Making; Social Perceptiveness; Complex Problem Solving; Critical Thinking; Writing.

Education and Training Programs: Law (LL.B., J.D.); Legal Professions and Studies, Other; Legal Studies, General. **Related Knowledge/Courses:** Sociology and Anthropology; Therapy and Counseling; Law and Government; Personnel and Human Resources; Psychology; Philosophy and Theology.

Archeologists

* Annual Earnings: $53,910
* Beginning Wage: $32,150
* Earnings Growth Potential: High (40.4%)
* Growth: 15.0%
* Annual Job Openings: 446
* Self-Employed: 6.1%
* Part-Time: 20.1%
* Job Security: Most secure
* Education/Training Required: Master's degree

The Department of Labor reports this information for the occupation Anthropologists and Archeologists. The job openings listed here are shared with other specializations within that occupation, including Anthropologists.

Industries in Which Income Is Highest

Industry	Average Annual Earnings	Number Employed
Federal, State, and Local Government	$63,970	1,600
Museums, Historical Sites, and Similar Institutions	$56,900	160
Professional, Scientific, and Technical Services	$48,350	2,940
Administrative and Support Services	$48,020	100
Educational Services	$44,350	300

Metropolitan Areas Where Income Is Highest

Metropolitan Area	Average Annual Earnings	Number Employed
Anchorage, AK	$67,090	50
Madison, WI	$65,880	30
Los Angeles–Long Beach–Santa Ana, CA	$65,580	130
Honolulu, HI	$62,410	220
Sacramento–Arden-Arcade–Roseville, CA	$60,400	90

Conduct research to reconstruct record of past human life and culture from human remains, artifacts, architectural features, and structures recovered through excavation, underwater recovery, or other means of discovery. Write, present, and publish reports that record site history, methodology, and artifact analysis results, along with recommendations for conserving and interpreting findings. Compare findings from one site with archeological data from other sites to find similarities or differences. Research, survey, or assess sites of past societies and cultures in search of answers to specific research questions. Study objects and structures recovered by excavation to identify, date, and authenticate them and to interpret their significance. Develop and test theories concerning the origin and development of past cultures. Consult site reports, existing artifacts, and topographic maps to identify archeological sites. Create a grid of each site and draw and update maps of unit profiles, stratum surfaces, features, and findings. Record the exact locations and conditions of artifacts uncovered in diggings or surveys, using drawings and photographs as necessary. Assess archeological sites for resource management, development, or conservation purposes and recommend methods for site protection. Describe artifacts' physical properties or attributes, such as the materials from which artifacts are made and their size, shape, function, and decoration. Teach archeology at colleges and universities. Collect artifacts made of stone, bone, metal, and other materials, placing them in bags and marking them to show where they were found. Create artifact typologies to organize and make sense of past material cultures. Lead field training sites and train field staff, students, and volunteers in excavation methods. Clean, restore, and preserve artifacts.

Other Considerations for Income: In the federal government, social scientists with a bachelor's degree and no experience often started at a yearly salary of $28,862 or $35,572 in 2007, depending on their college records.

Those with a master's degree could start at $43,731, and those with a Ph.D. degree could begin at $52,912, while some individuals with experience and an advanced degree could start at $63,417. Beginning salaries were higher in selected areas of the country where the prevailing local pay level was higher.

Personality Type: Investigative-Realistic-Artistic. **Career Cluster:** 15 Science, Technology, Engineering, and Mathematics. **Career Pathway:** 15.3 Science and Mathematics. **Skills:** Science; Management of Financial Resources; Writing; Management of Personnel Resources; Reading Comprehension; Active Learning; Management of Material Resources; Critical Thinking.

Education and Training Programs: Anthropology; Archeology; Classics and Classical Languages, Literatures, and Linguistics, General; Physical and Biological Anthropology. **Related Knowledge/Courses:** History and Archeology; Sociology and Anthropology; Geography; Philosophy and Theology; Foreign Language; English Language.

Architects, Except Landscape and Naval

- ❋ Annual Earnings: $70,320
- ❋ Beginning Wage: $41,320
- ❋ Earnings Growth Potential: High (41.2%)
- ❋ Growth: 17.7%
- ❋ Annual Job Openings: 11,324
- ❋ Self-Employed: 20.3%
- ❋ Part-Time: 6.1%
- ❋ Job Security: Less secure than most
- ❋ Education/Training Required: Bachelor's degree

Industries in Which Income Is Highest

Industry	Average Annual Earnings	Number Employed
Federal, State, and Local Government	$80,520	3,550
Educational Services	$73,010	1,100
Construction of Buildings	$71,870	4,690
Professional, Scientific, and Technical Services	$69,570	98,050

Metropolitan Areas Where Income Is Highest

Metropolitan Area	Average Annual Earnings	Number Employed
Bakersfield, CA	$110,480	130
Cape Coral–Fort Myers, FL	$100,170	80
Bridgeport-Stamford-Norwalk, CT	$88,210	290
Mobile, AL	$86,420	170
Springfield, MA-CT	$86,380	70

Plan and design structures such as private residences, office buildings, theaters, factories, and other structural property. Prepare information regarding design, structure specifications, materials, color, equipment, estimated costs, or construction time. Consult with client to determine functional and spatial requirements of structure. Direct activities of workers engaged in preparing drawings and specification documents. Plan layout of project. Prepare contract documents for building contractors. Prepare scale drawings. Integrate engineering element into unified design. Conduct periodic on-site observation of work during construction to monitor compliance with plans. Administer construction contracts. Represent client in obtaining bids and awarding construction contracts. Prepare operating and maintenance manuals, studies, and reports.

Other Considerations for Income: Earnings of partners in established architectural firms may fluctuate because of changing business conditions. Some architects may have difficulty establishing their own practices and may go through a period when their expenses are greater than their income, requiring substantial financial resources. Many firms pay tuition and fees toward continuing education requirements for their employees.

Personality Type: Artistic-Investigative. **Career Cluster:** 02 Architecture and Construction. **Career Pathway:** 02.1 Design/Pre-Construction. **Skills:** Operations Analysis; Management of Financial Resources; Complex Problem Solving; Management of Personnel Resources; Coordination; Negotiation; Persuasion; Science.

Education and Training Programs: Architectural History and Criticism, General; Architecture (BArch, BA/BS, MArch, MA/MS, PhD); Architecture and Related Services, Other; Environmental Design/Architecture. **Related Knowledge/Courses:** Design; Building and Construction; Engineering and Technology; Fine Arts; Sales and Marketing; Law and Government.

Architecture Teachers, Postsecondary

- ❀ Annual Earnings: $71,710
- ❀ Beginning Wage: $38,310
- ❀ Earnings Growth Potential: High (46.6%)
- ❀ Growth: 22.9%
- ❀ Annual Job Openings: 1,044
- ❀ Self-Employed: 0.4%
- ❀ Part-Time: 27.8%
- ❀ Job Security: Most secure
- ❀ Education/Training Required: Doctoral degree

Industries in Which Income Is Highest

Industry	Average Annual Earnings	Number Employed
Educational Services	$71,930	6,270

Metropolitan Areas Where Income Is Highest

Metropolitan Area	Average Annual Earnings	Number Employed
San Diego–Carlsbad–San Marcos, CA	$89,590	150
Boston-Cambridge-Quincy, MA-NH	$87,510	90
Washington-Arlington-Alexandria, DC-VA-MD-WV	$85,780	590
Philadelphia-Camden-Wilmington, PA-NJ-DE-MD	$79,830	100
New York–Northern New Jersey–Long Island, NY-NJ-PA	$79,690	1,030

Teach courses in architecture and architectural design, such as architectural environmental design, interior architecture/design, and landscape architecture. Evaluate and grade students' work, including work performed in design studios. Prepare and deliver lectures to undergraduate and/or graduate students on topics such as architectural design methods, aesthetics and design, and structures and materials. Prepare course materials such as syllabi, homework assignments, and handouts. Initiate, facilitate, and moderate classroom discussions. Plan, evaluate, and revise curricula, course content, and course materials and methods of instruction. Keep abreast of developments in their field by reading current literature, talking with colleagues, and participating in professional conferences. Maintain student attendance records, grades, and other required records. Maintain regularly scheduled office hours to advise and assist students. Compile, administer, and grade examinations or assign this work to others. Conduct research in a particular field of knowledge and publish findings in professional journals, books, and/or electronic media. Supervise undergraduate and/or graduate teaching, internship, and research work. Advise students on academic and vocational curricula and on career issues. Collaborate with colleagues to address teaching and research issues. Compile bibliographies of specialized materials for outside reading assignments. Serve on academic or administrative committees that deal with institutional policies, departmental matters, and academic issues. Participate in student recruitment, registration, and placement activities. Select and obtain materials and supplies such as textbooks and laboratory equipment. Write grant proposals to procure external research funding. Provide professional consulting services to government and/or industry. Perform administrative duties such as serving as department head. Act as advisers to student organizations. Participate in campus and community events.

Other Considerations for Income: Earnings for college faculty vary according to rank and type of institution, geographic area, and field. According to a 2006–2007 survey by the American Association of University Professors, salaries for full-time faculty averaged $73,207. By rank, the average was $98,974 for professors, $69,911 for associate professors, $58,662 for assistant professors, $42,609 for instructors, and $48,289 for lecturers. Faculty in 4-year institutions earn higher salaries, on average, than do those in 2-year schools. Many faculty members have significant earnings in addition to their base salary from consulting, teaching additional courses, research, writing for publication, or other employment. In addition, many college and university faculty enjoy unique benefits, including access to campus facilities, tuition waivers for dependents, housing and travel allowances, and paid leave for sabbaticals. Part-time faculty and instructors usually have fewer benefits than full-time faculty.

Personality Type: Social-Artistic. **Career Clusters:** 02 Architecture and Construction; 05 Education and Training; 15 Science, Technology, Engineering, and Mathematics. **Career Pathways:** 02.1 Design/Pre-Construction; 05.3 Teaching/Training; 15.1 Engineering and Technology. **Skills:** Technology Design; Operations Analysis; Instructing; Writing; Complex Problem Solving; Science; Speaking; Critical Thinking.

Education and Training Programs: Architectural Engineering; Architecture (BArch, BA/BS, MArch, MA/MS, PhD); City/Urban, Community and Regional Planning; Environmental Design/Architecture; Interior Architecture; Landscape Architecture (BS, BSLA, BLA, MSLA, MLA, PhD); Teacher Education and Professional Development, Specific Subject Areas, Other. **Related Knowledge/Courses:** Fine Arts; Building and Construction; Design; History and Archeology; Philosophy and Theology; Geography.

Area, Ethnic, and Cultural Studies Teachers, Postsecondary

- ❀ Annual Earnings: $61,490
- ❀ Beginning Wage: $33,420
- ❀ Earnings Growth Potential: High (45.6%)
- ❀ Growth: 22.9%
- ❀ Annual Job Openings: 1,252
- ❀ Self-Employed: 0.4%
- ❀ Part-Time: 27.8%
- ❀ Job Security: Most secure
- ❀ Education/Training Required: Doctoral degree

Industries in Which Income Is Highest

Industry	Average Annual Earnings	Number Employed
Educational Services	$61,650	7,460

Metropolitan Areas Where Income Is Highest

Metropolitan Area	Average Annual Earnings	Number Employed
San Francisco–Oakland–Fremont, CA	$104,740	140
San Diego–Carlsbad–San Marcos, CA	$95,130	90
Sacramento–Arden-Arcade–Roseville, CA	$86,830	90
Philadelphia-Camden-Wilmington, PA-NJ-DE-MD	$80,320	190
Rochester, NY	$80,250	130

Teach courses pertaining to the culture and development of an area (e.g., Latin America), an ethnic group, or any other group (e.g., women's studies, urban affairs). Keep abreast of developments in their field by reading current literature, talking with colleagues, and participating in professional conferences. Conduct research in a particular field of knowledge and publish findings in professional journals, books, and/or electronic media. Evaluate and grade students' classwork, assignments, and papers. Prepare course materials such as syllabi, homework assignments, and handouts. Prepare and deliver lectures to undergraduate and/or graduate students on topics such as race and ethnic relations, gender studies, and cross-cultural perspectives. Initiate, facilitate, and moderate classroom discussions. Compile, administer, and grade examinations or assign this work to others. Maintain regularly scheduled office hours in order to advise and assist students. Plan, evaluate, and revise curricula, course content, and course materials and methods of instruction. Maintain student attendance records, grades, and other required records. Advise students on academic and vocational curricula and on career issues. Supervise undergraduate and/or graduate teaching, internship, and research work. Select and obtain materials and supplies such as textbooks. Collaborate with colleagues to address teaching and research issues. Serve on academic or administrative committees that deal with institutional policies, departmental matters, and academic issues. Compile bibliographies of specialized materials for outside reading assignments. Write grant proposals to procure external research funding. Participate in campus and community events. Participate in student recruitment, registration, and placement activities. Act as advisers to student organizations. Incorporate experiential/site visit components into courses. Perform administrative duties such as serving as department head. Provide professional consulting services to government and/or industry.

Other Considerations for Income: Earnings for college faculty vary according to rank and type of institution, geographic area, and field. According to a 2006–2007 survey by the American Association of University Professors, salaries for full-time faculty averaged $73,207. By rank, the average was $98,974 for professors, $69,911 for associate professors, $58,662 for assistant professors, $42,609 for instructors, and $48,289 for lecturers. Faculty in 4-year institutions earn higher salaries, on average, than do those in 2-year schools. Many faculty members have significant earnings in addition to their base salary from consulting, teaching additional courses, research, writing for publication, or other employment. In addition, many college and university faculty enjoy unique benefits, including access to campus facilities, tuition waivers for dependents, housing and travel allowances, and paid leave for sabbaticals. Part-time faculty and instructors usually have fewer benefits than full-time faculty.

Personality Type: Social-Investigative-Artistic. **Career Clusters:** 10 Human Service; 15 Science, Technology, Engineering, and Mathematics. **Career Pathways:** 10.2 Counseling and Mental Health Services; 15.3 Science and Mathematics. **Skills:** Writing; Critical Thinking; Instructing; Persuasion; Active Learning; Learning Strategies; Speaking; Management of Financial Resources.

Education and Training Programs: African Studies; African-American/Black Studies; American Indian/Native American Studies; American/United States Studies/Civilization; Area Studies, Other; Asian Studies/Civilization; Asian-American Studies; Balkans Studies; Baltic Studies; Canadian Studies; Caribbean Studies; Chinese Studies; Commonwealth Studies; East Asian Studies; Ethnic, Cultural Minority, Gender, and Group Studies, Other; European Studies/Civilization; French Studies; Gay/Lesbian Studies; German Studies; Hispanic-American, **Related Knowledge/Courses:** History and Archeology; Sociology and Anthropology; Foreign Language; Philosophy and Theology; Geography; Education and Training.

Art Directors

❋ Annual Earnings: $76,980

❋ Beginning Wage: $40,730

❋ Earnings Growth Potential: High (47.1%)

❋ Growth: 9.0%

❋ Annual Job Openings: 9,719

❋ Self-Employed: 59.0%

❋ Part-Time: 22.5%

❋ Job Security: Less secure than most

❋ Education/Training Required: Work experience plus degree

Industries in Which Income Is Highest

Industry	Average Annual Earnings	Number Employed
Motion Picture and Sound Recording Industries	$89,190	1,910
Management of Companies and Enterprises	$86,610	1,070
Professional, Scientific, and Technical Services	$82,540	16,280
Publishing Industries (Except Internet)	$68,170	6,410
Performing Arts, Spectator Sports, and Related Industries	$58,200	1,260

Metropolitan Areas Where Income Is Highest

Metropolitan Area	Average Annual Earnings	Number Employed
San Jose–Sunnyvale–Santa Clara, CA	$110,270	400
New York–Northern New Jersey–Long Island, NY-NJ-PA	$97,900	5,680
Boston-Cambridge-Quincy, MA-NH	$95,140	1,090
San Francisco–Oakland–Fremont, CA	$94,220	1,700
Los Angeles–Long Beach–Santa Ana, CA	$93,300	4,110

Formulate design concepts and presentation approaches and direct workers engaged in art work, layout design, and copy writing for visual communications media, such as magazines, books, newspapers, and packaging. Formulate basic layout design or presentation approach and specify material details, such as style and size of type, photographs, graphics, animation, video, and sound. Review and approve proofs of printed copy and art and copy materials developed by staff members. Manage own accounts and projects, working within budget and scheduling requirements. Confer with creative, art, copy-writing, or production department heads to discuss client requirements and presentation concepts and to coordinate creative activities. Present final layouts to clients for approval. Confer with clients to determine objectives; budget; background information; and presentation approaches, styles, and techniques. Hire, train, and direct staff members who develop design concepts into art layouts or who prepare layouts for printing. Work with creative directors to develop design solutions. Review illustrative material to determine if it conforms to standards and specifications. Attend photo shoots and printing sessions to ensure that the products needed are obtained. Create custom illustrations or other graphic elements. Mark up, paste, and complete layouts and write typography instructions to prepare materials for typesetting or printing. Negotiate with printers and estimators to determine what services will be performed. Conceptualize and help design interfaces for multimedia games, products, and devices. Prepare detailed storyboards showing sequence and timing of story development for television production.

Other Considerations for Income: No additional information.

Personality Type: Artistic-Enterprising. **Career Cluster:** 03 Arts, Audio/Video Technology, and Communications. **Career Pathway:** 03.3 Visual Arts. **Skills:** Operations Analysis; Management of Financial Resources; Coordination; Negotiation; Persuasion; Service Orientation; Systems Evaluation; Management of Personnel Resources.

Education and Training Programs: Graphic Design; Intermedia/Multimedia. **Related Knowledge/Courses:** Fine Arts; Design; Communications and Media; Production and Processing; Computers and Electronics; Administration and Management.

Art, Drama, and Music Teachers, Postsecondary

* Annual Earnings: $57,820
* Beginning Wage: $31,170
* Earnings Growth Potential: High (46.1%)
* Growth: 22.9%
* Annual Job Openings: 12,707
* Self-Employed: 0.4%
* Part-Time: 27.8%
* Job Security: Most secure
* Education/Training Required: Doctoral degree

Industries in Which Income Is Highest

Industry	Average Annual Earnings	Number Employed
Educational Services	$57,830	76,600

Metropolitan Areas Where Income Is Highest

Metropolitan Area	Average Annual Earnings	Number Employed
San Diego–Carlsbad–San Marcos, CA	$93,700	940
Los Angeles–Long Beach–Santa Ana, CA	$84,150	4,090
Lubbock, TX	$80,900	240
Sacramento–Arden-Arcade–Roseville, CA	$78,620	490
San Francisco–Oakland–Fremont, CA	$77,130	1,980

Teach courses in drama; music; and the arts, including fine and applied art, such as painting and sculpture, or design and crafts. Evaluate and grade students' classwork, performances, projects, assignments, and papers. Explain and demonstrate artistic techniques. Prepare students for performances, exams, or assessments. Prepare and deliver lectures to undergraduate or graduate students on topics such as acting techniques, fundamentals of music, and art history. Organize performance groups and direct their rehearsals. Prepare course materials such as syllabi, homework assignments, and handouts. Initiate, facilitate, and moderate classroom discussions. Keep abreast of developments in their field by reading current literature, talking with colleagues, and participating in professional conferences. Advise students on academic and vocational curricula and on career issues. Maintain student attendance records, grades, and other required records. Conduct research in a particular field of knowledge and publish findings in professional journals, books, or electronic media. Supervise undergraduate and/or graduate teaching, internship, and research work. Plan, evaluate, and revise curricula, course content, and course materials and methods of instruction. Maintain regularly scheduled office hours to advise and assist students. Compile, administer, and grade examinations or assign this work to others. Participate in student recruitment, registration, and placement activities. Select and obtain materials and supplies such as textbooks and performance pieces. Collaborate with colleagues to address teaching and research issues. Serve on academic or administrative committees that deal with institutional policies, departmental matters, and academic issues. Participate in campus and community events. Keep students informed of community events such as plays and concerts. Compile bibliographies of specialized materials for outside reading assignments. Display students' work in schools, galleries, and exhibitions. Perform administrative duties such as serving as department head.

Other Considerations for Income: Earnings for college faculty vary according to rank and type of institution, geographic area, and field. According to a 2006–2007 survey by the American Association of University Professors, salaries for full-time faculty averaged $73,207. By rank, the average was $98,974 for professors, $69,911 for associate professors, $58,662 for assistant professors, $42,609 for instructors, and $48,289 for lecturers. Faculty in 4-year institutions earn higher salaries, on average, than do those in 2-year schools. Many faculty members have significant earnings in addition to their base salary from consulting, teaching additional courses, research, writing for publication, or other employment. In addition, many college and university faculty enjoy unique benefits, including access to campus facilities, tuition waivers for dependents, housing and travel allowances, and paid leave for sabbaticals. Part-time faculty and instructors usually have fewer benefits than full-time faculty.

Personality Type: Social-Artistic. **Career Clusters:** 03 Arts, Audio/Video Technology, and Communications. **Career Pathways:** 03.1 Audio and Video Technology and Film; 03.2 Printing Technology; 03.3 Visual Arts; 03.4 Performing Arts. **Skills:** Instructing; Social Perceptiveness; Speaking; Active Listening; Persuasion; Learning Strategies; Critical Thinking; Monitoring.

Education and Training Programs: Art History, Criticism, and Conservation; Art/Art Studies, General; Ceramic Arts and Ceramics; Cinematography and Film/Video Production; Commercial Photography; Conducting; Crafts/Craft Design, Folk Art and Artisanry; Dance, General; Design and Applied Arts, Other; Design and Visual Communications, General; Directing and Theatrical Production; Drama and Dramatics/Theatre Arts, General; Dramatic/Theatre Arts and Stagecraft, Other; Fashion/Apparel Design; Fiber, Textile and Weaving Arts; others. **Related Knowledge/Courses:** Fine Arts; History and Archeology; Philosophy and Theology; Education and Training; Communications and Media; Sociology and Anthropology.

Astronomers

- ❇ Annual Earnings: $101,300
- ❇ Beginning Wage: $45,330
- ❇ Earnings Growth Potential: Very high (55.3%)
- ❇ Growth: 5.6%
- ❇ Annual Job Openings: 128
- ❇ Self-Employed: 0.4%
- ❇ Part-Time: 5.2%
- ❇ Job Security: Less secure than most
- ❇ Education/Training Required: Doctoral degree

Industries in Which Income Is Highest

Industry	Average Annual Earnings	Number Employed
Federal, State, and Local Government	$127,960	450
Professional, Scientific, and Technical Services	$98,160	320
Educational Services	$70,610	510

Metropolitan Areas Where Income Is Highest

Metropolitan Area	Average Annual Earnings	Number Employed
Insufficient data available		

Observe, research, and interpret celestial and astronomical phenomena to increase basic knowledge and apply such information to practical problems. Study celestial phenomena, using a variety of ground-based and space-borne telescopes and scientific instruments. Analyze research data to determine its significance, using computers. Present research findings at scientific conferences and in papers written for scientific journals. Measure radio, infrared, gamma, and X-ray emissions from extraterrestrial sources. Develop theories based on personal observations or on observations and theories of other astronomers. Raise funds for scientific research. Collaborate with other astronomers to carry out research projects. Develop instrumentation and software for astronomical observation and analysis. Teach astronomy or astrophysics. Develop and modify astronomy-related programs for public presentation. Calculate orbits and determine sizes, shapes, brightness, and motions of different celestial bodies. Direct the operations of a planetarium.

Other Considerations for Income: No additional information.

Personality Type: Investigative-Artistic-Realistic. **Career Cluster:** 15 Science, Technology, Engineering, and Mathematics. **Career Pathway:** 15.3 Science and Mathematics. **Skills:** Science; Programming; Mathematics; Complex Problem Solving; Technology Design; Active Learning; Critical Thinking; Reading Comprehension.

Education and Training Programs: Astronomy; Astronomy and Astrophysics, Other; Astrophysics; Planetary Astronomy and Science. **Related Knowledge/Courses:** Physics; Mathematics; Engineering and Technology; Chemistry; Computers and Electronics; Education and Training.

Atmospheric and Space Scientists

❋ Annual Earnings: $81,290
❋ Beginning Wage: $38,990
❋ Earnings Growth Potential: Very high (52.0%)
❋ Growth: 10.6%
❋ Annual Job Openings: 735
❋ Self-Employed: 0.0%
❋ Part-Time: 5.2%
❋ Job Security: More secure than most
❋ Education/Training Required: Bachelor's degree

Industries in Which Income Is Highest

Industry	Average Annual Earnings	Number Employed
Federal, State, and Local Government	$89,540	3,270
Broadcasting (Except Internet)	$79,250	710
Educational Services	$78,580	960
Professional, Scientific, and Technical Services	$65,290	3,740

Metropolitan Areas Where Income Is Highest

Metropolitan Area	Average Annual Earnings	Number Employed
Baltimore-Towson, MD	$104,130	110
Detroit-Warren-Livonia, MI	$103,490	40
Washington-Arlington-Alexandria, DC-VA-MD-WV	$97,830	570
New York–Northern New Jersey–Long Island, NY-NJ-PA	$97,380	130
Sacramento–Arden-Arcade–Roseville, CA	$95,620	110

Investigate atmospheric phenomena and interpret meteorological data gathered by surface and air stations, satellites, and radar to prepare reports and forecasts for public and other uses. Study and interpret data, reports, maps, photographs, and charts to predict long- and short-range weather conditions, using computer models and knowledge of climate theory, physics, and mathematics. Broadcast weather conditions, forecasts, and severe weather warnings to the public via television, radio, and the Internet or provide this information to the news media. Gather data from sources such as surface and upper air stations, satellites, weather bureaus, and radar for use in meteorological reports and forecasts. Prepare forecasts and briefings to meet the needs of industry, business, government, and other groups. Apply meteorological knowledge to problems in areas including agriculture, pollution control, and water management and to issues such as global warming or ozone depletion. Conduct basic or applied meteorological research into the processes and determinants of atmospheric phenomena, weather, and climate. Operate computer graphic equipment to produce weather reports and maps for analysis, distribution, or use in weather broadcasts. Measure wind, temperature, and humidity in the upper atmosphere, using weather balloons. Develop and use weather forecasting tools such as mathematical and computer models. Direct forecasting services at weather stations or at radio or television broadcasting facilities. Research and analyze the impact of industrial projects and pollution on climate, air quality, and weather phenomena. Collect air samples from planes and ships over land and sea to study atmospheric composition. Conduct numerical simulations of climate conditions to understand and predict global and regional weather patterns. Collect and analyze historical climate information such as precipitation and temperature records help predict future weather and climate trends. Consult with agencies, professionals, or researchers regarding the use and interpretation of climatological information.

Other Considerations for Income: No additional information.

Personality Type: Investigative-Realistic. **Career Cluster:** 15 Science, Technology, Engineering, and Mathematics. **Career Pathway:** 15.3 Science and Mathematics. **Skills:** Science; Programming; Judgment and Decision Making; Operation Monitoring; Operations Analysis; Technology Design; Quality Control Analysis; Operation and Control.

Education and Training Programs: Atmospheric Chemistry and Climatology; Atmospheric Physics and Dynamics; Atmospheric Sciences and Meteorology, General; Atmospheric Sciences and Meteorology, Other; Meteorology. **Related Knowledge/Courses:** Geography; Physics; Mathematics; Computers and Electronics; Communications and Media; Customer and Personal Service.

Atmospheric, Earth, Marine, and Space Sciences Teachers, Postsecondary

- ❋ Annual Earnings: $76,050
- ❋ Beginning Wage: $41,910
- ❋ Earnings Growth Potential: High (44.9%)
- ❋ Growth: 22.9%
- ❋ Annual Job Openings: 1,553
- ❋ Self-Employed: 0.4%
- ❋ Part-Time: 27.8%
- ❋ Job Security: Most secure
- ❋ Education/Training Required: Doctoral degree

Industries in Which Income Is Highest

Industry	Average Annual Earnings	Number Employed
Educational Services	$74,980	9,360

Metropolitan Areas Where Income Is Highest

Metropolitan Area	Average Annual Earnings	Number Employed
Dallas–Fort Worth–Arlington, TX	$99,930	190
Boston-Cambridge-Quincy, MA-NH	$98,690	200
Los Angeles–Long Beach–Santa Ana, CA	$97,710	710
Columbus, OH	$88,100	120
Philadelphia-Camden-Wilmington, PA-NJ-DE-MD	$87,190	280

Teach courses in the physical sciences, except chemistry and physics. Conduct research in a particular field of knowledge and publish findings in professional journals, books, and/or electronic media. Write grant proposals to procure external research funding. Keep abreast of developments in their field by reading current literature, talking with colleagues, and participating in professional conferences. Supervise undergraduate and/or graduate teaching, internships, and research work. Prepare and deliver lectures to undergraduate and/or graduate students on topics such as structural geology, micrometeorology, and atmospheric thermodynamics. Supervise laboratory work and fieldwork. Evaluate and grade students' classwork, assignments, and papers. Prepare course materials such as syllabi, homework assignments, and handouts. Collaborate with colleagues to address teaching and research issues. Compile, administer, and grade examinations or assign this work to others. Plan, evaluate, and revise curricula, course content, course materials, and methods of instruction. Initiate, facilitate, and moderate classroom discussions. Maintain regularly scheduled office hours to advise and assist students. Advise students on academic and vocational curricula and on career issues. Maintain student attendance records, grades, and other required records. Participate in student recruitment, registration, and placement activities. Perform administrative duties such as serving as department head. Select and obtain materials and supplies such as textbooks and laboratory equipment. Serve on academic or administrative committees that deal with institutional policies, departmental matters, and academic issues. Compile bibliographies of specialized materials for outside reading assignments. Provide professional consulting services to government and/or industry. Act as adviser to student organizations. Participate in campus and community events.

Other Considerations for Income: Earnings for college faculty vary according to rank and type of institution, geographic area, and field. According to a 2006–2007 survey by the American Association of University Professors, salaries for full-time faculty averaged $73,207. By rank, the average was $98,974 for professors, $69,911 for associate professors, $58,662 for assistant professors, $42,609 for instructors, and $48,289 for lecturers. Faculty in 4-year institutions earn higher salaries, on average, than do those in 2-year schools. Many faculty members have significant earnings in addition to their base salary from consulting, teaching additional courses, research, writing for publication, or other employment. In addition, many college and university faculty enjoy unique benefits, including access to campus facilities, tuition waivers for dependents, housing and travel allowances, and paid leave for sabbaticals. Part-time faculty and instructors usually have fewer benefits than full-time faculty.

Personality Type: Social-Investigative. **Career Clusters:** 05 Education and Training; 15 Science, Technology, Engineering, and Mathematics. **Career Pathways:** 05.3 Teaching/Training; 15.3 Science and Mathematics. **Skills:** Science; Programming; Mathematics; Management of Financial Resources; Complex Problem Solving; Writing; Active Learning; Reading Comprehension.

Education and Training Programs: Acoustics; Astronomy; Astrophysics; Atmospheric Chemistry and Climatology; Atmospheric Physics and Dynamics; Atmospheric Sciences and Meteorology, General; Atmospheric Sciences and Meteorology, Other; Atomic/Molecular Physics; Condensed Matter and Materials Physics; Elementary Particle Physics; Geochemistry; Geochemistry and Petrology; Geological and Earth Sciences/Geosciences, Other; Geology/Earth Science, General; Geophysics and Seismology; Hydrology and Water Resources Science; Meteorology; others. **Related Knowledge/Courses:** Physics; Geography; Chemistry; Biology; Mathematics; Education and Training.

Audiologists

* Annual Earnings: $62,030
* Beginning Wage: $40,360
* Earnings Growth Potential: Low (34.9%)
* Growth: 9.8%
* Annual Job Openings: 980
* Self-Employed: 10.2%
* Part-Time: 28.3%
* Job Security: Most secure
* Education/Training Required: First professional degree

Industries in Which Income Is Highest

Industry	Average Annual Earnings	Number Employed
Hospitals	$66,120	1,520
Ambulatory Health Care Services	$62,690	6,350
Educational Services	$60,980	1,740
Health and Personal Care Stores	$57,260	2,220

Metropolitan Areas Where Income Is Highest

Metropolitan Area	Average Annual Earnings	Number Employed
Sacramento–Arden-Arcade–Roseville, CA	$82,620	110
New York–Northern New Jersey–Long Island, NY-NJ-PA	$77,400	630
Detroit-Warren-Livonia, MI	$73,040	200
San Diego–Carlsbad–San Marcos, CA	$72,960	120
Portland-Vancouver-Beaverton, OR-WA	$72,840	130

Assess and treat persons with hearing and related disorders. May fit hearing aids and provide auditory training. May perform research related to hearing problems. Evaluate hearing and speech/language disorders to determine diagnoses and courses of treatment. Administer hearing or speech/language evaluations, tests, or examinations to patients to collect information on type and degree of impairment, using specialized instruments and electronic equipment. Fit and dispense assistive devices, such as hearing aids. Maintain client records at all stages, including initial evaluation and discharge. Refer clients to additional medical or educational services if needed. Counsel and instruct clients in techniques to improve hearing or speech impairment, including sign language or lipreading. Monitor clients' progress and discharge them from treatment when goals are attained. Plan and conduct treatment programs for clients' hearing or speech problems, consulting with physicians, nurses, psychologists, and other health-care personnel as necessary. Recommend assistive devices according to clients' needs or nature of impairments. Participate in conferences or training to update or share knowledge of new hearing or speech disorder treatment methods or technologies. Instruct clients, parents, teachers, or employers in how to avoid behavior patterns that lead to miscommunication. Examine and clean patients' ear canals. Advise educators or other medical staff on speech or hearing topics. Educate and supervise audiology students and health-care personnel. Fit and tune cochlear implants, providing rehabilitation for adjustment to listening with implant amplification systems. Work with multidisciplinary teams to assess and rehabilitate recipients of implanted hearing devices. Develop and supervise hearing screening programs. Conduct or direct research on hearing or speech topics and report findings to help in the development of procedures, technology, or treatments. Measure noise levels in workplaces and conduct hearing protection programs in industry, schools, and communities.

Other Considerations for Income: Some employers may pay for continuing education courses.

Personality Type: Investigative-Social. **Career Cluster:** 08 Health Science. **Career Pathway:** 08.1 Therapeutic Services. **Skills:** Science; Social Perceptiveness; Equipment Selection; Service Orientation; Persuasion; Reading Comprehension; Technology Design; Equipment Maintenance.

Education and Training Programs: Audiology/Audiologist; Audiology/Audiologist and Speech-Language Pathology/Pathologist; Communication Disorders Sciences and Services, Other; Communication Disorders, General; Communication Sciences and Disorders, General. **Related Knowledge/Courses:** Therapy and Counseling; Medicine and Dentistry; Psychology; Sales and Marketing; Customer and Personal Service; Sociology and Anthropology.

Auditors

❋ Annual Earnings: $59,430
❋ Beginning Wage: $36,720
❋ Earnings Growth Potential: Medium (38.2%)
❋ Growth: 17.7%
❋ Annual Job Openings: 134,463
❋ Self-Employed: 9.5%
❋ Part-Time: 9.3%
❋ Job Security: More secure than most
❋ Education/Training Required: Bachelor's degree

The Department of Labor reports this information for the occupation Accountants and Auditors. The job openings listed here are shared with other specializations within that occupation, including Accountants.

Industries in Which Income Is Highest

Industry	Average Annual Earnings	Number Employed
Motion Picture and Sound Recording Industries	$67,080	3,530
Other Information Services	$66,360	1,720
Computer and Electronic Product Manufacturing	$64,390	13,550
Utilities	$63,880	7,510
Telecommunications	$63,710	7,950

Metropolitan Areas Where Income Is Highest

Metropolitan Area	Average Annual Earnings	Number Employed
San Jose–Sunnyvale–Santa Clara, CA	$74,950	10,600
New York–Northern New Jersey–Long Island, NY-NJ-PA	$73,910	104,320
Napa, CA	$72,670	340
Bridgeport-Stamford-Norwalk, CT	$72,310	7,240
San Francisco–Oakland–Fremont, CA	$71,320	23,190

Examine and analyze accounting records to determine financial status of establishment and prepare financial reports concerning operating procedures. Collect and analyze data to detect deficient controls; duplicated effort;

extravagance; fraud; or non-compliance with laws, regulations, and management policies. Prepare detailed reports on audit findings. Supervise auditing of establishments and determine scope of investigation required. Report to management about asset utilization and audit results and recommend changes in operations and financial activities. Inspect account books and accounting systems for efficiency, effectiveness, and use of accepted accounting procedures to record transactions. Examine records and interview workers to ensure recording of transactions and compliance with laws and regulations. Examine and evaluate financial and information systems, recommending controls to ensure system reliability and data integrity. Review data about material assets, net worth, liabilities, capital stock, surplus, income, and expenditures. Confer with company officials about financial and regulatory matters. Examine whether the organization's objectives are reflected in its management activities and whether employees understand the objectives. Prepare, analyze, and verify annual reports, financial statements, and other records, using accepted accounting and statistical procedures to assess financial condition and facilitate financial planning. Inspect cash on hand, notes receivable and payable, negotiable securities, and canceled checks to confirm records are accurate. Examine inventory to verify journal and ledger entries. Direct activities of personnel engaged in filing, recording, compiling, and transmitting financial records. Conduct pre-implementation audits to determine whether systems and programs under development will work as planned. Audit payroll and personnel records to determine unemployment insurance premiums, workers' compensation coverage, liabilities, and compliance with tax laws.

Other Considerations for Income: Salaries vary because of differences in size of firm, location, level of education, and professional credentials. Wage and salary accountants and auditors usually receive standard benefits, including health and medical insurance, life insurance, a 401(k) plan, and paid annual leave. High-level senior accountants may receive additional benefits, such as the use of a company car and an expense account.

Personality Type: Conventional-Enterprising-Investigative. **Career Cluster:** 04 Business, Management, and Administration. **Career Pathway:** 04.2 Business, Financial Management, and Accounting. **Skills:** Systems Analysis; Systems Evaluation; Management of Personnel Resources; Writing; Management of Financial Resources; Persuasion; Speaking; Mathematics.

Education and Training Programs: Accounting; Accounting and Business/Management; Accounting and Computer Science; Accounting and Finance; Auditing; Taxation. **Related Knowledge/Courses:** Economics and Accounting; Administration and Management; Personnel and Human Resources; Law and Government; Computers and Electronics; Mathematics.

Automotive Engineering Technicians

- ✸ Annual Earnings: $48,130
- ✸ Beginning Wage: $31,110
- ✸ Earnings Growth Potential: Medium (35.4%)
- ✸ Growth: 6.4%
- ✸ Annual Job Openings: 3,710
- ✸ Self-Employed: 0.8%
- ✸ Part-Time: 5.9%
- ✸ Job Security: No data available
- ✸ Education/Training Required: Associate degree

The Department of Labor reports this information for the occupation Mechanical Engineering Technicians. The job openings listed here are shared with other specializations within that occupation.

Industries in Which Income Is Highest

Industry	Average Annual Earnings	Number Employed
Merchant Wholesalers, Durable Goods	$49,030	1,580
Management of Companies and Enterprises	$48,690	1,100
Professional, Scientific, and Technical Services	$48,650	17,260
Transportation Equipment Manufacturing	$48,570	3,820
Computer and Electronic Product Manufacturing	$48,090	4,470

Metropolitan Areas Where Income Is Highest

Metropolitan Area	Average Annual Earnings	Number Employed
Oxnard–Thousand Oaks–Ventura, CA	$65,940	60
San Jose–Sunnyvale–Santa Clara, CA	$62,420	840
Greensboro–High Point, NC	$60,610	120
Portland-Vancouver-Beaverton, OR-WA	$60,020	420
Seattle-Tacoma-Bellevue, WA	$59,850	990

Assist engineers in determining the practicality of proposed product design changes and plan and carry out tests on experimental test devices and equipment for performance, durability, and efficiency. No task data available.

Other Considerations for Income: No additional information.

Personality Type: No data available. **Career Cluster:** 13 Manufacturing. **Career Pathway:** 13.3 Maintenance, Installation and Repair. **Skills:** No data available.

Education and Training Programs: Mechanical Engineering Related Technologies/Technicians, Other; Mechanical Engineering/Mechanical Technology/Technician. **Related Knowledge/Courses:** No data available.

Automotive Engineers

- ❋ Annual Earnings: $74,920
- ❋ Beginning Wage: $47,900
- ❋ Earnings Growth Potential: Medium (36.1%)
- ❋ Growth: 4.2%
- ❋ Annual Job Openings: 12,394
- ❋ Self-Employed: 2.2%
- ❋ Part-Time: 1.9%
- ❋ Job Security: No data available
- ❋ Education/Training Required: Bachelor's degree

The Department of Labor reports this information for the occupation Mechanical Engineers. The job openings listed here are shared with other specializations within that occupation, including Fuel Cell Engineers.

Industries in Which Income Is Highest

Industry	Average Annual Earnings	Number Employed
Federal, State, and Local Government	$86,810	11,330
Management of Companies and Enterprises	$83,970	6,280
Computer and Electronic Product Manufacturing	$80,330	22,300
Professional, Scientific, and Technical Services	$79,060	69,520
Paper Manufacturing	$78,340	1,330

Metropolitan Areas Where Income Is Highest

Metropolitan Area	Average Annual Earnings	Number Employed
San Jose–Sunnyvale–Santa Clara, CA	$98,770	4,250
Washington-Arlington-Alexandria, DC-VA-MD-WV	$96,800	5,430
Albuquerque, NM	$93,890	890
Boulder, CO	$93,730	950
Denver-Aurora, CO	$92,810	2,150

Develop new or improved designs for vehicle structural members, engines, transmissions, and other vehicle systems, using computer-assisted design technology. Direct building, modification, and testing of vehicle and components. No task data available.

Other Considerations for Income: As a group, engineers earn some of the highest average starting salaries among those holding bachelor's degrees. Separate earnings figures for Automotive Engineers are not available, but they are probably similar to those for Mechanical Engineers, who are paid in the low-to-middle range among the various kinds of engineers. According to a 2007 survey by the National Association of Colleges and Employers, average starting salaries for Mechanical Engineers were $54,128 with a bachelor's, $62,798 with a master's, and $72,763 with a Ph.D.

Personality Type: No data available. **Career Cluster:** 15 Science, Technology, Engineering, and Mathematics. **Career Pathway:** 15.1 Engineering and Technology. **Skills:** No data available.

Education and Training Program: Mechanical Engineering. **Related Knowledge/Courses:** No data available.

Aviation Inspectors

- ❋ Annual Earnings: $55,250
- ❋ Beginning Wage: $27,560
- ❋ Earnings Growth Potential: Very high (50.1%)
- ❋ Growth: 16.4%
- ❋ Annual Job Openings: 2,122
- ❋ Self-Employed: 5.9%
- ❋ Part-Time: 3.7%
- ❋ Job Security: More secure than most
- ❋ Education/Training Required: Work experience in a related occupation

The Department of Labor reports this information for the occupation Transportation Inspectors. The job openings listed here are shared with other specializations within that occupation, including Freight and Cargo Inspectors; and Transportation Vehicle, Equipment, and Systems Inspectors, Except Aviation.

Industries in Which Income Is Highest

Industry	Average Annual Earnings	Number Employed
Federal, State, and Local Government	$62,100	11,310
Air Transportation	$59,340	1,380
Rail Transportation	$52,220	3,920
Support Activities for Transportation	$41,720	2,830
Truck Transportation	$39,650	1,170

Metropolitan Areas Where Income Is Highest

Metropolitan Area	Average Annual Earnings	Number Employed
Milwaukee–Waukesha–West Allis, WI	$92,180	60
Minneapolis–St. Paul–Bloomington, MN-WI	$89,530	170
Denver-Aurora, CO	$89,370	180
Washington-Arlington-Alexandria, DC-VA-MD-WV	$88,780	440
Oklahoma City, OK	$87,430	190

Inspect aircraft, maintenance procedures, air navigational aids, air traffic controls, and communications equipment to ensure conformance with federal safety regulations. Inspect work of aircraft mechanics performing maintenance, modification, or repair and overhaul of aircraft and aircraft mechanical systems to ensure adherence to standards and procedures. Start aircraft and observe gauges, meters, and other instruments to detect evidence of malfunctions. Examine aircraft access plates and doors for security. Examine landing gear, tires, and exteriors of fuselage, wings, and engines for evidence of damage or corrosion and to determine whether repairs are needed. Prepare and maintain detailed repair, inspection, investigation, and certification records and reports. Inspect new, repaired, or modified aircraft to identify damage or defects and to assess airworthiness and conformance to standards, using checklists, hand tools, and test instruments. Examine maintenance records and flight logs to determine if service and maintenance checks and overhauls were performed at prescribed intervals. Recommend replacement, repair, or modification of aircraft equipment. Recommend changes in rules, policies, standards, and regulations based on knowledge of operating conditions, aircraft improvements, and other factors. Issue pilots' licenses to individuals meeting standards. Investigate air accidents and complaints to determine causes. Observe flight activities of pilots to assess flying skills and to ensure conformance to flight and safety regulations. Conduct flight test programs to test equipment, instruments, and systems under a variety of conditions, using both manual and automatic controls. Approve or deny issuance of certificates of airworthiness. Analyze training programs and conduct oral and written examinations to ensure the competency of persons operating, installing, and repairing aircraft equipment. Schedule and coordinate in-flight testing programs with ground crews and air traffic control to ensure availability of ground tracking, equipment monitoring, and related services.

Other Considerations for Income: No additional information.

Personality Type: Realistic-Conventional-Investigative. **Career Cluster:** 16 Transportation, Distribution, and Logistics. **Career Pathway:** 16.1 Transportation Operations. **Skills:** Systems Analysis; Systems Evaluation; Quality Control Analysis; Operation Monitoring; Troubleshooting; Operation and Control; Reading Comprehension; Judgment and Decision Making.

Education and Training Program: Aircraft Powerplant Technology/Technician. **Related Knowledge/Courses:** Mechanical; Physics; Transportation; Chemistry; Design; Law and Government.

Avionics Technicians

❋ Annual Earnings: $49,310
❋ Beginning Wage: $34,220
❋ Earnings Growth Potential: Low (30.6%)
❋ Growth: 8.1%
❋ Annual Job Openings: 1,193
❋ Self-Employed: 0.0%
❋ Part-Time: 0.0%
❋ Job Security: Less secure than most
❋ Education/Training Required: Postsecondary vocational training

Industries in Which Income Is Highest

Industry	Average Annual Earnings	Number Employed
Air Transportation	$57,580	1,950
Transportation Equipment Manufacturing	$49,640	6,520
Federal, State, and Local Government	$49,490	2,030
Support Activities for Transportation	$45,490	4,140

Metropolitan Areas Where Income Is Highest

Metropolitan Area	Average Annual Earnings	Number Employed
Riverside–San Bernardino–Ontario, CA	$63,000	60
Omaha–Council Bluffs, NE-IA	$60,450	260
Denver-Aurora, CO	$59,230	130
Bridgeport-Stamford-Norwalk, CT	$58,710	390
Indianapolis-Carmel, IN	$58,510	110

Install, inspect, test, adjust, or repair avionics equipment, such as radar, radio, navigation, and missile control systems in aircraft or space vehicles. Set up and operate ground support and test equipment to perform functional flight tests of electrical and electronic systems. Test and troubleshoot instruments, components, and assemblies, using circuit testers, oscilloscopes, and voltmeters. Keep records of maintenance and repair work. Coordinate work with that of engineers, technicians, and other aircraft maintenance personnel. Interpret flight test data to diagnose malfunctions and systemic performance problems. Install electrical and electronic components, assemblies, and systems in aircraft, using hand tools, power tools, and soldering irons. Adjust, repair, or replace malfunctioning components or assemblies, using hand tools and soldering irons. Connect components to assemblies such as radio systems, instruments, magnetos, inverters, and in-flight refueling systems, using hand tools and soldering irons. Assemble components such as switches, electrical controls, and junction boxes, using hand tools and soldering irons. Fabricate parts and test aids as required. Lay out installation of aircraft assemblies and systems, following documentation such as blueprints, manuals, and wiring diagrams. Assemble prototypes or models of circuits, instruments, and systems so that they can be used for testing. Operate computer-aided drafting and design applications to design avionics system modifications.

Other Considerations for Income: Technicians who graduate from an aviation maintenance technician school often earn higher starting salaries than individuals who receive training in the Armed Forces or on the job. Airline mechanics and their immediate families receive reduced-fare transportation on their own and most other airlines. About 3 in 10 aircraft and avionics equipment mechanics and service technicians are members of unions or covered by union agreements. The principal unions are the International Association of Machinists and Aerospace Workers, and the Transport Workers Union of America. Some mechanics are represented by the International Brotherhood of Teamsters.

Personality Type: Realistic-Investigative-Conventional. **Career Clusters:** 13 Manufacturing; 16 Transportation, Distribution, and Logistics. **Career Pathways:** 13.1 Production; 13.3 Maintenance, Installation, and Repair; 16.4 Facility and Mobile Equipment Maintenance. **Skills:** Installation; Repairing; Equipment Maintenance; Troubleshooting; Operation and Control; Operation Monitoring; Quality Control Analysis; Systems Evaluation.

Education and Training Programs: Airframe Mechanics and Aircraft Maintenance Technology/Technician; Avionics Maintenance Technology/Technician. **Related Knowledge/Courses:** Engineering and Technology; Mechanical; Computers and Electronics; Telecommunications; Production and Processing; Design.

Biochemists and Biophysicists

❋ Annual Earnings: $82,840
❋ Beginning Wage: $44,320
❋ Earnings Growth Potential: High (46.5%)
❋ Growth: 15.9%
❋ Annual Job Openings: 1,637
❋ Self-Employed: 2.5%
❋ Part-Time: 7.3%
❋ Job Security: More secure than most
❋ Education/Training Required: Doctoral degree

Industries in Which Income Is Highest

Industry	Average Annual Earnings	Number Employed
Chemical Manufacturing	$87,700	7,220
Professional, Scientific, and Technical Services	$85,370	11,030
Educational Services	$47,100	1,510

Metropolitan Areas Where Income Is Highest

Metropolitan Area	Average Annual Earnings	Number Employed
Trenton-Ewing, NJ	$105,970	60
San Jose–Sunnyvale–Santa Clara, CA	$96,680	610
Philadelphia-Camden-Wilmington, PA-NJ-DE-MD	$96,030	2,490
Riverside–San Bernardino–Ontario, CA	$95,760	120
New York–Northern New Jersey–Long Island, NY-NJ-PA	$94,430	2,790

Study the chemical composition and physical principles of living cells and organisms and their electrical and mechanical energy and related phenomena. May conduct research in order to further understanding of the complex chemical combinations and reactions involved in metabolism, reproduction, growth, and heredity. May determine the effects of foods, drugs, serums, hormones, and other substances on tissues and vital processes of living organisms. Design and perform experiments with equipment such as lasers, accelerators, and mass spectrometers. Analyze brain functions, such as learning, thinking, and memory, and analyze the dynamics of seeing and hearing. Share research findings by writing scientific articles and by making presentations at scientific conferences. Develop and test new drugs and medications intended for commercial distribution. Develop methods to process, store, and use foods, drugs, and chemical compounds. Develop new methods to study the mechanisms of biological processes. Examine the molecular and chemical aspects of immune system functioning. Investigate the nature, composition, and expression of genes and research how genetic engineering can impact these processes. Determine the three-dimensional structure of biological macromolecules. Prepare reports and recommendations based upon research outcomes. Design and build laboratory equipment needed for special research projects. Isolate, analyze, and synthesize vitamins, hormones, allergens, minerals, and enzymes and determine their effects on body functions. Research cancer treatment, using radiation and nuclear particles. Research transformations of substances in cells, using atomic isotopes. Study how light is absorbed in processes such as photosynthesis or vision. Analyze foods to determine their nutritional values and the effects of cooking, canning, and processing on these values. Study spatial configurations of submicroscopic molecules such as proteins, using X-rays and electron microscopes. Teach and advise undergraduate and graduate students and supervise their research. Investigate the transmission of electrical impulses along nerves and muscles. Research how characteristics of plants and animals are carried through successive generations. Investigate damage to cells and tissues caused by X-rays and nuclear particles.

Other Considerations for Income: According to the National Association of Colleges and Employers, beginning salary offers in 2007 averaged $34,953 a year for bachelor's degree recipients in biological and life sciences.

Personality Type: Investigative-Artistic-Realistic. **Career Clusters:** 01 Agriculture, Food and Natural Resource; 15 Science, Technology, Engineering, and Mathematics. **Career Pathways:** 01.2 Plant Systems; 15.3 Science and Mathematics. **Skills:** Science; Technology Design; Writing; Operations Analysis; Equipment Selection; Reading Comprehension; Troubleshooting; Quality Control Analysis.

Education and Training Programs: Biochemistry; Biochemistry and Molecular Biology; Biophysics; Cell/Cellular Biology and Anatomical Sciences, Other; Molecular Biochemistry; Molecular Biophysics; Soil Chemistry and

B

Physics; Soil Microbiology. **Related Knowledge/Courses:** Biology; Chemistry; Physics; Engineering and Technology; Medicine and Dentistry; Design.

Biofuels Production Managers

* Annual Earnings: $83,290
* Beginning Wage: $50,330
* Earnings Growth Potential: Medium (39.6%)
* Growth: –5.9%
* Annual Job Openings: 14,889
* Self-Employed: 2.0%
* Part-Time: 1.6%
* Job Security: No data available
* Education/Training Required: Work experience in a related occupation

The Department of Labor reports this information for the occupation Industrial Production Managers. The job openings listed here are shared with other specializations within that occupation, including Biomass Production Managers; Geothermal Production Managers; Hydroelectric Production Managers; Methane/Landfill Gas Collection System Operators; and Quality Control Systems Managers.

Industries in Which Income Is Highest

Industry	Average Annual Earnings	Number Employed
Oil and Gas Extraction	$104,890	1,590
Professional, Scientific, and Technical Services	$103,550	3,450
Petroleum and Coal Products Manufacturing	$103,100	1,220
Utilities	$101,110	1,740
Management of Companies and Enterprises	$99,660	6,180

Metropolitan Areas Where Income Is Highest

Metropolitan Area	Average Annual Earnings	Number Employed
Austin–Round Rock, TX	$112,900	690
Cedar Rapids, IA	$110,680	530
Leominster-Fitchburg-Gardner, MA	$107,340	70
Saginaw–Saginaw Township North, MI	$106,880	140
Ann Arbor, MI	$104,600	320

Manage operations at biofuel power-generation facilities. Collect and process information on plant performance, diagnose problems, and design corrective procedures. No task data available.

Other Considerations for Income: No additional information.

Personality Type: No data available. **Career Cluster:** 04 Business, Management, and Administration. **Career Pathway:** 04.1 Management. **Skills:** No data available.

Education and Training Programs: Business Administration and Management, General; Business/Commerce, General; Operations Management and Supervision. **Related Knowledge/Courses:** No data available.

Biofuels/Biodiesel Technology and Product Development Managers

* Annual Earnings: $115,270
* Beginning Wage: $73,420
* Earnings Growth Potential: Medium (36.3%)
* Growth: 7.3%
* Annual Job Openings: 7,404
* Self-Employed: 0.0%
* Part-Time: 2.0%
* Job Security: No data available
* Education/Training Required: Work experience plus degree

The Department of Labor reports this information for the occupation Engineering Managers. The job openings listed here are shared with other specializations within that occupation.

Industries in Which Income Is Highest

Industry	Average Annual Earnings	Number Employed
Computer and Electronic Product Manufacturing	$128,750	28,760
Merchant Wholesalers, Durable Goods	$122,340	2,520
Management of Companies and Enterprises	$120,490	6,630
Professional, Scientific, and Technical Services	$120,010	58,960
Telecommunications	$119,930	3,130

Metropolitan Areas Where Income Is Highest

Metropolitan Area	Average Annual Earnings	Number Employed
San Jose–Sunnyvale–Santa Clara, CA	$154,310	7,100
Midland, TX	$152,580	130
Boulder, CO	$146,290	680
Decatur, IL	$143,540	400
Poughkeepsie-Newburgh-Middletown, NY	$143,480	330

Define, plan, or execute biofuel/biodiesel research programs that evaluate alternative feedstock and process technologies with near-term commercial potential. No task data available.

Other Considerations for Income: Engineering Managers, especially those at higher levels, often receive more benefits—such as expense accounts, stock option plans, and bonuses—than do nonmanagerial workers in their organizations.

Personality Type: No data available. **Career Cluster:** 15 Science, Technology, Engineering, and Mathematics. **Career Pathways:** 15.1 Engineering and Technology; 15.3 Science and Mathematics. **Skills:** No data available.

Education and Training Programs: Agricultural Engineering; Bioengineering and Biomedical Engineering; Chemical Engineering; Engineering, Other; Manufacturing Engineering. **Related Knowledge/Courses:** No data available.

Biological Science Teachers, Postsecondary

- ❀ Annual Earnings: $70,650
- ❀ Beginning Wage: $38,830
- ❀ Earnings Growth Potential: High (45.0%)
- ❀ Growth: 22.9%
- ❀ Annual Job Openings: 9,039
- ❀ Self-Employed: 0.4%
- ❀ Part-Time: 27.8%
- ❀ Job Security: Most secure
- ❀ Education/Training Required: Doctoral degree

Industries in Which Income Is Highest

Industry	Average Annual Earnings	Number Employed
Educational Services	$70,680	51,340

Metropolitan Areas Where Income Is Highest

Metropolitan Area	Average Annual Earnings	Number Employed
Mobile, AL	$134,550	230
San Antonio, TX	$118,120	1,700
El Paso, TX	$111,110	260
Madison, WI	$100,130	190
Riverside–San Bernardino–Ontario, CA	$98,170	280

Teach courses in biological sciences. Prepare and deliver lectures to undergraduate and/or graduate students on topics such as molecular biology, marine biology, and botany. Evaluate and grade students' classwork, laboratory work, assignments, and papers. Prepare course materials such as syllabi, homework assignments, and handouts. Compile, administer, and grade examinations or assign this work to others. Supervise students' laboratory work. Keep abreast of developments in their field by reading current literature, talking with colleagues, and participating in professional conferences. Maintain student attendance records, grades, and other required records. Initiate, facilitate, and moderate classroom discussions. Plan, evaluate, and revise curricula, course content, course materials, and

B

methods of instruction. Advise students on academic and vocational curricula and on career issues. Maintain regularly scheduled office hours to advise and assist students. Supervise undergraduate and/or graduate teaching, internships, and research work. Select and obtain materials and supplies such as textbooks and laboratory equipment. Collaborate with colleagues to address teaching and research issues. Conduct research in a particular field of knowledge and publish findings in professional journals, books, and/or electronic media. Serve on academic or administrative committees that deal with institutional policies, departmental matters, and academic issues. Participate in student recruitment, registration, and placement activities. Write grant proposals to procure external research funding. Perform administrative duties such as serving as department head. Act as advisers to student organizations. Compile bibliographies of specialized materials for outside reading assignments. Participate in campus and community events. Provide professional consulting services to government and/or industry.

Other Considerations for Income: Earnings for college faculty vary according to rank and type of institution, geographic area, and field. According to a 2006–2007 survey by the American Association of University Professors, salaries for full-time faculty averaged $73,207. By rank, the average was $98,974 for professors, $69,911 for associate professors, $58,662 for assistant professors, $42,609 for instructors, and $48,289 for lecturers. Faculty in 4-year institutions earn higher salaries, on average, than do those in 2-year schools. Many faculty members have significant earnings in addition to their base salary from consulting, teaching additional courses, research, writing for publication, or other employment. In addition, many college and university faculty enjoy unique benefits, including access to campus facilities, tuition waivers for dependents, housing and travel allowances, and paid leave for sabbaticals. Part-time faculty and instructors usually have fewer benefits than full-time faculty.

Personality Type: Social-Investigative. **Career Clusters:** 01 Agriculture, Food and Natural Resource; 15 Science, Technology, Engineering, and Mathematics. **Career Pathways:** 01.5 Natural Resources Systems; 15.3 Science and Mathematics. **Skills:** Science; Instructing; Writing; Reading Comprehension; Learning Strategies; Speaking; Active Learning; Critical Thinking.

Education and Training Programs: Anatomy; Animal Physiology; Biochemistry; Biological and Biomedical Sciences, Other; Biology/Biological Sciences, General; Biom-

etry/Biometrics; Biophysics; Biotechnology; Botany/Plant Biology; Cell/Cellular Biology and Histology; Ecology; Ecology, Evolution, Systematics and Population Biology, Other; Entomology; Evolutionary Biology; Immunology; Marine Biology and Biological Oceanography; Microbiology, General; Molecular Biology; Nutrition Sciences; Parasitology; others. **Related Knowledge/Courses:** Biology; Chemistry; Education and Training; Medicine and Dentistry; Physics; Geography.

Biomass Production Managers

❋ Annual Earnings: $83,290
❋ Beginning Wage: $50,330
❋ Earnings Growth Potential: Medium (39.6%)
❋ Growth: –5.9%
❋ Annual Job Openings: 14,889
❋ Self-Employed: 2.0%
❋ Part-Time: 1.6%
❋ Job Security: No data available
❋ Education/Training Required: Work experience in a related occupation

The Department of Labor reports this information for the occupation Industrial Production Managers. The job openings listed here are shared with other specializations within that occupation, including Biofuels Production Managers; Geothermal Production Managers; Hydroelectric Production Managers; Methane/Landfill Gas Collection System Operators; and Quality Control Systems Managers.

Industries in Which Income Is Highest

Industry	Average Annual Earnings	Number Employed
Oil and Gas Extraction	$104,890	1,590
Professional, Scientific, and Technical Services	$103,550	3,450
Petroleum and Coal Products Manufacturing	$103,100	1,220
Utilities	$101,110	1,740
Management of Companies and Enterprises	$99,660	6,180

Metropolitan Areas Where Income Is Highest

Metropolitan Area	Average Annual Earnings	Number Employed
Austin–Round Rock, TX	$112,900	690
Cedar Rapids, IA	$110,680	530
Leominster-Fitchburg-Gardner, MA	$107,340	70
Saginaw–Saginaw Township North, MI	$106,880	140
Ann Arbor, MI	$104,600	320

Manage operations at biomass power-generation facilities. Direct work activities at plant, including supervision of operations and maintenance staff. No task data available.

Other Considerations for Income: No additional information.

Personality Type: No data available. **Career Cluster:** 04 Business, Management, and Administration. **Career Pathway:** 04.1 Management. **Skills:** No data available.

Education and Training Programs: Business Administration and Management, General; Business/Commerce, General; Operations Management and Supervision. **Related Knowledge/Courses:** No data available.

Biomedical Engineers

* Annual Earnings: $77,400
* Beginning Wage: $47,640
* Earnings Growth Potential: Medium (38.4%)
* Growth: 21.1%
* Annual Job Openings: 1,804
* Self-Employed: 0.0%
* Part-Time: 3.4%
* Job Security: More secure than most
* Education/Training Required: Bachelor's degree

Industries in Which Income Is Highest

Industry	Average Annual Earnings	Number Employed
Computer and Electronic Product Manufacturing	$84,150	1,360
Miscellaneous Manufacturing	$81,870	3,630
Professional, Scientific, and Technical Services	$81,350	3,580
Chemical Manufacturing	$76,470	2,530
Hospitals	$60,700	1,570

Metropolitan Areas Where Income Is Highest

Metropolitan Area	Average Annual Earnings	Number Employed
San Francisco–Oakland–Fremont, CA	$99,320	850
San Jose–Sunnyvale–Santa Clara, CA	$96,950	380
Minneapolis–St. Paul–Bloomington, MN-WI	$91,910	740
Denver-Aurora, CO	$90,000	140
Boston-Cambridge-Quincy, MA-NH	$85,690	1,110

Apply knowledge of engineering, biology, and biomechanical principles to the design, development, and evaluation of biological and health systems and products, such as artificial organs, prostheses, instrumentation, medical information systems, and health management and care delivery systems. Evaluate the safety, efficiency, and effectiveness of biomedical equipment. Install, adjust, maintain, and/or repair biomedical equipment. Advise hospital administrators on the planning, acquisition, and use of medical equipment. Advise and assist in the application of instrumentation in clinical environments. Develop models or computer simulations of human bio-behavioral systems in order to obtain data for measuring or controlling life processes. Research new materials to be used for products such as implanted artificial organs. Design and develop medical diagnostic and clinical instrumentation, equipment, and procedures, utilizing the principles of engineering and bio-behavioral sciences. Conduct research, along with life scientists, chemists, and medical scientists, on the engineering aspects of the biological systems of humans and animals. Teach biomedical engineering or disseminate knowledge about field through writing or consulting. Design and deliver technology to assist people with disabilities. Diagnose and

B

interpret bioelectric data, using signal-processing techniques. Adapt or design computer hardware or software for medical science uses. Analyze new medical procedures in order to forecast likely outcomes. Develop new applications for energy sources, such as using nuclear power for biomedical implants.

Other Considerations for Income: As a group, engineers earn some of the highest average starting salaries among those holding bachelor's degrees. Biomedical Engineers are paid in the middle range among the various kinds of engineers. According to a 2007 survey by the National Association of Colleges and Employers, average starting salaries for Biomedical Engineers were $51,356 with a bachelor's and $59,240 with a master's.

Personality Type: Investigative-Realistic. **Career Cluster:** 15 Science, Technology, Engineering, and Mathematics. **Career Pathway:** 15.1 Engineering and Technology. **Skills:** Technology Design; Science; Installation; Operations Analysis; Quality Control Analysis; Systems Evaluation; Troubleshooting; Management of Material Resources.

Education and Training Program: Bioengineering and Biomedical Engineering. **Related Knowledge/Courses:** Engineering and Technology; Computers and Electronics; Physics; Design; Mechanical; Chemistry.

Biostatisticians

❋ Annual Earnings: $72,610

❋ Beginning Wage: $39,740

❋ Earnings Growth Potential: High (45.3%)

❋ Growth: 8.5%

❋ Annual Job Openings: 3,433

❋ Self-Employed: 6.0%

❋ Part-Time: 13.1%

❋ Job Security: No data available

❋ Education/Training Required: Bachelor's degree

The Department of Labor reports this information for the occupation Statisticians. The job openings listed here are shared with other specializations within that occupation, including Clinical Data Managers.

Industries in Which Income Is Highest

Industry	Average Annual Earnings	Number Employed
Chemical Manufacturing	$89,980	1,340
Professional, Scientific, and Technical Services	$80,610	4,720
Federal, State, and Local Government	$75,430	6,120
Insurance Carriers and Related Activities	$63,020	2,000
Educational Services	$58,280	1,860

Metropolitan Areas Where Income Is Highest

Metropolitan Area	Average Annual Earnings	Number Employed
Oxnard–Thousand Oaks–Ventura, CA	$92,430	190
San Jose–Sunnyvale–Santa Clara, CA	$92,090	240
Washington-Arlington-Alexandria, DC-VA-MD-WV	$91,950	3,500
San Francisco–Oakland–Fremont, CA	$89,340	540
Chicago-Naperville-Joliet, IL-IN-WI	$86,600	480

Develop and apply biostatistical theory and methods to the study of life sciences. No task data available.

Other Considerations for Income: Some employers offer tuition reimbursement.

Personality Type: Investigative-Conventional. **Career Cluster:** 15 Science, Technology, Engineering, and Mathematics. **Career Pathway:** 15.3 Science and Mathematics. **Skills:** No data available.

Education and Training Programs: Applied Mathematics, General; Biostatistics; Business Statistics; Mathematical Statistics and Probability; Mathematics, General; Statistics, General; Statistics, Other. **Related Knowledge/Courses:** No data available.

Boilermakers

* Annual Earnings: $52,260
* Beginning Wage: $32,480
* Earnings Growth Potential: Medium (37.8%)
* Growth: 14.0%
* Annual Job Openings: 2,333
* Self-Employed: 0.2%
* Part-Time: 2.6%
* Job Security: Least secure
* Education/Training Required: Long-term on-the-job training

Industries in Which Income Is Highest

Industry	Average Annual Earnings	Number Employed
Construction of Buildings	$58,160	4,520

Metropolitan Areas Where Income Is Highest

Metropolitan Area	Average Annual Earnings	Number Employed
Los Angeles–Long Beach–Santa Ana, CA	$72,510	270
Chicago-Naperville-Joliet, IL-IN-WI	$63,740	1,200
Cincinnati-Middletown, OH-KY-IN	$62,350	140
Abilene, TX	$62,010	60
New York–Northern New Jersey– Long Island, NY-NJ-PA	$61,670	420

Construct, assemble, maintain, and repair stationary steam boilers and boiler house auxiliaries. Align structures or plate sections to assemble boiler frame tanks or vats, following blueprints. Work involves use of hand and power tools, plumb bobs, levels, wedges, dogs, or turnbuckles. Assist in testing assembled vessels. Direct cleaning of boilers and boiler furnaces. Inspect and repair boiler fittings, such as safety valves, regulators, automatic-control mechanisms, water columns, and auxiliary machines. Examine boilers, pressure vessels, tanks, and vats to locate defects such as leaks, weak spots, and defective sections so that they can be repaired. Bolt or arc-weld pressure vessel structures and parts together, using wrenches and welding equipment. Inspect assembled vessels and individual components, such as tubes, fittings, valves, controls, and auxiliary mechanisms, to locate any defects. Repair or replace defective pressure vessel parts, such as safety valves and regulators, using torches, jacks, caulking hammers, power saws, threading dies, welding equipment, and metalworking machinery. Attach rigging and signal crane or hoist operators to lift heavy frame and plate sections and other parts into place. Bell, bead with power hammers, or weld pressure vessel tube ends in order to ensure leakproof joints. Lay out plate, sheet steel, or other heavy metal and locate and mark bending and cutting lines, using protractors, compasses, and drawing instruments or templates. Install manholes, handholes, taps, tubes, valves, gauges, and feedwater connections in drums of water tube boilers, using hand tools. Study blueprints to determine locations, relationships, and dimensions of parts. Straighten or reshape bent pressure vessel plates and structure parts, using hammers, jacks, and torches. Shape seams, joints, and irregular edges of pressure vessel sections and structural parts in order to attain specified fit of parts, using cutting torches, hammers, files, and metalworking machines. Position, align, and secure structural parts and related assemblies to boiler frames, tanks, or vats of pressure vessels, following blueprints. Locate and mark reference points for columns or plates on boiler foundations, following blueprints and using straightedges, squares, transits, and measuring instruments.

Other Considerations for Income: Apprentices generally start at about half of journey-level wages, with wages gradually increasing to the journey wage as workers gain skills. Many boilermakers belong to labor unions, most to the International Brotherhood of Boilermakers. Other boilermakers are members of the International Association of machinists, the United Automobile Workers, or the United Steelworkers of America.

Personality Type: Realistic-Conventional. **Career Cluster:** 02 Architecture and Construction. **Career Pathway:** 02.2 Construction. **Skills:** Repairing; Installation; Equipment Maintenance; Operation Monitoring; Mathematics; Troubleshooting; Operation and Control; Equipment Selection.

Education and Training Program: Boilermaking/Boilermaker. **Related Knowledge/Courses:** Building and Construction; Mechanical; Engineering and Technology; Design; Physics; Transportation.

Broadcast News Analysts

❀ Annual Earnings: $51,260
❀ Beginning Wage: $23,470
❀ Earnings Growth Potential: Very high (54.2%)
❀ Growth: 6.0%
❀ Annual Job Openings: 1,444
❀ Self-Employed: 11.1%
❀ Part-Time: 17.3%
❀ Job Security: More secure than most
❀ Education/Training Required: Work experience plus degree

Industries in Which Income Is Highest

Industry	Average Annual Earnings	Number Employed
Broadcasting (Except Internet)	$52,440	5,800
Educational Services	$46,160	70
Other Information Services	$37,540	70

Metropolitan Areas Where Income Is Highest

Metropolitan Area	Average Annual Earnings	Number Employed
Dallas–Fort Worth–Arlington, TX	$99,960	60
Orlando-Kissimmee, FL	$94,290	60
Seattle-Tacoma-Bellevue, WA	$90,250	60
Sacramento–Arden-Arcade–Roseville, CA	$88,060	40
Baltimore-Towson, MD	$77,840	140

Analyze, interpret, and broadcast news received from various sources. Analyze and interpret news and information received from various sources in order to be able to broadcast the information. Write commentaries, columns, or scripts, using computers. Examine news items of local, national, and international significance to determine topics to address or obtain assignments from editorial staff members. Coordinate and serve as an anchor on news broadcast programs. Edit news material to ensure that it fits within available time or space. Select material most pertinent to presentation and organize this material into appropriate formats. Gather information and develop perspectives about news subjects through research, interviews, observation, and experience. Present news stories and introduce in-depth videotaped segments or live transmissions from on-the-scene reporters.

Other Considerations for Income: Broadcast News Analysts tend to be paid better than other workers in journalism.

Personality Type: Artistic-Social-Enterprising. **Career Cluster:** 03 Arts, Audio/Video Technology, and Communications. **Career Pathway:** 03.5 Journalism and Broadcasting. **Skills:** Writing; Time Management; Speaking; Management of Personnel Resources; Social Perceptiveness; Reading Comprehension; Operation and Control; Monitoring.

Education and Training Programs: Broadcast Journalism; Journalism; Political Communication; Radio and Television. **Related Knowledge/Courses:** Communications and Media; Telecommunications; English Language; Geography; Sociology and Anthropology; History and Archeology.

Budget Analysts

❀ Annual Earnings: $65,320
❀ Beginning Wage: $42,470
❀ Earnings Growth Potential: Medium (35.0%)
❀ Growth: 7.1%
❀ Annual Job Openings: 6,423
❀ Self-Employed: 0.0%
❀ Part-Time: 3.2%
❀ Job Security: Most secure
❀ Education/Training Required: Bachelor's degree

Industries in Which Income Is Highest

Industry	Average Annual Earnings	Number Employed
Computer and Electronic Product Manufacturing	$74,090	1,780
Transportation Equipment Manufacturing	$71,050	4,310
Professional, Scientific, and Technical Services	$70,650	6,980
Management of Companies and Enterprises	$70,460	4,520
Insurance Carriers and Related Activities	$68,670	1,520

Metropolitan Areas Where Income Is Highest

Metropolitan Area	Average Annual Earnings	Number Employed
San Jose–Sunnyvale–Santa Clara, CA	$92,270	1,380
San Francisco–Oakland–Fremont, CA	$85,190	1,930
Washington-Arlington-Alexandria, DC-VA-MD-WV	$81,340	5,120
Chicago-Naperville-Joliet, IL-IN-WI	$76,670	1,710
Dayton, OH	$76,570	260

Examine budget estimates for completeness, accuracy, and conformance with procedures and regulations. Analyze budgeting and accounting reports for the purpose of maintaining expenditure controls. Direct the preparation of regular and special budget reports. Consult with managers to ensure that budget adjustments are made in accordance with program changes. Match appropriations for specific programs with appropriations for broader programs, including items for emergency funds. Provide advice and technical assistance with cost analysis, fiscal allocation, and budget preparation. Summarize budgets and submit recommendations for the approval or disapproval of funds requests. Seek new ways to improve efficiency and increase profits. Review operating budgets to analyze trends affecting budget needs. Perform cost-benefit analyses to compare operating programs, review financial requests, or explore alternative financing methods. Interpret budget directives and establish policies for carrying out directives. Compile and analyze accounting records and other data to determine the financial resources required to implement a program. Testify before examining and fund-granting authorities, clarifying and promoting the proposed budgets.

Other Considerations for Income: Salaries of budget analysts vary widely by experience, education, and employer. According to a 2007 survey conducted by Robert Half International—a staffing services firm specializing in accounting and finance—starting salaries of financial, budget, treasury, and cost analysts in small companies ranged from $32,750 to $39,250. In large companies, starting salaries ranged from $36,500 to $43,750.

Personality Type: Conventional-Enterprising-Investigative. **Career Clusters:** 04 Business, Management, and Administration; 06 Finance. **Career Pathways:** 04.2 Business, Financial Management, and Accounting; 06.1 Financial and Investment Planning. **Skills:** Management of Financial Resources; Systems Analysis; Systems Evaluation.

Education and Training Programs: Accounting; Finance, General. **Related Knowledge/Courses:** Economics and Accounting; Clerical; Administration and Management; Mathematics; Personnel and Human Resources; Law and Government.

Business Intelligence Analysts

❋ Annual Earnings: $75,150
❋ Beginning Wage: $40,660
❋ Earnings Growth Potential: High (45.9%)
❋ Growth: 15.1%
❋ Annual Job Openings: 14,374
❋ Self-Employed: 6.6%
❋ Part-Time: 5.6%
❋ Job Security: No data available
❋ Education/Training Required: Work experience plus degree

The Department of Labor reports this information for the occupation Computer Specialists, All Other. The job openings listed here are shared with other specializations within that occupation, including Computer Systems Engineers/Architects; Data Warehousing Specialists; Database Architects; Document Management Specialists; Electronic Commerce Specialists; Geographic Information Systems Technicians; Geospatial Information Scientists and Technologists; Information Technology Project Managers; Network Designers; Software Quality Assurance Engineers and Testers; Video Game Designers; Web Administrators; and Web Developers.

Industries in Which Income Is Highest

Industry	Average Annual Earnings	Number Employed
Petroleum and Coal Products Manufacturing	$97,090	1,070
Transportation Equipment Manufacturing	$82,770	3,010
Oil and Gas Extraction	$81,350	1,710
Federal, State, and Local Government	$80,670	71,650
Management of Companies and Enterprises	$78,200	14,820

Metropolitan Areas Where Income Is Highest

Metropolitan Area	Average Annual Earnings	Number Employed
Washington-Arlington-Alexandria, DC-VA-MD-WV	$97,170	19,470
Atlantic City, NJ	$96,600	510
Pascagoula, MS	$95,430	60
San Jose–Sunnyvale–Santa Clara, CA	$92,710	3,580
Baltimore-Towson, MD	$89,730	5,650

Produce financial and market intelligence by querying data repositories and generating periodic reports. Devise methods for identifying data patterns and trends in available information sources. No task data available.

Other Considerations for Income: No additional information.

Personality Type: No data available. **Career Cluster:** 11 Information Technology. **Career Pathway:** 11.2 Information Support Services. **Skills:** No data available.

Education and Training Programs: Computer and Information Sciences and Support Services, Other; Computer and Information Sciences, General; Computer Engineering Technologies/Technicians, Other; Computer Engineering, General; Computer Science; Computer Software Engineering; Computer Systems Networking and Telecommunications; E-Commerce/Electronic Commerce; Information Science/Studies; Information Technology; System, Networking, and LAN/WAN Management/Manager; Web Page, Digital/Multimedia and Information Resources Design; others. **Related Knowledge/Courses:** No data available.

Business Teachers, Postsecondary

✸ Annual Earnings: $68,000
✸ Beginning Wage: $32,880
✸ Earnings Growth Potential: Very high (51.6%)
✸ Growth: 22.9%
✸ Annual Job Openings: 11,643
✸ Self-Employed: 0.4%
✸ Part-Time: 27.8%
✸ Job Security: Most secure
✸ Education/Training Required: Doctoral degree

Industries in Which Income Is Highest

Industry	Average Annual Earnings	Number Employed
Educational Services	$68,100	69,430

Metropolitan Areas Where Income Is Highest

Metropolitan Area	Average Annual Earnings	Number Employed
Worcester, MA-CT	$136,690	270
Ann Arbor, MI	$104,230	470
Winston-Salem, NC	$102,130	140
Grand Forks, ND-MN	$102,080	100
Stockton, CA	$97,070	110

Teach courses in business administration and management, such as accounting, finance, human resources, labor relations, marketing, and operations research. Prepare and deliver lectures to undergraduate and/or graduate students on topics such as financial accounting, principles of marketing, and operations management. Evaluate and grade students' classwork, assignments, and papers. Compile, administer, and grade examinations or assign this work to others. Prepare course materials such as syllabi, homework assignments, and handouts. Maintain student attendance records, grades, and other required records. Initiate, facilitate, and moderate classroom discussions. Plan, evaluate, and revise curricula, course content, and course materials and methods of instruction. Keep abreast of developments in their field by reading current literature, talking with colleagues, and participating in professional organizations and conferences. Maintain regularly scheduled office hours to advise and assist students. Advise students on academic and vocational curricula and on career issues. Select and obtain materials and supplies such as textbooks. Collaborate with colleagues to address teaching and research issues. Collaborate with members of the business community to improve programs, to develop new programs, and to provide student access to learning opportunities such as internships. Participate in student recruitment, registration, and placement activities. Serve on academic or administrative committees that deal with institutional policies, departmental matters, and academic issues. Participate in campus and community events. Compile bibliographies of specialized materials for outside reading assignments. Perform administrative duties such as serving as department head. Supervise undergraduate and/or graduate teaching, internship, and research work. Conduct research in a particular field of knowledge and publish findings in professional journals, books, and/or electronic media. Act as advisers to student organizations. Provide professional consulting services to government and/or industry.

Other Considerations for Income: Earnings for college faculty vary according to rank and type of institution, geographic area, and field. According to a 2006–2007 survey by the American Association of University Professors, salaries for full-time faculty averaged $73,207. By rank, the average was $98,974 for professors, $69,911 for associate professors, $58,662 for assistant professors, $42,609 for instructors, and $48,289 for lecturers. Faculty in 4-year institutions earn higher salaries, on average, than do those in 2-year schools. Many faculty members have significant earnings in addition to their base salary from consulting, teaching additional courses, research, writing for publication, or other employment. In addition, many college and university faculty enjoy unique benefits, including access to campus facilities, tuition waivers for dependents, housing and travel allowances, and paid leave for sabbaticals. Part-time faculty and instructors usually have fewer benefits than full-time faculty.

Personality Type: Social-Enterprising-Investigative. **Career Clusters:** 04 Business, Management, and Administration; 05 Education and Training; 06 Finance; 14 Marketing, Sales, and Service. **Career Pathways:** 04.1 Management; 04.2 Business Financial Management and Accounting; 04.2 Business, Financial Management, and Accounting; 04.3 Human Resources; 04.5 Marketing; 05.3 Teaching/Training; 06.1 Financial and Investment

Planning; 06.4 Insurance Services; 06.4 Insurance Services; 14.1 Management and Entrepreneurship; 14.5 Marketing Information Management and Research. **Skills:** Instructing; Learning Strategies; Writing; Monitoring; Speaking; Active Learning; Critical Thinking; Reading Comprehension.

Education and Training Programs: Accounting; Actuarial Science; Business Administration and Management, General; Business Statistics; Business Teacher Education; Business/Commerce, General; Business/Corporate Communications; Entrepreneurship/Entrepreneurial Studies; Finance, General; Financial Planning and Services; Franchising and Franchise Operations; Human Resources Management/Personnel Administration, General; Insurance; International Business/Trade/Commerce; International Finance; International Marketing; others. **Related Knowledge/Courses:** Economics and Accounting; Education and Training; Sociology and Anthropology; Sales and Marketing; Philosophy and Theology; English Language.

Captains, Mates, and Pilots of Water Vessels

See *Mates—Ship, Boat, and Barge; Pilots, Ship;* and *Ship and Boat Captains,* described separately.

Cartographers and Photogrammetrists

* Annual Earnings: $51,180
* Beginning Wage: $31,440
* Earnings Growth Potential: Medium (38.6%)
* Growth: 20.3%
* Annual Job Openings: 2,823
* Self-Employed: 3.4%
* Part-Time: 4.6%
* Job Security: Less secure than most
* Education/Training Required: Bachelor's degree

Industries in Which Income Is Highest

Industry	Average Annual Earnings	Number Employed
Federal, State, and Local Government	$54,280	4,170
Professional, Scientific, and Technical Services	$50,230	5,700

Metropolitan Areas Where Income Is Highest

Metropolitan Area	Average Annual Earnings	Number Employed
Washington-Arlington-Alexandria, DC-VA-MD-WV	$78,040	830
Las Vegas–Paradise, NV	$73,780	80
Denver-Aurora, CO	$71,760	580
San Francisco–Oakland–Fremont, CA	$68,220	190
Seattle-Tacoma-Bellevue, WA	$66,970	230

Collect, analyze, and interpret geographic information provided by geodetic surveys, aerial photographs, and satellite data. Research, study, and prepare maps and other spatial data in digital or graphic form for legal, social, political, educational, and design purposes. May work with Geographic Information Systems (GIS). May design and evaluate algorithms, data structures, and user interfaces for GIS and mapping systems. Identify, scale, and orient geodetic points, elevations, and other planimetric or topographic features, applying standard mathematical formulas. Collect information about specific features of the Earth, using aerial photography and other digital remote sensing techniques. Revise existing maps and charts, making all necessary corrections and adjustments. Compile data required for map preparation, including aerial photographs, survey notes, records, reports, and original maps. Inspect final compositions to ensure completeness and accuracy. Determine map content and layout, as well as production specifications such as scale, size, projection, and colors, and direct production to ensure that specifications are followed. Examine and analyze data from ground surveys, reports, aerial photographs, and satellite images to prepare topographic maps, aerial-photograph mosaics, and related charts. Select aerial photographic and remote sensing techniques and plotting equipment needed to meet required standards of accuracy. Delineate aerial photographic detail such as control points, hydrography, topography, and cultural features, using precision stereoplotting apparatus or drafting instruments.

Build and update digital databases. Prepare and alter trace maps, charts, tables, detailed drawings, and three-dimensional optical models of terrain, using stereoscopic plotting and computer graphics equipment. Determine guidelines that specify which source material is acceptable for use. Study legal records to establish boundaries of local, national, and international properties. Travel over photographed areas to observe, identify, record, and verify all relevant features.

Other Considerations for Income: No additional information.

Personality Type: Realistic-Investigative-Conventional. **Career Clusters:** 02 Architecture and Construction; 15 Science, Technology, Engineering, and Mathematics. **Career Pathways:** 02.1 Design/Pre-Construction; 15.3 Science and Mathematics. **Skills:** Science; Technology Design; Mathematics; Active Learning; Troubleshooting; Reading Comprehension; Operation and Control; Writing.

Education and Training Programs: Geographic Information Science and Cartography; Surveying Technology/Surveying. **Related Knowledge/Courses:** Geography; Design; Engineering and Technology; Computers and Electronics; Production and Processing; Mathematics.

Chemical Engineers

- ❈ Annual Earnings: $84,680
- ❈ Beginning Wage: $53,730
- ❈ Earnings Growth Potential: Medium (36.5%)
- ❈ Growth: 7.9%
- ❈ Annual Job Openings: 2,111
- ❈ Self-Employed: 1.9%
- ❈ Part-Time: 3.4%
- ❈ Job Security: More secure than most
- ❈ Education/Training Required: Bachelor's degree

Industries in Which Income Is Highest

Industry	Average Annual Earnings	Number Employed
Computer and Electronic Product Manufacturing	$89,890	1,550
Petroleum and Coal Products Manufacturing	$88,230	1,690
Federal, State, and Local Government	$87,950	1,350
Chemical Manufacturing	$86,030	9,720
Professional, Scientific, and Technical Services	$85,670	9,390

Metropolitan Areas Where Income Is Highest

Metropolitan Area	Average Annual Earnings	Number Employed
Oxnard–Thousand Oaks–Ventura, CA	$112,570	90
Syracuse, NY	$103,690	70
Houston–Sugar Land–Baytown, TX	$98,840	2,780
Kennewick-Richland-Pasco, WA	$98,580	230
Mobile, AL	$97,060	100

Design chemical plant equipment and devise processes for manufacturing chemicals and products such as gasoline, synthetic rubber, plastics, detergents, cement, paper, and pulp by applying principles and technology of chemistry, physics, and engineering. Perform tests throughout stages of production to determine degree of control over variables, including temperature, density, specific gravity, and pressure. Develop safety procedures to be employed by workers operating equipment or working in proximity to ongoing chemical reactions. Determine most effective arrangement of operations such as mixing, crushing, heat transfer, distillation, and drying. Prepare estimate of production costs and production progress reports for management. Direct activities of workers who operate or who are engaged in constructing and improving absorption, evaporation, or electromagnetic equipment. Perform laboratory studies of steps in manufacture of new product and test proposed process in small-scale operation such as a pilot plant. Develop processes to separate components of liquids or gases or generate electrical currents by using controlled chemical processes. Conduct research to develop new and improved chemical manufacturing processes. Design measurement and control systems for chemical plants based on data collected in laboratory experiments and in pilot plant operations. Design and plan layout of equipment.

Other Considerations for Income: As a group, engineers earn some of the highest average starting salaries among those holding bachelor's degrees. Chemical Engineers are paid in the middle range among the various kinds of engineers. According to a 2007 survey by the National Association of Colleges and Employers, average starting salaries for Chemical Engineers were $59,361 with a bachelor's, $68,561 with a master's, and $73,667 with a Ph.D.

Personality Type: Investigative-Realistic. **Career Cluster:** 15 Science, Technology, Engineering, and Mathematics. **Career Pathway:** 15.1 Engineering and Technology. **Skills:** Science; Technology Design; Troubleshooting; Programming; Operations Analysis; Installation; Systems Analysis; Mathematics.

Education and Training Program: Chemical Engineering. **Related Knowledge/Courses:** Engineering and Technology; Chemistry; Physics; Design; Biology; Production and Processing.

Chemical Plant and System Operators

❋ Annual Earnings: $52,480
❋ Beginning Wage: $34,960
❋ Earnings Growth Potential: Low (33.4%)
❋ Growth: –15.3%
❋ Annual Job Openings: 5,620
❋ Self-Employed: 0.1%
❋ Part-Time: 0.6%
❋ Job Security: Least secure
❋ Education/Training Required: Long-term on-the-job training

Industries in Which Income Is Highest

Industry	Average Annual Earnings	Number Employed
Chemical Manufacturing	$52,850	38,160
Petroleum and Coal Products Manufacturing	$51,820	3,160
Paper Manufacturing	$48,190	1,530

Metropolitan Areas Where Income Is Highest

Metropolitan Area	Average Annual Earnings	Number Employed
Beaumont–Port Arthur, TX	$63,780	1,230
Lake Charles, LA	$62,490	1,070
Los Angeles–Long Beach–Santa Ana, CA	$61,410	300
San Francisco–Oakland–Fremont, CA	$61,290	210
New Orleans–Metairie–Kenner, LA	$60,670	700

Control or operate an entire chemical process or system of machines. Move control settings to make necessary adjustments on equipment units affecting speeds of chemical reactions, quality, and yields. Monitor recording instruments, flowmeters, panel lights, and other indicators and listen for warning signals to verify conformity of process conditions. Control or operate chemical processes or systems of machines, using panelboards, control boards, or semi-automatic equipment. Record operating data such as process conditions, test results, and instrument readings. Confer with technical and supervisory personnel to report or resolve conditions affecting safety, efficiency, and product quality. Draw samples of products and conduct quality control tests to monitor processing and to ensure that standards are met. Regulate or shut down equipment during emergency situations as directed by supervisory personnel. Start pumps to wash and rinse reactor vessels; to exhaust gases and vapors; to regulate the flow of oil, steam, air, and perfume to towers; and to add products to converter or blending vessels. Interpret chemical reactions visible through sight glasses or on television monitors and review laboratory test reports for process adjustments. Patrol work areas to ensure that solutions in tanks and troughs are not in danger of overflowing. Notify maintenance, stationary-engineering, and other auxiliary personnel to correct equipment malfunctions and to adjust power, steam, water, or air supplies. Direct workers engaged in operating machinery that regulates the flow of materials and products. Inspect operating units such as towers, soap-spray storage tanks, scrubbers, collectors, and driers to ensure that all are functioning and to maintain maximum efficiency. Turn valves to regulate flow of products or byproducts through agitator tanks, storage drums, or neutralizer tanks. Calculate material requirements or yields according to formulas. Gauge tank levels, using calibrated rods. Repair and replace damaged equipment.

Other Considerations for Income: No additional information.

Personality Type: Realistic-Conventional. **Career Cluster:** 13 Manufacturing. **Career Pathway:** 13.2 Manufacturing Production Process Development. **Skills:** Operation Monitoring; Operation and Control; Troubleshooting; Science; Equipment Maintenance; Operations Analysis; Systems Analysis; Quality Control Analysis.

Education and Training Program: Chemical Technology/Technician. **Related Knowledge/Courses:** Production and Processing; Chemistry; Mechanical; Physics; Engineering and Technology; Public Safety and Security.

Chemistry Teachers, Postsecondary

* Annual Earnings: $67,240
* Beginning Wage: $38,960
* Earnings Growth Potential: High (42.1%)
* Growth: 22.9%
* Annual Job Openings: 3,405
* Self-Employed: 0.4%
* Part-Time: 27.8%
* Job Security: Most secure
* Education/Training Required: Doctoral degree

Industries in Which Income Is Highest

Industry	Average Annual Earnings	Number Employed
Educational Services	$66,890	19,440

Metropolitan Areas Where Income Is Highest

Metropolitan Area	Average Annual Earnings	Number Employed
Lubbock, TX	$96,770	70
Raleigh-Cary, NC	$94,120	210
San Diego–Carlsbad–San Marcos, CA	$91,230	430
Columbus, OH	$87,550	160
Austin–Round Rock, TX	$86,810	130

Teach courses pertaining to the chemical and physical properties and compositional changes of substances. Work may include instruction in the methods of qualitative and quantitative chemical analysis. Includes both teachers primarily engaged in teaching and those who do a combination of both teaching and research. Prepare and deliver lectures to undergraduate and/or graduate students on topics such as organic chemistry, analytical chemistry, and chemical separation. Supervise students' laboratory work. Evaluate and grade students' classwork, laboratory performance, assignments, and papers. Compile, administer, and grade examinations or assign this work to others. Maintain student attendance records, grades, and other required records. Prepare course materials such as syllabi, homework assignments, and handouts. Maintain regularly scheduled office hours to advise and assist students. Plan, evaluate, and revise curricula, course content, course materials, and methods of instruction. Supervise undergraduate and/or graduate teaching, internships, and research work. Keep abreast of developments in the field by reading current literature, talking with colleagues, and participating in professional conferences. Initiate, facilitate, and moderate classroom discussions. Select and obtain materials and supplies such as textbooks and laboratory equipment. Conduct research in a particular field of knowledge and publish findings in professional journals, books, and/or electronic media. Advise students on academic and vocational curricula and on career issues. Collaborate with colleagues to address teaching and research issues. Serve on academic or administrative committees that deal with institutional policies, departmental matters, and academic issues. Write grant proposals to procure external research funding. Participate in student recruitment, registration, and placement activities. Prepare and submit required reports related to instruction. Perform administrative duties such as serving as a department head. Act as advisers to student organizations. Compile bibliographies of specialized materials for outside reading assignments. Participate in campus and community events. Provide professional consulting services to government and/or industry.

Other Considerations for Income: Earnings for college faculty vary according to rank and type of institution, geographic area, and field. According to a 2006–2007 survey by the American Association of University Professors, salaries for full-time faculty averaged $73,207. By rank, the average was $98,974 for professors, $69,911 for associate professors, $58,662 for assistant professors, $42,609 for instructors, and $48,289 for lecturers. Faculty in 4-year institutions earn higher salaries, on average, than do those in 2-year schools. Many faculty members have significant earnings in addition to their base salary from consulting, teaching additional courses, research, writing for publication, or other employment. In addition, many college and university faculty enjoy unique benefits, including access to campus facilities, tuition waivers for dependents, housing and travel allowances, and paid leave for sabbaticals. Part-time faculty and instructors usually have fewer benefits than full-time faculty.

Personality Type: Social-Investigative-Realistic. **Career Cluster:** 15 Science, Technology, Engineering, and Mathematics. **Career Pathway:** 15.3 Science and Mathematics. **Skills:** Science; Mathematics; Instructing; Writing; Reading Comprehension; Active Learning; Technology Design; Complex Problem Solving.

Education and Training Programs: Analytical Chemistry; Chemical Physics; Chemistry, General; Chemistry, Other; Geochemistry; Inorganic Chemistry; Organic Chemistry; Physical Chemistry; Polymer Chemistry. **Related Knowledge/Courses:** Chemistry; Biology; Physics; Education and Training; Mathematics; English Language.

Chemists

- ❋ Annual Earnings: $66,230
- ❋ Beginning Wage: $37,840
- ❋ Earnings Growth Potential: High (42.9%)
- ❋ Growth: 9.1%
- ❋ Annual Job Openings: 9,024
- ❋ Self-Employed: 1.2%
- ❋ Part-Time: 3.9%
- ❋ Job Security: Less secure than most
- ❋ Education/Training Required: Bachelor's degree

Industries in Which Income Is Highest

Industry	Average Annual Earnings	Number Employed
Federal, State, and Local Government	$76,870	9,740
Management of Companies and Enterprises	$74,110	2,310
Merchant Wholesalers, Nondurable Goods	$69,160	1,920
Chemical Manufacturing	$65,890	29,300
Professional, Scientific, and Technical Services	$65,100	24,840

Metropolitan Areas Where Income Is Highest

Metropolitan Area	Average Annual Earnings	Number Employed
Washington-Arlington-Alexandria, DC-VA-MD-WV	$101,200	3,240
Bakersfield, CA	$89,060	140
Augusta–Richmond County, GA-SC	$89,020	220
Kennewick-Richland-Pasco, WA	$88,980	440
San Diego–Carlsbad–San Marcos, CA	$88,110	1,800

Conduct qualitative and quantitative chemical analyses or chemical experiments in laboratories for quality or process control or to develop new products or knowledge. Analyze organic and inorganic compounds to determine chemical and physical properties, composition, structure, relationships, and reactions, utilizing chromatography, spectroscopy, and spectrophotometry techniques. Develop, improve, and customize products, equipment, formulas, processes, and analytical methods. Compile and analyze test information to determine process or equipment operating efficiency and to diagnose malfunctions. Confer with scientists and engineers to conduct analyses of research projects, interpret test results, or develop nonstandard tests. Direct, coordinate, and advise personnel in test procedures for analyzing components and physical properties of materials. Induce changes in composition of substances by introducing heat, light, energy, and chemical catalysts for quantitative and qualitative analysis. Write technical papers and reports and prepare standards and specifications for processes, facilities, products, or tests. Study effects of various methods of processing, preserving, and packaging on composition and properties of foods. Prepare test solutions, compounds, and reagents for laboratory personnel to conduct test.

Other Considerations for Income: According to the National Association of Colleges and Employers, beginning salary offers in July 2007 for graduates with bachelor's degrees in chemistry averaged $41,506 a year.

Personality Type: Investigative-Realistic-Conventional. **Career Cluster:** 15 Science, Technology, Engineering, and Mathematics. **Career Pathway:** 15.3 Science and Mathematics. **Skills:** Science; Quality Control Analysis; Technology Design; Operation Monitoring; Equipment Selection; Management of Material Resources; Management of Financial Resources; Operations Analysis.

Education and Training Programs: Analytical Chemistry; Chemical Physics; Chemistry, General; Chemistry, Other; Inorganic Chemistry; Organic Chemistry; Physical Chemistry; Polymer Chemistry. **Related Knowledge/ Courses:** Chemistry; Physics; Mathematics; Production and Processing; Biology; Clerical.

Chief Executives

* Annual Earnings: $158,560
* Beginning Wage: $68,680
* Earnings Growth Potential: Very high (56.7%)
* Growth: 2.0%
* Annual Job Openings: 21,209
* Self-Employed: 22.0%
* Part-Time: 5.5%
* Job Security: More secure than most
* Education/Training Required: Work experience plus degree

Industries in Which Income Is Highest

Industry	Average Annual Earnings	Number Employed
Professional, Scientific, and Technical Services	$166,400+	30,080
Management of Companies and Enterprises	$166,400+	22,320
Merchant Wholesalers, Durable Goods	$166,400+	11,120
Credit Intermediation and Related Activities	$166,400+	9,580
Insurance Carriers and Related Activities	$166,400+	8,860

Metropolitan Areas Where Income Is Highest

Metropolitan Area	Average Annual Earnings	Number Employed
Boston-Cambridge-Quincy, MA-NH	$166,400+	15,300
Los Angeles–Long Beach–Santa Ana, CA	$166,400+	14,240
New York–Northern New Jersey–Long Island, NY-NJ-PA	$166,400+	12,160
Chicago-Naperville-Joliet, IL-IN-WI	$166,400+	11,670
Washington-Arlington-Alexandria, DC-VA-MD-WV	$166,400+	8,120

Determine and formulate policies and provide the overall direction of companies or private and public sector organizations within the guidelines set up by a board of directors or similar governing body. Plan, direct, or coordinate operational activities at the highest level of management with the help of subordinate executives and staff managers. Direct and coordinate an organization's financial and budget activities in order to fund operations, maximize investments, and increase efficiency. Confer with board members, organization officials, and staff members to discuss issues, coordinate activities, and resolve problems. Analyze operations to evaluate performance of a company and its staff in meeting objectives and to determine areas of potential cost reduction, program improvement, or policy change. Direct, plan, and implement policies, objectives, and activities of organizations or businesses in order to ensure continuing operations, to maximize returns on investments, and to increase productivity. Prepare budgets for approval, including those for funding and implementation of programs. Direct and coordinate activities of businesses or departments concerned with production, pricing, sales, and/or distribution of products. Negotiate or approve contracts and agreements with suppliers, distributors, federal and state agencies, and other organizational entities. Review reports submitted by staff members in order to recommend approval or to suggest changes. Appoint department heads or managers and assign or delegate responsibilities to them. Direct human resources activities, including the approval of human resource plans and activities, the selection of directors and other high-level staff, and establishment and organization of major departments. Preside over or serve on boards of directors, management committees, or other governing boards. Prepare and present reports concerning activities, expenses, budgets, government statutes and rulings, and other items affecting businesses or program services. Establish departmental responsibilities and coordinate functions among departments and sites. Implement corrective action plans to solve organizational or departmental problems.

Other Considerations for Income: Top executives are among the highest-paid workers in the U.S. economy. However, salary levels vary substantially, depending on the level of managerial responsibility; length of service; and type, size, and location of the firm. For example, a top manager in a very large corporation can earn significantly more than a counterpart in a small firm. In addition to salaries, total compensation often includes stock options and other performance bonuses. The use of executive dining rooms and company aircraft and cars, expense allowances, and company-paid insurance premiums and physical examinations also are among benefits commonly enjoyed by top executives in private industry. A number of chief executive officers also are provided with company-paid club memberships and other amenities.

Personality Type: Enterprising-Conventional. **Career Clusters:** 04 Business, Management, and Administration; 07 Government and Public Administration. **Career Pathways:** 04.1 Management; 07.1 Governance. **Skills:** Management of Financial Resources; Management of Material Resources; Judgment and Decision Making; Negotiation; Management of Personnel Resources; Systems Evaluation; Coordination; Operations Analysis.

Education and Training Programs: Business Administration and Management, General; Business/Commerce, General; Entrepreneurship/Entrepreneurial Studies; International Business/Trade/Commerce; International Relations and Affairs; Public Administration; Public Administration and Social Service Professions, Other; Public Policy Analysis, General; Transportation/Mobility Management. **Related Knowledge/Courses:** Economics and Accounting; Administration and Management; Sales and Marketing; Personnel and Human Resources; Law and Government; Medicine and Dentistry.

Chief Sustainability Officers

✸ Annual Earnings: $158,560
✸ Beginning Wage: $68,680
✸ Earnings Growth Potential: Very high (56.7%)
✸ Growth: 2.0%
✸ Annual Job Openings: 21,209
✸ Self-Employed: 22.0%
✸ Part-Time: 5.5%
✸ Job Security: No data available
✸ Education/Training Required: Work experience plus degree

The Department of Labor reports this information for the occupation Chief Executives. The job openings listed here are shared with other specializations within that occupation.

Industries in Which Income Is Highest

Industry	Average Annual Earnings	Number Employed
Professional, Scientific, and Technical Services	$166,400+	30,080
Management of Companies and Enterprises	$166,400+	22,320
Merchant Wholesalers, Durable Goods	$166,400+	11,120
Credit Intermediation and Related Activities	$166,400+	9,580
Insurance Carriers and Related Activities	$166,400+	8,860

Metropolitan Areas Where Income Is Highest

Metropolitan Area	Average Annual Earnings	Number Employed
Boston-Cambridge-Quincy, MA-NH	$166,400+	15,300
Los Angeles–Long Beach–Santa Ana, CA	$166,400+	14,240
New York–Northern New Jersey–Long Island, NY-NJ-PA	$166,400+	12,160
Chicago-Naperville-Joliet, IL-IN-WI	$166,400+	11,670
Washington-Arlington-Alexandria, DC-VA-MD-WV	$166,400+	8,120

Communicate and coordinate with management, shareholders, customers, and employees to address sustainability issues. Enact or oversee a corporate sustainability strategy. No task data available.

Other Considerations for Income: In addition to salaries, total compensation often includes stock options and other performance bonuses. The use of executive dining rooms and company aircraft and cars, expense allowances, and company-paid insurance premiums and physical examinations also are among benefits commonly enjoyed by executives in private industry. A number of executives also are provided with company-paid club memberships and other amenities.

Personality Type: No data available. **Career Clusters:** 04 Business, Management, and Administration; 07 Government and Public Administration; 16 Transportation, Distribution, and Logistics. **Career Pathways:** 04.1 Management; 07.1 Governance; 16.2 Logistics, Planning, and Management Services. **Skills:** No data available.

Education and Training Programs: Business Administration and Management, General; Business/Commerce, General; Entrepreneurship/Entrepreneurial Studies; International Business/Trade/Commerce; International Relations and Affairs; Public Administration; Public Administration and Social Service Professions, Other; Public Policy Analysis, General; Transportation/Mobility Management. **Related Knowledge/Courses:** No data available.

Chiropractors

✸ Annual Earnings: $66,490
✸ Beginning Wage: $32,380
✸ Earnings Growth Potential: Very high (51.3%)
✸ Growth: 14.4%
✸ Annual Job Openings: 3,179
✸ Self-Employed: 51.7%
✸ Part-Time: 23.6%
✸ Job Security: Most secure
✸ Education/Training Required: First professional degree

Industries in Which Income Is Highest

Industry	Average Annual Earnings	Number Employed
Ambulatory Health Care Services	$66,570	26,120

Metropolitan Areas Where Income Is Highest

Metropolitan Area	Average Annual Earnings	Number Employed
Charlotte-Gastonia-Concord, NC-SC	$128,390	90
Las Vegas–Paradise, NV	$121,740	230
Cincinnati-Middletown, OH-KY-IN	$118,650	270
Indianapolis-Carmel, IN	$99,070	110
Rockford, IL	$95,990	60

Adjust spinal column and other articulations of the body to correct abnormalities of the human body believed to be caused by interference with the nervous system. Examine patients to determine nature and extent of disorders. Manipulate spines or other involved areas. May utilize supplementary measures such as exercise, rest, water, light, heat, and nutritional therapy. Diagnose health problems by reviewing patients' health and medical histories; questioning, observing, and examining patients; and interpreting X-rays. Maintain accurate case histories of patients. Evaluate the functioning of the neuromuscularskeletal system and the spine, using systems of chiropractic diagnosis. Perform a series of manual adjustments to spines, or other articulations of the body, to correct musculoskeletal systems. Obtain and record patients' medical histories. Advise patients about recommended courses of treatment. Consult with and refer patients to appropriate health practitioners when necessary. Analyze X-rays to locate the sources of patients' difficulties and to rule out fractures or diseases as sources of problems. Counsel patients about nutrition, exercise, sleeping habits, stress management, and other matters. Arrange for diagnostic X-rays to be taken. Suggest and apply the use of supports such as straps, tapes, bandages, and braces if necessary.

Other Considerations for Income: In chiropractic, as in other types of independent practice, earnings are relatively low in the beginning and increase as the practice grows. Geographic location and the characteristics and qualifications of the practitioner also may influence earnings. Salaried chiropractors typically receive heath insurance

and retirement benefits from their employers, whereas self-employed chiropractors must provide for their own health insurance and retirement.

Personality Type: Social-Investigative-Realistic. **Career Cluster:** 08 Health Science. **Career Pathway:** 08.1 Therapeutic Services. **Skills:** Systems Analysis; Systems Evaluation; Service Orientation; Management of Personnel Resources; Writing.

Education and Training Program: Chiropractic (DC). **Related Knowledge/Courses:** Medicine and Dentistry; Therapy and Counseling; Biology; Psychology; Personnel and Human Resources; Sales and Marketing.

Civil Engineers

- Annual Earnings: $74,600
- Beginning Wage: $48,140
- Earnings Growth Potential: Medium (35.5%)
- Growth: 18.0%
- Annual Job Openings: 15,979
- Self-Employed: 4.9%
- Part-Time: 3.2%
- Job Security: Less secure than most
- Education/Training Required: Bachelor's degree

Industries in Which Income Is Highest

Industry	Average Annual Earnings	Number Employed
Management of Companies and Enterprises	$82,150	1,870
Utilities	$76,300	2,210
Real Estate	$75,430	1,060
Federal, State, and Local Government	$75,010	70,850
Professional, Scientific, and Technical Services	$74,680	140,330

Metropolitan Areas Where Income Is Highest

Metropolitan Area	Average Annual Earnings	Number Employed
Baton Rouge, LA	$96,260	1,370
San Jose–Sunnyvale–Santa Clara, CA	$93,020	1,560
Houston–Sugar Land–Baytown, TX	$92,640	13,920
Oxnard–Thousand Oaks–Ventura, CA	$91,210	720
Santa Rosa–Petaluma, CA	$90,820	280

Perform engineering duties in planning, designing, and overseeing construction and maintenance of building structures and facilities such as roads, railroads, airports, bridges, harbors, channels, dams, irrigation projects, pipelines, power plants, water and sewage systems, and waste disposal units. Includes architectural, structural, traffic, ocean, and geo-technical engineers. Manage and direct staff members and construction, operations, or maintenance activities at project site. Provide technical advice regarding design, construction, or program modifications and structural repairs to industrial and managerial personnel. Inspect project sites to monitor progress and ensure conformance to design specifications and safety or sanitation standards. Estimate quantities and cost of materials, equipment, or labor to determine project feasibility. Test soils and materials to determine the adequacy and strength of foundations, concrete, asphalt, or steel. Compute load and grade requirements, water flow rates, and material stress factors to determine design specifications. Plan and design transportation or hydraulic systems and structures, following construction and government standards and using design software and drawing tools. Analyze survey reports, maps, drawings, blueprints, aerial photography, and other topographical or geologic data to plan projects. Prepare or present public reports on topics such as bid proposals, deeds, environmental impact statements, or property and right-of-way descriptions. Direct or participate in surveying to lay out installations and establish reference points, grades, and elevations to guide construction. Conduct studies of traffic patterns or environmental conditions to identify engineering problems and assess the potential impact of projects.

Other Considerations for Income: As a group, engineers earn some of the highest average starting salaries among those holding bachelor's degrees. Civil Engineers are among the lower-paid of the various kinds of engineers. According to a 2007 survey by the National Association of Colleges and Employers, the average starting salary for Civil Engineers with a bachelor's were $48,509 with a bachelor's, $48,280 with a master's, and $62,275 with a Ph.D.

Personality Type: Realistic-Investigative-Conventional. **Career Cluster:** 15 Science, Technology, Engineering, and Mathematics. **Career Pathway:** 15.1 Engineering and Technology. **Skills:** Systems Analysis; Systems Evaluation; Mathematics; Management of Financial Resources; Management of Personnel Resources; Quality Control Analysis; Management of Material Resources; Complex Problem Solving.

Education and Training Programs: Civil Engineering, General; Civil Engineering, Other; Transportation and Highway Engineering; Water Resources Engineering. **Related Knowledge/Courses:** Engineering and Technology; Building and Construction; Design; Physics; Transportation; Mathematics.

Claims Adjusters, Examiners, and Investigators

See **Claims Examiners, Property and Casualty Insurance** and **Insurance Adjusters, Examiners, and Investigators,** described separately.

Claims Examiners, Property and Casualty Insurance

- ❀ Annual Earnings: $55,760
- ❀ Beginning Wage: $34,140
- ❀ Earnings Growth Potential: Medium (38.8%)
- ❀ Growth: 8.9%
- ❀ Annual Job Openings: 22,024
- ❀ Self-Employed: 3.5%
- ❀ Part-Time: 4.0%
- ❀ Job Security: Most secure
- ❀ Education/Training Required: Long-term on-the-job training

The Department of Labor reports this information for the occupation Claims Adjusters, Examiners, and Investigators. The job openings listed here are shared with other specializations within that occupation, including Insurance Adjusters, Examiners, and Investigators.

Industries in Which Income Is Highest

Industry	Average Annual Earnings	Number Employed
Federal, State, and Local Government	$62,000	50,470
Insurance Carriers and Related Activities	$54,330	204,500
Management of Companies and Enterprises	$53,840	5,980
Funds, Trusts, and Other Financial Vehicles	$53,780	4,810
Professional, Scientific, and Technical Services	$51,080	1,980

Metropolitan Areas Where Income Is Highest

Metropolitan Area	Average Annual Earnings	Number Employed
Poughkeepsie-Newburgh-Middletown, NY	$73,320	380
Asheville, NC	$72,940	120
Mobile, AL	$72,570	290
Salinas, CA	$71,650	130
Cape Coral–Fort Myers, FL	$71,030	130

Review settled insurance claims to determine that payments and settlements have been made in accordance with company practices and procedures. Report overpayments, underpayments, and other irregularities. Confer with legal counsel on claims requiring litigation. Investigate, evaluate, and settle claims, applying technical knowledge and human relations skills to effect fair and prompt disposal of cases and to contribute to a reduced loss ratio. Pay and process claims within designated authority level. Adjust reserves or provide reserve recommendations to ensure that reserve activities are consistent with corporate policies. Enter claim payments, reserves, and new claims on computer system, inputting concise yet sufficient file documentation. Resolve complex severe exposure claims, using high-service-oriented file handling. Maintain claim files such as records of settled claims and an inventory of claims requiring detailed analysis. Verify and analyze data used in settling claims to ensure that claims are valid and that settlements are made according to company practices and procedures. Examine claims investigated by insurance adjusters, further investigating questionable claims to determine whether to authorize payments. Present cases and participate in their discussion at claim committee meetings. Contact or interview claimants, doctors, medical specialists, or employers to get additional information. Confer with legal counsel on claims requiring litigation. Report overpayments, underpayments, and other irregularities. Communicate with reinsurance brokers to obtain information necessary for processing claims. Supervise claims adjusters to ensure that adjusters have followed proper methods. Conduct detailed bill reviews to implement sound litigation management and expense control. Prepare reports to be submitted to company's data-processing department.

Other Considerations for Income: No additional information.

Personality Type: Conventional-Enterprising. **Career Cluster:** 06 Finance. **Career Pathway:** 06.4 Insurance Services. **Skills:** Judgment and Decision Making; Writing; Persuasion; Negotiation; Reading Comprehension; Critical Thinking; Instructing; Active Listening.

Education and Training Programs: Health/Medical Claims Examiner; Insurance. **Related Knowledge/Courses:** Customer and Personal Service; Medicine and Dentistry; Clerical; Law and Government; Computers and Electronics; English Language.

Climate Change Analysts

- ❋ Annual Earnings: $59,750
- ❋ Beginning Wage: $36,310
- ❋ Earnings Growth Potential: Medium (39.2%)
- ❋ Growth: 25.1%
- ❋ Annual Job Openings: 6,961
- ❋ Self-Employed: 2.2%
- ❋ Part-Time: 5.3%
- ❋ Job Security: No data available
- ❋ Education/Training Required: Master's degree

The Department of Labor reports this information for the occupation Environmental Scientists and Specialists, Including Health. The job openings listed here are shared with other specializations within that occupation, including Environmental Restoration Planners; and Industrial Ecologists.

Industries in Which Income Is Highest

Industry	Average Annual Earnings	Number Employed
Utilities	$83,440	1,040
Professional, Scientific, and Technical Services	$61,330	35,270
Federal, State, and Local Government	$57,970	35,460
Educational Services	$57,170	2,840

Metropolitan Areas Where Income Is Highest

Metropolitan Area	Average Annual Earnings	Number Employed
Washington-Arlington-Alexandria, DC-VA-MD-WV	$89,540	3,750
San Jose–Sunnyvale–Santa Clara, CA	$82,970	390
Boston-Cambridge-Quincy, MA-NH	$82,930	2,110
Ann Arbor, MI	$80,300	210
Santa Rosa–Petaluma, CA	$79,330	380

Research and analyze policy developments related to climate change. Make climate-related recommendations for actions such as legislation, awareness campaigns, or fundraising approaches. No task data available.

Other Considerations for Income: According to the National Association of Colleges and Employers, beginning salary offers in July 2007 for graduates with bachelor's degrees in an environmental science averaged $38,336 a year.

Personality Type: No data available. **Career Cluster:** 01 Agriculture, Food and Natural Resource. **Career Pathway:** 01.5 Natural Resources Systems. **Skills:** No data available.

Education and Training Programs: Environmental Science; Environmental Studies. **Related Knowledge/ Courses:** No data available.

Clinical Data Managers

- ❋ Annual Earnings: $72,610
- ❋ Beginning Wage: $39,740
- ❋ Earnings Growth Potential: High (45.3%)
- ❋ Growth: 8.5%
- ❋ Annual Job Openings: 3,433
- ❋ Self-Employed: 6.0%
- ❋ Part-Time: 13.1%
- ❋ Job Security: No data available
- ❋ Education/Training Required: Bachelor's degree

The Department of Labor reports this information for the occupation Statisticians. The job openings listed here are shared with other specializations within that occupation, including Biostatisticians.

Industries in Which Income Is Highest

Industry	Average Annual Earnings	Number Employed
Chemical Manufacturing	$89,980	1,340
Professional, Scientific, and Technical Services	$80,610	4,720
Federal, State, and Local Government	$75,430	6,120
Insurance Carriers and Related Activities	$63,020	2,000
Educational Services	$58,280	1,860

Metropolitan Areas Where Income Is Highest

Metropolitan Area	Average Annual Earnings	Number Employed
Oxnard–Thousand Oaks–Ventura, CA	$92,430	190
San Jose–Sunnyvale–Santa Clara, CA	$92,090	240
Washington-Arlington-Alexandria, DC-VA-MD-WV	$91,950	3,500
San Francisco–Oakland–Fremont, CA	$89,340	540
Chicago-Naperville-Joliet, IL-IN-WI	$86,600	480

Apply knowledge of health care and database management to analyze clinical data and to identify and report trends. No task data available.

Other Considerations for Income: Some employers offer tuition reimbursement.

Personality Type: Conventional-Investigative. **Career Cluster:** 15 Science, Technology, Engineering, and Mathematics. **Career Pathway:** 15.3 Science and Mathematics. **Skills:** No data available.

Education and Training Programs: Applied Mathematics, General; Biostatistics; Business Statistics; Mathematical Statistics and Probability; Mathematics, General; Statistics, General; Statistics, Other. **Related Knowledge/ Courses:** No data available.

Clinical Nurse Specialists

- ❀ Annual Earnings: $80,240
- ❀ Beginning Wage: $48,300
- ❀ Earnings Growth Potential: Medium (39.8%)
- ❀ Growth: 16.4%
- ❀ Annual Job Openings: 31,877
- ❀ Self-Employed: 8.2%
- ❀ Part-Time: 5.5%
- ❀ Job Security: No data available
- ❀ Education/Training Required: Master's degree

The Department of Labor reports this information for the occupation Medical and Health Services Managers. The job openings listed here are shared with other specializations within that occupation.

Industries in Which Income Is Highest

Industry	Average Annual Earnings	Number Employed
Professional, Scientific, and Technical Services	$102,470	2,950
Insurance Carriers and Related Activities	$93,680	4,730
Management of Companies and Enterprises	$88,160	4,410
Hospitals	$86,850	105,870
Educational Services	$83,620	5,920

Metropolitan Areas Where Income Is Highest

Metropolitan Area	Average Annual Earnings	Number Employed
San Jose–Sunnyvale–Santa Clara, CA	$113,380	1,200
Olympia, WA	$106,660	90
Seattle-Tacoma-Bellevue, WA	$105,730	1,910
Rochester, MN	$104,820	300
New York–Northern New Jersey–Long Island, NY-NJ-PA	$100,600	23,010

Plan, direct, or coordinate daily patient care activities in a clinical practice. Ensure adherence to established clinical policies, protocols, regulations, and standards. No task data available.

Other Considerations for Income: No additional information.

Personality Type: Enterprising-Social-Conventional. **Career Cluster:** 08 Health Science. **Career Pathways:** 08.1 Therapeutic Services; 08.3 Health Informatics. **Skills:** No data available.

Education and Training Programs: Community Health and Preventive Medicine; Health and Medical Administrative Services, Other; Health Information/Medical Records Administration/Administrator; Health Services Administration; Health Unit Manager/Ward Supervisor; Health/Health Care Administration/Management; Hospital and Health Care Facilities Administration/Management; Public Health, General. **Related Knowledge/ Courses:** Medicine and Dentistry; Biology; Therapy and Counseling; Psychology; Sociology and Anthropology; Philosophy and Theology.

Clinical Psychologists

- ❀ Annual Earnings: $64,140
- ❀ Beginning Wage: $37,900
- ❀ Earnings Growth Potential: High (40.9%)
- ❀ Growth: 15.8%
- ❀ Annual Job Openings: 8,309
- ❀ Self-Employed: 34.2%
- ❀ Part-Time: 24.0%
- ❀ Job Security: Most secure
- ❀ Education/Training Required: Doctoral degree

C

The Department of Labor reports this information for the occupation Clinical, Counseling, and School Psychologists. The job openings listed here are shared with other specializations within that occupation, including Counseling Psychologists; and School Psychologists.

Industries in Which Income Is Highest

Industry	Average Annual Earnings	Number Employed
Administrative and Support Services	$72,400	1,140
Hospitals	$70,240	9,210
Professional, Scientific, and Technical Services	$70,010	1,020
Ambulatory Health Care Services	$65,810	19,180
Educational Services	$64,410	46,390

Metropolitan Areas Where Income Is Highest

Metropolitan Area	Average Annual Earnings	Number Employed
Vallejo-Fairfield, CA	$92,560	210
Dayton, OH	$91,750	210
Visalia-Porterville, CA	$90,930	80
Trenton-Ewing, NJ	$89,310	270
Stockton, CA	$87,780	130

Diagnose or evaluate mental and emotional disorders of individuals through observation, interview, and psychological tests and formulate and administer programs of treatment. Identify psychological, emotional, or behavioral issues and diagnose disorders, using information obtained from interviews, tests, records, and reference materials. Develop and implement individual treatment plans, specifying type, frequency, intensity, and duration of therapy. Interact with clients to assist them in gaining insight, defining goals, and planning action to achieve effective personal, social, educational, and vocational development and adjustment. Discuss the treatment of problems with clients. Utilize a variety of treatment methods such as psychotherapy, hypnosis, behavior modification, stress reduction therapy, psychodrama, and play therapy. Counsel individuals and groups regarding problems such as stress, substance abuse, and family situations to modify behavior or to improve personal, social, and vocational adjustment. Write reports on clients and maintain required paperwork. Evaluate the effectiveness of counseling or treatments and the accuracy and completeness of diagnoses; then modify plans and diagnoses as necessary. Obtain and study medical, psychological, social, and family histories by interviewing individuals, couples, or families and by reviewing records. Consult reference material such as textbooks, manuals, and journals to identify symptoms, make diagnoses, and develop approaches to treatment. Maintain current knowledge of relevant research. Observe individuals at play, in group interactions, or in other contexts to detect indications of mental deficiency, abnormal behavior, or maladjustment. Select, administer, score, and interpret psychological tests to obtain information on individuals' intelligence, achievements, interests, and personalities. Refer clients to other specialists, institutions, or support services as necessary. Develop, direct, and participate in training programs for staff and students.

Other Considerations for Income: No additional information.

Personality Type: Investigative-Social-Artistic. **Career Clusters:** 08 Health Science; 10 Human Service. **Career Pathways:** 08.1 Therapeutic Services; 08.3 Health Informatics; 10.2 Counseling and Mental Health Services. **Skills:** Social Perceptiveness; Service Orientation; Complex Problem Solving; Learning Strategies; Active Listening; Negotiation; Active Learning; Critical Thinking.

Education and Training Programs: Psychoanalysis and Psychotherapy; Psychology, General. **Related Knowledge/Courses:** Therapy and Counseling; Psychology; Sociology and Anthropology; Philosophy and Theology; Customer and Personal Service; Medicine and Dentistry.

Clinical Research Coordinators

- ❋ Annual Earnings: $112,800
- ❋ Beginning Wage: $65,960
- ❋ Earnings Growth Potential: High (41.5%)
- ❋ Growth: 11.4%
- ❋ Annual Job Openings: 3,661
- ❋ Self-Employed: 0.6%
- ❋ Part-Time: 4.4%
- ❋ Job Security: No data available
- ❋ Education/Training Required: Work experience in a related occupation

The Department of Labor reports this information for the occupation Natural Sciences Managers. The job openings listed here are shared with other specializations within that occupation, including Water Resource Specialists.

Industries in Which Income Is Highest

Industry	Average Annual Earnings	Number Employed
Chemical Manufacturing	$139,610	5,660
Management of Companies and Enterprises	$136,560	2,160
Professional, Scientific, and Technical Services	$125,560	16,240
Federal, State, and Local Government	$95,610	12,760
Educational Services	$91,920	1,990

Metropolitan Areas Where Income Is Highest

Metropolitan Area	Average Annual Earnings	Number Employed
San Jose–Sunnyvale–Santa Clara, CA	$166,400+	860
Philadelphia-Camden-Wilmington, PA-NJ-DE-MD	$162,090	1,740
New York–Northern New Jersey–Long Island, NY-NJ-PA	$149,910	3,540
San Francisco–Oakland–Fremont, CA	$149,110	2,250
San Diego–Carlsbad–San Marcos, CA	$141,210	1,300

Plan, direct, or coordinate clinical research projects. Direct the activities of workers engaged in clinical research projects to ensure compliance with protocols and overall clinical objectives. May evaluate and analyze clinical data. No task data available.

Other Considerations for Income: No additional information.

Personality Type: Enterprising-Investigative-Conventional. **Career Clusters:** 08 Health Science; 15 Science, Technology, Engineering, and Mathematics. **Career Pathways:** 08.5 Biotechnology Research and Development; 15.3 Science and Mathematics. **Skills:** No data available.

Education and Training Programs: Biometry/Biometrics; Biostatistics; Biotechnology; Cell/Cellular Biology and Anatomical Sciences, Other; Immunology; Medical Microbiology and Bacteriology; Microbiology, General; Nutrition Sciences; Parasitology; Pathology/Experimental Pathology; Pharmacology; Statistics, General; Toxicology; Virology. **Related Knowledge/Courses:** No data available.

Clinical, Counseling, and School Psychologists

See *Clinical Psychologists; Counseling Psychologists;* and *School Psychologists,* described separately.

Commercial and Industrial Designers

- ❋ Annual Earnings: $57,350
- ❋ Beginning Wage: $31,400
- ❋ Earnings Growth Potential: High (45.2%)
- ❋ Growth: 7.2%
- ❋ Annual Job Openings: 4,777
- ❋ Self-Employed: 29.8%
- ❋ Part-Time: 16.7%
- ❋ Job Security: Least secure
- ❋ Education/Training Required: Bachelor's degree

Industries in Which Income Is Highest

Industry	Average Annual Earnings	Number Employed
Transportation Equipment Manufacturing	$68,990	2,220
Management of Companies and Enterprises	$63,940	3,410
Merchant Wholesalers, Durable Goods	$60,510	1,860
Professional, Scientific, and Technical Services	$60,370	9,020
Machinery Manufacturing	$52,910	2,390

Metropolitan Areas Where Income Is Highest

Metropolitan Area	Average Annual Earnings	Number Employed
San Jose–Sunnyvale–Santa Clara, CA	$86,860	580
Ann Arbor, MI	$77,430	240
Minneapolis–St. Paul–Bloomington, MN-WI	$74,650	900
Portland–South Portland–Biddeford, ME	$71,210	110
San Francisco–Oakland–Fremont, CA	$70,190	980

Develop and design manufactured products, such as cars, home appliances, and children's toys. Combine artistic talent with research on product use, marketing, and materials to create the most functional and appealing product design. Prepare sketches of ideas, detailed drawings, illustrations, artwork, or blueprints, using drafting instruments, paints and brushes, or computer-aided design equipment. Direct and coordinate the fabrication of models or samples and the drafting of working drawings and specification sheets from sketches. Modify and refine designs, using working models, to conform with customer specifications, production limitations, or changes in design trends. Coordinate the look and function of product lines. Confer with engineering, marketing, production, or sales departments, or with customers, to establish and evaluate design concepts for manufactured products. Present designs and reports to customers or design committees for approval and discuss need for modification. Evaluate feasibility of design ideas based on factors such as appearance, safety, function, serviceability, budget, production costs/methods, and market characteristics. Read publications, attend showings, and study competing products and design styles and motifs to obtain perspective and generate design concepts. Research production specifications, costs, production materials, and manufacturing methods and provide cost estimates and itemized production requirements. Design graphic material for use as ornamentation, illustration, or advertising on manufactured materials and packaging or containers. Develop manufacturing procedures and monitor the manufacture of their designs in a factory to improve operations and product quality. Supervise assistants' work throughout the design process. Fabricate models or samples in paper, wood, glass, fabric, plastic, metal, or other materials, using hand or power tools. Investigate product characteristics such as the product's safety and handling qualities; its market appeal; how efficiently it can be produced; and ways of distributing, using, and maintaining it. Develop industrial standards and regulatory guidelines.

Other Considerations for Income: No additional information.

Personality Type: Artistic-Enterprising-Realistic. **Career Cluster:** 03 Arts, Audio/Video Technology, and Communications. **Career Pathways:** 03.1 Audio and Video Technology and Film; 03.3 Visual Arts. **Skills:** Technology Design; Operations Analysis; Quality Control Analysis; Troubleshooting; Equipment Selection; Installation; Systems Evaluation; Mathematics.

Education and Training Programs: Commercial and Advertising Art; Design and Applied Arts, Other; Design and Visual Communications, General; Industrial and Product Design. **Related Knowledge/Courses:** Design; Engineering and Technology; Mathematics; Physics; Mechanical; Production and Processing.

Commercial Pilots

- Annual Earnings: $65,340
- Beginning Wage: $32,020
- Earnings Growth Potential: Very high (51.0%)
- Growth: 13.2%
- Annual Job Openings: 1,425
- Self-Employed: 1.9%
- Part-Time: 14.2%
- Job Security: Least secure
- Education/Training Required: Postsecondary vocational training

Industries in Which Income Is Highest

Industry	Average Annual Earnings	Number Employed
Air Transportation	$66,710	12,360
Ambulatory Health Care Services	$61,000	2,290
Support Activities for Transportation	$57,640	2,960
Educational Services	$52,070	4,060
Support Activities for Agriculture and Forestry	$52,040	1,010

Metropolitan Areas Where Income Is Highest

Metropolitan Area	Average Annual Earnings	Number Employed
Atlanta–Sandy Springs–Marietta, GA	$155,780	1,350
Sebastian–Vero Beach, FL	$91,120	80
Charlotte-Gastonia-Concord, NC-SC	$87,340	180
Washington-Arlington-Alexandria, DC-VA-MD-WV	$85,510	280
Miami–Fort Lauderdale–Miami Beach, FL	$83,880	1,200

Pilot and navigate the flight of small fixed or rotary winged aircraft primarily for the transport of cargo and passengers. Requires Commercial Rating. Check aircraft prior to flights to ensure that the engines, controls, instruments, and other systems are functioning properly. Start engines, operate controls, and pilot airplanes to transport passengers, mail, or freight while adhering to flight plans, regulations, and procedures. Contact control towers for takeoff clearances, arrival instructions, and other information, using radio equipment. Monitor engine operation, fuel consumption, and functioning of aircraft systems during flights. Consider airport altitudes, outside temperatures, plane weights, and wind speeds and directions to calculate the speed needed to become airborne. Order changes in fuel supplies, loads, routes, or schedules to ensure safety of flights. Obtain and review data such as load weights, fuel supplies, weather conditions, and flight schedules to determine flight plans and to see if changes might be necessary. Plan flights, following government and company regulations, using aeronautical charts and navigation instruments. Use instrumentation to pilot aircraft when visibility is poor. Check baggage or cargo to ensure that it has been loaded correctly. Request changes in altitudes or routes as circumstances dictate. Choose routes, altitudes, and speeds that will provide the fastest, safest, and smoothest flights. Coordinate flight activities with ground crews and air-traffic control and inform crew members of flight and test procedures. Write specified information in flight records, such as flight times, altitudes flown, and fuel consumption. Teach company regulations and procedures to other pilots. Instruct other pilots and student pilots in aircraft operations. Co-pilot aircraft or perform captain's duties if required. File instrument flight plans with air traffic control so that flights can be coordinated with other air traffic.

Other Considerations for Income: Earnings of aircraft pilots and flight engineers vary greatly depending whether they work as airline or commercial pilots. Earnings of airline pilots are among the highest in the nation, and depend on factors such as the type, size, and maximum speed of the plane and the number of hours and miles flown. For example, pilots who fly jet aircraft usually earn higher salaries than pilots who fly turboprops. Airline pilots and flight engineers may earn extra pay for night and international flights. Airline pilots usually are eligible for life and health insurance plans. They also receive retirement benefits and, if they fail the FAA physical examination at some point in their careers, they get disability payments. In addition, pilots receive an expense allowance, or per diem, for every hour they are away from home. Some airlines also provide allowances to pilots for purchasing and cleaning their uniforms. As an additional benefit, pilots and their immediate families usually are entitled to free or reduced-fare transportation on their own and other airlines. More than half of all aircraft pilots are members of unions.

Personality Type: Realistic-Investigative-Enterprising. **Career Cluster:** 16 Transportation, Distribution, and Logistics. **Career Pathway:** 16.1 Transportation Operations. **Skills:** Operation Monitoring; Operation and Control; Troubleshooting; Judgment and Decision Making; Systems Evaluation; Critical Thinking; Systems Analysis; Equipment Maintenance.

Education and Training Programs: Airline/Commercial/Professional Pilot and Flight Crew; Flight Instructor. **Related Knowledge/Courses:** Transportation; Geography; Mechanical; Physics; Telecommunications; Psychology.

Communications Teachers, Postsecondary

- ❋ Annual Earnings: $57,760
- ❋ Beginning Wage: $31,720
- ❋ Earnings Growth Potential: High (45.1%)
- ❋ Growth: 22.9%
- ❋ Annual Job Openings: 4,074
- ❋ Self-Employed: 0.4%
- ❋ Part-Time: 27.8%
- ❋ Job Security: Most secure
- ❋ Education/Training Required: Doctoral degree

Industries in Which Income Is Highest

Industry	Average Annual Earnings	Number Employed
Educational Services	$57,740	24,320

Metropolitan Areas Where Income Is Highest

Metropolitan Area	Average Annual Earnings	Number Employed
Lubbock, TX	$90,250	90
San Diego–Carlsbad–San Marcos, CA	$89,930	340
Los Angeles–Long Beach–Santa Ana, CA	$82,700	780
Milwaukee–Waukesha–West Allis, WI	$80,310	210
Columbus, OH	$78,720	210

Teach courses in communications, such as organizational communications, public relations, radio/television broadcasting, and journalism. Evaluate and grade students' classwork, assignments, and papers. Prepare course materials such as syllabi, homework assignments, and handouts. Initiate, facilitate, and moderate classroom discussions. Prepare and deliver lectures to undergraduate or graduate students on topics such as public speaking, media criticism, and oral traditions. Compile, administer, and grade examinations or assign this work to others. Maintain student attendance records, grades, and other required records. Plan, evaluate, and revise curricula, course content, and course materials and methods of instruction. Maintain regularly scheduled office hours to advise and assist students. Keep abreast of developments in their field by reading current literature, talking with colleagues, and participating in professional conferences. Advise students on academic and vocational curricula and on career issues. Supervise undergraduate or graduate teaching, internship, and research work. Select and obtain materials and supplies such as textbooks. Collaborate with colleagues to address teaching and research issues. Conduct research in a particular field of knowledge and publish findings in professional journals, books, or electronic media. Participate in student recruitment, registration, and placement activities. Serve on academic or administrative committees that deal with institutional policies, departmental matters, and academic issues. Compile bibliographies of specialized materials for outside reading assignments. Act as advisers to student organizations. Participate in campus and community events. Perform administrative duties such as serving as department head. Write grant proposals to procure external research funding. Provide professional consulting services to government or industry.

Other Considerations for Income: Earnings for college faculty vary according to rank and type of institution, geographic area, and field. According to a 2006–2007 survey by the American Association of University Professors, salaries for full-time faculty averaged $73,207. By rank, the average was $98,974 for professors, $69,911 for associate professors, $58,662 for assistant professors, $42,609 for instructors, and $48,289 for lecturers. Faculty in 4-year institutions earn higher salaries, on average, than do those in 2-year schools. Many faculty members have significant earnings in addition to their base salary from consulting, teaching additional courses, research, writing for publication, or other employment. In addition, many college and university faculty enjoy unique benefits, including access to campus facilities, tuition waivers for dependents, housing and travel allowances, and paid leave for sabbaticals. Part-time faculty and instructors usually have fewer benefits than full-time faculty.

Personality Type: Social-Artistic. **Career Clusters:** 03 Arts, Audio/Video Technology, and Communications; 04 Business, Management, and Administration; 05 Education and Training. **Career Pathways:** 03.5 Journalism and Broadcasting; 04.1 Management; 04.5 Marketing; 05.3 Teaching/Training. **Skills:** Instructing; Writing; Persuasion; Learning Strategies; Monitoring; Speaking; Social Perceptiveness; Critical Thinking.

Education and Training Programs: Advertising; Broadcast Journalism; Communication, Journalism, and Related Programs, Other; Digital Communication and Media/Multimedia; Health Communication; Humanities/Humanistic Studies; Journalism; Journalism, Other; Mass Communication/Media Studies; Political Communication; Public Relations/Image Management; Radio and Television; Speech Communication and Rhetoric. **Related Knowledge/Courses:** Communications and Media; Education and Training; Philosophy and Theology; Sociology and Anthropology; English Language; History and Archeology.

Compensation and Benefits Managers

❋ Annual Earnings: $86,500
❋ Beginning Wage: $49,350
❋ Earnings Growth Potential: High (42.9%)
❋ Growth: 12.0%
❋ Annual Job Openings: 6,121
❋ Self-Employed: 1.4%
❋ Part-Time: 2.7%
❋ Job Security: More secure than most
❋ Education/Training Required: Work experience plus degree

Industries in Which Income Is Highest

Industry	Average Annual Earnings	Number Employed
Management of Companies and Enterprises	$94,230	6,270
Professional, Scientific, and Technical Services	$92,680	4,500
Insurance Carriers and Related Activities	$91,710	1,840
Credit Intermediation and Related Activities	$90,600	2,030
Educational Services	$86,900	1,370

Metropolitan Areas Where Income Is Highest

Metropolitan Area	Average Annual Earnings	Number Employed
San Jose–Sunnyvale–Santa Clara, CA	$127,620	390
New York–Northern New Jersey–Long Island, NY-NJ-PA	$110,390	3,450
Minneapolis–St. Paul–Bloomington, MN-WI	$107,930	460
Miami–Fort Lauderdale–Miami Beach, FL	$106,510	660
San Francisco–Oakland–Fremont, CA	$105,410	810

Plan, direct, or coordinate compensation and benefits activities and staff of an organization. Design, evaluate, and modify benefits policies to ensure that programs are current, competitive, and in compliance with legal requirements. Analyze compensation policies, government regulations, and prevailing wage rates to develop competitive compensation plans. Fulfill all reporting requirements of all relevant government rules and regulations, including the Employee Retirement Income Security Act (ERISA). Direct preparation and distribution of written and verbal information to inform employees of benefits, compensation, and personnel policies. Administer, direct, and review employee benefit programs, including the integration of benefit programs following mergers and acquisitions. Plan, direct, supervise, and coordinate work activities of subordinates and staff relating to employment, compensation, labor relations, and employee relations. Identify and implement benefits to increase the quality of life for employees by working with brokers and researching benefits issues. Manage the design and development of tools to assist employees in benefits selection and to guide managers through compensation decisions. Prepare detailed job descriptions and classification systems and define job levels and families in partnership with other managers. Prepare budgets for personnel operations. Formulate policies, procedures, and programs for recruitment, testing, placement, classification, orientation, benefits and compensation, and labor and industrial relations. Mediate between benefits providers and employees, such as by assisting in handling employees' benefits-related questions or taking suggestions. Develop methods to improve employment policies, processes, and practices and recommend changes to management. Study legislation, arbitration decisions, and collective bargaining contracts to assess industry trends. Maintain records and compile statistical reports concerning personnel-related data such as hires, transfers, performance appraisals, and absenteeism rates.

Other Considerations for Income: Compensation and Benefits Managers are among the lower-paid workers among human resource managers. According to a July 2007 salary survey conducted by the National Association of Colleges and Employers, bachelor's degree candidates majoring in human resources, including labor and industrial relations, received starting offers averaging $41,680 a year.

Personality Type: Enterprising-Conventional-Social. **Career Cluster:** 04 Business, Management, and Administration. **Career Pathway:** 04.3 Human Resources. **Skills:** Management of Financial Resources; Systems Analysis; Systems Evaluation; Management of Personnel Resources; Negotiation.

Education and Training Programs: Human Resources Management/Personnel Administration, General; Labor and Industrial Relations. **Related Knowledge/Cours-**

es: Personnel and Human Resources; Economics and Accounting; Administration and Management; Mathematics; Law and Government; Communications and Media.

Compensation, Benefits, and Job Analysis Specialists

- ❈ Annual Earnings: $53,860
- ❈ Beginning Wage: $34,080
- ❈ Earnings Growth Potential: Medium (36.7%)
- ❈ Growth: 18.4%
- ❈ Annual Job Openings: 18,761
- ❈ Self-Employed: 2.1%
- ❈ Part-Time: 7.6%
- ❈ Job Security: More secure than most
- ❈ Education/Training Required: Bachelor's degree

Industries in Which Income Is Highest

Industry	Average Annual Earnings	Number Employed
Telecommunications	$64,410	1,250
Transportation Equipment Manufacturing	$60,770	1,250
Computer and Electronic Product Manufacturing	$60,670	1,930
Publishing Industries (Except Internet)	$60,440	1,170
Professional, Scientific, and Technical Services	$59,610	14,240

Metropolitan Areas Where Income Is Highest

Metropolitan Area	Average Annual Earnings	Number Employed
Bloomington-Normal, IL	$110,630	350
San Jose–Sunnyvale–Santa Clara, CA	$73,760	850
Hartford–West Hartford–East Hartford, CT	$66,630	610
Terre Haute, IN	$66,580	80
Washington-Arlington-Alexandria, DC-VA-MD-WV	$64,710	3,490

Conduct programs of compensation and benefits and job analysis for employer. May specialize in specific areas, such as position classification and pension programs. Evaluate job positions, determining classification, exempt or non-exempt status, and salary. Ensure company compliance with federal and state laws, including reporting requirements. Advise managers and employees on state and federal employment regulations, collective agreements, benefit and compensation policies, personnel procedures, and classification programs. Plan, develop, evaluate, improve, and communicate methods and techniques for selecting, promoting, compensating, evaluating, and training workers. Provide advice on the resolution of classification and salary complaints. Prepare occupational classifications, job descriptions, and salary scales. Assist in preparing and maintaining personnel records and handbooks. Prepare reports such as organization and flow charts and career path reports to summarize job analysis and evaluation and compensation analysis information. Administer employee insurance, pension, and savings plans, working with insurance brokers and plan carriers. Negotiate collective agreements on behalf of employers or workers and mediate labor disputes and grievances. Develop, implement, administer, and evaluate personnel and labor relations programs, including performance appraisal, affirmative action, and employment equity programs. Perform multifactor data and cost analyses that may be used in areas such as support of collective bargaining agreements. Research employee benefit and health and safety practices and recommend changes or modifications to existing policies. Analyze organizational, occupational, and industrial data to facilitate organizational functions and provide technical information to business, industry, and government. Advise staff of individuals' qualifications. Assess need for and develop job analysis instruments and materials.

Other Considerations for Income: Compensation, Benefits, and Job Analysis Specialists are among the higher-paid workers among human resource specialists. According to a July 2007 salary survey conducted by the National Association of Colleges and Employers, bachelor's degree candidates majoring in human resources, including labor and industrial relations, received starting offers averaging $41,680 a year.

Personality Type: Conventional-Enterprising. **Career Cluster:** 04 Business, Management, and Administration. **Career Pathway:** 04.3 Human Resources. **Skills:** Service Orientation; Judgment and Decision Making; Management of Financial Resources; Persuasion; Active Listening; Negotiation; Monitoring; Coordination.

Education and Training Programs: Human Resources Management/Personnel Administration, General; Labor and Industrial Relations. **Related Knowledge/Courses:** Personnel and Human Resources; Economics and Accounting; Law and Government; English Language; Administration and Management; Mathematics.

Compliance Officers, Except Agriculture, Construction, Health and Safety, and Transportation

See *Coroners; Environmental Compliance Inspectors; Equal Opportunity Representatives and Officers; Government Property Inspectors and Investigators;* and *Licensing Examiners and Inspectors, described separately.*

Computer and Information Scientists, Research

- ❀ Annual Earnings: $97,970
- ❀ Beginning Wage: $57,480
- ❀ Earnings Growth Potential: High (41.3%)
- ❀ Growth: 21.5%
- ❀ Annual Job Openings: 2,901
- ❀ Self-Employed: 5.3%
- ❀ Part-Time: 5.6%
- ❀ Job Security: More secure than most
- ❀ Education/Training Required: Doctoral degree

Industries in Which Income Is Highest

Industry	Average Annual Earnings	Number Employed
Merchant Wholesalers, Durable Goods	$118,270	1,140
Publishing Industries (Except Internet)	$108,380	2,810
Professional, Scientific, and Technical Services	$99,100	12,220
Federal, State, and Local Government	$93,660	5,380
Educational Services	$65,200	1,530

Metropolitan Areas Where Income Is Highest

Metropolitan Area	Average Annual Earnings	Number Employed
San Jose–Sunnyvale–Santa Clara, CA	$122,590	1,050
Boston-Cambridge-Quincy, MA-NH	$121,260	1,390
Atlanta–Sandy Springs–Marietta, GA	$121,260	490
Columbia, SC	$119,980	70
Los Angeles–Long Beach–Santa Ana, CA	$117,510	830

Conduct research into fundamental computer and information science as theorists, designers, or inventors. Solve or develop solutions to problems in the field of computer hardware and software. Analyze problems to develop solutions involving computer hardware and software. Assign or schedule tasks in order to meet work priorities and goals. Evaluate project plans and proposals to assess feasibility issues. Apply theoretical expertise and innovation to create or apply new technology, such as adapting principles for applying computers to new uses. Consult with users, management, vendors, and technicians to determine computing needs and system requirements. Meet with managers, vendors, and others to solicit cooperation and resolve problems. Conduct logical analyses of business, scientific, engineering, and other technical problems, formulating mathematical models of problems for solution by computers. Develop and interpret organizational goals, policies, and procedures. Participate in staffing decisions and direct training of subordinates. Develop performance standards and evaluate work in light of established standards. Design computers and the software that runs them. Maintain network hardware and software, direct network security measures, and monitor networks to ensure availability to system users. Participate in multidisciplinary projects in areas such as virtual reality, human-computer interaction, or robotics. Approve, prepare, monitor, and adjust operational budgets. Direct daily operations of departments, coordinating project activities with other departments.

Other Considerations for Income: No additional information.

Personality Type: Investigative-Realistic-Conventional. **Career Cluster:** 11 Information Technology. **Career Pathways:** 11.1 Network Systems; 11.2 Information Support Services; 11.2 Information Support Services; 11.3 Interactive Media; 11.4 Programming and Software Development. **Skills:** Programming; Science; Systems Analysis; Operations Analysis; Technology Design; Active Learning; Complex Problem Solving; Mathematics.

Education and Training Programs: Artificial Intelligence; Computer and Information Sciences and Support Services, Other; Computer and Information Sciences, General; Computer Science; Computer Systems Analysis/Analyst; Information Science/Studies; Medical Informatics. **Related Knowledge/Courses:** Computers and Electronics; Telecommunications; Engineering and Technology; Mathematics; Education and Training; Design.

Computer and Information Systems Managers

❈ Annual Earnings: $112,210
❈ Beginning Wage: $68,750
❈ Earnings Growth Potential: Medium (38.7%)
❈ Growth: 16.4%
❈ Annual Job Openings: 30,887
❈ Self-Employed: 1.4%
❈ Part-Time: 2.1%
❈ Job Security: Least secure
❈ Education/Training Required: Work experience plus degree

Industries in Which Income Is Highest

Industry	Average Annual Earnings	Number Employed
Securities, Commodity Contracts, and Other Financial Investments and Related Activities	$136,590	8,530
Other Information Services	$133,120	2,930
Computer and Electronic Product Manufacturing	$127,530	11,080
Publishing Industries (Except Internet)	$123,800	11,990
Merchant Wholesalers, Durable Goods	$121,710	12,500

Metropolitan Areas Where Income Is Highest

Metropolitan Area	Average Annual Earnings	Number Employed
San Jose–Sunnyvale–Santa Clara, CA	$154,810	7,370
Poughkeepsie-Newburgh-Middletown, NY	$135,060	600
New York–Northern New Jersey–Long Island, NY-NJ-PA	$134,570	27,360
San Francisco–Oakland–Fremont, CA	$133,570	8,230
Salinas, CA	$131,470	200

Plan, direct, or coordinate activities in such fields as electronic data processing, information systems, systems analysis, and computer programming. Review project plans to plan and coordinate project activity. Manage backup, security, and user help systems. Develop and interpret organizational goals, policies, and procedures. Develop computer information resources, providing for data security and control, strategic computing, and disaster recovery. Consult with users, management, vendors, and technicians to assess computing needs and system requirements. Stay abreast of advances in technology. Meet with department heads, managers, supervisors, vendors, and others to solicit cooperation and resolve problems. Provide users with technical support for computer problems. Recruit, hire, train, and supervise staff or participate in staffing decisions. Evaluate data processing proposals to assess project feasibility and requirements. Review and approve all systems charts and programs prior to their implementation. Control operational budget and expenditures. Direct daily operations of department, analyzing workflow, establishing priorities, developing standards, and setting deadlines. Assign and review the work of systems analysts, programmers, and other computer-related workers. Evaluate the organization's technology use and needs and recommend improvements such as hardware and software upgrades. Prepare and review operational reports or project progress reports. Purchase necessary equipment.

Other Considerations for Income: Earnings for computer and information systems managers vary by specialty and level of responsibility. The Robert Half Technology 2007 Salary Guide lists the following annual salary ranges for various computer and information systems manager positions: Chief Technology Officer (CTO), $101,000–$157,750; Chief Security Officer, $97,500–$141,000; Vice President of Information Technology, $107,500–$157,750; Information Technology Manager, Technical Services Manager, $62,500–$88,250. In addition, computer and information systems managers, especially those at higher levels, often receive employment-related benefits, such as expense accounts, stock option plans, and bonuses.

Personality Type: Enterprising-Conventional-Investigative. **Career Clusters:** 04 Business, Management, and Administration; 11 Information Technology. **Career Pathways:** 04.1 Management; 04.4 Business Analysis; 11.1 Network Systems; 11.2 Information Support Services. **Skills:** Systems Evaluation; Programming; Systems Analysis; Management of Financial Resources; Management of Material Resources; Management of Personnel Resources; Operation Monitoring; Negotiation.

Education and Training Programs: Computer and Information Sciences, General; Computer Science; Information Resources Management/CIO Training; Information Science/Studies; Knowledge Management; Management Information Systems, General; Network and System Administration/Administrator; Operations Management and Supervision. **Related Knowledge/Courses:** Telecommunications; Computers and Electronics; Economics and Accounting; Production and Processing; Personnel and Human Resources; Administration and Management.

Computer Hardware Engineers

❋ Annual Earnings: $97,400
❋ Beginning Wage: $59,170
❋ Earnings Growth Potential: Medium (39.3%)
❋ Growth: 4.6%
❋ Annual Job Openings: 3,572
❋ Self-Employed: 3.6%
❋ Part-Time: 2.7%
❋ Job Security: Less secure than most
❋ Education/Training Required: Bachelor's degree

Industries in Which Income Is Highest

Industry	Average Annual Earnings	Number Employed
Computer and Electronic Product Manufacturing	$98,980	30,780
Professional, Scientific, and Technical Services	$98,150	24,350
Merchant Wholesalers, Durable Goods	$94,600	4,030
Federal, State, and Local Government	$93,450	4,280
Administrative and Support Services	$83,190	1,770

Metropolitan Areas Where Income Is Highest

Metropolitan Area	Average Annual Earnings	Number Employed
San Jose–Sunnyvale–Santa Clara, CA	$119,260	10,350
Santa Barbara–Santa Maria, CA	$116,070	100
New York–Northern New Jersey–Long Island, NY-NJ-PA	$114,990	3,450
Boulder, CO	$112,680	1,850
San Francisco–Oakland–Fremont, CA	$110,700	2,910

Research, design, develop, and test computer or computer-related equipment for commercial, industrial, military, or scientific use. May supervise the manufacturing and installation of computer or computer-related equipment and components. Update knowledge and skills to keep up with rapid advancements in computer technology. Provide technical support to designers, marketing and sales departments, suppliers, engineers, and other team members throughout the product development and implementation process. Test and verify hardware and support peripherals to ensure that they meet specifications and requirements, analyzing and recording test data. Monitor functioning of equipment and make necessary modifications to ensure system operates in conformance with specifications. Analyze information to determine, recommend, and plan layout, including type of computers and peripheral equipment modifications. Build, test, and modify product prototypes, using working models or theoretical models constructed using computer simulation. Analyze user needs and recommend appropriate hardware. Direct technicians, engineering designers, or other technical support personnel as needed. Confer with engineering staff and consult specifications to evaluate interface between hardware and software and operational

C

and performance requirements of overall system. Select hardware and material, assuring compliance with specifications and product requirements. Store, retrieve, and manipulate data for analysis of system capabilities and requirements. Write detailed functional specifications that document the hardware development process and support hardware introduction. Specify power supply requirements and configuration, drawing on system performance expectations and design specifications. Provide training and support to system designers and users. Assemble and modify existing pieces of equipment to meet special needs. Evaluate factors such as reporting formats required, cost constraints, and need for security restrictions to determine hardware configuration.

Other Considerations for Income: As a group, engineers earn some of the highest average starting salaries among those holding bachelor's degrees. Computer Hardware Engineers are among the better-paid of the various kinds of engineers. According to a 2007 survey by the National Association of Colleges and Employers, average starting salaries for Computer Engineers (both hardware and software) were $56,201 with a bachelor's, $60,000 with a master's, and $92,500 with a Ph.D.

Personality Type: Investigative-Realistic-Conventional. **Career Clusters:** 11 Information Technology; 15 Science, Technology, Engineering, and Mathematics. **Career Pathways:** 11.4 Programming and Software Development; 15.1 Engineering and Technology. **Skills:** Programming; Operations Analysis; Systems Analysis; Systems Evaluation; Troubleshooting; Technology Design; Science; Quality Control Analysis.

Education and Training Programs: Computer Engineering, General; Computer Hardware Engineering. **Related Knowledge/Courses:** Computers and Electronics; Engineering and Technology; Telecommunications; Design; Physics; Communications and Media.

Computer Programmers

- ❋ Annual Earnings: $69,620
- ❋ Beginning Wage: $40,080
- ❋ Earnings Growth Potential: High (42.4%)
- ❋ Growth: –4.1%
- ❋ Annual Job Openings: 27,937
- ❋ Self-Employed: 3.9%
- ❋ Part-Time: 4.7%
- ❋ Job Security: More secure than most
- ❋ Education/Training Required: Bachelor's degree

Industries in Which Income Is Highest

Industry	Average Annual Earnings	Number Employed
Securities, Commodity Contracts, and Other Financial Investments and Related Activities	$81,430	5,260
Computer and Electronic Product Manufacturing	$81,140	7,150
Publishing Industries (Except Internet)	$78,780	21,550
Merchant Wholesalers, Durable Goods	$78,240	15,530
Chemical Manufacturing	$77,210	2,340

Metropolitan Areas Where Income Is Highest

Metropolitan Area	Average Annual Earnings	Number Employed
Fayetteville, NC	$112,500	220
San Jose–Sunnyvale–Santa Clara, CA	$99,810	5,840
Rochester, MN	$97,030	480
Vallejo-Fairfield, CA	$92,120	70
Seattle-Tacoma-Bellevue, WA	$88,430	9,410

Convert project specifications and statements of problems and procedures to detailed logical flow charts for coding into computer language. Develop and write computer programs to store, locate, and retrieve specific documents, data, and information. May program Web sites. Correct errors by making appropriate changes and rechecking the program to ensure that the desired results are produced. Conduct trial runs of programs and software applications to be sure that they will produce the desired information and that the instructions are correct. Compile and write documentation of program development and subsequent revisions, inserting comments in the coded instructions so others can understand the program. Write, update, and maintain computer programs or software packages to handle specific jobs such as tracking inventory, storing or retrieving data, or controlling other equipment. Consult with managerial, engineering, and technical personnel to clarify program intent, identify problems, and suggest changes. Perform or direct revision, repair, or expansion of existing programs to increase operating efficiency or adapt to new requirements. Write, analyze, review, and rewrite programs, using workflow chart and diagram and applying knowledge of computer capabilities, subject matter, and symbolic logic. Write or contribute to instructions or manuals to guide end users. Investigate whether networks, workstations, the central processing unit of the system, or peripheral equipment are responding to a program's instructions. Prepare detailed workflow charts and diagrams that describe input, output, and logical operation and convert them into a series of instructions coded in a computer language. Perform systems analysis and programming tasks to maintain and control the use of computer systems software as a systems programmer. Consult with and assist computer operators or system analysts to define and resolve problems in running computer programs. Assign, coordinate, and review work and activities of programming personnel. Collaborate with computer manufacturers and other users to develop new programming methods. Train subordinates in programming and program coding.

Other Considerations for Income: According to the National Association of Colleges and Employers, starting salary offers for computer programmers averaged $49,928 per year in 2007.

Personality Type: Investigative-Conventional. **Career Cluster:** 11 Information Technology. **Career Pathways:** 11.1 Network Systems; 11.3 Interactive Media; 11.4 Programming and Software Development. **Skills:** Programming; Operations Analysis; Technology Design; Systems Analysis; Troubleshooting; Installation; Complex Problem Solving; Systems Evaluation.

Education and Training Programs: Artificial Intelligence; Bioinformatics; Computer Graphics; Computer Programming, Specific Applications; Computer Programming, Vendor/Product Certification; Computer Programming/Programmer, General; E-Commerce/Electronic Commerce; Management Information Systems, General; Medical Informatics; Medical Office Computer Specialist/

Assistant Training; Web Page, Digital/Multimedia and Information Resources Design; Web/Multimedia Management and Webmaster. **Related Knowledge/Courses:** Computers and Electronics; Mathematics; Design; Administration and Management; English Language; Communications and Media.

Computer Science Teachers, Postsecondary

- ❋ Annual Earnings: $66,440
- ❋ Beginning Wage: $35,320
- ❋ Earnings Growth Potential: High (46.8%)
- ❋ Growth: 22.9%
- ❋ Annual Job Openings: 5,820
- ❋ Self-Employed: 0.4%
- ❋ Part-Time: 27.8%
- ❋ Job Security: Most secure
- ❋ Education/Training Required: Doctoral degree

Industries in Which Income Is Highest

Industry	Average Annual Earnings	Number Employed
Educational Services	$66,660	32,280

Metropolitan Areas Where Income Is Highest

Metropolitan Area	Average Annual Earnings	Number Employed
Lubbock, TX	$117,320	60
Sioux Falls, SD	$106,360	60
Madison, WI	$99,820	100
Portland-Vancouver-Beaverton, OR-WA	$98,910	180
Providence–Fall River–Warwick, RI-MA	$96,870	110

Teach courses in computer science. May specialize in a field of computer science, such as the design and function of computers or operations and research analysis. Evaluate and grade students' classwork, laboratory work, assignments, and papers. Maintain student attendance records, grades, and other required records. Prepare and deliver lectures to undergraduate and/or graduate students on topics such as programming, data structures, and software design. Prepare course materials such as syllabi, homework assignments, and handouts. Compile, administer, and grade examinations or assign this work to others. Keep abreast of developments in their field by reading current literature, talking with colleagues, and participating in professional conferences. Initiate, facilitate, and moderate classroom discussions. Plan, evaluate, and revise curricula, course content, and course materials and methods of instruction. Supervise students' laboratory work. Maintain regularly scheduled office hours to advise and assist students. Select and obtain materials and supplies such as textbooks and laboratory equipment. Advise students on academic and vocational curricula and on career issues. Participate in student recruitment, registration, and placement activities. Collaborate with colleagues to address teaching and research issues. Serve on academic or administrative committees that deal with institutional policies, departmental matters, and academic issues. Act as advisers to student organizations. Supervise undergraduate and/or graduate teaching, internship, and research work. Perform administrative duties such as serving as department head. Conduct research in a particular field of knowledge and publish findings in professional journals, books, and/or electronic media. Direct research of other teachers or of graduate students working for advanced academic degrees. Provide professional consulting services to government and/or industry. Participate in campus and community events. Compile bibliographies of specialized materials for outside reading assignments. Write grant proposals to procure external research funding.

Other Considerations for Income: Earnings for college faculty vary according to rank and type of institution, geographic area, and field. According to a 2006–2007 survey by the American Association of University Professors, salaries for full-time faculty averaged $73,207. By rank, the average was $98,974 for professors, $69,911 for associate professors, $58,662 for assistant professors, $42,609 for instructors, and $48,289 for lecturers. Faculty in 4-year institutions earn higher salaries, on average, than do those in 2-year schools. Many faculty members have significant earnings in addition to their base salary from consulting, teaching additional courses, research, writing for publication, or other employment. In addition, many college and university faculty enjoy unique benefits, including access to campus facilities, tuition waivers for dependents, housing and travel allowances, and paid leave for sabbaticals. Part-time faculty and instructors usually have fewer benefits than full-time faculty.

Personality Type: Social-Investigative-Conventional. **Career Cluster:** 11 Information Technology. **Career Pathways:** 11.1 Network Systems; 11.2 Information Support Services; 11.4 Programming and Software Development. **Skills:** Programming; Operations Analysis; Instructing; Technology Design; Mathematics; Science; Learning Strategies; Complex Problem Solving.

Education and Training Programs: Computer and Information Sciences, General; Computer Programming/Programmer, General; Computer Science; Computer Systems Analysis/Analyst; Information Science/Studies. **Related Knowledge/Courses:** Computers and Electronics; Education and Training; Telecommunications; Mathematics; Engineering and Technology; English Language.

Computer Security Specialists

- ❋ Annual Earnings: $66,310
- ❋ Beginning Wage: $41,000
- ❋ Earnings Growth Potential: Medium (38.2%)
- ❋ Growth: 27.0%
- ❋ Annual Job Openings: 37,010
- ❋ Self-Employed: 0.4%
- ❋ Part-Time: 3.1%
- ❋ Job Security: More secure than most
- ❋ Education/Training Required: Bachelor's degree

The Department of Labor reports this information for the occupation Network and Computer Systems Administrators. The job openings listed here are shared with other specializations within that occupation.

Industries in Which Income Is Highest

Industry	Average Annual Earnings	Number Employed
Securities, Commodity Contracts, and Other Financial Investments and Related Activities	$78,300	5,540
Other Information Services	$77,430	2,130
Publishing Industries (Except Internet)	$74,360	9,130
Computer and Electronic Product Manufacturing	$71,770	5,550
Chemical Manufacturing	$71,690	2,170

Metropolitan Areas Where Income Is Highest

Metropolitan Area	Average Annual Earnings	Number Employed
San Jose–Sunnyvale–Santa Clara, CA	$97,520	3,630
Vallejo-Fairfield, CA	$86,920	170
San Francisco–Oakland–Fremont, CA	$85,280	8,060
New York–Northern New Jersey–Long Island, NY-NJ-PA	$80,560	22,440
Bridgeport-Stamford-Norwalk, CT	$80,230	1,260

Plan, coordinate, and implement security measures for information systems to regulate access to computer data files and prevent unauthorized modification, destruction, or disclosure of information. Train users and promote security awareness to ensure system security and to improve server and network efficiency. Develop plans to safeguard computer files against accidental or unauthorized modification, destruction, or disclosure and to meet emergency data processing needs. Confer with users to discuss issues such as computer data access needs, security violations, and programming changes. Monitor current reports of computer viruses to determine when to update virus protection systems. Modify computer security files to incorporate new software, correct errors, or change individual access status. Coordinate implementation of computer system plan with establishment personnel and outside vendors. Monitor use of data files and regulate access to safeguard information in computer files. Perform risk assessments and execute tests of data-processing system to ensure functioning of data-processing activities and security measures. Encrypt data transmissions and erect firewalls to conceal confidential information as it is being transmitted and to keep out tainted digital transfers. Document computer security and emergency measures policies, procedures, and tests. Review violations of computer security procedures and discuss procedures with violators to ensure violations are not repeated. Maintain permanent fleet cryptologic and carry-on direct support systems required in special land, sea surface, and subsurface operations.

Other Considerations for Income: No additional information.

Personality Type: Conventional-Investigative-Realistic. **Career Cluster:** 11 Information Technology. **Career Pathway:** 11.4 Programming and Software Development. **Skills:** Systems Evaluation; Systems Analysis; Operations Analysis; Programming; Installation; Management of Material Resources; Troubleshooting; Management of Financial Resources.

Education and Training Programs: Computer and Information Sciences and Support Services, Other; Computer and Information Sciences, General; Computer and Information Systems Security/Information Assurance; Computer Systems Analysis/Analyst; Computer Systems Networking and Telecommunications; Information Science/Studies; Network and System Administration/Administrator; System, Networking, and LAN/WAN Management/Manager. **Related Knowledge/Courses:** Telecommunications; Computers and Electronics; Engineering and Technology; Education and Training; Design; Public Safety and Security.

Computer Software Engineers, Applications

- ❀ Annual Earnings: $85,430
- ❀ Beginning Wage: $53,720
- ❀ Earnings Growth Potential: Medium (37.1%)
- ❀ Growth: 44.6%
- ❀ Annual Job Openings: 58,690
- ❀ Self-Employed: 2.0%
- ❀ Part-Time: 2.6%
- ❀ Job Security: More secure than most
- ❀ Education/Training Required: Bachelor's degree

Industries in Which Income Is Highest

Industry	Average Annual Earnings	Number Employed
Securities, Commodity Contracts, and Other Financial Investments and Related Activities	$94,410	14,120
Computer and Electronic Product Manufacturing	$92,970	31,560
Merchant Wholesalers, Durable Goods	$91,470	19,610
Other Information Services	$89,980	4,230
Credit Intermediation and Related Activities	$89,890	11,890

Metropolitan Areas Where Income Is Highest

Metropolitan Area	Average Annual Earnings	Number Employed
San Jose–Sunnyvale–Santa Clara, CA	$107,560	17,990
Salinas, CA	$107,440	230
Barnstable Town, MA	$105,030	60
San Francisco–Oakland–Fremont, CA	$100,560	18,360
Poughkeepsie-Newburgh-Middletown, NY	$96,380	490

Develop, create, and modify general computer applications software or specialized utility programs. Analyze user needs and develop software solutions. Design software or customize software for client use with the aim of optimizing operational efficiency. May analyze and design databases within an application area, working individually or coordinating database development as part of a team. Confer with systems analysts, engineers, programmers, and others to design system and to obtain information on project limitations and capabilities, performance requirements, and interfaces. Modify existing software to correct errors, allow it to adapt to new hardware, or improve its performance. Analyze user needs and software requirements to determine feasibility of design within time and cost constraints. Consult with customers about software system design and maintenance. Coordinate software system installation and monitor equipment functioning to ensure specifications are met. Design, develop, and modify software systems, using scientific analysis and mathematical models to predict and measure outcome and consequences of design. Develop and direct software system testing and validation procedures, programming, and documentation. Analyze information to determine, recommend, and plan computer specifications and layouts and peripheral equipment modifications. Supervise the work of programmers, technologists, and technicians and other engineering and scientific personnel. Obtain and evaluate information on factors such as reporting formats required, costs, and security needs to determine hardware configuration. Determine system performance standards. Train users to use new or modified equipment. Store, retrieve, and manipulate data for analysis of system capabilities and requirements. Specify power supply requirements and configuration. Recommend purchase of equipment to control dust, temperature, and humidity in area of system installation.

Other Considerations for Income: According to the National Association of Colleges and Employers, start-

ing salary offers for graduates with a bachelor's degree in computer engineering averaged $56,201 in 2007. Starting salary offers for graduates with a bachelor's degree in computer science averaged $53,396.

Personality Type: Investigative-Realistic-Conventional. **Career Clusters:** 11 Information Technology; 15 Science, Technology, Engineering, and Mathematics. **Career Pathways:** 11.1 Network Systems; 11.2 Information Support Services; 11.3 Interactive Media; 11.4 Programming and Software Development; 15.3 Science and Mathematics. **Skills:** Programming; Troubleshooting; Technology Design; Systems Analysis; Quality Control Analysis; Operations Analysis; Installation; Complex Problem Solving.

Education and Training Programs: Artificial Intelligence; Bioinformatics; Computer Engineering Technologies/Technicians, Other; Computer Engineering, General; Computer Science; Computer Software Engineering; Information Technology; Medical Illustration and Informatics, Other; Medical Informatics. **Related Knowledge/Courses:** Computers and Electronics; Mathematics; Engineering and Technology; Design; English Language.

Computer Software Engineers, Systems Software

- ❋ Annual Earnings: $92,430
- ❋ Beginning Wage: $57,810
- ❋ Earnings Growth Potential: Medium (37.5%)
- ❋ Growth: 28.2%
- ❋ Annual Job Openings: 33,139
- ❋ Self-Employed: 2.1%
- ❋ Part-Time: 2.6%
- ❋ Job Security: More secure than most
- ❋ Education/Training Required: Bachelor's degree

Industries in Which Income Is Highest

Industry	Average Annual Earnings	Number Employed
Other Information Services	$107,240	6,910
Securities, Commodity Contracts, and Other Financial Investments and Related Activities	$98,230	5,380
Computer and Electronic Product Manufacturing	$97,450	53,340
Merchant Wholesalers, Durable Goods	$95,210	18,090
Publishing Industries (Except Internet)	$93,510	26,640

Metropolitan Areas Where Income Is Highest

Metropolitan Area	Average Annual Earnings	Number Employed
San Jose–Sunnyvale–Santa Clara, CA	$114,930	26,400
Rapid City, SD	$111,670	70
Santa Rosa–Petaluma, CA	$108,930	600
Stockton, CA	$105,260	120
Boulder, CO	$104,480	2,720

Research, design, develop, and test operating systems–level software, compilers, and network distribution software for medical, industrial, military, communications, aerospace, business, scientific, and general computing applications. Set operational specifications and formulate and analyze software requirements. Apply principles and techniques of computer science, engineering, and mathematical analysis. Modify existing software to correct errors, to adapt it to new hardware, or to upgrade interfaces and improve performance. Design and develop software systems, using scientific analysis and mathematical models to predict and measure outcome and consequences of design. Consult with engineering staff to evaluate interface between hardware and software, develop specifications and performance requirements, and resolve customer problems. Analyze information to determine, recommend, and plan installation of a new system or modification of an existing system. Develop and direct software system testing and validation procedures. Direct software programming and development of documentation. Consult with customers or other departments on project status, proposals, and technical issues such as software system design and maintenance. Advise customer about, or perform, maintenance of software

system. Coordinate installation of software system. Monitor functioning of equipment to ensure system operates in conformance with specifications. Store, retrieve, and manipulate data for analysis of system capabilities and requirements. Confer with data processing and project managers to obtain information on limitations and capabilities for data-processing projects. Prepare reports and correspondence concerning project specifications, activities, and status. Evaluate factors such as reporting formats required, cost constraints, and need for security restrictions to determine hardware configuration. Supervise and assign work to programmers, designers, technologists and technicians, and other engineering and scientific personnel. Train users to use new or modified equipment. Utilize microcontrollers to develop control signals; implement control algorithms; and measure process variables such as temperatures, pressures, and positions. Recommend purchase of equipment to control dust, temperature, and humidity in area of system installation. Specify power supply requirements and configuration.

Other Considerations for Income: According to the National Association of Colleges and Employers, starting salary offers for graduates with a bachelor's degree in computer engineering averaged $56,201 in 2007. Starting salary offers for graduates with a bachelor's degree in computer science averaged $53,396.

Personality Type: Investigative-Conventional-Realistic. **Career Cluster:** 11 Information Technology. **Career Pathways:** 11.1 Network Systems; 11.2 Information Support Services; 11.3 Interactive Media; 11.4 Programming and Software Development. **Skills:** Programming; Technology Design; Systems Analysis; Troubleshooting; Operations Analysis; Complex Problem Solving; Science; Mathematics.

Education and Training Programs: Artificial Intelligence; Computer Engineering Technologies/Technicians, Other; Computer Engineering, General; Computer Science; Information Science/Studies; Information Technology. **Related Knowledge/Courses:** Computers and Electronics; Engineering and Technology; Design; Telecommunications; Mathematics; Communications and Media.

Computer Specialists, All Other

See *Business Intelligence Analysts; Computer Systems Engineers/Architects; Data Warehousing Specialists; Database Architects; Document Management Spe-*

cialists; Electronic Commerce Specialists; Geographic Information Systems Technicians; Geospatial Information Scientists and Technologists; Information Technology Project Managers; Information Technology Project Managers; Network Designers; Software Quality Assurance Engineers and Testers; Video Game Designers; Web Administrators; and *Web Developers, described separately.*

Computer Systems Analysts

❋ Annual Earnings: $75,500

❋ Beginning Wage: $45,390

❋ Earnings Growth Potential: Medium (39.9%)

❋ Growth: 29.0%

❋ Annual Job Openings: 63,166

❋ Self-Employed: 5.8%

❋ Part-Time: 5.6%

❋ Job Security: More secure than most

❋ Education/Training Required: Bachelor's degree

Industries in Which Income Is Highest

Industry	Average Annual Earnings	Number Employed
Securities, Commodity Contracts, and Other Financial Investments and Related Activities	$87,080	9,010
Computer and Electronic Product Manufacturing	$86,360	12,510
Merchant Wholesalers, Durable Goods	$86,350	23,300
Electrical Equipment, Appliance, and Component Manufacturing	$80,100	1,020
Other Information Services	$79,910	1,280

Metropolitan Areas Where Income Is Highest

Metropolitan Area	Average Annual Earnings	Number Employed
Manchester, NH	$96,100	530
Bridgeport-Stamford-Norwalk, CT	$92,910	1,940
Bloomington-Normal, IL	$90,560	950
Washington-Arlington-Alexandria, DC-VA-MD-WV	$89,870	33,600
Salinas, CA	$89,430	320

Analyze science, engineering, business, and all other data-processing problems for application to electronic data-processing systems. Analyze user requirements, procedures, and problems to automate or improve existing systems and review computer system capabilities, workflow, and scheduling limitations. May analyze or recommend commercially available software. May supervise computer programmers. Provide staff and users with assistance solving computer-related problems, such as malfunctions and program problems. Test, maintain, and monitor computer programs and systems, including coordinating the installation of computer programs and systems. Use object-oriented programming languages as well as client and server applications development processes and multimedia and Internet technology. Confer with clients regarding the nature of the information processing or computation needs a computer program is to address. Coordinate and link the computer systems within an organization to increase compatibility and so information can be shared. Consult with management to ensure agreement on system principles. Expand or modify system to serve new purposes or improve workflow. Interview or survey workers, observe job performance, or perform the job to determine what information is processed and how it is processed. Determine computer software or hardware needed to set up or alter system. Train staff and users to work with computer systems and programs. Analyze information processing or computation needs and plan and design computer systems, using techniques such as structured analysis, data modeling, and information engineering. Assess the usefulness of pre-developed application packages and adapt them to a user environment. Define the goals of the system and devise flow charts and diagrams describing logical operational steps of programs. Develop, document, and revise system design procedures, test procedures, and quality standards. Review and analyze computer printouts and performance indicators to locate code problems; correct errors by correcting code. Recommend new equipment or software packages. Read manuals, periodicals, and technical reports to learn how to develop programs that meet staff and user requirements. Supervise computer programmers or other systems analysts or serve as project leaders for particular systems projects.

Other Considerations for Income: According to the National Association of Colleges and Employers, starting offers for graduates with a bachelor's degree in computer science averaged $53,396 in 2007. Starting offers for graduates with a bachelor's degree in information sciences and systems averaged $50,852. For those with a degree in management information systems/business data processing, starting offers averaged $47,648.

Personality Type: Investigative-Conventional-Realistic. **Career Cluster:** 11 Information Technology. **Career Pathways:** 11.2 Information Support Services; 11.3 Interactive Media; 11.4 Programming and Software Development. **Skills:** Installation; Quality Control Analysis; Technology Design; Programming; Systems Analysis; Troubleshooting; Operations Analysis; Systems Evaluation.

Education and Training Programs: Computer and Information Sciences, General; Computer Systems Analysis/Analyst; Information Technology; Web/Multimedia Management and Webmaster. **Related Knowledge/Courses:** Computers and Electronics; Engineering and Technology; Mathematics; Telecommunications; Clerical; English Language.

Computer Systems Engineers/ Architects

⚜ Annual Earnings: $75,150
⚜ Beginning Wage: $40,660
⚜ Earnings Growth Potential: High (45.9%)
⚜ Growth: 15.1%
⚜ Annual Job Openings: 14,374
⚜ Self-Employed: 6.6%
⚜ Part-Time: 5.6%
⚜ Job Security: More secure than most
⚜ Education/Training Required: Bachelor's degree

The Department of Labor reports this information for the occupation Computer Specialists, All Other. The job openings listed here are shared with other specializations within

that occupation, including Business Intelligence Analysts; Data Warehousing Specialists; Database Architects; Document Management Specialists; Electronic Commerce Specialists; Geographic Information Systems Technicians; Geospatial Information Scientists and Technologists; Information Technology Project Managers; Network Designers; Software Quality Assurance Engineers and Testers; Video Game Designers; Web Administrators; and Web Developers.

Industries in Which Income Is Highest

Industry	Average Annual Earnings	Number Employed
Petroleum and Coal Products Manufacturing	$97,090	1,070
Transportation Equipment Manufacturing	$82,770	3,010
Oil and Gas Extraction	$81,350	1,710
Federal, State, and Local Government	$80,670	71,650
Management of Companies and Enterprises	$78,200	14,820

Metropolitan Areas Where Income Is Highest

Metropolitan Area	Average Annual Earnings	Number Employed
Washington-Arlington-Alexandria, DC-VA-MD-WV	$97,170	19,470
Atlantic City, NJ	$96,600	510
Pascagoula, MS	$95,430	60
San Jose–Sunnyvale–Santa Clara, CA	$92,710	3,580
Baltimore-Towson, MD	$89,730	5,650

Design and develop solutions to complex applications problems, system administration issues, or network concerns. Perform systems management and integration functions. Communicate with staff or clients to understand specific system requirements. Provide advice on project costs, design concepts, or design changes. Document design specifications, installation instructions, and other system-related information. Verify stability, interoperability, portability, security, or scalability of system architecture. Collaborate with engineers or software developers to select appropriate design solutions or ensure the compatibility of system components. Provide technical guidance or support for the development or troubleshooting of systems. Evaluate current or emerging technologies to consider factors such as cost, portability, compatibility, or usability. Identify system data, hardware, or software components required to meet user needs. Provide guidelines for implementing secure systems to customers or installation teams. Monitor system operation to detect potential problems. Direct the analysis, development, and operation of complete computer systems. Investigate system component suitability for specified purposes and make recommendations regarding component use. Perform ongoing hardware and software maintenance operations, including installing or upgrading hardware or software. Develop or approve project plans, schedules, or budgets. Configure servers to meet functional specifications. Design and conduct hardware or software tests. Define and analyze objectives, scope, issues, or organizational impact of information systems. Develop system engineering, software engineering, system integration, or distributed system architectures. Establish functional or system standards to ensure that operational requirements, quality requirements, and design constraints are addressed. Evaluate existing systems to determine effectiveness and suggest changes to meet organizational requirements. Research, test, or verify proper functioning of software patches and fixes. Communicate project information through presentations, technical reports, or white papers.

Other Considerations for Income: According to the National Association of Colleges and Employers, starting salary offers for graduates with a bachelor's degree in computer engineering averaged $56,201 in 2007. Starting salary offers for graduates with a bachelor's degree in computer science averaged $53,396.

Personality Type: Investigative-Realistic-Conventional. **Career Cluster:** 11 Information Technology. **Career Pathway:** 11.4 Programming and Software Development. **Skills:** Programming; Systems Evaluation; Technology Design; Systems Analysis; Troubleshooting; Operations Analysis; Installation; Science.

Education and Training Programs: Computer and Information Sciences and Support Services, Other; Computer and Information Sciences, General; Computer Engineering Technologies/Technicians, Other; Computer Engineering, General; Computer Science; Computer Software Engineering; Computer Systems Networking and Telecommunications; E-Commerce/Electronic Commerce; Information Science/Studies; Information Technology; System, Networking, and LAN/WAN Management/Manager; Web Page, Digital/Multimedia and Information Resources Design; others. **Related Knowledge/Courses:** Computers and Electronics; Engineering and Technology; Telecommunications; Design; Mathematics; Sales and Marketing.

Conservation Scientists

See *Park Naturalists; Range Managers; and Soil and Water Conservationists, described separately.*

Construction and Building Inspectors

* Annual Earnings: $50,180
* Beginning Wage: $31,270
* Earnings Growth Potential: Medium (37.7%)
* Growth: 18.2%
* Annual Job Openings: 12,606
* Self-Employed: 9.4%
* Part-Time: 4.6%
* Job Security: More secure than most
* Education/Training Required: Work experience in a related occupation

Industries in Which Income Is Highest

Industry	Average Annual Earnings	Number Employed
Construction of Buildings	$57,620	2,430
Heavy and Civil Engineering Construction	$51,930	1,370
Federal, State, and Local Government	$50,320	54,710
Professional, Scientific, and Technical Services	$49,600	31,040
Administrative and Support Services	$45,710	1,090

Metropolitan Areas Where Income Is Highest

Metropolitan Area	Average Annual Earnings	Number Employed
San Jose–Sunnyvale–Santa Clara, CA	$80,060	510
Anchorage, AK	$74,790	120
Los Angeles–Long Beach–Santa Ana, CA	$74,410	4,070
San Francisco–Oakland–Fremont, CA	$72,960	1,190
Salinas, CA	$70,000	70

Inspect structures using engineering skills to determine structural soundness and compliance with specifications, building codes, and other regulations. Inspections may be general in nature or may be limited to a specific area, such as electrical systems or plumbing. Issue violation notices and stop-work orders, conferring with owners, violators, and authorities to explain regulations and recommend rectifications. Inspect bridges, dams, highways, buildings, wiring, plumbing, electrical circuits, sewers, heating systems, and foundations during and after construction for structural quality, general safety, and conformance to specifications and codes. Approve and sign plans that meet required specifications. Review and interpret plans, blueprints, site layouts, specifications, and construction methods to ensure compliance to legal requirements and safety regulations. Monitor installation of plumbing, wiring, equipment, and appliances to ensure that installation is performed properly and is in compliance with applicable regulations. Inspect and monitor construction sites to ensure adherence to safety standards, building codes, and specifications. Measure dimensions and verify level, alignment, and elevation of structures and fixtures to ensure compliance to building plans and codes. Maintain daily logs and supplement inspection records with photographs. Use survey instruments, metering devices, tape measures, and test equipment such as concrete strength measurers to perform inspections. Train, direct, and supervise other construction inspectors. Issue permits for construction, relocation, demolition, and occupancy. Examine lifting and conveying devices such as elevators, escalators, moving sidewalks, lifts and hoists, inclined railways, ski lifts, and amusement rides to ensure safety and proper functioning. Compute estimates of work completed or of needed renovations or upgrades and approve payment for contractors. Evaluate premises for cleanliness, including proper garbage disposal and lack of vermin infestation.

Other Considerations for Income: Building inspectors, including plan examiners, generally earn the highest salaries. Salaries in large metropolitan areas are substantially higher than those in small jurisdictions. Benefits vary by place of employment. Those working for the government and private companies typically receive standard benefits, including health and medical insurance, a retirement plan, and paid annual leave. Those who are self-employed may have to provide their own benefits. More than a quarter of all construction and building inspectors belonged to a union in 2006.

Personality Type: Realistic-Conventional-Investigative. **Career Cluster:** 02 Architecture and Construction. **Career Pathway:** 02.2 Construction. **Skills:** Systems Analysis; Systems Evaluation; Quality Control Analysis; Operation Monitoring.

Education and Training Program: Building/Home/Construction Inspection/Inspector. **Related Knowledge/Courses:** Building and Construction; Engineering and Technology; Design; Physics; Public Safety and Security; Mechanical.

Construction Managers

* Annual Earnings: $79,860
* Beginning Wage: $47,000
* Earnings Growth Potential: High (41.1%)
* Growth: 15.7%
* Annual Job Openings: 44,158
* Self-Employed: 56.3%
* Part-Time: 4.9%
* Job Security: Least secure
* Education/Training Required: Bachelor's degree

Industries in Which Income Is Highest

Industry	Average Annual Earnings	Number Employed
Real Estate	$89,660	4,850
Management of Companies and Enterprises	$88,570	3,000
Administrative and Support Services	$87,090	2,070
Professional, Scientific, and Technical Services	$85,430	12,130
Heavy and Civil Engineering Construction	$82,920	24,160

Metropolitan Areas Where Income Is Highest

Metropolitan Area	Average Annual Earnings	Number Employed
Port St. Lucie–Fort Pierce, FL	$120,630	190
Poughkeepsie-Newburgh-Middletown, NY	$119,840	410
Napa, CA	$118,110	150
Salinas, CA	$117,300	150
New York–Northern New Jersey– Long Island, NY-NJ-PA	$117,150	14,380

Plan, direct, coordinate, or budget, usually through subordinate supervisory personnel, activities concerned with the construction and maintenance of structures, facilities, and systems. Participate in the conceptual development of a construction project and oversee its organization, scheduling, and implementation. Schedule the project in logical steps and budget time required to meet deadlines. Confer with supervisory personnel, owners, contractors, and design professionals to discuss and resolve matters such as work procedures, complaints, and construction problems. Prepare contracts and negotiate revisions, changes, and additions to contractual agreements with architects, consultants, clients, suppliers, and subcontractors. Prepare and submit budget estimates and progress and cost tracking reports. Interpret and explain plans and contract terms to administrative staff, workers, and clients, representing the owner or developer. Plan, organize, and direct activities concerned with the construction and maintenance of structures, facilities, and systems. Take actions to deal with the results of delays, bad weather, or emergencies at construction sites. Inspect and review projects to monitor compliance with building and safety codes and other regulations. Study job specifications to determine appropriate construction methods. Select, contract, and oversee workers who complete specific pieces of the project, such as painting or plumbing. Obtain all necessary permits and licenses. Direct and supervise workers. Develop and implement quality control programs. Investigate damage, accidents, or delays at construction sites to ensure that proper procedures are being carried out. Determine labor requirements and dispatch workers to construction sites. Evaluate construction methods and determine cost-effectiveness of plans, using computers. Requisition supplies and materials to complete construction projects. Direct acquisition of land for construction projects.

Other Considerations for Income: Earnings of salaried construction managers and self-employed independent construction contractors vary depending upon the size and nature of the construction project, its geographic location, and economic conditions. In addition to typical benefits, many salaried construction managers receive bonuses and use of company motor vehicles.

Personality Type: Enterprising-Realistic-Conventional. **Career Clusters:** 02 Architecture and Construction; 04 Business, Management, and Administration. **Career Pathways:** 02.2 Construction; 04.1 Management. **Skills:** Management of Financial Resources; Management of Material Resources; Management of Personnel Resources; Systems Analysis; Systems Evaluation; Negotiation; Operation Monitoring; Persuasion.

Education and Training Programs: Business Administration and Management, General; Business/Commerce, General; Construction Engineering Technology/Technician; Operations Management and Supervision. **Related Knowledge/Courses:** Building and Construction; Design; Engineering and Technology; Mechanical; Administration and Management; Personnel and Human Resources.

Copy Writers

* Annual Earnings: $53,070
* Beginning Wage: $28,020
* Earnings Growth Potential: High (47.2%)
* Growth: 12.8%
* Annual Job Openings: 24,023
* Self-Employed: 65.9%
* Part-Time: 21.8%
* Job Security: More secure than most
* Education/Training Required: Bachelor's degree

The Department of Labor reports this information for the occupation Writers and Authors. The job openings listed here are shared with other specializations within that occupation, including Poets, Lyricists, and Creative Writers.

Industries in Which Income Is Highest

Industry	Average Annual Earnings	Number Employed
Motion Picture and Sound Recording Industries	$69,400	2,500
Federal, State, and Local Government	$65,970	1,850
Professional, Scientific, and Technical Services	$60,130	11,050
Performing Arts, Spectator Sports, and Related Industries	$59,720	2,690
Management of Companies and Enterprises	$53,600	1,190

Metropolitan Areas Where Income Is Highest

Metropolitan Area	Average Annual Earnings	Number Employed
San Diego–Carlsbad–San Marcos, CA	$78,930	510
Los Angeles–Long Beach–Santa Ana, CA	$75,530	4,040
Washington-Arlington-Alexandria, DC-VA-MD-WV	$70,740	2,700
San Jose–Sunnyvale–Santa Clara, CA	$66,490	260
New York–Northern New Jersey–Long Island, NY-NJ-PA	$65,580	6,110

Write advertising copy for use by publication or broadcast media to promote sale of goods and services. Write advertising copy for use by publication, broadcast, or Internet media to promote the sale of goods and services. Present drafts and ideas to clients. Discuss the product, advertising themes and methods, and any changes that should be made in advertising copy with the client. Consult with sales, media, and marketing representatives to obtain information on product or service and discuss style and length of advertising copy. Vary language and tone of messages based on product and medium. Edit or rewrite existing copy as necessary and submit copy for approval by supervisor. Write to customers in their terms and on their level so that the advertiser's sales message is more readily received. Write articles; bulletins; sales letters; speeches; and other related informative, marketing, and promotional material. Invent names for products and write the slogans that appear on packaging, brochures, and other promotional material. Review advertising trends, consumer surveys, and other data regarding marketing of goods and services to determine the best way to promote products. Develop advertising campaigns for a wide range of clients, working with an advertising agency's creative director and art director to determine the best way to present advertising information. Conduct research and interviews to determine which of a product's selling features should be promoted.

Other Considerations for Income: No additional information.

Personality Type: Enterprising-Artistic. **Career Cluster:** 03 Arts, Audio/Video Technology, and Communications. **Career Pathway:** 03.5 Journalism and Broadcasting. **Skills:** Persuasion; Technology Design; Equipment Selection; Quality Control Analysis; Time Management; Writing; Active Listening; Negotiation.

Education and Training Programs: Broadcast Journalism; Business/Corporate Communications; Communication, Journalism, and Related Programs, Other; Family and Consumer Sciences/Human Sciences Communication; Journalism; Mass Communication/Media Studies; Playwriting and Screenwriting; Speech Communication and Rhetoric. **Related Knowledge/Courses:** Sales and Marketing; Communications and Media; English Language; Computers and Electronics; Clerical; Administration and Management.

Coroners

- ❀ Annual Earnings: $48,890
- ❀ Beginning Wage: $29,490
- ❀ Earnings Growth Potential: Medium (39.7%)
- ❀ Growth: 4.9%
- ❀ Annual Job Openings: 15,841
- ❀ Self-Employed: 0.4%
- ❀ Part-Time: 5.0%
- ❀ Job Security: More secure than most
- ❀ Education/Training Required: Work experience in a related occupation

The Department of Labor reports this information for the occupation Compliance Officers, Except Agriculture, Construction, Health and Safety, and Transportation. The job openings listed here are shared with other specializations within that occupation, including Environmental Compliance Inspectors; Equal Opportunity Representatives and Officers; Government Property Inspectors and Investigators; Licensing Examiners and Inspectors; and Regulatory Affairs Specialists.

Industries in Which Income Is Highest

Industry	Average Annual Earnings	Number Employed
Postal Service	$77,500	1,970
Utilities	$74,890	1,880
Securities, Commodity Contracts, and Other Financial Investments and Related Activities	$70,720	6,480
Telecommunications	$64,400	2,560
Chemical Manufacturing	$61,920	3,910

Metropolitan Areas Where Income Is Highest

Metropolitan Area	Average Annual Earnings	Number Employed
Brunswick, GA	$83,080	500
Bridgeport-Stamford-Norwalk, CT	$73,120	640
Warner Robins, GA	$69,670	80
San Francisco–Oakland–Fremont, CA	$67,520	4,370
Hartford–West Hartford–East Hartford, CT	$67,460	1,420

Direct activities such as autopsies, pathological and toxicological analyses, and inquests relating to the investigation of deaths occurring within a legal jurisdiction to determine cause of death or to fix responsibility for accidental, violent, or unexplained deaths. Perform medico-legal examinations and autopsies, conducting preliminary examinations of the body in order to identify victims, to locate signs of trauma, and to identify factors that would indicate time of death. Inquire into the cause, manner, and circumstances of human deaths and establish the identities of deceased persons. Direct activities of workers who conduct autopsies, perform pathological and toxicological analyses, and prepare documents for permanent records. Complete death certificates, including the assignment of a cause and manner of death. Observe and record the positions and conditions of bodies and of related evidence. Collect and document any pertinent medical history information. Observe, record, and preserve any objects or personal property related to deaths, including objects such as medication containers and suicide notes. Complete reports and forms required to finalize cases. Remove or supervise removal of bodies from death scenes, using the proper equipment and supplies, and arrange for transportation to morgues. Testify at inquests, hearings, and court trials. Interview persons present at death scenes to obtain information useful in determining the manner of death. Provide information concerning the circumstances of death to relatives of the deceased. Locate and document information regarding the next of kin, including their relationship to the deceased and the status of notification attempts. Confer with officials of public health and law enforcement agencies in order to coordinate interdepartmental activities. Inventory personal effects, such as jewelry or wallets, that are recovered from bodies. Coordinate the release of personal effects to authorized persons and facilitate the disposition of unclaimed corpses and personal effects. Arrange for the next of kin to be notified of deaths. Record the disposition of minor children, as well as details of arrangements made for their care.

Other Considerations for Income: Earnings vary widely and depend partly on the work load, which in turn may depend on the local crime rate.

Personality Type: Investigative-Realistic-Conventional. **Career Cluster:** 12 Law, Public Safety, Corrections, and Security. **Career Pathway:** 12.6 Inspection Services. **Skills:** Science; Management of Financial Resources; Reading Comprehension; Critical Thinking; Management of Personnel Resources; Speaking; Management of Material Resources; Writing.

Education and Training Program: Public Administration. **Related Knowledge/Courses:** Medicine and Dentistry; Biology; Psychology; Therapy and Counseling; Chemistry; Law and Government.

Cost Estimators

- ❋ Annual Earnings: $56,510
- ❋ Beginning Wage: $33,150
- ❋ Earnings Growth Potential: High (41.3%)
- ❋ Growth: 18.5%
- ❋ Annual Job Openings: 38,379
- ❋ Self-Employed: 1.1%
- ❋ Part-Time: 5.8%
- ❋ Job Security: Less secure than most
- ❋ Education/Training Required: Bachelor's degree

Industries in Which Income Is Highest

Industry	Average Annual Earnings	Number Employed
Utilities	$72,130	1,180
Transportation Equipment Manufacturing	$66,050	2,680
Professional, Scientific, and Technical Services	$63,320	9,070
Heavy and Civil Engineering Construction	$63,160	12,070
Management of Companies and Enterprises	$62,250	2,590

Metropolitan Areas Where Income Is Highest

Metropolitan Area	Average Annual Earnings	Number Employed
San Francisco–Oakland–Fremont, CA	$78,290	3,870
Bridgeport-Stamford-Norwalk, CT	$75,910	460
Napa, CA	$75,760	120
Santa Rosa–Petaluma, CA	$74,200	560
Atlantic City, NJ	$72,910	180

Prepare cost estimates for product manufacturing, construction projects, or services to aid management in bidding on or determining prices of products or services. May specialize according to particular service performed or type of product manufactured. Consult with clients, vendors, personnel in other departments, or construction foremen to discuss and formulate estimates and resolve issues. Analyze blueprints and other documentation to prepare time, cost, materials, and labor estimates. Prepare estimates for use in selecting vendors or subcontractors. Confer with engineers, architects, owners, contractors, and subcontractors on changes and adjustments to cost estimates. Prepare estimates used by management for purposes such as planning, organizing, and scheduling work. Prepare cost and expenditure statements and other necessary documentation at regular intervals for the duration of the project. Assess cost-effectiveness of products, projects, or services, tracking actual costs relative to bids as projects develop. Set up cost-monitoring and cost-reporting systems and procedures. Conduct special studies to develop and establish standard hour and related cost data or to effect cost reductions. Review material and labor requirements to decide whether it is more cost-effective to produce or purchase components. Prepare and maintain a directory of suppliers, contractors, and subcontractors.

Establish and maintain tendering processes and conduct negotiations. Visit sites and record information about access, drainage and topography, and availability of services such as water and electricity.

Other Considerations for Income: Salaries of cost estimators vary widely by experience, education, size of firm, and industry. According to a July 2007 salary survey by the National Association of Colleges and Employers, those with bachelor's degrees in construction science/management received job offers averaging $46,930 a year.

Personality Type: Conventional-Enterprising. **Career Clusters:** 02 Architecture and Construction; 04 Business, Management, and Administration; 13 Manufacturing; 15 Science, Technology, Engineering, and Mathematics. **Career Pathways:** 02.2 Construction; 04.1 Management; 13.1 Production; 15.1 Engineering and Technology. **Skills:** Management of Financial Resources; Systems Analysis; Management of Material Resources; Mathematics; Systems Evaluation; Persuasion; Complex Problem Solving; Negotiation.

Education and Training Programs: Business Administration and Management, General; Business/Commerce, General; Construction Engineering; Construction Engineering Technology/Technician; Manufacturing Engineering; Materials Engineering; Mechanical Engineering. **Related Knowledge/Courses:** Engineering and Technology; Mathematics; Economics and Accounting; Building and Construction; Design; Computers and Electronics.

Counseling Psychologists

- ❊ Annual Earnings: $64,140
- ❊ Beginning Wage: $37,900
- ❊ Earnings Growth Potential: High (40.9%)
- ❊ Growth: 15.8%
- ❊ Annual Job Openings: 8,309
- ❊ Self-Employed: 34.2%
- ❊ Part-Time: 24.0%
- ❊ Job Security: Most secure
- ❊ Education/Training Required: Doctoral degree

The Department of Labor reports this information for the occupation Clinical, Counseling, and School Psychologists. The job openings listed here are shared with other specializations within that occupation, including Clinical Psychologists; and School Psychologists.

Industries in Which Income Is Highest

Industry	Average Annual Earnings	Number Employed
Administrative and Support Services	$72,400	1,140
Hospitals	$70,240	9,210
Professional, Scientific, and Technical Services	$70,010	1,020
Ambulatory Health Care Services	$65,810	19,180
Educational Services	$64,410	46,390

Metropolitan Areas Where Income Is Highest

Metropolitan Area	Average Annual Earnings	Number Employed
Vallejo-Fairfield, CA	$92,560	210
Dayton, OH	$91,750	210
Visalia-Porterville, CA	$90,930	80
Trenton-Ewing, NJ	$89,310	270
Stockton, CA	$87,780	130

Assess and evaluate individuals' problems through the use of case history, interview, and observation and provide individual or group counseling services to assist individuals in achieving more effective personal, social, educational, and vocational development and adjustment. Collect information about individuals or clients, using interviews, case histories, observational techniques, and other assessment methods. Counsel individuals, groups, or families to help them understand problems, define goals, and develop realistic action plans. Develop therapeutic and treatment plans based on clients' interests, abilities, and needs. Consult with other professionals to discuss therapies, treatments, counseling resources, or techniques and to share occupational information. Analyze data such as interview notes, test results, and reference manuals in order to identify symptoms and to diagnose the nature of clients' problems. Advise clients on how they could be helped by counseling. Evaluate the results of counseling methods to determine the reliability and validity of treatments. Provide consulting services to schools, social service agencies, and businesses. Refer clients to specialists or to other institutions for non-counseling treatment of problems. Select, administer, and interpret psychological tests to assess intelligence, aptitudes, abilities, or interests. Conduct research to develop or improve diagnostic or therapeutic counseling techniques.

Other Considerations for Income: Earnings of Clinical, Counseling, and School Psychologists tend to be lower than those of Industrial-Organizational Psychologists.

Personality Type: Social-Investigative-Artistic. **Career Clusters:** 08 Health Science; 10 Human Service. **Career Pathways:** 08.1 Therapeutic Services; 10.2 Counseling and Mental Health Services. **Skills:** Social Perceptiveness; Active Listening; Persuasion; Service Orientation; Coordination; Monitoring; Negotiation; Learning Strategies.

Education and Training Programs: Psychoanalysis and Psychotherapy; Psychology, General. **Related Knowledge/Courses:** Therapy and Counseling; Philosophy and Theology; Sociology and Anthropology; Psychology; English Language; Customer and Personal Service.

Court Reporters

- ❇ Annual Earnings: $49,710
- ❇ Beginning Wage: $25,360
- ❇ Earnings Growth Potential: High (49.0%)
- ❇ Growth: 24.5%
- ❇ Annual Job Openings: 2,620
- ❇ Self-Employed: 7.9%
- ❇ Part-Time: 13.6%
- ❇ Job Security: Most secure
- ❇ Education/Training Required: Postsecondary vocational training

Industries in Which Income Is Highest

Industry	Average Annual Earnings	Number Employed
Federal, State, and Local Government	$53,280	11,030
Administrative and Support Services	$44,770	6,580

Metropolitan Areas Where Income Is Highest

Metropolitan Area	Average Annual Earnings	Number Employed
Portland-Vancouver-Beaverton, OR-WA	$90,490	90
New York–Northern New Jersey–Long Island, NY-NJ-PA	$80,690	1,010
Providence–Fall River–Warwick, RI-MA	$69,560	70
Denver-Aurora, CO	$64,680	300
Sacramento–Arden-Arcade–Roseville, CA	$64,560	210

Use verbatim methods and equipment to capture, store, retrieve, and transcribe pretrial and trial proceedings or other information. Includes stenocaptioners who operate computerized stenographic captioning equipment to provide captions of live or prerecorded broadcasts for hearing-impaired viewers. Take notes in shorthand or use a stenotype or shorthand machine that prints letters on a paper tape. Provide transcripts of proceedings upon request of judges, lawyers, or the public. Record verbatim proceedings of courts, legislative assemblies, committee meetings, and other proceedings, using computerized recording equipment, electronic stenograph machines, or stenomasks. Transcribe recorded proceedings in accordance with established formats. Ask speakers to clarify inaudible statements. File a legible transcript of records of a court case with the court clerk's office. File and store shorthand notes of court session. Respond to requests during court sessions to read portions of the proceedings already recorded. Record depositions and other proceedings for attorneys. Verify accuracy of transcripts by checking copies against original records of proceedings and accuracy of rulings by checking with judges. Record symbols on computer disks or CD-ROM; then translate and display them as text in computer-aided transcription process.

Other Considerations for Income: Compensation and compensation methods for court reporters vary with the type of reporting job, the experience of the individual reporter, the level of certification achieved, and the region of the country. Official court reporters earn a salary and a per-page fee for transcripts. Many salaried court reporters supplement their income by doing freelance work. Freelance court reporters are paid per job and receive a per-page fee for transcripts. Communication Access Real-time Translation providers are paid by the hour. Captioners receive a salary and benefits if they work as employees of a captioning company; captioners working as independent contractors are paid by the hour.

Personality Type: Conventional-Enterprising. **Career Cluster:** 12 Law, Public Safety, Corrections, and Security. **Career Pathway:** 12.5 Legal Services. **Skills:** Reading Comprehension; Active Listening; Equipment Selection; Operation and Control; Equipment Maintenance; Operation Monitoring; Operations Analysis; Installation.

Education and Training Programs: Court Reporting/Court Reporter; Journalism; Mass Communication/Media Studies; Speech Communication and Rhetoric. **Related Knowledge/Courses:** Clerical; English Language; Law and Government; Computers and Electronics; Production and Processing; Customer and Personal Service.

Credit Analysts

- ❋ Annual Earnings: $55,250
- ❋ Beginning Wage: $32,290
- ❋ Earnings Growth Potential: High (41.6%)
- ❋ Growth: 1.9%
- ❋ Annual Job Openings: 3,180
- ❋ Self-Employed: 0.0%
- ❋ Part-Time: 5.3%
- ❋ Job Security: Less secure than most
- ❋ Education/Training Required: Bachelor's degree

Industries in Which Income Is Highest

Industry	Average Annual Earnings	Number Employed
Securities, Commodity Contracts, and Other Financial Investments and Related Activities	$75,150	3,200
Motor Vehicle and Parts Dealers	$69,430	7,020
Professional, Scientific, and Technical Services	$60,340	1,800
Merchant Wholesalers, Durable Goods	$54,120	1,580
Management of Companies and Enterprises	$53,490	6,540

Metropolitan Areas Where Income Is Highest

Metropolitan Area	Average Annual Earnings	Number Employed
Stockton, CA	$87,290	60
New York–Northern New Jersey–Long Island, NY-NJ-PA	$85,850	6,990
San Francisco–Oakland–Fremont, CA	$77,720	1,440
Poughkeepsie-Newburgh-Middletown, NY	$75,480	70
Denver-Aurora, CO	$74,770	760

Analyze current credit data and financial statements of individuals or firms to determine the degree of risk involved in extending credit or lending money. Prepare reports with this credit information for use in decision-making. Evaluate customer records and recommend payment plans based on earnings, savings data, payment history, and purchase activity. Confer with credit association and other business representatives to exchange credit information. Complete loan applications, including credit analyses and summaries of loan requests, and submit to loan committees for approval. Generate financial ratios, using computer programs, to evaluate customers' financial status. Review individual or commercial customer files to identify and select delinquent accounts for collection. Compare liquidity, profitability, and credit histories of establishments being evaluated with those of similar establishments in the same industries and geographic locations. Consult with customers to resolve complaints and verify financial and credit transactions. Analyze financial data such as income growth, quality of management, and market share to determine expected profitability of loans.

Other Considerations for Income: No additional information.

Personality Type: Conventional-Enterprising. **Career Clusters:** 04 Business, Management, and Administration; 06 Finance. **Career Pathways:** 04.2 Business, Financial Management, and Accounting; 06.1 Financial and Investment Planning. **Skills:** Speaking; Writing; Operations Analysis; Active Listening; Negotiation; Judgment and Decision Making; Systems Evaluation; Monitoring.

Education and Training Programs: Accounting; Credit Management; Finance, General. **Related Knowledge/Courses:** Economics and Accounting; Clerical; Mathematics; Law and Government; English Language.

Criminal Investigators and Special Agents

* Annual Earnings: $60,910
* Beginning Wage: $36,500
* Earnings Growth Potential: High (40.1%)
* Growth: 17.3%
* Annual Job Openings: 14,746
* Self-Employed: 0.3%
* Part-Time: 2.2%
* Job Security: Most secure
* Education/Training Required: Work experience in a related occupation

The Department of Labor reports this information for the occupation Detectives and Criminal Investigators. The job openings listed here are shared with other specializations within that occupation, including Immigration and Customs Inspectors; Intelligence Analysts; Police Detectives; and Police Identification and Records Officers.

Industries in Which Income Is Highest

Industry	Average Annual Earnings	Number Employed
Federal, State, and Local Government	$60,780	103,680

Metropolitan Areas Where Income Is Highest

Metropolitan Area	Average Annual Earnings	Number Employed
San Jose–Sunnyvale–Santa Clara, CA	$92,430	310
Washington-Arlington-Alexandria, DC-VA-MD-WV	$88,440	4,590
Springfield, MA-CT	$82,690	60
Brunswick, GA	$80,960	350
New Haven, CT	$79,550	200

Investigate alleged or suspected criminal violations of federal, state, or local laws to determine if evidence is sufficient to recommend prosecution. Record evidence and documents, using equipment such as cameras and photocopy machines. Obtain and verify evidence by interviewing and observing suspects and witnesses or by analyzing records. Examine records to locate links in chains of evidence or information. Prepare reports that detail investigation findings. Determine scope, timing, and direction of investigations. Collaborate with other offices and agencies to exchange information and coordinate activities. Testify before grand juries concerning criminal activity investigations. Analyze evidence in laboratories or in the field. Investigate organized crime, public corruption, financial crime, copyright infringement, civil rights violations, bank robbery, extortion, kidnapping, and other violations of federal or state statutes. Identify case issues and evidence needed, based on analysis of charges, complaints, or allegations of law violations. Obtain and use search and arrest warrants. Serve subpoenas or other official papers. Collaborate with other authorities on activities such as surveillance, transcription, and research. Develop relationships with informants to obtain information related to cases. Search for and collect evidence such as fingerprints, using investigative equipment. Collect and record physical information about arrested suspects, including fingerprints, height and weight measurements, and photographs. Compare crime scene fingerprints with those from suspects or fingerprint files to identify perpetrators, using computers. Administer counter-terrorism and counter-narcotics reward programs. Provide protection for individuals such as government leaders, political candidates, and visiting foreign dignitaries. Perform undercover assignments and maintain surveillance, including monitoring authorized wiretaps. Manage security programs designed to protect personnel, facilities, and information. Issue security clearances.

Other Considerations for Income: Total earnings for local, state, and special police and detectives frequently exceed the stated salary because of payments for overtime, which can be significant. In addition to the common benefits—paid vacation, sick leave, and medical and life insurance—most police and sheriffs' departments provide officers with special allowances for uniforms. Because police officers usually are covered by liberal pension plans, many retire at half pay after 25 or 30 years of service.

Personality Type: Enterprising-Investigative. **Career Cluster:** 12 Law, Public Safety, Corrections, and Security. **Career Pathway:** 12.4 Law Enforcement Services. **Skills:** Negotiation; Operations Analysis; Programming; Judgment and Decision Making; Service Orientation; Complex Problem Solving; Equipment Selection; Persuasion.

Education and Training Programs: Criminal Justice/ Police Science; Criminalistics and Criminal Science.

Related Knowledge/Courses: Law and Government; Psychology; Geography; Public Safety and Security; Clerical; Telecommunications.

Criminal Justice and Law Enforcement Teachers, Postsecondary

❀ Annual Earnings: $53,640
❀ Beginning Wage: $30,430
❀ Earnings Growth Potential: High (43.3%)
❀ Growth: 22.9%
❀ Annual Job Openings: 1,911
❀ Self-Employed: 0.4%
❀ Part-Time: 27.8%
❀ Job Security: Most secure
❀ Education/Training Required: Doctoral degree

Industries in Which Income Is Highest

Industry	Average Annual Earnings	Number Employed
Educational Services	$53,750	11,440

Metropolitan Areas Where Income Is Highest

Metropolitan Area	Average Annual Earnings	Number Employed
San Diego–Carlsbad–San Marcos, CA	$87,700	160
Los Angeles–Long Beach–Santa Ana, CA	$86,170	350
Pittsburgh, PA	$76,350	100
Milwaukee–Waukesha–West Allis, WI	$67,500	100
Philadelphia-Camden-Wilmington, PA-NJ-DE-MD	$65,700	170

Teach courses in criminal justice, corrections, and law enforcement administration. Initiate, facilitate, and moderate classroom discussions. Keep abreast of developments in their field by reading current literature, talking with colleagues, and participating in professional conferences. Evaluate and grade students' classwork, assignments, and papers. Compile, administer, and grade examinations or assign this work to others. Prepare and deliver lectures to undergraduate or graduate students on topics such as criminal law, defensive policing, and investigation techniques. Prepare course materials such as syllabi, homework assignments, and handouts. Conduct research in a particular field of knowledge and publish findings in professional journals, books, and/or electronic media. Plan, evaluate, and revise curricula, course content, and course materials and methods of instruction. Supervise undergraduate and/or graduate teaching, internship, and research work. Maintain student attendance records, grades, and other required records. Select and obtain materials and supplies such as textbooks. Advise students on academic and vocational curricula and on career issues. Maintain regularly scheduled office hours to advise and assist students. Collaborate with colleagues to address teaching and research issues. Write grant proposals to procure external research funding. Serve on academic or administrative committees that deal with institutional policies, departmental matters, and academic issues. Compile bibliographies of specialized materials for outside reading assignments. Participate in student recruitment, registration, and placement activities. Provide professional consulting services to government and/or industry. Perform administrative duties such as serving as department head. Participate in campus and community events. Act as advisers to student organizations.

Other Considerations for Income: Earnings for college faculty vary according to rank and type of institution, geographic area, and field. According to a 2006–2007 survey by the American Association of University Professors, salaries for full-time faculty averaged $73,207. By rank, the average was $98,974 for professors, $69,911 for associate professors, $58,662 for assistant professors, $42,609 for instructors, and $48,289 for lecturers. Faculty in 4-year institutions earn higher salaries, on average, than do those in 2-year schools. Many faculty members have significant earnings in addition to their base salary from consulting, teaching additional courses, research, writing for publication, or other employment. In addition, many college and university faculty enjoy unique benefits, including access to campus facilities, tuition waivers for dependents, housing and travel allowances, and paid leave for sabbaticals. Part-time faculty and instructors usually have fewer benefits than full-time faculty.

Personality Type: Social-Investigative. **Career Clusters:** 05 Education and Training; 12 Law, Public Safety, Corrections, and Security. **Career Pathways:** 05.3 Teaching/Training; 12.1 Correction Services; 12.3 Security and Protective Services; 12.4 Law Enforcement Services. **Skills:** Writing; Critical Thinking; Instructing; Active Learning; Reading Comprehension; Persuasion; Speaking; Science.

Education and Training Programs: Corrections; Corrections Administration; Corrections and Criminal Justice, Other; Criminal Justice/Law Enforcement Administration; Criminal Justice/Police Science; Criminal Justice/Safety Studies; Criminalistics and Criminal Science; Forensic Science and Technology; Juvenile Corrections; Security and Loss Prevention Services; Teacher Education and Professional Development, Specific Subject Areas, Other. **Related Knowledge/Courses:** Sociology and Anthropology; Philosophy and Theology; History and Archeology; Law and Government; English Language; Education and Training.

Critical Care Nurses

❋ Annual Earnings: $62,450
❋ Beginning Wage: $43,410
❋ Earnings Growth Potential: Low (30.5%)
❋ Growth: 23.5%
❋ Annual Job Openings: 233,499
❋ Self-Employed: 0.8%
❋ Part-Time: 21.8%
❋ Job Security: No data available
❋ Education/Training Required: Master's degree

The Department of Labor reports this information for the occupation Registered Nurses. The job openings listed here are shared with other specializations within that occupation, including Acute Care Nurses; and Advanced Practice Psychiatric Nurses.

Industries in Which Income Is Highest

Industry	Average Annual Earnings	Number Employed
Administrative and Support Services	$67,720	98,770
Religious, Grantmaking, Civic, Professional, and Similar Organizations	$64,540	2,030
Federal, State, and Local Government	$64,340	144,990
Merchant Wholesalers, Nondurable Goods	$64,150	1,010
Hospitals	$63,890	1,535,440

Metropolitan Areas Where Income Is Highest

Metropolitan Area	Average Annual Earnings	Number Employed
San Jose–Sunnyvale–Santa Clara, CA	$109,110	14,590
San Francisco–Oakland–Fremont, CA	$97,590	32,780
Modesto, CA	$91,910	3,040
Vallejo-Fairfield, CA	$88,500	3,010
Napa, CA	$88,030	1,430

Provide advanced nursing care for patients in critical or coronary care units. No task data available.

Other Considerations for Income: Many employers offer flexible work schedules, child care, educational benefits, and bonuses.

Personality Type: Social-Investigative-Realistic. **Career Cluster:** 08 Health Science. **Career Pathway:** 08.1 Therapeutic Services. **Skills:** No data available.

Education and Training Program: Critical Care Nursing. **Related Knowledge/Courses:** Medicine and Dentistry; Biology; Psychology; Therapy and Counseling; Sociology and Anthropology; Philosophy and Theology.

Crop and Livestock Managers

- ❋ Annual Earnings: $56,230
- ❋ Beginning Wage: $31,350
- ❋ Earnings Growth Potential: High (44.2%)
- ❋ Growth: 1.1%
- ❋ Annual Job Openings: 18,101
- ❋ Self-Employed: 0.0%
- ❋ Part-Time: 9.3%
- ❋ Job Security: More secure than most
- ❋ Education/Training Required: Work experience plus degree

The Department of Labor reports this information for the occupation Farm, Ranch, and Other Agricultural Managers. The job openings listed here are shared with other specializations within that occupation, including Aquacultural Managers; and Nursery and Greenhouse Managers.

Industries in Which Income Is Highest

Industry	Average Annual Earnings	Number Employed
Management of Companies and Enterprises	$79,060	160
Merchant Wholesalers, Nondurable Goods	$63,250	180
Forestry and Logging	$62,970	40
Federal, State, and Local Government	$62,360	350
Food Manufacturing	$60,360	60

Metropolitan Areas Where Income Is Highest

Metropolitan Area	Average Annual Earnings	Number Employed
Yuma, AZ	$84,050	70
Port St. Lucie–Fort Pierce, FL	$73,340	40
Salinas, CA	$72,050	140
Santa Barbara–Santa Maria, CA	$69,170	40
Visalia-Porterville, CA	$68,110	80

Direct and coordinate, through subordinate supervisory personnel, activities of workers engaged in agricultural crop production for corporations, cooperatives, or other owners. Record information such as production figures, farm management practices, and parent stock data and prepare financial and operational reports. Confer with buyers to arrange for the sale of crops. Contract with farmers or independent owners for raising of crops or for management of crop production. Evaluate financial statements and make budget proposals. Analyze soil to determine types and quantities of fertilizer required for maximum production. Purchase machinery, equipment, and supplies, such as tractors, seed, fertilizer, and chemicals. Analyze market conditions to determine acreage allocations. Direct and coordinate worker activities such as planting, irrigation, chemical application, harvesting, and grading. Inspect orchards and fields to determine maturity dates of crops or to estimate potential crop damage from weather. Hire, discharge, transfer, and promote workers. Enforce applicable safety regulations. Negotiate with bank officials to obtain credit. Plan and direct development and production of hybrid plant varieties with high yields or with disease or insect resistance. Inspect equipment to ensure proper functioning. Determine procedural changes in drying, grading, storage, and shipment processes in order to provide greater efficiency and accuracy. Coordinate growing activities with activities of related departments such as engineering, equipment maintenance, and packing.

Other Considerations for Income: No additional information.

Personality Type: Enterprising-Realistic-Conventional. **Career Cluster:** 01 Agriculture, Food and Natural Resource. **Career Pathways:** 01.1 Food Products and Processing Systems; 01.2 Plant Systems; 01.3 Animal Systems. **Skills:** Management of Financial Resources; Negotiation; Management of Material Resources; Science; Persuasion; Judgment and Decision Making; Mathematics; Management of Personnel Resources.

Education and Training Programs: Agribusiness/Agricultural Business Operations; Agricultural Animal Breeding; Agricultural Business and Management, General; Agricultural Business and Management, Other; Agricultural Production Operations, General; Agricultural Production Operations, Other; Animal Nutrition; Animal/Livestock Husbandry and Production; Crop Production; Dairy Husbandry and Production; Dairy Science; Farm/Farm and Ranch Management; Greenhouse Operations and Management; Horse Husbandry/Equine Science and Management; others. **Related Knowledge/Courses:** Food Production; Economics and Accounting; Biology; Geography; Sales and Marketing; Chemistry.

Cytogenetic Technologists

❊ Annual Earnings: $53,500
❊ Beginning Wage: $36,180
❊ Earnings Growth Potential: Low (32.4%)
❊ Growth: 12.4%
❊ Annual Job Openings: 11,457
❊ Self-Employed: 0.7%
❊ Part-Time: 14.3%
❊ Job Security: No data available
❊ Education/Training Required: Bachelor's degree

The Department of Labor reports this information for the occupation Medical and Clinical Laboratory Technologists. The job openings listed here are shared with other specializations within that occupation, including Cytotechnologists; and Histotechnologists and Histologic Technicians.

Industries in Which Income Is Highest

Industry	Average Annual Earnings	Number Employed
Federal, State, and Local Government	$58,080	7,470
Hospitals	$54,250	102,390
Professional, Scientific, and Technical Services	$51,920	2,950
Ambulatory Health Care Services	$51,670	43,900
Educational Services	$48,080	6,900

Metropolitan Areas Where Income Is Highest

Metropolitan Area	Average Annual Earnings	Number Employed
Salinas, CA	$90,210	80
San Jose–Sunnyvale–Santa Clara, CA	$82,200	920
Santa Barbara–Santa Maria, CA	$78,910	120
Chico, CA	$75,570	90
Santa Rosa–Petaluma, CA	$75,140	200

Analyze chromosomes found in biological specimens such as amniotic fluids, bone marrow, and blood to aid in the study, diagnosis, or treatment of genetic diseases. No task data available.

Other Considerations for Income: Cytogenetic Technologists are better paid than most other specialists in clinical laboratory technology.

Personality Type: Investigative-Realistic-Conventional. **Career Cluster:** 08 Health Science. **Career Pathway:** 08.2 Diagnostics Services. **Skills:** No data available.

Education and Training Programs: Clinical Laboratory Science/Medical Technology/Technologist; Cytogenetics/Genetics/Clinical Genetics Technology/Technologist. **Related Knowledge/Courses:** No data available.

Cytotechnologists

- ❋ Annual Earnings: $53,500
- ❋ Beginning Wage: $36,180
- ❋ Earnings Growth Potential: Low (32.4%)
- ❋ Growth: 12.4%
- ❋ Annual Job Openings: 11,457
- ❋ Self-Employed: 0.7%
- ❋ Part-Time: 14.3%
- ❋ Job Security: No data available
- ❋ Education/Training Required: Bachelor's degree

The Department of Labor reports this information for the occupation Medical and Clinical Laboratory Technologists. The job openings listed here are shared with other specializations within that occupation, including Cytogenetic Technologists; and Histotechnologists and Histologic Technicians.

Industries in Which Income Is Highest

Industry	Average Annual Earnings	Number Employed
Federal, State, and Local Government	$58,080	7,470
Hospitals	$54,250	102,390
Professional, Scientific, and Technical Services	$51,920	2,950
Ambulatory Health Care Services	$51,670	43,900
Educational Services	$48,080	6,900

Metropolitan Areas Where Income Is Highest

Metropolitan Area	Average Annual Earnings	Number Employed
Salinas, CA	$90,210	80
San Jose–Sunnyvale–Santa Clara, CA	$82,200	920
Santa Barbara–Santa Maria, CA	$78,910	120
Chico, CA	$75,570	90
Santa Rosa–Petaluma, CA	$75,140	200

Stain, mount, and study cells to detect evidence of cancer, hormonal abnormalities, and other pathological conditions, following established standards and practices. No task data available.

Other Considerations for Income: Cytotechnologists are better paid than most other specialists in clinical laboratory technology.

Personality Type: Investigative-Realistic. **Career Cluster:** 08 Health Science. **Career Pathway:** 08.2 Diagnostics Services. **Skills:** No data available.

Education and Training Programs: Clinical Laboratory Science/Medical Technology/Technologist; Cytotechnology/Cytotechnologist. **Related Knowledge/Courses:** No data available.

Data Warehousing Specialists

- ❋ Annual Earnings: $75,150
- ❋ Beginning Wage: $40,660
- ❋ Earnings Growth Potential: High (45.9%)
- ❋ Growth: 15.1%
- ❋ Annual Job Openings: 14,374
- ❋ Self-Employed: 6.6%
- ❋ Part-Time: 5.6%
- ❋ Job Security: No data available
- ❋ Education/Training Required: Associate degree

The Department of Labor reports this information for the occupation Computer Specialists, All Other. The job openings listed here are shared with other specializations within that occupation, including Business Intelligence Analysts; Computer Systems Engineers/Architects; Database Architects; Document Management Specialists; Electronic Commerce Specialists; Geographic Information Systems Technicians; Geospatial Information Scientists and Technologists; Information Technology Project Managers; Network Designers; Software Quality Assurance Engineers and Testers; Video Game Designers; Web Administrators; and Web Developers.

Industries in Which Income Is Highest

Industry	Average Annual Earnings	Number Employed
Petroleum and Coal Products Manufacturing	$97,090	1,070
Transportation Equipment Manufacturing	$82,770	3,010
Oil and Gas Extraction	$81,350	1,710
Federal, State, and Local Government	$80,670	71,650
Management of Companies and Enterprises	$78,200	14,820

Metropolitan Areas Where Income Is Highest

Metropolitan Area	Average Annual Earnings	Number Employed
Washington-Arlington-Alexandria, DC-VA-MD-WV	$97,170	19,470
Atlantic City, NJ	$96,600	510
Pascagoula, MS	$95,430	60
San Jose–Sunnyvale–Santa Clara, CA	$92,710	3,580
Baltimore-Towson, MD	$89,730	5,650

Design, model, or implement corporate data warehousing activities. Program and configure warehouses of database information and provide support to warehouse users. No task data available.

Other Considerations for Income: No additional information.

Personality Type: No data available. **Career Cluster:** 11 Information Technology. **Career Pathway:** 11.2 Information Support Services. **Skills:** No data available.

Education and Training Programs: Computer and Information Sciences and Support Services, Other; Computer and Information Sciences, General; Computer Engineering Technologies/Technicians, Other; Computer Engineering, General; Computer Science; Computer Software Engineering; Computer Systems Networking and Telecommunications; E-Commerce/Electronic Commerce; Information Science/Studies; Information Technology; System, Networking, and LAN/WAN Management/Manager; Web Page, Digital/Multimedia and Information Resources Design; others. **Related Knowledge/Courses:** No data available.

Database Administrators

✳ Annual Earnings: $69,740
✳ Beginning Wage: $39,900
✳ Earnings Growth Potential: High (42.8%)
✳ Growth: 28.6%
✳ Annual Job Openings: 8,258
✳ Self-Employed: 1.3%
✳ Part-Time: 5.3%
✳ Job Security: More secure than most
✳ Education/Training Required: Bachelor's degree

Industries in Which Income Is Highest

Industry	Average Annual Earnings	Number Employed
Securities, Commodity Contracts, and Other Financial Investments and Related Activities	$83,010	3,940
Insurance Carriers and Related Activities	$75,880	5,370
Computer and Electronic Product Manufacturing	$75,790	2,940
Management of Companies and Enterprises	$74,730	8,600
Data Processing, Hosting and Related Services	$74,230	2,760

Metropolitan Areas Where Income Is Highest

Metropolitan Area	Average Annual Earnings	Number Employed
Stockton, CA	$89,340	70
San Francisco–Oakland–Fremont, CA	$89,120	2,520
Trenton-Ewing, NJ	$85,560	300
Los Angeles–Long Beach–Santa Ana, CA	$84,720	5,930
Las Vegas–Paradise, NV	$82,350	230

Coordinate changes to computer databases. Test and implement the databases, applying knowledge of database management systems. May plan, coordinate, and implement security measures to safeguard computer databases. Test programs or databases, correct errors, and make necessary modifications. Modify existing databases and database management systems or direct programmers and analysts to make changes. Plan, coordinate, and implement security measures to safeguard information in computer files against accidental or unauthorized damage, modification, or disclosure. Work as part of project teams to coordinate database development and determine project scope and limitations. Write and code logical and physical database descriptions and specify identifiers of database to management system or direct others in coding descriptions. Train users and answer questions. Specify users and user access levels for each segment of databases. Approve, schedule, plan, and supervise the installation and testing of new products and improvements to computer systems such as the installation of new databases. Review project requests describing database user needs to estimate time and cost required to accomplish project. Develop standards and guidelines to guide the use and acquisition of software and to protect vulnerable information. Review procedures in database management system manuals for making changes to database. Develop methods for integrating different products so they work properly together such as customizing commercial databases to fit specific needs. Develop data models describing data elements and how they are used, following procedures and using pen, template, or computer software. Select and enter codes to monitor database performances and to create production databases. Establish and calculate optimum values for database parameters, using manuals and calculators. Revise company definition of data as defined in data dictionary. Review workflow charts developed by programmer analysts to understand tasks computer will perform, such as updating records. Identify and evaluate industry trends in database systems to serve as a source of information and advice for upper management.

Other Considerations for Income: Database Administrators are better paid than most other computer specialists.

Personality Type: Conventional-Investigative. **Career Clusters:** 04 Business, Management, and Administration; 11 Information Technology. **Career Pathways:** 04.4 Business Analysis; 11.2 Information Support Services; 11.4 Programming and Software Development. **Skills:** Programming; Systems Analysis; Systems Evaluation; Management of Personnel Resources; Operation Monitoring; Complex Problem Solving; Troubleshooting; Judgment and Decision Making.

Education and Training Programs: Computer and Information Sciences, General; Computer and Information Systems Security/Information Assurance; Computer Systems Analysis/Analyst; Data Modeling/Warehousing and Database Administration; Management Information

Systems, General. **Related Knowledge/Courses:** Computers and Electronics; Telecommunications; Clerical; Communications and Media; Engineering and Technology; Mathematics.

Database Architects

* Annual Earnings: $75,150
* Beginning Wage: $40,660
* Earnings Growth Potential: High (45.9%)
* Growth: 15.1%
* Annual Job Openings: 14,374
* Self-Employed: 6.6%
* Part-Time: 5.6%
* Job Security: No data available
* Education/Training Required: Bachelor's degree

The Department of Labor reports this information for the occupation Computer Specialists, All Other. The job openings listed here are shared with other specializations within that occupation, including Business Intelligence Analysts; Computer Systems Engineers/Architects; Data Warehousing Specialists; Document Management Specialists; Electronic Commerce Specialists; Geographic Information Systems Technicians; Geospatial Information Scientists and Technologists; Information Technology Project Managers; Network Designers; Software Quality Assurance Engineers and Testers; Video Game Designers; Web Administrators; and Web Developers.

Industries in Which Income Is Highest

Industry	Average Annual Earnings	Number Employed
Petroleum and Coal Products Manufacturing	$97,090	1,070
Transportation Equipment Manufacturing	$82,770	3,010
Oil and Gas Extraction	$81,350	1,710
Federal, State, and Local Government	$80,670	71,650
Management of Companies and Enterprises	$78,200	14,820

Metropolitan Areas Where Income Is Highest

Metropolitan Area	Average Annual Earnings	Number Employed
Washington-Arlington-Alexandria, DC-VA-MD-WV	$97,170	19,470
Atlantic City, NJ	$96,600	510
Pascagoula, MS	$95,430	60
San Jose–Sunnyvale–Santa Clara, CA	$92,710	3,580
Baltimore-Towson, MD	$89,730	5,650

Design strategies for enterprise database systems and set standards for operations, programming, and security. Design and construct large relational databases. Integrate new systems with existing warehouse structure and refine system performance and functionality. No task data available.

Other Considerations for Income: Database Architects are better paid than most other computer specialists.

Personality Type: No data available. **Career Cluster:** 11 Information Technology. **Career Pathway:** 11.4 Programming and Software Development. **Skills:** No data available.

Education and Training Programs: Computer and Information Sciences and Support Services, Other; Computer and Information Sciences, General; Computer Engineering Technologies/Technicians, Other; Computer Engineering, General; Computer Science; Computer Software Engineering; Computer Systems Networking and Telecommunications; E-Commerce/Electronic Commerce; Information Science/Studies; Information Technology; System, Networking, and LAN/WAN Management/Manager; Web Page, Digital/Multimedia and Information Resources Design; others. **Related Knowledge/Courses:** No data available.

Dental Hygienists

❋ Annual Earnings: $66,570
❋ Beginning Wage: $44,180
❋ Earnings Growth Potential: Low (33.6%)
❋ Growth: 30.1%
❋ Annual Job Openings: 10,433
❋ Self-Employed: 0.1%
❋ Part-Time: 58.7%
❋ Job Security: Most secure
❋ Education/Training Required: Associate degree

Industries in Which Income Is Highest

Industry	Average Annual Earnings	Number Employed
Administrative and Support Services	$69,560	2,000
Ambulatory Health Care Services	$66,770	168,260
Federal, State, and Local Government	$50,550	1,250

Metropolitan Areas Where Income Is Highest

Metropolitan Area	Average Annual Earnings	Number Employed
Santa Rosa–Petaluma, CA	$118,700	360
San Francisco–Oakland–Fremont, CA	$106,900	3,470
Vallejo-Fairfield, CA	$99,340	250
Merced, CA	$98,640	100
Salinas, CA	$98,320	120

Clean teeth and examine oral areas, head, and neck for signs of oral disease. May educate patients on oral hygiene, take and develop X-rays, or apply fluoride or sealants. Clean calcareous deposits, accretions, and stains from teeth and beneath margins of gums, using dental instruments. Feel and visually examine gums for sores and signs of disease. Chart conditions of decay and disease for diagnosis and treatment by dentist. Feel lymph nodes under patient's chin to detect swelling or tenderness that could indicate presence of oral cancer. Apply fluorides and other cavity-preventing agents to arrest dental decay. Examine gums, using probes, to locate periodontal recessed gums and signs of gum disease. Expose and develop X-ray film. Provide clinical services and health education to improve and maintain oral health of school-children. Remove excess cement from coronal surfaces of teeth. Make impressions for study casts. Place, carve, and finish amalgam restorations. Administer local anesthetic agents. Conduct dental health clinics for community groups to augment services of dentist. Remove sutures and dressings. Place and remove rubber dams, matrices, and temporary restorations.

Other Considerations for Income: Earnings vary by geographic location, employment setting, and years of experience. Dental hygienists may be paid on an hourly, daily, salary, or commission basis. Benefits vary substantially by practice setting and may be contingent upon full-time employment. According to the American Dental Association, 86 percent of hygienists receive hospital and medical benefits.

Personality Type: Social-Realistic-Conventional. **Career Cluster:** 08 Health Science. **Career Pathway:** 08.1 Therapeutic Services. **Skills:** Active Learning; Science; Reading Comprehension; Time Management; Equipment Selection; Persuasion; Social Perceptiveness; Writing.

Education and Training Program: Dental Hygiene/ Hygienist. **Related Knowledge/Courses:** Medicine and Dentistry; Psychology; Therapy and Counseling; Chemistry; Biology; Sales and Marketing.

Dentists, General

- ❋ Annual Earnings: $142,870
- ❋ Beginning Wage: $71,870
- ❋ Earnings Growth Potential: High (49.7%)
- ❋ Growth: 9.2%
- ❋ Annual Job Openings: 7,106
- ❋ Self-Employed: 36.6%
- ❋ Part-Time: 25.9%
- ❋ Job Security: Less secure than most
- ❋ Education/Training Required: First professional degree

Industries in Which Income Is Highest

Industry	Average Annual Earnings	Number Employed
Ambulatory Health Care Services	$145,810	81,810
Federal, State, and Local Government	$119,180	1,860

Metropolitan Areas Where Income Is Highest

Metropolitan Area	Average Annual Earnings	Number Employed
Dallas–Fort Worth–Arlington, TX	$166,400+	1,780
Atlanta–Sandy Springs–Marietta, GA	$166,400+	1,600
Seattle-Tacoma-Bellevue, WA	$166,400+	1,080
St. Louis, MO-IL	$166,400+	860
Charlotte-Gastonia-Concord, NC-SC	$166,400+	630

Diagnose and treat diseases, injuries, and malformations of teeth and gums and related oral structures. May treat diseases of nerve, pulp, and other dental tissues affecting vitality of teeth. Use masks, gloves, and safety glasses to protect themselves and their patients from infectious diseases. Administer anesthetics to limit the amount of pain experienced by patients during procedures. Examine teeth, gums, and related tissues, using dental instruments, X-rays, and other diagnostic equipment, to evaluate dental health, diagnose diseases or abnormalities, and plan appropriate treatments. Formulate plan of treatment for patient's teeth and mouth tissue. Use air turbine and hand instruments, dental appliances, and surgical implements. Advise and instruct patients regarding preventive dental care, the causes and treatment of dental problems, and oral health-care services. Design, make, and fit prosthodontic appliances such as space maintainers, bridges, and dentures or write fabrication instructions or prescriptions for denturists and dental technicians. Diagnose and treat diseases, injuries, and malformations of teeth, gums, and related oral structures and provide preventive and corrective services. Fill pulp chamber and canal with endodontic materials. Write prescriptions for antibiotics and other medications. Analyze and evaluate dental needs to determine changes and trends in patterns of dental disease. Treat exposure of pulp by pulp capping, removal of pulp from pulp chamber, or root canal, using dental instruments. Eliminate irritating margins of fillings and correct occlusions, using dental instruments. Perform oral and periodontal surgery on the jaw or mouth. Remove diseased tissue, using surgical instruments. Apply fluoride and sealants to teeth. Manage business, employing and supervising staff and handling paperwork and insurance claims. Bleach, clean, or polish teeth to restore natural color. Plan, organize, and maintain dental health programs. Produce and evaluate dental health educational materials.

Other Considerations for Income: Self-employed dentists in private practice tend to earn more than do salaried dentists. Dentists who are salaried often receive benefits paid by their employer, with health insurance and malpractice insurance being among the most common. However, like other business owners, self-employed dentists must provide their own health insurance, life insurance, retirement plans, and other benefits.

Personality Type: Investigative-Realistic-Social. **Career Cluster:** 08 Health Science. **Career Pathway:** 08.1 Therapeutic Services. **Skills:** Science; Management of Financial Resources; Management of Material Resources; Equipment Selection; Complex Problem Solving; Reading Comprehension; Service Orientation; Judgment and Decision Making.

Education and Training Programs: Advanced General Dentistry (Cert., MS, PhD); Dental Public Health and Education (Cert., MS/MPH, PhD/DPH); Dental Public Health Specialty; Dentistry (DDS, DMD); Pediatric Dentistry Residency Program; Pediatric Dentistry/Pedodontics (Cert., MS, PhD). **Related Knowledge/Courses:** Medicine and Dentistry; Biology; Psychology; Chemistry; Personnel and Human Resources; Economics and Accounting.

Dermatologists

❋ Annual Earnings: $166,400+

❋ Beginning Wage: $49,710

❋ Earnings Growth Potential: Cannot be calculated

❋ Growth: 14.2%

❋ Annual Job Openings: 38,027

❋ Self-Employed: 14.7%

❋ Part-Time: 8.1%

❋ Job Security: No data available

❋ Education/Training Required: First professional degree

The Department of Labor reports this information for the occupation Physicians and Surgeons. The job openings listed here are shared with other specializations within that occupation, including Allergists and Immunologists; Anesthesiologists; Family and General Practitioners; Hospitalists; Internists, General; Neurologists; Nuclear Medicine Physicians; Obstetricians and Gynecologists; Ophthalmologists; Pathologists; Pediatricians, General; Physical Medicine and Rehabilitation Physicians; Preventive Medicine Physicians; Psychiatrists; Radiologists; Sports Medicine Physicians; Surgeons; and Urologists.

Industries in Which Income Is Highest

Industry	Average Annual Earnings	Number Employed
Ambulatory Health Care Services	$166,400+	147,400
Administrative and Support Services	$166,400+	1,310
Federal, State, and Local Government	$162,300	28,180
Professional, Scientific, and Technical Services	$107,470	1,210
Hospitals	$72,130	72,490

Metropolitan Areas Where Income Is Highest

Metropolitan Area	Average Annual Earnings	Number Employed
Los Angeles–Long Beach–Santa Ana, CA	$166,400+	8,810
Boston-Cambridge-Quincy, MA-NH	$166,400+	6,380
Dallas–Fort Worth–Arlington, TX	$166,400+	4,950
Tampa–St. Petersburg–Clearwater, FL	$166,400+	3,810
Portland-Vancouver-Beaverton, OR-WA	$166,400+	3,180

Diagnose, treat, and help prevent diseases or other conditions of the skin. No task data available.

Other Considerations for Income: Earnings of physicians and surgeons are among the highest of any occupation. Separate earnings figures for Dermatologists are not available.

Personality Type: Investigative-Social-Realistic. **Career Cluster:** 08 Health Science. **Career Pathway:** 08.1 Therapeutic Services. **Skills:** No data available.

Education and Training Program: Dermatology Residency Program. **Related Knowledge/Courses:** No data available.

Detectives and Criminal Investigators

See *Criminal Investigators and Special Agents; Immigration and Customs Inspectors; Intelligence Analysts; Police Detectives;* and *Police Identification and Records Officers,* described separately.

Diagnostic Medical Sonographers

⚜ Annual Earnings: $61,980
⚜ Beginning Wage: $43,600
⚜ Earnings Growth Potential: Low (29.7%)
⚜ Growth: 19.1%
⚜ Annual Job Openings: 3,211
⚜ Self-Employed: 1.1%
⚜ Part-Time: 17.3%
⚜ Job Security: Most secure
⚜ Education/Training Required: Associate degree

Industries in Which Income Is Highest

Industry	Average Annual Earnings	Number Employed
Hospitals	$61,890	29,310
Ambulatory Health Care Services	$61,660	18,150

Metropolitan Areas Where Income Is Highest

Metropolitan Area	Average Annual Earnings	Number Employed
Worcester, MA-CT	$88,410	90
San Jose–Sunnyvale–Santa Clara, CA	$87,360	290
San Francisco–Oakland–Fremont, CA	$81,560	590
Santa Rosa–Petaluma, CA	$79,060	70
Portland-Vancouver-Beaverton, OR-WA	$78,550	270

Produce ultrasonic recordings of internal organs for use by physicians. Provide sonograms and oral or written summaries of technical findings to physicians for use in medical diagnosis. Decide which images to include, looking for differences between healthy and pathological areas. Operate ultrasound equipment to produce and record images of the motion, shape, and composition of blood, organs, tissues, and bodily masses such as fluid accumulations. Select appropriate equipment settings and adjust patient positions to obtain the best sites and angles. Observe screens during scans to ensure that images produced are satisfactory for diagnostic purposes, making adjustments to equipment as required. Prepare patients for exams by explaining procedures, transferring them to ultrasound tables, scrubbing skin and applying gel, and positioning them properly. Observe and care for patients throughout examinations to ensure their safety and comfort. Obtain and record accurate patient histories, including prior test results and information from physical examinations. Determine whether scope of exams should be extended, based on findings. Maintain records that include patient information; sonographs and interpretations; files of correspondence; publications and regulations; or quality assurance records such as pathology, biopsy, or post-operative reports. Record and store suitable images, using camera unit connected to the ultrasound equipment. Coordinate work with physicians and other health-care team members, including providing assistance during invasive procedures. Perform clerical duties such as scheduling exams and special procedures, keeping records, and archiving computerized images. Perform legal and ethical duties, including preparing safety and accident reports, obtaining written consent from patients to perform invasive procedures, and reporting symptoms of abuse and neglect. Clean, check, and maintain sonographic equipment, submitting maintenance requests or performing minor repairs as necessary.

Other Considerations for Income: No additional information.

Personality Type: Investigative-Social-Realistic. **Career Cluster:** 08 Health Science. **Career Pathways:** 08.1 Therapeutic Services; 08.2 Diagnostics Services. **Skills:** Operation Monitoring; Operation and Control; Quality Control Analysis; Equipment Maintenance.

Education and Training Programs: Allied Health Diagnostic, Intervention, and Treatment Professions, Other; Diagnostic Medical Sonography/Sonographer and Ultrasound Technician Training. **Related Knowledge/Courses:** Medicine and Dentistry; Physics; Biology; Customer and Personal Service; Psychology; Clerical.

Dietitians and Nutritionists

* Annual Earnings: $50,590
* Beginning Wage: $31,460
* Earnings Growth Potential: Medium (37.8%)
* Growth: 8.6%
* Annual Job Openings: 4,996
* Self-Employed: 7.9%
* Part-Time: 27.0%
* Job Security: Most secure
* Education/Training Required: Bachelor's degree

Industries in Which Income Is Highest

Industry	Average Annual Earnings	Number Employed
Ambulatory Health Care Services	$53,210	8,660
Federal, State, and Local Government	$51,660	8,360
Hospitals	$51,500	20,210
Nursing and Residential Care Facilities	$50,240	6,030
Food Services and Drinking Places	$46,280	3,750

Metropolitan Areas Where Income Is Highest

Metropolitan Area	Average Annual Earnings	Number Employed
San Jose–Sunnyvale–Santa Clara, CA	$79,400	370
San Francisco–Oakland–Fremont, CA	$72,460	670
Bridgeport-Stamford-Norwalk, CT	$67,700	140
Stockton, CA	$66,610	80
Santa Rosa–Petaluma, CA	$63,800	60

Plan and conduct food service or nutritional programs to assist in the promotion of health and control of disease. May supervise activities of a department providing quantity food services, counsel individuals, or conduct nutritional research. Assess nutritional needs, diet restrictions, and current health plans to develop and implement dietary-care plans and provide nutritional counseling. Consult with physicians and health-care personnel to determine nutritional needs and diet restrictions of patient or client. Advise patients and their families on nutritional principles, dietary plans and diet modifications, and food selection and preparation. Counsel individuals and groups on basic rules of good nutrition, healthy eating habits, and nutrition monitoring to improve their quality of life. Monitor food service operations to ensure conformance to nutritional, safety, sanitation, and quality standards. Coordinate recipe development and standardization and develop new menus for independent food service operations. Develop policies for food service or nutritional programs to assist in health promotion and disease control. Inspect meals served for conformance to prescribed diets and standards of palatability and appearance. Develop curriculum and prepare manuals, visual aids, course outlines, and other materials used in teaching. Prepare and administer budgets for food, equipment, and supplies. Purchase food in accordance with health and safety codes. Select, train, and supervise workers who plan, prepare, and serve meals. Manage quantity food service departments or clinical and community nutrition services. Coordinate diet counseling services. Advise food service managers and organizations on sanitation, safety procedures, menu development, budgeting, and planning to assist with the establishment, operation, and evaluation of food service facilities and nutrition programs. Organize, develop, analyze, test, and prepare special meals such as low-fat, low-cholesterol, and chemical-free meals. Plan, conduct, and evaluate dietary, nutritional, and epidemiological research.

Other Considerations for Income: Earnings tend to be highest for dietitians working in food and nutrition management and in education and research.

Personality Type: Investigative-Social. **Career Clusters:** 05 Education and Training; 08 Health Science; 15 Science, Technology, Engineering, and Mathematics. **Career Pathways:** 05.3 Teaching/Training; 08.1 Therapeutic Services; 08.4 Support Services; 15.3 Science and Mathematics. **Skills:** Science; Writing; Social Perceptiveness; Instructing; Speaking; Reading Comprehension; Learning Strategies; Persuasion.

Education and Training Programs: Clinical Nutrition/Nutritionist; Dietetics and Clinical Nutrition Services, Other; Dietetics/Dietitian (RD); Foods, Nutrition, and Related Services, Other; Foods, Nutrition, and Wellness Studies, General; Foodservice Systems Administration/Management; Human Nutrition; Nutrition Sciences. **Related Knowledge/Courses:** Therapy and Counseling; Biology; Sociology and Anthropology; Medicine and Dentistry; Food Production; Chemistry.

Directors—Stage, Motion Pictures, Television, and Radio

❀ Annual Earnings: $64,430
❀ Beginning Wage: $30,250
❀ Earnings Growth Potential: Very high (53.0%)
❀ Growth: 11.1%
❀ Annual Job Openings: 8,992
❀ Self-Employed: 29.5%
❀ Part-Time: 9.0%
❀ Job Security: More secure than most
❀ Education/Training Required: Work experience plus degree

The Department of Labor reports this information for the occupation Producers and Directors. The job openings listed here are shared with other specializations within that occupation, including Producers, Program Directors, Talent Directors, and Technical Directors/Managers.

Industries in Which Income Is Highest

Industry	Average Annual Earnings	Number Employed
Professional, Scientific, and Technical Services	$87,270	6,370
Motion Picture and Sound Recording Industries	$85,900	24,890
Publishing Industries (Except Internet)	$68,350	1,170
Federal, State, and Local Government	$62,950	1,860
Broadcasting (Except Internet)	$58,340	27,400

Metropolitan Areas Where Income Is Highest

Metropolitan Area	Average Annual Earnings	Number Employed
Oxnard–Thousand Oaks–Ventura, CA	$104,940	190
Los Angeles–Long Beach–Santa Ana, CA	$103,490	15,150
New York–Northern New Jersey–Long Island, NY-NJ-PA	$97,940	13,430
San Francisco–Oakland–Fremont, CA	$79,300	1,500
Washington-Arlington-Alexandria, DC-VA-MD-WV	$74,730	2,620

Interpret script, conduct rehearsals, and direct activities of cast and technical crew for stage, motion pictures, television, or radio programs. Direct live broadcasts, films and recordings, or non-broadcast programming for public entertainment or education. Supervise and coordinate the work of camera, lighting, design, and sound crew members. Study and research scripts to determine how they should be directed. Cut and edit film or tape to integrate component parts into desired sequences. Collaborate with film and sound editors during the post-production process as films are edited and soundtracks are added. Confer with technical directors, managers, crew members, and writers to discuss details of production, such as photography, script, music, sets, and costumes. Plan details such as framing, composition, camera movement, sound, and actor movement for each shot or scene. Communicate to actors the approach, characterization, and movement needed for each scene in such a way that rehearsals and takes are minimized. Establish pace of programs and sequences of scenes according to time requirements and cast and set accessibility. Choose settings and locations for films and determine how scenes will be shot in these settings. Identify and approve equipment and elements required for productions, such as scenery, lights, props, costumes, choreography, and music. Compile scripts, program notes, and other material related to productions. Perform producers' duties such as securing financial backing, establishing and administering budgets, and recruiting cast and crew. Select plays or scripts for production and determine how material should be interpreted and performed. Compile cue words and phrases; cue announcers, cast members, and technicians during performances. Consult with writers, producers, or actors about script changes or "workshop" scripts, through rehearsal with writers and actors, to create final drafts. Collaborate with producers to hire crew members such as art directors, cinematographers, and costumer designers. Review film daily to check on work in progress and to plan for future filming.

Other Considerations for Income: The most successful producers and directors may have extraordinarily high earnings but for others, because earnings may be erratic, many supplement their income by holding jobs in other fields. Directing a production at a dinner theater generally will pay less than directing one at a summer theater, but has more potential for generating income from royalties. Regional theaters may hire directors for longer periods, increasing compensation accordingly. The highest-paid directors work on Broadway and commonly earn over $50,000 per show. However, they also receive payment

D

in the form of royalties—a negotiated percentage of gross box office receipts—that can exceed their contract fee for long-running box office successes.

Personality Type: Enterprising-Artistic. **Career Cluster:** 03 Arts, Audio/Video Technology, and Communications. **Career Pathways:** 03.4 Performing Arts; 03.5 Journalism and Broadcasting. **Skills:** Management of Personnel Resources; Time Management; Judgment and Decision Making; Operations Analysis; Equipment Selection; Active Listening; Speaking; Critical Thinking.

Education and Training Programs: Cinematography and Film/Video Production; Directing and Theatrical Production; Drama and Dramatics/Theatre Arts, General; Dramatic/Theatre Arts and Stagecraft, Other; Film/Cinema/Video Studies; Radio and Television. **Related Knowledge/Courses:** Communications and Media; Telecommunications; Fine Arts; Geography; Computers and Electronics; Education and Training.

Document Management Specialists

- ❋ Annual Earnings: $75,150
- ❋ Beginning Wage: $40,660
- ❋ Earnings Growth Potential: High (45.9%)
- ❋ Growth: 15.1%
- ❋ Annual Job Openings: 14,374
- ❋ Self-Employed: 6.6%
- ❋ Part-Time: 5.6%
- ❋ Job Security: No data available
- ❋ Education/Training Required: Work experience in a related occupation

The Department of Labor reports this information for the occupation Computer Specialists, All Other. The job openings listed here are shared with other specializations within that occupation, including Business Intelligence Analysts; Computer Systems Engineers/Architects; Data Warehousing Specialists; Database Architects; Electronic Commerce Specialists; Geographic Information Systems Technicians; Geospatial Information Scientists and Technologists; Information Technology Project Managers; Network Designers; Software Quality Assurance Engineers and Testers; Video Game Designers; Web Administrators; and Web Developers.

Industries in Which Income Is Highest

Industry	Average Annual Earnings	Number Employed
Petroleum and Coal Products Manufacturing	$97,090	1,070
Transportation Equipment Manufacturing	$82,770	3,010
Oil and Gas Extraction	$81,350	1,710
Federal, State, and Local Government	$80,670	71,650
Management of Companies and Enterprises	$78,200	14,820

Metropolitan Areas Where Income Is Highest

Metropolitan Area	Average Annual Earnings	Number Employed
Washington-Arlington-Alexandria, DC-VA-MD-WV	$97,170	19,470
Atlantic City, NJ	$96,600	510
Pascagoula, MS	$95,430	60
San Jose–Sunnyvale–Santa Clara, CA	$92,710	3,580
Baltimore-Towson, MD	$89,730	5,650

Implement and administer enterprise-wide document management procedures for the capture, storage, retrieval, sharing, and destruction of electronic records and documents. No task data available.

Other Considerations for Income: No additional information.

Personality Type: No data available. **Career Cluster:** 11 Information Technology. **Career Pathway:** 11.2 Information Support Services. **Skills:** No data available.

Education and Training Programs: Computer and Information Sciences and Support Services, Other; Computer and Information Sciences, General; Computer Engineering Technologies/Technicians, Other; Computer Engineering, General; Computer Science; Computer Software Engineering; Computer Systems Networking and Telecommunications; E-Commerce/Electronic Commerce; Information Science/Studies; Information Technology; System, Networking, and LAN/WAN Management/Manager; Web Page, Digital/Multimedia and Information Resources Design; others. **Related Knowledge/Courses:** No data available.

Economics Teachers, Postsecondary

❋ Annual Earnings: $80,130
❋ Beginning Wage: $43,720
❋ Earnings Growth Potential: High (45.4%)
❋ Growth: 22.9%
❋ Annual Job Openings: 2,208
❋ Self-Employed: 0.4%
❋ Part-Time: 27.8%
❋ Job Security: Most secure
❋ Education/Training Required: Doctoral degree

Industries in Which Income Is Highest

Industry	Average Annual Earnings	Number Employed
Educational Services	$80,140	12,540

Metropolitan Areas Where Income Is Highest

Metropolitan Area	Average Annual Earnings	Number Employed
Providence–Fall River–Warwick, RI-MA	$109,060	90
Ann Arbor, MI	$104,660	80
Riverside–San Bernardino–Ontario, CA	$102,510	80
Columbus, OH	$97,460	100
Philadelphia-Camden-Wilmington, PA-NJ-DE-MD	$97,020	290

Teach courses in economics. Prepare and deliver lectures to undergraduate and/or graduate students on topics such as econometrics, price theory, and macroeconomics. Prepare course materials such as syllabi, homework assignments, and handouts. Evaluate and grade students' classwork, assignments, and papers. Compile, administer, and grade examinations or assign this work to others. Keep abreast of developments in their field by reading current literature, talking with colleagues, and participating in professional conferences. Maintain student attendance records, grades, and other required records. Initiate, facilitate, and moderate classroom discussions. Maintain regularly scheduled office hours in order to advise and assist students. Select and obtain materials and supplies such as textbooks. Plan, evaluate, and revise curricula, course content, and course materials and methods of instruction. Conduct research in a particular field of knowledge and publish findings in professional journals, books, and/or electronic media. Supervise undergraduate and/or graduate teaching, internship, and research work. Advise students on academic and vocational curricula and on career issues. Serve on academic or administrative committees that deal with institutional policies, departmental matters, and academic issues. Collaborate with colleagues to address teaching and research issues. Compile bibliographies of specialized materials for outside reading assignments. Participate in student recruitment, registration, and placement activities. Perform administrative duties such as serving as department head. Write grant proposals to procure external research funding. Participate in campus and community events. Provide professional consulting services to government and/or industry. Act as advisers to student organizations.

Other Considerations for Income: Earnings for college faculty vary according to rank and type of institution, geographic area, and field. According to a 2006–2007 survey by the American Association of University Professors, salaries for full-time faculty averaged $73,207. By rank, the average was $98,974 for professors, $69,911 for associate professors, $58,662 for assistant professors, $42,609 for instructors, and $48,289 for lecturers. Faculty in 4-year institutions earn higher salaries, on average, than do those in 2-year schools. Many faculty members have significant earnings in addition to their base salary from consulting, teaching additional courses, research, writing for publication, or other employment. In addition, many college and university faculty enjoy unique benefits, including access to campus facilities, tuition waivers for dependents, housing and travel allowances, and paid leave for sabbaticals. Part-time faculty and instructors usually have fewer benefits than full-time faculty.

Personality Type: Social-Investigative. **Career Clusters:** 04 Business, Management, and Administration; 15 Science, Technology, Engineering, and Mathematics. **Career Pathways:** 04.1 Management; 15.3 Science and Mathematics. **Skills:** Mathematics; Writing; Speaking; Instructing; Reading Comprehension; Critical Thinking; Learning Strategies; Active Learning.

Education and Training Programs: Applied Economics; Business/Managerial Economics; Development Economics and International Development; Econometrics and Quantitative Economics; Economics, General; Economics, Other; Humanities/Humanistic Studies; International Economics; Social Science Teacher Education. **Related Knowledge/Courses:** Economics and Accounting; History and Archeology; Mathematics; Philosophy and Theology; Education and Training; English Language.

Economists

* Annual Earnings: $83,590
* Beginning Wage: $44,050
* Earnings Growth Potential: High (47.3%)
* Growth: 7.5%
* Annual Job Openings: 1,555
* Self-Employed: 6.5%
* Part-Time: 3.3%
* Job Security: Most secure
* Education/Training Required: Master's degree

Industries in Which Income Is Highest

Industry	Average Annual Earnings	Number Employed
Professional, Scientific, and Technical Services	$91,680	3,250
Federal, State, and Local Government	$82,140	7,090

Metropolitan Areas Where Income Is Highest

Metropolitan Area	Average Annual Earnings	Number Employed
Washington-Arlington-Alexandria, DC-VA-MD-WV	$107,190	4,670
New York–Northern New Jersey–Long Island, NY-NJ-PA	$100,280	310
Los Angeles–Long Beach–Santa Ana, CA	$99,620	190
San Francisco–Oakland–Fremont, CA	$99,400	210
Portland-Vancouver-Beaverton, OR-WA	$91,230	130

Conduct research, prepare reports, or formulate plans to aid in solution of economic problems arising from production and distribution of goods and services. May collect and process economic and statistical data, using econometric and sampling techniques. Study eco-

nomic and statistical data in area of specialization, such as finance, labor, or agriculture. Provide advice and consultation on economic relationships to businesses, public and private agencies, and other employers. Compile, analyze, and report data to explain economic phenomena and forecast market trends, applying mathematical models and statistical techniques. Formulate recommendations, policies, or plans to solve economic problems or to interpret markets. Develop economic guidelines and standards and prepare points of view used in forecasting trends and formulating economic policy. Testify at regulatory or legislative hearings concerning the estimated effects of changes in legislation or public policy and present recommendations based on cost-benefit analyses. Supervise research projects and students' study projects. Forecast production and consumption of renewable resources and supply, consumption, and depletion of non-renewable resources. Teach theories, principles, and methods of economics.

Other Considerations for Income: In the federal government, having a doctoral degree can mean a starting salary $10,000 higher than for someone with a master's degree.

Personality Type: Investigative-Conventional-Enterprising. **Career Clusters:** 01 Agriculture, Food and Natural Resource; 04 Business, Management, and Administration; 15 Science, Technology, Engineering, and Mathematics. **Career Pathways:** 01.2 Plant Systems; 04.1 Management; 15.3 Science and Mathematics. **Skills:** Mathematics; Programming; Persuasion; Judgment and Decision Making; Complex Problem Solving; Writing; Critical Thinking; Systems Analysis.

Education and Training Programs: Agricultural Economics; Applied Economics; Business/Managerial Economics; Development Economics and International Development; Econometrics and Quantitative Economics; Economics, General; Economics, Other; International Economics. **Related Knowledge/Courses:** Economics and Accounting; Mathematics; Geography; Sales and Marketing; Computers and Electronics; English Language.

Editors

* Annual Earnings: $49,990
* Beginning Wage: $28,090
* Earnings Growth Potential: High (43.8%)
* Growth: 2.3%
* Annual Job Openings: 20,193
* Self-Employed: 13.4%
* Part-Time: 14.6%
* Job Security: Most secure
* Education/Training Required: Bachelor's degree

Industries in Which Income Is Highest

Industry	Average Annual Earnings	Number Employed
Motion Picture and Sound Recording Industries	$53,420	3,310
Professional, Scientific, and Technical Services	$53,110	8,560
Management of Companies and Enterprises	$52,090	1,970
Broadcasting (Except Internet)	$50,730	4,090
Other Information Services	$50,110	5,160

Metropolitan Areas Where Income Is Highest

Metropolitan Area	Average Annual Earnings	Number Employed
Naples–Marco Island, FL	$104,010	80
Manchester, NH	$74,360	80
Providence–Fall River–Warwick, RI-MA	$67,630	270
Seattle-Tacoma-Bellevue, WA	$65,140	1,090
New York–Northern New Jersey–Long Island, NY-NJ-PA	$65,070	18,430

Perform variety of editorial duties, such as laying out, indexing, and revising content of written materials, in preparation for final publication. Prepare, rewrite, and edit copy to improve readability or supervise others who do this work. Read copy or proof to detect and correct errors in spelling, punctuation, and syntax. Allocate print space for story text, photos, and illustrations according to space parameters and copy significance, using knowledge of layout principles. Plan the contents of publications according to the publication's style, editorial policy, and publishing requirements. Verify facts, dates, and statistics, using standard reference sources. Review and approve proofs submitted by composing room prior to publication production. Develop story or content ideas, considering reader or audience appeal. Oversee publication production, including artwork, layout, computer typesetting, and printing, ensuring adherence to deadlines and budget requirements. Confer with management and editorial staff members regarding placement and emphasis of developing news stories. Assign topics, events, and stories to individual writers or reporters for coverage. Read, evaluate, and edit manuscripts or other materials submitted for publication and confer with authors regarding changes in content, style or organization, or publication. Monitor news-gathering operations to ensure utilization of all news sources, such as press releases, telephone contacts, radio, television, wire services, and other reporters. Meet frequently with artists, typesetters, layout personnel, marketing directors, and production managers to discuss projects and resolve problems. Supervise and coordinate work of reporters and other editors. Make manuscript acceptance or revision recommendations to the publisher. Select local, state, national, and international news items received from wire services based on assessment of items' significance and interest value. Interview and hire writers and reporters or negotiate contracts, royalties, and payments for authors or freelancers.

Other Considerations for Income: No additional information.

Personality Type: Artistic-Enterprising-Conventional. **Career Cluster:** 03 Arts, Audio/Video Technology, and Communications. **Career Pathway:** 03.5 Journalism and Broadcasting. **Skills:** Writing; Reading Comprehension; Active Listening; Judgment and Decision Making; Critical Thinking; Time Management; Persuasion; Active Learning.

Education and Training Programs: Broadcast Journalism; Business/Corporate Communications; Communication, Journalism, and Related Programs, Other; English Language and Literature, General; Family and Consumer Sciences/Human Sciences Communication; Journalism; Mass Communication/Media Studies; Publishing. **Related Knowledge/Courses:** Communications and Media; History and Archeology; Geography; Fine Arts; English Language; Clerical.

Education Administrators, Elementary and Secondary School

- ❋ Annual Earnings: $83,880
- ❋ Beginning Wage: $55,580
- ❋ Earnings Growth Potential: Low (33.7%)
- ❋ Growth: 7.6%
- ❋ Annual Job Openings: 27,143
- ❋ Self-Employed: 3.3%
- ❋ Part-Time: 8.3%
- ❋ Job Security: Most secure
- ❋ Education/Training Required: Work experience plus degree

Industries in Which Income Is Highest

Industry	Average Annual Earnings	Number Employed
Federal, State, and Local Government	$88,150	1,850
Educational Services	$83,910	215,700

Metropolitan Areas Where Income Is Highest

Metropolitan Area	Average Annual Earnings	Number Employed
Bridgeport-Stamford-Norwalk, CT	$115,940	870
San Diego–Carlsbad–San Marcos, CA	$113,880	1,820
New Haven, CT	$112,350	550
Los Angeles–Long Beach–Santa Ana, CA	$110,970	6,540
Danbury, CT	$110,070	110

Plan, direct, or coordinate the academic, clerical, or auxiliary activities of public or private elementary or secondary-level schools. Review and approve new programs or recommend modifications to existing programs, submitting program proposals for school board approval as necessary. Prepare, maintain, or oversee the preparation and maintenance of attendance, activity, planning, or personnel reports and records. Confer with parents and staff to discuss educational activities, policies, and student behavioral or learning problems. Prepare and submit budget requests and recommendations or grant proposals to solicit program funding. Direct and coordinate school

maintenance services and the use of school facilities. Counsel and provide guidance to students regarding personal, academic, vocational, or behavioral issues. Organize and direct committees of specialists, volunteers, and staff to provide technical and advisory assistance for programs. Teach classes or courses to students. Advocate for new schools to be built or for existing facilities to be repaired or remodeled. Plan and develop instructional methods and content for educational, vocational, or student activity programs. Develop partnerships with businesses, communities, and other organizations to help meet identified educational needs and to provide school-to-work programs. Direct and coordinate activities of teachers, administrators, and support staff at schools, public agencies, and institutions. Evaluate curricula, teaching methods, and programs to determine their effectiveness, efficiency, and utilization and to ensure that school activities comply with federal, state, and local regulations. Set educational standards and goals and help establish policies and procedures to carry them out. Recruit, hire, train, and evaluate primary and supplemental staff. Enforce discipline and attendance rules. Observe teaching methods and examine learning materials to evaluate and standardize curricula and teaching techniques and to determine areas where improvement is needed.

Other Considerations for Income: Salaries of education administrators depend on several factors, including the location and enrollment level in the school or school district. According to a survey of public schools, conducted by the Educational Research Service, average salaries for principals and assistant principals in the 2006–2007 school year were $82,414 for elementary school, $87,866 for junior high school or middle school, and $92,965 for senior high school. Benefits for education administrators are generally very good. Many get 4 or 5 weeks of vacation every year and have generous health and pension packages. Many colleges and universities offer free tuition to employees and their families.

Personality Type: Enterprising-Social-Conventional. **Career Cluster:** 05 Education and Training. **Career Pathway:** 05.1 Administration and Administrative Support. **Skills:** Management of Personnel Resources; Management of Financial Resources; Negotiation; Learning Strategies; Monitoring; Management of Material Resources; Systems Evaluation; Social Perceptiveness.

Education and Training Programs: Educational Administration and Supervision, Other; Educational Leadership and Administration, General; Educational, Instructional, and Curriculum Supervision; Elementary and Middle

School Administration/Principalship; Secondary School Administration/Principalship. **Related Knowledge/Courses:** Therapy and Counseling; Education and Training; Personnel and Human Resources; Psychology; Sociology and Anthropology; History and Archeology.

Education Administrators, Postsecondary

* Annual Earnings: $80,670
* Beginning Wage: $45,050
* Earnings Growth Potential: High (44.2%)
* Growth: 14.2%
* Annual Job Openings: 17,121
* Self-Employed: 3.3%
* Part-Time: 8.3%
* Job Security: Most secure
* Education/Training Required: Work experience plus degree

Industries in Which Income Is Highest

Industry	Average Annual Earnings	Number Employed
Educational Services	$80,550	95,940

Metropolitan Areas Where Income Is Highest

Metropolitan Area	Average Annual Earnings	Number Employed
Albuquerque, NM	$144,240	190
Lubbock, TX	$140,120	100
Hartford–West Hartford–East Hartford, CT	$121,630	610
El Paso, TX	$112,110	260
Norwich–New London, CT-RI	$111,450	60

Plan, direct, or coordinate research, instructional, student administration and services, and other educational activities at postsecondary institutions, including universities, colleges, and junior and community colleges. Recruit, hire, train, and terminate departmental personnel. Plan, administer, and control budgets; maintain financial records; and produce financial reports.

Represent institutions at community and campus events, in meetings with other institution personnel, and during accreditation processes. Participate in faculty and college committee activities. Provide assistance to faculty and staff in duties such as teaching classes, conducting orientation programs, issuing transcripts, and scheduling events. Establish operational policies and procedures and make any necessary modifications, based on analysis of operations, demographics, and other research information. Confer with other academic staff to explain and formulate admission requirements and course credit policies. Appoint individuals to faculty positions and evaluate their performance. Direct activities of administrative departments such as admissions, registration, and career services. Develop curricula and recommend curricula revisions and additions. Determine course schedules and coordinate teaching assignments and room assignments to ensure optimum use of buildings and equipment. Consult with government regulatory and licensing agencies to ensure the institution's conformance with applicable standards. Direct, coordinate, and evaluate the activities of personnel engaged in administering academic institutions, departments, and/or alumni organizations. Teach courses within their department. Participate in student recruitment, selection, and admission, making admissions recommendations when required to do so. Review student misconduct reports requiring disciplinary action and counsel students regarding such reports. Supervise coaches. Assess and collect tuition and fees. Direct scholarship, fellowship, and loan programs, performing activities such as selecting recipients and distributing aid. Coordinate the production and dissemination of university publications such as course catalogs and class schedules.

Other Considerations for Income: According to the College and University Professional Association for Human Resources, median annual salaries for selected administrators in higher education in 2006–2007 ranged from $66,008 for a registrar to $140,595 for a chief academic officer. Deans of academic departments tend to earn more if the students in their departments are preparing for better-paying careers (e.g., in business). Benefits for education administrators are generally very good. Many get 4 or 5 weeks of vacation every year and have generous health and pension packages. Many colleges and universities offer free tuition to employees and their families.

Personality Type: Enterprising-Conventional-Social. **Career Cluster:** 05 Education and Training. **Career Pathway:** 05.1 Administration and Administrative Support. **Skills:** Management of Financial Resources; Management of Personnel Resources; Systems Evaluation;

Persuasion; Monitoring; Judgment and Decision Making; Operations Analysis; Management of Material Resources.

Education and Training Programs: Community College Education; Educational Administration and Supervision, Other; Educational Leadership and Administration, General; Educational, Instructional, and Curriculum Supervision; Higher Education/Higher Education Administration. **Related Knowledge/Courses:** Personnel and Human Resources; Education and Training; Sociology and Anthropology; Administration and Management; Philosophy and Theology; Sales and Marketing.

Education Teachers, Postsecondary

❋ Annual Earnings: $56,400
❋ Beginning Wage: $29,510
❋ Earnings Growth Potential: High (47.7%)
❋ Growth: 22.9%
❋ Annual Job Openings: 9,359
❋ Self-Employed: 0.4%
❋ Part-Time: 27.8%
❋ Job Security: Most secure
❋ Education/Training Required: Doctoral degree

Industries in Which Income Is Highest

Industry	Average Annual Earnings	Number Employed
Educational Services	$56,410	55,760

Metropolitan Areas Where Income Is Highest

Metropolitan Area	Average Annual Earnings	Number Employed
Lubbock, TX	$80,010	300
San Francisco–Oakland–Fremont, CA	$78,110	1,000
Santa Barbara–Santa Maria, CA	$75,410	80
San Diego–Carlsbad–San Marcos, CA	$75,080	490
Riverside–San Bernardino–Ontario, CA	$72,210	340

Teach courses pertaining to education, such as counseling, curriculum, guidance, instruction, teacher education, and teaching English as a second language. Prepare course materials such as syllabi, homework assignments, and handouts. Prepare and deliver lectures to undergraduate and/or graduate students on topics such as children's literature, learning and development, and reading instruction. Initiate, facilitate, and moderate classroom discussions. Evaluate and grade students' classwork, assignments, and papers. Plan, evaluate, and revise curricula, course content, and course materials and methods of instruction. Supervise students' fieldwork, internship, and research work. Keep abreast of developments in their field by reading current literature, talking with colleagues, and participating in professional conferences. Advise students on academic and vocational curricula and on career issues. Maintain regularly scheduled office hours to advise and assist students. Maintain student attendance records, grades, and other required records. Collaborate with colleagues to address teaching and research issues. Compile, administer, and grade examinations or assign this work to others. Conduct research in a particular field of knowledge and publish findings in professional journals, books, or electronic media. Select and obtain materials and supplies such as textbooks. Participate in student recruitment, registration, and placement activities. Advise and instruct teachers employed in school systems by providing activities such as in-service seminars. Serve on academic or administrative committees that deal with institutional policies, departmental matters, and academic issues. Compile bibliographies of specialized materials for outside reading assignments. Write grant proposals to procure external research funding. Participate in campus and community events. Perform administrative duties such as serving as department head. Act as advisers to student organizations. Provide professional consulting services to government and/or industry.

Other Considerations for Income: Earnings for college faculty vary according to rank and type of institution, geographic area, and field. According to a 2006–2007 survey by the American Association of University Professors, salaries for full-time faculty averaged $73,207. By rank, the average was $98,974 for professors, $69,911 for associate professors, $58,662 for assistant professors, $42,609 for instructors, and $48,289 for lecturers. Faculty in 4-year institutions earn higher salaries, on average, than do those in 2-year schools. Many faculty members have significant earnings in addition to their base salary from consulting, teaching additional courses, research, writing for publication, or other employment. In addition, many college and university faculty enjoy unique benefits, including access to campus facilities, tuition waivers for dependents, housing and travel allowances, and paid leave for sabbaticals. Part-time faculty and instructors usually have fewer benefits than full-time faculty.

Personality Type: Social-Artistic-Investigative. **Career Cluster:** 05 Education and Training. **Career Pathway:** 05.3 Teaching/Training. **Skills:** Learning Strategies; Instructing; Writing; Social Perceptiveness; Speaking; Persuasion; Science; Monitoring.

Education and Training Programs: Agricultural Teacher Education; Art Teacher Education; Biology Teacher Education; Business Teacher Education; Chemistry Teacher Education; Computer Teacher Education; Drama and Dance Teacher Education; Driver and Safety Teacher Education; Education, General; English/Language Arts Teacher Education; Family and Consumer Sciences/Home Economics Teacher Education; Foreign Language Teacher Education; French Language Teacher Education; Geography Teacher Education; German Language Teacher Education; others. **Related Knowledge/Courses:** Therapy and Counseling; Education and Training; Sociology and Anthropology; Philosophy and Theology; Psychology; English Language.

Educational, Vocational, and School Counselors

❀ Annual Earnings: $51,050
❀ Beginning Wage: $29,360
❀ Earnings Growth Potential: High (42.5%)
❀ Growth: 12.6%
❀ Annual Job Openings: 54,025
❀ Self-Employed: 6.1%
❀ Part-Time: 15.4%
❀ Job Security: Most secure
❀ Education/Training Required: Master's degree

Industries in Which Income Is Highest

Industry	Average Annual Earnings	Number Employed
Educational Services	$54,140	193,240
Federal, State, and Local Government	$49,580	10,630
Management of Companies and Enterprises	$47,530	1,510
Ambulatory Health Care Services	$38,870	1,100
Religious, Grantmaking, Civic, Professional, and Similar Organizations	$36,440	1,770

Metropolitan Areas Where Income Is Highest

Metropolitan Area	Average Annual Earnings	Number Employed
Modesto, CA	$73,520	290
Cape Coral–Fort Myers, FL	$73,350	290
San Jose–Sunnyvale–Santa Clara, CA	$70,780	1,490
Danville, VA	$69,610	100
Las Cruces, NM	$69,090	130

Counsel individuals and provide group educational and vocational guidance services. Counsel students regarding educational issues such as course and program selection, class scheduling, school adjustment, truancy, study habits, and career planning. Counsel individuals to help them understand and overcome personal, social, or behavioral problems affecting their educational or vocational situations. Maintain accurate and complete student records as required by laws, district policies, and administrative regulations. Confer with parents or guardians, teachers, other counselors, and administrators to resolve students' behavioral, academic, and other problems. Provide crisis intervention to students when difficult situations occur at schools. Identify cases involving domestic abuse or other family problems affecting students' development. Meet with parents and guardians to discuss their children's progress and to determine their priorities for their children and their resource needs. Prepare students for later educational experiences by encouraging them to explore learning opportunities and to persevere with challenging tasks. Encourage students and/or parents to seek additional assistance from mental health professionals when necessary. Observe and evaluate students' performance, behavior, social development, and physical health. Enforce all administration policies and rules governing students. Meet with other professionals to discuss individual students' needs and progress. Provide students with information on such topics as college degree programs and admission requirements, financial aid opportunities, trade and technical schools, and apprenticeship programs. Evaluate individuals' abilities, interests, and personality characteristics, using tests, records, interviews, and professional sources. Collaborate with teachers and administrators in the development, evaluation, and revision of school programs. Establish and enforce behavioral rules and procedures to maintain order among students.

Other Considerations for Income: Counselors working for schools tend to earn less than self-employed counselors who have well-established practices or counselors employed in group practices.

Personality Type: Social. **Career Cluster:** 05 Education and Training. **Career Pathway:** 05.2 Professional Support Services. **Skills:** Social Perceptiveness; Service Orientation; Negotiation; Active Listening; Persuasion; Writing; Learning Strategies; Monitoring.

Education and Training Programs: College Student Counseling and Personnel Services; Counselor Education/School Counseling and Guidance Services. **Related Knowledge/Courses:** Therapy and Counseling; Psychology; Sociology and Anthropology; Education and Training; Philosophy and Theology; Clerical.

Electrical and Electronic Engineering Technicians

See *Electronics Engineering Technicians* and *Electrical Engineering Technicians,* described separately.

Electrical and Electronics Drafters

See *Electrical Drafters* and *Electronic Drafters,* described separately.

Electrical and Electronics Repairers, Commercial and Industrial Equipment

- ❊ Annual Earnings: $48,430
- ❊ Beginning Wage: $29,920
- ❊ Earnings Growth Potential: Medium (38.2%)
- ❊ Growth: 6.8%
- ❊ Annual Job Openings: 6,607
- ❊ Self-Employed: 0.0%
- ❊ Part-Time: 0.6%
- ❊ Job Security: Most secure
- ❊ Education/Training Required: Postsecondary vocational training

Industries in Which Income Is Highest

Industry	Average Annual Earnings	Number Employed
Utilities	$59,560	1,030
Paper Manufacturing	$52,720	2,180
Federal, State, and Local Government	$52,460	13,080
Telecommunications	$51,710	3,600
Professional, Scientific, and Technical Services	$51,700	2,400

Metropolitan Areas Where Income Is Highest

Metropolitan Area	Average Annual Earnings	Number Employed
Sacramento–Arden-Arcade–Roseville, CA	$85,150	240
Kennewick-Richland-Pasco, WA	$82,260	80
San Francisco–Oakland–Fremont, CA	$70,750	600
Anchorage, AK	$70,370	100
Decatur, AL	$69,160	130

Repair, test, adjust, or install electronic equipment, such as industrial controls, transmitters, and antennas. Perform scheduled preventive maintenance tasks, such as checking, cleaning, and repairing equipment, to detect and prevent problems. Examine work orders and converse with equipment operators to detect equipment problems and to ascertain whether mechanical or human errors contributed to the problems. Operate equipment to demonstrate proper use and to analyze malfunctions. Set up and test industrial equipment to ensure that it functions properly. Test faulty equipment to diagnose malfunctions, using test equipment and software and applying knowledge of the functional operation of electronic units and systems. Repair and adjust equipment, machines, and defective components, replacing worn parts such as gaskets and seals in watertight electrical equipment. Calibrate testing instruments and installed or repaired equipment to prescribed specifications. Advise management regarding customer satisfaction, product performance, and suggestions for product improvements. Study blueprints, schematics, manuals, and other specifications to determine installation procedures. Inspect components of industrial equipment for accurate assembly and installation and for defects such as loose connections and frayed wires. Maintain equipment logs that record performance problems, repairs, calibrations, and tests. Coordinate efforts with other workers involved in installing and maintaining equipment or components. Maintain inventory of spare parts. Consult with customers, supervisors, and engineers to plan layout of equipment and to resolve problems in system operation and maintenance. Install repaired equipment in various settings, such as industrial or military establishments. Send defective units to the manufacturer or to a specialized repair shop for repair. Determine feasibility of using standardized equipment and develop specifications for equipment required to perform additional functions.

Other Considerations for Income: Electrical and Electronics Repairers, Commercial and Industrial Equipment, are paid in the middle range of earnings, compared to those of other electrical and electronic repair specializations.

Personality Type: Realistic-Investigative-Conventional. **Career Cluster:** 13 Manufacturing. **Career Pathway:** 13.3 Maintenance, Installation and Repair. **Skills:** Installation; Repairing; Operation Monitoring; Troubleshooting; Equipment Maintenance; Operation and Control; Systems Analysis; Science.

Education and Training Programs: Computer Installation and Repair Technology/Technician; Industrial Electronics Technology/Technician. **Related Knowledge/Courses:** Mechanical; Computers and Electronics; Engineering and Technology; Design; Telecommunications; Physics.

Electrical and Electronics Repairers, Powerhouse, Substation, and Relay

- ❋ Annual Earnings: $61,040
- ❋ Beginning Wage: $43,480
- ❋ Earnings Growth Potential: Low (28.8%)
- ❋ Growth: –4.7%
- ❋ Annual Job Openings: 1,591
- ❋ Self-Employed: 0.0%
- ❋ Part-Time: 0.6%
- ❋ Job Security: Most secure
- ❋ Education/Training Required: Postsecondary vocational training

Industries in Which Income Is Highest

Industry	Average Annual Earnings	Number Employed
Utilities	$61,790	18,070
Federal, State, and Local Government	$59,760	2,380

Metropolitan Areas Where Income Is Highest

Metropolitan Area	Average Annual Earnings	Number Employed
Milwaukee–Waukesha–West Allis, WI	$74,980	270
Syracuse, NY	$74,470	280
Riverside–San Bernardino–Ontario, CA	$73,320	60
Phoenix-Mesa-Scottsdale, AZ	$71,850	60
Minneapolis–St. Paul–Bloomington, MN-WI	$71,640	130

Inspect, test, repair, or maintain electrical equipment in generating stations, substations, and in-service relays. Construct, test, maintain, and repair substation relay and control systems. Inspect and test equipment and circuits to identify malfunctions or defects, using wiring diagrams and testing devices such as ohmmeters, voltmeters, or ammeters. Consult manuals, schematics, wiring diagrams, and engineering personnel to troubleshoot and solve equipment problems and to determine optimum equipment functioning. Notify facility personnel of equipment shutdowns. Open and close switches to isolate defective relays; then perform adjustments or repairs. Prepare and maintain records detailing tests, repairs, and maintenance. Analyze test data to diagnose malfunctions, to determine performance characteristics of systems, and to evaluate effects of system modifications. Test insulators and bushings of equipment by inducing voltage across insulation, testing current, and calculating insulation loss. Repair, replace, and clean equipment and components such as circuit breakers, brushes, and commutators. Disconnect voltage regulators, bolts, and screws and connect replacement regulators to high-voltage lines. Schedule and supervise the construction and testing of special devices and the implementation of unique monitoring or control systems. Run signal quality and connectivity tests for individual cables and record results. Schedule and supervise splicing or termination of cables in color-code order. Test oil in circuit breakers and transformers for dielectric strength, refilling oil periodically. Maintain inventories of spare parts for all equipment, requisitioning parts as necessary. Set forms and pour concrete footings for installation of heavy equipment.

Other Considerations for Income: Electrical and Electronics Repairers, Powerhouse, Substation, and Relay, are paid better than workers in other electrical and electronic repair specializations.

Personality Type: Realistic-Conventional. **Career Cluster:** 13 Manufacturing. **Career Pathway:** 13.3 Maintenance, Installation, and Repair. **Skills:** Installation; Repairing; Equipment Maintenance; Troubleshooting; Operation Monitoring; Operation and Control; Science; Operations Analysis.

Education and Training Program: Mechanic and Repair Technologies/Technicians, Other. **Related Knowledge/Courses:** Mechanical; Design; Telecommunications; Building and Construction; Physics; Public Safety and Security.

Electrical Drafters

❈ Annual Earnings: $51,320
❈ Beginning Wage: $32,050
❈ Earnings Growth Potential: Medium (37.5%)
❈ Growth: 4.1%
❈ Annual Job Openings: 4,786
❈ Self-Employed: 5.7%
❈ Part-Time: 5.9%
❈ Job Security: Less secure than most
❈ Education/Training Required: Postsecondary vocational training

The Department of Labor reports this information for the occupation Electrical and Electronics Drafters. The job openings listed here are shared with other specializations within that occupation, including Electronic Drafters.

Industries in Which Income Is Highest

Industry	Average Annual Earnings	Number Employed
Transportation Equipment Manufacturing	$62,900	1,220
Utilities	$61,240	2,240
Telecommunications	$54,440	1,740
Computer and Electronic Product Manufacturing	$53,780	4,750
Specialty Trade Contractors	$51,390	6,000

Metropolitan Areas Where Income Is Highest

Metropolitan Area	Average Annual Earnings	Number Employed
Boulder, CO	$66,920	80
Greenville, SC	$65,880	150
Buffalo–Niagara Falls, NY	$65,540	100
Phoenix-Mesa-Scottsdale, AZ	$65,490	350
Seattle-Tacoma-Bellevue, WA	$65,310	980

Develop specifications and instructions for installation of voltage transformers, overhead or underground cables, and related electrical equipment used to conduct electrical energy from transmission lines or high-voltage distribution lines to consumers. Use computer-aided drafting equipment and/or conventional drafting stations; technical handbooks; tables; calculators; and traditional drafting tools such as boards, pencils, protractors, and T-squares. Draft working drawings, wiring diagrams, wiring connection specifications, or cross-sections of underground cables as required for instructions to installation crew. Confer with engineering staff and other personnel to resolve problems. Draw master sketches to scale, showing relation of proposed installations to existing facilities and exact specifications and dimensions. Measure factors that affect installation and arrangement of equipment, such as distances to be spanned by wire and cable. Assemble documentation packages and produce drawing sets, which are then checked by an engineer or an architect. Review completed construction drawings and cost estimates for accuracy and conformity to standards and regulations. Prepare and interpret specifications, calculating weights, volumes, and stress factors. Explain drawings to production or construction teams and provide adjustments as necessary. Supervise and train other technologists, technicians, and drafters. Study work order requests to determine type of service, such as lighting or power, demanded by installation. Visit proposed installation sites and draw rough sketches of location. Determine the order of work and the method of presentation, such as orthographic or isometric drawing. Reproduce working drawings on copy machines or trace drawings in ink. Write technical reports and draw charts that display statistics and data.

Other Considerations for Income: Electrical and electronic drafters have the highest earnings of the main drafting specialties.

Personality Type: Realistic-Investigative-Conventional. **Career Cluster:** 02 Architecture and Construction. **Career Pathway:** 02.1 Design/Pre-Construction. **Skills:** Mathematics; Installation; Active Learning; Critical Thinking; Equipment Selection; Technology Design; Quality Control Analysis; Operations Analysis.

Education and Training Program: Electrical/Electronics Drafting and Electrical/Electronics CAD/CADD. **Related Knowledge/Courses:** Design; Engineering and Technology; Building and Construction; Telecommunications; Computers and Electronics; Clerical.

Electrical Engineering Technicians

❀ Annual Earnings: $53,240
❀ Beginning Wage: $32,490
❀ Earnings Growth Potential: Medium (39.0%)
❀ Growth: 3.6%
❀ Annual Job Openings: 12,583
❀ Self-Employed: 0.9%
❀ Part-Time: 5.9%
❀ Job Security: More secure than most
❀ Education/Training Required: Associate degree

The Department of Labor reports this information for the occupation Electrical and Electronic Engineering Technicians. The job openings listed here are shared with other specializations within that occupation, including Electronics Engineering Technicians.

Industries in Which Income Is Highest

Industry	Average Annual Earnings	Number Employed
Federal, State, and Local Government	$67,180	12,640
Utilities	$59,570	7,370
Wholesale Electronic Markets and Agents and Brokers	$58,480	1,760
Chemical Manufacturing	$57,690	1,300
Postal Service	$57,600	7,690

Metropolitan Areas Where Income Is Highest

Metropolitan Area	Average Annual Earnings	Number Employed
Anchorage, AK	$75,070	220
Bremerton-Silverdale, WA	$73,860	210
Bakersfield, CA	$73,820	570
Kennewick-Richland-Pasco, WA	$68,490	160
Norwich–New London, CT-RI	$68,280	430

Apply electrical theory and related knowledge to test and modify developmental or operational electrical machinery and electrical control equipment and

E

circuitry in industrial or commercial plants and laboratories. Usually work under direction of engineering staff. Assemble electrical and electronic systems and prototypes according to engineering data and knowledge of electrical principles, using hand tools and measuring instruments. Provide technical assistance and resolution when electrical or engineering problems are encountered before, during, and after construction. Install and maintain electrical control systems and solid state equipment. Modify electrical prototypes, parts, assemblies, and systems to correct functional deviations. Set up and operate test equipment to evaluate performance of developmental parts, assemblies, or systems under simulated operating conditions and record results. Collaborate with electrical engineers and other personnel to identify, define, and solve developmental problems. Build, calibrate, maintain, troubleshoot, and repair electrical instruments or testing equipment. Analyze and interpret test information to resolve design-related problems. Write commissioning procedures for electrical installations. Prepare project cost and work-time estimates. Evaluate engineering proposals, shop drawings, and design comments for sound electrical engineering practice and conformance with established safety and design criteria and recommend approval or disapproval. Draw or modify diagrams and write engineering specifications to clarify design details and functional criteria of experimental electronics units. Conduct inspections for quality control and assurance programs, reporting findings and recommendations. Prepare contracts and initiate, review, and coordinate modifications to contract specifications and plans throughout the construction process. Plan, schedule, and monitor work of support personnel to assist supervisor. Review existing electrical engineering criteria to identify necessary revisions, deletions, or amendments to outdated material. Perform supervisory duties such as recommending work assignments, approving leaves, and completing performance evaluations.

Other Considerations for Income: Electrical Engineering Technicians are among the best-paid of the various kinds of engineering technicians.

Personality Type: Realistic-Investigative-Conventional. **Career Cluster:** 13 Manufacturing. **Career Pathways:** 13.2 Manufacturing Production Process Development; 13.3 Maintenance, Installation and Repair. **Skills:** Repairing; Installation; Troubleshooting; Science; Operations Analysis; Technology Design; Equipment Maintenance; Mathematics.

Education and Training Programs: Computer Engineering Technology/Technician; Computer Technology/

Computer Systems Technology; Electrical and Electronic Engineering Technologies/Technicians, Other; Electrical, Electronic and Communications Engineering Technology/Technician; Telecommunications Technology/Technician. **Related Knowledge/Courses:** Engineering and Technology; Design; Computers and Electronics; Physics; Mechanical; Telecommunications.

Electrical Engineers

- ❋ Annual Earnings: $82,160
- ❋ Beginning Wage: $52,990
- ❋ Earnings Growth Potential: Medium (35.5%)
- ❋ Growth: 6.3%
- ❋ Annual Job Openings: 6,806
- ❋ Self-Employed: 2.1%
- ❋ Part-Time: 2.0%
- ❋ Job Security: More secure than most
- ❋ Education/Training Required: Bachelor's degree

Industries in Which Income Is Highest

Industry	Average Annual Earnings	Number Employed
Fabricated Metal Product Manufacturing	$87,250	1,670
Computer and Electronic Product Manufacturing	$86,360	33,520
Professional, Scientific, and Technical Services	$84,720	50,300
Federal, State, and Local Government	$84,360	7,070
Utilities	$82,940	12,680

Metropolitan Areas Where Income Is Highest

Metropolitan Area	Average Annual Earnings	Number Employed
Santa Cruz–Watsonville, CA	$111,530	100
San Jose–Sunnyvale–Santa Clara, CA	$104,930	5,300
Rochester, MN	$100,140	90
Santa Barbara–Santa Maria, CA	$96,190	410
Sacramento–Arden-Arcade–Roseville, CA	$95,460	990

Design, develop, test, or supervise the manufacturing and installation of electrical equipment, components, or systems for commercial, industrial, military, or scientific use. Confer with engineers, customers, and others to discuss existing or potential engineering projects and products. Design, implement, maintain, and improve electrical instruments, equipment, facilities, components, products, and systems for commercial, industrial, and domestic purposes. Operate computer-assisted engineering and design software and equipment to perform engineering tasks. Direct and coordinate manufacturing, construction, installation, maintenance, support, documentation, and testing activities to ensure compliance with specifications, codes, and customer requirements. Perform detailed calculations to compute and establish manufacturing, construction, and installation standards and specifications. Inspect completed installations and observe operations to ensure conformance to design and equipment specifications and compliance with operational and safety standards. Plan and implement research methodology and procedures to apply principles of electrical theory to engineering projects. Prepare specifications for purchase of materials and equipment. Supervise and train project team members as necessary. Investigate and test vendors' and competitors' products. Oversee project production efforts to assure projects are completed satisfactorily, on time, and within budget. Prepare and study technical drawings, specifications of electrical systems, and topographical maps to ensure that installation and operations conform to standards and customer requirements. Investigate customer or public complaints, determine nature and extent of problem, and recommend remedial measures. Plan layout of electric-power-generating plants and distribution lines and stations. Assist in developing capital project programs for new equipment and major repairs. Develop budgets, estimating labor, material, and construction costs. Compile data and write reports regarding existing and potential engineering studies and projects.

Other Considerations for Income: As a group, engineers earn some of the highest average starting salaries among those holding bachelor's degrees. Electrical Engineers are paid in the middle range among the various kinds of engineers. According to a 2007 survey by the National Association of Colleges and Employers, average starting salaries for Electrical/Electronics and Communications Engineers were $55,292 with a bachelor's, $66,309 with a master's, and $75,982 with a Ph.D.

Personality Type: Investigative-Realistic. **Career Cluster:** 15 Science, Technology, Engineering, and Mathematics. **Career Pathway:** 15.1 Engineering and Technology.

Skills: Technology Design; Systems Analysis; Science; Troubleshooting; Systems Evaluation; Equipment Selection; Management of Material Resources; Programming.

Education and Training Program: Electrical and Electronics Engineering. **Related Knowledge/Courses:** Design; Engineering and Technology; Physics; Computers and Electronics; Mathematics; Mechanical.

Electrical Power-Line Installers and Repairers

- ❈ Annual Earnings: $55,100
- ❈ Beginning Wage: $31,420
- ❈ Earnings Growth Potential: High (43.0%)
- ❈ Growth: 7.2%
- ❈ Annual Job Openings: 6,401
- ❈ Self-Employed: 0.6%
- ❈ Part-Time: 1.3%
- ❈ Job Security: More secure than most
- ❈ Education/Training Required: Long-term on-the-job training

Industries in Which Income Is Highest

Industry	Average Annual Earnings	Number Employed
Utilities	$58,960	54,090
Management of Companies and Enterprises	$56,400	1,900
Federal, State, and Local Government	$54,240	14,790
Specialty Trade Contractors	$52,290	6,790
Heavy and Civil Engineering Construction	$45,390	31,460

Metropolitan Areas Where Income Is Highest

Metropolitan Area	Average Annual Earnings	Number Employed
Fresno, CA	$93,470	190
Visalia-Porterville, CA	$89,630	110
Merced, CA	$87,740	70
Riverside–San Bernardino–Ontario, CA	$83,180	1,470
Bakersfield, CA	$82,130	670

Install or repair cables or wires used in electrical power or distribution systems. May erect poles and light- or heavy-duty transmission towers. Adhere to safety practices and procedures, such as checking equipment regularly and erecting barriers around work areas. Open switches or attach grounding devices to remove electrical hazards from disturbed or fallen lines or to facilitate repairs. Climb poles or use truck-mounted buckets to access equipment. Place insulating or fireproofing materials over conductors and joints. Install, maintain, and repair electrical distribution and transmission systems, including conduits; cables; wires; and related equipment such as transformers, circuit breakers, and switches. Identify defective sectionalizing devices, circuit breakers, fuses, voltage regulators, transformers, switches, relays, or wiring, using wiring diagrams and electrical-testing instruments. Drive vehicles equipped with tools and materials to job sites. Coordinate work assignment preparation and completion with other workers. String wire conductors and cables between poles, towers, trenches, pylons, and buildings, setting lines in place and using winches to adjust tension. Inspect and test power lines and auxiliary equipment to locate and identify problems, using reading and testing instruments. Test conductors according to electrical diagrams and specifications to identify corresponding conductors and to prevent incorrect connections. Replace damaged poles with new poles and straighten the poles. Install watt-hour meters and connect service drops between power lines and consumers' facilities. Attach crossarms, insulators, and auxiliary equipment to poles prior to installing them. Travel in trucks, helicopters, and airplanes to inspect lines for freedom from obstruction and adequacy of insulation. Dig holes, using augers, and set poles, using cranes and power equipment. Trim trees that could be hazardous to the functioning of cables or wires.

Other Considerations for Income: Earnings for line installers and repairers are higher than those in most other occupations that do not require postsecondary education. Many line installers and repairers belong to unions, principally the Communications Workers of America, the International Brotherhood of Electrical Workers, and the Utility Workers Union of America. For these workers, union contracts set wage rates, wage increases, and the time needed to advance from one job level to the next. Good health, education, and vacation benefits are common in the occupation.

Personality Type: Realistic-Investigative-Conventional. **Career Cluster:** 02 Architecture and Construction. **Career Pathway:** 02.2 Construction. **Skills:** Repairing; Installation; Equipment Maintenance; Operation Monitoring; Troubleshooting; Operation and Control; Equipment Selection; Technology Design.

Education and Training Programs: Electrical and Power Transmission Installation/Installer, General; Electrical and Power Transmission Installers, Other; Lineworker. **Related Knowledge/Courses:** Building and Construction; Mechanical; Customer and Personal Service; Engineering and Technology; Transportation; Design.

Electronic Commerce Specialists

* Annual Earnings: $75,150
* Beginning Wage: $40,660
* Earnings Growth Potential: High (45.9%)
* Growth: 15.1%
* Annual Job Openings: 14,374
* Self-Employed: 6.6%
* Part-Time: 5.6%
* Job Security: No data available
* Education/Training Required: Work experience in a related occupation

The Department of Labor reports this information for the occupation Computer Specialists, All Other. The job openings listed here are shared with other specializations within that occupation, including Business Intelligence Analysts; Computer Systems Engineers/Architects; Data Warehousing Specialists; Database Architects; Document Management Specialists; Geographic Information Systems Technicians; Geospatial Information Scientists and Technologists; Information Technology Project Managers; Network Designers; Software Quality Assurance Engineers and Testers; Video Game Designers; Web Administrators; and Web Developers.

Industries in Which Income Is Highest

Industry	Average Annual Earnings	Number Employed
Petroleum and Coal Products Manufacturing	$97,090	1,070
Transportation Equipment Manufacturing	$82,770	3,010
Oil and Gas Extraction	$81,350	1,710
Federal, State, and Local Government	$80,670	71,650
Management of Companies and Enterprises	$78,200	14,820

Metropolitan Areas Where Income Is Highest

Metropolitan Area	Average Annual Earnings	Number Employed
Washington-Arlington-Alexandria, DC-VA-MD-WV	$97,170	19,470
Atlantic City, NJ	$96,600	510
Pascagoula, MS	$95,430	60
San Jose–Sunnyvale–Santa Clara, CA	$92,710	3,580
Baltimore-Towson, MD	$89,730	5,650

Market products on proprietary Web sites. Produce online advertising. Determine Web site content and design. Analyze customer preferences and online sales. No task data available.

Other Considerations for Income: No additional information.

Personality Type: No data available. **Career Cluster:** 11 Information Technology. **Career Pathway:** 11.2 Information Support Services. **Skills:** No data available.

Education and Training Programs: Computer and Information Sciences and Support Services, Other; Computer and Information Sciences, General; Computer Engineering Technologies/Technicians, Other; Computer Engineering, General; Computer Science; Computer Software Engineering; Computer Systems Networking and Telecommunications; E-Commerce/Electronic Commerce; Information Science/Studies; Information Technology; System, Networking, and LAN/WAN Management/Manager; Web Page, Digital/Multimedia and Information Resources Design; others. **Related Knowledge/Courses:** No data available.

Electronic Drafters

- ❈ Annual Earnings: $51,320
- ❈ Beginning Wage: $32,050
- ❈ Earnings Growth Potential: Medium (37.5%)
- ❈ Growth: 4.1%
- ❈ Annual Job Openings: 4,786
- ❈ Self-Employed: 5.7%
- ❈ Part-Time: 5.9%
- ❈ Job Security: Less secure than most
- ❈ Education/Training Required: Postsecondary vocational training

The Department of Labor reports this information for the occupation Electrical and Electronics Drafters. The job openings listed here are shared with other specializations within that occupation, including Electrical Drafters.

Industries in Which Income Is Highest

Industry	Average Annual Earnings	Number Employed
Transportation Equipment Manufacturing	$62,900	1,220
Utilities	$61,240	2,240
Telecommunications	$54,440	1,740
Computer and Electronic Product Manufacturing	$53,780	4,750
Specialty Trade Contractors	$51,390	6,000

Metropolitan Areas Where Income Is Highest

Metropolitan Area	Average Annual Earnings	Number Employed
Boulder, CO	$66,920	80
Greenville, SC	$65,880	150
Buffalo–Niagara Falls, NY	$65,540	100
Phoenix-Mesa-Scottsdale, AZ	$65,490	350
Seattle-Tacoma-Bellevue, WA	$65,310	980

Draw wiring diagrams, circuit board assembly diagrams, schematics, and layout drawings used for manufacture, installation, and repair of electronic equipment. Draft detail and assembly drawings of design components, circuitry, and printed circuit boards, using computer-assisted equipment or standard drafting techniques and devices. Consult with engineers to discuss and interpret design concepts and determine requirements of detailed working drawings. Locate files relating to specified design project in database library, load program into computer, and record completed job data. Examine electronic schematics and supporting documents to develop, compute, and verify specifications for drafting data, such as configuration of parts, dimensions, and tolerances. Supervise and coordinate work activities of workers engaged in drafting, designing layouts, assembling, and testing printed circuit boards. Compare logic element configuration on display screen with engineering schematics and calculate figures to convert, redesign, and modify element. Review work orders and procedural manuals and confer with vendors and design staff to resolve problems and modify design. Review blueprints to determine customer requirements and consult with assembler regarding schematics, wiring procedures, and conductor paths. Train students to use drafting machines and to prepare schematic diagrams, block diagrams, control drawings, logic diagrams, integrated circuit drawings, and interconnection diagrams. Generate computer tapes of final layout design to produce layered photo masks and photo plotting design onto film. Select drill size to drill test head, according to test design and specifications, and submit guide layout to designated department. Key and program specified commands and engineering specifications into computer system to change functions and test final layout. Copy drawings of printed circuit board fabrication, using print machine or blueprinting procedure. Plot electrical test points on layout sheets and draw schematics for wiring test fixture heads to frames.

Other Considerations for Income: Electrical and electronic drafters have the highest earnings of the main drafting specialties.

Personality Type: Conventional-Realistic-Investigative. **Career Cluster:** 02 Architecture and Construction. **Career Pathway:** 02.1 Design/Pre-Construction. **Skills:** Technology Design; Operations Analysis; Installation; Equipment Selection; Mathematics; Coordination; Negotiation; Complex Problem Solving.

Education and Training Program: Electrical/Electronics Drafting and Electrical/Electronics CAD/CADD. **Related Knowledge/Courses:** Design; Engineering and Technology; Mechanical; Physics; Telecommunications; Mathematics.

Electronics Engineering Technicians

※ Annual Earnings: $53,240
※ Beginning Wage: $32,490
※ Earnings Growth Potential: Medium (39.0%)
※ Growth: 3.6%
※ Annual Job Openings: 12,583
※ Self-Employed: 0.9%
※ Part-Time: 5.9%
※ Job Security: More secure than most
※ Education/Training Required: Associate degree

The Department of Labor reports this information for the occupation Electrical and Electronic Engineering Technicians. The job openings listed here are shared with other specializations within that occupation, including Electrical Engineering Technicians.

Industries in Which Income Is Highest

Industry	Average Annual Earnings	Number Employed
Federal, State, and Local Government	$67,180	12,640
Utilities	$59,570	7,370
Wholesale Electronic Markets and Agents and Brokers	$58,480	1,760
Chemical Manufacturing	$57,690	1,300
Postal Service	$57,600	7,690

Metropolitan Areas Where Income Is Highest

Metropolitan Area	Average Annual Earnings	Number Employed
Anchorage, AK	$75,070	220
Bremerton-Silverdale, WA	$73,860	210
Bakersfield, CA	$73,820	570
Kennewick-Richland-Pasco, WA	$68,490	160
Norwich–New London, CT-RI	$68,280	430

Lay out, build, test, troubleshoot, repair, and modify developmental and production electronic components, parts, equipment, and systems, such as computer equipment, missile control instrumentation, electron tubes, test equipment, and machine tool numerical controls, applying principles and theories of electronics, electrical circuitry, engineering mathematics, electronic and electrical testing, and physics. Usually work under direction of engineering staff. Read blueprints, wiring diagrams, schematic drawings, and engineering instructions for assembling electronics units, applying knowledge of electronic theory and components. Test electronics units, using standard test equipment, and analyze results to evaluate performance and determine need for adjustment. Perform preventative maintenance and calibration of equipment and systems. Assemble, test, and maintain circuitry or electronic components according to engineering instructions, technical manuals, and knowledge of electronics, using hand and power tools. Adjust and replace defective or improperly functioning circuitry and electronics components, using hand tools and soldering iron. Write reports and record data on testing techniques, laboratory equipment, and specifications to assist engineers. Identify and resolve equipment malfunctions, working with manufacturers and field representatives as necessary to procure replacement parts. Provide user applications and engineering support and recommendations for new and existing equipment with regard to installation, upgrades, and enhancement. Maintain system logs and manuals to document testing and operation of equipment. Provide customer support and education, working with users to identify needs, determine sources of problems, and provide information on product use. Maintain working knowledge of state-of-the-art tools or software by reading or by attending conferences, workshops, or other training. Build prototypes from rough sketches or plans. Design basic circuitry and draft sketches for clarification of details and design documentation under engineers' direction, using drafting instruments and computer-aided design (CAD) equipment. Procure parts and maintain inventory and related documentation. Research equipment and component needs, sources, competitive prices, delivery times, and ongoing operational costs. Write computer or microprocessor software programs.

Other Considerations for Income: Electronics Engineering Technicians are among the best-paid of the various kinds of engineering technicians.

Personality Type: Realistic-Investigative. **Career Cluster:** 13 Manufacturing. **Career Pathway:** 13.3 Maintenance, Installation and Repair. **Skills:** Repairing; Equipment Maintenance; Operation Monitoring; Troubleshooting; Systems Analysis; Quality Control Analysis; Systems Evaluation.

Education and Training Programs: Computer Engineering Technology/Technician; Computer Technology/Computer Systems Technology; Electrical and Electronic Engineering Technologies/Technicians, Other; Electrical, Electronic and Communications Engineering Technology/Technician; Telecommunications Technology/Technician. **Related Knowledge/Courses:** Telecommunications; Engineering and Technology; Design; Mechanical; Computers and Electronics; Physics.

Electronics Engineers, Except Computer

* Annual Earnings: $86,370
* Beginning Wage: $55,330
* Earnings Growth Potential: Medium (35.9%)
* Growth: 3.7%
* Annual Job Openings: 5,699
* Self-Employed: 2.2%
* Part-Time: 2.0%
* Job Security: More secure than most
* Education/Training Required: Bachelor's degree

Industries in Which Income Is Highest

Industry	Average Annual Earnings	Number Employed
Federal, State, and Local Government	$94,670	17,330
Transportation Equipment Manufacturing	$92,510	4,780
Professional, Scientific, and Technical Services	$89,350	26,300
Computer and Electronic Product Manufacturing	$88,590	35,720
Management of Companies and Enterprises	$85,980	4,200

E

Metropolitan Areas Where Income Is Highest

Metropolitan Area	Average Annual Earnings	Number Employed
Tucson, AZ	$111,210	900
Durham, NC	$106,990	530
Utica-Rome, NY	$106,730	230
San Jose–Sunnyvale–Santa Clara, CA	$105,950	7,290
Trenton-Ewing, NJ	$104,960	230

Research, design, develop, and test electronic components and systems for commercial, industrial, military, or scientific use, utilizing knowledge of electronic theory and materials properties. Design electronic circuits and components for use in fields such as telecommunications, aerospace guidance and propulsion control, acoustics, or instruments and controls. Design electronic components, software, products, or systems for commercial, industrial, medical, military, or scientific applications. Provide technical support and instruction to staff or customers regarding equipment standards, assisting with specific, difficult in-service engineering. Operate computer-assisted engineering and design software and equipment to perform engineering tasks. Analyze system requirements, capacity, cost, and customer needs to determine feasibility of project and develop system plan. Confer with engineers, customers, vendors, or others to discuss existing and potential engineering projects or products. Review and evaluate work of others inside and outside the organization to ensure effectiveness, technical adequacy, and compatibility in the resolution of complex engineering problems. Determine material and equipment needs and order supplies. Inspect electronic equipment, instruments, products, and systems to ensure conformance to specifications, safety standards, and applicable codes and regulations. Evaluate operational systems, prototypes, and proposals and recommend repair or design modifications based on factors such as environment, service, cost, and system capabilities. Prepare documentation containing information such as confidential descriptions and specifications of proprietary hardware and software, product development and introduction schedules, product costs, and information about product performance weaknesses. Direct and coordinate activities concerned with manufacture, construction, installation, maintenance, operation, and modification of electronic equipment, products, and systems. Develop and perform operational, maintenance, and testing procedures for electronic products, components, equipment, and systems. Plan and develop applications and modifications for electronic properties used in components, products, and systems to improve technical performance.

Other Considerations for Income: As a group, engineers earn some of the highest average starting salaries among those holding bachelor's degrees. Electronics Engineers are paid in the middle range among the various kinds of engineers. According to a 2007 survey by the National Association of Colleges and Employers, average starting salaries for Electrical/Electronics and Communications Engineers were $55,292 with a bachelor's, $66,309 with a master's, and $75,982 with a Ph.D.

Personality Type: Investigative-Realistic. **Career Cluster:** 15 Science, Technology, Engineering, and Mathematics. **Career Pathway:** 15.1 Engineering and Technology. **Skills:** Troubleshooting; Installation; Science; Operations Analysis; Technology Design; Equipment Selection; Systems Evaluation; Quality Control Analysis.

Education and Training Program: Electrical and Electronics Engineering. **Related Knowledge/Courses:** Engineering and Technology; Design; Physics; Computers and Electronics; Telecommunications; Production and Processing.

Elementary School Teachers, Except Special Education

- ❋ Annual Earnings: $49,330
- ❋ Beginning Wage: $33,400
- ❋ Earnings Growth Potential: Low (32.3%)
- ❋ Growth: 13.6%
- ❋ Annual Job Openings: 181,612
- ❋ Self-Employed: 0.0%
- ❋ Part-Time: 9.5%
- ❋ Job Security: More secure than most
- ❋ Education/Training Required: Bachelor's degree

Industries in Which Income Is Highest

Industry	Average Annual Earnings	Number Employed
Educational Services	$49,370	1,529,330
Administrative and Support Services	$45,550	7,920
Social Assistance	$40,580	1,510
Religious, Grantmaking, Civic, Professional, and Similar Organizations	$37,620	2,820

Metropolitan Areas Where Income Is Highest

Metropolitan Area	Average Annual Earnings	Number Employed
Kingston, NY	$70,440	940
Napa, CA	$69,300	700
Yuba City, CA	$69,170	920
Fresno, CA	$67,290	5,400
Modesto, CA	$66,790	2,800

Teach pupils in public or private schools at the elementary level basic academic, social, and other formative skills. Establish and enforce rules for behavior and procedures for maintaining order among the students for whom they are responsible. Observe and evaluate students' performance, behavior, social development, and physical health. Prepare materials and classrooms for class activities. Adapt teaching methods and instructional materials to meet students' varying needs and interests. Plan and conduct activities for a balanced program of instruction, demonstration, and work time that provides students with opportunities to observe, question, and investigate. Instruct students individually and in groups, using various teaching methods such as lectures, discussions, and demonstrations. Establish clear objectives for all lessons, units, and projects and communicate those objectives to students. Assign and grade classwork and homework. Read books to entire classes or small groups. Prepare, administer, and grade tests and assignments in order to evaluate students' progress. Confer with parents or guardians, teachers, counselors, and administrators to resolve students' behavioral and academic problems. Meet with parents and guardians to discuss their children's progress and to determine their priorities for their children and their resource needs. Prepare students for later grades by encouraging them to explore learning opportunities and to persevere with challenging tasks. Maintain accurate and complete student records as required by laws, district policies, and administrative regulations. Guide and counsel students with adjustment or academic problems or special academic interests. Prepare and implement remedial programs for students requiring extra help. Prepare objectives and outlines for courses of study, following curriculum guidelines or requirements of states and schools. Provide a variety of materials and resources for children to explore, manipulate, and use, both in learning activities and in imaginative play. Enforce administration policies and rules governing students.

Other Considerations for Income: Teachers can boost their earnings in a number of ways. In some schools, teachers receive extra pay for coaching sports and working with students in extracurricular activities. Getting a master's degree or national certification often results in a raise in pay, as does acting as a mentor. Some teachers earn extra income during the summer by teaching summer school or performing other jobs in the school system. Although private school teachers generally earn less than public school teachers, they may be given other benefits, such as free or subsidized housing.

Personality Type: Social-Artistic-Conventional. **Career Cluster:** 05 Education and Training. **Career Pathway:** 05.3 Teaching/Training. **Skills:** Instructing; Learning Strategies; Monitoring; Social Perceptiveness; Speaking; Persuasion; Writing; Service Orientation.

Education and Training Programs: Elementary Education and Teaching; Teacher Education, Multiple Levels. **Related Knowledge/Courses:** Geography; History and Archeology; Sociology and Anthropology; Therapy and Counseling; Philosophy and Theology; Education and Training.

E

Elevator Installers and Repairers

❋ Annual Earnings: $69,380
❋ Beginning Wage: $40,300
❋ Earnings Growth Potential: High (41.9%)
❋ Growth: 8.8%
❋ Annual Job Openings: 2,850
❋ Self-Employed: 0.0%
❋ Part-Time: 0.4%
❋ Job Security: Least secure
❋ Education/Training Required: Long-term on-the-job training

Industries in Which Income Is Highest

Industry	Average Annual Earnings	Number Employed
Specialty Trade Contractors	$69,600	23,480

Metropolitan Areas Where Income Is Highest

Metropolitan Area	Average Annual Earnings	Number Employed
Albany-Schenectady-Troy, NY	$93,110	90
Portland-Vancouver-Beaverton, OR-WA	$88,780	270
San Francisco–Oakland–Fremont, CA	$88,550	430
Boston-Cambridge-Quincy, MA-NH	$86,760	530
Honolulu, HI	$86,690	390

Assemble, install, repair, or maintain electric or hydraulic freight or passenger elevators, escalators, or dumbwaiters. Assemble, install, repair, and maintain elevators, escalators, moving sidewalks, and dumbwaiters, using hand and power tools and testing devices such as test lamps, ammeters, and voltmeters. Test newly installed equipment to ensure that it meets specifications such as stopping at floors for set amounts of time. Check that safety regulations and building codes are met and complete service reports verifying conformance to standards. Locate malfunctions in brakes, motors, switches, and signal and control systems, using test equipment. Connect electrical wiring to control panels and electric motors. Read and interpret blueprints to determine the layout of system components, frameworks, and foundations and to select installation equipment. Adjust safety controls; counterweights; door mechanisms; and components such as valves, ratchets, seals, and brake linings. Inspect wiring connections, control panel hookups, door installations, and alignments and clearances of cars and hoistways to ensure that equipment will operate properly. Disassemble defective units and repair or replace parts such as locks, gears, cables, and electric wiring. Maintain log books that detail all repairs and checks performed. Participate in additional training to keep skills up to date. Attach guide shoes and rollers to minimize the lateral motion of cars as they travel through shafts. Connect car frames to counterweights, using steel cables. Bolt or weld steel rails to the walls of shafts to guide elevators, working from scaffolding or platforms. Assemble elevator cars, installing each car's platform, walls, and doors. Install outer doors and door frames at elevator entrances on each floor of a structure. Install electrical wires and controls by attaching conduit along shaft walls from floor to floor and then pulling plastic-covered wires through the conduit. Cut prefabricated sections of framework, rails, and other components to specified dimensions.

Other Considerations for Income: Earnings of elevator installers and repairers are among the highest of all construction trades. Earnings for members of the International Union of Elevator Constructors vary based on the local and specialty. Check with a local in your area for exact wages. About 3 out of 4 elevator installers and repairers were members of unions or covered by a union contract, one of the highest proportions of all occupations. The largest numbers were members of the International Union of Elevator Constructors. In addition to free continuing education, elevator installers and repairers receive basic benefits enjoyed by most other workers.

Personality Type: Realistic-Investigative-Conventional. **Career Cluster:** 13 Manufacturing. **Career Pathway:** 13.3 Maintenance, Installation and Repair. **Skills:** Installation; Repairing; Equipment Maintenance; Troubleshooting; Quality Control Analysis; Technology Design; Equipment Selection; Science.

Education and Training Program: Industrial Mechanics and Maintenance Technology. **Related Knowledge/Courses:** Building and Construction; Mechanical; Physics; Design; Engineering and Technology; Public Safety and Security.

Emergency Management Specialists

❋ Annual Earnings: $50,460
❋ Beginning Wage: $27,640
❋ Earnings Growth Potential: High (45.2%)
❋ Growth: 12.3%
❋ Annual Job Openings: 1,538
❋ Self-Employed: 0.1%
❋ Part-Time: 9.6%
❋ Job Security: More secure than most
❋ Education/Training Required: Work experience in a related occupation

Industries in Which Income Is Highest

Industry	Average Annual Earnings	Number Employed
Hospitals	$54,060	1,080
Federal, State, and Local Government	$48,140	7,940

Metropolitan Areas Where Income Is Highest

Metropolitan Area	Average Annual Earnings	Number Employed
San Francisco–Oakland–Fremont, CA	$80,290	90
Los Angeles–Long Beach–Santa Ana, CA	$79,140	140
Knoxville, TN	$76,270	120
Washington-Arlington-Alexandria, DC-VA-MD-WV	$74,650	280
Portland-Vancouver-Beaverton, OR-WA	$72,020	60

Coordinate disaster response or crisis management activities, provide disaster-preparedness training, and prepare emergency plans and procedures for natural (e.g., hurricanes, floods, earthquakes), wartime, or technological (e.g., nuclear power plant emergencies, hazardous materials spills) disasters or hostage situations. Keep informed of activities or changes that could affect the likelihood of an emergency, as well as those that could affect response efforts and details of plan implementation. Prepare plans that outline operating procedures to be used in response to disasters or emergencies such as hurricanes, nuclear accidents, and terrorist attacks and in recovery from these events. Propose alteration of emergency response procedures based on regulatory changes, technological changes, or knowledge gained from outcomes of previous emergency situations. Maintain and update all resource materials associated with emergency-preparedness plans. Coordinate disaster response or crisis management activities such as ordering evacuations, opening public shelters, and implementing special needs plans and programs. Develop and maintain liaisons with municipalities, county departments, and similar entities in order to facilitate plan development, response effort coordination, and exchanges of personnel and equipment. Keep informed of federal, state, and local regulations affecting emergency plans and ensure that plans adhere to these regulations. Design and administer emergency and disaster-preparedness training courses that teach people how to effectively respond to major emergencies and disasters. Prepare emergency situation status reports that describe response and recovery efforts, needs, and preliminary damage assessments. Inspect facilities and equipment such as emergency management centers and communications equipment to determine their operational and functional capabilities in emergency situations. Consult with officials of local and area governments, schools, hospitals, and other institutions in order to determine their needs and capabilities in the event of a natural disaster or other emergency. Develop and perform tests and evaluations of emergency management plans in accordance with state and federal regulations.

Other Considerations for Income: No additional information.

Personality Type: Social-Enterprising. **Career Clusters:** 07 Government and Public Administration; 10 Human Service. **Career Pathways:** 07.1 Governance; 10.3 Family and Community Services. **Skills:** Management of Material Resources; Service Orientation; Judgment and Decision Making; Complex Problem Solving; Coordination; Operations Analysis; Management of Financial Resources; Writing.

Education and Training Programs: Community Organization and Advocacy; Public Administration. **Related Knowledge/Courses:** Public Safety and Security; Customer and Personal Service; Education and Training; Law and Government; Physics; Telecommunications.

E

Engineering Managers

❈ Annual Earnings: $115,270
❈ Beginning Wage: $73,420
❈ Earnings Growth Potential: Medium (36.3%)
❈ Growth: 7.3%
❈ Annual Job Openings: 7,404
❈ Self-Employed: 0.0%
❈ Part-Time: 2.0%
❈ Job Security: Less secure than most
❈ Education/Training Required: Work experience plus degree

Industries in Which Income Is Highest

Industry	Average Annual Earnings	Number Employed
Computer and Electronic Product Manufacturing	$128,750	28,760
Merchant Wholesalers, Durable Goods	$122,340	2,520
Management of Companies and Enterprises	$120,490	6,630
Professional, Scientific, and Technical Services	$120,010	58,960
Telecommunications	$119,930	3,130

Metropolitan Areas Where Income Is Highest

Metropolitan Area	Average Annual Earnings	Number Employed
San Jose–Sunnyvale–Santa Clara, CA	$154,310	7,100
Midland, TX	$152,580	130
Boulder, CO	$146,290	680
Decatur, IL	$143,540	400
Poughkeepsie-Newburgh-Middletown, NY	$143,480	330

Plan, direct, or coordinate activities or research and development in such fields as architecture and engineering. Coordinate and direct projects, making detailed plans to accomplish goals and directing the integration of technical activities. Consult or negotiate with clients to prepare project specifications. Present and explain proposals, reports, and findings to clients. Direct, review, and approve product design and changes. Recruit employ-ees; assign, direct, and evaluate their work; and oversee the development and maintenance of staff competence. Perform administrative functions such as reviewing and writing reports, approving expenditures, enforcing rules, and making decisions about the purchase of materials or services. Prepare budgets, bids, and contracts and direct the negotiation of research contracts. Analyze technology, resource needs, and market demand to plan and assess the feasibility of projects. Confer with management, production, and marketing staff to discuss project specifications and procedures. Review and recommend or approve contracts and cost estimates. Develop and implement policies, standards, and procedures for the engineering and technical work performed in the department, service, laboratory, or firm. Plan and direct the installation, testing, operation, maintenance, and repair of facilities and equipment. Administer highway planning, construction, and maintenance. Confer with and report to officials and the public to provide information and solicit support for projects. Set scientific and technical goals within broad outlines provided by top management. Direct the engineering of water control, treatment, and distribution projects. Plan, direct, and coordinate survey work with other staff activities; certify survey work; and write land legal descriptions.

Other Considerations for Income: Engineering Managers, especially those at higher levels, often receive more benefits—such as expense accounts, stock option plans, and bonuses—than do nonmanagerial workers in their organizations.

Personality Type: Enterprising-Realistic-Investigative. **Career Clusters:** 02 Architecture and Construction; 11 Information Technology; 15 Science, Technology, Engineering, and Mathematics. **Career Pathways:** 02.1 Design/Pre-Construction; 11.4 Programming and Software Development; 15.1 Engineering and Technology; 15.3 Science and Mathematics. **Skills:** Management of Financial Resources; Systems Analysis; Systems Evaluation; Management of Personnel Resources; Management of Material Resources; Mathematics; Complex Problem Solving; Negotiation.

Education and Training Programs: Aerospace, Aeronautical and Astronautical/Space Engineering; Agricultural Engineering; Architectural Engineering; Architecture (BArch, BA/BS, MArch, MA/MS, PhD); Bioengineering and Biomedical Engineering; Ceramic Sciences and Engineering; Chemical Engineering; City/Urban, Community and Regional Planning; Civil Engineering, General; Civil Engineering, Other; Computer Engineering, General; Computer Engineering, Other; Computer Hardware Engineering; Computer Software Engineering; others. **Related Knowledge/Courses:** Engineering and Technology; Design; Physics; Building and Construction; Computers and Electronics; Mathematics.

Engineering Teachers, Postsecondary

- ❀ Annual Earnings: $82,810
- ❀ Beginning Wage: $45,150
- ❀ Earnings Growth Potential: High (45.5%)
- ❀ Growth: 22.9%
- ❀ Annual Job Openings: 5,565
- ❀ Self-Employed: 0.4%
- ❀ Part-Time: 27.8%
- ❀ Job Security: Most secure
- ❀ Education/Training Required: Doctoral degree

Industries in Which Income Is Highest

Industry	Average Annual Earnings	Number Employed
Educational Services	$82,810	31,980

Metropolitan Areas Where Income Is Highest

Metropolitan Area	Average Annual Earnings	Number Employed
Raleigh-Cary, NC	$114,070	220
Philadelphia-Camden-Wilmington, PA-NJ-DE-MD	$107,480	880
Sacramento–Arden-Arcade–Roseville, CA	$104,330	70
Columbus, OH	$103,820	310
Boston-Cambridge-Quincy, MA-NH	$101,310	870

Teach courses pertaining to the application of physical laws and principles of engineering for the development of machines, materials, instruments, processes, and services. Includes teachers of subjects such as chemical, civil, electrical, industrial, mechanical, mineral, and petroleum engineering. Includes both teachers primar-ily engaged in teaching and those who do a combination of both teaching and research.** Prepare and deliver lectures to undergraduate and/or graduate students on topics such as mechanics, hydraulics, and robotics. Keep abreast of developments in their field by reading current literature, talking with colleagues, and participating in professional conferences. Supervise undergraduate and/or graduate teaching, internship, and research work. Evaluate and grade students' classwork, laboratory work, assignments, and papers. Conduct research in a particular field of knowledge and publish findings in professional journals, books, and/or electronic media. Prepare course materials such as syllabi, homework assignments, and handouts. Compile, administer, and grade examinations or assign this work to others. Write grant proposals to procure external research funding. Supervise students' laboratory work. Initiate, facilitate, and moderate class discussions. Maintain regularly scheduled office hours to advise and assist students. Plan, evaluate, and revise curricula, course content, and course materials and methods of instruction. Advise students on academic and vocational curricula and on career issues. Maintain student attendance records, grades, and other required records. Collaborate with colleagues to address teaching and research issues. Select and obtain materials and supplies such as textbooks and laboratory equipment. Participate in student recruitment, registration, and placement activities. Serve on academic or administrative committees that deal with institutional policies, departmental matters, and academic issues. Perform administrative duties such as serving as department head. Provide professional consulting services to government and/or industry. Compile bibliographies of specialized materials for outside reading assignments. Act as advisers to student organizations. Participate in campus and community events.

Other Considerations for Income: Earnings for college faculty vary according to rank and type of institution, geographic area, and field. According to a 2006–2007 survey by the American Association of University Professors, salaries for full-time faculty averaged $73,207. By rank, the average was $98,974 for professors, $69,911 for associate professors, $58,662 for assistant professors, $42,609 for instructors, and $48,289 for lecturers. Faculty in 4-year institutions earn higher salaries, on average, than do those in 2-year schools. Many faculty members have significant earnings in addition to their base salary from consulting, teaching additional courses, research, writing for publication, or other employment. In addition, many college and university faculty enjoy unique benefits, including access to campus facilities, tuition waivers for dependents, hous-

E

ing and travel allowances, and paid leave for sabbaticals. Part-time faculty and instructors usually have fewer benefits than full-time faculty.

Personality Type: Investigative-Realistic-Social. **Career Clusters:** 02 Architecture and Construction; 05 Education and Training; 11 Information Technology; 15 Science, Technology, Engineering, and Mathematics. **Career Pathways:** 02.1 Design/Pre-Construction; 05.3 Teaching/Training; 11.4 Programming and Software Development; 15.1 Engineering and Technology; 15.3 Science and Mathematics. **Skills:** Science; Programming; Mathematics; Technology Design; Complex Problem Solving; Management of Financial Resources; Critical Thinking; Operations Analysis.

Education and Training Programs: Aerospace, Aeronautical and Astronautical/Space Engineering; Agricultural Engineering; Architectural Engineering; Bioengineering and Biomedical Engineering; Ceramic Sciences and Engineering; Chemical Engineering; Civil Engineering, General; Civil Engineering, Other; Computer Engineering, General; Computer Engineering, Other; Computer Hardware Engineering; Computer Software Engineering; Construction Engineering; Electrical and Electronics Engineering; Engineering Mechanics; others. **Related Knowledge/Courses:** Engineering and Technology; Physics; Design; Mathematics; Education and Training; Telecommunications.

English Language and Literature Teachers, Postsecondary

* Annual Earnings: $56,380
* Beginning Wage: $32,290
* Earnings Growth Potential: High (42.7%)
* Growth: 22.9%
* Annual Job Openings: 10,475
* Self-Employed: 0.4%
* Part-Time: 27.8%
* Job Security: Most secure
* Education/Training Required: Doctoral degree

Industries in Which Income Is Highest

Industry	Average Annual Earnings	Number Employed
Educational Services	$56,380	62,210

Metropolitan Areas Where Income Is Highest

Metropolitan Area	Average Annual Earnings	Number Employed
San Diego–Carlsbad–San Marcos, CA	$84,980	650
Columbus, OH	$79,890	400
Lubbock, TX	$79,100	160
San Jose–Sunnyvale–Santa Clara, CA	$78,130	340
Los Angeles–Long Beach–Santa Ana, CA	$77,940	2,610

Teach courses in English language and literature, including linguistics and comparative literature. Initiate, facilitate, and moderate classroom discussions. Evaluate and grade students' classwork, assignments, and papers. Prepare course materials such as syllabi, homework assignments, and handouts. Prepare and deliver lectures to undergraduate and graduate students on topics such as poetry, novel structure, and translation and adaptation. Maintain student attendance records, grades, and other required records. Plan, evaluate, and revise curricula, course content, and course materials and methods of instruction. Compile, administer, and grade examinations or assign this work to others. Maintain regularly scheduled office hours in order to advise and assist students. Keep abreast of developments in their field by reading current literature, talking with colleagues, and participating in professional conferences. Select and obtain materials and supplies such as textbooks. Advise students on academic and vocational curricula and on career issues. Conduct research in a particular field of knowledge and publish findings in professional journals, books, or electronic media. Collaborate with colleagues to address teaching and research issues. Serve on academic or administrative committees that deal with institutional policies, departmental matters, and academic issues. Participate in campus and community events. Participate in student recruitment, registration, and placement activities. Compile bibliographies of specialized materials for outside reading assignments. Supervise undergraduate and/or graduate teaching, internship, and research work. Provide assistance to students in college writing centers. Perform administrative duties such as serving as department head. Recruit, train, and supervise student writing instructors. Act as advisers to student organizations. Write grant proposals to procure external research funding. Provide professional consulting services to government or industry.

Other Considerations for Income: Earnings for college faculty vary according to rank and type of institution, geographic area, and field. According to a 2006–2007 survey by the American Association of University Professors, salaries for full-time faculty averaged $73,207. By rank, the average was $98,974 for professors, $69,911 for associate professors, $58,662 for assistant professors, $42,609 for instructors, and $48,289 for lecturers. Faculty in 4-year institutions earn higher salaries, on average, than do those in 2-year schools. Many faculty members have significant earnings in addition to their base salary from consulting, teaching additional courses, research, writing for publication, or other employment. In addition, many college and university faculty enjoy unique benefits, including access to campus facilities, tuition waivers for dependents, housing and travel allowances, and paid leave for sabbaticals. Part-time faculty and instructors usually have fewer benefits than full-time faculty.

Personality Type: Social-Artistic-Investigative. **Career Clusters:** 03 Arts, Audio/Video Technology, and Communications; 05 Education and Training. **Career Pathways:** 03.5 Journalism and Broadcasting; 05.3 Teaching/Training. **Skills:** Instructing; Writing; Learning Strategies; Social Perceptiveness; Reading Comprehension; Persuasion; Critical Thinking; Active Learning.

Education and Training Programs: Comparative Literature; English Language and Literature, General; English Language and Literature/Letters, Other; Humanities/Humanistic Studies. **Related Knowledge/Courses:** Philosophy and Theology; History and Archeology; English Language; Education and Training; Fine Arts; Sociology and Anthropology.

Environmental Compliance Inspectors

- ❊ Annual Earnings: $48,890
- ❊ Beginning Wage: $29,490
- ❊ Earnings Growth Potential: Medium (39.7%)
- ❊ Growth: 4.9%
- ❊ Annual Job Openings: 15,841
- ❊ Self-Employed: 0.4%
- ❊ Part-Time: 5.0%
- ❊ Job Security: More secure than most
- ❊ Education/Training Required: Long-term on-the-job training

The Department of Labor reports this information for the occupation Compliance Officers, Except Agriculture, Construction, Health and Safety, and Transportation. The job openings listed here are shared with other specializations within that occupation, including Coroners; Equal Opportunity Representatives and Officers; Government Property Inspectors and Investigators; Licensing Examiners and Inspectors; and Regulatory Affairs Specialists.

Industries in Which Income Is Highest

Industry	Average Annual Earnings	Number Employed
Postal Service	$77,500	1,970
Utilities	$74,890	1,880
Securities, Commodity Contracts, and Other Financial Investments and Related Activities	$70,720	6,480
Telecommunications	$64,400	2,560
Chemical Manufacturing	$61,920	3,910

Metropolitan Areas Where Income Is Highest

Metropolitan Area	Average Annual Earnings	Number Employed
Brunswick, GA	$83,080	500
Bridgeport-Stamford-Norwalk, CT	$73,120	640
Warner Robins, GA	$69,670	80
San Francisco–Oakland–Fremont, CA	$67,520	4,370
Hartford–West Hartford–East Hartford, CT	$67,460	1,420

E

Inspect and investigate sources of pollution to protect the public and environment and ensure conformance with federal, state, and local regulations and ordinances. Determine the nature of code violations and actions to be taken and issue written notices of violation; participate in enforcement hearings as necessary. Examine permits, licenses, applications, and records to ensure compliance with licensing requirements. Prepare, organize, and maintain inspection records. Interview individuals to determine the nature of suspected violations and to obtain evidence of violations. Prepare written, oral, tabular, and graphic reports summarizing requirements and regulations, including enforcement and chain of custody documentation. Monitor follow-up actions in cases where violations were found and review compliance monitoring reports. Investigate complaints and suspected violations regarding illegal dumping, pollution, pesticides, product quality, or labeling laws. Inspect waste pretreatment, treatment, and disposal facilities and systems for conformance to federal, state, or local regulations. Inform individuals and groups of pollution control regulations and inspection findings and explain how problems can be corrected. Determine sampling locations and methods and collect water or wastewater samples for analysis, preserving samples with appropriate containers and preservation methods. Verify that hazardous chemicals are handled, stored, and disposed of in accordance with regulations. Research and keep informed of pertinent information and developments in areas such as EPA laws and regulations. Determine which sites and violation reports to investigate and coordinate compliance and enforcement activities with other government agencies. Observe and record field conditions, gathering, interpreting, and reporting data such as flow meter readings and chemical levels. Learn and observe proper safety precautions, rules, regulations, and practices so that unsafe conditions can be recognized and proper safety protocols implemented. Evaluate label information for accuracy and conformance to regulatory requirements.

Other Considerations for Income: No additional information.

Personality Type: Conventional-Investigative-Realistic. **Career Cluster:** 12 Law, Public Safety, Corrections, and Security. **Career Pathway:** 12.6 Inspection Services. **Skills:** Science; Negotiation; Writing; Reading Comprehension; Mathematics; Active Listening; Persuasion; Operation Monitoring.

Education and Training Program: Natural Resources Management and Policy, Other. **Related Knowledge/**

Courses: Biology; Chemistry; Law and Government; Geography; Physics; Engineering and Technology.

Environmental Economists

- ❋ Annual Earnings: $83,590
- ❋ Beginning Wage: $44,050
- ❋ Earnings Growth Potential: High (47.3%)
- ❋ Growth: 7.5%
- ❋ Annual Job Openings: 1,555
- ❋ Self-Employed: 6.5%
- ❋ Part-Time: 3.3%
- ❋ Job Security: No data available
- ❋ Education/Training Required: Master's degree

The Department of Labor reports this information for the occupation Economists. The job openings listed here are shared with other specializations within that occupation.

Industries in Which Income Is Highest

Industry	Average Annual Earnings	Number Employed
Professional, Scientific, and Technical Services	$91,680	3,250
Federal, State, and Local Government	$82,140	7,090

Metropolitan Areas Where Income Is Highest

Metropolitan Area	Average Annual Earnings	Number Employed
Washington-Arlington-Alexandria, DC-VA-MD-WV	$107,190	4,670
New York–Northern New Jersey–Long Island, NY-NJ-PA	$100,280	310
Los Angeles–Long Beach–Santa Ana, CA	$99,620	190
San Francisco–Oakland–Fremont, CA	$99,400	210
Portland-Vancouver-Beaverton, OR-WA	$91,230	130

Assess and quantify the benefits of environmental alternatives, such as use of renewable energy resources. No task data available.

Other Considerations for Income: In the federal government, having a doctoral degree can mean a starting salary $10,000 higher than for someone with a master's degree.

Personality Type: No data available. **Career Clusters:** 01 Agriculture, Food and Natural Resource; 04 Business, Management, and Administration; 15 Science, Technology, Engineering, and Mathematics. **Career Pathways:** 01.2 Plant Systems; 04.1 Management; 15.3 Science and Mathematics. **Skills:** No data available.

Education and Training Programs: Agricultural Economics; Applied Economics; Business/Managerial Economics; Development Economics and International Development; Econometrics and Quantitative Economics; Economics, General; Economics, Other; International Economics. **Related Knowledge/Courses:** No data available.

Environmental Engineers

* Annual Earnings: $74,020
* Beginning Wage: $45,310
* Earnings Growth Potential: Medium (38.8%)
* Growth: 25.4%
* Annual Job Openings: 5,003
* Self-Employed: 2.7%
* Part-Time: 3.0%
* Job Security: Most secure
* Education/Training Required: Bachelor's degree

Industries in Which Income Is Highest

Industry	Average Annual Earnings	Number Employed
Waste Management and Remediation Services	$75,860	2,370
Professional, Scientific, and Technical Services	$74,410	27,540
Federal, State, and Local Government	$71,410	15,660

Metropolitan Areas Where Income Is Highest

Metropolitan Area	Average Annual Earnings	Number Employed
Oxnard–Thousand Oaks–Ventura, CA	$99,230	90
Bakersfield, CA	$97,740	80
San Francisco–Oakland–Fremont, CA	$96,080	960
Bradenton-Sarasota-Venice, FL	$92,800	110
Durham, NC	$91,420	190

Design, plan, or perform engineering duties in the prevention, control, and remediation of environmental health hazards, using various engineering disciplines. Work may include waste treatment, site remediation, or pollution control technology. Collaborate with environmental scientists, planners, hazardous waste technicians, engineers, and other specialists and experts in law and business to address environmental problems. Inspect industrial and municipal facilities and programs to evaluate operational effectiveness and ensure compliance with environmental regulations. Prepare, review, and update environmental investigation and recommendation reports. Design and supervise the development of systems processes or equipment for control, management, or remediation of water, air, or soil quality. Provide environmental engineering assistance in network analysis, regulatory analysis, and planning or reviewing database development. Obtain, update, and maintain plans, permits, and standard operating procedures. Provide technical-level support for environmental remediation and litigation projects, including remediation system design and determination of regulatory applicability. Monitor progress of environmental improvement programs. Inform company employees and other interested parties of environmental issues. Advise corporations and government agencies of procedures to follow in cleaning up contaminated sites to protect people and the environment. Develop proposed project objectives and targets and report to management on progress in attaining them. Request bids from suppliers or consultants. Advise industries and government agencies about environmental policies and standards. Assess the existing or potential environmental impact of land use projects on air, water, and land. Assist in budget implementation, forecasts, and administration. Serve on teams conducting multimedia inspections at complex facilities, providing assistance with planning, quality assurance, safety inspection protocols, and sampling. Coordinate and manage environmental protection programs and projects,

E

assigning and evaluating work. Maintain, write, and revise quality assurance documentation and procedures.

Other Considerations for Income: As a group, engineers earn some of the highest average starting salaries among those holding bachelor's degrees. Environmental Engineers are paid in the middle range among the various kinds of engineers. According to a 2007 survey by the National Association of Colleges and Employers, average starting salaries for Environmental or Environmental Health Engineers were $47,960 with a bachelor's.

Personality Type: Investigative-Realistic-Conventional. **Career Cluster:** 15 Science, Technology, Engineering, and Mathematics. **Career Pathway:** 15.1 Engineering and Technology. **Skills:** Systems Analysis; Systems Evaluation; Quality Control Analysis; Mathematics; Complex Problem Solving; Operation Monitoring; Management of Financial Resources; Judgment and Decision Making.

Education and Training Program: Environmental/Environmental Health Engineering. **Related Knowledge/Courses:** Engineering and Technology; Physics; Design; Chemistry; Building and Construction; Biology.

Environmental Restoration Planners

※ Annual Earnings: $59,750

※ Beginning Wage: $36,310

※ Earnings Growth Potential: Medium (39.2%)

※ Growth: 25.1%

※ Annual Job Openings: 6,961

※ Self-Employed: 2.2%

※ Part-Time: 5.3%

※ Job Security: No data available

※ Education/Training Required: Master's degree

The Department of Labor reports this information for the occupation Environmental Scientists and Specialists, Including Health. The job openings listed here are shared with other specializations within that occupation, including Climate Change Analysts; Environmental Scientists and Specialists, Including Health; and Industrial Ecologists.

Industries in Which Income Is Highest

Industry	Average Annual Earnings	Number Employed
Utilities	$83,440	1,040
Professional, Scientific, and Technical Services	$61,330	35,270
Federal, State, and Local Government	$57,970	35,460
Educational Services	$57,170	2,840

Metropolitan Areas Where Income Is Highest

Metropolitan Area	Average Annual Earnings	Number Employed
Washington-Arlington-Alexandria, DC-VA-MD-WV	$89,540	3,750
San Jose–Sunnyvale–Santa Clara, CA	$82,970	390
Boston-Cambridge-Quincy, MA-NH	$82,930	2,110
Ann Arbor, MI	$80,300	210
Santa Rosa–Petaluma, CA	$79,330	380

Collaborate with field and biology staff to oversee the implementation of restoration projects and to develop new products. Process and synthesize complex scientific data into practical strategies for restoration, monitoring, or management. No task data available.

Other Considerations for Income: According to the National Association of Colleges and Employers, beginning salary offers in July 2007 for graduates with bachelor's degrees in an environmental science averaged $38,336 a year.

Personality Type: No data available. **Career Cluster:** 01 Agriculture, Food and Natural Resource. **Career Pathway:** 01.5 Natural Resources Systems. **Skills:** No data available.

Education and Training Programs: Environmental Science; Environmental Studies. **Related Knowledge/Courses:** No data available.

Environmental Science Teachers, Postsecondary

❋ Annual Earnings: $65,130
❋ Beginning Wage: $31,550
❋ Earnings Growth Potential: Very high (51.6%)
❋ Growth: 22.9%
❋ Annual Job Openings: 769
❋ Self-Employed: 0.4%
❋ Part-Time: 27.8%
❋ Job Security: Most secure
❋ Education/Training Required: Doctoral degree

Industries in Which Income Is Highest

Industry	Average Annual Earnings	Number Employed
Educational Services	$65,360	4,840

Metropolitan Areas Where Income Is Highest

Metropolitan Area	Average Annual Earnings	Number Employed
San Diego–Carlsbad–San Marcos, CA	$111,650	40
Philadelphia-Camden-Wilmington, PA-NJ-DE-MD	$99,240	160
Minneapolis–St. Paul–Bloomington, MN-WI	$98,330	40
Riverside–San Bernardino–Ontario, CA	$89,470	60
Los Angeles–Long Beach–Santa Ana, CA	$86,420	70

Teach courses in environmental science. Supervise undergraduate and/or graduate teaching, internship, and research work. Conduct research in a particular field of knowledge and publish findings in professional journals, books, and/or electronic media. Keep abreast of developments in their field by reading current literature, talking with colleagues, and participating in professional conferences. Evaluate and grade students' classwork, laboratory work, assignments, and papers. Write grant proposals to procure external research funding. Supervise students' laboratory work and fieldwork. Prepare course materials such as syllabi, homework assignments, and handouts. Plan, evaluate, and revise curricula, course content, and course materials and methods of instruction. Compile, administer, and grade examinations or assign this work to others. Initiate, facilitate, and moderate classroom discussions. Advise students on academic and vocational curricula and on career issues. Prepare and deliver lectures to undergraduate and/or graduate students on topics such as hazardous waste management, industrial safety, and environmental toxicology. Maintain student attendance records, grades, and other required records. Select and obtain materials and supplies such as textbooks and laboratory equipment. Maintain regularly scheduled office hours in order to advise and assist students. Collaborate with colleagues to address teaching and research issues. Perform administrative duties such as serving as department head. Participate in student recruitment, registration, and placement activities. Provide professional consulting services to government and/or industry. Serve on academic or administrative committees that deal with institutional policies, departmental matters, and academic issues. Compile bibliographies of specialized materials for outside reading assignments. Participate in campus and community events. Act as advisers to student organizations.

Other Considerations for Income: Earnings for college faculty vary according to rank and type of institution, geographic area, and field. According to a 2006–2007 survey by the American Association of University Professors, salaries for full-time faculty averaged $73,207. By rank, the average was $98,974 for professors, $69,911 for associate professors, $58,662 for assistant professors, $42,609 for instructors, and $48,289 for lecturers. Faculty in 4-year institutions earn higher salaries, on average, than do those in 2-year schools. Many faculty members have significant earnings in addition to their base salary from consulting, teaching additional courses, research, writing for publication, or other employment. In addition, many college and university faculty enjoy unique benefits, including access to campus facilities, tuition waivers for dependents, housing and travel allowances, and paid leave for sabbaticals. Part-time faculty and instructors usually have fewer benefits than full-time faculty.

Personality Type: Social-Investigative-Artistic. **Career Clusters:** 01 Agriculture, Food and Natural Resource; 05 Education and Training. **Career Pathways:** 01.5 Natural Resources Systems; 05.3 Teaching/Training. **Skills:** Science; Writing; Reading Comprehension; Instructing; Mathematics; Management of Financial Resources; Programming; Critical Thinking.

Education and Training Programs: Environmental Science; Environmental Studies; Science Teacher Education/

General Science Teacher Education. **Related Knowledge/ Courses:** Biology; Geography; Chemistry; Education and Training; Physics; History and Archeology.

Environmental Scientists and Specialists, Including Health

❀ Annual Earnings: $59,750

❀ Beginning Wage: $36,310

❀ Earnings Growth Potential: Medium (39.2%)

❀ Growth: 25.1%

❀ Annual Job Openings: 6,961

❀ Self-Employed: 2.2%

❀ Part-Time: 5.3%

❀ Job Security: More secure than most

❀ Education/Training Required: Master's degree

Industries in Which Income Is Highest

Industry	Average Annual Earnings	Number Employed
Utilities	$83,440	1,040
Professional, Scientific, and Technical Services	$61,330	35,270
Federal, State, and Local Government	$57,970	35,460
Educational Services	$57,170	2,840

Metropolitan Areas Where Income Is Highest

Metropolitan Area	Average Annual Earnings	Number Employed
Washington-Arlington-Alexandria, DC-VA-MD-WV	$89,540	3,750
San Jose–Sunnyvale–Santa Clara, CA	$82,970	390
Boston-Cambridge-Quincy, MA-NH	$82,930	2,110
Ann Arbor, MI	$80,300	210
Santa Rosa–Petaluma, CA	$79,330	380

Conduct research or perform investigation for the purpose of identifying, abating, or eliminating sources of pollutants or hazards that affect either the environment or the health of the population. Using knowledge of various scientific disciplines, may collect, synthesize, study, report, and take action based on data derived from measurements or observations of air, food, soil, water, and other sources. Collect, synthesize, analyze, manage, and report environmental data such as pollution emission measurements, atmospheric monitoring measurements, meteorological and mineralogical information, and soil or water samples. Analyze data to determine validity, quality, and scientific significance, and to interpret correlations between human activities and environmental effects. Communicate scientific and technical information to the public, organizations, or internal audiences through oral briefings, written documents, workshops, conferences, training sessions, or public hearings. Provide scientific and technical guidance, support, coordination, and oversight to governmental agencies, environmental programs, industry, or the public. Process and review environmental permits, licenses, and related materials. Review and implement environmental technical standards, guidelines, policies, and formal regulations that meet all appropriate requirements. Prepare charts or graphs from data samples, providing summary information on the environmental relevance of the data. Determine data collection methods to be employed in research projects and surveys. Investigate and report on accidents affecting the environment. Research sources of pollution to determine their effects on the environment and to develop theories or methods of pollution abatement or control. Provide advice on proper standards and regulations or the development of policies, strategies, and codes of practice for environmental management. Monitor effects of pollution and land degradation, and recommend means of prevention or control. Supervise or train students, environmental technologists, technicians, or other related staff. Evaluate violations or problems discovered during inspections to determine appropriate regulatory actions or to provide advice on the development and prosecution of regulatory cases. Conduct environmental audits and inspections, and investigations of violations.

Other Considerations for Income: According to the National Association of Colleges and Employers, beginning salary offers in July 2007 for graduates with bachelor's degrees in an environmental science averaged $38,336 a year.

Personality Type: Investigative-Realistic-Conventional. **Career Cluster:** 01 Agriculture, Food and Natural Resource. **Career Pathway:** 01.5 Natural Resources Systems. **Skills:** Science; Programming; Systems Analysis; Systems Evaluation; Reading Comprehension; Writing; Complex Problem Solving; Management of Personnel Resources.

Education and Training Programs: Environmental Science; Environmental Studies. **Related Knowledge/ Courses:** Biology; Geography; Chemistry; Physics; Law and Government; Engineering and Technology.

Epidemiologists

- ❀ Annual Earnings: $61,360
- ❀ Beginning Wage: $40,480
- ❀ Earnings Growth Potential: Low (34.0%)
- ❀ Growth: 13.6%
- ❀ Annual Job Openings: 503
- ❀ Self-Employed: 2.6%
- ❀ Part-Time: 5.9%
- ❀ Job Security: More secure than most
- ❀ Education/Training Required: Master's degree

Industries in Which Income Is Highest

Industry	Average Annual Earnings	Number Employed
Professional, Scientific, and Technical Services	$70,400	520
Hospitals	$66,890	620
Federal, State, and Local Government	$57,690	2,530
Educational Services	$57,290	380

Metropolitan Areas Where Income Is Highest

Metropolitan Area	Average Annual Earnings	Number Employed
San Francisco–Oakland–Fremont, CA	$99,980	60
Durham, NC	$84,050	50
Washington-Arlington-Alexandria, DC-VA-MD-WV	$73,980	170
Hartford–West Hartford–East Hartford, CT	$72,900	110
Chicago-Naperville-Joliet, IL-IN-WI	$69,960	110

Investigate and describe the determinants and distribution of disease, disability, and other health outcomes and develop the means for prevention and control. Monitor and report incidents of infectious diseases to local and state health agencies. Plan and direct studies to investigate human or animal disease, preventive methods, and treatments for disease. Communicate research findings on various types of diseases to health practitioners, policy makers, and the public. Provide expertise in the design, management, and evaluation of study protocols and health status questionnaires, sample selection, and analysis. Oversee public health programs, including statistical analysis, health care planning, surveillance systems, and public health improvement. Investigate diseases or parasites to determine cause and risk factors, progress, life cycle, or mode of transmission. Educate healthcare workers, patients, and the public about infectious and communicable diseases, including disease transmission and prevention. Conduct research to develop methodologies, instrumentation, and procedures for medical application, analyzing data and presenting findings. Identify and analyze public health issues related to foodborne parasitic diseases and their impact on public policies or scientific studies or surveys. Supervise professional, technical, and clerical personnel. Plan, administer, and evaluate health safety standards and programs to improve public health, conferring with health department, industry personnel, physicians, and others. Prepare and analyze samples to study effects of drugs, gases, pesticides, or microorganisms on cell structure and tissue. Consult with and advise physicians, educators, researchers, government health officials, and others regarding medical applications of sciences such as physics, biology, and chemistry. Teach principles of medicine and medical and laboratory procedures to physicians, residents, students, and technicians. Standardize drug dosages, methods of immunization, and procedures for manufacture of drugs and medicinal compounds.

Other Considerations for Income: No additional information.

Personality Type: Investigative-Social. **Career Clusters:** 10 Human Service; 15 Science, Technology, Engineering, and Mathematics. **Career Pathways:** 10.2 Counseling and Mental Health Services; 15.3 Science and Mathematics. **Skills:** Systems Analysis; Systems Evaluation; Reading Comprehension; Complex Problem Solving; Judgment and Decision Making; Management of Personnel Resources; Science; Writing.

Education and Training Programs: Cell/Cellular Biology and Histology; Epidemiology; Medical Scientist. **Related Knowledge/Courses:** Biology; Medicine and Dentistry; Sociology and Anthropology; Geography; Mathematics; Education and Training.

Equal Opportunity Representatives and Officers

❀ Annual Earnings: $48,890
❀ Beginning Wage: $29,490
❀ Earnings Growth Potential: Medium (39.7%)
❀ Growth: 4.9%
❀ Annual Job Openings: 15,841
❀ Self-Employed: 0.4%
❀ Part-Time: 5.0%
❀ Job Security: More secure than most
❀ Education/Training Required: Long-term on-the-job training

The Department of Labor reports this information for the occupation Compliance Officers, Except Agriculture, Construction, Health and Safety, and Transportation. The job openings listed here are shared with other specializations within that occupation, including Coroners; Environmental Compliance Inspectors; Government Property Inspectors and Investigators; Licensing Examiners and Inspectors; and Regulatory Affairs Specialists.

Industries in Which Income Is Highest

Industry	Average Annual Earnings	Number Employed
Postal Service	$77,500	1,970
Utilities	$74,890	1,880
Securities, Commodity Contracts, and Other Financial Investments and Related Activities	$70,720	6,480
Telecommunications	$64,400	2,560
Chemical Manufacturing	$61,920	3,910

Metropolitan Areas Where Income Is Highest

Metropolitan Area	Average Annual Earnings	Number Employed
Brunswick, GA	$83,080	500
Bridgeport-Stamford-Norwalk, CT	$73,120	640
Warner Robins, GA	$69,670	80
San Francisco–Oakland–Fremont, CA	$67,520	4,370
Hartford–West Hartford–East Hartford, CT	$67,460	1,420

Monitor and evaluate compliance with equal opportunity laws, guidelines, and policies to ensure that employment practices and contracting arrangements give equal opportunity without regard to race, religion, color, national origin, sex, age, or disability. Investigate employment practices and alleged violations of laws to document and correct discriminatory factors. Interpret civil rights laws and equal opportunity regulations for individuals and employers. Study equal opportunity complaints to clarify issues. Meet with persons involved in equal opportunity complaints to verify case information and to arbitrate and settle disputes. Coordinate, monitor, and revise complaint procedures to ensure timely processing and review of complaints. Prepare reports of selection, survey, and other statistics and recommendations for corrective action. Conduct surveys and evaluate findings to determine whether systematic discrimination exists. Develop guidelines for nondiscriminatory employment practices and monitor their implementation and impact. Review company contracts to determine actions required to meet governmental equal opportunity provisions. Counsel newly hired members of minority and disadvantaged groups, informing them about details of civil rights laws. Provide information, technical assistance, and training to supervisors, managers, and employees on topics such as employee supervision, hiring, grievance procedures, and staff development. Verify that all job descriptions are submitted for review and approval and that descriptions meet regulatory standards. Act as liaisons between minority placement agencies and employers or between job search committees and other equal opportunity administrators. Consult with community representatives to develop technical assistance agreements in accordance with governmental regulations. Meet with job search committees or coordinators to explain the role of the equal opportunity coordinator, to provide resources for advertising, and to explain expectations for future contacts. Participate in the recruitment of employees through job fairs, career days, and advertising plans.

Other Considerations for Income: No additional information.

Personality Type: Social-Enterprising-Conventional. **Career Cluster:** 12 Law, Public Safety, Corrections, and Security. **Career Pathway:** 12.6 Inspection Services. **Skills:** Negotiation; Persuasion; Social Perceptiveness; Complex Problem Solving; Service Orientation; Judgment and Decision Making; Writing; Active Listening.

Education and Training Program: Public Administration and Social Service Professions, Other. **Related**

Knowledge/Courses: Law and Government; Personnel and Human Resources; Clerical; English Language; Customer and Personal Service; Administration and Management.

Family and General Practitioners

❋ Annual Earnings: $157,250

❋ Beginning Wage: $73,370

❋ Earnings Growth Potential: Very high (53.3%)

❋ Growth: 14.2%

❋ Annual Job Openings: 38,027

❋ Self-Employed: 14.7%

❋ Part-Time: 8.1%

❋ Job Security: Most secure

❋ Education/Training Required: First professional degree

The Department of Labor reports this information for the occupation Physicians and Surgeons. The job openings listed here are shared with other specializations within that occupation, including Allergists and Immunologists; Anesthesiologists; Dermatologists; Hospitalists; Internists, General; Neurologists; Nuclear Medicine Physicians; Obstetricians and Gynecologists; Ophthalmologists; Pathologists; Pediatricians, General; Physical Medicine and Rehabilitation Physicians; Preventive Medicine Physicians; Psychiatrists; Radiologists; Sports Medicine Physicians; Surgeons; and Urologists.

Industries in Which Income Is Highest

Industry	Average Annual Earnings	Number Employed
Ambulatory Health Care Services	$162,300	77,540
Hospitals	$150,650	18,410
Educational Services	$134,350	2,330
Federal, State, and Local Government	$117,260	6,340

Metropolitan Areas Where Income Is Highest

Metropolitan Area	Average Annual Earnings	Number Employed
Detroit-Warren-Livonia, MI	$166,400+	2,790
Pittsburgh, PA	$166,400+	1,640
Atlanta–Sandy Springs–Marietta, GA	$166,400+	1,480
Boston-Cambridge-Quincy, MA-NH	$166,400+	1,330
Dallas–Fort Worth–Arlington, TX	$166,400+	1,220

Diagnose, treat, and help prevent diseases and injuries that commonly occur in the general population. Prescribe or administer treatment, therapy, medication, vaccination, and other specialized medical care to treat or prevent illness, disease, or injury. Order, perform, and interpret tests and analyze records, reports, and examination information to diagnose patients' condition. Monitor the patients' conditions and progress and re-evaluate treatments as necessary. Explain procedures and discuss test results or prescribed treatments with patients. Collect, record, and maintain patient information, such as medical history, reports, and examination results. Advise patients and community members concerning diet, activity, hygiene, and disease prevention. Refer patients to medical specialists or other practitioners when necessary. Direct and coordinate activities of nurses, students, assistants, specialists, therapists, and other medical staff. Coordinate work with nurses, social workers, rehabilitation therapists, pharmacists, psychologists, and other health-care providers. Deliver babies. Operate on patients to remove, repair, or improve functioning of diseased or injured body parts and systems. Plan, implement, or administer health programs or standards in hospital, business, or community for information, prevention, or treatment of injury or illness. Prepare reports for government or management of birth, death, and disease statistics; workforce evaluations; or medical status of individuals. Conduct research to study anatomy and develop or test medications, treatments, or procedures to prevent or control disease or injury.

Other Considerations for Income: Earnings of physicians and surgeons are among the highest of any occupation, but Family and General Practitioners are among the lowest-paid physicians. The Medical Group Management Association's Physician Compensation and Production Survey of 2005 reported earnings of $137,119 for Family and General Practitioners with less than two years in their specialty and $156,010 for those with more than one year in their specialty. These figures cover salary, bonus and incentive payments, research stipends, honoraria, and distribution of profits. Self-employed physicians—those who own or are part owners of their medical practice—generally have higher median incomes than salaried physicians, but their must provide for their own health insurance and retirement.

Personality Type: Investigative-Social. **Career Clusters:** 08 Health Science; 15 Science, Technology, Engineering, and Mathematics. **Career Pathways:** 08.1 Therapeutic Services; 15.3 Science and Mathematics. **Skills:** Science; Social Perceptiveness; Reading Comprehension; Complex Problem Solving; Persuasion; Service Orientation; Management of Financial Resources; Active Learning.

Education and Training Programs: Medicine (MD); Osteopathic Medicine/Osteopathy (DO). **Related Knowledge/Courses:** Medicine and Dentistry; Therapy and Counseling; Biology; Psychology; Sociology and Anthropology; Chemistry.

Farm, Ranch, and Other Agricultural Managers

See *Aquacultural Managers; Crop and Livestock Managers;* and *Nursery and Greenhouse Managers,* described separately.

Fashion Designers

* Annual Earnings: $61,160
* Beginning Wage: $32,150
* Earnings Growth Potential: High (47.4%)
* Growth: 5.0%
* Annual Job Openings: 1,968
* Self-Employed: 23.6%
* Part-Time: 16.7%
* Job Security: Least secure
* Education/Training Required: Associate degree

Industries in Which Income Is Highest

Industry	Average Annual Earnings	Number Employed
Management of Companies and Enterprises	$72,560	1,360
Apparel Manufacturing	$67,250	3,020
Merchant Wholesalers, Nondurable Goods	$61,360	7,340
Professional, Scientific, and Technical Services	$59,520	1,330

Metropolitan Areas Where Income Is Highest

Metropolitan Area	Average Annual Earnings	Number Employed
Portland–South Portland–Biddeford, ME	$81,940	60
San Francisco–Oakland–Fremont, CA	$76,310	420
New York–Northern New Jersey–Long Island, NY-NJ-PA	$70,000	7,410
Los Angeles–Long Beach–Santa Ana, CA	$63,500	2,980
Seattle-Tacoma-Bellevue, WA	$59,830	100

Design clothing and accessories. Create original garments or design garments that follow well-established fashion trends. May develop the line of color and kinds of materials. Examine sample garments on and off models, then modify designs to achieve desired effects. Determine prices for styles. Select materials and production techniques to be used for products. Draw patterns for articles designed, then cut patterns and cut material according to patterns, using measuring instruments and scissors. Design custom clothing and accessories for individuals, retailers, or theatrical, television, or film productions. Attend fashion shows and review garment magazines and manuals to gather information about fashion trends and consumer preferences. Develop a group of products and/or accessories and market them through venues such as boutiques or mail-order catalogs. Test fabrics or oversee testing so that garment-care labels can be created. Visit textile showrooms to keep up to date on the latest fabrics. Sew together sections of material to form mockups or samples of garments or articles, using sewing equipment. Research the styles and periods of clothing needed for film or theatrical productions. Direct and coordinate workers involved in drawing and cutting patterns and constructing samples or finished garments. Purchase new or used clothing and accessory items as needed to complete designs.

Provide sample garments to agents and sales representatives and arrange for showings of sample garments at sales meetings or fashion shows. Identify target markets for designs, looking at factors such as age, gender, and socio-economic status. Read scripts and consult directors and other production staff to develop design concepts and plan productions. Confer with sales and management executives or with clients to discuss design ideas. Collaborate with other designers to coordinate special products and designs. Sketch rough and detailed drawings of apparel or accessories and write specifications such as color schemes, construction, material types, and accessory requirements. Adapt other designers' ideas for the mass market.

Other Considerations for Income: Earnings in fashion design can vary widely based on the employer and years of experience. Starting salaries in fashion design tend to be very low until designers are established in the industry. Salaried fashion designers usually earn higher and more stable incomes than self-employed or freelance designers. However, a few of the most successful self-employed fashion designers may earn many times the salary of the highest paid salaried designers. Self-employed fashion designers must provide their own benefits and retirement.

Personality Type: Artistic-Enterprising-Realistic. **Career Clusters:** 03 Arts, Audio/Video Technology, and Communications; 13 Manufacturing. **Career Pathways:** 03.3 Visual Arts; 13.2 Manufacturing Production Process Development. **Skills:** Technology Design; Operations Analysis; Quality Control Analysis; Negotiation; Time Management; Systems Evaluation; Mathematics; Active Learning.

Education and Training Programs: Apparel and Textile Manufacture; Fashion and Fabric Consultant; Fashion/Apparel Design; Textile Science. **Related Knowledge/Courses:** Fine Arts; Design; Sales and Marketing; Production and Processing; Communications and Media; Administration and Management.

Film and Video Editors

- ❋ Annual Earnings: $50,560
- ❋ Beginning Wage: $24,640
- ❋ Earnings Growth Potential: Very high (51.3%)
- ❋ Growth: 12.7%
- ❋ Annual Job Openings: 2,707
- ❋ Self-Employed: 15.9%
- ❋ Part-Time: 18.9%
- ❋ Job Security: Most secure
- ❋ Education/Training Required: Bachelor's degree

Industries in Which Income Is Highest

Industry	Average Annual Earnings	Number Employed
Motion Picture and Sound Recording Industries	$55,960	12,830
Professional, Scientific, and Technical Services	$41,700	1,110
Broadcasting (Except Internet)	$39,940	3,010

Metropolitan Areas Where Income Is Highest

Metropolitan Area	Average Annual Earnings	Number Employed
Los Angeles–Long Beach–Santa Ana, CA	$68,200	5,620
Boston-Cambridge-Quincy, MA-NH	$68,090	340
San Francisco–Oakland–Fremont, CA	$60,970	640
Denver-Aurora, CO	$60,280	230
New York–Northern New Jersey–Long Island, NY-NJ-PA	$58,940	2,390

Edit motion picture soundtracks, film, and video. Cut shot sequences to different angles at specific points in scenes, making each individual cut as fluid and seamless as possible. Study scripts to become familiar with production concepts and requirements. Edit films and videotapes to insert music, dialogue, and sound effects; to arrange films into sequences; and to correct errors, using editing equipment. Select and combine the most effective shots of each scene to form a logical and smoothly running story. Mark frames where a particular shot or piece of sound is to begin or end. Determine the specific audio and visual effects and music necessary to complete films. Verify key numbers and time codes on materials. Organize and string together raw footage into a continuous whole according to scripts or the instructions of directors and producers. Review assembled films or edited videotapes on screens or monitors to determine if corrections are necessary. Program computerized graphic effects. Review footage sequence by sequence to become familiar with it before assembling it into a final product. Set up and operate computer editing systems, electronic titling systems, video switching equipment, and digital video effects units to produce a final product. Record needed sounds or obtain them from sound effects libraries. Confer with producers and directors concerning layout or editing approaches needed to increase dramatic or entertainment value of productions. Manipulate plot, score, sound, and graphics to make the parts into a continuous whole, working closely with people in audio, visual, music, optical, or special effects departments. Supervise and coordinate activities of workers engaged in film editing, assembling, and recording activities. Trim film segments to specified lengths and reassemble segments in sequences that present stories with maximum effect. Develop post-production models for films. Piece sounds together to develop film soundtracks.

Other Considerations for Income: No additional information.

Personality Type: Artistic-Enterprising-Investigative. **Career Cluster:** 03 Arts, Audio/Video Technology, and Communications. **Career Pathways:** 03.1 Audio and Video Technology and Film; 03.5 Journalism and Broadcasting; 03.6 Telecommunications. **Skills:** Equipment Selection; Operation and Control; Operations Analysis; Equipment Maintenance; Installation; Troubleshooting; Operation Monitoring; Active Learning.

Education and Training Programs: Audiovisual Communications Technologies/Technicians, Other; Cinematography and Film/Video Production; Communications Technology/Technician; Photojournalism; Radio and Television; Radio and Television Broadcasting Technology/Technician. **Related Knowledge/Courses:** Fine Arts; Communications and Media; Design; Computers and Electronics; Telecommunications; Production and Processing.

Financial Analysts

❋ Annual Earnings: $73,150
❋ Beginning Wage: $43,440
❋ Earnings Growth Potential: High (40.6%)
❋ Growth: 33.8%
❋ Annual Job Openings: 29,317
❋ Self-Employed: 8.3%
❋ Part-Time: 7.1%
❋ Job Security: Least secure
❋ Education/Training Required: Bachelor's degree

Industries in Which Income Is Highest

Industry	Average Annual Earnings	Number Employed
Securities, Commodity Contracts, and Other Financial Investments and Related Activities	$86,630	63,610
Computer and Electronic Product Manufacturing	$76,530	8,070
Publishing Industries (Except Internet)	$75,810	2,500
Utilities	$75,690	1,870
Merchant Wholesalers, Durable Goods	$74,010	2,570

Metropolitan Areas Where Income Is Highest

Metropolitan Area	Average Annual Earnings	Number Employed
Bridgeport-Stamford-Norwalk, CT	$99,460	3,360
San Francisco–Oakland–Fremont, CA	$95,620	6,620
New York–Northern New Jersey–Long Island, NY-NJ-PA	$91,360	41,500
Olympia, WA	$89,020	60
San Jose–Sunnyvale–Santa Clara, CA	$87,420	3,340

Conduct quantitative analyses of information affecting investment programs of public or private institutions. Assemble spreadsheets and draw charts and graphs used to illustrate technical reports, using computer. Analyze financial information to produce forecasts of business, industry, and economic conditions for use in making investment decisions. Maintain knowledge and stay abreast of developments in the fields of industrial technology, business, finance, and economic theory. Interpret data affecting investment programs, such as price, yield, stability, future trends in investment risks, and economic influences. Monitor fundamental economic, industrial, and corporate developments through the analysis of information obtained from financial publications and services, investment banking firms, government agencies, trade publications, company sources, and personal interviews. Recommend investments and investment timing to companies, investment firm staff, or the investing public. Determine the prices at which securities should be syndicated and offered to the public. Prepare plans of action for investment based on financial analyses. Evaluate and compare the relative quality of various securities in a given industry. Present oral and written reports on general economic trends, individual corporations, and entire industries. Contact brokers and purchase investments for companies according to company policy. Collaborate with investment bankers to attract new corporate clients to securities firms.

Other Considerations for Income: The bonuses that many financial analysts receive in addition to their salary can be a significant part of their total earnings. Usually, the bonus is based on how well their predictions compare to the actual performance of a benchmark investment.

Personality Type: Conventional-Investigative-Enterprising. **Career Clusters:** 04 Business, Management, and Administration; 06 Finance. **Career Pathways:** 04.2 Business, Financial Management, and Accounting; 06.1 Financial and Investment Planning. **Skills:** Management of Financial Resources; Judgment and Decision Making; Mathematics; Systems Evaluation; Programming; Complex Problem Solving; Operations Analysis; Systems Analysis.

Education and Training Programs: Accounting and Business/Management; Accounting and Finance; Finance, General. **Related Knowledge/Courses:** Economics and Accounting; Mathematics; Law and Government; Clerical; Administration and Management; English Language.

Financial Examiners

- ❀ Annual Earnings: $70,930
- ❀ Beginning Wage: $38,870
- ❀ Earnings Growth Potential: High (45.2%)
- ❀ Growth: 10.7%
- ❀ Annual Job Openings: 2,449
- ❀ Self-Employed: 0.0%
- ❀ Part-Time: 9.3%
- ❀ Job Security: More secure than most
- ❀ Education/Training Required: Bachelor's degree

Industries in Which Income Is Highest

Industry	Average Annual Earnings	Number Employed
Monetary Authorities—Central Bank	$84,850	1,200
Management of Companies and Enterprises	$76,690	1,690
Federal, State, and Local Government	$76,420	9,660
Securities, Commodity Contracts, and Other Financial Investments and Related Activities	$75,480	4,300
Insurance Carriers and Related Activities	$64,450	1,490

Metropolitan Areas Where Income Is Highest

Metropolitan Area	Average Annual Earnings	Number Employed
Springfield, MA-CT	$105,660	70
San Francisco–Oakland–Fremont, CA	$99,180	800
Washington-Arlington-Alexandria, DC-VA-MD-WV	$98,610	670
Richmond, VA	$97,580	150
Charlotte-Gastonia-Concord, NC-SC	$95,620	500

Enforce or ensure compliance with laws and regulations governing financial and securities institutions and financial and real estate transactions. May examine, verify correctness of, or establish authenticity of records. Investigate activities of institutions in order to enforce laws and regulations and to ensure legality of transactions and operations or financial solvency. Review and analyze new, proposed, or revised laws, regulations, policies, and procedures in order to interpret their meaning and determine their impact. Plan, supervise, and review work of assigned subordinates. Recommend actions to ensure compliance with laws and regulations or to protect solvency of institutions. Examine the minutes of meetings of directors, stockholders, and committees in order to investigate the specific authority extended at various levels of management. Prepare reports, exhibits, and other supporting schedules that detail an institution's safety and soundness, compliance with laws and regulations, and recommended solutions to questionable financial conditions. Review balance sheets, operating income and expense accounts, and loan documentation in order to confirm institution assets and liabilities. Review audit reports of internal and external auditors in order to monitor adequacy of scope of reports or to discover specific weaknesses in internal routines. Train other examiners in the financial examination process. Establish guidelines for procedures and policies that comply with new and revised regulations and direct their implementation. Direct and participate in formal and informal meetings with bank directors, trustees, senior management, counsels, outside accountants, and consultants in order to gather information and discuss findings. Verify and inspect cash reserves, assigned collateral, and bank-owned securities in order to check internal control procedures. Review applications for mergers, acquisitions, establishment of new institutions, acceptance in Federal Reserve System, or registration of securities sales in order to determine their public interest value and conformance to regulations and recommend acceptance or rejection.

Other Considerations for Income: No additional information.

Personality Type: Enterprising-Conventional. **Career Clusters:** 04 Business, Management, and Administration; 07 Government and Public Administration. **Career Pathways:** 04.2 Business, Financial Management, and Accounting; 07.5 Revenue and Taxation. **Skills:** Quality Control Analysis; Monitoring; Management of Financial Resources; Systems Analysis; Systems Evaluation; Operations Analysis; Writing; Reading Comprehension.

Education and Training Programs: Accounting; Taxation. **Related Knowledge/Courses:** Economics and Accounting; Law and Government; Clerical; Mathematics; English Language; Administration and Management.

Financial Managers

See *Financial Managers, Branch or Department* and *Treasurers and Controllers,* described separately.

Financial Managers, Branch or Department

- ❀ Annual Earnings: $99,330
- ❀ Beginning Wage: $53,860
- ❀ Earnings Growth Potential: High (45.8%)
- ❀ Growth: 12.6%
- ❀ Annual Job Openings: 57,589
- ❀ Self-Employed: 4.6%
- ❀ Part-Time: 4.2%
- ❀ Job Security: Less secure than most
- ❀ Education/Training Required: Work experience plus degree

The Department of Labor reports this information for the occupation Financial Managers. The job openings listed here are shared with other specializations within that occupation, including Treasurers and Controllers.

Industries in Which Income Is Highest

Industry	Average Annual Earnings	Number Employed
Securities, Commodity Contracts, and Other Financial Investments and Related Activities	$138,090	39,480
Motion Picture and Sound Recording Industries	$129,160	1,730
Publishing Industries (Except Internet)	$118,510	5,260
Telecommunications	$115,570	3,140
Management of Companies and Enterprises	$115,520	46,420

Metropolitan Areas Where Income Is Highest

Metropolitan Area	Average Annual Earnings	Number Employed
San Jose–Sunnyvale–Santa Clara, CA	$135,000	5,540
New York–Northern New Jersey–Long Island, NY-NJ-PA	$134,500	62,030
San Francisco–Oakland–Fremont, CA	$125,600	13,220
Boulder, CO	$122,720	300
Bridgeport-Stamford-Norwalk, CT	$115,410	4,700

Direct and coordinate financial activities of workers in a branch, office, or department of an establishment, such as branch bank, brokerage firm, risk and insurance department, or credit department. Establish and maintain relationships with individual and business customers and provide assistance with problems these customers may encounter. Examine, evaluate, and process loan applications. Plan, direct, and coordinate the activities of workers in branches, offices, or departments of such establishments as branch banks, brokerage firms, risk and insurance departments, or credit departments. Oversee the flow of cash and financial instruments. Recruit staff members and oversee training programs. Network within communities to find and attract new business. Approve or reject, or coordinate the approval and rejection of, lines of credit and commercial, real estate, and personal loans. Prepare financial and regulatory reports required by laws, regulations, and boards of directors. Establish procedures for custody and control of assets, records, loan collateral, and securities in order to ensure safekeeping. Review collection reports to determine the status of collections and the amounts of outstanding balances. Prepare operational and risk reports for management analysis. Evaluate financial reporting systems, accounting and collection procedures, and investment activities and make recommendations for changes to procedures, operating systems, budgets, and other financial control functions. Plan, direct, and coordinate risk and insurance programs of establishments to control risks and losses. Submit delinquent accounts to attorneys or outside agencies for collection. Communicate with stockholders and other investors to provide information and to raise capital. Evaluate data pertaining to costs in order to plan budgets. Analyze and classify risks and investments to determine their potential impacts on companies. Review reports of securities transactions and price lists in order to analyze market conditions. Develop and analyze information to assess the current and future financial status of firms.

Other Considerations for Income: Large organizations often pay more than small ones, and salary levels also can depend on the type of industry and location. Many financial managers in both public and private industry receive additional compensation in the form of bonuses, which, like salaries, vary substantially by size of firm. Deferred compensation in the form of stock options is becoming more common, especially for senior-level executives.

Personality Type: Enterprising-Conventional. **Career Clusters:** 04 Business, Management, and Administration; 06 Finance. **Career Pathways:** 04.2 Business, Financial Management, and Accounting; 06.1 Financial and Investment Planning. **Skills:** Management of Personnel Resources; Management of Financial Resources; Service Orientation; Time Management; Persuasion; Negotiation; Instructing; Systems Evaluation.

Education and Training Programs: Accounting and Business/Management; Accounting and Finance; Credit Management; Finance and Financial Management Services, Other; Finance, General; International Finance; Public Finance. **Related Knowledge/Courses:** Economics and Accounting; Sales and Marketing; Personnel and Human Resources; Clerical; Customer and Personal Service; Mathematics.

Fire Inspectors

- ❋ Annual Earnings: $53,030
- ❋ Beginning Wage: $32,680
- ❋ Earnings Growth Potential: Medium (38.4%)
- ❋ Growth: 11.0%
- ❋ Annual Job Openings: 644
- ❋ Self-Employed: 0.0%
- ❋ Part-Time: 2.2%
- ❋ Job Security: Most secure
- ❋ Education/Training Required: Work experience in a related occupation

The Department of Labor reports this information for the occupation Fire Inspectors and Investigators. The job openings listed here are shared with other specializations within that occupation, including Fire Investigators.

Industries in Which Income Is Highest

Industry	Average Annual Earnings	Number Employed
Federal, State, and Local Government	$53,240	11,850

Metropolitan Areas Where Income Is Highest

Metropolitan Area	Average Annual Earnings	Number Employed
Los Angeles–Long Beach–Santa Ana, CA	$94,120	240
San Francisco–Oakland–Fremont, CA	$93,080	90
Seattle-Tacoma-Bellevue, WA	$77,820	150
Tulsa, OK	$76,120	60
Sacramento–Arden-Arcade–Roseville, CA	$74,920	80

Inspect buildings and equipment to detect fire hazards and enforce state and local regulations. Inspect buildings to locate hazardous conditions and fire code violations such as accumulations of combustible material, electrical wiring problems, and inadequate or non-functional fire exits. Identify corrective actions necessary to bring properties into compliance with applicable fire codes, laws, regulations, and standards and explain these measures to property owners or their representatives. Conduct inspections and acceptance testing of newly installed fire protection systems. Inspect and test fire protection or fire detection systems to verify that such systems are installed in accordance with appropriate laws, codes, ordinances, regulations, and standards. Conduct fire code compliance follow-ups to ensure that corrective actions have been taken in cases where violations were found. Inspect properties that store, handle, and use hazardous materials to ensure compliance with laws, codes, and regulations; issue hazardous materials permits to facilities found in compliance. Write detailed reports of fire inspections performed, fire code violations observed, and corrective recommendations offered. Review blueprints and plans for new or remodeled buildings to ensure the structures meet fire safety codes. Develop or review fire exit plans. Attend training classes to maintain current knowledge of fire prevention, safety, and firefighting procedures. Present and explain fire code requirements and fire prevention information to architects, contractors, attorneys, engineers, developers, fire service personnel, and the general public. Conduct fire exit drills to monitor and evaluate evacuation procedures. Inspect liquefied petroleum installations, storage containers, and transportation and delivery systems for compliance with fire laws. Search for clues as to the cause of a fire after the fire is completely extinguished. Develop and coordinate fire prevention programs such as false alarm billing, fire inspection reporting, and hazardous materials management.

Other Considerations for Income: No additional information.

Personality Type: Conventional-Realistic. **Career Cluster:** 12 Law, Public Safety, Corrections, and Security. **Career Pathway:** 12.2 Emergency and Fire Management Services. **Skills:** Science; Persuasion; Operations Analysis; Service Orientation; Negotiation; Operation Monitoring; Writing; Complex Problem Solving.

Education and Training Programs: Fire Prevention and Safety Technology/Technician; Fire Science/Fire-fighting. **Related Knowledge/Courses:** Building and Construction; Public Safety and Security; Chemistry; Law and Government; Physics; Customer and Personal Service.

Fire Inspectors and Investigators

See *Fire Inspectors* and *Fire Investigators,* described *separately.*

Fire Investigators

- ❋ Annual Earnings: $53,030
- ❋ Beginning Wage: $32,680
- ❋ Earnings Growth Potential: Medium (38.4%)
- ❋ Growth: 11.0%
- ❋ Annual Job Openings: 644
- ❋ Self-Employed: 0.0%
- ❋ Part-Time: 2.2%
- ❋ Job Security: Most secure
- ❋ Education/Training Required: Work experience in a related occupation

The Department of Labor reports this information for the occupation Fire Inspectors and Investigators. The job openings listed here are shared with other specializations within that occupation, including Fire Inspectors.

Industries in Which Income Is Highest

Industry	Average Annual Earnings	Number Employed
Federal, State, and Local Government	$53,240	11,850

Metropolitan Areas Where Income Is Highest

Metropolitan Area	Average Annual Earnings	Number Employed
Los Angeles–Long Beach–Santa Ana, CA	$94,120	240
San Francisco–Oakland–Fremont, CA	$93,080	90
Seattle-Tacoma-Bellevue, WA	$77,820	150
Tulsa, OK	$76,120	60
Sacramento–Arden-Arcade–Roseville, CA	$74,920	80

Conduct investigations to determine causes of fires and explosions. Package collected pieces of evidence in securely closed containers such as bags, crates, or boxes to protect them. Examine fire sites and collect evidence such as glass, metal fragments, charred wood, and accelerant residue for use in determining the cause of a fire. Instruct children about the dangers of fire. Analyze evidence and other information to determine probable cause of fire or explosion. Photograph damage and evidence related to causes of fires or explosions to document investigation findings. Subpoena and interview witnesses, property owners, and building occupants to obtain information and sworn testimony. Swear out warrants and arrest and process suspected arsonists. Testify in court cases involving fires, suspected arson, and false alarms. Prepare and maintain reports of investigation results and records of convicted arsonists and arson suspects. Test sites and materials to establish facts such as burn patterns and flash points of materials, using test equipment. Conduct internal investigation to determine negligence and violation of laws and regulations by fire department employees. Dust evidence or portions of fire scenes for latent fingerprints.

Other Considerations for Income: No additional information.

Personality Type: Investigative-Realistic-Conventional. **Career Cluster:** 12 Law, Public Safety, Corrections, and Security. **Career Pathway:** 12.2 Emergency and Fire Management Services. **Skills:** Science; Equipment Maintenance; Management of Personnel Resources; Operation and Control; Equipment Selection; Repairing; Judgment and Decision Making; Operations Analysis.

Education and Training Programs: Fire Prevention and Safety Technology/Technician; Fire Science/Fire-fighting. **Related Knowledge/Courses:** Building and Construction; Public Safety and Security; Physics; Chemistry; Mechanical; Law and Government.

Fire-Prevention and Protection Engineers

* Annual Earnings: $72,490
* Beginning Wage: $43,540
* Earnings Growth Potential: Medium (39.9%)
* Growth: 9.6%
* Annual Job Openings: 1,105
* Self-Employed: 1.1%
* Part-Time: 2.0%
* Job Security: More secure than most
* Education/Training Required: Bachelor's degree

The Department of Labor reports this information for the occupation Health and Safety Engineers, Except Mining Safety Engineers and Inspectors. The job openings listed here are shared with other specializations within that occupation, including Industrial Safety and Health Engineers; and Product Safety Engineers.

Industries in Which Income Is Highest

Industry	Average Annual Earnings	Number Employed
Federal, State, and Local Government	$79,770	3,870
Professional, Scientific, and Technical Services	$77,660	4,000
Chemical Manufacturing	$75,550	2,360
Waste Management and Remediation Services	$72,380	1,210
Heavy and Civil Engineering Construction	$65,140	1,860

Metropolitan Areas Where Income Is Highest

Metropolitan Area	Average Annual Earnings	Number Employed
San Jose–Sunnyvale–Santa Clara, CA	$94,140	160
Kennewick-Richland-Pasco, WA	$90,170	120
Chicago-Naperville-Joliet, IL-IN-WI	$88,820	1,140
Knoxville, TN	$88,170	90
Huntsville, AL	$86,540	100

Research causes of fires, determine fire protection methods, and design or recommend materials or equipment such as structural components or fire-detection equipment to assist organizations in safeguarding life and property against fire, explosion, and related hazards. Design fire detection equipment, alarm systems, and fire extinguishing devices and systems. Inspect buildings or building designs to determine fire protection system requirements and potential problems in areas such as water supplies, exit locations, and construction materials. Advise architects, builders, and other construction personnel on fire prevention equipment and techniques and on fire code and standard interpretation and compliance. Prepare and write reports detailing specific fire prevention and protection issues, such as work performed and proposed review schedules. Determine causes of fires and ways in which they could have been prevented. Direct the purchase, modification, installation, maintenance, and operation of fire protection systems. Consult with authorities to discuss safety regulations and to recommend changes as necessary. Develop plans for the prevention of destruction by fire, wind, and water. Study the relationships between ignition sources and materials to determine how fires start. Attend workshops, seminars, or conferences to present or obtain information regarding fire prevention and protection. Develop training materials and conduct training sessions on fire protection. Evaluate fire department performance and the laws and regulations affecting fire prevention or fire safety. Conduct research on fire retardants and the fire safety of materials and devices.

Other Considerations for Income: As a group, engineers earn some of the highest average starting salaries among those holding bachelor's degrees. Separate earnings figures for Fire-Prevention and Protection Engineers are not available, but they are probably similar to those for Health and Safety Engineers, who are among the lowest-paid of the various kinds of engineers.

Personality Type: Investigative-Realistic-Enterprising. **Career Cluster:** 15 Science, Technology, Engineering, and Mathematics. **Career Pathway:** 15.1 Engineering and Technology. **Skills:** Science; Management of Financial Resources; Operations Analysis; Mathematics; Systems Analysis; Negotiation; Complex Problem Solving; Management of Personnel Resources.

Education and Training Program: Environmental/Environmental Health Engineering. **Related Knowledge/Courses:** Design; Engineering and Technology; Building and Construction; Physics; Chemistry; Public Safety and Security.

First-Line Supervisors/ Managers of Construction Trades and Extraction Workers

* Annual Earnings: $58,140
* Beginning Wage: $35,790
* Earnings Growth Potential: Medium (38.4%)
* Growth: 9.1%
* Annual Job Openings: 82,923
* Self-Employed: 24.4%
* Part-Time: 3.0%
* Job Security: Least secure
* Education/Training Required: Work experience in a related occupation

Industries in Which Income Is Highest

Industry	Average Annual Earnings	Number Employed
Utilities	$68,240	3,830
Mining (Except Oil and Gas)	$66,950	8,510
Oil and Gas Extraction	$65,680	3,400
Professional, Scientific, and Technical Services	$65,320	4,770
Support Activities for Mining	$63,280	15,450

Metropolitan Areas Where Income Is Highest

Metropolitan Area	Average Annual Earnings	Number Employed
San Francisco–Oakland–Fremont, CA	$84,020	8,600
Anchorage, AK	$83,780	540
San Jose–Sunnyvale–Santa Clara, CA	$79,870	3,150
Chicago-Naperville-Joliet, IL-IN-WI	$78,490	10,610
Vallejo-Fairfield, CA	$77,460	580

Directly supervise and coordinate activities of construction or extraction workers. Examine and inspect work progress, equipment, and construction sites to verify safety and to ensure that specifications are met. Read specifications such as blueprints to determine construction requirements and to plan procedures. Estimate material and worker requirements to complete jobs. Supervise, coordinate, and schedule the activities of construction or extractive workers. Confer with managerial and technical personnel, other departments, and contractors in order to resolve problems and to coordinate activities. Coordinate work activities with other construction project activities. Locate, measure, and mark site locations and placement of structures and equipment, using measuring and marking equipment. Order or requisition materials and supplies. Record information such as personnel, production, and operational data on specified forms and reports. Assign work to employees based on material and worker requirements of specific jobs. Provide assistance to workers engaged in construction or extraction activities, using hand tools and equipment. Train workers in construction methods, operation of equipment, safety procedures, and company policies. Analyze worker and production problems and recommend solutions such as improving production methods or implementing motivational plans. Arrange for repairs of equipment and machinery. Suggest or initiate personnel actions such as promotions, transfers, and hires.

Other Considerations for Income: No additional information.

Personality Type: Enterprising-Realistic-Conventional. **Career Cluster:** 02 Architecture and Construction. **Career Pathway:** 02.2 Construction. **Skills:** Management of Material Resources; Installation; Equipment Maintenance; Repairing; Coordination; Equipment Selection; Management of Personnel Resources; Mathematics.

Education and Training Programs: Blasting/Blaster; Building/Construction Finishing, Management, and Inspection, Other; Building/Construction Site Management/Manager; Building/Home/Construction Inspection/Inspector; Building/Property Maintenance; Carpentry/Carpenter; Concrete Finishing/Concrete Finisher; Construction Trades, Other; Drywall Installation/Drywaller; Electrical and Power Transmission Installation/Installer, General; Electrical and Power Transmission Installers, Other; Electrician; Glazier; Lineworker; Mason/Masonry. **Related Knowledge/Courses:** Building and Construction; Mechanical; Design; Engineering and Technology; Production and Processing; Public Safety and Security.

First-Line Supervisors/ Managers of Correctional Officers

- ❀ Annual Earnings: $57,380
- ❀ Beginning Wage: $32,300
- ❀ Earnings Growth Potential: High (43.7%)
- ❀ Growth: 12.5%
- ❀ Annual Job Openings: 4,180
- ❀ Self-Employed: 0.0%
- ❀ Part-Time: 0.0%
- ❀ Job Security: Most secure
- ❀ Education/Training Required: Work experience in a related occupation

Industries in Which Income Is Highest

Industry	Average Annual Earnings	Number Employed
Federal, State, and Local Government	$57,820	39,420
Administrative and Support Services	$40,380	1,260

Metropolitan Areas Where Income Is Highest

Metropolitan Area	Average Annual Earnings	Number Employed
Sacramento–Arden-Arcade–Roseville, CA	$86,770	590
San Francisco–Oakland–Fremont, CA	$86,130	260
Riverside–San Bernardino–Ontario, CA	$81,410	690
Bakersfield, CA	$80,990	550
Los Angeles–Long Beach–Santa Ana, CA	$77,500	400

Supervise and coordinate activities of correctional officers and jailers. Take, receive, and check periodic inmate counts. Maintain order, discipline, and security within assigned areas in accordance with relevant rules, regulations, policies, and laws. Respond to emergencies such as escapes. Maintain knowledge of, comply with, and enforce all institutional policies, rules, procedures, and regulations. Supervise and direct the work of correctional officers to ensure the safe custody, discipline, and welfare of inmates. Restrain, secure, and control offenders, using chemical agents, firearms, and other weapons of force as necessary. Supervise and perform searches of inmates and their quarters to locate contraband items. Monitor behavior of subordinates to ensure alert, courteous, and professional behavior toward inmates, parolees, fellow employees, visitors, and the public. Complete administrative paperwork and supervise the preparation and maintenance of records, forms, and reports. Instruct employees and provide on-the-job training. Conduct roll calls of correctional officers. Supervise activities such as searches, shakedowns, riot control, and institutional tours. Carry injured offenders or employees to safety and provide emergency first aid when necessary. Supervise and provide security for offenders performing tasks such as construction, maintenance, laundry, food service, and other industrial or agricultural operations. Develop work and security procedures. Set up employee work schedules. Resolve problems between inmates. Read and review offender information to identify issues that require special attention. Rate behavior of inmates, promoting acceptable attitudes and behaviors to those with low ratings. Transfer and transport offenders on foot or by driving vehicles such as trailers, vans, and buses. Examine incoming and outgoing mail to ensure conformance with regulations. Convey correctional officers' and inmates' complaints to superiors.

Other Considerations for Income: According to the Federal Bureau of Prisons, the starting salary for federal correctional officers was $28,862 a year in 2007. Starting federal salaries were slightly higher in areas where prevailing local pay levels were higher. In addition to typical benefits, correctional officers employed in the public sector usually are provided with uniforms or a clothing allowance to purchase their own uniforms. Civil service systems or merit boards cover officers employed by the federal government and most state governments. Their retirement coverage entitles correctional officers to retire at age 50 after 20 years of service or at any age with 25 years of service.

Personality Type: Enterprising-Conventional-Realistic. **Career Cluster:** 12 Law, Public Safety, Corrections, and Security. **Career Pathway:** 12.1 Correction Services. **Skills:** Social Perceptiveness; Negotiation; Management of Personnel Resources; Persuasion; Monitoring; Writing; Service Orientation; Complex Problem Solving.

Education and Training Programs: Corrections; Corrections Administration. **Related Knowledge/Courses:** Public Safety and Security; Psychology; Therapy and Counseling; Personnel and Human Resources; Clerical; Law and Government.

First-Line Supervisors/ Managers of Fire Fighting and Prevention Workers

See *Forest Fire Fighting and Prevention Supervisors* and *Municipal Fire Fighting and Prevention Supervisors,* described separately.

First-Line Supervisors/ Managers of Mechanics, Installers, and Repairers

* Annual Earnings: $57,300
* Beginning Wage: $34,830
* Earnings Growth Potential: Medium (39.2%)
* Growth: 7.3%
* Annual Job Openings: 24,361
* Self-Employed: 1.5%
* Part-Time: 0.9%
* Job Security: Less secure than most
* Education/Training Required: Work experience in a related occupation

Industries in Which Income Is Highest

Industry	Average Annual Earnings	Number Employed
Petroleum and Coal Products Manufacturing	$74,010	1,530
Utilities	$72,300	15,480
Postal Service	$71,970	3,180
Telecommunications	$70,440	17,600
Air Transportation	$70,330	3,090

Metropolitan Areas Where Income Is Highest

Metropolitan Area	Average Annual Earnings	Number Employed
Fairbanks, AK	$76,300	160
Bremerton-Silverdale, WA	$75,770	690
San Jose–Sunnyvale–Santa Clara, CA	$73,780	2,190
Kokomo, IN	$72,870	250
Anchorage, AK	$72,390	570

Supervise and coordinate the activities of mechanics, installers, and repairers. Determine schedules, sequences, and assignments for work activities, based on work priority, quantity of equipment, and skill of personnel. Monitor employees' work levels and review work performance. Monitor tool and part inventories and the condition and maintenance of shops to ensure adequate working conditions. Recommend or initiate personnel actions such as hires, promotions, transfers, discharges, and disciplinary measures. Investigate accidents and injuries, and prepare reports of findings. Compile operational and personnel records such as time and production records, inventory data, repair and maintenance statistics, and test results. Develop, implement, and evaluate maintenance policies and procedures. Counsel employees about work-related issues and assist employees to correct job-skill deficiencies. Examine objects, systems, or facilities, and analyze information to determine needed installations, services, or repairs. Conduct or arrange for worker training in safety, repair, and maintenance techniques, operational procedures, or equipment use. Inspect and monitor work areas, examine tools and equipment, and provide employee safety training to prevent, detect, and correct unsafe conditions or violations of procedures and safety rules. Inspect, test, and measure completed work, using devices such as hand tools and gauges to verify conformance to standards and repair requirements. Requisition materials and supplies such as tools, equipment, and replacement parts. Participate in budget preparation and administration, coordinating purchasing and documentation, and monitoring departmental expenditures. Perform skilled repair and maintenance operations, using equipment such as hand and power tools, hydraulic presses and shears, and welding equipment. Meet with vendors and suppliers to discuss products used in repair work. Compute estimates and actual costs of factors such as materials, labor, and outside contractors.

Other Considerations for Income: No additional information.

Personality Type: Enterprising-Conventional-Realistic. **Career Cluster:** 13 Manufacturing. **Career Pathway:** 13.1 Production. **Skills:** Repairing; Management of Financial Resources; Systems Analysis; Equipment Maintenance; Management of Personnel Resources; Quality Control Analysis; Management of Material Resources; Operation Monitoring.

Education and Training Program: Operations Management and Supervision. **Related Knowledge/Courses:** Mechanical; Personnel and Human Resources; Production and Processing; Engineering and Technology; Building and Construction; Economics and Accounting.

First-Line Supervisors/ Managers of Non-Retail Sales Workers

* Annual Earnings: $68,100
* Beginning Wage: $36,830
* Earnings Growth Potential: High (45.9%)
* Growth: 3.7%
* Annual Job Openings: 48,883
* Self-Employed: 45.4%
* Part-Time: 5.3%
* Job Security: Least secure
* Education/Training Required: Work experience in a related occupation

Industries in Which Income Is Highest

Industry	Average Annual Earnings	Number Employed
Securities, Commodity Contracts, and Other Financial Investments and Related Activities	$89,190	4,930
Computer and Electronic Product Manufacturing	$83,020	3,440
Professional, Scientific, and Technical Services	$82,160	19,470
Wholesale Electronic Markets and Agents and Brokers	$81,100	15,760
Chemical Manufacturing	$79,940	1,910

Metropolitan Areas Where Income Is Highest

Metropolitan Area	Average Annual Earnings	Number Employed
New York–Northern New Jersey–Long Island, NY-NJ-PA	$93,070	24,910
Ocean City, NJ	$92,820	80
San Jose–Sunnyvale–Santa Clara, CA	$91,790	2,340
Salisbury, MD	$88,110	90
Springfield, OH	$87,730	60

Directly supervise and coordinate activities of sales workers other than retail sales workers. May perform duties such as budgeting, accounting, and personnel work in addition to supervisory duties. Listen to and resolve customer complaints regarding services, products, or personnel. Monitor sales staff performance to ensure that goals are met. Hire, train, and evaluate personnel. Confer with company officials to develop methods and procedures to increase sales, expand markets, and promote business. Direct and supervise employees engaged in sales, inventory-taking, reconciling cash receipts, or performing specific services such as pumping gasoline for customers. Provide staff with assistance in performing difficult or complicated duties. Plan and prepare work schedules and assign employees to specific duties. Attend company meetings to exchange product information and coordinate work activities with other departments. Prepare sales and inventory reports for management and budget departments. Formulate pricing policies on merchandise according to profitability requirements. Examine merchandise to ensure correct pricing and display and ensure that it functions as advertised. Analyze details of sales territories to assess their growth potential and to set quotas. Visit retailers and sales representatives to promote products and gather information. Keep records pertaining to purchases, sales, and requisitions. Coordinate sales promotion activities and prepare merchandise displays and advertising copy. Prepare rental or lease agreements, specifying charges and payment procedures for use of machinery, tools, or other items. Inventory stock and reorder when inventories drop to specified levels. Examine products purchased for resale or received for storage to determine product condition.

Other Considerations for Income: Salaries of sales worker supervisors vary substantially, depending on a worker's level of responsibility and length of service and the type, size, and location of the firm. Compensation systems also vary by type of establishment and by merchandise sold. Many supervisors receive a commission or a combination of salary and commission. Under a commission system, supervisors receive a percentage of sales. Thus, these supervisors' earnings depend on their ability to sell their product and the condition of the economy. Those who sell large amounts of merchandise or exceed sales goals often receive bonuses or other awards.

Personality Type: Enterprising-Conventional-Social. **Career Cluster:** 14 Marketing, Sales, and Service. **Career Pathway:** 14.2 Professional Sales and Marketing. **Skills:** Management of Personnel Resources; Negotiation; Persuasion; Time Management; Operations Analysis; Social Perceptiveness; Monitoring; Judgment and Decision Making.

Education and Training Programs: Business, Management, Marketing, and Related Support Services, Other; General Merchandising, Sales, and Related Marketing Operations, Other; Special Products Marketing Operations, Other; Specialized Merchandising, Sales, and Marketing Operations, Other. **Related Knowledge/Courses:** Sales and Marketing; Economics and Accounting; Personnel and Human Resources; Administration and Management; Mathematics; Education and Training.

First-Line Supervisors/ Managers of Police and Detectives

* Annual Earnings: $75,490
* Beginning Wage: $46,000
* Earnings Growth Potential: Medium (39.1%)
* Growth: 9.2%
* Annual Job Openings: 9,373
* Self-Employed: 0.0%
* Part-Time: 0.8%
* Job Security: Most secure
* Education/Training Required: Work experience in a related occupation

Industries in Which Income Is Highest

Industry	Average Annual Earnings	Number Employed
Federal, State, and Local Government	$75,740	90,600
Educational Services	$63,390	1,970

Metropolitan Areas Where Income Is Highest

Metropolitan Area	Average Annual Earnings	Number Employed
San Jose–Sunnyvale–Santa Clara, CA	$125,320	190
Los Angeles–Long Beach–Santa Ana, CA	$111,420	2,800
Riverside–San Bernardino–Ontario, CA	$110,360	300
Santa Cruz–Watsonville, CA	$108,810	60
San Francisco–Oakland–Fremont, CA	$107,050	850

Supervise and coordinate activities of members of police force. Supervise and coordinate the investigation of criminal cases, offering guidance and expertise to investigators, and ensuring that procedures are conducted in accordance with laws and regulations. Maintain logs, prepare reports, and direct the preparation, handling, and maintenance of departmental records. Explain police operations to subordinates to assist them in performing their job duties. Cooperate with court personnel and officials from other law enforcement agencies and testify in court as necessary. Review contents of written orders to ensure adherence to legal requirements. Investigate and resolve personnel problems within organization and charges of misconduct against staff. Direct collection, preparation, and handling of evidence and personal property of prisoners. Inform personnel of changes in regulations and policies, implications of new or amended laws, and new techniques of police work. Train staff in proper police work procedures. Monitor and evaluate the job performance of subordinates, and authorize promotions and transfers. Prepare work schedules and assign duties to subordinates. Conduct raids and order detention of witnesses and suspects for questioning. Discipline staff for violation of departmental rules and regulations. Develop, implement, and revise departmental policies and procedures. Inspect facilities, supplies, vehicles, and equipment to ensure conformance to standards. Requisition and issue equipment and supplies. Meet with civic, educational, and community groups to develop community programs and events, and to discuss law enforcement subjects. Prepare news releases and respond to police correspondence. Prepare budgets and manage expenditures of department funds. Direct release or transfer of prisoners.

Other Considerations for Income: According to the International City-County Management Association's annual Police and Fire Personnel, Salaries, and Expenditures Survey, average salaries for sworn full-time positions in 2006 were $44,160–$55,183 for police corporals, $53,734–$63,564 for sergeants, and $59,940–$72,454 for lieutenants. In addition to the common benefits—paid vacation, sick leave, and medical and life insurance—most police and sheriffs' departments provide officers with special allowances for uniforms. Because police officers usually are covered by liberal pension plans, many retire at half pay after 25 or 30 years of service.

Personality Type: Enterprising-Social-Conventional. **Career Cluster:** 12 Law, Public Safety, Corrections, and Security. **Career Pathways:** 12.1 Correction Services; 12.4 Law Enforcement Services. **Skills:** Management of Personnel Resources; Management of Financial Resources; Persuasion; Systems Analysis; Systems Evaluation; Monitoring; Negotiation; Management of Material Resources.

Education and Training Programs: Corrections; Criminal Justice/Law Enforcement Administration; Criminal Justice/Safety Studies. **Related Knowledge/Courses:** Public Safety and Security; Law and Government; Psychology; Sociology and Anthropology; Therapy and Counseling; Personnel and Human Resources.

First-Line Supervisors/ Managers of Production and Operating Workers

❀ Annual Earnings: $50,440
❀ Beginning Wage: $30,780
❀ Earnings Growth Potential: Medium (39.0%)
❀ Growth: –4.8%
❀ Annual Job Openings: 46,144
❀ Self-Employed: 2.4%
❀ Part-Time: 1.9%
❀ Job Security: Least secure
❀ Education/Training Required: Work experience in a related occupation

Industries in Which Income Is Highest

Industry	Average Annual Earnings	Number Employed
Utilities	$74,010	11,020
Petroleum and Coal Products Manufacturing	$67,490	5,490
Oil and Gas Extraction	$67,450	1,830
Pipeline Transportation	$62,300	1,060
Mining (Except Oil and Gas)	$60,240	2,600

Metropolitan Areas Where Income Is Highest

Metropolitan Area	Average Annual Earnings	Number Employed
Fairbanks, AK	$73,550	80
Bremerton-Silverdale, WA	$72,410	380
Flint, MI	$71,890	630
Corvallis, OR	$69,930	150
Kokomo, IN	$69,910	430

Supervise and coordinate the activities of production and operating workers, such as inspectors, precision workers, machine setters and operators, assemblers, fabricators, and plant and system operators. Enforce safety and sanitation regulations. Direct and coordinate the activities of employees engaged in the production or processing of goods, such as inspectors, machine setters, and fabricators. Read and analyze charts, work orders, production schedules, and other records and reports to determine production requirements and to evaluate current production estimates and outputs. Confer with other supervisors to coordinate operations and activities within or between departments. Plan and establish work schedules, assignments, and production sequences to meet production goals. Inspect materials, products, or equipment to detect defects or malfunctions. Demonstrate equipment operations and work and safety procedures to new employees or assign employees to experienced workers for training. Observe work and monitor gauges, dials, and other indicators to ensure that operators conform to production or processing standards. Interpret specifications, blueprints, job orders, and company policies and procedures for workers. Confer with management or subordinates to resolve worker problems, complaints, or grievances. Maintain operations data such as time, production, and cost records and prepare management reports of production results. Recommend or implement measures to motivate employees and to improve production methods, equipment performance, product quality, or efficiency. Determine standards, budgets, production goals, and rates based on company policies, equipment and labor availability, and workloads. Requisition materials, supplies, equipment parts, or repair services. Recommend personnel actions such as hirings and promotions. Set up and adjust machines and equipment. Calculate labor and equipment requirements and production specifications, using standard formulas. Plan and develop new products and production processes.

Other Considerations for Income: No additional information.

Personality Type: Enterprising-Realistic-Conventional. **Career Cluster:** 13 Manufacturing. **Career Pathway:** 13.1 Production. **Skills:** Management of Personnel Resources; Operation Monitoring; Operation and Control; Quality Control Analysis; Operations Analysis; Systems Analysis; Monitoring; Systems Evaluation.

Education and Training Program: Operations Management and Supervision. **Related Knowledge/Courses:** Production and Processing; Mechanical; Personnel and Human Resources; Engineering and Technology; Administration and Management; Psychology.

First-Line Supervisors/ Managers of Transportation and Material-Moving Machine and Vehicle Operators

* Annual Earnings: $51,320
* Beginning Wage: $30,940
* Earnings Growth Potential: Medium (39.7%)
* Growth: 10.2%
* Annual Job Openings: 16,580
* Self-Employed: 1.5%
* Part-Time: 5.3%
* Job Security: More secure than most
* Education/Training Required: Work experience in a related occupation

Industries in Which Income Is Highest

Industry	Average Annual Earnings	Number Employed
Postal Service	$66,380	7,050
Rail Transportation	$61,190	2,310
Couriers and Messengers	$58,640	10,160
Air Transportation	$58,630	2,390
Federal, State, and Local Government	$58,230	17,270

Metropolitan Areas Where Income Is Highest

Metropolitan Area	Average Annual Earnings	Number Employed
Fairbanks, AK	$76,080	60
Longview, WA	$73,250	100
Saginaw–Saginaw Township North, MI	$69,890	170
Redding, CA	$65,900	140
Anchorage, AK	$65,480	190

Directly supervise and coordinate activities of transportation and material-moving machine and vehicle operators and helpers. Enforce safety rules and regulations. Plan work assignments and equipment allocations to meet transportation, operations, or production goals. Confer with customers, supervisors, contractors, and other personnel to exchange information and to resolve problems. Direct workers in transportation or related services, such as pumping, moving, storing, and loading and unloading of materials or people. Resolve worker problems or collaborate with employees to assist in problem resolution. Review orders, production schedules, blueprints, and shipping and receiving notices to determine work sequences and material shipping dates, types, volumes, and destinations. Monitor fieldwork to ensure that it is being performed properly and that materials are being used as they should be. Recommend and implement measures to improve worker motivation, equipment performance, work methods, and customer services. Maintain or verify records of time, materials, expenditures, and crew activities. Interpret transportation and tariff regulations, shipping orders, safety regulations, and company policies and procedures for workers. Explain and demonstrate work tasks to new workers or assign workers to more experienced workers for further training. Prepare, compile, and submit reports on work activities, operations, production, and work-related accidents. Recommend or implement personnel actions such as employee selection, evaluation, and rewards or disciplinary actions. Requisition needed personnel, supplies, equipment, parts, or repair services. Inspect or test materials, stock, vehicles, equipment, and facilities to ensure that they are safe, are free of defects, and meet specifications. Plan and establish transportation routes. Compute and estimate cash, payroll, transportation, personnel, and storage requirements. Dispatch personnel and vehicles in response to telephone or radio reports of emergencies. Perform or schedule repairs and preventive maintenance of vehicles and other equipment.

Other Considerations for Income: No additional information.

Personality Type: Enterprising-Conventional-Realistic. **Career Cluster:** 16 Transportation, Distribution, and Logistics. **Career Pathway:** 16.1 Transportation Operations. **Skills:** Management of Personnel Resources; Management of Financial Resources; Management of Material Resources; Social Perceptiveness; Operations Analysis; Equipment Selection; Systems Evaluation; Monitoring.

Education and Training Programs: No related CIP programs; this job is learned through work experience in a related occupation. **Related Knowledge/Courses:** Transportation; Production and Processing; Personnel and Human Resources; Customer and Personal Service; Public Safety and Security; Administration and Management.

Fish and Game Wardens

- ❊ Annual Earnings: $48,930
- ❊ Beginning Wage: $30,400
- ❊ Earnings Growth Potential: Medium (37.9%)
- ❊ Growth: –0.2%
- ❊ Annual Job Openings: 576
- ❊ Self-Employed: 0.0%
- ❊ Part-Time: 1.1%
- ❊ Job Security: Most secure
- ❊ Education/Training Required: Associate degree

Industries in Which Income Is Highest

Industry	Average Annual Earnings	Number Employed
Federal, State, and Local Government	$48,930	7,720

Metropolitan Areas Where Income Is Highest

Metropolitan Area	Average Annual Earnings	Number Employed
New York–Northern New Jersey–Long Island, NY-NJ-PA	$61,990	40
Providence–Fall River–Warwick, RI-MA	$53,340	60
Boise City–Nampa, ID	$51,780	40
Tallahassee, FL	$39,090	40
Atlanta–Sandy Springs–Marietta, GA	$32,210	160

Patrol assigned area to prevent fish and game law violations. Investigate reports of damage to crops or property by wildlife. Compile biological data. Patrol assigned areas by car, boat, airplane, or horse or on foot to enforce game, fish, or boating laws and to manage wildlife programs, lakes, or land. Investigate hunting accidents and reports of fish and game law violations and issue warnings or citations and file reports as necessary. Serve warrants, make arrests, and compile and present evidence for court actions. Protect and preserve native wildlife, plants, and ecosystems. Promote and provide hunter and trapper safety training. Seize equipment used in fish and game law violations and arrange for disposition of fish or game illegally taken or possessed. Provide assistance to other local law enforcement agencies as required. Address schools, civic groups, sporting clubs, and the media to disseminate information concerning wildlife conservation and regulations. Recommend revisions or changes in hunting and trapping regulations or seasons and in animal management programs so that wildlife balances and habitats can be maintained. Inspect commercial operations relating to fish and wildlife, recreation, and protected areas. Collect and report information on populations and conditions of fish and wildlife in their habitats, availability of game food and cover, and suspected pollution. Survey areas and compile figures of bag counts of hunters to determine the effectiveness of control measures. Participate in search-and-rescue operations and in firefighting efforts. Investigate crop, property, or habitat damage or destruction or instances of water pollution to determine causes and to advise property owners of preventive measures. Design and implement control measures to prevent or counteract damage caused by wildlife or people. Document and detail the extent of crop, property, or habitat damage and make financial loss estimates and compensation recommendations. Supervise the activities of seasonal workers. Issue licenses, permits, and other documentation. Provide advice and information to park and reserve visitors.

Other Considerations for Income: No additional information.

Personality Type: Realistic-Investigative. **Career Cluster:** 01 Agriculture, Food and Natural Resource. **Career Pathway:** 01.5 Natural Resources Systems. **Skills:** Equipment Maintenance; Persuasion; Science; Social Perceptiveness; Speaking; Writing; Repairing; Negotiation.

Education and Training Programs: Fishing and Fisheries Sciences and Management; Natural Resource Economics; Wildlife, Fish and Wildlands Science and Management. **Related Knowledge/Courses:** Biology; Law and Government; Geography; Public Safety and Security; Psychology; Sociology and Anthropology.

Food Scientists and Technologists

* Annual Earnings: $59,520
* Beginning Wage: $33,790
* Earnings Growth Potential: High (43.2%)
* Growth: 10.3%
* Annual Job Openings: 663
* Self-Employed: 16.3%
* Part-Time: 11.4%
* Job Security: Most secure
* Education/Training Required: Bachelor's degree

Industries in Which Income Is Highest

Industry	Average Annual Earnings	Number Employed
Professional, Scientific, and Technical Services	$64,950	1,940
Food Manufacturing	$56,270	5,290

Metropolitan Areas Where Income Is Highest

Metropolitan Area	Average Annual Earnings	Number Employed
Washington-Arlington-Alexandria, DC-VA-MD-WV	$94,220	150
New York–Northern New Jersey–Long Island, NY-NJ-PA	$81,210	500
Philadelphia-Camden-Wilmington, PA-NJ-DE-MD	$80,020	150
Buffalo–Niagara Falls, NY	$78,790	130
Dallas–Fort Worth-Arlington, TX	$72,510	290

Use chemistry, microbiology, engineering, and other sciences to study the principles underlying the processing and deterioration of foods; analyze food content to determine levels of vitamins, fat, sugar, and protein; discover new food sources; research ways to make processed foods safe, palatable, and healthful; and apply food science knowledge to determine the best ways to process, package, preserve, store, and distribute food. Test new products for flavor, texture, color, nutritional content, and adherence to government and industry standards. Check raw ingredients for maturity or stability for processing and finished products for safety, quality, and nutritional value. Confer with process engineers, plant operators, flavor experts, and packaging and marketing specialists in order to resolve problems in product development. Evaluate food processing and storage operations and assist in the development of quality assurance programs for such operations. Study methods to improve aspects of foods such as chemical composition, flavor, color, texture, nutritional value, and convenience. Study the structure and composition of food or the changes foods undergo in storage and processing. Develop new or improved ways of preserving, processing, packaging, storing, and delivering foods, using knowledge of chemistry, microbiology, and other sciences. Develop food standards and production specifications, safety and sanitary regulations, and waste management and water supply specifications. Demonstrate products to clients. Inspect food processing areas in order to ensure compliance with government regulations and standards for sanitation, safety, quality, and waste management standards. Search for substitutes for harmful or undesirable additives, such as nitrites.

Other Considerations for Income: No additional information.

Personality Type: Investigative-Realistic-Conventional. **Career Cluster:** 01 Agriculture, Food and Natural Resource. **Career Pathways:** 01.1 Food Products and Processing Systems; 01.2 Plant Systems; 01.7 Agribusiness Systems. **Skills:** Quality Control Analysis; Science; Troubleshooting; Operations Analysis; Reading Comprehension; Mathematics; Operation Monitoring; Monitoring.

Education and Training Programs: Agriculture, General; Food Science; Food Technology and Processing; International Agriculture. **Related Knowledge/Courses:** Food Production; Chemistry; Production and Processing; Biology; Physics; Mathematics.

Foreign Language and Literature Teachers, Postsecondary

❊ Annual Earnings: $55,570
❊ Beginning Wage: $31,480
❊ Earnings Growth Potential: High (43.4%)
❊ Growth: 22.9%
❊ Annual Job Openings: 4,317
❊ Self-Employed: 0.4%
❊ Part-Time: 27.8%
❊ Job Security: Most secure
❊ Education/Training Required: Doctoral degree

Industries in Which Income Is Highest

Industry	Average Annual Earnings	Number Employed
Educational Services	$55,560	26,370

Metropolitan Areas Where Income Is Highest

Metropolitan Area	Average Annual Earnings	Number Employed
Poughkeepsie-Newburgh-Middletown, NY	$77,690	60
Sacramento–Arden-Arcade–Roseville, CA	$76,200	110
Providence–Fall River–Warwick, RI-MA	$74,580	180
Lubbock, TX	$72,170	120
Los Angeles–Long Beach–Santa Ana, CA	$71,410	1,300

Teach courses in foreign (i.e., other than English) languages and literature. Evaluate and grade students' classwork, assignments, and papers. Prepare course materials such as syllabi, homework assignments, and handouts. Initiate, facilitate, and moderate classroom discussions. Maintain student attendance records, grades, and other required records. Compile, administer, and grade examinations or assign this work to others. Plan, evaluate, and revise curricula, course content, and course materials and methods of instruction. Prepare and deliver lectures to undergraduate and graduate students on topics such as how to speak and write a foreign language and the cultural aspects of areas where a particular language is used. Maintain regularly scheduled office hours to advise and assist students. Select and obtain materials and supplies such as textbooks. Keep abreast of developments in their field by reading current literature, talking with colleagues, and participating in professional organizations and activities. Advise students on academic and vocational curricula and on career issues. Conduct research in a particular field of knowledge and publish findings in scholarly journals, books, and/or electronic media. Collaborate with colleagues to address teaching and research issues. Serve on academic or administrative committees that deal with institutional policies, departmental matters, and academic issues. Participate in student recruitment, registration, and placement activities. Compile bibliographies of specialized materials for outside reading assignments. Participate in campus and community events. Act as advisers to student organizations. Perform administrative duties such as serving as department head. Supervise undergraduate and graduate teaching, internship, and research work. Write grant proposals to procure external research funding. Provide professional consulting services to government or industry.

Other Considerations for Income: Earnings for college faculty vary according to rank and type of institution, geographic area, and field. According to a 2006–2007 survey by the American Association of University Professors, salaries for full-time faculty averaged $73,207. By rank, the average was $98,974 for professors, $69,911 for associate professors, $58,662 for assistant professors, $42,609 for instructors, and $48,289 for lecturers. Faculty in 4-year institutions earn higher salaries, on average, than do those in 2-year schools. Many faculty members have significant earnings in addition to their base salary from consulting, teaching additional courses, research, writing for publication, or other employment. In addition, many college and university faculty enjoy unique benefits, including access to campus facilities, tuition waivers for dependents, housing and travel allowances, and paid leave for sabbaticals. Part-time faculty and instructors usually have fewer benefits than full-time faculty.

Personality Type: Social-Artistic-Investigative. **Career Cluster:** 05 Education and Training. **Career Pathway:** 05.3 Teaching/Training. **Skills:** Learning Strategies; Instructing; Writing; Reading Comprehension; Speaking; Persuasion; Social Perceptiveness; Critical Thinking.

Education and Training Programs: African Languages, Literatures, and Linguistics; Albanian Language and Literature; American Indian/Native American Languages,

Literatures, and Linguistics; Ancient Near Eastern and Biblical Languages, Literatures, and Linguistics; Ancient/Classical Greek Language and Literature; Arabic Language and Literature; Australian/Oceanic/Pacific Languages, Literatures, and Linguistics; Baltic Languages, Literatures, and Linguistics; Bengali Language and Literature; others. **Related Knowledge/Courses:** Foreign Language; Philosophy and Theology; History and Archeology; Sociology and Anthropology; Geography; English Language.

Forensic Science Technicians

- ❀ Annual Earnings: $49,860
- ❀ Beginning Wage: $30,990
- ❀ Earnings Growth Potential: Medium (37.8%)
- ❀ Growth: 30.7%
- ❀ Annual Job Openings: 3,074
- ❀ Self-Employed: 1.3%
- ❀ Part-Time: 19.4%
- ❀ Job Security: Less secure than most
- ❀ Education/Training Required: Bachelor's degree

Industries in Which Income Is Highest

Industry	Average Annual Earnings	Number Employed
Federal, State, and Local Government	$50,360	10,340

Metropolitan Areas Where Income Is Highest

Metropolitan Area	Average Annual Earnings	Number Employed
Los Angeles–Long Beach–Santa Ana, CA	$71,590	510
Washington-Arlington-Alexandria, DC-VA-MD-WV	$61,240	480
San Diego–Carlsbad–San Marcos, CA	$60,190	160
Chicago-Naperville-Joliet, IL-IN-WI	$60,000	490
New York–Northern New Jersey–Long Island, NY-NJ-PA	$59,100	380

Collect, identify, classify, and analyze physical evidence related to criminal investigations. Perform tests on weapons or substances such as fiber, hair, and tissue to determine significance to investigation. May testify as expert witnesses on evidence or crime laboratory techniques. May serve as specialists in area of expertise, such as ballistics, fingerprinting, handwriting, or biochemistry. Testify in court about investigative and analytical methods and findings. Keep records and prepare reports detailing findings, investigative methods, and laboratory techniques. Interpret laboratory findings and test results to identify and classify substances, materials, and other evidence collected at crime scenes. Operate and maintain laboratory equipment and apparatus. Prepare solutions, reagents, and sample formulations needed for laboratory work. Analyze and classify biological fluids, using DNA typing or serological techniques. Collect evidence from crime scenes, storing it in conditions that preserve its integrity. Identify and quantify drugs and poisons found in biological fluids and tissues, in foods, and at crime scenes. Analyze handwritten and machine-produced textual evidence to decipher altered or obliterated text or to determine authorship, age, or source. Reconstruct crime scenes to determine relationships among pieces of evidence. Examine DNA samples to determine if they match other samples. Collect impressions of dust from surfaces to obtain and identify fingerprints. Analyze gunshot residue and bullet paths to determine how shootings occurred. Visit morgues, examine scenes of crimes, or contact other sources to obtain evidence or information to be used in investigations. Examine physical evidence such as hair, fiber, wood, or soil residues to obtain information about its source and composition. Determine types of bullets used in shooting and whether they were fired from a specific weapon. Examine firearms to determine mechanical condition and legal status, performing restoration work on damaged firearms to obtain information such as serial numbers. Confer with ballistics, fingerprinting, handwriting, document, electronics, medical, chemical, or metallurgical experts concerning evidence and its interpretation. Interpret the pharmacological effects of a drug or a combination of drugs on an individual.

Other Considerations for Income: No additional information.

Personality Type: Investigative-Realistic-Conventional. **Career Cluster:** 12 Law, Public Safety, Corrections, and Security. **Career Pathway:** 12.4 Law Enforcement Services. **Skills:** Science; Quality Control Analysis; Troubleshooting; Speaking; Equipment Selection; Active Learning; Reading Comprehension; Monitoring.

Education and Training Program: Forensic Science and Technology. **Related Knowledge/Courses:** Chemistry;

Biology; Clerical; Law and Government; Design; Customer and Personal Service.

Forest Fire Fighting and Prevention Supervisors

❋ Annual Earnings: $67,440
❋ Beginning Wage: $40,850
❋ Earnings Growth Potential: Medium (39.4%)
❋ Growth: 11.5%
❋ Annual Job Openings: 3,771
❋ Self-Employed: 0.0%
❋ Part-Time: 0.4%
❋ Job Security: Most secure
❋ Education/Training Required: Work experience in a related occupation

The Department of Labor reports this information for the occupation First-Line Supervisors/Managers of Fire Fighting and Prevention Workers. The job openings listed here are shared with other specializations within that occupation, including Municipal Fire Fighting and Prevention Supervisors.

Industries in Which Income Is Highest

Industry	Average Annual Earnings	Number Employed
Federal, State, and Local Government	$67,760	52,280

Metropolitan Areas Where Income Is Highest

Metropolitan Area	Average Annual Earnings	Number Employed
San Francisco–Oakland–Fremont, CA	$122,310	570
Chicago-Naperville-Joliet, IL-IN-WI	$107,630	2,580
Atlantic City, NJ	$106,650	110
San Jose–Sunnyvale–Santa Clara, CA	$93,900	140
Trenton-Ewing, NJ	$92,560	140

Supervise fire fighters who control and suppress fires in forests or vacant public land. Communicate fire details to superiors, subordinates, and interagency dispatch centers, using two-way radios. Serve as working leader of an engine, hand, helicopter, or prescribed fire crew of three or more firefighters. Maintain fire suppression equipment in good condition, checking equipment periodically to ensure that it is ready for use. Evaluate size, location, and condition of forest fires in order to request and dispatch crews and position equipment so fires can be contained safely and effectively. Operate wildland fire engines and hoselays. Direct and supervise prescribed burn projects and prepare post-burn reports analyzing burn conditions and results. Monitor prescribed burns to ensure that they are conducted safely and effectively. Identify staff training and development needs to ensure that appropriate training can be arranged. Maintain knowledge of forest fire laws and fire prevention techniques and tactics. Recommend equipment modifications or new equipment purchases. Perform administrative duties such as compiling and maintaining records, completing forms, preparing reports, and composing correspondence. Recruit and hire forest fire-fighting personnel. Train workers in such skills as parachute jumping, fire suppression, aerial observation, and radio communication, both in the classroom and on the job. Review and evaluate employee performance. Observe fires and crews from air to determine fire-fighting force requirements and to note changing conditions that will affect fire-fighting efforts. Inspect all stations, uniforms, equipment, and recreation areas to ensure compliance with safety standards, taking corrective action as necessary. Schedule employee work assignments and set work priorities. Regulate open burning by issuing burning permits, inspecting problem sites, issuing citations for violations of laws and ordinances, and educating the public in proper burning practices.

Other Considerations for Income: Fire fighters receive benefits that usually include medical and liability insurance, vacation and sick leave, and some paid holidays. Almost all fire departments provide protective clothing (helmets, boots, and coats) and breathing apparatus, and many also provide dress uniforms. Fire fighters generally are covered by pension plans, often providing retirement at half pay after 25 years of service or if the individual is disabled in the line of duty.

Personality Type: Enterprising-Realistic-Conventional. **Career Cluster:** 12 Law, Public Safety, Corrections, and Security. **Career Pathway:** 12.2 Emergency and Fire Management Services. **Skills:** Equipment Maintenance; Repairing; Operation Monitoring; Management of Personnel Resources; Operation and Control; Science; Management of Material Resources; Equipment Selection.

Education and Training Programs: Fire Prevention and Safety Technology/Technician; Fire Services Administration. **Related Knowledge/Courses:** Public Safety and Security; Building and Construction; Mechanical; Customer and Personal Service; Personnel and Human Resources; Transportation.

Foresters

❋ Annual Earnings: $53,750
❋ Beginning Wage: $34,710
❋ Earnings Growth Potential: Medium (35.4%)
❋ Growth: 5.1%
❋ Annual Job Openings: 772
❋ Self-Employed: 4.2%
❋ Part-Time: 4.9%
❋ Job Security: More secure than most
❋ Education/Training Required: Bachelor's degree

Industries in Which Income Is Highest

Industry	Average Annual Earnings	Number Employed
Wood Product Manufacturing	$55,760	1,180
Federal, State, and Local Government	$51,980	6,410

Metropolitan Areas Where Income Is Highest

Metropolitan Area	Average Annual Earnings	Number Employed
Washington-Arlington-Alexandria, DC-VA-MD-WV	$76,250	70
Sacramento–Arden-Arcade–Roseville, CA	$71,240	90
Redding, CA	$67,670	60
Portland-Vancouver-Beaverton, OR-WA	$63,350	140
Eugene-Springfield, OR	$62,330	110

Manage forested lands for economic, recreational, and conservation purposes. May inventory the type, amount, and location of standing timber; appraise the timber's worth; negotiate the purchase; and draw up contracts for procurement. May determine how to conserve wildlife habitats, creek beds, water quality, and soil stability and how best to comply with environ- mental regulations. **May devise plans for planting and growing new trees, monitor trees for healthy growth, and determine the best time for harvesting. Develop forest management plans for public and privately-owned forested lands.** Monitor contract compliance and results of forestry activities to assure adherence to government regulations. Establish short- and long-term plans for management of forest lands and forest resources. Supervise activities of other forestry workers. Choose and prepare sites for new trees, using controlled burning, bulldozers, or herbicides to clear weeds, brush, and logging debris. Plan and supervise forestry projects, such as determining the type, number, and placement of trees to be planted; managing tree nurseries; thinning forest; and monitoring growth of new seedlings. Negotiate terms and conditions of agreements and contracts for forest harvesting, forest management, and leasing of forest lands. Direct and participate in forest-fire suppression. Determine methods of cutting and removing timber with minimum waste and environmental damage. Analyze effect of forest conditions on tree growth rates and tree species prevalence and the yield, duration, seed production, growth viability, and germination of different species. Monitor forest-cleared lands to ensure that they are reclaimed to their most suitable end use. Plan and implement projects for conservation of wildlife habitats and soil and water quality. Plan and direct forest surveys and related studies and prepare reports and recommendations. Perform inspections of forests or forest nurseries. Map forest area soils and vegetation to estimate the amount of standing timber and future value and growth. Conduct public educational programs on forest care and conservation. Procure timber from private landowners. Subcontract with loggers or pulpwood cutters for tree removal and to aid in road layout. Plan cutting programs and manage timber sales from harvested areas, helping companies to achieve production goals. Monitor wildlife populations and assess the impacts of forest operations on population and habitats.

Other Considerations for Income: In private industry, starting salaries for students with a bachelor's degree were comparable with starting salaries in the federal government, but starting salaries in state and local governments were usually lower. Conservation scientists and foresters who work for federal, state, and local governments and large private firms generally receive more generous benefits than do those working for smaller firms. Governments usually have good pension, health, and leave plans.

Personality Type: Realistic-Investigative-Enterprising. **Career Cluster:** 01 Agriculture, Food and Natural Resource. **Career Pathway:** 01.5 Natural Resources

Systems. **Skills:** Management of Financial Resources; Science; Programming; Operations Analysis; Quality Control Analysis; Mathematics; Coordination; Systems Analysis.

Education and Training Programs: Forest Management/Forest Resources Management; Forest Resources Production and Management; Forest Sciences and Biology; Forestry, General; Forestry, Other; Natural Resources and Conservation, Other; Natural Resources Management and Policy; Natural Resources Management and Policy, Other; Natural Resources/Conservation, General; Urban Forestry; Wood Science and Wood Products/Pulp and Paper Technology. **Related Knowledge/Courses:** Biology; Geography; Mathematics; Law and Government; English Language; Computers and Electronics.

Forestry and Conservation Science Teachers, Postsecondary

- ❊ Annual Earnings: $62,140
- ❊ Beginning Wage: $36,980
- ❊ Earnings Growth Potential: High (40.5%)
- ❊ Growth: 22.9%
- ❊ Annual Job Openings: 454
- ❊ Self-Employed: 0.4%
- ❊ Part-Time: 27.8%
- ❊ Job Security: Most secure
- ❊ Education/Training Required: Doctoral degree

Industries in Which Income Is Highest

Industry	Average Annual Earnings	Number Employed
Educational Services	$62,180	2,440

Metropolitan Areas Where Income Is Highest

Metropolitan Area	Average Annual Earnings	Number Employed
Insufficient data available		

Teach courses in environmental and conservation science. Conduct research in a particular field of knowledge and publish findings in books, professional journals, and/or electronic media. Keep abreast of developments in their field by reading current literature, talking with colleagues, and participating in professional conferences. Prepare and deliver lectures to undergraduate and/or graduate students on topics such as forest resource policy, forest pathology, and mapping. Evaluate and grade students' classwork, assignments, and papers. Write grant proposals to procure external research funding. Supervise undergraduate and/or graduate teaching, internship, and research work. Plan, evaluate, and revise curricula, course content, and course materials and methods of instruction. Prepare course materials such as syllabi, homework assignments, and handouts. Compile, administer, and grade examinations or assign this work to others. Advise students on academic and vocational curricula and on career issues. Initiate, facilitate, and moderate classroom discussions. Supervise students' laboratory work and fieldwork. Maintain student attendance records, grades, and other required records. Collaborate with colleagues to address teaching and research issues. Maintain regularly scheduled office hours in order to advise and assist students. Select and obtain materials and supplies such as textbooks and laboratory equipment. Participate in student recruitment, registration, and placement activities. Serve on academic or administrative committees that deal with institutional policies, departmental matters, and academic issues. Provide professional consulting services to government and/or industry. Perform administrative duties such as serving as department head. Compile bibliographies of specialized materials for outside reading assignments. Act as advisers to student organizations. Participate in campus and community events.

Other Considerations for Income: Earnings for college faculty vary according to rank and type of institution, geographic area, and field. According to a 2006–2007 survey by the American Association of University Professors, salaries for full-time faculty averaged $73,207. By rank, the average was $98,974 for professors, $69,911 for associate professors, $58,662 for assistant professors, $42,609 for instructors, and $48,289 for lecturers. Faculty in 4-year institutions earn higher salaries, on average, than do those in 2-year schools. Many faculty members have significant earnings in addition to their base salary from consulting, teaching additional courses, research, writing for publication, or other employment. In addition, many college and university faculty enjoy unique benefits, including access to campus facilities, tuition waivers for dependents, housing and travel allowances, and paid leave for sabbaticals. Part-time faculty and instructors usually have fewer benefits than full-time faculty.

Personality Type: Social-Investigative-Realistic. **Career Clusters:** 01 Agriculture, Food, and Natural Resource; 05 Education and Training; 05 Education and Training. **Career Pathways:** 01.5 Natural Resources Systems; 05.3 Teaching/Training. **Skills:** Science; Management of Financial Resources; Writing; Instructing; Mathematics; Management of Personnel Resources; Complex Problem Solving; Active Learning.

Education and Training Program: Science Teacher Education/General Science Teacher Education. **Related Knowledge/Courses:** Biology; Geography; Education and Training; Mathematics; History and Archeology; Chemistry.

Freight and Cargo Inspectors

* Annual Earnings: $55,250
* Beginning Wage: $27,560
* Earnings Growth Potential: Very high (50.1%)
* Growth: 16.4%
* Annual Job Openings: 2,122
* Self-Employed: 5.9%
* Part-Time: 3.7%
* Job Security: More secure than most
* Education/Training Required: Work experience in a related occupation

The Department of Labor reports this information for the occupation Transportation Inspectors. The job openings listed here are shared with other specializations within that occupation, including Aviation Inspectors; and Transportation Vehicle, Equipment, and Systems Inspectors, Except Aviation.

Industries in Which Income Is Highest

Industry	Average Annual Earnings	Number Employed
Federal, State, and Local Government	$62,100	11,310
Air Transportation	$59,340	1,380
Rail Transportation	$52,220	3,920
Support Activities for Transportation	$41,720	2,830
Truck Transportation	$39,650	1,170

Metropolitan Areas Where Income Is Highest

Metropolitan Area	Average Annual Earnings	Number Employed
Milwaukee–Waukesha–West Allis, WI	$92,180	60
Minneapolis–St. Paul–Bloomington, MN-WI	$89,530	170
Denver-Aurora, CO	$89,370	180
Washington-Arlington-Alexandria, DC-VA-MD-WV	$88,780	440
Oklahoma City, OK	$87,430	190

Inspect the handling, storage, and stowing of freight and cargoes. Prepare and submit reports after completion of freight shipments. Inspect shipments to ensure that freight is securely braced and blocked. Record details about freight conditions, handling of freight, and any problems encountered. Advise crews in techniques of stowing dangerous and heavy cargo. Observe loading of freight to ensure that crews comply with procedures. Recommend remedial procedures to correct any violations found during inspections. Inspect loaded cargo, cargo lashed to decks or in storage facilities, and cargo handling devices to determine compliance with health and safety regulations and need for maintenance. Measure ships' holds and depths of fuel and water in tanks, using sounding lines and tape measures. Notify workers of any special treatment required for shipments. Direct crews to reload freight or to insert additional bracing or packing as necessary. Check temperatures and humidities of shipping and storage areas to ensure that they are at appropriate levels to protect cargo. Determine cargo transportation capabilities by reading documents that set forth cargo loading and securing procedures, capacities, and stability factors. Read draft markings to determine depths of vessels in water. Issue certificates of compliance for vessels without violations. Write certificates of admeasurement that list details such as designs, lengths, depths, and breadths of vessels, and methods of propulsion. Calculate gross and net tonnage, hold capacities, volumes of stored fuel and water, cargo weights, and ship stability factors, using mathematical formulas. Post warning signs on vehicles containing explosives or flammable or radioactive materials. Measure heights and widths of loads to ensure they will pass over bridges or through tunnels on scheduled routes. Time rolls of ships, using stopwatches. Determine types of licenses and safety equipment required, and compute applicable fees such as tolls and wharfage fees.

Other Considerations for Income: No additional information.

Personality Type: Realistic-Conventional. **Career Cluster:** 16 Transportation, Distribution, and Logistics. **Career Pathway:** 16.1 Transportation Operations. **Skills:** Operation Monitoring; Quality Control Analysis; Science; Mathematics; Writing; Service Orientation; Equipment Selection; Troubleshooting.

Education and Training Programs: No related CIP programs; this job is learned through work experience in a related occupation. **Related Knowledge/Courses:** Transportation; Engineering and Technology; Public Safety and Security; Physics; Geography; Mechanical.

Fuel Cell Engineers

❋ Annual Earnings: $74,920
❋ Beginning Wage: $47,900
❋ Earnings Growth Potential: Medium (36.1%)
❋ Growth: 4.2%
❋ Annual Job Openings: 12,394
❋ Self-Employed: 2.2%
❋ Part-Time: 1.9%
❋ Job Security: No data available
❋ Education/Training Required: Bachelor's degree

The Department of Labor reports this information for the occupation Mechanical Engineers. The job openings listed here are shared with other specializations within that occupation, including Automotive Engineers.

Industries in Which Income Is Highest

Industry	Average Annual Earnings	Number Employed
Federal, State, and Local Government	$86,810	11,330
Management of Companies and Enterprises	$83,970	6,280
Computer and Electronic Product Manufacturing	$80,330	22,300
Professional, Scientific, and Technical Services	$79,060	69,520
Paper Manufacturing	$78,340	1,330

Metropolitan Areas Where Income Is Highest

Metropolitan Area	Average Annual Earnings	Number Employed
San Jose–Sunnyvale–Santa Clara, CA	$98,770	4,250
Washington-Arlington-Alexandria, DC-VA-MD-WV	$96,800	5,430
Albuquerque, NM	$93,890	890
Boulder, CO	$93,730	950
Denver-Aurora, CO	$92,810	2,150

Design, evaluate, modify, and construct fuel cell components and systems for transportation, stationary, or portable applications. No task data available.

Other Considerations for Income: As a group, engineers earn some of the highest average starting salaries among those holding bachelor's degrees. Separate earnings figures for Fuel Cell Engineers are not available, but they are probably similar to those for Mechanical Engineers, who are paid in the low-to-middle range among the various kinds of engineers. According to a 2007 survey by the National Association of Colleges and Employers, average starting salaries for Mechanical Engineers were $54,128 with a bachelor's, $62,798 with a master's, and $72,763 with a Ph.D.

Personality Type: No data available. **Career Cluster:** 15 Science, Technology, Engineering, and Mathematics. **Career Pathway:** 15.1 Engineering and Technology. **Skills:** No data available.

Education and Training Program: Mechanical Engineering. **Related Knowledge/Courses:** No data available.

Funeral Directors

❋ Annual Earnings: $52,210
❋ Beginning Wage: $29,910
❋ Earnings Growth Potential: High (42.7%)
❋ Growth: 12.5%
❋ Annual Job Openings: 3,939
❋ Self-Employed: 19.7%
❋ Part-Time: 8.5%
❋ Job Security: Most secure
❋ Education/Training Required: Associate degree

Industries in Which Income Is Highest

Industry	Average Annual Earnings	Number Employed
Personal and Laundry Services	$51,790	25,180

Metropolitan Areas Where Income Is Highest

Metropolitan Area	Average Annual Earnings	Number Employed
Seattle-Tacoma-Bellevue, WA	$79,930	70
Boston-Cambridge-Quincy, MA-NH	$77,950	420
Providence–Fall River–Warwick, RI-MA	$77,530	100
Salt Lake City, UT	$75,410	70
Trenton-Ewing, NJ	$73,420	80

Perform various tasks to arrange and direct funeral services, such as coordinating transportation of bodies to mortuaries for embalming, interviewing families or other authorized people to arrange details, selecting pallbearers, procuring officials for religious rites, and providing transportation for mourners. Obtain information needed to complete legal documents such as death certificates and burial permits. Oversee the preparation and care of the remains of people who have died. Consult with families or friends of the deceased to arrange funeral details such as obituary notice wording, casket selection, and plans for services. Plan, schedule, and coordinate funerals, burials, and cremations, arranging details such as floral delivery and the time and place of services. Perform embalming duties as necessary. Arrange for clergy members to perform needed services. Contact cemeteries to schedule the opening and closing of graves. Provide information on funeral service options, products, and merchandise and maintain a casket display area. Close caskets and lead funeral corteges to churches or burial sites. Offer counsel and comfort to bereaved families and friends. Inform survivors of benefits for which they may be eligible. Discuss and negotiate prearranged funerals with clients. Maintain financial records, order merchandise, and prepare accounts. Provide or arrange transportation between sites for the remains, mourners, pallbearers, clergy, and flowers. Plan placement of caskets at funeral sites and place and adjust lights, fixtures, and floral displays. Direct preparations and shipment of bodies for out-of-state burials. Manage funeral home operations, including the hiring, training, and supervision of embalmers, funeral attendants, or other staff. Clean funeral home facilities and grounds. Arrange for pallbearers and inform pallbearers and honorary groups of their duties. Receive and usher people to their seats for services. Participate in community activities for funeral home promotion or other purposes.

Other Considerations for Income: Salaries of funeral directors depend on the number of years of experience in funeral service, the number of services performed, the number of facilities operated, the area of the country, and the director's level of formal education. Funeral directors in large cities usually earn more than their counterparts in small towns and rural areas.

Personality Type: Enterprising-Social-Conventional. **Career Cluster:** 10 Human Service. **Career Pathway:** 10.4 Personal Care Services. **Skills:** Management of Personnel Resources; Social Perceptiveness; Management of Financial Resources; Service Orientation; Systems Evaluation; Systems Analysis; Negotiation; Persuasion.

Education and Training Programs: Funeral Direction/Service; Funeral Service and Mortuary Science, General. **Related Knowledge/Courses:** Philosophy and Theology; Chemistry; Therapy and Counseling; Customer and Personal Service; Biology; Sales and Marketing.

Gaming Managers

- Annual Earnings: $68,290
- Beginning Wage: $40,520
- Earnings Growth Potential: High (40.7%)
- Growth: 24.4%
- Annual Job Openings: 549
- Self-Employed: 16.3%
- Part-Time: 4.5%
- Job Security: Less secure than most
- Education/Training Required: Work experience in a related occupation

Industries in Which Income Is Highest

Industry	Average Annual Earnings	Number Employed
Accommodation	$71,720	1,050
Management of Companies and Enterprises	$70,660	40
Federal, State, and Local Government	$68,120	1,330
Performing Arts, Spectator Sports, and Related Industries	$66,340	50
Amusement, Gambling, and Recreation Industries	$66,080	1,250

Metropolitan Areas Where Income Is Highest

Metropolitan Area	Average Annual Earnings	Number Employed
Los Angeles–Long Beach–Santa Ana, CA	$88,000	60
Reno-Sparks, NV	$83,940	80
Chicago-Naperville-Joliet, IL-IN-WI	$83,760	90
San Diego–Carlsbad–San Marcos, CA	$83,230	70
Las Vegas–Paradise, NV	$82,200	390

Plan, organize, direct, control, or coordinate gaming operations in a casino. Formulate gaming policies for their area of responsibility. Resolve customer complaints regarding problems such as payout errors. Remove suspected cheaters, such as card counters and other players who may have systems that shift the odds of winning to their favor. Maintain familiarity with all games used at a facility, as well as strategies and tricks employed in those games. Train new workers and evaluate their performance. Circulate among gaming tables to ensure that operations are conducted properly, that dealers follow house rules, and that players are not cheating. Explain and interpret house rules, such as game rules and betting limits. Monitor staffing levels to ensure that games and tables are adequately staffed for each shift, arranging for staff rotations and breaks and locating substitute employees as necessary. Interview and hire workers. Prepare work schedules and station assignments and keep attendance records. Direct the distribution of complimentary hotel rooms, meals, and other discounts or free items given to players based on their length of play and betting totals. Establish policies on issues such as the type of gambling offered and the odds, the extension of credit, and the serving of food and beverages. Track supplies of money to tables and perform any required paperwork. Set and maintain a bank and table limit for each game. Monitor credit extended to players. Review operational expenses, budget estimates, betting accounts, and collection reports for accuracy. Record, collect, and pay off bets, issuing receipts as necessary. Direct workers compiling summary sheets that show wager amounts and payoffs for races and events. Notify board attendants of table vacancies so that waiting patrons can play.

Other Considerations for Income: No additional information.

Personality Type: Enterprising-Conventional. **Career Cluster:** 09 Hospitality and Tourism. **Career Pathway:** 09.1 Restaurants and Food/Beverage Services. **Skills:** Management of Personnel Resources; Management of Financial Resources; Systems Evaluation; Service Orientation; Negotiation; Operations Analysis; Social Perceptiveness; Mathematics.

Education and Training Program: Personal and Culinary Services, Other. **Related Knowledge/Courses:** Sales and Marketing; Personnel and Human Resources; Customer and Personal Service; Administration and Management; Economics and Accounting; Mathematics.

Gas Plant Operators

- ❋ Annual Earnings: $55,760
- ❋ Beginning Wage: $35,390
- ❋ Earnings Growth Potential: Medium (36.5%)
- ❋ Growth: –9.9%
- ❋ Annual Job Openings: 1,332
- ❋ Self-Employed: 0.1%
- ❋ Part-Time: 0.6%
- ❋ Job Security: More secure than most
- ❋ Education/Training Required: Long-term on-the-job training

Industries in Which Income Is Highest

Industry	Average Annual Earnings	Number Employed
Utilities	$56,680	5,990
Pipeline Transportation	$55,460	3,780
Chemical Manufacturing	$55,070	1,640
Oil and Gas Extraction	$54,910	1,870

Metropolitan Areas Where Income Is Highest

Metropolitan Area	Average Annual Earnings	Number Employed
Boston-Cambridge-Quincy, MA-NH	$73,870	620
Riverside–San Bernardino–Ontario, CA	$73,120	270
New York–Northern New Jersey–Long Island, NY-NJ-PA	$68,880	340
Washington-Arlington-Alexandria, DC-VA-MD-WV	$59,320	190
Philadelphia-Camden-Wilmington, PA-NJ-DE-MD	$58,610	210

Distribute or process gas for utility companies and others by controlling compressors to maintain specified pressures on main pipelines. Determine causes of abnormal pressure variances and make corrective recommendations such as installation of pipes to relieve overloading. Distribute or process gas for utility companies or industrial plants, using panel boards, control boards, and semi-automatic equipment. Start and shut down plant equipment. Test gas, chemicals, and air during processing to assess factors such as purity and moisture content and to detect quality problems or gas or chemical leaks. Adjust temperature, pressure, vacuum, level, flow rate, and transfer of gas to maintain processes at required levels or to correct problems. Change charts in recording meters. Calculate gas ratios to detect deviations from specifications, using testing apparatus. Clean, maintain, and repair equipment, using hand tools, or request that repair and maintenance work be performed. Collaborate with other operators to solve unit problems. Monitor equipment functioning; observe temperature, level, and flow gauges; and perform regular unit checks to ensure that all equipment is operating as it should. Control fractioning columns, compressors, purifying towers, heat exchangers, and related equipment to extract nitrogen and oxygen from air. Control equipment to regulate flow and pressure of gas to feedlines of boilers, furnaces, and related steam-generating or heating equipment. Operate construction equipment to install and maintain gas distribution systems. Signal or direct workers who tend auxiliary equipment. Record, review, and compile operations records; test results; and gauge readings such as temperatures, pressures, concentrations, and flows. Read logsheets to determine product demand and disposition or to detect malfunctions. Monitor transportation and storage of flammable and other potentially dangerous products to ensure that safety guidelines are followed. Contact maintenance crews when necessary.

Other Considerations for Income: No additional information.

Personality Type: Realistic-Conventional. **Career Cluster:** 13 Manufacturing. **Career Pathway:** 13.1 Production. **Skills:** Operation Monitoring; Operation and Control; Repairing; Equipment Maintenance; Science; Operations Analysis; Troubleshooting; Quality Control Analysis.

Education and Training Program: Mechanic and Repair Technologies/Technicians, Other. **Related Knowledge/Courses:** Mechanical; Physics; Building and Construction; Chemistry; Public Safety and Security; Engineering and Technology.

General and Operations Managers

- ❋ Annual Earnings: $91,570
- ❋ Beginning Wage: $45,410
- ❋ Earnings Growth Potential: Very high (50.4%)
- ❋ Growth: 1.5%
- ❋ Annual Job Openings: 112,072
- ❋ Self-Employed: 0.9%
- ❋ Part-Time: 3.2%
- ❋ Job Security: More secure than most
- ❋ Education/Training Required: Work experience plus degree

Industries in Which Income Is Highest

Industry	Average Annual Earnings	Number Employed
Securities, Commodity Contracts, and Other Financial Investments and Related Activities	$152,660	16,160
Other Information Services	$133,920	3,240
Computer and Electronic Product Manufacturing	$129,230	18,540
Professional, Scientific, and Technical Services	$128,290	155,920
Chemical Manufacturing	$123,400	14,100

Metropolitan Areas Where Income Is Highest

Metropolitan Area	Average Annual Earnings	Number Employed
Trenton-Ewing, NJ	$154,320	2,080
Bridgeport-Stamford-Norwalk, CT	$143,270	9,170
New York–Northern New Jersey–Long Island, NY-NJ-PA	$135,720	96,220
San Jose–Sunnyvale–Santa Clara, CA	$132,290	16,490
Seattle-Tacoma-Bellevue, WA	$128,620	12,620

Plan, direct, or coordinate the operations of companies or public- and private-sector organizations. Duties and responsibilities include formulating policies, managing daily operations, and planning the use of materials and human resources, but are too diverse and general in nature to be classified in any one functional area of management or administration, such as personnel, purchasing, or administrative services. Includes owners and managers who head small business establishments whose duties are primarily managerial. Oversee activities directly related to making products or providing services. Direct and coordinate activities of businesses or departments concerned with the production, pricing, sales, or distribution of products. Review financial statements, sales and activity reports, and other performance data to measure productivity and goal achievement and to determine areas needing cost reduction and program improvement. Manage staff, preparing work schedules and assigning specific duties. Direct and coordinate organization's financial and budget activities to fund operations, maximize investments, and increase efficiency. Establish and implement departmental policies, goals, objectives, and procedures, conferring with board members, organization officials, and staff members as necessary. Determine staffing requirements and interview, hire, and train new employees or oversee those personnel processes. Plan and direct activities such as sales promotions, coordinating with other department heads as required. Determine goods and services to be sold and set prices and credit terms based on forecasts of customer demand. Monitor businesses and agencies to ensure that they efficiently and effectively provide needed services while staying within budgetary limits. Locate, select, and procure merchandise for resale, representing management in purchase negotiations. Perform sales floor work such as greeting and assisting customers, stocking shelves, and taking inventory. Manage the movement of goods into and out of production facilities. Develop and implement product marketing strategies, including advertising campaigns and sales promotions. Recommend locations for new facilities or oversee the remodeling of current facilities. Direct non-merchandising departments of businesses such as advertising and purchasing. Plan store layouts and design displays.

Other Considerations for Income: In addition to salaries, total compensation often includes stock options and other performance bonuses. The use of executive dining rooms and company aircraft and cars, expense allowances, and company-paid insurance premiums and physical examinations also are among benefits commonly enjoyed by executives in private industry. A number of executives also are provided with company-paid club memberships and other amenities.

Personality Type: Enterprising-Conventional-Social. **Career Clusters:** 04 Business, Management, and Administration; 07 Government and Public Administration. **Career Pathways:** 04.1 Management; 07.1 Governance. **Skills:** Systems Analysis; Management of Material Resources; Management of Personnel Resources; Management of Financial Resources; Systems Evaluation; Negotiation; Operation Monitoring; Persuasion.

Education and Training Programs: Business Administration and Management, General; Entrepreneurship/Entrepreneurial Studies; International Business/Trade/Commerce; Public Administration. **Related Knowledge/Courses:** Economics and Accounting; Personnel and Human Resources; Administration and Management; Sales and Marketing; Clerical; Building and Construction.

Geodetic Surveyors

* Annual Earnings: $52,980
* Beginning Wage: $29,600
* Earnings Growth Potential: High (44.1%)
* Growth: 23.7%
* Annual Job Openings: 14,305
* Self-Employed: 3.7%
* Part-Time: 4.6%
* Job Security: No data available
* Education/Training Required: Bachelor's degree

The Department of Labor reports this information for the occupation Surveyors. The job openings listed here are shared with other specializations within that occupation.

Industries in Which Income Is Highest

Industry	Average Annual Earnings	Number Employed
Federal, State, and Local Government	$61,320	5,460
Construction of Buildings	$55,000	1,130
Professional, Scientific, and Technical Services	$52,030	44,470
Heavy and Civil Engineering Construction	$51,480	2,280

Metropolitan Areas Where Income Is Highest

Metropolitan Area	Average Annual Earnings	Number Employed
Santa Barbara–Santa Maria, CA	$97,710	90
Yuba City, CA	$82,070	90
Anchorage, AK	$80,620	350
Los Angeles–Long Beach–Santa Ana, CA	$76,720	2,030
Stockton, CA	$76,200	80

Measure large areas of the Earth's surface, using satellite observations, global navigation satellite systems (GNSS), light detection and ranging (LIDAR), or related sources. No task data available.

Other Considerations for Income: No additional information.

Personality Type: Investigative-Conventional-Realistic. **Career Cluster:** 02 Architecture and Construction. **Career Pathway:** 02.1 Design/Pre-Construction. **Skills:** No data available.

Education and Training Program: Surveying Technology/Surveying. **Related Knowledge/Courses:** No data available.

Geographers

* Annual Earnings: $66,600
* Beginning Wage: $38,780
* Earnings Growth Potential: High (41.8%)
* Growth: 6.1%
* Annual Job Openings: 75
* Self-Employed: 5.3%
* Part-Time: 20.1%
* Job Security: More secure than most
* Education/Training Required: Master's degree

Industries in Which Income Is Highest

Industry	Average Annual Earnings	Number Employed
Federal, State, and Local Government	$71,030	740
Professional, Scientific, and Technical Services	$57,930	230
Educational Services	$40,100	90

Metropolitan Areas Where Income Is Highest

Metropolitan Area	Average Annual Earnings	Number Employed
Washington-Arlington-Alexandria, DC-VA-MD-WV	$80,090	210
Pittsburgh, PA	$50,870	50

Study nature and use of areas of earth's surface, relating and interpreting interactions of physical and cultural phenomena. Conduct research on physical aspects of a region, including land forms, climates, soils, plants, and animals, and conduct research on the spatial implications of human activities within a given

area, including social characteristics, economic activities, and political organization, as well as researching interdependence between regions at scales ranging from local to global. Create and modify maps, graphs, or diagrams, using geographical information software and related equipment and principles of cartography such as coordinate systems, longitude, latitude, elevation, topography, and map scales. Write and present reports of research findings. Develop, operate, and maintain geographical information (GIS) computer systems, including hardware, software, plotters, digitizers, printers, and video cameras. Locate and obtain existing geographic information databases. Analyze geographic distributions of physical and cultural phenomena on local, regional, continental, or global scales. Teach geography. Gather and compile geographic data from sources including censuses, field observations, satellite imagery, aerial photographs, and existing maps. Conduct fieldwork at outdoor sites. Study the economic, political, and cultural characteristics of a specific region's population. Provide consulting services in fields including resource development and management, business location and market area analysis, environmental hazards, regional cultural history, and urban social planning. Collect data on physical characteristics of specified areas, such as geological formations, climates, and vegetation, using surveying or meteorological equipment. Provide geographical information systems support to the private and public sectors.

Other Considerations for Income: In the federal government, social scientists with a bachelor's degree and no experience often started at a yearly salary of $28,862 or $35,572 in 2007, depending on their college records. Those with a master's degree could start at $43,731, and those with a Ph.D. degree could begin at $52,912, while some individuals with experience and an advanced degree could start at $63,417. Beginning salaries were higher in selected areas of the country where the prevailing local pay level was higher.

Personality Type: Investigative-Realistic-Artistic. **Career Cluster:** 15 Science, Technology, Engineering, and Mathematics. **Career Pathway:** 15.3 Science and Mathematics. **Skills:** Systems Analysis; Systems Evaluation; Writing; Reading Comprehension; Science; Management of Personnel Resources; Complex Problem Solving; Speaking.

Education and Training Program: Geography. **Related Knowledge/Courses:** Geography; Sociology and Anthropology; History and Archeology; Philosophy and Theology; Foreign Language; Biology.

Geographic Information Systems Technicians

❋ Annual Earnings: $75,150
❋ Beginning Wage: $40,660
❋ Earnings Growth Potential: High (45.9%)
❋ Growth: 15.1%
❋ Annual Job Openings: 14,374
❋ Self-Employed: 6.6%
❋ Part-Time: 5.6%
❋ Job Security: No data available
❋ Education/Training Required: Associate degree

The Department of Labor reports this information for the occupation Computer Specialists, All Other. The job openings listed here are shared with other specializations within that occupation, including Business Intelligence Analysts; Computer Systems Engineers/Architects; Data Warehousing Specialists; Database Architects; Document Management Specialists; Electronic Commerce Specialists; Geospatial Information Scientists and Technologists; Information Technology Project Managers; Network Designers; Software Quality Assurance Engineers and Testers; Video Game Designers; Web Administrators; and Web Developers.

Industries in Which Income Is Highest

Industry	Average Annual Earnings	Number Employed
Petroleum and Coal Products Manufacturing	$97,090	1,070
Transportation Equipment Manufacturing	$82,770	3,010
Oil and Gas Extraction	$81,350	1,710
Federal, State, and Local Government	$80,670	71,650
Management of Companies and Enterprises	$78,200	14,820

Metropolitan Areas Where Income Is Highest

Metropolitan Area	Average Annual Earnings	Number Employed
Washington-Arlington-Alexandria, DC-VA-MD-WV	$97,170	19,470
Atlantic City, NJ	$96,600	510
Pascagoula, MS	$95,430	60
San Jose–Sunnyvale–Santa Clara, CA	$92,710	3,580
Baltimore-Towson, MD	$89,730	5,650

Assist scientists, technologists, and related professionals in building, maintaining, modifying, and using geographic information systems (GIS) databases. May also perform some custom application development and provide user support. No task data available.

Other Considerations for Income: No additional information.

Personality Type: Investigative-Realistic-Conventional. **Career Cluster:** 11 Information Technology. **Career Pathway:** 11.4 Programming and Software Development. **Skills:** No data available.

Education and Training Programs: Computer and Information Sciences and Support Services, Other; Computer and Information Sciences, General; Computer Engineering Technologies/Technicians, Other; Computer Engineering, General; Computer Science; Computer Software Engineering; Computer Systems Networking and Telecommunications; E-Commerce/Electronic Commerce; Information Science/Studies; Information Technology; System, Networking, and LAN/WAN Management/Manager; Web Page, Digital/Multimedia and Information Resources Design; others. **Related Knowledge/Courses:** No data available.

Geography Teachers, Postsecondary

- ❀ Annual Earnings: $62,880
- ❀ Beginning Wage: $36,250
- ❀ Earnings Growth Potential: High (42.4%)
- ❀ Growth: 22.9%
- ❀ Annual Job Openings: 697
- ❀ Self-Employed: 0.4%
- ❀ Part-Time: 27.8%
- ❀ Job Security: Most secure
- ❀ Education/Training Required: Doctoral degree

Industries in Which Income Is Highest

Industry	Average Annual Earnings	Number Employed
Educational Services	$62,880	4,030

Metropolitan Areas Where Income Is Highest

Metropolitan Area	Average Annual Earnings	Number Employed
San Jose–Sunnyvale–Santa Clara, CA	$98,950	30
Los Angeles–Long Beach–Santa Ana, CA	$90,000	60
Philadelphia-Camden-Wilmington, PA-NJ-DE-MD	$80,300	110
Detroit-Warren-Livonia, MI	$76,890	40
New York–Northern New Jersey–Long Island, NY-NJ-PA	$72,630	50

Teach courses in geography. Prepare and deliver lectures to undergraduate and/or graduate students on topics such as urbanization, environmental systems, and cultural geography. Evaluate and grade students' classwork, assignments, and papers. Compile, administer, and grade examinations or assign this work to others. Initiate, facilitate, and moderate classroom discussions. Maintain student attendance records, grades, and other required records. Prepare course materials such as syllabi, homework assignments, and handouts. Keep abreast of developments in their field by reading current literature, talking with colleagues, and participating in professional conferences.

Supervise undergraduate and/or graduate teaching, internship, and research work. Plan, evaluate, and revise curricula, course content, and course materials and methods of instruction. Maintain regularly scheduled office hours to advise and assist students. Supervise students' laboratory work and fieldwork. Conduct research in a particular field of knowledge and publish findings in professional journals, books, and electronic media. Collaborate with colleagues to address teaching and research issues. Select and obtain materials and supplies such as textbooks. Advise students on academic and vocational curricula and on career issues. Serve on academic or administrative committees that deal with institutional policies, departmental matters, and academic issues. Participate in student recruitment, registration, and placement activities. Participate in campus and community events. Compile bibliographies of specialized materials for outside reading assignments. Perform administrative duties such as serving as department head. Write grant proposals to procure external research funding. Maintain geographic information systems laboratories, performing duties such as updating software. Perform spatial analysis and modeling, using geographic information system techniques. Act as advisers to student organizations.

Other Considerations for Income: Earnings for college faculty vary according to rank and type of institution, geographic area, and field. According to a 2006–2007 survey by the American Association of University Professors, salaries for full-time faculty averaged $73,207. By rank, the average was $98,974 for professors, $69,911 for associate professors, $58,662 for assistant professors, $42,609 for instructors, and $48,289 for lecturers. Faculty in 4-year institutions earn higher salaries, on average, than do those in 2-year schools. Many faculty members have significant earnings in addition to their base salary from consulting, teaching additional courses, research, writing for publication, or other employment. In addition, many college and university faculty enjoy unique benefits, including access to campus facilities, tuition waivers for dependents, housing and travel allowances, and paid leave for sabbaticals. Part-time faculty and instructors usually have fewer benefits than full-time faculty.

Personality Type: Social-Investigative. **Career Clusters:** 05 Education and Training; 15 Science, Technology, Engineering, and Mathematics. **Career Pathways:** 05.3 Teaching/Training; 15.3 Science and Mathematics. **Skills:** Science; Writing; Instructing; Learning Strategies; Reading Comprehension; Speaking; Critical Thinking; Active Learning.

Education and Training Programs: Geography; Geography Teacher Education; Humanities/Humanistic Studies. **Related Knowledge/Courses:** Geography; Sociology and Anthropology; History and Archeology; Philosophy and Theology; Education and Training; Communications and Media.

Geological and Petroleum Technicians

See *Geological Sample Test Technicians* and *Geophysical Data Technicians,* described separately.

Geological Sample Test Technicians

- ❀ Annual Earnings: $53,360
- ❀ Beginning Wage: $26,630
- ❀ Earnings Growth Potential: Very high (50.1%)
- ❀ Growth: 8.6%
- ❀ Annual Job Openings: 1,895
- ❀ Self-Employed: 0.0%
- ❀ Part-Time: 1.0%
- ❀ Job Security: Less secure than most
- ❀ Education/Training Required: Associate degree

The Department of Labor reports this information for the occupation Geological and Petroleum Technicians. The job openings listed here are shared with other specializations within that occupation, including Geophysical Data Technicians.

Industries in Which Income Is Highest

Industry	Average Annual Earnings	Number Employed
Petroleum and Coal Products Manufacturing	$68,180	1,340
Oil and Gas Extraction	$61,670	4,900
Support Activities for Mining	$42,160	2,950
Professional, Scientific, and Technical Services	$37,950	3,680

Metropolitan Areas Where Income Is Highest

Metropolitan Area	Average Annual Earnings	Number Employed
San Francisco–Oakland–Fremont, CA	$80,220	630
Houston–Sugar Land–Baytown, TX	$67,640	3,080
Bakersfield, CA	$64,260	130
Denver-Aurora, CO	$63,960	670
New Orleans–Metairie–Kenner, LA	$61,940	550

Test and analyze geological samples, crude oil, or petroleum products to detect presence of petroleum, gas, or mineral deposits indicating potential for exploration and production or to determine physical and chemical properties to ensure that products meet quality standards. Test and analyze samples in order to determine their content and characteristics, using laboratory apparatus and testing equipment. Collect and prepare solid and fluid samples for analysis. Assemble, operate, and maintain field and laboratory testing, measuring, and mechanical equipment, working as part of a crew when required. Compile and record testing and operational data for review and further analysis. Adjust and repair testing, electrical, and mechanical equipment and devices. Supervise well exploration and drilling activities and well completions. Inspect engines for wear and defective parts, using equipment and measuring devices. Prepare notes, sketches, geological maps, and cross sections. Participate in geological, geophysical, geochemical, hydrographic, or oceanographic surveys; prospecting field trips; exploratory drilling; well logging; or underground mine survey programs. Plot information from aerial photographs, well logs, section descriptions, and other databases. Assess the environmental impacts of development projects on subsurface materials. Collaborate with hydrogeologists to evaluate groundwater and well circulation. Prepare, transcribe, and/or analyze seismic, gravimetric, well log, or other geophysical and survey data. Participate in the evaluation of possible mining locations.

Other Considerations for Income: No additional information.

Personality Type: Realistic-Investigative-Conventional. **Career Cluster:** 01 Agriculture, Food and Natural Resource. **Career Pathway:** 01.5 Natural Resources Systems. **Skills:** Science; Equipment Maintenance; Operation Monitoring; Quality Control Analysis; Mathematics; Operations Analysis; Installation; Operation and Control.

Education and Training Program: Petroleum Technology/Technician. **Related Knowledge/Courses:** Chemistry; Geography; Physics; Mechanical; Mathematics; Computers and Electronics.

Geophysical Data Technicians

- ❋ Annual Earnings: $53,360
- ❋ Beginning Wage: $26,630
- ❋ Earnings Growth Potential: Very high (50.1%)
- ❋ Growth: 8.6%
- ❋ Annual Job Openings: 1,895
- ❋ Self-Employed: 0.0%
- ❋ Part-Time: 1.0%
- ❋ Job Security: Less secure than most
- ❋ Education/Training Required: Associate degree

The Department of Labor reports this information for the occupation Geological and Petroleum Technicians. The job openings listed here are shared with other specializations within that occupation, including Geological Sample Test Technicians.

Industries in Which Income Is Highest

Industry	Average Annual Earnings	Number Employed
Petroleum and Coal Products Manufacturing	$68,180	1,340
Oil and Gas Extraction	$61,670	4,900
Support Activities for Mining	$42,160	2,950
Professional, Scientific, and Technical Services	$37,950	3,680

Metropolitan Areas Where Income Is Highest

Metropolitan Area	Average Annual Earnings	Number Employed
San Francisco–Oakland–Fremont, CA	$80,220	630
Houston–Sugar Land–Baytown, TX	$67,640	3,080
Bakersfield, CA	$64,260	130
Denver-Aurora, CO	$63,960	670
New Orleans–Metairie–Kenner, LA	$61,940	550

Measure, record, and evaluate geological data by using sonic, electronic, electrical, seismic, or gravity-measuring instruments to prospect for oil or gas. May collect and evaluate core samples and cuttings. Prepare notes, sketches, geological maps, and cross-sections. Read and study reports in order to compile information and data for geological and geophysical prospecting. Interview individuals and research public databases in order to obtain information. Assemble, maintain, and distribute information for library or record systems. Operate and adjust equipment and apparatus used to obtain geological data. Plan and direct activities of workers who operate equipment to collect data. Set up or direct setup of instruments used to collect geological data. Record readings in order to compile data used in prospecting for oil or gas. Supervise oil, water, and gas well drilling activities. Collect samples and cuttings, using equipment and hand tools. Develop and print photographic recordings of information, using equipment. Measure geological characteristics used in prospecting for oil or gas, using measuring instruments. Evaluate and interpret core samples and cuttings and other geological data used in prospecting for oil or gas. Diagnose and repair malfunctioning instruments and equipment, using manufacturers' manuals and hand tools. Prepare and attach packing instructions to shipping containers. Develop and design packing materials and handling procedures for shipping of objects.

Other Considerations for Income: No additional information.

Personality Type: Conventional-Realistic-Investigative. **Career Cluster:** 01 Agriculture, Food and Natural Resource. **Career Pathway:** 01.5 Natural Resources Systems. **Skills:** Science; Technology Design; Mathematics; Operations Analysis; Operation Monitoring; Persuasion; Equipment Selection; Management of Financial Resources.

Education and Training Program: Petroleum Technology/Technician. **Related Knowledge/Courses:** Geography; Engineering and Technology; Physics; Computers and Electronics; Mathematics; Chemistry.

Geoscientists, Except Hydrologists and Geographers

- ❀ Annual Earnings: $79,160
- ❀ Beginning Wage: $41,700
- ❀ Earnings Growth Potential: High (47.3%)
- ❀ Growth: 21.9%
- ❀ Annual Job Openings: 2,471
- ❀ Self-Employed: 2.2%
- ❀ Part-Time: 5.3%
- ❀ Job Security: Most secure
- ❀ Education/Training Required: Master's degree

Industries in Which Income Is Highest

Industry	Average Annual Earnings	Number Employed
Oil and Gas Extraction	$127,560	5,810
Support Activities for Mining	$86,280	1,830
Federal, State, and Local Government	$72,890	5,220
Educational Services	$66,560	1,290
Professional, Scientific, and Technical Services	$66,310	14,200

Metropolitan Areas Where Income Is Highest

Metropolitan Area	Average Annual Earnings	Number Employed
Houston–Sugar Land–Baytown, TX	$128,040	5,200
San Antonio, TX	$114,670	250
Oklahoma City, OK	$112,460	640
Corpus Christi, TX	$108,900	500
Bakersfield, CA	$105,310	150

Study the composition, structure, and other physical aspects of the Earth. May use knowledge of geology, physics, and mathematics in exploration for oil, gas, minerals, or underground water or in waste disposal, land reclamation, or other environmental problems. May study the Earth's internal composition, atmospheres, and oceans and its magnetic, electrical, and gravitational forces. Includes mineralogists, crystallographers, paleontologists, stratigraphers, geodesists,

and seismologists. Analyze and interpret geological, geochemical, and geophysical information from sources such as survey data, well logs, bore holes, and aerial photos. Locate and estimate probable natural gas, oil, and mineral ore deposits and underground water resources, using aerial photographs, charts, or research and survey results. Plan and conduct geological, geochemical, and geophysical field studies and surveys, sample collection, or drilling and testing programs used to collect data for research or application. Analyze and interpret geological data, using computer software. Search for and review research articles or environmental, historical, and technical reports. Assess ground and surface water movement to provide advice regarding issues such as waste management, route and site selection, and the restoration of contaminated sites. Prepare geological maps, cross-sectional diagrams, charts, and reports concerning mineral extraction, land use, and resource management, using results of field work and laboratory research. Investigate the composition, structure, and history of the Earth's crust through the collection, examination, measurement, and classification of soils, minerals, rocks, or fossil remains. Conduct geological and geophysical studies to provide information for use in regional development, site selection, and development of public works projects. Measure characteristics of the Earth, such as gravity and magnetic fields, using equipment such as seismographs, gravimeters, torsion balances, and magnetometers. Inspect construction projects to analyze engineering problems, applying geological knowledge and using test equipment and drilling machinery. Design geological mine maps, monitor mine structural integrity, or advise and monitor mining crews. Identify risks for natural disasters such as mudslides, earthquakes, and volcanic eruptions, providing advice on mitigation of potential damage.

Other Considerations for Income: The petroleum, mineral, and mining industries offer higher salaries, but less job security, than other industries because economic downturns sometimes cause layoffs. According to the National Association of Colleges and Employers, beginning salary offers in July 2007 for graduates with bachelor's degrees in geology and related sciences averaged $40,786 a year.

Personality Type: Investigative-Realistic. **Career Cluster:** 15 Science, Technology, Engineering, and Mathematics. **Career Pathway:** 15.3 Science and Mathematics. **Skills:** Systems Analysis; Science; Systems Evaluation; Reading Comprehension; Writing; Management of Personnel Resources.

Education and Training Programs: Geochemistry; Geochemistry and Petrology; Geological and Earth Sciences/Geosciences, Other; Geology/Earth Science, General; Geophysics and Seismology; Oceanography, Chemical and Physical; Paleontology. **Related Knowledge/Courses:** Geography; Engineering and Technology; Physics; Chemistry; Mathematics; Design.

Geospatial Information Scientists and Technologists

- ❋ Annual Earnings: $75,150
- ❋ Beginning Wage: $40,660
- ❋ Earnings Growth Potential: High (45.9%)
- ❋ Growth: 15.1%
- ❋ Annual Job Openings: 14,374
- ❋ Self-Employed: 6.6%
- ❋ Part-Time: 5.6%
- ❋ Job Security: No data available
- ❋ Education/Training Required: Bachelor's degree

The Department of Labor reports this information for the occupation Computer Specialists, All Other. The job openings listed here are shared with other specializations within that occupation, including Business Intelligence Analysts; Computer Systems Engineers/Architects; Data Warehousing Specialists; Database Architects; Document Management Specialists; Electronic Commerce Specialists; Geographic Information Systems Technicians; Information Technology Project Managers; Network Designers; Software Quality Assurance Engineers and Testers; Video Game Designers; Web Administrators; and Web Developers.

Industries in Which Income Is Highest

Industry	Average Annual Earnings	Number Employed
Petroleum and Coal Products Manufacturing	$97,090	1,070
Transportation Equipment Manufacturing	$82,770	3,010
Oil and Gas Extraction	$81,350	1,710
Federal, State, and Local Government	$80,670	71,650
Management of Companies and Enterprises	$78,200	14,820

Metropolitan Areas Where Income Is Highest

Metropolitan Area	Average Annual Earnings	Number Employed
Washington-Arlington-Alexandria, DC-VA-MD-WV	$97,170	19,470
Atlantic City, NJ	$96,600	510
Pascagoula, MS	$95,430	60
San Jose–Sunnyvale–Santa Clara, CA	$92,710	3,580
Baltimore-Towson, MD	$89,730	5,650

Research and develop geospatial technologies. May produce databases, perform applications programming, or coordinate projects. May specialize in areas such as agriculture, mining, health care, retail trade, urban planning, or military intelligence. No task data available.

Other Considerations for Income: No additional information.

Personality Type: Investigative-Realistic-Conventional. **Career Cluster:** 11 Information Technology. **Career Pathway:** 11.4 Programming and Software Development. **Skills:** No data available.

Education and Training Programs: Computer and Information Sciences and Support Services, Other; Computer and Information Sciences, General; Computer Engineering Technologies/Technicians, Other; Computer Engineering, General; Computer Science; Computer Software Engineering; Computer Systems Networking and Telecommunications; E-Commerce/Electronic Commerce; Information Science/Studies; Information Technology; System, Networking, and LAN/WAN Management/Manager; Web Page, Digital/Multimedia and Information Resources Design; others. **Related Knowledge/Courses:** Geography; Computers and Electronics; Design; Engineering and Technology; Mathematics; Education and Training.

Geothermal Production Managers

❋ Annual Earnings: $83,290
❋ Beginning Wage: $50,330
❋ Earnings Growth Potential: Medium (39.6%)
❋ Growth: –5.9%
❋ Annual Job Openings: 14,889
❋ Self-Employed: 2.0%
❋ Part-Time: 1.6%
❋ Job Security: No data available
❋ Education/Training Required: Work experience in a related occupation

The Department of Labor reports this information for the occupation Industrial Production Managers. The job openings listed here are shared with other specializations within that occupation, including Biofuels Production Managers; Biomass Production Managers; Hydroelectric Production Managers; Methane/Landfill Gas Collection System Operators; and Quality Control Systems Managers.

Industries in Which Income Is Highest

Industry	Average Annual Earnings	Number Employed
Oil and Gas Extraction	$104,890	1,590
Professional, Scientific, and Technical Services	$103,550	3,450
Petroleum and Coal Products Manufacturing	$103,100	1,220
Utilities	$101,110	1,740
Management of Companies and Enterprises	$99,660	6,180

Metropolitan Areas Where Income Is Highest

Metropolitan Area	Average Annual Earnings	Number Employed
Austin–Round Rock, TX	$112,900	690
Cedar Rapids, IA	$110,680	530
Leominster-Fitchburg-Gardner, MA	$107,340	70
Saginaw–Saginaw Township North, MI	$106,880	140
Ann Arbor, MI	$104,600	320

Manage operations at geothermal power generation facilities. Maintain and monitor geothermal plant equipment for efficient and safe plant operations. No task data available.

Other Considerations for Income: No additional information.

Personality Type: No data available. **Career Cluster:** 04 Business, Management, and Administration. **Career Pathway:** 04.1 Management. **Skills:** No data available.

Education and Training Programs: Business Administration and Management, General; Business/Commerce, General; Operations Management and Supervision. **Related Knowledge/Courses:** No data available.

Government Property Inspectors and Investigators

* ❋ Annual Earnings: $48,890
* ❋ Beginning Wage: $29,490
* ❋ Earnings Growth Potential: Medium (39.7%)
* ❋ Growth: 4.9%
* ❋ Annual Job Openings: 15,841
* ❋ Self-Employed: 0.4%
* ❋ Part-Time: 5.0%
* ❋ Job Security: More secure than most
* ❋ Education/Training Required: Long-term on-the-job training

The Department of Labor reports this information for the occupation Compliance Officers, Except Agriculture, Construction, Health and Safety, and Transportation. The job openings listed here are shared with other specializations within that occupation, including Coroners; Environmental Compliance Inspectors; Equal Opportunity Representatives and Officers; Licensing Examiners and Inspectors; and Regulatory Affairs Specialists.

Industries in Which Income Is Highest

Industry Earnings	Average Annual Earnings	Number Employed
Postal Service	$77,500	1,970
Utilities	$74,890	1,880
Securities, Commodity Contracts, and Other Financial Investments and Related Activities	$70,720	6,480
Telecommunications	$64,400	2,560
Chemical Manufacturing	$61,920	3,910

Metropolitan Areas Where Income Is Highest

Metropolitan Area	Average Annual Earnings	Number Employed
Brunswick, GA	$83,080	500
Bridgeport-Stamford-Norwalk, CT	$73,120	640
Warner Robins, GA	$69,670	80
San Francisco–Oakland–Fremont, CA	$67,520	4,370
Hartford–West Hartford–East Hartford, CT	$67,460	1,420

Investigate or inspect government property to ensure compliance with contract agreements and government regulations. Prepare correspondence, reports of inspections or investigations, and recommendations for action. Inspect government-owned equipment and materials in the possession of private contractors to ensure compliance with contracts and regulations and to prevent misuse. Examine records, reports, and documents to establish facts and detect discrepancies. Inspect manufactured or processed products to ensure compliance with contract specifications and legal requirements. Locate and interview plaintiffs, witnesses, or representatives of business or government to gather facts relevant to inspections or alleged violations. Recommend legal or administrative action to protect government property. Submit samples of products to government laboratories for testing as required. Coordinate with and assist law enforcement agencies in matters of mutual concern. Testify in court or at administrative proceedings concerning findings of investigations. Collect, identify, evaluate, and preserve case evidence. Monitor investigations of suspected offenders to ensure that they are conducted in accordance with constitutional requirements. Investigate applications for special licenses or permits, as well as alleged violations of licenses or permits.

Other Considerations for Income: No additional information.

Personality Type: Conventional-Enterprising-Realistic. **Career Cluster:** 12 Law, Public Safety, Corrections, and Security. **Career Pathway:** 12.6 Inspection Services. **Skills:** Quality Control Analysis; Technology Design; Science; Troubleshooting; Equipment Selection; Coordination; Operation and Control; Service Orientation.

Education and Training Program: Building/Home/Construction Inspection/Inspector. **Related Knowledge/Courses:** Building and Construction; Engineering and Technology; Public Safety and Security; Mechanical; Transportation; Computers and Electronics.

Green Marketers

* Annual Earnings: $80,220
* Beginning Wage: $40,090
* Earnings Growth Potential: High (50.0%)
* Growth: 6.2%
* Annual Job Openings: 2,955
* Self-Employed: 13.4%
* Part-Time: 4.8%
* Job Security: No data available
* Education/Training Required: Work experience plus degree

The Department of Labor reports this information for the occupation Advertising and Promotions Managers. The job openings listed here are shared with other specializations within that occupation.

Industries in Which Income Is Highest

Industry	Average Annual Earnings	Number Employed
Professional, Scientific, and Technical Services	$102,310	9,300
Management of Companies and Enterprises	$85,950	3,470
Publishing Industries (Except Internet)	$80,770	3,320
Broadcasting (Except Internet)	$79,060	1,810
Merchant Wholesalers, Nondurable Goods	$78,610	2,330

Metropolitan Areas Where Income Is Highest

Metropolitan Area	Average Annual Earnings	Number Employed
New York–Northern New Jersey–Long Island, NY-NJ-PA	$127,920	5,670
Minneapolis–St. Paul–Bloomington, MN-WI	$107,790	300
Jacksonville, FL	$107,600	110
Trenton-Ewing, NJ	$103,360	60
Cleveland-Elyria-Mentor, OH	$103,040	170

Create and implement methods to market green products and services. No task data available.

Other Considerations for Income: Salary levels vary substantially, depending upon the level of managerial responsibility, length of service, education, size of firm, location, and industry. For example, manufacturing firms usually pay these managers higher salaries than nonmanufacturing firms. Many managers earn bonuses equal to 10 percent or more of their salaries.

Personality Type: No data available. **Career Clusters:** 04 Business, Management, and Administration; 14 Marketing, Sales, and Service. **Career Pathways:** 04.1 Management; 04.5 Marketing; 14.1 Management and Entrepreneurship. **Skills:** No data available.

Education and Training Programs: Advertising; Marketing/Marketing Management, General; Public Relations/Image Management. **Related Knowledge/Courses:** No data available.

Health and Safety Engineers, Except Mining Safety Engineers and Inspectors

See *Fire-Prevention and Protection Engineers; Industrial Safety and Health Engineers;* and *Product Safety Engineers,* described separately.

Health Specialties Teachers, Postsecondary

- ❋ Annual Earnings: $84,390
- ❋ Beginning Wage: $38,610
- ❋ Earnings Growth Potential: Very high (54.2%)
- ❋ Growth: 22.9%
- ❋ Annual Job Openings: 19,617
- ❋ Self-Employed: 0.4%
- ❋ Part-Time: 27.8%
- ❋ Job Security: Most secure
- ❋ Education/Training Required: Doctoral degree

Industries in Which Income Is Highest

Industry	Average Annual Earnings	Number Employed
Hospitals	$94,760	5,990
Educational Services	$83,860	117,880

Metropolitan Areas Where Income Is Highest

Metropolitan Area	Average Annual Earnings	Number Employed
Rochester, NY	$148,920	430
Baltimore-Towson, MD	$122,640	4,210
New York–Northern New Jersey–Long Island, NY-NJ-PA	$118,540	7,440
Santa Rosa–Petaluma, CA	$109,290	170
Houston–Sugar Land–Baytown, TX	$106,340	5,210

Teach courses in health specialties, such as veterinary medicine, dentistry, pharmacy, therapy, laboratory technology, and public health. Initiate, facilitate, and moderate classroom discussions. Keep abreast of developments in their field by reading current literature, talking with colleagues, and participating in professional conferences. Compile, administer, and grade examinations or assign this work to others. Evaluate and grade students' classwork, assignments, and papers. Prepare course materials such as syllabi, homework assignments, and handouts. Prepare and deliver lectures to undergraduate or graduate students on topics such as public health, stress management, and worksite health promotion. Plan, evaluate, and revise curricula, course content, and course materials and methods of instruction. Supervise undergraduate or graduate teaching, internship, and research work. Conduct research in a particular field of knowledge and publish findings in professional journals, books, or electronic media. Collaborate with colleagues to address teaching and research issues. Supervise laboratory sessions. Maintain student attendance records, grades, and other required records. Maintain regularly scheduled office hours in order to advise and assist students. Advise students on academic and vocational curricula and on career issues. Participate in student recruitment, registration, and placement activities. Write grant proposals to procure external research funding. Serve on academic or administrative committees that deal with institutional policies, departmental matters, and academic issues. Select and obtain materials and supplies such as textbooks and laboratory equipment. Act as advisers to student organizations. Perform administrative duties such as serving as department head. Compile bibliographies of specialized materials for outside reading assignments. Provide professional consulting services to government and industry. Participate in campus and community events.

Other Considerations for Income: Earnings for college faculty vary according to rank and type of institution, geographic area, and field. According to a 2006–2007 survey by the American Association of University Professors, salaries for full-time faculty averaged $73,207. By rank, the average was $98,974 for professors, $69,911 for associate professors, $58,662 for assistant professors, $42,609 for instructors, and $48,289 for lecturers. Faculty in 4-year institutions earn higher salaries, on average, than do those in 2-year schools. Many faculty members have significant earnings in addition to their base salary from consulting, teaching additional courses, research, writing for publication, or other employment. In addition, many college and university faculty enjoy unique benefits, including access to campus facilities, tuition waivers for dependents, housing and travel allowances, and paid leave for sabbaticals. Part-time faculty and instructors usually have fewer benefits than full-time faculty.

Personality Type: Social-Investigative. **Career Cluster:** 15 Science, Technology, Engineering, and Mathematics. **Career Pathway:** 15.3 Science and Mathematics. **Skills:** Science; Instructing; Writing; Reading Comprehension; Learning Strategies; Complex Problem Solving; Critical Thinking; Speaking.

Education and Training Programs: Allied Health and Medical Assisting Services, Other; Allied Health Diagnostic, Intervention, and Treatment Professions, Other; Art Therapy/Therapist; Asian Bodywork Therapy; Audiology/Audiologist; Audiology/Audiologist and Speech-Language Pathology/Pathologist; Biostatistics; Blood Bank Technology Specialist Training; Cardiovascular Technology/Technologist; Chiropractic (DC); Clinical Laboratory Science/Medical Technology/Technologist; Clinical/Medical Laboratory Assistant Training; others. **Related Knowledge/Courses:** Biology; Medicine and Dentistry; Education and Training; Therapy and Counseling; Sociology and Anthropology; Psychology.

Historians

* Annual Earnings: $54,530
* Beginning Wage: $25,670
* Earnings Growth Potential: Very high (52.9%)
* Growth: 7.8%
* Annual Job Openings: 245
* Self-Employed: 5.2%
* Part-Time: 20.1%
* Job Security: Most secure
* Education/Training Required: Master's degree

Industries in Which Income Is Highest

Industry	Average Annual Earnings	Number Employed
Professional, Scientific, and Technical Services	$65,970	830
Federal, State, and Local Government	$51,040	2,100
Educational Services	$49,850	100
Museums, Historical Sites, and Similar Institutions	$44,140	210

Metropolitan Areas Where Income Is Highest

Metropolitan Area	Average Annual Earnings	Number Employed
Washington-Arlington-Alexandria, DC-VA-MD-WV	$78,810	570
Trenton-Ewing, NJ	$70,040	50
New York–Northern New Jersey–Long Island, NY-NJ-PA	$67,570	210
Boston-Cambridge-Quincy, MA-NH	$51,610	80
Milwaukee–Waukesha–West Allis, WI	$47,300	50

Research, analyze, record, and interpret the past as recorded in sources such as government and institutional records; newspapers and other periodicals; photographs; interviews; films; and unpublished manuscripts, such as personal diaries and letters. Gather historical data from sources such as archives, court records, diaries, news files, and photographs, as well as collect data sources such as books, pamphlets, and periodicals. Organize data and analyze and interpret its authenticity and relative significance. Trace historical development in a particular field, such as social, cultural, political, or diplomatic history. Conduct historical research as a basis for the identification, conservation, and reconstruction of historic places and materials. Teach and conduct research in colleges, universities, museums, and other research agencies and schools. Conduct historical research and publish or present findings and theories. Speak to various groups, organizations, and clubs to promote the aims and activities of historical societies. Prepare publications and exhibits or review those prepared by others in order to ensure their historical accuracy. Research the history of a particular country or region or of a specific time period. Determine which topics to research or pursue research topics specified by clients or employers. Present historical accounts in terms of individuals or social, ethnic, political, economic, or geographic groupings. Organize information for publication and for other means of dissemination, such as use in CD-ROMs or Internet sites. Research and prepare manuscripts in support of public programming and the development of exhibits at historic sites, museums, libraries, and archives. Advise or consult with individuals and institutions regarding issues such as the historical authenticity of materials or the customs of a specific historical period. Translate or request translation of reference materials. Collect detailed information on individuals for use in biographies. Interview people in order to gather information about historical events and to record oral histories. Recommend actions related to historical art, such as which items to add to a collection or which items to display in an exhibit.

Other Considerations for Income: In the federal government, social scientists with a bachelor's degree and no experience often started at a yearly salary of $28,862 or $35,572 in 2007, depending on their college records. Those with a master's degree could start at $43,731, and those with a Ph.D. degree could begin at $52,912, while some individuals with experience and an advanced degree could start at $63,417. Beginning salaries were higher in selected areas of the country where the prevailing local pay level was higher.

Personality Type: Investigative. **Career Clusters:** 03 Arts, Audio/Video Technology, and Communications; 05 Education and Training; 15 Science, Technology, Engineering, and Mathematics. **Career Pathways:** 03.1 Audio and Video Technology and Film; 05.3 Teaching/Training; 15.3 Science and Mathematics. **Skills:** Reading Comprehension; Management of Financial Resources; Writing; Management of Personnel Resources; Speaking; Social Perceptiveness; Active Listening; Time Management.

Education and Training Programs: American History (United States); Ancient Studies/Civilization; Architectural History and Criticism, General; Asian History; Canadian History; Classical, Ancient Mediterranean and Near Eastern Studies and Archaeology; Cultural Resource Management and Policy Analysis; European History; Historic Preservation and Conservation; Historic Preservation and Conservation, Other; History and Philosophy of Science and Technology; History, General; History, Other; Holocaust and Related Studies; others. **Related Knowledge/Courses:** History and Archeology; Computers and Electronics; English Language; Geography; Communications and Media; Clerical.

History Teachers, Postsecondary

* Annual Earnings: $62,000
* Beginning Wage: $34,230
* Earnings Growth Potential: High (44.8%)
* Growth: 22.9%
* Annual Job Openings: 3,570
* Self-Employed: 0.4%
* Part-Time: 27.8%
* Job Security: Most secure
* Education/Training Required: Doctoral degree

Industries in Which Income Is Highest

Industry	Average Annual Earnings	Number Employed
Educational Services	$62,000	21,020

Metropolitan Areas Where Income Is Highest

Metropolitan Area	Average Annual Earnings	Number Employed
Los Angeles–Long Beach–Santa Ana, CA	$83,210	520
Riverside–San Bernardino–Ontario, CA	$80,300	140
San Diego–Carlsbad–San Marcos, CA	$79,900	270
Houston–Sugar Land–Baytown, TX	$78,690	290
Baltimore-Towson, MD	$78,230	190

Teach courses in human history and historiography. Prepare and deliver lectures to undergraduate and/or graduate students on topics such as ancient history, postwar civilizations, and the history of third-world countries. Evaluate and grade students' classwork, assignments, and papers. Prepare course materials such as syllabi, homework assignments, and handouts. Compile, administer, and grade examinations or assign this work to others. Initiate, facilitate, and moderate classroom discussions. Keep abreast of developments in their field by reading current literature, talking with colleagues, and participating in professional conferences. Plan, evaluate, and revise curricula, course content, and course materials and methods of instruction. Maintain student attendance records, grades, and other required records. Maintain regularly scheduled office hours to advise and assist students. Conduct research in a particular field of knowledge and publish findings in professional journals, books, or electronic media. Select and obtain materials and supplies such as textbooks. Advise students on academic and vocational curricula and on career issues. Collaborate with colleagues to address teaching and research issues. Serve on academic or administrative committees that deal with institutional policies, departmental matters, and academic issues. Participate in campus and community events. Act as advisers to student organizations. Participate in student recruitment, registration, and placement activities. Compile bibliographies of specialized materials for outside reading assignments. Supervise undergraduate and graduate teaching, internship, and research work. Perform administrative duties such as serving as department head. Write grant proposals to procure external research funding. Provide professional consulting services to government, educational institutions, and industry.

Other Considerations for Income: Earnings for college faculty vary according to rank and type of institution, geographic area, and field. According to a 2006–2007 survey by the American Association of University Professors, salaries for full-time faculty averaged $73,207. By rank, the average was $98,974 for professors, $69,911 for associate professors, $58,662 for assistant professors, $42,609 for instructors, and $48,289 for lecturers. Faculty in 4-year institutions earn higher salaries, on average, than do those in 2-year schools. Many faculty members have significant earnings in addition to their base salary from consulting, teaching additional courses, research, writing for publication, or other employment. In addition, many college and university faculty enjoy unique benefits, including access to campus facilities, tuition waivers for dependents, housing and travel allowances, and paid leave for sabbaticals. Part-time faculty and instructors usually have fewer benefits than full-time faculty.

Personality Type: Social-Investigative-Artistic. **Career Clusters:** 05 Education and Training; 15 Science, Technology, Engineering, and Mathematics. **Career Pathways:** 05.3 Teaching/Training; 15.3 Science and Mathematics. **Skills:** Writing; Instructing; Learning Strategies; Reading Comprehension; Speaking; Critical Thinking; Persuasion; Active Learning.

Education and Training Programs: American History (United States); Asian History; Canadian History; European History; History and Philosophy of Science and Technology; History, General; History, Other; Humani-

ties/Humanistic Studies; Public/Applied History. **Related Knowledge/Courses:** History and Archeology; Philosophy and Theology; Geography; Sociology and Anthropology; Education and Training; English Language.

Histotechnologists and Histologic Technicians

- ❋ Annual Earnings: $53,500
- ❋ Beginning Wage: $36,180
- ❋ Earnings Growth Potential: Low (32.4%)
- ❋ Growth: 12.4%
- ❋ Annual Job Openings: 11,457
- ❋ Self-Employed: 0.7%
- ❋ Part-Time: 14.3%
- ❋ Job Security: No data available
- ❋ Education/Training Required: Associate degree

The Department of Labor reports this information for the occupation Medical and Clinical Laboratory Technologists. The job openings listed here are shared with other specializations within that occupation, including Cytogenetic Technologists; and Cytotechnologists.

Industries in Which Income Is Highest

Industry	Average Annual Earnings	Number Employed
Federal, State, and Local Government	$58,080	7,470
Hospitals	$54,250	102,390
Professional, Scientific, and Technical Services	$51,920	2,950
Ambulatory Health Care Services	$51,670	43,900
Educational Services	$48,080	6,900

Metropolitan Areas Where Income Is Highest

Metropolitan Area	Average Annual Earnings	Number Employed
Salinas, CA	$90,210	80
San Jose–Sunnyvale–Santa Clara, CA	$82,200	920
Santa Barbara–Santa Maria, CA	$78,910	120
Chico, CA	$75,570	90
Santa Rosa–Petaluma, CA	$75,140	200

Prepare histologic slides from tissue sections for microscopic examination and diagnosis by pathologists. May assist in research studies. No task data available.

Other Considerations for Income: Histotechnologists are better paid than most other specialists in clinical laboratory technology. Histologic Technicians are paid less well than most.

Personality Type: Realistic-Investigative-Conventional. **Career Cluster:** 08 Health Science. **Career Pathway:** 08.2 Diagnostics Services. **Skills:** No data available.

Education and Training Programs: Clinical Laboratory Science/Medical Technology/Technologist; Histologic Technology/Histotechnologist. **Related Knowledge/Courses:** No data available.

Home Economics Teachers, Postsecondary

❋ Annual Earnings: $64,210
❋ Beginning Wage: $33,930
❋ Earnings Growth Potential: High (47.2%)
❋ Growth: 22.9%
❋ Annual Job Openings: 820
❋ Self-Employed: 0.4%
❋ Part-Time: 27.8%
❋ Job Security: Most secure
❋ Education/Training Required: Doctoral degree

Industries in Which Income Is Highest

Industry	Average Annual Earnings	Number Employed
Educational Services	$64,230	4,820

Metropolitan Areas Where Income Is Highest

Metropolitan Area	Average Annual Earnings	Number Employed
Sacramento–Arden-Arcade–Roseville, CA	$106,530	60
Los Angeles–Long Beach–Santa Ana, CA	$99,390	170
Riverside–San Bernardino–Ontario, CA	$94,880	60
San Francisco–Oakland–Fremont, CA	$86,780	140
San Diego–Carlsbad–San Marcos, CA	$84,980	170

Teach courses in child care, family relations, finance, nutrition, and related subjects as pertaining to home management. Evaluate and grade students' classwork, laboratory work, projects, assignments, and papers. Initiate, facilitate, and moderate classroom discussions. Prepare and deliver lectures to undergraduate or graduate students on topics such as food science, nutrition, and child care. Prepare course materials such as syllabi, homework assignments, and handouts. Keep abreast of developments in their field by reading current literature, talking with colleagues, and participating in professional conferences. Maintain student attendance records, grades, and other required records. Plan, evaluate, and revise curricula, course content, and course materials and methods of instruction. Compile, administer, and grade examinations or assign this work to others. Advise students on academic and vocational curricula and on career issues. Maintain regularly scheduled office hours to advise and assist students. Supervise undergraduate or graduate teaching, internship, and research work. Select and obtain materials and supplies such as textbooks. Conduct research in a particular field of knowledge and publish findings in professional journals, books, and/or electronic media. Collaborate with colleagues to address teaching and research issues. Act as advisers to student organizations. Participate in student recruitment, registration, and placement activities. Serve on academic or administrative committees that deal with institutional policies, departmental matters, and academic issues. Participate in campus and community events. Compile bibliographies of specialized materials for outside reading assignments. Perform administrative duties such as serving as department head. Write grant proposals to procure external research funding. Provide professional consulting services to government and industry.

Other Considerations for Income: Earnings for college faculty vary according to rank and type of institution, geographic area, and field. According to a 2006–2007 survey by the American Association of University Professors, salaries for full-time faculty averaged $73,207. By rank, the average was $98,974 for professors, $69,911 for associate professors, $58,662 for assistant professors, $42,609 for instructors, and $48,289 for lecturers. Faculty in 4-year institutions earn higher salaries, on average, than do those in 2-year schools. Many faculty members have significant earnings in addition to their base salary from consulting, teaching additional courses, research, writing for publication, or other employment. In addition, many college and university faculty enjoy unique benefits, including access to campus facilities, tuition waivers for dependents, housing and travel allowances, and paid leave for sabbaticals. Part-time faculty and instructors usually have fewer benefits than full-time faculty.

Personality Type: Social-Investigative-Artistic. **Career Clusters:** 05 Education and Training; 08 Health Science; 10 Human Service. **Career Pathways:** 05.3 Teaching/Training; 08.4 Support Services; 10.1 Early Childhood Development and Services; 10.3 Family and Community Services; 10.5 Consumer Services Career. **Skills:** Writing; Instructing; Learning Strategies; Service Orientation; Active Learning; Operations Analysis; Social Perceptiveness; Speaking.

Education and Training Programs: Business Family and Consumer Sciences/Human Sciences; Child Care and Support Services Management; Family and Consumer Sciences/Human Sciences, General; Foodservice Systems Administration/Management; Human Development and Family Studies, General. **Related Knowledge/Courses:** Sociology and Anthropology; Philosophy and Theology; Education and Training; Therapy and Counseling; Psychology; English Language.

Hospitalists

- ❀ Annual Earnings: $166,400+
- ❀ Beginning Wage: $49,710
- ❀ Earnings Growth Potential: Cannot be calculated
- ❀ Growth: 14.2%
- ❀ Annual Job Openings: 38,027
- ❀ Self-Employed: 14.7%
- ❀ Part-Time: 8.1%
- ❀ Job Security: No data available
- ❀ Education/Training Required: First professional degree

The Department of Labor reports this information for the occupation Physicians and Surgeons. The job openings listed

here are shared with other specializations within that occupation, including Allergists and Immunologists; Anesthesiologists; Dermatologists; Family and General Practitioners; Internists, General; Neurologists; Nuclear Medicine Physicians; Obstetricians and Gynecologists; Ophthalmologists; Pathologists; Pediatricians, General; Physical Medicine and Rehabilitation Physicians; Preventive Medicine Physicians; Psychiatrists; Radiologists; Sports Medicine Physicians; Surgeons; and Urologists.

Industries in Which Income Is Highest

Industry Earnings	Average Annual Earnings	Number Employed
Ambulatory Health Care Services	$166,400+	147,400
Administrative and Support Services	$166,400+	1,310
Federal, State, and Local Government	$162,300	28,180
Professional, Scientific, and Technical Services	$107,470	1,210
Hospitals	$72,130	72,490

Metropolitan Areas Where Income Is Highest

Metropolitan Area	Average Annual Earnings	Number Employed
Los Angeles–Long Beach–Santa Ana, CA	$166,400+	8,810
Boston-Cambridge-Quincy, MA-NH	$166,400+	6,380
Dallas–Fort Worth–Arlington, TX	$166,400+	4,950
Tampa–St. Petersburg–Clearwater, FL	$166,400+	3,810
Portland-Vancouver-Beaverton, OR-WA	$166,400+	3,180

Provide inpatient care predominantly in settings such as medical wards, acute care units, intensive care units, rehabilitation centers, or emergency rooms. Manage and coordinate patient care throughout treatment. No task data available.

Other Considerations for Income: Earnings of physicians and surgeons are among the highest of any occupation. Separate earnings figures for Hospitalists are not available.

Personality Type: Social-Investigative. **Career Cluster:** 08 Health Science. **Career Pathway:** 08.1 Therapeutic Services. **Skills:** No data available.

Education and Training Program: Medicine (MD). **Related Knowledge/Courses:** No data available.

Human Factors Engineers and Ergonomists

- ❋ Annual Earnings: $73,820
- ❋ Beginning Wage: $47,720
- ❋ Earnings Growth Potential: Medium (35.4%)
- ❋ Growth: 20.3%
- ❋ Annual Job Openings: 11,272
- ❋ Self-Employed: 0.9%
- ❋ Part-Time: 2.0%
- ❋ Job Security: No data available
- ❋ Education/Training Required: Bachelor's degree

The Department of Labor reports this information for the occupation Industrial Engineers. The job openings listed here are shared with other specializations within that occupation.

Industries in Which Income Is Highest

Industry	Average Annual Earnings	Number Employed
Oil and Gas Extraction	$89,120	1,160
Petroleum and Coal Products Manufacturing	$84,620	1,160
Management of Companies and Enterprises	$81,830	10,240
Federal, State, and Local Government	$81,270	1,590
Professional, Scientific, and Technical Services	$79,800	29,430

Metropolitan Areas Where Income Is Highest

Metropolitan Area	Average Annual Earnings	Number Employed
San Jose–Sunnyvale–Santa Clara, CA	$96,770	3,530
Anchorage, AK	$96,620	80
Victoria, TX	$95,470	140
Lafayette, LA	$94,560	80
Bakersfield, CA	$92,410	230

Design objects, facilities, and environments to optimize human well-being and overall system performance, applying theory, principles, and data regarding the relationship between humans and respective technology. Investigate and analyze characteristics of human behavior and performance as it relates to the use of technology. No task data available.

Other Considerations for Income: As a group, engineers earn some of the highest average starting salaries among those holding bachelor's degrees. Separate earnings figures for Human Factors Engineers and Ergonomists are not available, but they are probably similar to those for Industrial Engineers, who are paid in the low-to-middle range among the various kinds of engineers. According to a 2007 survey by the National Association of Colleges and Employers, average starting salaries for Industrial and Manufacturing Engineers were $55,067 with a bachelor's, $64,759 with a master's, and $77,364 with a Ph.D.

Personality Type: No data available. **Career Cluster:** 15 Science, Technology, Engineering, and Mathematics. **Career Pathway:** 15.1 Engineering and Technology. **Skills:** No data available.

Education and Training Program: Industrial Engineering. **Related Knowledge/Courses:** No data available.

Hydroelectric Production Managers

- ❋ Annual Earnings: $83,290
- ❋ Beginning Wage: $50,330
- ❋ Earnings Growth Potential: Medium (39.6%)
- ❋ Growth: –5.9%
- ❋ Annual Job Openings: 14,889
- ❋ Self-Employed: 2.0%
- ❋ Part-Time: 1.6%
- ❋ Job Security: No data available
- ❋ Education/Training Required: Work experience in a related occupation

The Department of Labor reports this information for the occupation Industrial Production Managers. The job openings listed here are shared with other specializations within that occupation, including Biofuels Production Managers; Biomass Production Managers; Geothermal Production Managers; Methane/Landfill Gas Collection System Operators; and Quality Control Systems Managers.

H

Industries in Which Income Is Highest

Industry	Average Annual Earnings	Number Employed
Oil and Gas Extraction	$104,890	1,590
Professional, Scientific, and Technical Services	$103,550	3,450
Petroleum and Coal Products Manufacturing	$103,100	1,220
Utilities	$101,110	1,740
Management of Companies and Enterprises	$99,660	6,180

Metropolitan Areas Where Income Is Highest

Metropolitan Area	Average Annual Earnings	Number Employed
Austin–Round Rock, TX	$112,900	690
Cedar Rapids, IA	$110,680	530
Leominster-Fitchburg-Gardner, MA	$107,340	70
Saginaw–Saginaw Township North, MI	$106,880	140
Ann Arbor, MI	$104,600	320

Manage operations at hydroelectric power-generation facilities. Maintain and monitor hydroelectric plant equipment for efficient and safe plant operations. No task data available.

Other Considerations for Income: No additional information.

Personality Type: No data available. **Career Cluster:** 04 Business, Management, and Administration. **Career Pathway:** 04.1 Management. **Skills:** No data available.

Education and Training Programs: Business Administration and Management, General; Business/Commerce, General; Operations Management and Supervision. **Related Knowledge/Courses:** No data available.

Hydrologists

* Annual Earnings: $71,450
* Beginning Wage: $44,410
* Earnings Growth Potential: Medium (37.8%)
* Growth: 24.3%
* Annual Job Openings: 687
* Self-Employed: 2.4%
* Part-Time: 5.3%
* Job Security: More secure than most
* Education/Training Required: Master's degree

Industries in Which Income Is Highest

Industry	Average Annual Earnings	Number Employed
Professional, Scientific, and Technical Services	$72,120	3,740
Federal, State, and Local Government	$70,710	3,710
Educational Services	$58,700	30

Metropolitan Areas Where Income Is Highest

Metropolitan Area	Average Annual Earnings	Number Employed
Los Angeles–Long Beach–Santa Ana, CA	$90,640	130
Boston-Cambridge-Quincy, MA-NH	$87,220	100
Sacramento–Arden-Arcade–Roseville, CA	$85,480	220
Trenton-Ewing, NJ	$84,230	60
Portland-Vancouver-Beaverton, OR-WA	$83,770	140

Research the distribution, circulation, and physical properties of underground and surface waters; study the form and intensity of precipitation, its rate of infiltration into the soil, its movement through the earth, and its return to the ocean and atmosphere. Study and document quantities, distribution, disposition, and development of underground and surface waters. Draft final reports describing research results, including illustrations, appendices, maps, and other attachments. Coordinate and supervise the work of professional and technical staff, including research assistants, technologists, and technicians. Prepare hydrogeologic evaluations of known or suspected hazardous waste sites and land treatment and feedlot facilities. Design and conduct scientific hydrogeological investigations to ensure that accurate and appropriate information is available for use in water resource management decisions. Study public water supply issues, including flood and drought risks, water quality, wastewater, and impacts on wetland habitats. Collect and analyze water samples as part of field investigations and/or to validate data from automatic monitors. Apply research findings to help minimize the environmental impacts of pollution, water-borne diseases, erosion, and sedimentation. Measure and graph phenomena such as lake levels, stream flows, and changes in water volumes. Investigate complaints or conflicts related to the alteration of public waters, gathering information, recommending alternatives, informing participants of progress, and preparing draft orders. Develop or modify methods of conducting hydrologic studies. Answer questions and provide technical assistance and information to contractors and/or the public regarding issues such as well drilling, code requirements, hydrology, and geology. Install, maintain, and calibrate instruments such as those that monitor water levels, rainfall, and sediments. Evaluate data and provide recommendations regarding the feasibility of municipal projects such as hydroelectric power plants, irrigation systems, flood warning systems, and waste treatment facilities. Conduct short-term and long-term climate assessments and study storm occurrences.

Other Considerations for Income: According to the National Association of Colleges and Employers, beginning salary offers in July 2007 for graduates with bachelor's degrees in an environmental science averaged $38,336 a year.

Personality Type: Investigative-Realistic. **Career Cluster:** 15 Science, Technology, Engineering, and Mathematics. **Career Pathway:** 15.3 Science and Mathematics. **Skills:** Science; Programming; Management of Financial Resources; Mathematics; Management of Personnel Resources; Complex Problem Solving; Systems Analysis; Management of Material Resources.

Education and Training Programs: Geology/Earth Science, General; Hydrology and Water Resources Science; Oceanography, Chemical and Physical. **Related Knowledge/Courses:** Geography; Physics; Engineering and Technology; Biology; Chemistry; Mathematics.

Immigration and Customs Inspectors

* Annual Earnings: $60,910
* Beginning Wage: $36,500
* Earnings Growth Potential: High (40.1%)
* Growth: 17.3%
* Annual Job Openings: 14,746
* Self-Employed: 0.3%
* Part-Time: 2.2%
* Job Security: Most secure
* Education/Training Required: Work experience in a related occupation

The Department of Labor reports this information for the occupation Detectives and Criminal Investigators. The job openings listed here are shared with other specializations within that occupation, including Criminal Investigators and Special Agents; Intelligence Analysts; Police Detectives; and Police Identification and Records Officers.

Industries in Which Income Is Highest

Industry	Average Annual Earnings	Number Employed
Federal, State, and Local Government	$60,780	103,680

Metropolitan Areas Where Income Is Highest

Metropolitan Area	Average Annual Earnings	Number Employed
San Jose–Sunnyvale–Santa Clara, CA	$92,430	310
Washington-Arlington-Alexandria, DC-VA-MD-WV	$88,440	4,590
Springfield, MA-CT	$82,690	60
Brunswick, GA	$80,960	350
New Haven, CT	$79,550	200

Investigate and inspect persons, common carriers, goods, and merchandise arriving in or departing from the United States or moving between states to detect violations of immigration and customs laws and regulations. Examine immigration applications, visas, and passports and interview persons to determine eligibility for admission, residence, and travel in U.S. Detain persons found to be in violation of customs or immigration laws and arrange for legal action such as deportation. Locate and seize contraband or undeclared merchandise and vehicles, aircraft, or boats that contain such merchandise. Interpret and explain laws and regulations to travelers, prospective immigrants, shippers, and manufacturers. Inspect cargo, baggage, and personal articles entering or leaving U.S. for compliance with revenue laws and U.S. Customs Service regulations. Record and report job-related activities, findings, transactions, violations, discrepancies, and decisions. Institute civil and criminal prosecutions and cooperate with other law enforcement agencies in the investigation and prosecution of those in violation of immigration or customs laws. Testify regarding decisions at immigration appeals or in federal court. Determine duty and taxes to be paid on goods. Collect samples of merchandise for examination, appraisal, or testing. Investigate applications for duty refunds and petition for remission or mitigation of penalties when warranted.

Other Considerations for Income: No additional information.

Personality Type: Conventional-Enterprising-Realistic. **Career Cluster:** 12 Law, Public Safety, Corrections, and Security. **Career Pathway:** 12.4 Law Enforcement Services. **Skills:** Persuasion; Operations Analysis; Equipment Selection; Negotiation; Speaking; Social Perceptiveness; Active Listening; Judgment and Decision Making.

Education and Training Programs: Criminal Justice/ Police Science; Criminalistics and Criminal Science. **Related Knowledge/Courses:** Public Safety and Security; Law and Government; Foreign Language; Geography; Customer and Personal Service; Philosophy and Theology.

Industrial Ecologists

❋ Annual Earnings: $59,750
❋ Beginning Wage: $36,310
❋ Earnings Growth Potential: Medium (39.2%)
❋ Growth: 25.1%
❋ Annual Job Openings: 6,961
❋ Self-Employed: 2.2%
❋ Part-Time: 5.3%
❋ Job Security: No data available
❋ Education/Training Required: Master's degree

The Department of Labor reports this information for the occupation Environmental Scientists and Specialists, Including Health. The job openings listed here are shared with other specializations within that occupation, including Climate Change Analysts; and Environmental Restoration Planners.

Industries in Which Income Is Highest

Industry	Average Annual Earnings	Number Employed
Utilities	$83,440	1,040
Professional, Scientific, and Technical Services	$61,330	35,270
Federal, State, and Local Government	$57,970	35,460
Educational Services	$57,170	2,840

Metropolitan Areas Where Income Is Highest

Metropolitan Area	Average Annual Earnings	Number Employed
Washington-Arlington-Alexandria, DC-VA-MD-WV	$89,540	3,750
San Jose–Sunnyvale–Santa Clara, CA	$82,970	390
Boston-Cambridge-Quincy, MA-NH	$82,930	2,110
Ann Arbor, MI	$80,300	210
Santa Rosa–Petaluma, CA	$79,330	380

Study or investigate industrial production and natural ecosystems to achieve high production, sustainable resources, and environmental safety or protection. May apply principles and activities of natural ecosystems to develop models for industrial systems. No task data available.

Other Considerations for Income: According to the National Association of Colleges and Employers, beginning salary offers in July 2007 for graduates with bachelor's degrees in an environmental science averaged $38,336 a year.

Personality Type: No data available. **Career Cluster:** 01 Agriculture, Food and Natural Resource. **Career Pathway:** 01.5 Natural Resources Systems. **Skills:** No data available.

Education and Training Programs: Environmental Science; Environmental Studies. **Related Knowledge/ Courses:** No data available.

Industrial Engineers

❋ Annual Earnings: $73,820
❋ Beginning Wage: $47,720
❋ Earnings Growth Potential: Medium (35.4%)
❋ Growth: 20.3%
❋ Annual Job Openings: 11,272
❋ Self-Employed: 0.9%
❋ Part-Time: 2.0%
❋ Job Security: More secure than most
❋ Education/Training Required: Bachelor's degree

Industries in Which Income Is Highest

Industry	Average Annual Earnings	Number Employed
Oil and Gas Extraction	$89,120	1,160
Petroleum and Coal Products Manufacturing	$84,620	1,160
Management of Companies and Enterprises	$81,830	10,240
Federal, State, and Local Government	$81,270	1,590
Professional, Scientific, and Technical Services	$79,800	29,430

Metropolitan Areas Where Income Is Highest

Metropolitan Area	Average Annual Earnings	Number Employed
San Jose–Sunnyvale–Santa Clara, CA	$96,770	3,530
Anchorage, AK	$96,620	80
Victoria, TX	$95,470	140
Lafayette, LA	$94,560	80
Bakersfield, CA	$92,410	230

Design, develop, test, and evaluate integrated systems for managing industrial production processes, including human work factors, quality control, inventory control, logistics and material flow, cost analysis, and production coordination. Analyze statistical data and product specifications to determine standards and establish quality and reliability objectives of finished product. Develop manufacturing methods, labor utilization standards, and cost analysis systems to promote efficient staff and facility utilization. Recommend methods for improving utilization of personnel, material, and utilities. Plan and establish sequence of operations to fabricate and assemble parts or products and to promote efficient utilization. Apply statistical methods and perform mathematical calculations to determine manufacturing processes, staff requirements, and production standards. Coordinate quality control objectives and activities to resolve production problems, maximize product reliability, and minimize cost. Confer with vendors, staff, and management personnel regarding purchases, procedures, product specifications, manufacturing capabilities, and project status. Draft and design layout of equipment, materials, and workspace to illustrate maximum efficiency, using drafting tools and computer. Review production schedules, engineering specifications, orders, and related information to obtain knowledge of manufacturing methods, procedures, and activities. Communicate with management and user personnel to develop production and design standards. Estimate production cost and effect of product design changes for management review, action, and control. Formulate sampling procedures and designs and develop forms and instructions for recording, evaluating, and reporting quality and reliability data. Record or oversee recording of information to ensure currency of engineering drawings and documentation of production problems. Study operations sequence, material flow, functional statements, organization charts, and project information to determine worker functions and responsibilities. Direct workers engaged in product measurement, inspection, and testing activities to ensure quality control and reliability.

Other Considerations for Income: As a group, engineers earn some of the highest average starting salaries among those holding bachelor's degrees. Industrial Engineers are paid in the low-to-middle range among the various kinds of engineers. According to a 2007 survey by the National Association of Colleges and Employers, average starting salaries for Industrial and Manufacturing Engineers were $55,067 with a bachelor's, $64,759 with a master's, and $77,364 with a Ph.D.

Personality Type: Investigative-Conventional-Enterprising. **Career Cluster:** 15 Science, Technology, Engineering, and Mathematics. **Career Pathway:** 15.1 Engineering and Technology. **Skills:** Equipment Selection; Technology Design; Troubleshooting; Installation; Systems Analysis; Mathematics; Judgment and Decision Making; Negotiation.

Education and Training Program: Industrial Engineering. **Related Knowledge/Courses:** Engineering and Technology; Design; Production and Processing; Mechanical; Physics; Mathematics.

Industrial Production Managers

* ❈ Annual Earnings: $83,290
* ❈ Beginning Wage: $50,330
* ❈ Earnings Growth Potential: Medium (39.6%)
* ❈ Growth: –5.9%
* ❈ Annual Job Openings: 14,889
* ❈ Self-Employed: 2.0%
* ❈ Part-Time: 1.6%
* ❈ Job Security: More secure than most
* ❈ Education/Training Required: Work experience in a related occupation

Industries in Which Income Is Highest

Industry	Average Annual Earnings	Number Employed
Oil and Gas Extraction	$104,890	1,590
Professional, Scientific, and Technical Services	$103,550	3,450
Petroleum and Coal Products Manufacturing	$103,100	1,220
Utilities	$101,110	1,740
Management of Companies and Enterprises	$99,660	6,180

Metropolitan Areas Where Income Is Highest

Metropolitan Area	Average Annual Earnings	Number Employed
Austin–Round Rock, TX	$112,900	690
Cedar Rapids, IA	$110,680	530
Leominster-Fitchburg-Gardner, MA	$107,340	70
Saginaw–Saginaw Township North, MI	$106,880	140
Ann Arbor, MI	$104,600	320

Plan, direct, or coordinate the work activities and resources necessary for manufacturing products in accordance with specifications for cost, quality, and quantity. Direct and coordinate production, processing, distribution, and marketing activities of industrial organization. Review processing schedules and production orders to make decisions concerning inventory requirements, staffing requirements, work procedures, and duty assignments, considering budgetary limitations and time constraints. Review operations and confer with technical or administrative staff to resolve production or processing problems. Develop and implement production tracking and quality control systems, analyzing reports on production, quality control, maintenance, and other aspects of operations to detect problems. Hire, train, evaluate, and discharge staff, and resolve personnel grievances. Set and monitor product standards, examining samples of raw products or directing testing during processing, to ensure finished products are of prescribed quality. Prepare and maintain production reports and personnel records. Coordinate and recommend procedures for maintenance or modification of facilities and equipment, including the replacement of machines. Initiate and coordinate inventory and cost control programs. Institute employee suggestion or involvement programs. Maintain current knowledge of the quality control field, relying on current literature pertaining to materials use, technological advances, and statistical studies. Review plans and confer with research and support staff to develop new products and processes. Develop budgets and approve expenditures for supplies, materials, and human resources, ensuring that materials, labor, and equipment are used efficiently to meet production targets. Negotiate prices of materials with suppliers.

Other Considerations for Income: No additional information.

Personality Type: Enterprising-Conventional. **Career Cluster:** 04 Business, Management, and Administration. **Career Pathway:** 04.1 Management. **Skills:** Management of Personnel Resources; Management of Financial Resources; Systems Analysis; Operation Monitoring; Management of Material Resources; Systems Evaluation; Monitoring; Judgment and Decision Making.

Education and Training Programs: Business Administration and Management, General; Business/Commerce, General; Operations Management and Supervision. **Related Knowledge/Courses:** Production and Processing; Mechanical; Administration and Management; Design; Personnel and Human Resources; Engineering and Technology.

Industrial Safety and Health Engineers

❋ Annual Earnings: $72,490
❋ Beginning Wage: $43,540
❋ Earnings Growth Potential: Medium (39.9%)
❋ Growth: 9.6%
❋ Annual Job Openings: 1,105
❋ Self-Employed: 1.1%
❋ Part-Time: 2.0%
❋ Job Security: More secure than most
❋ Education/Training Required: Bachelor's degree

The Department of Labor reports this information for the occupation Health and Safety Engineers, Except Mining Safety Engineers and Inspectors. The job openings listed here are shared with other specializations within that occupation, including Fire-Prevention and Protection Engineers; and Product Safety Engineers.

Industries in Which Income Is Highest

Industry	Average Annual Earnings	Number Employed
Federal, State, and Local Government	$79,770	3,870
Professional, Scientific, and Technical Services	$77,660	4,000
Chemical Manufacturing	$75,550	2,360
Waste Management and Remediation Services	$72,380	1,210
Heavy and Civil Engineering Construction	$65,140	1,860

Metropolitan Areas Where Income Is Highest

Metropolitan Area	Average Annual Earnings	Number Employed
San Jose–Sunnyvale–Santa Clara, CA	$94,140	160
Kennewick-Richland-Pasco, WA	$90,170	120
Chicago-Naperville-Joliet, IL-IN-WI	$88,820	1,140
Knoxville, TN	$88,170	90
Huntsville, AL	$86,540	100

Plan, implement, and coordinate safety programs requiring application of engineering principles and technology to prevent or correct unsafe environmental working conditions. Investigate industrial accidents, injuries, or occupational diseases to determine causes and preventive measures. Report or review findings from accident investigations, facilities inspections, or environmental testing. Maintain and apply knowledge of current policies, regulations, and industrial processes. Inspect facilities, machinery, and safety equipment to identify and correct potential hazards and to ensure safety regulation compliance. Conduct or coordinate worker training in areas such as safety laws and regulations, hazardous condition monitoring, and use of safety equipment. Review employee safety programs to determine their adequacy. Interview employers and employees to obtain information about work environments and workplace incidents. Review plans and specifications for construction of new machinery or equipment to determine whether all safety requirements have been met. Compile, analyze, and interpret statistical data related to occupational illnesses and accidents. Interpret safety regulations for others interested in industrial safety, such as safety engineers, labor representatives, and safety inspectors. Recommend process and product safety features that will reduce employees' exposure to chemical, physical, and biological work hazards. Conduct or direct testing of air quality, noise, temperature, or radiation levels to verify compliance with health and safety regulations. Provide technical advice and guidance to organizations on how to handle health-related problems and make needed changes. Confer with medical professionals to assess health risks and to develop ways to manage health issues and concerns. Install safety devices on machinery or direct device installation. Maintain liaisons with outside organizations such as fire departments, mutual aid societies, and rescue teams so that emergency responses can be facilitated. Evaluate adequacy of actions taken to correct health inspection violations. Write and revise safety regulations and codes.

Other Considerations for Income: As a group, engineers earn some of the highest average starting salaries among those holding bachelor's degrees. Separate earnings figures for Industrial Safety and Health Engineers are not available, but they are probably similar to those for Health and Safety Engineers, who are among the lowest-paid of the various kinds of engineers.

Personality Type: Investigative-Conventional-Realistic. **Career Cluster:** 15 Science, Technology, Engineering, and Mathematics. **Career Pathway:** 15.1 Engineering and Technology. **Skills:** Management of Financial Resources; Science; Systems Analysis; Persuasion; Operations

Analysis; Systems Evaluation; Management of Material Resources; Management of Personnel Resources.

Education and Training Program: Environmental/Environmental Health Engineering. **Related Knowledge/Courses:** Building and Construction; Physics; Chemistry; Biology; Engineering and Technology; Education and Training.

Industrial-Organizational Psychologists

❈ Annual Earnings: $77,010
❈ Beginning Wage: $38,690
❈ Earnings Growth Potential: High (49.8%)
❈ Growth: 21.3%
❈ Annual Job Openings: 118
❈ Self-Employed: 39.3%
❈ Part-Time: 24.0%
❈ Job Security: Most secure
❈ Education/Training Required: Master's degree

Industries in Which Income Is Highest

Industry	Average Annual Earnings	Number Employed
Computer and Electronic Product Manufacturing	$88,380	50
Management of Companies and Enterprises	$80,700	50
Professional, Scientific, and Technical Services	$77,700	840
Federal, State, and Local Government	$54,270	80

Metropolitan Areas Where Income Is Highest

Metropolitan Area	Average Annual Earnings	Number Employed

Insufficient data available

Apply principles of psychology to personnel, administration, management, sales, and marketing problems. Activities may include policy planning; employee screening, training, and development; and organizational development and analysis. May work with management to reorganize the work setting to improve worker productivity. Develop and implement employee selection and placement programs. Analyze job requirements and content to establish criteria for classification, selection, training, and other related personnel functions. Develop interview techniques, rating scales, and psychological tests used to assess skills, abilities, and interests for the purpose of employee selection, placement, and promotion. Advise management concerning personnel, managerial, and marketing policies and practices and their potential effects on organizational effectiveness and efficiency. Analyze data, using statistical methods and applications, to evaluate the outcomes and effectiveness of workplace programs. Assess employee performance. Observe and interview workers to obtain information about the physical, mental, and educational requirements of jobs as well as information about aspects such as job satisfaction. Write reports on research findings and implications to contribute to general knowledge and to suggest potential changes in organizational functioning. Facilitate organizational development and change. Identify training and development needs. Formulate and implement training programs, applying principles of learning and individual differences. Study organizational effectiveness, productivity, and efficiency, including the nature of workplace supervision and leadership. Conduct research studies of physical work environments, organizational structures, communication systems, group interactions, morale, and motivation to assess organizational functioning. Counsel workers about job and career-related issues. Study consumers' reactions to new products and package designs, and to advertising efforts, using surveys and tests. Participate in mediation and dispute resolution.

Other Considerations for Income: Earnings of Industrial-Organizational Psychologists tend to be higher than those of Clinical, Counseling, and School Psychologists.

Personality Type: Investigative-Enterprising-Artistic. **Career Cluster:** 08 Health Science. **Career Pathway:** 08.1 Therapeutic Services. **Skills:** Science; Systems Evaluation; Judgment and Decision Making; Writing; Monitoring; Time Management; Coordination; Critical Thinking.

Education and Training Program: Psychology, General. **Related Knowledge/Courses:** Personnel and Human Resources; Psychology; Sociology and Anthropology; Education and Training; Therapy and Counseling; Mathematics.

Informatics Nurse Specialists

❋ Annual Earnings: $75,500
❋ Beginning Wage: $45,390
❋ Earnings Growth Potential: Medium (39.9%)
❋ Growth: 29.0%
❋ Annual Job Openings: 63,166
❋ Self-Employed: 5.8%
❋ Part-Time: 5.6%
❋ Job Security: No data available
❋ Education/Training Required: Bachelor's degree

The Department of Labor reports this information for the occupation Computer Systems Analysts. The job openings listed here are shared with other specializations within that occupation.

Industries in Which Income Is Highest

Industry	Average Annual Earnings	Number Employed
Securities, Commodity Contracts, and Other Financial Investments and Related Activities	$87,080	9,010
Computer and Electronic Product Manufacturing	$86,360	12,510
Merchant Wholesalers, Durable Goods	$86,350	23,300
Electrical Equipment, Appliance, and Component Manufacturing	$80,100	1,020
Other Information Services	$79,910	1,280

Metropolitan Areas Where Income Is Highest

Metropolitan Area	Average Annual Earnings	Number Employed
Manchester, NH	$96,100	530
Bridgeport-Stamford-Norwalk, CT	$92,910	1,940
Bloomington-Normal, IL	$90,560	950
Washington-Arlington-Alexandria, DC-VA-MD-WV	$89,870	33,600
Salinas, CA	$89,430	320

Apply knowledge of nursing and informatics to assist in the design, development, and ongoing modification of computerized health-care systems. May educate staff and assist in problem solving to promote the implementation of the health-care system. No task data available.

Other Considerations for Income: Educational background can affect earnings. Those with a bachelor of science in nursing and graduate training in computer science can expect the best earnings.

Personality Type: Social-Investigative. **Career Cluster:** 08 Health Science. **Career Pathways:** 08.1 Therapeutic Services; 08.3 Health Informatics. **Skills:** No data available.

Education and Training Programs: Computer and Information Sciences, General; Computer Systems Analysis/Analyst; Information Technology; Web/Multimedia Management and Webmaster. **Related Knowledge/Courses:** Medicine and Dentistry; Sociology and Anthropology; Education and Training; Engineering and Technology; Computers and Electronics; Clerical.

Information Technology Project Managers

❋ Annual Earnings: $75,150
❋ Beginning Wage: $40,660
❋ Earnings Growth Potential: High (45.9%)
❋ Growth: 15.1%
❋ Annual Job Openings: 14,374
❋ Self-Employed: 6.6%
❋ Part-Time: 5.6%
❋ Job Security: No data available
❋ Education/Training Required: Work experience plus degree

The Department of Labor reports this information for the occupation Computer Specialists, All Other. The job openings listed here are shared with other specializations within that occupation, including Business Intelligence Analysts; Computer Systems Engineers/Architects; Data Warehousing Specialists; Database Architects; Document Management Specialists; Electronic Commerce Specialists; Geographic Information Systems Technicians; Geospatial Information Scientists and Technologists; Network Designers; Software Quality Assurance Engineers and Testers; Video Game Designers; Web Administrators; and Web Developers.

Industries in Which Income Is Highest

Industry	Average Annual Earnings	Number Employed
Petroleum and Coal Products Manufacturing	$97,090	1,070
Transportation Equipment Manufacturing	$82,770	3,010
Oil and Gas Extraction	$81,350	1,710
Federal, State, and Local Government	$80,670	71,650
Management of Companies and Enterprises	$78,200	14,820

Metropolitan Areas Where Income Is Highest

Metropolitan Area	Average Annual Earnings	Number Employed
Washington-Arlington-Alexandria, DC-VA-MD-WV	$97,170	19,470
Atlantic City, NJ	$96,600	510
Pascagoula, MS	$95,430	60
San Jose–Sunnyvale–Santa Clara, CA	$92,710	3,580
Baltimore-Towson, MD	$89,730	5,650

Plan, initiate, and manage information technology (IT) projects. Lead and guide the work of technical staff. Serve as liaison between business and technical aspects of projects. Plan project stages and assess business implications for each stage. Monitor progress to assure deadlines, standards, and cost targets are met. No task data available.

Other Considerations for Income: Very experienced managers may work on a project-by-project basis and be able to negotiate compensation for each project.

Personality Type: No data available. **Career Cluster:** 11 Information Technology. **Career Pathway:** 11.4 Programming and Software Development. **Skills:** No data available.

Education and Training Programs: Computer and Information Sciences and Support Services, Other; Computer and Information Sciences, General; Computer Engineering Technologies/Technicians, Other; Computer Engineering, General; Computer Science; Computer Software Engineering; Computer Systems Networking and Telecommunications; E-Commerce/Electronic Commerce; Information Science/Studies; Information Technology; System, Networking, and LAN/WAN Management/Manager; Web Page, Digital/Multimedia and Informa-

tion Resources Design; others. **Related Knowledge/Courses:** No data available.

Instructional Coordinators

- ❀ Annual Earnings: $56,880
- ❀ Beginning Wage: $31,800
- ❀ Earnings Growth Potential: High (44.1%)
- ❀ Growth: 22.5%
- ❀ Annual Job Openings: 21,294
- ❀ Self-Employed: 3.1%
- ❀ Part-Time: 19.7%
- ❀ Job Security: Most secure
- ❀ Education/Training Required: Master's degree

Industries in Which Income Is Highest

Industry	Average Annual Earnings	Number Employed
Federal, State, and Local Government	$60,700	14,690
Educational Services	$58,930	88,890
Professional, Scientific, and Technical Services	$58,460	2,090
Religious, Grantmaking, Civic, Professional, and Similar Organizations	$45,160	2,080
Management of Companies and Enterprises	$42,920	1,070

Metropolitan Areas Where Income Is Highest

Metropolitan Area	Average Annual Earnings	Number Employed
Poughkeepsie-Newburgh-Middletown, NY	$89,480	230
Visalia-Porterville, CA	$88,360	130
Hartford–West Hartford–East Hartford, CT	$84,980	520
Trenton-Ewing, NJ	$77,040	650
San Diego–Carlsbad–San Marcos, CA	$76,320	2,100

Develop instructional material, coordinate educational content, and incorporate current technology in specialized fields that provide guidelines to educators and

instructors for developing curricula and conducting courses. Conduct or participate in workshops, committees, and conferences designed to promote the intellectual, social, and physical welfare of students. Plan and conduct teacher training programs and conferences dealing with new classroom procedures, instructional materials and equipment, and teaching aids. Advise teaching and administrative staff in curriculum development, use of materials and equipment, and implementation of state and federal programs and procedures. Recommend, order, or authorize purchase of instructional materials, supplies, equipment, and visual aids designed to meet student educational needs and district standards. Interpret and enforce provisions of state education codes and rules and regulations of state education boards. Confer with members of educational committees and advisory groups to obtain knowledge of subject areas and to relate curriculum materials to specific subjects, individual student needs, and occupational areas. Organize production and design of curriculum materials. Research, evaluate, and prepare recommendations on curricula, instructional methods, and materials for school systems. Observe work of teaching staff to evaluate performance and to recommend changes that could strengthen teaching skills. Develop instructional materials to be used by educators and instructors. Prepare grant proposals, budgets, and program policies and goals or assist in their preparation. Develop tests, questionnaires, and procedures that measure the effectiveness of curricula and use these tools to determine whether program objectives are being met. Update the content of educational programs to ensure that students are being trained with equipment and processes that are technologically current. Address public audiences to explain program objectives and to elicit support. Advise and teach students. Prepare or approve manuals, guidelines, and reports on state educational policies and practices for distribution to school districts.

Other Considerations for Income: No additional information.

Personality Type: Social-Investigative-Enterprising. **Career Cluster:** 05 Education and Training. **Career Pathways:** 05.1 Administration and Administrative Support; 05.3 Teaching/Training. **Skills:** Management of Financial Resources; Learning Strategies; Monitoring; Social Perceptiveness; Coordination; Time Management; Management of Personnel Resources; Persuasion.

Education and Training Programs: Curriculum and Instruction; Educational/Instructional Technology. **Related Knowledge/Courses:** Education and Training; Sociology and Anthropology; English Language; Personnel and Human Resources; Communications and Media; Psychology.

Instructional Designers and Technologists

- ❋ Annual Earnings: $56,880
- ❋ Beginning Wage: $31,800
- ❋ Earnings Growth Potential: High (44.1%)
- ❋ Growth: 22.5%
- ❋ Annual Job Openings: 21,294
- ❋ Self-Employed: 3.1%
- ❋ Part-Time: 19.7%
- ❋ Job Security: No data available
- ❋ Education/Training Required: Bachelor's degree

The Department of Labor reports this information for the occupation Instructional Coordinators. The job openings listed here are shared with other specializations within that occupation.

Industries in Which Income Is Highest

Industry	Average Annual Earnings	Number Employed
Federal, State, and Local Government	$60,700	14,690
Educational Services	$58,930	88,890
Professional, Scientific, and Technical Services	$58,460	2,090
Religious, Grantmaking, Civic, Professional, and Similar Organizations	$45,160	2,080
Management of Companies and Enterprises	$42,920	1,070

Metropolitan Areas Where Income Is Highest

Metropolitan Area	Average Annual Earnings	Number Employed
Poughkeepsie-Newburgh-Middletown, NY	$89,480	230
Visalia-Porterville, CA	$88,360	130
Hartford–West Hartford–East Hartford, CT	$84,980	520
Trenton-Ewing, NJ	$77,040	650
San Diego–Carlsbad–San Marcos, CA	$76,320	2,100

Develop instructional materials and products and assist in the technology-based redesign of courses. Assist faculty in learning about, becoming proficient in, and applying instructional technology. No task data available.

Other Considerations for Income: No additional information.

Personality Type: No data available. Career Cluster: 05 Education and Training. Career Pathways: 05.1 Administration and Administrative Support; 05.3 Teaching/Training. Skills: No data available.

Education and Training Programs: Curriculum and Instruction; Educational/Instructional Technology. Related Knowledge/Courses: No data available.

Insurance Adjusters, Examiners, and Investigators

- ❀ Annual Earnings: $55,760
- ❀ Beginning Wage: $34,140
- ❀ Earnings Growth Potential: Medium (38.8%)
- ❀ Growth: 8.9%
- ❀ Annual Job Openings: 22,024
- ❀ Self-Employed: 3.5%
- ❀ Part-Time: 4.0%
- ❀ Job Security: Most secure
- ❀ Education/Training Required: Long-term on-the-job training

The Department of Labor reports this information for the occupation Claims Adjusters, Examiners, and Investigators. The job openings listed here are shared with other specializations within that occupation, including Claims Examiners, Property and Casualty Insurance.

Industries in Which Income Is Highest

Industry	Average Annual Earnings	Number Employed
Federal, State, and Local Government	$62,000	50,470
Insurance Carriers and Related Activities	$54,330	204,500
Management of Companies and Enterprises	$53,840	5,980
Funds, Trusts, and Other Financial Vehicles	$53,780	4,810
Professional, Scientific, and Technical Services	$51,080	1,980

Metropolitan Areas Where Income Is Highest

Metropolitan Area	Average Annual Earnings	Number Employed
Poughkeepsie-Newburgh-Middletown, NY	$73,320	380
Asheville, NC	$72,940	120
Mobile, AL	$72,570	290
Salinas, CA	$71,650	130
Cape Coral–Fort Myers, FL	$71,030	130

Investigate, analyze, and determine the extent of insurance company's liability concerning personal, casualty, or property loss or damages and attempt to effect settlement with claimants. Correspond with or interview medical specialists, agents, witnesses, or claimants to compile information. Calculate benefit payments and approve payment of claims within a certain monetary limit. Interview or correspond with claimant and witnesses, consult police and hospital records, and inspect property damage to determine extent of liability. Investigate and assess damage to property. Examine claims forms and other records to determine insurance coverage. Analyze information gathered by investigation and report findings and recommendations. Negotiate claim settlements and recommend litigation when settlement cannot be negotiated. Collect evidence to support contested claims in court. Prepare report of findings of investigation. Interview or correspond with agents and claimants to correct errors or omissions and to investigate questionable claims. Refer questionable claims to investigator or claims adjuster for investigation or settlement. Examine titles to property to determine validity and act as company agent in transactions with property owners. Obtain credit information from banks and other credit services. Communicate with former associates to verify employment record and to obtain background information regarding persons or businesses applying for credit.

Other Considerations for Income: Earnings of claims adjusters, examiners, and investigators vary significantly. Many claims adjusters, especially those who work for insurance companies, receive additional bonuses or benefits as part of their job. Adjusters often are furnished a laptop computer, a cellular telephone, and a company car or are reimbursed for the use of their own vehicle for business purposes.

Personality Type: Conventional-Enterprising. **Career Cluster:** 06 Finance. **Career Pathway:** 06.4 Insurance Services. **Skills:** Negotiation; Persuasion; Judgment and Decision Making; Time Management; Management of Financial Resources; Reading Comprehension; Writing; Critical Thinking.

Education and Training Programs: Health/Medical Claims Examiner; Insurance. **Related Knowledge/Courses:** Customer and Personal Service; Clerical; English Language; Building and Construction; Law and Government; Mathematics.

Insurance Appraisers, Auto Damage

- ❋ Annual Earnings: $53,440
- ❋ Beginning Wage: $36,500
- ❋ Earnings Growth Potential: Low (31.7%)
- ❋ Growth: 12.5%
- ❋ Annual Job Openings: 1,030
- ❋ Self-Employed: 4.1%
- ❋ Part-Time: 4.0%
- ❋ Job Security: Most secure
- ❋ Education/Training Required: Postsecondary vocational training

Industries in Which Income Is Highest

Industry	Average Annual Earnings	Number Employed
Insurance Carriers and Related Activities	$53,520	10,170

Metropolitan Areas Where Income Is Highest

Metropolitan Area	Average Annual Earnings	Number Employed
Boston-Cambridge-Quincy, MA-NH	$59,960	480
Sacramento–Arden-Arcade–Roseville, CA	$59,960	180
Seattle-Tacoma-Bellevue, WA	$59,540	70
Philadelphia-Camden-Wilmington, PA-NJ-DE-MD	$58,900	170
Worcester, MA-CT	$57,470	110

Appraise automobile or other vehicle damage to determine cost of repair for insurance claim settlement and seek agreement with automotive repair shop on cost of repair. Prepare insurance forms to indicate repair cost or cost estimates and recommendations. Estimate parts and labor to repair damage, using standard automotive labor and parts-cost manuals and knowledge of automotive repair. Review repair-cost estimates with automobile-repair shop to secure agreement on cost of repairs. Examine damaged vehicle to determine extent of structural, body, mechanical, electrical, or interior damage. Evaluate practicality of repair as opposed to payment of market value of vehicle before accident. Determine salvage value on total-loss vehicle. Prepare insurance forms to indicate repair-cost estimates and recommendations. Arrange to have damage appraised by another appraiser to resolve disagreement with shop on repair cost.

Other Considerations for Income: No additional information.

Personality Type: Conventional-Realistic-Enterprising. **Career Cluster:** 06 Finance. **Career Pathway:** 06.4 Insurance Services. **Skills:** Negotiation; Service Orientation; Persuasion; Judgment and Decision Making; Active Listening; Time Management; Speaking; Equipment Selection.

Education and Training Program: Insurance. **Related Knowledge/Courses:** Customer and Personal Service; Law and Government; Medicine and Dentistry; Transportation; Computers and Electronics; Telecommunications.

Insurance Underwriters

❈ Annual Earnings: $56,790
❈ Beginning Wage: $35,010
❈ Earnings Growth Potential: Medium (38.4%)
❈ Growth: 6.3%
❈ Annual Job Openings: 6,880
❈ Self-Employed: 0.0%
❈ Part-Time: 3.6%
❈ Job Security: Most secure
❈ Education/Training Required: Bachelor's degree

Industries in Which Income Is Highest

Industry	Average Annual Earnings	Number Employed
Credit Intermediation and Related Activities	$58,130	4,910
Funds, Trusts, and Other Financial Vehicles	$56,770	1,110
Insurance Carriers and Related Activities	$56,740	86,440
Management of Companies and Enterprises	$56,490	3,460

Metropolitan Areas Where Income Is Highest

Metropolitan Area	Average Annual Earnings	Number Employed
New York–Northern New Jersey–Long Island, NY-NJ-PA	$71,960	8,890
Boston-Cambridge-Quincy, MA-NH	$67,560	1,780
Santa Rosa–Petaluma, CA	$66,980	130
Reading, PA	$66,930	90
San Francisco–Oakland–Fremont, CA	$66,000	1,510

Review individual applications for insurance to evaluate degree of risk involved and determine acceptance of applications. Examine documents to determine degree of risk from such factors as applicant financial standing and value and condition of property. Decline excessive risks. Write to field representatives, medical personnel, and others to obtain further information, quote rates, or explain company underwriting policies. Evaluate possibility of losses due to catastrophe or excessive insurance. Decrease value of policy when risk is substandard and specify applicable endorsements or apply rating to ensure safe profitable distribution of risks, using reference materials. Review company records to determine amount of insurance in force on single risk or group of closely related risks. Authorize reinsurance of policy when risk is high.

Other Considerations for Income: Insurance companies usually provide better-than-average benefits, including retirement plans and employer-financed group life and health insurance. Insurance companies usually pay tuition for underwriting courses that their trainees complete, and some also offer salary incentives.

Personality Type: Conventional-Enterprising-Investigative. **Career Cluster:** 06 Finance. **Career Pathway:** 06.4 Insurance Services. **Skills:** Writing; Service Orientation; Speaking; Active Listening; Learning Strategies; Active Learning; Monitoring; Persuasion.

Education and Training Program: Insurance. **Related Knowledge/Courses:** Medicine and Dentistry; Economics and Accounting; Clerical; Therapy and Counseling; Sales and Marketing; Biology.

Intelligence Analysts

❈ Annual Earnings: $60,910
❈ Beginning Wage: $36,500
❈ Earnings Growth Potential: High (40.1%)
❈ Growth: 17.3%
❈ Annual Job Openings: 14,746
❈ Self-Employed: 0.3%
❈ Part-Time: 2.2%
❈ Job Security: No data available
❈ Education/Training Required: Work experience plus degree

The Department of Labor reports this information for the occupation Detectives and Criminal Investigators. The job openings listed here are shared with other specializations within that occupation, including Criminal Investigators and Special Agents; Immigration and Customs Inspectors; Intelligence Analysts; Police Detectives; and Police Identification and Records Officers.

Industries in Which Income Is Highest

Industry	Average Annual Earnings	Number Employed
Federal, State, and Local Government	$60,780	103,680

Metropolitan Areas Where Income Is Highest

Metropolitan Area	Average Annual Earnings	Number Employed
San Jose–Sunnyvale–Santa Clara, CA	$92,430	310
Washington-Arlington-Alexandria, DC-VA-MD-WV	$88,440	4,590
Springfield, MA-CT	$82,690	60
Brunswick, GA	$80,960	350
New Haven, CT	$79,550	200

Gather, analyze, and evaluate information from a variety of sources, such as law enforcement databases, surveillance, intelligence networks, and geographic information systems. Use data to anticipate and prevent organized crime activities, such as terrorism. No task data available.

Other Considerations for Income: Federal law provides special salary rates to federal employees who serve in law enforcement. Additionally, federal special agents and inspectors receive law enforcement availability pay (LEAP)—equal to 25 percent of the agent's grade and step—awarded because of the large amount of overtime that these agents are expected to work. For example, in 2007, FBI agents entered federal service as GS-10 employees on the pay scale at a base salary of $48,159, yet they earned about $60,199 a year with availability pay. They could advance to the GS-13 grade level in field nonsupervisory assignments at a base salary of $75,414, which was worth $94,268 with availability pay. FBI supervisory, management, and executive positions in grades GS-14 and GS-15 paid a base salary of about $89,115 and $104,826 a year, respectively, which amounted to $111,394 or $131,033 per year including availability pay. Salaries were slightly higher in selected areas where the prevailing local pay level was higher. Because federal agents may be eligible for a special law enforcement benefits package, applicants should ask their recruiter for more information.

Personality Type: No data available. **Career Cluster:** 12 Law, Public Safety, Corrections, and Security. **Career**

Pathway: 12.4 Law Enforcement Services. **Skills:** No data available.

Education and Training Program: Criminalistics and Criminal Science. **Related Knowledge/Courses:** No data available.

Internists, General

- ❀ Annual Earnings: $166,400+
- ❀ Beginning Wage: $91,940
- ❀ Earnings Growth Potential: Cannot be calculated
- ❀ Growth: 14.2%
- ❀ Annual Job Openings: 38,027
- ❀ Self-Employed: 14.7%
- ❀ Part-Time: 8.1%
- ❀ Job Security: Most secure
- ❀ Education/Training Required: First professional degree

The Department of Labor reports this information for the occupation Physicians and Surgeons. The job openings listed here are shared with other specializations within that occupation, including Allergists and Immunologists; Anesthesiologists; Dermatologists; Family and General Practitioners; Hospitalists; Neurologists; Nuclear Medicine Physicians; Obstetricians and Gynecologists; Ophthalmologists; Pathologists; Pediatricians, General; Physical Medicine and Rehabilitation Physicians; Preventive Medicine Physicians; Psychiatrists; Radiologists; Sports Medicine Physicians; Surgeons; and Urologists.

Industries in Which Income Is Highest

Industry	Average Annual Earnings	Number Employed
Ambulatory Health Care Services	$166,400+	36,990
Hospitals	$162,190	8,300
Educational Services	$125,220	1,120

Metropolitan Areas Where Income Is Highest

Metropolitan Area	Average Annual Earnings	Number Employed
Boston-Cambridge-Quincy, MA-NH	$166,400+	2,150
Atlanta–Sandy Springs–Marietta, GA	$166,400+	1,790
Chicago-Naperville-Joliet, IL-IN-WI	$166,400+	1,790
San Francisco–Oakland–Fremont, CA	$166,400+	1,090
Minneapolis–St. Paul–Bloomington, MN-WI	$166,400+	820

Diagnose and provide non-surgical treatment of diseases and injuries of internal organ systems. Provide care mainly for adults who have a wide range of problems associated with the internal organs. Treat internal disorders, such as hypertension; heart disease; diabetes; and problems of the lung, brain, kidney, and gastrointestinal tract. Analyze records, reports, test results, or examination information to diagnose medical condition of patient. Prescribe or administer medication, therapy, and other specialized medical care to treat or prevent illness, disease, or injury. Provide and manage long-term, comprehensive medical care, including diagnosis and non-surgical treatment of diseases, for adult patients in an office or hospital. Manage and treat common health problems, such as infections, influenza and pneumonia, as well as serious, chronic, and complex illnesses, in adolescents, adults, and the elderly. Monitor patients' conditions and progress and re-evaluate treatments as necessary. Collect, record, and maintain patient information, such as medical history, reports, and examination results. Make diagnoses when different illnesses occur together or in situations where the diagnosis may be obscure. Explain procedures and discuss test results or prescribed treatments with patients. Advise patients and community members concerning diet, activity, hygiene, and disease prevention. Refer patient to medical specialist or other practitioner when necessary. Immunize patients to protect them from preventable diseases. Advise surgeon of a patient's risk status and recommend appropriate intervention to minimize risk. Direct and coordinate activities of nurses, students, assistants, specialists, therapists, and other medical staff. Provide consulting services to other doctors caring for patients with special or difficult problems. Operate on patients to remove, repair, or improve functioning of diseased or injured body parts and systems. Plan, implement, or administer health programs in hospitals, businesses, or communities for prevention and treatment of injuries or illnesses.

Other Considerations for Income: Earnings of physicians and surgeons are among the highest of any occupation; Internists are in the middle range of earners among medical specialists. The Medical Group Management Association's Physician Compensation and Production Survey of 2005 reported earnings of $141,912 for Internists with less than two years in their specialty and $166,420 for those with more than one year in their specialty. These figures cover salary, bonus and incentive payments, research stipends, honoraria, and distribution of profits. Self-employed physicians—those who own or are part owners of their medical practice—generally have higher median incomes than salaried physicians, but their must provide for their own health insurance and retirement.

Personality Type: Investigative-Social-Realistic. **Career Cluster:** 08 Health Science. **Career Pathway:** 08.1 Therapeutic Services. **Skills:** Science; Judgment and Decision Making; Complex Problem Solving; Reading Comprehension; Social Perceptiveness; Service Orientation; Management of Financial Resources; Persuasion.

Education and Training Program: Medicine (MD). **Related Knowledge/Courses:** Medicine and Dentistry; Biology; Therapy and Counseling; Psychology; Chemistry; Education and Training.

Judges, Magistrate Judges, and Magistrates

- ❊ Annual Earnings: $110,220
- ❊ Beginning Wage: $32,290
- ❊ Earnings Growth Potential: Very high (70.7%)
- ❊ Growth: 5.1%
- ❊ Annual Job Openings: 1,567
- ❊ Self-Employed: 0.0%
- ❊ Part-Time: 5.9%
- ❊ Job Security: Most secure
- ❊ Education/Training Required: Work experience plus degree

Industries in Which Income Is Highest

Industry	Average Annual Earnings	Number Employed
Federal, State, and Local Government	$110,220	25,470

Metropolitan Areas Where Income Is Highest

Metropolitan Area	Average Annual Earnings	Number Employed
Providence–Fall River–Warwick, RI-MA	$166,400+	90
Hartford–West Hartford–East Hartford, CT	$149,930	100
Trenton-Ewing, NJ	$144,950	60
Wichita, KS	$142,590	60
St. Louis, MO-IL	$141,850	120

Arbitrate, advise, adjudicate, or administer justice in a court of law. May sentence defendant in criminal cases according to government statutes. May determine liability of defendant in civil cases. May issue marriage licenses and perform wedding ceremonies. Instruct juries on applicable laws, direct juries to deduce the facts from the evidence presented, and hear their verdicts. Sentence defendants in criminal cases on conviction by jury according to applicable government statutes. Rule on admissibility of evidence and methods of conducting testimony. Preside over hearings and listen to allegations made by plaintiffs to determine whether the evidence supports the charges. Read documents on pleadings and motions to ascertain facts and issues. Interpret and enforce rules of procedure or establish new rules in situations where there are no procedures already established by law. Monitor proceedings to ensure that all applicable rules and procedures are followed. Advise attorneys, juries, litigants, and court personnel regarding conduct, issues, and proceedings. Research legal issues and write opinions on the issues. Conduct preliminary hearings to decide issues such as whether there is reasonable and probable cause to hold defendants in felony cases. Write decisions on cases. Award compensation for damages to litigants in civil cases in relation to findings by juries or by the court. Settle disputes between opposing attorneys. Supervise other judges, court officers, and the court's administrative staff. Impose restrictions upon parties in civil cases until trials can be held. Rule on custody and access disputes and enforce court orders regarding custody and support of children.

Grant divorces and divide assets between spouses. Participate in judicial tribunals to help resolve disputes. Perform wedding ceremonies.

Other Considerations for Income: Most salaried judges are provided health, life, and dental insurance; pension plans; judicial immunity protection; expense accounts; vacation, holiday, and sick leave; and contributions to retirement plans made on their behalf. In many states, judicial compensation committees, which make recommendations on the amount of salary increases, determine judicial salaries. States without commissions have statutes that regulate judicial salaries, link judicial salaries to the increases in pay for federal judges, or adjust annual pay according to the change in the Consumer Price Index, calculated by the U.S. Bureau of Labor Statistics.

Personality Type: Enterprising-Social. **Career Cluster:** 12 Law, Public Safety, Corrections, and Security. **Career Pathway:** 12.5 Legal Services. **Skills:** Judgment and Decision Making; Persuasion; Negotiation; Critical Thinking; Active Listening; Reading Comprehension; Social Perceptiveness; Management of Personnel Resources.

Education and Training Programs: Law (LL.B., J.D.); Legal Professions and Studies, Other; Legal Studies, General. **Related Knowledge/Courses:** Law and Government; Therapy and Counseling; Philosophy and Theology; English Language; Psychology; Sociology and Anthropology.

Landscape Architects

* Annual Earnings: $58,960
* Beginning Wage: $36,520
* Earnings Growth Potential: Medium (38.1%)
* Growth: 16.4%
* Annual Job Openings: 2,342
* Self-Employed: 18.5%
* Part-Time: 6.1%
* Job Security: Less secure than most
* Education/Training Required: Bachelor's degree

Industries in Which Income Is Highest

Industry	Average Annual Earnings	Number Employed
Federal, State, and Local Government	$73,900	1,950
Professional, Scientific, and Technical Services	$59,710	13,930
Administrative and Support Services	$47,970	3,380

Metropolitan Areas Where Income Is Highest

Metropolitan Area	Average Annual Earnings	Number Employed
San Luis Obispo–Paso Robles, CA	$80,620	60
Dallas–Fort Worth–Arlington, TX	$79,710	270
Riverside–San Bernardino–Ontario, CA	$78,010	100
Hartford–West Hartford–East Hartford, CT	$77,950	220
Sacramento–Arden-Arcade–Roseville, CA	$77,330	260

Plan and design land areas for such projects as parks and other recreational facilities; airports; highways; hospitals; schools; land subdivisions; and commercial, industrial, and residential sites. Prepare site plans, specifications, and cost estimates for land development, coordinating arrangement of existing and proposed land features and structures. Confer with clients, engineering personnel, and architects on overall program. Compile and analyze data on conditions such as location, drainage, and location of structures for environmental reports and landscaping plans. Inspect landscape work to ensure compliance with specifications, approve quality of materials and work, and advise client and construction personnel.

Other Considerations for Income: No additional information.

Personality Type: Artistic-Investigative-Realistic. **Career Cluster:** 02 Architecture and Construction. **Career Pathway:** 02.1 Design/Pre-Construction. **Skills:** Operations Analysis; Management of Financial Resources; Coordination; Mathematics; Complex Problem Solving; Social Perceptiveness; Persuasion; Writing.

Education and Training Programs: Environmental Design/Architecture; Landscape Architecture (BS, BSLA, BLA, MSLA, MLA, PhD). **Related Knowledge/Courses:** Design; Geography; Building and Construction; Fine Arts; Biology; Engineering and Technology.

Law Teachers, Postsecondary

❀ Annual Earnings: $93,210
❀ Beginning Wage: $40,810
❀ Earnings Growth Potential: Very high (56.2%)
❀ Growth: 22.9%
❀ Annual Job Openings: 2,169
❀ Self-Employed: 0.4%
❀ Part-Time: 27.8%
❀ Job Security: Most secure
❀ Education/Training Required: First professional degree

Industries in Which Income Is Highest

Industry	Average Annual Earnings	Number Employed
Educational Services	$93,200	12,470

Metropolitan Areas Where Income Is Highest

Metropolitan Area	Average Annual Earnings	Number Employed
Columbus, OH	$127,830	70
Buffalo–Niagara Falls, NY	$118,250	60
Dallas–Fort Worth–Arlington, TX	$106,670	80
Washington-Arlington-Alexandria, DC-VA-MD-WV	$100,050	1,080
Minneapolis–St. Paul–Bloomington, MN-WI	$98,310	190

Teach courses in law. Evaluate and grade students' classwork, assignments, papers, and oral presentations. Compile, administer, and grade examinations or assign this work to others. Prepare and deliver lectures to undergraduate or graduate students on topics such as civil procedure, contracts, and torts. Initiate, facilitate, and moderate classroom discussions. Prepare course materials such as syllabi, homework assignments, and handouts. Keep abreast of developments in their field by reading current literature, talking with colleagues, and participating in professional conferences. Plan, evaluate, and revise curricula, course content, and course materials and methods of instruction. Maintain regularly scheduled office hours to advise and assist students. Conduct research in a particular field of knowledge and publish findings in professional journals, books, or electronic media. Advise students on academic and vocational curricula and on career issues. Supervise undergraduate and/or graduate teaching, internship, and research work. Select and obtain materials and supplies such as textbooks. Maintain student attendance records, grades, and other required records. Serve on academic or administrative committees that deal with institutional policies, departmental matters, and academic issues. Perform administrative duties such as serving as department head. Collaborate with colleagues to address teaching and research issues. Participate in student recruitment, registration, and placement activities. Compile bibliographies of specialized materials for outside reading assignments. Participate in campus and community events. Act as advisers to student organizations. Assign cases for students to hear and try. Provide professional consulting services to government or industry. Write grant proposals to procure external research funding.

Other Considerations for Income: Earnings for college faculty vary according to rank and type of institution, geographic area, and field. According to a 2006–2007 survey by the American Association of University Professors, salaries for full-time faculty averaged $73,207. By rank, the average was $98,974 for professors, $69,911 for associate professors, $58,662 for assistant professors, $42,609 for instructors, and $48,289 for lecturers. Faculty in 4-year institutions earn higher salaries, on average, than do those in 2-year schools. Many faculty members have significant earnings in addition to their base salary from consulting, teaching additional courses, research, writing for publication, or other employment. In addition, many college and university faculty enjoy unique benefits, including access to campus facilities, tuition waivers for dependents, housing and travel allowances, and paid leave for sabbaticals. Part-time faculty and instructors usually have fewer benefits than full-time faculty.

Personality Type: Social-Investigative-Enterprising. **Career Clusters:** 05 Education and Training; 12 Law, Public Safety, Corrections, and Security. **Career Pathway:** 05.3 Teaching/Training; 12.5 Legal Services. **Skills:** Instructing; Critical Thinking; Writing; Reading Comprehension; Speaking; Persuasion; Active Listening; Learning Strategies.

Education and Training Program: Law (LL.B., J.D.). **Related Knowledge/Courses:** Law and Government; English Language; History and Archeology; Education and Training; Philosophy and Theology; Communications and Media.

Lawyers

- ❀ Annual Earnings: $110,590
- ❀ Beginning Wage: $54,460
- ❀ Earnings Growth Potential: Very high (50.8%)
- ❀ Growth: 11.0%
- ❀ Annual Job Openings: 49,445
- ❀ Self-Employed: 26.7%
- ❀ Part-Time: 5.9%
- ❀ Job Security: Less secure than most
- ❀ Education/Training Required: First professional degree

Industries in Which Income Is Highest

Industry	Average Annual Earnings	Number Employed
Computer and Electronic Product Manufacturing	$156,790	1,400
Securities, Commodity Contracts, and Other Financial Investments and Related Activities	$151,640	4,060
Telecommunications	$150,590	1,510
Management of Companies and Enterprises	$145,770	13,830
Publishing Industries (Except Internet)	$144,750	1,380

Metropolitan Areas Where Income Is Highest

Metropolitan Area	Average Annual Earnings	Number Employed
San Jose–Sunnyvale–Santa Clara, CA	$166,400+	4,040
Rockford, IL	$166,400+	300
Rocky Mount, NC	$157,990	70
Santa Rosa–Petaluma, CA	$148,590	440
Chattanooga, TN-GA	$145,090	810

Represent clients in criminal and civil litigation and other legal proceedings, draw up legal documents, and manage or advise clients on legal transactions. May specialize in a single area or may practice broadly in many areas of law. Advise clients concerning business transactions, claim liability, advisability of prosecuting or defending lawsuits, or legal rights and obligations. Interpret laws, rulings, and regulations for individuals and businesses. Analyze the probable outcomes of cases, using knowledge of legal precedents. Present and summarize cases to judges and juries. Gather evidence to formulate defense or to initiate legal actions by such means as interviewing clients and witnesses to ascertain the facts of a case. Evaluate findings and develop strategies and arguments in preparation for presentation of cases. Represent clients in court or before government agencies. Examine legal data to determine advisability of defending or prosecuting lawsuit. Select jurors, argue motions, meet with judges, and question witnesses during the course of a trial. Present evidence to defend clients or prosecute defendants in criminal or civil litigation. Study Constitution, statutes, decisions, regulations, and ordinances of quasi-judicial bodies to determine ramifications for cases. Prepare and draft legal documents, such as wills, deeds, patent applications, mortgages, leases, and contracts. Prepare legal briefs and opinions and file appeals in state and federal courts of appeal. Negotiate settlements of civil disputes. Confer with colleagues with specialties in appropriate areas of legal issue to establish and verify bases for legal proceedings. Search for and examine public and other legal records to write opinions or establish ownership. Supervise legal assistants. Perform administrative and management functions related to the practice of law. Act as agent, trustee, guardian, or executor for businesses or individuals. Probate wills and represent and advise executors and administrators of estates. Help develop federal and state programs, draft and interpret laws and legislation, and establish enforcement procedures.

Other Considerations for Income: Salaries of experienced attorneys vary widely according to the type, size, and location of their employer. Lawyers who own their own practices usually earn less than those who are partners in law firms. Lawyers starting their own practice may need to work part time in other occupations to supplement their income until their practice is well established. Most salaried lawyers are provided health and life insurance, and contributions are made to retirement plans on their behalf. Lawyers who practice independently are covered only if they arrange and pay for such benefits themselves.

Personality Type: Enterprising-Investigative. **Career Cluster:** 12 Law, Public Safety, Corrections, and Security. **Career Pathway:** 12.5 Legal Services. **Skills:** Persuasion; Negotiation; Writing; Judgment and Decision Making; Critical Thinking; Speaking; Reading Comprehension; Active Listening.

Education and Training Programs: Advanced Legal Research/Studies, General (LL.M., M.C.L., M.L.I., M.S.L., J.S.D./S.J.D.); American/U.S. Law/Legal Studies/Jurisprudence (LL.M., M.C.J., J.S.D./S.J.D.); Banking, Corporate, Finance, and Securities Law (LL.M., J.S.D./S.J.D.); Canadian Law/Legal Studies/Jurisprudence (LL.M., M.C.J., J.S.D./S.J.D.); Comparative Law (LL.M., M.C.L., J.S.D./S.J.D.); Energy, Environment, and Natural Resources Law (LL.M., M.S., J.S.D./S.J.D.); Health Law (LL.M., M.J., J.S.D./S.J.D.); others. **Related Knowledge/Courses:** Law and Government; English Language; Personnel and Human Resources; Customer and Personal Service; Economics and Accounting; Administration and Management.

Librarians

- ❋ Annual Earnings: $52,530
- ❋ Beginning Wage: $33,190
- ❋ Earnings Growth Potential: Medium (36.8%)
- ❋ Growth: 3.6%
- ❋ Annual Job Openings: 18,945
- ❋ Self-Employed: 0.6%
- ❋ Part-Time: 21.2%
- ❋ Job Security: Most secure
- ❋ Education/Training Required: Master's degree

Industries in Which Income Is Highest

Industry	Average Annual Earnings	Number Employed
Professional, Scientific, and Technical Services	$59,670	3,230
Educational Services	$54,740	89,080
Hospitals	$51,480	1,270
Federal, State, and Local Government	$48,840	46,540
Other Information Services	$48,060	7,010

Metropolitan Areas Where Income Is Highest

Metropolitan Area	Average Annual Earnings	Number Employed
San Jose–Sunnyvale–Santa Clara, CA	$75,230	740
Santa Barbara–Santa Maria, CA	$70,140	130
Stockton, CA	$68,830	90
San Francisco–Oakland–Fremont, CA	$68,120	1,810
Colorado Springs, CO	$68,050	280

Administer libraries and perform related library services. Work in a variety of settings, including public libraries, schools, colleges and universities, museums, corporations, government agencies, law firms, nonprofit organizations, and health-care providers. Tasks may include selecting, acquiring, cataloguing, classifying, circulating, and maintaining library materials and furnishing reference, bibliographical, and readers' advisory services. May perform in-depth, strategic research and synthesize, analyze, edit, and filter information. May set up or work with databases and information systems to catalogue and access information. Search standard reference materials, including online sources and the Internet, to answer patrons' reference questions. Analyze patrons' requests to determine needed information and assist in furnishing or locating that information. Teach library patrons to search for information by using databases. Keep records of circulation and materials. Supervise budgeting, planning, and personnel activities. Check books in and out of the library. Explain use of library facilities, resources, equipment, and services and provide information about library policies. Review and evaluate resource material, such as book reviews and catalogs, to select and order print, audiovisual, and electronic resources. Code, classify, and catalog books, publications, films, audiovisual aids, and other library materials based on subject matter or standard library classification systems. Locate unusual or unique information in response to specific requests. Direct and train library staff in duties such as receiving, shelving, researching, cataloging, and equipment use. Respond to customer complaints, taking action as necessary. Organize collections of books, publications, documents, audiovisual aids, and other reference materials for convenient access. Develop library policies and procedures. Evaluate materials to determine outdated or unused items to be discarded. Develop information access aids such as indexes and annotated bibliographies, Web pages, electronic pathfinders, and online tutorials. Plan and deliver client-centered programs and services such as special services for corporate clients, storytelling for children, newsletters, or programs for special groups. Compile lists of books, periodicals, articles, and audiovisual materials on particular subjects. Arrange for interlibrary loans of materials not available in a particular library. Assemble and arrange display materials.

Other Considerations for Income: Salaries of librarians vary according to the individual's qualifications and the type, size, and location of the library. Librarians with primarily administrative duties often have greater earnings. About 1 in 4 librarians are a member of a union or are covered under a union contract.

Personality Type: Conventional-Social-Enterprising. **Career Cluster:** 05 Education and Training. **Career Pathways:** 05.2 Professional Support Services; 05.3 Teaching/Training. **Skills:** Management of Financial Resources; Management of Material Resources; Learning Strategies; Equipment Selection; Service Orientation; Systems Evaluation; Persuasion; Monitoring.

Education and Training Programs: Library and Information Science; Library Science, Other; School Librarian/School Library Media Specialist. **Related Knowledge/Courses:** History and Archeology; Sociology and Anthropology; Clerical; Education and Training; Philosophy and Theology; English Language.

Library Science Teachers, Postsecondary

* Annual Earnings: $58,570
* Beginning Wage: $36,570
* Earnings Growth Potential: Medium (37.6%)
* Growth: 22.9%
* Annual Job Openings: 702
* Self-Employed: 0.4%
* Part-Time: 27.8%
* Job Security: Most secure
* Education/Training Required: Doctoral degree

Industries in Which Income Is Highest

Industry	Average Annual Earnings	Number Employed
Educational Services	$58,570	3,960

Metropolitan Areas Where Income Is Highest

Metropolitan Area	Average Annual Earnings	Number Employed
San Francisco–Oakland–Fremont, CA	$92,410	50
Los Angeles–Long Beach–Santa Ana, CA	$77,240	100
New York–Northern New Jersey–Long Island, NY-NJ-PA	$69,910	260
Columbus, OH	$63,310	90
Minneapolis–St. Paul–Bloomington, MN-WI	$61,260	40

Teach courses in library science. Prepare course materials such as syllabi, homework assignments, and handouts. Prepare and deliver lectures to undergraduate or graduate students on topics such as collection development, archival methods, and indexing and abstracting. Evaluate and grade students' classwork, assignments, and papers. Keep abreast of developments in their field by reading current literature, talking with colleagues, and participating in professional conferences. Initiate, facilitate, and moderate classroom discussions. Plan, evaluate, and revise curricula, course content, and course materials and methods of instruction. Conduct research in a particular field of knowledge and publish findings in professional journals, books, and/or electronic media. Maintain student attendance records, grades, and other required records. Collaborate with colleagues to address teaching and research issues. Advise students on academic and vocational curricula and on career issues. Compile, administer, and grade examinations or assign this work to others. Supervise undergraduate or graduate teaching, internship, and research work. Maintain regularly scheduled office hours in order to advise and assist students. Write grant proposals to procure external research funding. Select and obtain materials and supplies such as textbooks. Serve on academic or administrative committees that deal with institutional policies, departmental matters, and academic issues. Compile bibliographies of specialized materials for outside reading assignments. Participate in student recruitment, registration, and placement activities. Perform administrative duties such as serving as department head. Participate in campus and community events. Act as advisers to student organizations. Provide professional consulting services to government and/or industry.

Other Considerations for Income: Earnings for college faculty vary according to rank and type of institution, geographic area, and field. According to a 2006–2007 survey by the American Association of University Professors, salaries for full-time faculty averaged $73,207. By rank, the average was $98,974 for professors, $69,911 for associate professors, $58,662 for assistant professors, $42,609 for instructors, and $48,289 for lecturers. Faculty in 4-year institutions earn higher salaries, on average, than do those in 2-year schools. Many faculty members have significant earnings in addition to their base salary from consulting, teaching additional courses, research, writing for publication, or other employment. In addition, many college and university faculty enjoy unique benefits, including access to campus facilities, tuition waivers for dependents, housing and travel allowances, and paid leave for sabbaticals. Part-time faculty and instructors usually have fewer benefits than full-time faculty.

Personality Type: Social-Investigative-Conventional. **Career Cluster:** 05 Education and Training. **Career Pathways:** 05.2 Professional Support Services; 05.3 Teaching/Training. **Skills:** Writing; Learning Strategies; Instructing; Reading Comprehension; Active Learning; Operations Analysis; Speaking; Monitoring.

Education and Training Programs: Humanities/Humanistic Studies; Library and Information Science; Teacher Education and Professional Development, Specific Subject Areas, Other. **Related Knowledge/Courses:** Education and Training; Sociology and Anthropology; Communications and Media; English Language; History and Archeology; Philosophy and Theology.

Licensing Examiners and Inspectors

❈ Annual Earnings: $48,890
❈ Beginning Wage: $29,490
❈ Earnings Growth Potential: Medium (39.7%)
❈ Growth: 4.9%
❈ Annual Job Openings: 15,841
❈ Self-Employed: 0.4%
❈ Part-Time: 5.0%
❈ Job Security: More secure than most
❈ Education/Training Required: Long-term on-the-job training

The Department of Labor reports this information for the occupation Compliance Officers, Except Agriculture, Construction, Health and Safety, and Transportation. The job openings listed here are shared with other specializations within that occupation, including Coroners; Environmental Compliance Inspectors; Equal Opportunity Representatives and Officers; Government Property Inspectors and Investigators; and Regulatory Affairs Specialists.

Industries in Which Income Is Highest

Industry	Average Annual Earnings	Number Employed
Postal Service	$77,500	1,970
Utilities	$74,890	1,880
Securities, Commodity Contracts, and Other Financial Investments and Related Activities	$70,720	6,480
Telecommunications	$64,400	2,560
Chemical Manufacturing	$61,920	3,910

Metropolitan Areas Where Income Is Highest

Metropolitan Area	Average Annual Earnings	Number Employed
Brunswick, GA	$83,080	500
Bridgeport-Stamford-Norwalk, CT	$73,120	640
Warner Robins, GA	$69,670	80
San Francisco–Oakland–Fremont, CA	$67,520	4,370
Hartford–West Hartford–East Hartford, CT	$67,460	1,420

Examine, evaluate, and investigate eligibility for, conformity with, or liability under licenses or permits. Issue licenses to individuals meeting standards. Evaluate applications, records, and documents in order to gather information about eligibility or liability issues. Administer oral, written, road, or flight tests to license applicants. Score tests and observe equipment operation and control in order to rate ability of applicants. Advise licensees and other individuals or groups concerning licensing, permit, or passport regulations. Warn violators of infractions or penalties. Prepare reports of activities, evaluations, recommendations, and decisions. Prepare correspondence to inform concerned parties of licensing decisions and of appeals processes. Confer with and interview officials, technical or professional specialists, and applicants in order to obtain information or to clarify facts relevant to licensing decisions. Report law or regulation violations to appropriate boards and agencies. Visit establishments to verify that valid licenses and permits are displayed and that licensing standards are being upheld.

Other Considerations for Income: No additional information.

Personality Type: Conventional-Enterprising. **Career Cluster:** 12 Law, Public Safety, Corrections, and Security. **Career Pathway:** 12.6 Inspection Services. **Skills:** Speaking; Service Orientation; Judgment and Decision Making; Active Listening; Reading Comprehension.

Education and Training Program: Public Administration and Social Service Professions, Other. **Related Knowledge/Courses:** Clerical; Customer and Personal Service; Law and Government; Foreign Language; Psychology; Public Safety and Security.

Loan Officers

❈ Annual Earnings: $54,700
❈ Beginning Wage: $30,850
❈ Earnings Growth Potential: High (43.6%)
❈ Growth: 11.5%
❈ Annual Job Openings: 54,237
❈ Self-Employed: 2.9%
❈ Part-Time: 6.6%
❈ Job Security: Less secure than most
❈ Education/Training Required: Bachelor's degree

Industries in Which Income Is Highest

Industry	Average Annual Earnings	Number Employed
Federal, State, and Local Government	$67,360	4,810
Securities, Commodity Contracts, and Other Financial Investments and Related Activities	$64,090	4,440
Real Estate	$60,910	4,890
Administrative and Support Services	$60,160	1,440
Professional, Scientific, and Technical Services	$60,010	3,620

Metropolitan Areas Where Income Is Highest

Metropolitan Area	Average Annual Earnings	Number Employed
Atlantic City, NJ	$90,280	80
Waco, TX	$80,180	160
Auburn-Opelika, AL	$79,750	80
Springfield, MA-CT	$76,700	320
Winchester, VA-WV	$76,570	170

Evaluate, authorize, or recommend approval of commercial, real estate, or credit loans. Advise borrowers on financial status and methods of payments. Includes mortgage loan officers and agents, collection analysts, loan servicing officers, and loan underwriters. Meet with applicants to obtain information for loan applications and to answer questions about the process. Approve loans within specified limits and refer loan applications outside those limits to management for approval. Analyze applicants' financial status, credit, and property evaluations to determine feasibility of granting loans. Explain to customers the different types of loans and credit options that are available, as well as the terms of those services. Obtain and compile copies of loan applicants' credit histories, corporate financial statements, and other financial information. Review and update credit and loan files. Review loan agreements to ensure that they are complete and accurate according to policy. Compute payment schedules. Stay abreast of new types of loans and other financial services and products to better meet customers' needs. Submit applications to credit analysts for verification and recommendation. Handle customer complaints and take appropriate action to resolve them. Work with clients to identify their financial goals and to find ways of reaching those goals. Confer with underwriters to aid in resolving mortgage application problems. Negotiate payment arrangements with customers who have delinquent loans. Market bank products to individuals and firms, promoting bank services that may meet customers' needs. Supervise loan personnel. Set credit policies, credit lines, procedures, and standards in conjunction with senior managers. Provide special services such as investment banking for clients with more specialized needs. Analyze potential loan markets and develop referral networks to locate prospects for loans. Prepare reports to send to customers whose accounts are delinquent and forward irreconcilable accounts for collector action. Arrange for maintenance and liquidation of delinquent properties. Interview, hire, and train new employees. Petition courts to transfer titles and deeds of collateral to banks.

Other Considerations for Income: The form of compensation for loan officers varies. Most are paid a commission based on the number of loans they originate. Some institutions pay only salaries, while others pay their loan officers a salary plus a commission or bonus based on the number of loans originated. Loan officers who are paid on commission usually earn more than those who earn only a salary, and those who work for smaller banks generally earn less than those employed by larger institutions. According to a salary survey conducted by Robert Half International, a staffing services firm specializing in accounting and finance, consumer loan officers, referred to as personal bankers, with 1 to 3 years of experience earned between $30,750 and $36,250 in 2007, and commercial loan officers with 1 to 3 years of experience made between $45,750 and $70,250. Commercial loan officers with more than 3 years of experience made between $61,750 and $100,750, and consumer loan officers earned between $36,250 and $51,250. Earnings of loan officers with graduate degrees or professional certifications are higher. Banks and other lenders sometimes may offer their loan officers free checking privileges and somewhat lower interest rates on personal loans.

Personality Type: Conventional-Enterprising-Social. **Career Cluster:** 06 Finance. **Career Pathway:** 06.1 Financial and Investment Planning. **Skills:** Persuasion; Social Perceptiveness; Service Orientation; Complex Problem Solving; Negotiation; Instructing; Speaking; Judgment and Decision Making.

Education and Training Programs: Credit Management; Finance, General. **Related Knowledge/Courses:** Economics and Accounting; Sales and Marketing; Law and Government; English Language; Mathematics; Customer and Personal Service.

Locomotive Engineers

❀ Annual Earnings: $48,440
❀ Beginning Wage: $32,670
❀ Earnings Growth Potential: Low (32.6%)
❀ Growth: 2.9%
❀ Annual Job Openings: 3,548
❀ Self-Employed: 0.0%
❀ Part-Time: 1.7%
❀ Job Security: Less secure than most
❀ Education/Training Required: Moderate-term on-the-job training

The Department of Labor reports this information for the occupation Locomotive Engineers and Operators. The job openings listed here are shared with other specializations within that occupation, including Locomotive Firers; and Rail Yard Engineers, Dinkey Operators, and Hostlers.

Industries in Which Income Is Highest

Industry	Average Annual Earnings	Number Employed
Federal, State, and Local Government	$57,180	1,430
Rail Transportation	$48,370	40,250

Metropolitan Areas Where Income Is Highest

Metropolitan Area	Average Annual Earnings	Number Employed
New York–Northern New Jersey– Long Island, NY-NJ-PA	$52,640	900
Los Angeles–Long Beach–Santa Ana, CA	$50,500	380
Houston–Sugar Land–Baytown, TX	$31,260	70

Drive electric, diesel-electric, steam, or gas-turbine-electric locomotives to transport passengers or freight. Interpret train orders, electronic or manual signals, and railroad rules and regulations. Monitor gauges and meters that measure speed, amperage, battery charge, and air pressure in brake lines and in main reservoirs. Interpret train orders, signals, and railroad rules and regulations that govern the operation of locomotives. Observe tracks to detect obstructions. Receive starting signals from conductors; then move controls such as throttles and air brakes to drive electric, diesel-electric, steam, or gas-turbine-electric locomotives. Confer with conductors or traffic control center personnel via radiophones to issue or receive information concerning stops, delays, or oncoming trains. Operate locomotives to transport freight or passengers between stations and to assemble and disassemble trains within rail yards. Respond to emergency conditions or breakdowns, following applicable safety procedures and rules. Check to ensure that brake examination tests are conducted at shunting stations. Call out train signals to assistants in order to verify meanings. Inspect locomotives to verify adequate fuel, sand, water, and other supplies before each run and to check for mechanical problems. Prepare reports regarding any problems encountered, such as accidents, signaling problems, unscheduled stops, or delays. Check to ensure that documentation, including procedure manuals and logbooks, is in the driver's cab and available for staff use. Inspect locomotives after runs to detect damaged or defective equipment. Drive diesel-electric rail-detector cars to transport rail-flaw-detecting machines over tracks. Monitor train loading procedures to ensure that freight and rolling stock are loaded or unloaded without damage.

Other Considerations for Income: Most railroad transportation workers are paid according to miles traveled or hours worked, whichever leads to higher earnings. Factors such as seniority, job assignments, and location impact potential earnings. Seventy-four percent of railroad transportation workers are members of unions compared to 12 percent for all occupations. Many different railroad unions represent various crafts on the railroads. Among the largest of the railroad employee unions are the United Transportation Union and the Brotherhood of Locomotive Engineers and Trainmen.

Personality Type: Realistic-Conventional. **Career Cluster:** 16 Transportation, Distribution, and Logistics. **Career Pathway:** 16.1 Transportation Operations. **Skills:** Operation Monitoring; Operation and Control; Troubleshooting; Instructing; Active Listening; Equipment Maintenance; Service Orientation; Quality Control Analysis.

Education and Training Program: Transportation and Materials Moving, Other. **Related Knowledge/Courses:** Transportation; Mechanical; Public Safety and Security.

Locomotive Firers

❋ Annual Earnings: $48,190
❋ Beginning Wage: $30,310
❋ Earnings Growth Potential: Medium (37.1%)
❋ Growth: 2.9%
❋ Annual Job Openings: 3,548
❋ Self-Employed: 0.0%
❋ Part-Time: 1.7%
❋ Job Security: Less secure than most
❋ Education/Training Required: Moderate-term on-the-job training

The Department of Labor reports this information for the occupation Locomotive Engineers and Operators. The job openings listed here are shared with other specializations within that occupation, including Locomotive Engineers; and Rail Yard Engineers, Dinkey Operators, and Hostlers.

Industries in Which Income Is Highest

Industry	Average Annual Earnings	Number Employed
Rail Transportation	$47,960	920

Metropolitan Areas Where Income Is Highest

Metropolitan Area	Average Annual Earnings	Number Employed

No data available.

Monitor locomotive instruments and watch for dragging equipment, obstacles on rights-of-way, and train signals during run. Watch for and relay traffic signals from yard workers to yard engineer in railroad yard. Signal other workers to set brakes and to throw track switches when switching cars from trains to way stations. Monitor oil, temperature, and pressure gauges on dashboards to determine whether engines are operating safely and efficiently. Check to see that trains are equipped with supplies such as fuel, water, and sand. Inspect locomotives to detect damaged or worn parts. Operate locomotives in emergency situations. Receive signals from workers in rear of train and relay that information to engineers. Start diesel engines to warm engines before runs. Observe train signals along routes and verify their meanings for engineers. Observe tracks from left sides of locomotives to detect obstructions on tracks. Monitor trains as they go around curves to detect dragging equipment and smoking journal boxes.

Other Considerations for Income: Most railroad transportation workers are paid according to miles traveled or hours worked, whichever leads to higher earnings. Factors such as seniority, job assignments, and location impact potential earnings. Seventy-four percent of railroad transportation workers are members of unions compared to 12 percent for all occupations. Many different railroad unions represent various crafts on the railroads. Among the largest of the railroad employee unions are the United Transportation Union and the Brotherhood of Locomotive Engineers and Trainmen.

Personality Type: Realistic-Conventional. **Career Cluster:** 16 Transportation, Distribution, and Logistics. **Career Pathway:** 16.1 Transportation Operations. **Skills:** Operation Monitoring; Operation and Control.

Education and Training Program: Transportation and Materials Moving, Other. **Related Knowledge/Courses:** Transportation; Mechanical; Public Safety and Security; Physics.

Logisticians

❋ Annual Earnings: $66,480
❋ Beginning Wage: $39,500
❋ Earnings Growth Potential: High (40.6%)
❋ Growth: 17.3%
❋ Annual Job Openings: 9,671
❋ Self-Employed: 1.5%
❋ Part-Time: 3.6%
❋ Job Security: More secure than most
❋ Education/Training Required: Bachelor's degree

Industries in Which Income Is Highest

Industry	Average Annual Earnings	Number Employed
Utilities	$73,600	1,520
Federal, State, and Local Government	$73,340	23,750
Telecommunications	$71,310	1,760
Computer and Electronic Product Manufacturing	$70,600	6,360
Management of Companies and Enterprises	$67,770	7,950

Metropolitan Areas Where Income Is Highest

Metropolitan Area	Average Annual Earnings	Number Employed
Dayton, OH	$80,990	570
San Jose–Sunnyvale–Santa Clara, CA	$80,690	1,640
Oxnard–Thousand Oaks–Ventura, CA	$80,630	410
Washington-Arlington-Alexandria, DC-VA-MD-WV	$80,460	4,280
Huntsville, AL	$79,510	1,810

Analyze and coordinate the logistical functions of a firm or organization. Responsible for the entire life cycle of a product, including acquisition, distribution, internal allocation, delivery, and final disposal of resources. Maintain and develop positive business relationships with a customer's key personnel involved in or directly relevant to a logistics activity. Develop an understanding of customers' needs and take actions to ensure that such needs are met. Direct availability and allocation of materials, supplies, and finished products. Collaborate with other departments as necessary to meet customer requirements, to take advantage of sales opportunities, or, in the case of shortages, to minimize negative impacts on a business. Protect and control proprietary materials. Review logistics performance with customers against targets, benchmarks, and service agreements. Develop and implement technical project management tools such as plans, schedules, and responsibility and compliance matrices. Direct team activities, establishing task priorities, scheduling and tracking work assignments, providing guidance, and ensuring the availability of resources. Report project plans, progress, and results. Direct and support the compilation and analysis of technical source data necessary for product development. Explain proposed solutions to customers, management, or other interested parties through written proposals and oral presentations. Provide project management services, including the provision and analysis of technical data. Develop proposals that include documentation for estimates. Plan, organize, and execute logistics support activities such as maintenance planning, repair analysis, and test equipment recommendations. Participate in the assessment and review of design alternatives and design change proposal impacts. Support the development of training materials and technical manuals. Stay informed of logistics technology advances and apply appropriate technology in order to improve logistics processes. Redesign the movement of goods in order to maximize value and minimize costs.

Other Considerations for Income: No additional information.

Personality Type: Enterprising-Conventional. **Career Clusters:** 04 Business, Management, and Administration; 16 Transportation, Distribution, and Logistics. **Career Pathways:** 04.1 Management; 16.2 Logistics, Planning, and Management Services. **Skills:** Management of Financial Resources; Management of Material Resources; Systems Analysis; Operations Analysis; Management of Personnel Resources; Service Orientation; Persuasion; Technology Design.

Education and Training Programs: Logistics, Materials, and Supply Chain Management; Operations Management and Supervision; Transportation/Mobility Management. **Related Knowledge/Courses:** Telecommunications; Geography; Computers and Electronics; Economics and Accounting; Administration and Management; Public Safety and Security.

Logistics Analysts

- ❋ Annual Earnings: $66,480
- ❋ Beginning Wage: $39,500
- ❋ Earnings Growth Potential: High (40.6%)
- ❋ Growth: 17.3%
- ❋ Annual Job Openings: 9,671
- ❋ Self-Employed: 1.5%
- ❋ Part-Time: 3.6%
- ❋ Job Security: No data available
- ❋ Education/Training Required: Bachelor's degree

The Department of Labor reports this information for the occupation Logisticians. The job openings listed here are shared with other specializations within that occupation, including Logistics Engineers.

Industries in Which Income Is Highest

Industry	Average Annual Earnings	Number Employed
Utilities	$73,600	1,520
Federal, State, and Local Government	$73,340	23,750
Telecommunications	$71,310	1,760
Computer and Electronic Product Manufacturing	$70,600	6,360
Management of Companies and Enterprises	$67,770	7,950

Metropolitan Areas Where Income Is Highest

Metropolitan Area	Average Annual Earnings	Number Employed
Dayton, OH	$80,990	570
San Jose–Sunnyvale–Santa Clara, CA	$80,690	1,640
Oxnard–Thousand Oaks–Ventura, CA	$80,630	410
Washington-Arlington-Alexandria, DC-VA-MD-WV	$80,460	4,280
Huntsville, AL	$79,510	1,810

Analyze product delivery or supply chain processes to identify or recommend changes. May manage route activity, including invoicing, electronic bills, and shipment tracing. No task data available.

Other Considerations for Income: No additional information.

Personality Type: Conventional-Enterprising-Investigative. **Career Clusters:** 04 Business, Management, and Administration; 16 Transportation, Distribution, and Logistics. **Career Pathways:** 04.1 Management; 16.2 Logistics, Planning, and Management Services. **Skills:** No data available.

Education and Training Programs: Logistics, Materials, and Supply Chain Management; Operations Management and Supervision; Transportation/Mobility Management. **Related Knowledge/Courses:** No data available.

Logistics Engineers

❋ Annual Earnings: $66,480
❋ Beginning Wage: $39,500
❋ Earnings Growth Potential: High (40.6%)
❋ Growth: 17.3%
❋ Annual Job Openings: 9,671
❋ Self-Employed: 1.5%
❋ Part-Time: 3.6%
❋ Job Security: No data available
❋ Education/Training Required: Bachelor's degree

The Department of Labor reports this information for the occupation Logisticians. The job openings listed here are shared with other specializations within that occupation, including Logistics Analysts.

Industries in Which Income Is Highest

Industry	Average Annual Earnings	Number Employed
Utilities	$73,600	1,520
Federal, State, and Local Government	$73,340	23,750
Telecommunications	$71,310	1,760
Computer and Electronic Product Manufacturing	$70,600	6,360
Management of Companies and Enterprises	$67,770	7,950

Metropolitan Areas Where Income Is Highest

Metropolitan Area	Average Annual Earnings	Number Employed
Dayton, OH	$80,990	570
San Jose–Sunnyvale–Santa Clara, CA	$80,690	1,640
Oxnard–Thousand Oaks–Ventura, CA	$80,630	410
Washington-Arlington-Alexandria, DC-VA-MD-WV	$80,460	4,280
Huntsville, AL	$79,510	1,810

Design and analyze operational solutions for projects such as transportation optimization, network modeling, process and methods analysis, cost containment, capacity enhancement, routing and shipment opti-

mization, and information management. No task data available.

Other Considerations for Income: No additional information.

Personality Type: Investigative-Conventional-Realistic. **Career Clusters:** 04 Business, Management, and Administration; 15 Science, Technology, Engineering, and Mathematics; 16 Transportation, Distribution, and Logistics. **Career Pathways:** 04.1 Management; 15.1 Engineering and Technology; 16.2 Logistics, Planning, and Management Services. **Skills:** No data available.

Education and Training Programs: Logistics, Materials, and Supply Chain Management; Operations Management and Supervision; Transportation/Mobility Management. **Related Knowledge/Courses:** No data available.

Low Vision Therapists, Orientation and Mobility Specialists, and Vision Rehabilitation Therapists

❀ Annual Earnings: $66,780
❀ Beginning Wage: $42,820
❀ Earnings Growth Potential: Medium (35.9%)
❀ Growth: 23.1%
❀ Annual Job Openings: 8,338
❀ Self-Employed: 8.6%
❀ Part-Time: 29.8%
❀ Job Security: No data available
❀ Education/Training Required: Master's degree

The Department of Labor reports this information for the occupation Occupational Therapists. The job openings listed here are shared with other specializations within that occupation.

Industries in Which Income Is Highest

Industry	Average Annual Earnings	Number Employed
Administrative and Support Services	$76,890	1,480
Nursing and Residential Care Facilities	$71,350	10,670
Ambulatory Health Care Services	$69,870	29,860
Hospitals	$67,790	28,540
Educational Services	$60,150	13,090

Metropolitan Areas Where Income Is Highest

Metropolitan Area	Average Annual Earnings	Number Employed
Naples–Marco Island, FL	$96,120	80
Valdosta, GA	$89,280	70
Las Vegas–Paradise, NV	$88,090	430
Chico, CA	$86,610	70
San Francisco–Oakland–Fremont, CA	$85,770	950

Provide therapy to patients with visual impairments to improve their functioning in daily life activities. May train patients in activities such as computer use, communication skills, or home management skills. No task data available.

Other Considerations for Income: No additional information.

Personality Type: Social-Investigative-Realistic. **Career Cluster:** 08 Health Science. **Career Pathway:** 08.1 Therapeutic Services. **Skills:** No data available.

Education and Training Program: Occupational Therapy/Therapist. **Related Knowledge/Courses:** No data available.

Management Analysts

❋ Annual Earnings: $73,570
❋ Beginning Wage: $41,910
❋ Earnings Growth Potential: High (43.0%)
❋ Growth: 21.9%
❋ Annual Job Openings: 125,669
❋ Self-Employed: 27.0%
❋ Part-Time: 13.2%
❋ Job Security: More secure than most
❋ Education/Training Required: Work experience plus degree

Industries in Which Income Is Highest

Industry	Average Annual Earnings	Number Employed
Merchant Wholesalers, Durable Goods	$91,390	9,650
Publishing Industries (Except Internet)	$84,310	5,770
Other Information Services	$81,520	1,130
Professional, Scientific, and Technical Services	$81,290	210,420
Computer and Electronic Product Manufacturing	$78,090	6,420

Metropolitan Areas Where Income Is Highest

Metropolitan Area	Average Annual Earnings	Number Employed
Odessa, TX	$145,390	110
Naples–Marco Island, FL	$142,120	380
Portsmouth, NH-ME	$107,930	250
Punta Gorda, FL	$102,830	160
Idaho Falls, ID	$98,180	180

Conduct organizational studies and evaluations, design systems and procedures, conduct work simplifications and measurement studies, and prepare operations and procedures manuals to assist management in operating more efficiently and effectively. Includes program analysts and management consultants. Gather and organize information on problems or procedures. Analyze data gathered and develop solutions or alternative methods of proceeding. Confer with personnel concerned to ensure successful functioning of newly implemented systems or procedures. Develop and implement records management program for filing, protection, and retrieval of records and assure compliance with program. Review forms and reports and confer with management and users about format, distribution, and purpose and to identify problems and improvements. Document findings of study and prepare recommendations for implementation of new systems, procedures, or organizational changes. Interview personnel and conduct on-site observation to ascertain unit functions; work performed; and methods, equipment, and personnel used. Prepare manuals and train workers in use of new forms, reports, procedures, or equipment according to organizational policy. Design, evaluate, recommend, and approve changes of forms and reports. Plan study of work problems and procedures, such as organizational change, communications, information flow, integrated production methods, inventory control, or cost analysis. Recommend purchase of storage equipment and design area layout to locate equipment in space available.

Other Considerations for Income: Salaries for management analysts vary widely by years of experience and education, geographic location, specific expertise, and size of employer. Generally, management analysts employed in large firms or in metropolitan areas have the highest salaries. Salaried management analysts usually receive common benefits, such as health and life insurance, a retirement plan, vacation, and sick leave, as well as less common benefits, such as profit sharing and bonuses for outstanding work. In addition, all travel expenses usually are reimbursed by the employer. Self-employed consultants have to maintain their own office and provide their own benefits.

Personality Type: Investigative-Enterprising-Conventional. **Career Cluster:** 04 Business, Management, and Administration. **Career Pathway:** 04.1 Management. **Skills:** Operations Analysis; Installation; Systems Evaluation; Management of Financial Resources; Quality Control Analysis; Operation and Control; Systems Analysis; Equipment Maintenance.

Education and Training Programs: Business Administration and Management, General; Business/Commerce, General. **Related Knowledge/Courses:** Personnel and Human Resources; Clerical; Sales and Marketing; Economics and Accounting; Customer and Personal Service; Administration and Management.

Marine Architects

- ❋ Annual Earnings: $74,140
- ❋ Beginning Wage: $43,070
- ❋ Earnings Growth Potential: High (41.9%)
- ❋ Growth: 10.9%
- ❋ Annual Job Openings: 495
- ❋ Self-Employed: 12.4%
- ❋ Part-Time: 2.6%
- ❋ Job Security: Less secure than most
- ❋ Education/Training Required: Bachelor's degree

The Department of Labor reports this information for the occupation Marine Engineers and Naval Architects. The job openings listed here are shared with other specializations within that occupation, including Marine Engineers.

Industries in Which Income Is Highest

Industry	Average Annual Earnings	Number Employed
Administrative and Support Services	$120,480	40
Federal, State, and Local Government	$93,940	990
Water Transportation	$82,150	520
Transportation Equipment Manufacturing	$79,390	910
Educational Services	$68,770	50

Metropolitan Areas Where Income Is Highest

Metropolitan Area	Average Annual Earnings	Number Employed
Washington-Arlington-Alexandria, DC-VA-MD-WV	$105,730	830
Boston-Cambridge-Quincy, MA-NH	$94,800	50
Philadelphia-Camden-Wilmington, PA-NJ-DE-MD	$90,930	90
Seattle-Tacoma-Bellevue, WA	$80,110	290
New Orleans–Metairie–Kenner, LA	$74,290	110

Design and oversee construction and repair of marine craft and floating structures such as ships, barges, tugs, dredges, submarines, torpedoes, floats, and buoys. May confer with marine engineers. Design complete hull and superstructure according to specifications and test data and in conformity with standards of safety, efficiency, and economy. Design layout of craft interior, including cargo space, passenger compartments, ladder wells, and elevators. Study design proposals and specifications to establish basic characteristics of craft, such as size, weight, speed, propulsion, displacement, and draft. Confer with marine engineering personnel to establish arrangement of boiler room equipment and propulsion machinery, heating and ventilating systems, refrigeration equipment, piping, and other functional equipment. Evaluate performance of craft during dock and sea trials to determine design changes and conformance with national and international standards. Oversee construction and testing of prototype in model basin and develop sectional and waterline curves of hull to establish center of gravity, ideal hull form, and buoyancy and stability data.

Other Considerations for Income: As a group, engineers earn some of the highest average starting salaries among those holding bachelor's degrees. Marine Architects are paid in the middle range among the various kinds of engineers. Separate earnings figures for Marine Architects with various degrees are not available.

Personality Type: Investigative-Realistic-Artistic. **Career Cluster:** 15 Science, Technology, Engineering, and Mathematics. **Career Pathway:** 15.1 Engineering and Technology. **Skills:** Science; Mathematics; Operations Analysis; Technology Design; Complex Problem Solving; Equipment Selection; Installation; Systems Analysis.

Education and Training Program: Naval Architecture and Marine Engineering. **Related Knowledge/Courses:** Engineering and Technology; Design; Physics; Building and Construction; Mechanical; Production and Processing.

Marine Engineers

- ❋ Annual Earnings: $74,140
- ❋ Beginning Wage: $43,070
- ❋ Earnings Growth Potential: High (41.9%)
- ❋ Growth: 10.9%
- ❋ Annual Job Openings: 495
- ❋ Self-Employed: 12.4%
- ❋ Part-Time: 2.6%
- ❋ Job Security: Less secure than most
- ❋ Education/Training Required: Bachelor's degree

The Department of Labor reports this information for the occupation Marine Engineers and Naval Architects. The job openings listed here are shared with other specializations within that occupation, including Marine Architects.

Industries in Which Income Is Highest

Industry	Average Annual Earnings	Number Employed
Administrative and Support Services	$120,480	40
Federal, State, and Local Government	$93,940	990
Water Transportation	$82,150	520
Transportation Equipment Manufacturing	$79,390	910
Educational Services	$68,770	50

Metropolitan Areas Where Income Is Highest

Metropolitan Area	Average Annual Earnings	Number Employed
Washington-Arlington-Alexandria, DC-VA-MD-WV	$105,730	830
Boston-Cambridge-Quincy, MA-NH	$94,800	50
Philadelphia-Camden-Wilmington, PA-NJ-DE-MD	$90,930	90
Seattle-Tacoma-Bellevue, WA	$80,110	290
New Orleans–Metairie–Kenner, LA	$74,290	110

Design, develop, and take responsibility for the installation of ship machinery and related equipment, including propulsion machines and power supply systems. Prepare, or direct the preparation of, product or system layouts and detailed drawings and schematics. Inspect marine equipment and machinery in order to draw up work requests and job specifications. Conduct analytical, environmental, operational, or performance studies in order to develop designs for products such as marine engines, equipment, and structures. Design and oversee testing, installation, and repair of marine apparatus and equipment. Prepare plans, estimates, design and construction schedules, and contract specifications, including any special provisions. Investigate and observe tests on machinery and equipment for compliance with standards. Coordinate activities with regulatory bodies in order to ensure repairs and alterations are at minimum cost consistent with safety. Prepare technical reports for use by engineering, management, or sales personnel.

Conduct environmental, operational, or performance tests on marine machinery and equipment. Maintain contact with, and formulate reports for, contractors and clients to ensure completion of work at minimum cost. Evaluate operation of marine equipment during acceptance testing and shakedown cruises. Analyze data in order to determine feasibility of product proposals. Determine conditions under which tests are to be conducted, as well as sequences and phases of test operations. Procure materials needed to repair marine equipment and machinery. Confer with research personnel to clarify or resolve problems and to develop or modify designs. Review work requests and compare them with previous work completed on ships to ensure that costs are economically sound. Act as liaisons between ships' captains and shore personnel to ensure that schedules and budgets are maintained and that ships are operated safely and efficiently. Perform monitoring activities to ensure that ships comply with international regulations and standards for lifesaving equipment and pollution preventatives.

Other Considerations for Income: As a group, engineers earn some of the highest average starting salaries among those holding bachelor's degrees. Marine Engineers are paid in the middle range among the various kinds of engineers. Separate earnings figures for Marine Engineers with various degrees are not available.

Personality Type: Investigative-Realistic. **Career Cluster:** 15 Science, Technology, Engineering, and Mathematics. **Career Pathway:** 15.1 Engineering and Technology. **Skills:** Science; Technology Design; Installation; Mathematics; Operations Analysis; Equipment Selection; Systems Analysis; Troubleshooting.

Education and Training Program: Naval Architecture and Marine Engineering. **Related Knowledge/Courses:** Engineering and Technology; Design; Mechanical; Physics; Building and Construction; Computers and Electronics.

Marine Engineers and Naval Architects

See *Marine Architects* and *Marine Engineers, described separately.*

Market Research Analysts

* ❋ Annual Earnings: $61,070
* ❋ Beginning Wage: $33,770
* ❋ Earnings Growth Potential: High (44.7%)
* ❋ Growth: 20.1%
* ❋ Annual Job Openings: 45,015
* ❋ Self-Employed: 6.6%
* ❋ Part-Time: 12.5%
* ❋ Job Security: Less secure than most
* ❋ Education/Training Required: Bachelor's degree

Industries in Which Income Is Highest

Industry	Average Annual Earnings	Number Employed
Computer and Electronic Product Manufacturing	$85,920	7,470
Transportation Equipment Manufacturing	$79,600	1,480
Publishing Industries (Except Internet)	$78,080	11,840
Telecommunications	$76,350	6,910
Merchant Wholesalers, Durable Goods	$67,840	10,110

Metropolitan Areas Where Income Is Highest

Metropolitan Area	Average Annual Earnings	Number Employed
San Jose–Sunnyvale–Santa Clara, CA	$100,070	5,170
Spartanburg, SC	$99,660	60
Seattle-Tacoma-Bellevue, WA	$91,040	7,560
Durham, NC	$86,440	690
Austin–Round Rock, TX	$81,380	2,440

Research market conditions in local, regional, or national areas to determine potential sales of a product or service. May gather information on competitors, prices, sales, and methods of marketing and distribution. May use survey results to create a marketing campaign based on regional preferences and buying habits. Collect and analyze data on customer demographics, preferences, needs, and buying habits to identify potential markets and factors affecting product demand. Prepare reports of findings, illustrating data graphically and translating complex findings into written text. Measure and assess customer and employee satisfaction. Forecast and track marketing and sales trends, analyzing collected data. Seek and provide information to help companies determine their position in the marketplace. Measure the effectiveness of marketing, advertising, and communications programs and strategies. Conduct research on consumer opinions and marketing strategies, collaborating with marketing professionals, statisticians, pollsters, and other professionals. Attend staff conferences to provide management with information and proposals concerning the promotion, distribution, design, and pricing of company products or services. Gather data on competitors and analyze their prices, sales, and method of marketing and distribution. Monitor industry statistics and follow trends in trade literature. Devise and evaluate methods and procedures for collecting data, such as surveys, opinion polls, or questionnaires, or arrange to obtain existing data. Develop and implement procedures for identifying advertising needs. Direct trained survey interviewers.

Other Considerations for Income: No additional information.

Personality Type: Investigative-Enterprising-Conventional. **Career Clusters:** 04 Business, Management, and Administration; 14 Marketing, Sales, and Service; 15 Science, Technology, Engineering, and Mathematics. **Career Pathways:** 04.1 Management; 14.5 Marketing Information Management and Research; 15.3 Science and Mathematics. **Skills:** Writing; Negotiation; Persuasion; Judgment and Decision Making; Reading Comprehension; Management of Financial Resources; Coordination; Active Listening.

Education and Training Programs: Applied Economics; Business/Managerial Economics; Econometrics and Quantitative Economics; Economics, General; International Economics; Marketing Research. **Related Knowledge/Courses:** Sales and Marketing; Clerical; Sociology and Anthropology; Economics and Accounting; Computers and Electronics; Personnel and Human Resources.

Marketing Managers

❊ Annual Earnings: $108,580
❊ Beginning Wage: $55,270
❊ Earnings Growth Potential: High (49.1%)
❊ Growth: 14.4%
❊ Annual Job Openings: 20,189
❊ Self-Employed: 2.3%
❊ Part-Time: 4.1%
❊ Job Security: Least secure
❊ Education/Training Required: Work experience plus degree

Industries in Which Income Is Highest

Industry	Average Annual Earnings	Number Employed
Motion Picture and Sound Recording Industries	$147,080	1,720
Other Information Services	$130,740	1,110
Securities, Commodity Contracts, and Other Financial Investments and Related Activities	$128,670	6,910
Computer and Electronic Product Manufacturing	$123,790	9,770
Merchant Wholesalers, Nondurable Goods	$121,070	3,470

Metropolitan Areas Where Income Is Highest

Metropolitan Area	Average Annual Earnings	Number Employed
San Jose–Sunnyvale–Santa Clara, CA	$148,680	5,590
San Francisco–Oakland–Fremont, CA	$140,480	6,580
Modesto, CA	$136,560	160
New York–Northern New Jersey–Long Island, NY-NJ-PA	$136,350	17,850
Salinas, CA	$133,920	240

Determine the demand for products and services offered by firms and their competitors and identify potential customers. Develop pricing strategies with the goal of maximizing firms' profits or shares of the market while ensuring that firms' customers are satisfied. Oversee product development or monitor trends that indicate the need for new products and services. Formulate, direct, and coordinate marketing activities and policies to promote products and services, working with advertising and promotion managers. Identify, develop, and evaluate marketing strategies, based on knowledge of establishment objectives, market characteristics, and cost and markup factors. Direct the hiring, training, and performance evaluations of marketing and sales staff and oversee their daily activities. Evaluate the financial aspects of product development, such as budgets, expenditures, research and development appropriations, and return-on-investment and profit-loss projections. Develop pricing strategies, balancing firm objectives and customer satisfaction. Compile lists describing product or service offerings. Initiate market research studies and analyze their findings. Use sales forecasting and strategic planning to ensure the sale and profitability of products, lines, or services, analyzing business developments and monitoring market trends. Coordinate and participate in promotional activities and trade shows, working with developers, advertisers, and production managers to market products and services. Consult with buying personnel to gain advice regarding the types of products or services expected to be in demand. Conduct economic and commercial surveys to identify potential markets for products and services. Select products and accessories to be displayed at trade or special production shows. Negotiate contracts with vendors and distributors to manage product distribution, establishing distribution networks and developing distribution strategies. Consult with product development personnel on product specifications such as design, color, and packaging. Advise businesses and other groups on local, national, and international factors affecting the buying and selling of products and services. Confer with legal staff to resolve problems such as copyright infringement and royalty sharing with outside producers and distributors.

Other Considerations for Income: Salary levels vary substantially, depending upon the level of managerial responsibility, length of service, education, size of firm, location, and industry. For example, manufacturing firms usually pay these managers higher salaries than nonmanufacturing firms. Many managers earn bonuses equal to 10 percent or more of their salaries.

Personality Type: Enterprising-Conventional. **Career Cluster:** 14 Marketing, Sales, and Service. **Career Pathways:** 14.1 Management and Entrepreneurship; 14.2 Professional Sales and Marketing; 14.5 Marketing Information Management and Research. **Skills:** Management of Financial Resources; Systems Analysis; Systems Evaluation; Management of Personnel Resources; Negotiation; Persuasion; Management of Material Resources; Social Perceptiveness.

Education and Training Programs: Apparel and Textile Marketing Management; Consumer Merchandising/ Retailing Management; International Marketing; Marketing Research; Marketing, Other; Marketing/Marketing Management, General. **Related Knowledge/Courses:** Sales and Marketing; Personnel and Human Resources; Customer and Personal Service; Communications and Media; Economics and Accounting; Sociology and Anthropology.

Materials Engineers

* Annual Earnings: $81,820
* Beginning Wage: $51,420
* Earnings Growth Potential: Medium (37.2%)
* Growth: 4.0%
* Annual Job Openings: 1,390
* Self-Employed: 0.0%
* Part-Time: 3.2%
* Job Security: More secure than most
* Education/Training Required: Bachelor's degree

Industries in Which Income Is Highest

Industry	Average Annual Earnings	Number Employed
Federal, State, and Local Government	$96,130	1,610
Transportation Equipment Manufacturing	$87,530	3,820
Professional, Scientific, and Technical Services	$84,420	3,950
Machinery Manufacturing	$82,070	1,250
Computer and Electronic Product Manufacturing	$81,690	4,630

Metropolitan Areas Where Income Is Highest

Metropolitan Area	Average Annual Earnings	Number Employed
Washington-Arlington-Alexandria, DC-VA-MD-WV	$112,210	510
Rochester, NY	$109,860	100
Dayton, OH	$101,070	450
San Jose–Sunnyvale–Santa Clara, CA	$100,520	750
St. Louis, MO-IL	$95,570	330

Evaluate materials and develop machinery and processes to manufacture materials for use in products that must meet specialized design and performance specifications. Develop new uses for known materials. Includes those working with composite materials or specializing in one type of material, such as graphite, metal and metal alloys, ceramics and glass, plastics and polymers, and naturally occurring materials. Analyze product failure data and laboratory test results in order to determine causes of problems and develop solutions. Monitor material performance and evaluate material deterioration. Supervise the work of technologists, technicians, and other engineers and scientists. Design and direct the testing and/or control of processing procedures. Evaluate technical specifications and economic factors relating to process or product design objectives. Conduct or supervise tests on raw materials or finished products in order to ensure their quality. Perform managerial functions such as preparing proposals and budgets, analyzing labor costs, and writing reports. Solve problems in a number of engineering fields, such as mechanical, chemical, electrical, civil, nuclear, and aerospace. Plan and evaluate new projects, consulting with other engineers and corporate executives as necessary. Review new product plans and make recommendations for material selection based on design objectives, such as strength, weight, heat resistance, electrical conductivity, and cost. Design processing plants and equipment. Modify properties of metal alloys, using thermal and mechanical treatments. Guide technical staff engaged in developing materials for specific uses in projected products or devices. Plan and implement laboratory operations for the purpose of developing material and fabrication procedures that meet cost, product specification, and performance standards. Determine appropriate methods for fabricating and joining materials. Conduct training sessions on new material products, applications, or manufacturing methods for customers and their employees. Supervise production and testing processes in industrial settings such as metal refining facilities, smelting or foundry operations, or non-metallic materials production operations. Write for technical magazines, journals, and trade association publications. Replicate the characteristics of materials and their components with computers.

Other Considerations for Income: As a group, engineers earn some of the highest average starting salaries among those holding bachelor's degrees. Materials Engineers are paid in the middle range among the various kinds of engineers. According to a 2007 survey by the National Association of Colleges and Employers, average starting salaries for Materials Engineers were $56,233 with a bachelor's.

Personality Type: Investigative-Realistic-Enterprising. **Career Cluster:** 15 Science, Technology, Engineering, and Mathematics. **Career Pathway:** 15.1 Engineering and Technology. **Skills:** Science; Mathematics; Quality Control Analysis; Equipment Selection; Reading Comprehension; Technology Design; Troubleshooting; Complex Problem Solving.

Education and Training Programs: Ceramic Sciences and Engineering; Materials Engineering; Metallurgical Engineering. **Related Knowledge/Courses:** Engineering and Technology; Chemistry; Physics; Design; Mathematics; Mechanical.

Materials Scientists

- ❀ Annual Earnings: $80,230
- ❀ Beginning Wage: $43,670
- ❀ Earnings Growth Potential: High (45.6%)
- ❀ Growth: 8.7%
- ❀ Annual Job Openings: 1,039
- ❀ Self-Employed: 1.0%
- ❀ Part-Time: 3.9%
- ❀ Job Security: Less secure than most
- ❀ Education/Training Required: Bachelor's degree

Industries in Which Income Is Highest

Industry	Average Annual Earnings	Number Employed
Federal, State, and Local Government	$91,630	110
Miscellaneous Manufacturing	$90,680	160
Management of Companies and Enterprises	$86,500	1,640
Nonmetallic Mineral Product Manufacturing	$86,500	90
Computer and Electronic Product Manufacturing	$86,250	500

Metropolitan Areas Where Income Is Highest

Metropolitan Area	Average Annual Earnings	Number Employed
San Francisco–Oakland–Fremont, CA	$105,350	80
San Jose–Sunnyvale–Santa Clara, CA	$97,840	80
Dayton, OH	$96,130	60
Boston-Cambridge-Quincy, MA-NH	$94,270	360
Chicago-Naperville-Joliet, IL-IN-WI	$91,860	860

Research and study the structures and chemical properties of various natural and manmade materials, including metals, alloys, rubber, ceramics, semiconductors, polymers, and glass. Determine ways to strengthen or combine materials or develop new materials with new or specific properties for use in a variety of products and applications. Plan laboratory experiments to confirm feasibility of processes and techniques used in the production of materials having special characteristics. Confer with customers in order to determine how materials can be tailored to suit their needs. Conduct research into the structures and properties of materials such as metals, alloys, polymers, and ceramics to obtain information that could be used to develop new products or enhance existing ones. Prepare reports of materials study findings for the use of other scientists and requestors. Devise testing methods to evaluate the effects of various conditions on particular materials. Determine ways to strengthen or combine materials or develop new materials with new or specific properties for use in a variety of products and applications. Recommend materials for reliable performance in various environments. Test individual parts and products to ensure that manufacturer and governmental quality and safety standards are met. Visit suppliers of materials or users of products to gather specific information. Research methods of processing, forming, and firing materials to develop such products as ceramic fillings for teeth, unbreakable dinner plates, and telescope lenses. Study the nature, structure, and physical properties of metals and their alloys and their responses to applied forces. Monitor production processes to ensure that equipment is used efficiently and that projects are completed within appropriate time frames and budgets. Test material samples for tolerance under tension, compression, and shear to determine the cause of metal failures. Test metals to determine whether they meet specifications of mechanical strength; strength-weight ratio; ductility; magnetic and electrical properties; and resistance to abrasion, corrosion, heat, and cold. Teach in colleges and universities.

Other Considerations for Income: According to the National Association of Colleges and Employers, beginning salary offers in July 2007 for graduates with bachelor's degrees in chemistry averaged $41,506 a year.

Personality Type: Investigative-Realistic. **Career Cluster:** 15 Science, Technology, Engineering, and Mathematics. **Career Pathway:** 15.3 Science and Mathematics. **Skills:** Science; Programming; Technology Design; Quality Control Analysis; Equipment Selection; Mathematics; Installation; Troubleshooting.

Education and Training Program: Materials Science. **Related Knowledge/Courses:** Chemistry; Engineering and Technology; Mathematics; Physics; Production and Processing; Administration and Management.

Mates—Ship, Boat, and Barge

* Annual Earnings: $61,960
* Beginning Wage: $29,330
* Earnings Growth Potential: Very high (52.7%)
* Growth: 17.9%
* Annual Job Openings: 2,665
* Self-Employed: 6.8%
* Part-Time: 4.8%
* Job Security: Least secure
* Education/Training Required: Work experience in a related occupation

The Department of Labor reports this information for the occupation Captains, Mates, and Pilots of Water Vessels. The job openings listed here are shared with other specializations

within that occupation, including Pilots, Ship; and Ship and Boat Captains.

Industries in Which Income Is Highest

Industry	Average Annual Earnings	Number Employed
Support Activities for Transportation	$67,910	9,510
Water Transportation	$67,040	11,640
Federal, State, and Local Government	$55,620	2,180
Scenic and Sightseeing Transportation	$38,380	3,660

Metropolitan Areas Where Income Is Highest

Metropolitan Area	Average Annual Earnings	Number Employed
Detroit-Warren-Livonia, MI	$137,730	60
Memphis, TN-MS-AR	$89,540	190
Houston–Sugar Land–Baytown, TX	$79,320	1,530
Baton Rouge, LA	$78,360	480
Houma–Bayou Cane–Thibodaux, LA	$75,570	3,350

Supervise and coordinate activities of crew aboard ships, boats, barges, or dredges. Determine geographical position of ship, using lorans, azimuths of celestial bodies, or computers, and use this information to determine the course and speed of the ship. Observe water from ship's masthead to advise on navigational direction. Supervise crews in cleaning and maintaining decks, superstructures, and bridges. Supervise crew members in the repair or replacement of defective gear and equipment. Steer vessels, using navigational devices such as compasses and sextants and navigational aids such as lighthouses and buoys. Inspect equipment such as cargo-handling gear, lifesaving equipment, visual-signaling equipment, and fishing, towing, or dredging gear to detect problems. Arrange for ships to be stocked, fueled, and repaired. Assume command of vessel in the event that ship's master becomes incapacitated. Participate in activities related to maintenance of vessel security. Stand watches on vessel during specified periods while vessel is under way. Observe loading and unloading of cargo and equipment to ensure that handling and storage are performed according to specifications.

Other Considerations for Income: Because companies provide food and housing at sea and it is difficult to spend money while working, the workers are able to save a large portion of their pay. The rate of unionization for marine transportation workers is about 16 percent, higher than the average for all occupations. Unionization rates vary by region. In unionized areas, merchant marine officers and seamen, both veterans and beginners, are hired for voyages through union hiring halls or directly by shipping companies. Hiring halls rank the candidates by the length of time the person has been out of work and fill open slots accordingly. Most major seaports have hiring halls.

Personality Type: Enterprising-Realistic-Conventional. **Career Cluster:** 16 Transportation, Distribution, and Logistics. **Career Pathway:** 16.1 Transportation Operations. **Skills:** Equipment Maintenance; Repairing; Operation and Control; Operation Monitoring; Troubleshooting; Installation; Equipment Selection; Judgment and Decision Making.

Education and Training Programs: Commercial Fishing; Marine Science/Merchant Marine Officer; Marine Transportation, Other. **Related Knowledge/Courses:** Transportation; Geography; Public Safety and Security; Telecommunications; Personnel and Human Resources; Mechanical.

Mathematical Science Teachers, Postsecondary

- ❊ Annual Earnings: $61,120
- ❊ Beginning Wage: $33,800
- ❊ Earnings Growth Potential: High (44.7%)
- ❊ Growth: 22.9%
- ❊ Annual Job Openings: 7,663
- ❊ Self-Employed: 0.4%
- ❊ Part-Time: 27.8%
- ❊ Job Security: Most secure
- ❊ Education/Training Required: Doctoral degree

Industries in Which Income Is Highest

Industry	Average Annual Earnings	Number Employed
Educational Services	$61,100	45,660

Metropolitan Areas Where Income Is Highest

Metropolitan Area	Average Annual Earnings	Number Employed
San Diego–Carlsbad–San Marcos, CA	$95,360	680
Lubbock, TX	$95,060	140
Madison, WI	$91,460	140
San Francisco–Oakland–Fremont, CA	$90,560	660
Columbus, OH	$89,640	360

Teach courses pertaining to mathematical concepts, statistics, and actuarial science and to the application of original and standardized mathematical techniques in solving specific problems and situations. Evaluate and grade students' classwork, assignments, and papers. Compile, administer, and grade examinations or assign this work to others. Prepare and deliver lectures to undergraduate and/or graduate students on topics such as linear algebra, differential equations, and discrete mathematics. Prepare course materials such as syllabi, homework assignments, and handouts. Maintain student attendance records, grades, and other required records. Maintain regularly scheduled office hours to advise and assist students. Plan, evaluate, and revise curricula, course content, and course materials and methods of instruction. Initiate, facilitate, and moderate classroom discussions. Select and obtain materials and supplies such as textbooks. Keep abreast of developments in their field by reading current literature, talking with colleagues, and participating in professional conferences. Advise students on academic and vocational curricula and on career issues. Collaborate with colleagues to address teaching and research issues. Serve on academic or administrative committees that deal with institutional policies, departmental matters, and academic issues. Participate in student recruitment, registration, and placement activities. Perform administrative duties such as serving as department head. Conduct research in a particular field of knowledge and publish findings in books, professional journals, and/or electronic media. Supervise undergraduate and/or graduate teaching, internship, and research work. Act as advisers to student organizations. Participate in campus and community events. Write grant proposals to procure external research funding. Compile bibliographies of specialized materials for outside reading assignments. Provide professional consulting services to government and/or industry.

Other Considerations for Income: Earnings for college faculty vary according to rank and type of institution, geographic area, and field. According to a 2006–2007 survey by the American Association of University Professors, salaries for full-time faculty averaged $73,207. By rank, the average was $98,974 for professors, $69,911 for associate professors, $58,662 for assistant professors, $42,609 for instructors, and $48,289 for lecturers. Faculty in 4-year institutions earn higher salaries, on average, than do those in 2-year schools. Many faculty members have significant earnings in addition to their base salary from consulting, teaching additional courses, research, writing for publication, or other employment. In addition, many college and university faculty enjoy unique benefits, including access to campus facilities, tuition waivers for dependents, housing and travel allowances, and paid leave for sabbaticals. Part-time faculty and instructors usually have fewer benefits than full-time faculty.

Personality Type: Social-Investigative-Artistic. **Career Clusters:**05 Education and Training; 15 Science, Technology, Engineering, and Mathematics. **Career Pathways:**05.3 Teaching/Training; 15.3 Science and Mathematics. **Skills:** Mathematics; Instructing; Science; Learning Strategies; Critical Thinking; Complex Problem Solving; Speaking; Reading Comprehension.

Education and Training Programs: Algebra and Number Theory; Analysis and Functional Analysis; Applied Mathematics, General; Business Statistics; Geometry/ Geometric Analysis; Logic; Mathematical Statistics and Probability; Mathematics and Statistics, Other; Mathematics, General; Mathematics, Other; Statistics, General; Topology and Foundations. **Related Knowledge/ Courses:** Mathematics; Education and Training; Physics; Computers and Electronics; English Language; Communications and Media.

Mathematicians

- ❀ Annual Earnings: $95,150
- ❀ Beginning Wage: $53,570
- ❀ Earnings Growth Potential: High (43.7%)
- ❀ Growth: 10.2%
- ❀ Annual Job Openings: 473
- ❀ Self-Employed: 0.0%
- ❀ Part-Time: 5.6%
- ❀ Job Security: Most secure
- ❀ Education/Training Required: Doctoral degree

Industries in Which Income Is Highest

Industry	Average Annual Earnings	Number Employed
Professional, Scientific, and Technical Services	$100,010	1,200
Federal, State, and Local Government	$99,740	1,000
Insurance Carriers and Related Activities	$91,530	60
Educational Services	$63,190	360

Metropolitan Areas Where Income Is Highest

Metropolitan Area	Average Annual Earnings	Number Employed
Washington-Arlington-Alexandria, DC-VA-MD-WV	$123,910	370
San Diego–Carlsbad–San Marcos, CA	$112,850	90
Huntsville, AL	$98,250	50
Baltimore-Towson, MD	$91,800	140
New York–Northern New Jersey–Long Island, NY-NJ-PA	$90,340	160

Conduct research in fundamental mathematics or in application of mathematical techniques to science, management, and other fields. Solve or direct solutions to problems in various fields by mathematical methods. Apply mathematical theories and techniques to the solution of practical problems in business, engineering, the sciences, or other fields. Develop computational methods for solving problems that occur in areas of science and engineering or that come from applications in business or industry. Maintain knowledge in the field by reading professional journals, talking with other mathematicians, and attending professional conferences. Perform computations and apply methods of numerical analysis to data. Develop mathematical or statistical models of phenomena to be used for analysis or for computational simulation. Assemble sets of assumptions and explore the consequences of each set. Address the relationships of quantities, magnitudes, and forms through the use of numbers and symbols. Develop new principles and new relationships between existing mathematical principles to advance mathematical science. Design, analyze, and decipher encryption systems designed to transmit military, political, financial, or law-enforcement-related information in code. Conduct research to extend mathematical knowledge in traditional areas, such as algebra, geometry, probability, and logic.

Other Considerations for Income: In early 2007, the average annual salary for mathematicians employed by the federal government in supervisory, nonsupervisory, and managerial positions was $93,539; for mathematical statisticians, $96,121; and for cryptanalysts, the average was $90,435.

Personality Type: Investigative-Conventional-Artistic. **Career Cluster:** 15 Science, Technology, Engineering, and Mathematics. **Career Pathway:** 15.3 Science and Mathematics. **Skills:** Programming; Science; Mathematics; Complex Problem Solving; Operations Analysis; Critical Thinking; Reading Comprehension; Active Learning.

Education and Training Programs: Algebra and Number Theory; Analysis and Functional Analysis; Applied Mathematics, General; Applied Mathematics, Other; Computational Mathematics; Geometry/Geometric Analysis; Logic; Mathematical Statistics and Probability; Mathematics and Statistics, Other; Mathematics, General; Mathematics, Other; Topology and Foundations. **Related Knowledge/Courses:** Mathematics; Physics; Computers and Electronics; Engineering and Technology; English Language.

Mechanical Engineering Technicians

❋ Annual Earnings: $48,130
❋ Beginning Wage: $31,110
❋ Earnings Growth Potential: Medium (35.4%)
❋ Growth: 6.4%
❋ Annual Job Openings: 3,710
❋ Self-Employed: 0.8%
❋ Part-Time: 5.9%
❋ Job Security: More secure than most
❋ Education/Training Required: Associate degree

Industries in Which Income Is Highest

Industry	Average Annual Earnings	Number Employed
Merchant Wholesalers, Durable Goods	$49,030	1,580
Management of Companies and Enterprises	$48,690	1,100
Professional, Scientific, and Technical Services	$48,650	17,260
Transportation Equipment Manufacturing	$48,570	3,820
Computer and Electronic Product Manufacturing	$48,090	4,470

Metropolitan Areas Where Income Is Highest

Metropolitan Area	Average Annual Earnings	Number Employed
Oxnard–Thousand Oaks–Ventura, CA	$65,940	60
San Jose–Sunnyvale–Santa Clara, CA	$62,420	840
Greensboro–High Point, NC	$60,610	120
Portland-Vancouver-Beaverton, OR-WA	$60,020	420
Seattle-Tacoma-Bellevue, WA	$59,850	990

Apply theory and principles of mechanical engineering to modify, develop, and test machinery and equipment under direction of engineering staff or physical scientists. Prepare parts sketches and write work orders and purchase requests to be furnished by outside contractors. Draft detail drawing or sketch for drafting room completion or to request parts fabrication by machine, sheet, or wood shops. Review project instructions and blueprints to ascertain test specifications, procedures, and objectives and test nature of technical problems such as redesign. Review project instructions and specifications to identify, modify, and plan requirements fabrication, assembly, and testing. Devise, fabricate, and assemble new or modified mechanical components for products such as industrial machinery or equipment and measuring instruments. Discuss changes in design, method of manufacture and assembly, and drafting techniques and procedures with staff and coordinate corrections. Set up and conduct tests of complete units and components under operational conditions to investigate proposals for improving equipment performance. Inspect lines and figures for clarity and return erroneous drawings to designer for correction. Analyze test results in relation to design or rated specifications and test objectives and modify or adjust equipment to meet specifications. Evaluate tool drawing designs by measuring drawing dimensions and comparing with original specifications for form and function, using engineering skills. Confer with technicians, submit reports of test results to engineering department, and recommend design or material changes. Calculate required capacities for equipment of proposed system to obtain specified performance and submit data to engineering personnel for approval. Record test procedures and results, numerical and graphical data, and recommendations for changes in product or test methods. Read dials and meters to determine amperage, voltage, and electrical output and input at specific operating temperature to analyze parts performance.

Other Considerations for Income: Mechanical Engineering Technicians are paid in the middle range of earnings, compared to those of other kinds of engineering technicians.

Personality Type: Realistic-Investigative. **Career Clusters:** 01 Agriculture, Food and Natural Resource; 13 Manufacturing. **Career Pathways:** 01.5 Natural Resources Systems; 13.3 Maintenance, Installation and Repair. **Skills:** Installation; Troubleshooting; Technology Design; Operations Analysis; Equipment Selection; Science; Mathematics; Systems Evaluation.

Education and Training Programs: Mechanical Engineering Related Technologies/Technicians, Other; Mechanical Engineering/Mechanical Technology/Technician. **Related Knowledge/Courses:** Mechanical; Design; Engineering and Technology; Physics; Production and Processing; Chemistry.

Mechanical Engineers

- ❋ Annual Earnings: $74,920
- ❋ Beginning Wage: $47,900
- ❋ Earnings Growth Potential: Medium (36.1%)
- ❋ Growth: 4.2%
- ❋ Annual Job Openings: 12,394
- ❋ Self-Employed: 2.2%
- ❋ Part-Time: 1.9%
- ❋ Job Security: More secure than most
- ❋ Education/Training Required: Bachelor's degree

Industries in Which Income Is Highest

Industry	Average Annual Earnings	Number Employed
Federal, State, and Local Government	$86,810	11,330
Management of Companies and Enterprises	$83,970	6,280
Computer and Electronic Product Manufacturing	$80,330	22,300
Professional, Scientific, and Technical Services	$79,060	69,520
Paper Manufacturing	$78,340	1,330

Metropolitan Areas Where Income Is Highest

Metropolitan Area	Average Annual Earnings	Number Employed
San Jose–Sunnyvale–Santa Clara, CA	$98,770	4,250
Washington-Arlington-Alexandria, DC-VA-MD-WV	$96,800	5,430
Albuquerque, NM	$93,890	890
Boulder, CO	$93,730	950
Denver-Aurora, CO	$92,810	2,150

Perform engineering duties in planning and designing tools, engines, machines, and other mechanically functioning equipment. Oversee installation, operation, maintenance, and repair of such equipment as centralized heat, gas, water, and steam systems. Read and interpret blueprints, technical drawings, schematics, and computer-generated reports. Confer with engineers and other personnel to implement operating procedures, resolve system malfunctions, and provide technical information. Research and analyze customer design proposals, specifications, manuals, and other data to evaluate the feasibility, cost, and maintenance requirements of designs or applications. Specify system components or direct modification of products to ensure conformance with engineering design and performance specifications. Research, design, evaluate, install, operate, and maintain mechanical products, equipment, systems, and processes to meet requirements, applying knowledge of engineering principles. Investigate equipment failures and difficulties to diagnose faulty operation and to make recommendations to maintenance crew. Assist drafters in developing the structural design of products, using drafting tools, computer-assisted design (CAD), or drafting equipment and software. Provide feedback to design engineers on customer problems and needs. Oversee installation, operation, maintenance, and repair to ensure that machines and equipment are installed and functioning according to specifications. Conduct research that tests and analyzes the feasibility, design, operation, and performance of equipment, components, and systems. Recommend design modifications to eliminate machine or system malfunctions. Develop and test models of alternate designs and processing methods to assess feasibility, operating condition effects, possible new applications, and necessity of modification. Develop, coordinate, and monitor all aspects of production, including selection of manufacturing methods, fabrication, and operation of product designs. Estimate costs and submit bids for engineering, construction, or extraction projects and prepare contract documents.

Other Considerations for Income: As a group, engineers earn some of the highest average starting salaries among those holding bachelor's degrees. Mechanical Engineers are paid in the low-to-middle range among the various kinds of engineers. According to a 2007 survey by the National Association of Colleges and Employers, average starting salaries for Mechanical Engineers were $54,128 with a bachelor's, $62,798 with a master's, and $72,763 with a Ph.D.

Personality Type: Investigative-Realistic-Conventional. **Career Cluster:** 15 Science, Technology, Engineering, and Mathematics. **Career Pathway:** 15.1 Engineering and Technology. **Skills:** Science; Operations Analysis; Installation; Complex Problem Solving; Mathematics; Systems Analysis; Judgment and Decision Making; Coordination.

Education and Training Program: Mechanical Engineering. **Related Knowledge/Courses:** Design; Engineering and Technology; Physics; Mechanical; Production and Processing; Mathematics.

Medical and Clinical Laboratory Technologists

❀ Annual Earnings: $53,500
❀ Beginning Wage: $36,180
❀ Earnings Growth Potential: Low (32.4%)
❀ Growth: 12.4%
❀ Annual Job Openings: 11,457
❀ Self-Employed: 0.7%
❀ Part-Time: 14.3%
❀ Job Security: Most secure
❀ Education/Training Required: Bachelor's degree

Industries in Which Income Is Highest

Industry	Average Annual Earnings	Number Employed
Federal, State, and Local Government	$58,080	7,470
Hospitals	$54,250	102,390
Professional, Scientific, and Technical Services	$51,920	2,950
Ambulatory Health Care Services	$51,670	43,900
Educational Services	$48,080	6,900

Metropolitan Areas Where Income Is Highest

Metropolitan Area	Average Annual Earnings	Number Employed
Salinas, CA	$90,210	80
San Jose–Sunnyvale–Santa Clara, CA	$82,200	920
Santa Barbara–Santa Maria, CA	$78,910	120
Chico, CA	$75,570	90
Santa Rosa–Petaluma, CA	$75,140	200

Perform complex medical laboratory tests for diagnosis, treatment, and prevention of disease. May train or supervise staff. Conduct chemical analysis of bodily fluids, including blood, urine, and spinal fluid, to determine presence of normal and abnormal components. Analyze laboratory findings to check the accuracy of the results. Enter data from analysis of medical tests and clinical results into computer for storage. Operate, calibrate, and maintain equipment used in quantitative and qualitative analysis, such as spectrophotometers, calorimeters, flame photometers, and computer-controlled analyzers. Establish and monitor quality assurance programs and activities to ensure the accuracy of laboratory results. Set up, clean, and maintain laboratory equipment. Provide technical information about test results to physicians, family members, and researchers. Supervise, train, and direct lab assistants, medical and clinical laboratory technicians and technologists, and other medical laboratory workers engaged in laboratory testing. Collect and study blood samples to determine the number of cells, their morphology, or their blood group, blood type, and compatibility for transfusion purposes, using microscopic techniques. Analyze samples of biological material for chemical content or reaction. Cultivate, isolate, and assist in identifying microbial organisms, and perform various tests on these microorganisms. Obtain, cut, stain, and mount biological material on slides for microscopic study and diagnosis, following standard laboratory procedures. Select and prepare specimen and media for cell culture, using aseptic technique and knowledge of medium components and cell requirements. Develop, standardize, evaluate, and modify procedures, techniques, and tests used in the analysis of specimens and in medical laboratory experiments. Harvest cell cultures at optimum time based on knowledge of cell cycle differences and culture conditions. Conduct medical research under direction of microbiologist or biochemist.

Other Considerations for Income: Earnings vary widely, depending on specialization and type of laboratory.

Personality Type: Investigative-Realistic-Conventional. **Career Cluster:** 08 Health Science. **Career Pathway:** 08.2 Diagnostics Services. **Skills:** Science; Operation Monitoring; Quality Control Analysis; Equipment Maintenance; Management of Personnel Resources; Systems Analysis; Operation and Control.

Education and Training Programs: Clinical Laboratory Science/Medical Technology/Technologist; Clinical/Medical Laboratory Science and Allied Professions, Other; Cytogenetics/Genetics/Clinical Genetics Technology/Technologist; Cytotechnology/Cytotechnologist; Histologic Technology/Histotechnologist; Renal/Dialysis Technologist/Technician. **Related Knowledge/Courses:** Biology; Chemistry; Medicine and Dentistry; Mechanical; Clerical; Mathematics.

Medical and Health Services Managers

* Annual Earnings: $80,240
* Beginning Wage: $48,300
* Earnings Growth Potential: Medium (39.8%)
* Growth: 16.4%
* Annual Job Openings: 31,877
* Self-Employed: 8.2%
* Part-Time: 5.5%
* Job Security: Most secure
* Education/Training Required: Work experience plus degree

Industries in Which Income Is Highest

Industry	Average Annual Earnings	Number Employed
Professional, Scientific, and Technical Services	$102,470	2,950
Insurance Carriers and Related Activities	$93,680	4,730
Management of Companies and Enterprises	$88,160	4,410
Hospitals	$86,850	105,870
Educational Services	$83,620	5,920

Metropolitan Areas Where Income Is Highest

Metropolitan Area	Average Annual Earnings	Number Employed
San Jose–Sunnyvale–Santa Clara, CA	$113,380	1,200
Olympia, WA	$106,660	90
Seattle-Tacoma-Bellevue, WA	$105,730	1,910
Rochester, MN	$104,820	300
New York–Northern New Jersey–Long Island, NY-NJ-PA	$100,600	23,010

Plan, direct, or coordinate medicine and health services in hospitals, clinics, managed care organizations, public health agencies, or similar organizations. Conduct and administer fiscal operations, including accounting, planning budgets, authorizing expenditures, establishing rates for services, and coordinating financial reporting. Direct, supervise, and evaluate work activities of medical, nursing, technical, clerical, service, maintenance, and other personnel. Maintain communication between governing boards, medical staff, and department heads by attending board meetings and coordinating interdepartmental functioning. Review and analyze facility activities and data to aid planning and cash and risk management and to improve service utilization. Plan, implement, and administer programs and services in a health-care or medical facility, including personnel administration, training, and coordination of medical, nursing, and physical plant staff. Direct or conduct recruitment, hiring, and training of personnel. Establish work schedules and assignments for staff, according to workload, space, and equipment availability. Maintain awareness of advances in medicine, computerized diagnostic and treatment equipment, data processing technology, government regulations, health insurance changes, and financing options. Monitor the use of diagnostic services, inpatient beds, facilities, and staff to ensure effective use of resources and assess the need for additional staff, equipment, and services. Develop and maintain computerized record management systems to store and process data such as personnel activities and information and to produce reports. Establish and evaluate objectives and evaluative operational criteria for units they manage. Prepare activity reports to inform management of the status and implementation plans of programs, services, and quality initiatives. Inspect facilities and recommend building or equipment modifications to ensure emergency readiness and compliance with access, safety, and sanitation regulations. Develop and implement organizational policies and procedures for the facility or medical unit.

Other Considerations for Income: Earnings of medical and health services managers vary by type and size of the facility and by level of responsibility. Salaries are highest in orthopedics and cardiology, lowest in family practice.

Personality Type: Enterprising-Conventional-Social. **Career Cluster:** 08 Health Science. **Career Pathways:** 08.1 Therapeutic Services; 08.2 Diagnostics Services; 08.3 Health Informatics. **Skills:** Management of Financial Resources; Management of Personnel Resources; Systems Evaluation; Management of Material Resources; Systems Analysis; Negotiation; Judgment and Decision Making; Social Perceptiveness.

Education and Training Programs: Community Health and Preventive Medicine; Health and Medical Administrative Services, Other; Health Information/Medical Records Administration/Administrator; Health Services Administration; Health Unit Manager/Ward Supervisor; Health/Health Care Administration/Management;

Hospital and Health Care Facilities Administration/Management; Public Health, General. **Related Knowledge/ Courses:** Economics and Accounting; Personnel and Human Resources; Administration and Management; Sales and Marketing; Medicine and Dentistry; Law and Government.

Medical Scientists, Except Epidemiologists

* Annual Earnings: $72,590
* Beginning Wage: $39,870
* Earnings Growth Potential: High (45.1%)
* Growth: 20.2%
* Annual Job Openings: 10,596
* Self-Employed: 2.0%
* Part-Time: 5.9%
* Job Security: More secure than most
* Education/Training Required: Doctoral degree

Industries in Which Income Is Highest

Industry	Average Annual Earnings	Number Employed
Management of Companies and Enterprises	$91,180	2,050
Merchant Wholesalers, Nondurable Goods	$90,640	2,440
Federal, State, and Local Government	$89,010	1,910
Chemical Manufacturing	$87,600	14,300
Professional, Scientific, and Technical Services	$78,990	38,010

Metropolitan Areas Where Income Is Highest

Metropolitan Area	Average Annual Earnings	Number Employed
Vallejo-Fairfield, CA	$115,070	80
Burlington–South Burlington, VT	$97,300	260
San Jose–Sunnyvale–Santa Clara, CA	$95,710	2,740
Washington-Arlington-Alexandria, DC-VA-MD-WV	$94,370	2,400
Santa Rosa–Petaluma, CA	$92,630	60

Conduct research dealing with the understanding of human diseases and the improvement of human health. Engage in clinical investigation or other research, production, technical writing, or related activities. Conduct research to develop methodologies, instrumentation, and procedures for medical application, analyzing data and presenting findings. Plan and direct studies to investigate human or animal disease, preventive methods, and treatments for disease. Follow strict safety procedures when handling toxic materials to avoid contamination. Evaluate effects of drugs, gases, pesticides, parasites, and microorganisms at various levels. Teach principles of medicine and medical and laboratory procedures to physicians, residents, students, and technicians. Prepare and analyze organ, tissue, and cell samples to identify toxicity, bacteria, or microorganisms or to study cell structure. Standardize drug dosages, methods of immunization, and procedures for manufacture of drugs and medicinal compounds. Investigate cause, progress, life cycle, or mode of transmission of diseases or parasites. Confer with health department, industry personnel, physicians, and others to develop health safety standards and public health improvement programs. Study animal and human health and physiological processes. Consult with and advise physicians, educators, researchers, and others regarding medical applications of physics, biology, and chemistry. Use equipment such as atomic absorption spectrometers, electron microscopes, flow cytometers, and chromatography systems.

Other Considerations for Income: No additional information.

Personality Type: Investigative-Realistic-Artistic. **Career Clusters:** 08 Health Science; 15 Science, Technology, Engineering, and Mathematics. **Career Pathways:** 08.1 Therapeutic Services; 15.3 Science and Mathematics. **Skills:** Science; Management of Financial Resources; Judgment and Decision Making; Reading Comprehension; Writing; Time Management; Complex Problem Solving; Active Listening.

Education and Training Programs: Anatomy; Biochemistry; Biomedical Sciences, General; Biophysics; Biostatistics; Cardiovascular Science; Cell Physiology; Cell/Cellular Biology and Histology; Endocrinology; Environmental Toxicology; Epidemiology; Exercise Physiology; Human/Medical Genetics; Immunology; Medical Microbiology and Bacteriology; Medical Scientist; Molecular Biology; Molecular Pharmacology; Molecular Physiology; Molecular Toxicology; Neuropharmacology; Oncology and Cancer Biology; Pathology/Experimental Pathology;

others. **Related Knowledge/Courses:** Biology; Medicine and Dentistry; Chemistry; Communications and Media; Personnel and Human Resources; Mathematics.

Methane/Landfill Gas Collection System Operators

- ❀ Annual Earnings: $83,290
- ❀ Beginning Wage: $50,330
- ❀ Earnings Growth Potential: Medium (39.6%)
- ❀ Growth: –5.9%
- ❀ Annual Job Openings: 14,889
- ❀ Self-Employed: 2.0%
- ❀ Part-Time: 1.6%
- ❀ Job Security: No data available
- ❀ Education/Training Required: Work experience in a related occupation

The Department of Labor reports this information for the occupation Industrial Production Managers. The job openings listed here are shared with other specializations within that occupation, including Biofuels Production Managers; Biomass Production Managers; Geothermal Production Managers; Hydroelectric Production Managers; and Quality Control Systems Managers.

Industries in Which Income Is Highest

Industry	Average Annual Earnings	Number Employed
Oil and Gas Extraction	$104,890	1,590
Professional, Scientific, and Technical Services	$103,550	3,450
Petroleum and Coal Products Manufacturing	$103,100	1,220
Utilities	$101,110	1,740
Management of Companies and Enterprises	$99,660	6,180

Metropolitan Areas Where Income Is Highest

Metropolitan Area	Average Annual Earnings	Number Employed
Austin–Round Rock, TX	$112,900	690
Cedar Rapids, IA	$110,680	530
Leominster-Fitchburg-Gardner, MA	$107,340	70
Saginaw–Saginaw Township North, MI	$106,880	140
Ann Arbor, MI	$104,600	320

Direct daily operations, maintenance, or repair of landfill gas projects, including maintenance of daily logs, determination of service priorities, and compliance with reporting requirements. No task data available.

Other Considerations for Income: No additional information.

Personality Type: No data available. **Career Cluster:** 04 Business, Management, and Administration. **Career Pathway:** 04.1 Management. **Skills:** No data available.

Education and Training Programs: Business Administration and Management, General; Business/Commerce, General; Operations Management and Supervision. **Related Knowledge/Courses:** No data available.

Microbiologists

❋ Annual Earnings: $64,350

❋ Beginning Wage: $38,240

❋ Earnings Growth Potential: High (40.6%)

❋ Growth: 11.2%

❋ Annual Job Openings: 1,306

❋ Self-Employed: 2.7%

❋ Part-Time: 7.3%

❋ Job Security: More secure than most

❋ Education/Training Required: Doctoral degree

Industries in Which Income Is Highest

Industry	Average Annual Earnings	Number Employed
Federal, State, and Local Government	$69,370	4,410
Professional, Scientific, and Technical Services	$67,830	4,740
Chemical Manufacturing	$64,230	3,460
Educational Services	$46,430	1,180

Metropolitan Areas Where Income Is Highest

Metropolitan Area	Average Annual Earnings	Number Employed
Washington-Arlington-Alexandria, DC-VA-MD-WV	$92,660	1,590
Riverside–San Bernardino–Ontario, CA	$89,330	80
New Haven, CT	$85,830	80
San Jose–Sunnyvale–Santa Clara, CA	$84,880	140
Atlanta–Sandy Springs–Marietta, GA	$84,720	420

Investigate the growth, structure, development, and other characteristics of microscopic organisms, such as bacteria, algae, or fungi. Includes medical microbiologists who study the relationship between organisms and disease or the effects of antibiotics on microorganisms. Prepare technical reports and recommendations based upon research outcomes. Supervise biological technologists and technicians and other scientists. Provide laboratory services for health departments, for community environmental health programs, and for physicians needing information for diagnosis and treatment. Use a variety of specialized equipment such as electron microscopes, gas chromatographs, and high pressure liquid chromatographs, electrophoresis units, thermocyclers, fluorescence activated cell sorters and phosphoimagers. Examine physiological, morphological, and cultural characteristics, using microscopes, to identify and classify microorganisms in human, water, and food specimens. Study growth, structure, development, and general characteristics of bacteria and other microorganisms to understand their relationships to human, plant, and animal health. Isolate and maintain cultures of bacteria or other microorganisms in prescribed or developed media, controlling moisture, aeration, temperature, and nutrition. Observe action of microorganisms upon living tissues of plants, higher animals, and other microorganisms, and on dead organic matter.

Study the structure and function of human, animal, and plant tissues, cells, pathogens, and toxins. Conduct chemical analyses of substances such as acids, alcohols, and enzymes. Monitor and perform tests on water, food, and the environment to detect harmful microorganisms or to obtain information about sources of pollution, contamination, or infection. Develop new products and procedures for sterilization, food and pharmaceutical supply preservation, or microbial contamination detection. Research use of bacteria and microorganisms to develop vitamins, antibiotics, amino acids, grain alcohol, sugars, and polymers.

Other Considerations for Income: According to the National Association of Colleges and Employers, beginning salary offers in 2007 averaged $34,953 a year for bachelor's degree recipients in biological and life sciences.

Personality Type: Investigative-Realistic. **Career Cluster:** 15 Science, Technology, Engineering, and Mathematics. **Career Pathway:** 15.3 Science and Mathematics. **Skills:** Science; Systems Analysis; Systems Evaluation; Management of Personnel Resources; Active Learning; Reading Comprehension; Writing; Judgment and Decision Making.

Education and Training Programs: Biochemistry and Molecular Biology; Cell/Cellular Biology and Anatomical Sciences, Other; Microbiology, General; Soil Microbiology; Structural Biology. **Related Knowledge/Courses:** Biology; Chemistry; Medicine and Dentistry; English Language; Education and Training; Mathematics.

Middle School Teachers, Except Special and Vocational Education

- ❀ Annual Earnings: $49,700
- ❀ Beginning Wage: $34,020
- ❀ Earnings Growth Potential: Low (31.5%)
- ❀ Growth: 11.2%
- ❀ Annual Job Openings: 75,270
- ❀ Self-Employed: 0.0%
- ❀ Part-Time: 9.5%
- ❀ Job Security: Most secure
- ❀ Education/Training Required: Bachelor's degree

Industries in Which Income Is Highest

Industry	Average Annual Earnings	Number Employed
Educational Services	$49,740	656,480
Administrative and Support Services	$42,830	3,690

Metropolitan Areas Where Income Is Highest

Metropolitan Area	Average Annual Earnings	Number Employed
Napa, CA	$74,680	490
Modesto, CA	$72,500	900
San Jose–Sunnyvale–Santa Clara, CA	$71,110	3,480
Hartford–West Hartford–East Hartford, CT	$67,300	3,290
Oxnard–Thousand Oaks–Ventura, CA	$67,090	1,710

Teach students in public or private schools in one or more subjects at the middle, intermediate, or junior high level, which falls between elementary and senior high school as defined by applicable state laws and regulations. Establish and enforce rules for behavior and procedures for maintaining order among the students for whom they are responsible. Adapt teaching methods and instructional materials to meet students' varying needs and interests. Instruct through lectures, discussions, and demonstrations in one or more subjects such as English, mathematics, or social studies. Prepare, administer, and grade tests and assignments to evaluate students' progress. Establish clear objectives for all lessons, units, and projects and communicate these objectives to students. Plan and conduct activities for a balanced program of instruction, demonstration, and work time that provides students with opportunities to observe, question, and investigate. Maintain accurate, complete, and correct student records as required by laws, district policies, and administrative regulations. Observe and evaluate students' performance, behavior, social development, and physical health. Assign lessons and correct homework. Prepare materials and classrooms for class activities. Enforce all administration policies and rules governing students. Confer with parents or guardians, other teachers, counselors, and administrators to resolve students' behavioral and academic problems. Prepare students for later grades by encouraging them to explore learning opportunities and to persevere with challenging tasks. Prepare objectives and outlines for courses of study, following curriculum guidelines or requirements of states and schools. Guide and counsel students with adjustment or academic problems or special academic interests. Meet with parents and guardians to discuss their children's progress and to determine their priorities for their children and their resource needs. Meet with other professionals to discuss individual students' needs and progress. Prepare and implement remedial programs for students requiring extra help.

Other Considerations for Income: Teachers can boost their earnings in a number of ways. In some schools, teachers receive extra pay for coaching sports and working with students in extracurricular activities. Getting a master's degree or national certification often results in a raise in pay, as does acting as a mentor. Some teachers earn extra income during the summer by teaching summer school or performing other jobs in the school system. Although private school teachers generally earn less than public school teachers, they may be given other benefits, such as free or subsidized housing.

Personality Type: Social-Artistic. **Career Cluster:** 05 Education and Training. **Career Pathway:** 05.3 Teaching/Training. **Skills:** Learning Strategies; Instructing; Monitoring; Social Perceptiveness; Time Management; Persuasion; Negotiation; Speaking.

Education and Training Programs: Art Teacher Education; Computer Teacher Education; English/Language Arts Teacher Education; Family and Consumer Sciences/Home Economics Teacher Education; Foreign Language Teacher Education; Health Occupations Teacher Education; Health Teacher Education; History Teacher Education; Junior High/Intermediate/Middle School Education and Teaching; Mathematics Teacher Education; Music Teacher Education; Physical Education Teaching and Coaching; Reading Teacher Education; others. **Related Knowledge/Courses:** Sociology and Anthropology; History and Archeology; Philosophy and Theology; Education and Training; Therapy and Counseling; Geography.

Mining and Geological Engineers, Including Mining Safety Engineers

❊ Annual Earnings: $75,960
❊ Beginning Wage: $45,020
❊ Earnings Growth Potential: High (40.7%)
❊ Growth: 10.0%
❊ Annual Job Openings: 456
❊ Self-Employed: 0.0%
❊ Part-Time: 5.3%
❊ Job Security: Less secure than most
❊ Education/Training Required: Bachelor's degree

Industries in Which Income Is Highest

Industry	Average Annual Earnings	Number Employed
Management of Companies and Enterprises	$87,010	320
Oil and Gas Extraction	$84,440	990
Federal, State, and Local Government	$84,040	550
Support Activities for Mining	$81,130	290
Professional, Scientific, and Technical Services	$72,570	2,320

Metropolitan Areas Where Income Is Highest

Metropolitan Area	Average Annual Earnings	Number Employed
Tulsa, OK	$108,180	60
Denver-Aurora, CO	$97,280	300
Tuscaloosa, AL	$90,870	40
Spokane, WA	$89,500	40
Houston–Sugar Land–Baytown, TX	$82,480	600

Determine the location and plan the extraction of coal, metallic ores, nonmetallic minerals, and building materials such as stone and gravel. Inspect mining areas for unsafe structures, equipment, and working conditions. Select locations and plan underground or surface mining operations, specifying processes, labor usage, and equipment that will result in safe, economical, and environmentally sound extraction of minerals and ores.

Examine maps, deposits, drilling locations, or mines to determine the location, size, accessibility, contents, value, and potential profitability of mineral, oil, and gas deposits. Supervise and coordinate the work of technicians, technologists, survey personnel, engineers, scientists, and other mine personnel. Prepare schedules, reports, and estimates of the costs involved in developing and operating mines. Monitor mine production rates to assess operational effectiveness. Design, implement, and monitor the development of mines, facilities, systems, or equipment. Select or develop mineral location, extraction, and production methods based on factors such as safety, cost, and deposit characteristics. Prepare technical reports for use by mining, engineering, and management personnel. Implement and coordinate mine safety programs, including the design and maintenance of protective and rescue equipment and safety devices. Test air to detect toxic gases and recommend measures to remove them, such as installation of ventilation shafts. Design, develop, and implement computer applications for use in mining operations such as mine design, modeling, or mapping or for monitoring mine conditions. Select or devise materials-handling methods and equipment to transport ore, waste materials, and mineral products efficiently and economically. Devise solutions to problems of land reclamation and water and air pollution, such as methods of storing excavated soil and returning exhausted mine sites to natural states. Lay out, direct, and supervise mine construction operations, such as the construction of shafts and tunnels. Evaluate data to develop new mining products, equipment, or processes.

Other Considerations for Income: As a group, engineers earn some of the highest average starting salaries among those holding bachelor's degrees. Mining and Geological Engineers are paid in the middle range among the various kinds of engineers. According to a 2007 survey by the National Association of Colleges and Employers, average starting salaries for Mining and Mineral Engineers were $54,381 with a bachelor's.

Personality Type: Investigative-Realistic-Enterprising. **Career Cluster:** 15 Science, Technology, Engineering, and Mathematics. **Career Pathway:** 15.1 Engineering and Technology. **Skills:** Operations Analysis; Science; Programming; Management of Financial Resources; Mathematics; Management of Material Resources; Systems Analysis; Technology Design.

Education and Training Program: Mining and Mineral Engineering. **Related Knowledge/Courses:** Engineering and Technology; Design; Chemistry; Physics; Production and Processing; Geography.

Multi-Media Artists and Animators

* Annual Earnings: $56,330
* Beginning Wage: $31,570
* Earnings Growth Potential: High (44.0%)
* Growth: 25.8%
* Annual Job Openings: 13,182
* Self-Employed: 69.7%
* Part-Time: 22.5%
* Job Security: Less secure than most
* Education/Training Required: Bachelor's degree

Industries in Which Income Is Highest

Industry	Average Annual Earnings	Number Employed
Other Information Services	$74,690	1,030
Motion Picture and Sound Recording Industries	$65,550	9,060
Publishing Industries (Except Internet)	$55,940	3,760
Professional, Scientific, and Technical Services	$54,330	10,610
Performing Arts, Spectator Sports, and Related Industries	$49,850	1,130

Metropolitan Areas Where Income Is Highest

Metropolitan Area	Average Annual Earnings	Number Employed
San Jose–Sunnyvale–Santa Clara, CA	$95,570	520
San Francisco–Oakland–Fremont, CA	$76,360	1,990
Austin–Round Rock, TX	$75,590	400
Los Angeles–Long Beach–Santa Ana, CA	$70,430	6,790
Seattle-Tacoma-Bellevue, WA	$60,200	1,350

Create special effects, animation, or other visual images, using film, video, computers, or other electronic tools and media, for use in products or creations such as computer games, movies, music videos, and commercials. Design complex graphics and animation, using independent judgment, creativity, and computer equipment. Create two-dimensional and three-dimensional images depicting objects in motion or illustrating a process, using computer animation or modeling programs.

Make objects or characters appear lifelike by manipulating light, color, texture, shadow, and transparency or manipulating static images to give the illusion of motion. Apply story development, directing, cinematography, and editing to animation to create storyboards that show the flow of the animation and map out key scenes and characters. Assemble, typeset, scan, and produce digital camera-ready art or film negatives and printer's proofs. Script, plan, and create animated narrative sequences under tight deadlines, using computer software and hand-drawing techniques. Create basic designs, drawings, and illustrations for product labels, cartons, direct mail, or television. Create pen-and-paper images to be scanned, edited, colored, textured, or animated by computer. Develop briefings, brochures, multimedia presentations, Web pages, promotional products, technical illustrations, and computer artwork for use in products, technical manuals, literature, newsletters, and slide shows. Use models to simulate the behavior of animated objects in the finished sequence. Create and install special effects as required by the script, mixing chemicals and fabricating needed parts from wood, metal, plaster, and clay. Participate in design and production of multimedia campaigns, handling budgeting and scheduling and assisting with such responsibilities as production coordination, background design, and progress tracking. Convert real objects to animated objects through modeling, using techniques such as optical scanning. Implement and maintain configuration control systems.

Other Considerations for Income: Earnings for self-employed artists vary widely. Some charge only a nominal fee while they gain experience and build a reputation for their work. Others can earn more than salaried artists. Many, however, find it difficult to rely solely on income earned from selling paintings or other works of art. Like other self-employed workers, freelance artists must provide their own benefits.

Personality Type: Artistic-Investigative. **Career Clusters:** 03 Arts, Audio/Video Technology, and Communications; 11 Information Technology. **Career Pathways:** 03.1 Audio and Video Technology and Film; 03.2 Printing Technology; 03.3 Visual Arts; 11.1 Network Systems. **Skills:** Operations Analysis; Technology Design; Time Management; Judgment and Decision Making; Science; Reading Comprehension; Active Listening; Programming.

Education and Training Programs: Animation, Interactive Technology, Video Graphics and Special Effects; Drawing; Graphic Design; Intermedia/Multimedia; Painting; Printmaking; Web Page, Digital/Multimedia

and Information Resources Design. **Related Knowledge/Courses:** Fine Arts; Design; Computers and Electronics; Communications and Media; English Language.

Municipal Fire Fighting and Prevention Supervisors

* Annual Earnings: $67,440
* Beginning Wage: $40,850
* Earnings Growth Potential: Medium (39.4%)
* Growth: 11.5%
* Annual Job Openings: 3,771
* Self-Employed: 0.0%
* Part-Time: 0.4%
* Job Security: Most secure
* Education/Training Required: Work experience in a related occupation

The Department of Labor reports this information for the occupation First-Line Supervisors/Managers of Fire Fighting and Prevention Workers. The job openings listed here are shared with other specializations within that occupation, including Forest Fire Fighting and Prevention Supervisors.

Industries in Which Income Is Highest

Industry	Average Annual Earnings	Number Employed
Federal, State, and Local Government	$67,760	52,280

Metropolitan Areas Where Income Is Highest

Metropolitan Area	Average Annual Earnings	Number Employed
San Francisco–Oakland–Fremont, CA	$122,310	570
Chicago-Naperville-Joliet, IL-IN-WI	$107,630	2,580
Atlantic City, NJ	$106,650	110
San Jose–Sunnyvale–Santa Clara, CA	$93,900	140
Trenton-Ewing, NJ	$92,560	140

Supervise fire fighters who control and extinguish municipal fires, protect life and property, and conduct rescue efforts. Assign firefighters to jobs at strategic locations to facilitate rescue of persons and maximize application of extinguishing agents. Provide emergency medical services as required and perform light to heavy rescue functions at emergencies. Assess nature and extent of fire, condition of building, danger to adjacent buildings, and water supply status to determine crew or company requirements. Instruct and drill fire department personnel in assigned duties, including firefighting, medical care, hazardous materials response, fire prevention, and related subjects. Evaluate the performance of assigned firefighting personnel. Direct the training of firefighters, assigning of instructors to training classes, and providing of supervisors with reports on training progress and status. Prepare activity reports listing fire call locations, actions taken, fire types and probable causes, damage estimates, and situation dispositions. Maintain required maps and records. Attend in-service training classes to remain current in knowledge of codes, laws, ordinances, and regulations. Evaluate fire station procedures to ensure efficiency and enforcement of departmental regulations. Direct firefighters in station maintenance duties and participate in these duties. Compile and maintain equipment and personnel records, including accident reports. Direct investigation of cases of suspected arson, hazards, and false alarms and submit reports outlining findings. Recommend personnel actions related to disciplinary procedures, performance, leaves of absence, and grievances. Supervise and participate in the inspection of properties to ensure that they are in compliance with applicable fire codes, ordinances, laws, regulations, and standards. Write and submit proposals for repair, modification, or replacement of firefighting equipment. Coordinate the distribution of fire prevention promotional materials.

Other Considerations for Income: Fire fighters receive benefits that usually include medical and liability insurance, vacation and sick leave, and some paid holidays. Almost all fire departments provide protective clothing (helmets, boots, and coats) and breathing apparatus, and many also provide dress uniforms. Fire fighters generally are covered by pension plans, often providing retirement at half pay after 25 years of service or if the individual is disabled in the line of duty.

Personality Type: Enterprising-Realistic-Social. **Career Cluster:** 12 Law, Public Safety, Corrections, and Security. **Career Pathway:** 12.2 Emergency and Fire Management Services. **Skills:** Equipment Maintenance; Management of Personnel Resources; Service Orientation; Operation Monitoring; Management of Material Resources; Operation and Control; Coordination; Equipment Selection.

Education and Training Programs: Fire Prevention and Safety Technology/Technician; Fire Services Administration. **Related Knowledge/Courses:** Building and Construction; Public Safety and Security; Medicine and Dentistry; Chemistry; Mechanical; Personnel and Human Resources.

Natural Sciences Managers

- ✳ Annual Earnings: $112,800
- ✳ Beginning Wage: $65,960
- ✳ Earnings Growth Potential: High (41.5%)
- ✳ Growth: 11.4%
- ✳ Annual Job Openings: 3,661
- ✳ Self-Employed: 0.6%
- ✳ Part-Time: 4.4%
- ✳ Job Security: Less secure than most
- ✳ Education/Training Required: Work experience plus degree

Industries in Which Income Is Highest

Industry	Average Annual Earnings	Number Employed
Chemical Manufacturing	$139,610	5,660
Management of Companies and Enterprises	$136,560	2,160
Professional, Scientific, and Technical Services	$125,560	16,240
Federal, State, and Local Government	$95,610	12,760
Educational Services	$91,920	1,990

Metropolitan Areas Where Income Is Highest

Metropolitan Area	Average Annual Earnings	Number Employed
San Jose–Sunnyvale–Santa Clara, CA	$166,400+	860
Philadelphia-Camden-Wilmington, PA-NJ-DE-MD	$162,090	1,740
New York–Northern New Jersey–Long Island, NY-NJ-PA	$149,910	3,540
San Francisco–Oakland–Fremont, CA	$149,110	2,250
San Diego–Carlsbad–San Marcos, CA	$141,210	1,300

Plan, direct, or coordinate activities in such fields as life sciences, physical sciences, mathematics, and statistics and research and development in these fields. Confer with scientists, engineers, regulators, and others to plan and review projects and to provide technical assistance. Develop client relationships and communicate with clients to explain proposals, present research findings, establish specifications, or discuss project status. Plan and direct research, development, and production activities. Prepare project proposals. Design and coordinate successive phases of problem analysis, solution proposals, and testing. Review project activities and prepare and review research, testing, and operational reports. Hire, supervise, and evaluate engineers, technicians, researchers, and other staff. Determine scientific and technical goals within broad outlines provided by top management and make detailed plans to accomplish these goals. Develop and implement policies, standards, and procedures for the architectural, scientific, and technical work performed to ensure regulatory compliance and operations enhancement. Develop innovative technology and train staff for its implementation. Provide for stewardship of plant and animal resources and habitats, studying land use; monitoring animal populations; and providing shelter, resources, and medical treatment for animals. Conduct own research in field of expertise. Recruit personnel and oversee the development and maintenance of staff competence. Advise and assist in obtaining patents or meeting other legal requirements. Prepare and administer budget, approve and review expenditures, and prepare financial reports. Make presentations at professional meetings to further knowledge in the field.

Other Considerations for Income: Natural Sciences Managers, especially those at higher levels, often receive more benefits—such as expense accounts, stock option plans, and bonuses—than do nonmanagerial workers in their organizations.

Personality Type: Enterprising-Investigative. **Career Clusters:** 04 Business, Management, and Administration; 10 Human Service; 15 Science, Technology, Engineering, and Mathematics. **Career Pathways:** 04.2 Business, Financial Management, and Accounting; 04.4 Business Analysis; 10.2 Counseling and Mental Health Services; 15.3 Science and Mathematics. **Skills:** Science; Mathematics; Active Learning; Reading Comprehension; Writing; Management of Personnel Resources; Complex Problem Solving; Critical Thinking.

Education and Training Programs: Acoustics; Algebra and Number Theory; Analysis and Functional Analysis; Analytical Chemistry; Anatomy; Animal Genetics; Animal Physiology; Applied Mathematics, General; Applied Mathematics, Other; Astronomy; Astrophysics; Atmospheric Chemistry and Climatology; Atmospheric Physics and Dynamics; Atmospheric Sciences and Meteorology, General; Atmospheric Sciences and Meteorology, Other; Atomic/Molecular Physics; Biochemistry; Biological and Biomedical Sciences, Other; others. **Related Knowledge/Courses:** Biology; Chemistry; Engineering and Technology; Law and Government; Administration and Management; Physics.

Network and Computer Systems Administrators

- ❋ Annual Earnings: $66,310
- ❋ Beginning Wage: $41,000
- ❋ Earnings Growth Potential: Medium (38.2%)
- ❋ Growth: 27.0%
- ❋ Annual Job Openings: 37,010
- ❋ Self-Employed: 0.4%
- ❋ Part-Time: 3.1%
- ❋ Job Security: More secure than most
- ❋ Education/Training Required: Bachelor's degree

Industries in Which Income Is Highest

Industry	Average Annual Earnings	Number Employed
Securities, Commodity Contracts, and Other Financial Investments and Related Activities	$78,300	5,540
Other Information Services	$77,430	2,130
Publishing Industries (Except Internet)	$74,360	9,130
Computer and Electronic Product Manufacturing	$71,770	5,550
Chemical Manufacturing	$71,690	2,170

Metropolitan Areas Where Income Is Highest

Metropolitan Area	Average Annual Earnings	Number Employed
San Jose–Sunnyvale–Santa Clara, CA	$97,520	3,630
Vallejo-Fairfield, CA	$86,920	170
San Francisco–Oakland–Fremont, CA	$85,280	8,060
New York–Northern New Jersey–Long Island, NY-NJ-PA	$80,560	22,440
Bridgeport-Stamford-Norwalk, CT	$80,230	1,260

Install, configure, and support organizations' local area networks (LANs), wide area networks (WANs), and Internet systems or segments of network systems. Maintain network hardware and software. Monitor networks to ensure network availability to all system users and perform necessary maintenance to support network availability. May supervise other network support and client server specialists and plan, coordinate, and implement network security measures. Maintain and administer computer networks and related computing environments, including computer hardware, systems software, applications software, and all configurations. Perform data backups and disaster recovery operations. Diagnose, troubleshoot, and resolve hardware, software, or other network and system problems and replace defective components when necessary. Plan, coordinate, and implement network security measures to protect data, software, and hardware. Configure, monitor, and maintain e-mail applications or virus protection software. Operate master consoles to monitor the performance of computer systems and networks and to coordinate computer network access and use. Load computer tapes and disks and install software and printer paper or forms. Design, configure, and test computer hardware, networking software, and operating system software. Monitor network performance to determine whether adjustments need to be made and to determine where changes will need to be made in the future. Confer with network users about how to solve existing system problems. Research new technologies by attending seminars, reading trade articles, or taking classes and implement or recommend the implementation of new technologies. Analyze equipment performance records to determine the need for repair or replacement. Implement and provide technical support for voice services and equipment such as private branch exchanges, voice mail systems, and telecom systems. Maintain inventories of parts for emergency repairs. Recommend changes to improve systems and network configurations and determine hardware

or software requirements related to such changes. Gather data pertaining to customer needs and use the information to identify, predict, interpret, and evaluate system and network requirements. Train people in computer system use. Coordinate with vendors and with company personnel to facilitate purchases.

Other Considerations for Income: According to Robert Half Technology, starting salaries in 2007 ranged from $50,000 to $75,750.

Personality Type: Investigative-Realistic-Conventional. **Career Cluster:** 11 Information Technology. **Career Pathways:** 11.1 Network Systems; 11.2 Information Support Services; 11.4 Programming and Software Development. **Skills:** Programming; Systems Evaluation; Systems Analysis; Operation Monitoring; Repairing; Quality Control Analysis; Troubleshooting; Equipment Maintenance.

Education and Training Programs: Computer and Information Sciences and Support Services, Other; Computer and Information Sciences, General; Computer and Information Systems Security/Information Assurance; Computer Systems Analysis/Analyst; Computer Systems Networking and Telecommunications; Information Science/Studies; Network and System Administration/Administrator; System, Networking, and LAN/WAN Management/Manager. **Related Knowledge/Courses:** Telecommunications; Computers and Electronics; Clerical; Administration and Management; Engineering and Technology.

Network Designers

* Annual Earnings: $75,150
* Beginning Wage: $40,660
* Earnings Growth Potential: High (45.9%)
* Growth: 15.1%
* Annual Job Openings: 14,374
* Self-Employed: 6.6%
* Part-Time: 5.6%
* Job Security: More secure than most
* Education/Training Required: Bachelor's degree

The Department of Labor reports this information for the occupation Computer Specialists, All Other. The job openings listed here are shared with other specializations within that occupation, including Business Intelligence Analysts; Computer Systems Engineers/Architects; Data Warehousing Specialists;

Database Architects; Document Management Specialists; Electronic Commerce Specialists; Geographic Information Systems Technicians; Geospatial Information Scientists and Technologists; Information Technology Project Managers; Software Quality Assurance Engineers and Testers; Video Game Designers; Web Administrators; and Web Developers.

Industries in Which Income Is Highest

Industry	Average Annual Earnings	Number Employed
Petroleum and Coal Products Manufacturing	$97,090	1,070
Transportation Equipment Manufacturing	$82,770	3,010
Oil and Gas Extraction	$81,350	1,710
Federal, State, and Local Government	$80,670	71,650
Management of Companies and Enterprises	$78,200	14,820

Metropolitan Areas Where Income Is Highest

Metropolitan Area	Average Annual Earnings	Number Employed
Washington-Arlington-Alexandria, DC-VA-MD-WV	$97,170	19,470
Atlantic City, NJ	$96,600	510
Pascagoula, MS	$95,430	60
San Jose–Sunnyvale–Santa Clara, CA	$92,710	3,580
Baltimore-Towson, MD	$89,730	5,650

Determine user requirements and design specifications for computer networks. Plan and implement network upgrades. Develop network-related documentation. Design, build, or operate equipment configuration prototypes, including network hardware, software, servers, or server operation systems. Coordinate network operations, maintenance, repairs, or upgrades. Adjust network sizes to meet volume or capacity demands. Communicate with vendors to gather information about products, to alert them to future needs, to resolve problems, or to address system maintenance issues. Coordinate installation of new equipment. Coordinate network or design activities with designers of associated networks. Design, organize, and deliver product awareness, skills transfer, and product education sessions for staff and suppliers. Determine specific network hardware or software require-ments, such as platforms, interfaces, bandwidths, or routine schemas. Develop disaster recovery plans. Communicate with customers, sales staff, or marketing staff to determine customer needs. Explain design specifications to integration or test engineers. Develop plans or budgets for network equipment replacement. Prepare design presentations and proposals for staff or customers. Supervise engineers and other staff in the design or implementation of network solutions. Use network computer-aided design (CAD) software packages to optimize network designs. Develop or maintain project reporting systems. Participate in network technology upgrade or expansion projects, including installation of hardware and software and integration testing. Research and test new or modified hardware or software products to determine performance and interoperability. Develop and implement solutions for network problems. Prepare or monitor project schedules, budgets, or cost control systems. Monitor and analyze network performance and data input/output reports to detect problems, identify inefficient use of computer resources, or perform capacity planning.

Other Considerations for Income: No additional information.

Personality Type: Conventional-Investigative-Realistic. **Career Cluster:** 11 Information Technology. **Career Pathway:** 11.4 Programming and Software Development. **Skills:** No data available.

Education and Training Programs: Computer and Information Sciences and Support Services, Other; Computer and Information Sciences, General; Computer Engineering Technologies/Technicians, Other; Computer Engineering, General; Computer Science; Computer Software Engineering; Computer Systems Networking and Telecommunications; E-Commerce/Electronic Commerce; Information Science/Studies; Information Technology; System, Networking, and LAN/WAN Management/Manager; Web Page, Digital/Multimedia and Information Resources Design; others. **Related Knowledge/Courses:** Telecommunications; Design; Computers and Electronics; Engineering and Technology; Administration and Management; Mathematics.

Network Systems and Data Communications Analysts

❊ Annual Earnings: $71,100
❊ Beginning Wage: $41,660
❊ Earnings Growth Potential: High (41.4%)
❊ Growth: 53.4%
❊ Annual Job Openings: 35,086
❊ Self-Employed: 17.5%
❊ Part-Time: 8.6%
❊ Job Security: More secure than most
❊ Education/Training Required: Bachelor's degree

Industries in Which Income Is Highest

Industry	Average Annual Earnings	Number Employed
Securities, Commodity Contracts, and Other Financial Investments and Related Activities	$83,780	4,540
Transportation Equipment Manufacturing	$81,960	1,260
Computer and Electronic Product Manufacturing	$78,230	4,590
Utilities	$76,970	1,460
Telecommunications	$75,870	30,630

Metropolitan Areas Where Income Is Highest

Metropolitan Area	Average Annual Earnings	Number Employed
San Jose–Sunnyvale–Santa Clara, CA	$95,390	3,480
Seattle-Tacoma-Bellevue, WA	$83,240	5,890
New York–Northern New Jersey–Long Island, NY-NJ-PA	$82,810	21,360
Washington-Arlington-Alexandria, DC-VA-MD-WV	$82,750	16,110
San Francisco–Oakland–Fremont, CA	$82,530	6,020

Analyze, design, test, and evaluate network systems, such as local area networks (LAN); wide area networks (WAN); and Internet, intranet, and other data communications systems. Perform network modeling, analysis, and planning. Research and recommend network and data communications hardware and software. Includes telecommunications specialists who deal with the interfacing of computer and communications equipment. May supervise computer programmers. Maintain needed files by adding and deleting files on the network server and backing up files to guarantee their safety in the event of problems with the network. Monitor system performance and provide security measures, troubleshooting, and maintenance as needed. Assist users to diagnose and solve data communication problems. Set up user accounts, regulating and monitoring file access to ensure confidentiality and proper use. Design and implement systems, network configurations, and network architecture, including hardware and software technology, site locations, and integration of technologies. Maintain the peripherals, such as printers, that are connected to the network. Identify areas of operation that need upgraded equipment such as modems, fiber-optic cables, and telephone wires. Train users in use of equipment. Develop and write procedures for installation, use, and troubleshooting of communications hardware and software. Adapt and modify existing software to meet specific needs. Work with other engineers, systems analysts, programmers, technicians, scientists, and top-level managers in the design, testing, and evaluation of systems. Test and evaluate hardware and software to determine efficiency, reliability, and compatibility with existing system and make purchase recommendations. Read technical manuals and brochures to determine which equipment meets establishment requirements. Consult customers, visit workplaces, or conduct surveys to determine present and future user needs. Visit vendors, attend conferences or training, and study technical journals to keep up with changes in technology.

Other Considerations for Income: Network Systems and Data Communications Analysts are paid in the middle range of earnings, compared to those of other computer specialists.

Personality Type: Investigative-Conventional. **Career Cluster:** 11 Information Technology. **Career Pathways:** 11.1 Network Systems; 11.2 Information Support Services; 11.4 Programming and Software Development. **Skills:** Installation; Technology Design; Troubleshooting; Systems Analysis; Programming; Systems Evaluation; Management of Material Resources; Operations Analysis.

Education and Training Programs: Computer and Information Sciences, General; Computer and Information Systems Security/Information Assurance; Computer Systems Analysis/Analyst; Computer Systems Networking and Telecommunications; Information Technology. **Related Knowledge/Courses:** Telecommunications; Computers and Electronics; Engineering and Technology; Design; Communications and Media; Clerical.

Neurologists

- ❋ Annual Earnings: $166,400+
- ❋ Beginning Wage: $49,710
- ❋ Earnings Growth Potential: Cannot be calculated
- ❋ Growth: 14.2%
- ❋ Annual Job Openings: 38,027
- ❋ Self-Employed: 14.7%
- ❋ Part-Time: 8.1%
- ❋ Job Security: No data available
- ❋ Education/Training Required: First professional degree

The Department of Labor reports this information for the occupation Physicians and Surgeons. The job openings listed here are shared with other specializations within that occupation, including Allergists and Immunologists; Anesthesiologists; Dermatologists; Family and General Practitioners; Hospitalists; Internists, General; Nuclear Medicine Physicians; Obstetricians and Gynecologists; Ophthalmologists; Pathologists; Pediatricians, General; Physical Medicine and Rehabilitation Physicians; Preventive Medicine Physicians; Psychiatrists; Radiologists; Sports Medicine Physicians; Surgeons; and Urologists.

Industries in Which Income Is Highest

Industry	Average Annual Earnings	Number Employed
Ambulatory Health Care Services	$166,400+	147,400
Administrative and Support Services	$166,400+	1,310
Federal, State, and Local Government	$162,300	28,180
Professional, Scientific, and Technical Services	$107,470	1,210
Hospitals	$72,130	72,490

Metropolitan Areas Where Income Is Highest

Metropolitan Area	Average Annual Earnings	Number Employed
Los Angeles–Long Beach–Santa Ana, CA	$166,400+	8,810
Boston-Cambridge-Quincy, MA-NH	$166,400+	6,380
Dallas–Fort Worth–Arlington, TX	$166,400+	4,950
Tampa–St. Petersburg–Clearwater, FL	$166,400+	3,810
Portland-Vancouver-Beaverton, OR-WA	$166,400+	3,180

Diagnose, treat, and help prevent diseases and disorders of the nervous system. No task data available.

Other Considerations for Income: Earnings of physicians and surgeons are among the highest of any occupation. Separate earnings figures for Neurologists are not available, but they earn roughly the same as Obstetricians and Gynecologists, who are in the middle range of earners among medical specialists. The Medical Group Management Association's Physician Compensation and Production Survey of 2005 reported earnings of $203,270 for Obstetricians and Gynecologists with less than two years in their specialty and $247,348 for those with more than one year in their specialty. These figures cover salary, bonus and incentive payments, research stipends, honoraria, and distribution of profits. Self-employed physicians—those who own or are part owners of their medical practice—generally have higher median incomes than salaried physicians, but their must provide for their own health insurance and retirement.

Personality Type: Investigative-Social-Realistic. **Career Cluster:** 08 Health Science. **Career Pathway:** 08.1 Therapeutic Services. **Skills:** No data available.

Education and Training Program: Neurology Residency Program. **Related Knowledge/Courses:** No data available.

Nuclear Engineers

❋ Annual Earnings: $97,080
❋ Beginning Wage: $68,300
❋ Earnings Growth Potential: Low (29.6%)
❋ Growth: 7.2%
❋ Annual Job Openings: 1,046
❋ Self-Employed: 0.0%
❋ Part-Time: 2.9%
❋ Job Security: More secure than most
❋ Education/Training Required: Bachelor's degree

Industries in Which Income Is Highest

Industry	Average Annual Earnings	Number Employed
Professional, Scientific, and Technical Services	$103,820	5,700
Utilities	$95,540	6,980

Metropolitan Areas Where Income Is Highest

Metropolitan Area	Average Annual Earnings	Number Employed
Washington-Arlington-Alexandria, DC-VA-MD-WV	$121,870	480
Knoxville, TN	$109,210	140
Richmond, VA	$103,050	670
Baltimore-Towson, MD	$100,400	60
Kennewick-Richland-Pasco, WA	$96,620	340

Conduct research on nuclear engineering problems or apply principles and theory of nuclear science to problems concerned with release, control, and utilization of nuclear energy and nuclear waste disposal. Examine accidents to obtain data that can be used to design preventive measures. Monitor nuclear facility operations to identify any design, construction, or operation practices that violate safety regulations and laws or that could jeopardize the safety of operations. Keep abreast of developments and changes in the nuclear field by reading technical journals and by independent study and research. Perform experiments that will provide information about acceptable methods of nuclear material usage, nuclear fuel reclamation, and waste disposal. Design and oversee construction and operation of nuclear reactors and power plants and nuclear fuels reprocessing and reclamation systems. Design and develop nuclear equipment such as reactor cores, radiation shielding, and associated instrumentation and control mechanisms. Initiate corrective actions or order plant shutdowns in emergency situations. Recommend preventive measures to be taken in the handling of nuclear technology, based on data obtained from operations monitoring or from evaluation of test results. Write operational instructions to be used in nuclear plant operation and nuclear fuel and waste handling and disposal. Conduct tests of nuclear fuel behavior and cycles and performance of nuclear machinery and equipment to optimize performance of existing plants. Direct operating and maintenance activities of operational nuclear power plants to ensure efficiency and conformity to safety standards. Synthesize analyses of test results and use the results to prepare technical reports of findings and recommendations. Prepare construction project proposals that include cost estimates and discuss proposals with interested parties such as vendors, contractors, and nuclear facility review boards. Analyze available data and consult with other scientists to determine parameters of experimentation and suitability of analytical models.

Other Considerations for Income: As a group, engineers earn some of the highest average starting salaries among those holding bachelor's degrees. Nuclear Engineers are among the best-paid of the various kinds of engineers. According to a 2007 survey by the National Association of Colleges and Employers, average starting salaries for Nuclear Engineers were $56,587 with a bachelor's and $59,167 with a master's.

Personality Type: Investigative-Realistic-Conventional. **Career Cluster:** 15 Science, Technology, Engineering, and Mathematics. **Career Pathway:** 15.1 Engineering and Technology. **Skills:** Operation Monitoring; Technology Design; Systems Evaluation; Systems Analysis; Operations Analysis; Quality Control Analysis; Mathematics; Science.

Education and Training Program: Nuclear Engineering. **Related Knowledge/Courses:** Engineering and Technology; Physics; Design; Chemistry; Mechanical; Building and Construction.

Nuclear Equipment Operation Technicians

❋ Annual Earnings: $67,890
❋ Beginning Wage: $40,310
❋ Earnings Growth Potential: High (40.6%)
❋ Growth: 6.7%
❋ Annual Job Openings: 1,021
❋ Self-Employed: 0.0%
❋ Part-Time: 3.9%
❋ Job Security: More secure than most
❋ Education/Training Required: Associate degree

The Department of Labor reports this information for the occupation Nuclear Technicians. The job openings listed here are shared with other specializations within that occupation, including Nuclear Monitoring Technicians.

Industries in Which Income Is Highest

Industry	Average Annual Earnings	Number Employed
Utilities	$71,450	3,260
Hospitals	$56,030	50
Professional, Scientific, and Technical Services	$55,630	1,660
Educational Services	$53,470	70

Metropolitan Areas Where Income Is Highest

Metropolitan Area	Average Annual Earnings	Number Employed
New York–Northern New Jersey–Long Island, NY-NJ-PA	$70,790	510
Boston-Cambridge-Quincy, MA-NH	$61,090	80
Los Angeles–Long Beach–Santa Ana, CA	$52,320	50

Operate equipment used for the release, control, and utilization of nuclear energy to assist scientists in laboratory and production activities. Follow policies and procedures for radiation workers to ensure personnel safety. Modify, devise, and maintain equipment used in operations. Set control panel switches, according to standard procedures, to route electric power from sources and direct particle beams through injector units. Submit computations to supervisors for review. Calculate equipment operating factors, such as radiation times, dosages, temperatures, gamma intensities, and pressures, using standard formulas and conversion tables. Perform testing, maintenance, repair, and upgrading of accelerator systems. Warn maintenance workers of radiation hazards and direct workers to vacate hazardous areas. Monitor instruments, gauges, and recording devices in control rooms during operation of equipment under direction of nuclear experimenters. Write summaries of activities and record experimental data, such as accelerator performance, systems status, particle beam specification, and beam conditions obtained.

Other Considerations for Income: No additional information.

Personality Type: Realistic-Conventional-Investigative. **Career Clusters:** 08 Health Science; 13 Manufacturing; 15 Science, Technology, Engineering, and Mathematics. **Career Pathways:** 08.2 Diagnostics Services; 13.3 Maintenance, Installation and Repair; 15.1 Engineering and Technology. **Skills:** Operation Monitoring; Operation and Control; Science; Mathematics; Equipment Maintenance; Quality Control Analysis; Troubleshooting; Reading Comprehension.

Education and Training Programs: Industrial Radiologic Technology/Technician; Nuclear and Industrial Radiologic Technologies/Technicians, Other; Nuclear Engineering Technology/Technician; Nuclear/Nuclear Power Technology/Technician; Radiation Protection/Health Physics Technician Training. **Related Knowledge/Courses:** Physics; Chemistry; Engineering and Technology; Public Safety and Security; Mechanical; Telecommunications.

Nuclear Medicine Physicians

❊ Annual Earnings: $166,400+

❊ Beginning Wage: $49,710

❊ Earnings Growth Potential: Cannot be calculated

❊ Growth: 14.2%

❊ Annual Job Openings: 38,027

❊ Self-Employed: 14.7%

❊ Part-Time: 8.1%

❊ Job Security: No data available

❊ Education/Training Required: First professional degree

The Department of Labor reports this information for the occupation Physicians and Surgeons. The job openings listed here are shared with other specializations within that occupation, including Allergists and Immunologists; Anesthesiologists; Dermatologists; Family and General Practitioners; Hospitalists; Internists, General; Neurologists; Obstetricians and Gynecologists; Ophthalmologists; Pathologists; Pediatricians, General; Physical Medicine and Rehabilitation Physicians; Preventive Medicine Physicians; Psychiatrists; Radiologists; Sports Medicine Physicians; Surgeons; and Urologists.

Industries in Which Income Is Highest

Industry	Average Annual Earnings	Number Employed
Ambulatory Health Care Services	$166,400+	147,400
Administrative and Support Services	$166,400+	1,310
Federal, State, and Local Government	$162,300	28,180
Professional, Scientific, and Technical Services	$107,470	1,210
Hospitals	$72,130	72,490

Metropolitan Areas Where Income Is Highest

Metropolitan Area	Average Annual Earnings	Number Employed
Los Angeles–Long Beach–Santa Ana, CA	$166,400+	8,810
Boston-Cambridge-Quincy, MA-NH	$166,400+	6,380
Dallas–Fort Worth–Arlington, TX	$166,400+	4,950
Tampa–St. Petersburg–Clearwater, FL	$166,400+	3,810
Portland-Vancouver-Beaverton, OR-WA	$166,400+	3,180

Diagnose and treat diseases, using radioactive materials and techniques. May monitor radionuclide preparation, administration, and disposition. No task data available.

Other Considerations for Income: Earnings of physicians and surgeons are among the highest of any occupation. Separate earnings figures for Nuclear Medicine Physicians are not available.

Personality Type: Investigative-Social. **Career Cluster:** 08 Health Science. **Career Pathway:** 08.1 Therapeutic Services. **Skills:** No data available.

Education and Training Program: Nuclear Medicine Residency Program. **Related Knowledge/Courses:** No data available.

Nuclear Medicine Technologists

❊ Annual Earnings: $66,660

❊ Beginning Wage: $48,450

❊ Earnings Growth Potential: Low (27.3%)

❊ Growth: 14.8%

❊ Annual Job Openings: 1,290

❊ Self-Employed: 1.0%

❊ Part-Time: 17.3%

❊ Job Security: Most secure

❊ Education/Training Required: Associate degree

Industries in Which Income Is Highest

Industry	Average Annual Earnings	Number Employed
Ambulatory Health Care Services	$67,220	6,650
Hospitals	$66,410	14,020

Metropolitan Areas Where Income Is Highest

Metropolitan Area	Average Annual Earnings	Number Employed
San Francisco–Oakland–Fremont, CA	$94,420	160
Fresno, CA	$91,190	60
Sacramento–Arden-Arcade–Roseville, CA	$90,670	120
San Jose–Sunnyvale–Santa Clara, CA	$90,110	80
Modesto, CA	$87,960	60

Prepare, administer, and measure radioactive isotopes in therapeutic, diagnostic, and tracer studies, using a variety of radioisotope equipment. Prepare stock solutions of radioactive materials and calculate doses to be administered by radiologists. Subject patients to radiation. Execute blood volume, red cell survival, and fat absorption studies, following standard laboratory techniques. Detect and map radiopharmaceuticals in patients' bodies, using a camera to produce photographic or computer images. Administer radiopharmaceuticals or radiation intravenously to detect or treat diseases, using radioisotope equipment, under direction of a physician. Produce computer-generated or film images for interpretation by physicians. Calculate, measure, and record radiation dosages or radiopharmaceuticals received, used, and disposed, using computers and following physicians' prescriptions. Perform quality control checks on laboratory equipment and cameras. Maintain and calibrate radioisotope and laboratory equipment. Dispose of radioactive materials and store radiopharmaceuticals, following radiation safety procedures. Process cardiac function studies, using computers. Prepare stock radiopharmaceuticals, adhering to safety standards that minimize radiation exposure to workers and patients. Record and process results of procedures. Explain test procedures and safety precautions to patients and provide them with assistance during test procedures. Gather information on patients' illnesses and medical histories to guide choices of diagnostic procedures for therapies. Measure glandular activity, blood volume, red cell survival, and radioactivity of patient, using scanners, Geiger counters, scintillation counters, and other laboratory equipment. Train and supervise student or subordinate nuclear medicine technologists. Position radiation fields, radiation beams, and patients to allow for most effective treatment of patients' diseases, using computers. Add radioactive substances to biological specimens such as blood, urine, and feces to determine therapeutic drug or hormone levels. Develop treatment procedures for nuclear medicine treatment programs.

Other Considerations for Income: No additional information.

Personality Type: Investigative-Realistic-Social. **Career Cluster:** 08 Health Science. **Career Pathways:** 08.1 Therapeutic Services; 08.2 Diagnostics Services. **Skills:** Operation Monitoring; Quality Control Analysis.

Education and Training Programs: Nuclear Medical Technology/Technologist; Radiation Protection/Health Physics Technician Training. **Related Knowledge/ Courses:** Medicine and Dentistry; Biology; Chemistry; Physics; Customer and Personal Service; Therapy and Counseling.

Nuclear Monitoring Technicians

- ❋ Annual Earnings: $67,890
- ❋ Beginning Wage: $40,310
- ❋ Earnings Growth Potential: High (40.6%)
- ❋ Growth: 6.7%
- ❋ Annual Job Openings: 1,021
- ❋ Self-Employed: 0.0%
- ❋ Part-Time: 3.9%
- ❋ Job Security: More secure than most
- ❋ Education/Training Required: Associate degree

The Department of Labor reports this information for the occupation Nuclear Technicians. The job openings listed here are shared with other specializations within that occupation, including Nuclear Equipment Operation Technicians.

Industries in Which Income Is Highest

Industry	Average Annual Earnings	Number Employed
Utilities	$71,450	3,260
Hospitals	$56,030	50
Professional, Scientific, and Technical Services	$55,630	1,660
Educational Services	$53,470	70

Metropolitan Areas Where Income Is Highest

Metropolitan Area	Average Annual Earnings	Number Employed
New York–Northern New Jersey–Long Island, NY-NJ-PA	$70,790	510
Boston-Cambridge-Quincy, MA-NH	$61,090	80
Los Angeles–Long Beach–Santa Ana, CA	$52,320	50

Collect and test samples to monitor results of nuclear experiments and contamination of humans, facilities, and environment. Calculate safe radiation exposure times for personnel, using plant contamination readings and prescribed safe levels of radiation. Provide initial response to abnormal events and to alarms from radiation monitoring equipment. Monitor personnel in order to determine the amounts and intensities of radiation exposure. Inform supervisors when individual exposures or area radiation levels approach maximum permissible limits. Instruct personnel in radiation safety procedures and demonstrate use of protective clothing and equipment. Determine intensities and types of radiation in work areas, equipment, and materials, using radiation detectors and other instruments. Collect samples of air, water, gases, and solids to determine radioactivity levels of contamination. Set up equipment that automatically detects area radiation deviations and test detection equipment to ensure its accuracy. Determine or recommend radioactive decontamination procedures according to the size and nature of equipment and the degree of contamination. Decontaminate objects by cleaning with soap or solvents or by abrading with wire brushes, buffing wheels, or sandblasting machines. Place radioactive waste, such as sweepings and broken sample bottles, into containers for disposal. Calibrate and maintain chemical instrumentation sensing elements and sampling system equipment, using calibration instruments and hand tools. Place irradiated nuclear fuel materials in environmental chambers for testing and observe reactions through cell windows. Enter data into computers in order to record characteristics of nuclear events and locating coordinates of particles. Operate manipulators from outside cells to move specimens into and out of shielded containers, to remove specimens from cells, or to place specimens on benches or equipment workstations. Prepare reports describing contamination tests, material and equipment decontaminated, and methods used in decontamination processes.

Other Considerations for Income: No additional information.

Personality Type: Realistic-Conventional-Investigative. **Career Clusters:** 08 Health Science; 13 Manufacturing; 15 Science, Technology, Engineering, and Mathematics. **Career Pathways:** 08.1 Therapeutic Services; 13.2 Manufacturing Production Process Development; 13.3 Maintenance, Installation and Repair; 15.1 Engineering and Technology. **Skills:** Science; Operation Monitoring; Equipment Maintenance; Mathematics; Operation and Control; Equipment Selection; Technology Design; Systems Analysis.

Education and Training Programs: Industrial Radiologic Technology/Technician; Nuclear and Industrial Radiologic Technologies/Technicians, Other; Nuclear Engineering Technology/Technician; Nuclear/Nuclear Power Technology/Technician; Radiation Protection/Health Physics Technician Training. **Related Knowledge/Courses:** Physics; Chemistry; Public Safety and Security; Engineering and Technology; Design; Biology.

Nuclear Power Reactor Operators

❋ Annual Earnings: $73,320
❋ Beginning Wage: $55,730
❋ Earnings Growth Potential: Very low (24.0%)
❋ Growth: 10.6%
❋ Annual Job Openings: 233
❋ Self-Employed: 0.0%
❋ Part-Time: 0.6%
❋ Job Security: Most secure
❋ Education/Training Required: Long-term on-the-job training

Industries in Which Income Is Highest

Industry	Average Annual Earnings	Number Employed
Utilities	$73,440	4,450
Educational Services	$46,980	70

Metropolitan Areas Where Income Is Highest

Metropolitan Area	Average Annual Earnings	Number Employed

Insufficient data available

Control nuclear reactors. Adjust controls to position rod and to regulate flux level, reactor period, coolant temperature, and rate of power flow, following standard procedures. Respond to system or unit abnormalities, diagnosing the cause and recommending or taking corrective action. Monitor all systems for normal running conditions, performing activities such as checking gauges to assess output or assess the effects of generator loading on other equipment. Implement operational procedures such as those controlling startup and shutdown activities. Note malfunctions of equipment, instruments, or controls and report these conditions to supervisors. Monitor and operate boilers, turbines, wells, and auxiliary power plant equipment. Dispatch orders and instructions to personnel through radiotelephone or intercommunication systems to coordinate auxiliary equipment operation. Record operating data such as the results of surveillance tests. Participate in nuclear fuel element handling activities such as preparation, transfer, loading, and unloading. Conduct inspections and operations outside of control rooms as necessary. Direct reactor operators in emergency situations in accordance with emergency operating procedures. Authorize maintenance activities on units and changes in equipment and system operational status.

Other Considerations for Income: No additional information.

Personality Type: Realistic-Conventional-Enterprising. **Career Cluster:** 13 Manufacturing. **Career Pathways:** 13.1 Production; 13.3 Maintenance, Installation and Repair. **Skills:** Operation Monitoring; Operation and Control; Science; Systems Analysis; Troubleshooting; Equipment Maintenance; Quality Control Analysis; Reading Comprehension.

Education and Training Program: Nuclear/Nuclear Power Technology/Technician. **Related Knowledge/Courses:** Physics; Engineering and Technology; Chemistry; Mechanical; Public Safety and Security; Design.

Nuclear Technicians

See *Nuclear Equipment Operation Technicians and Nuclear Monitoring Technicians,* described separately.

Nursery and Greenhouse Managers

※ Annual Earnings: $56,230
※ Beginning Wage: $31,350
※ Earnings Growth Potential: High (44.2%)
※ Growth: 1.1%
※ Annual Job Openings: 18,101
※ Self-Employed: 0.0%
※ Part-Time: 9.3%
※ Job Security: More secure than most
※ Education/Training Required: Work experience plus degree

The Department of Labor reports this information for the occupation Farm, Ranch, and Other Agricultural Managers. The job openings listed here are shared with other specializations within that occupation, including Aquacultural Managers; and Crop and Livestock Managers.

Industries in Which Income Is Highest

Industry	Average Annual Earnings	Number Employed
Management of Companies and Enterprises	$79,060	160
Merchant Wholesalers, Nondurable Goods	$63,250	180
Forestry and Logging	$62,970	40
Federal, State, and Local Government	$62,360	350
Food Manufacturing	$60,360	60

Metropolitan Areas Where Income Is Highest

Metropolitan Area	Average Annual Earnings	Number Employed
Yuma, AZ	$84,050	70
Port St. Lucie–Fort Pierce, FL	$73,340	40
Salinas, CA	$72,050	140
Santa Barbara–Santa Maria, CA	$69,170	40
Visalia-Porterville, CA	$68,110	80

Plan, organize, direct, control, and coordinate activities of workers engaged in propagating, cultivating, and harvesting horticultural specialties, such as trees, shrubs, flowers, mushrooms, and other plants. Construct structures and accessories such as greenhouses and benches. Coordinate clerical, recordkeeping, inventory, requisitioning, and marketing activities. Cut and prune trees, shrubs, flowers, and plants. Graft plants. Inspect facilities and equipment for signs of disrepair, and perform necessary maintenance work. Position and regulate plant irrigation systems, and program environmental and irrigation control computers. Provide information to customers on the care of trees, shrubs, flowers, plants, and lawns. Confer with horticultural personnel in order to plan facility renovations or additions. Determine plant growing conditions such as in greenhouses, hydroponic environments, or natural settings, and set planting and care schedules. Prepare soil for planting, and plant or transplant seeds, bulbs, and cuttings. Negotiate contracts such as those for land leases or tree purchases. Apply pesticides and fertilizers to plants. Tour work areas to observe work being done, to inspect crops, and to evaluate plant and soil conditions. Hire employees, and train them in gardening techniques. Select and purchase seeds, plant nutrients, disease control chemicals, and garden and lawn care equipment. Manage nurseries that grow horticultural plants for sale to trade or retail customers, for display or exhibition, or for research. Assign work schedules and duties to nursery or greenhouse staffs, and supervise their work. Determine types and quantities of horticultural plants to be grown, based on budgets, projected sales volumes, and/or executive directives. Explain and enforce safety regulations and policies. Identify plants as well as problems such as diseases, weeds, and insect pests.

Other Considerations for Income: No additional information.

Personality Type: Enterprising-Realistic-Conventional. **Career Cluster:** 01 Agriculture, Food and Natural Resource. **Career Pathway:** 01.2 Plant Systems. **Skills:** Management of Financial Resources; Management of Material Resources; Science; Management of Personnel Resources; Systems Evaluation; Installation; Operation Monitoring; Equipment Maintenance.

Education and Training Programs: Agribusiness/Agricultural Business Operations; Agricultural Animal Breeding; Agricultural Business and Management, General; Agricultural Business and Management, Other; Agricultural Production Operations, General; Agricultural Production Operations, Other; Animal Nutrition; Animal/Livestock Husbandry and Production; Crop Production; Dairy Husbandry and Production; Dairy Science; Farm/Farm and Ranch Management; Greenhouse Operations and Management; Horse Husbandry/Equine Science and Management; others. **Related Knowledge/Courses:** Biology; Production and Processing; Sales and Marketing; Chemistry; Personnel and Human Resources; Design.

Nursing Instructors and Teachers, Postsecondary

* Annual Earnings: $59,210
* Beginning Wage: $37,190
* Earnings Growth Potential: Medium (37.2%)
* Growth: 22.9%
* Annual Job Openings: 7,337
* Self-Employed: 0.4%
* Part-Time: 27.8%
* Job Security: Most secure
* Education/Training Required: Doctoral degree

Industries in Which Income Is Highest

Industry	Average Annual Earnings	Number Employed
Hospitals	$72,060	4,200
Educational Services	$57,820	42,250

Metropolitan Areas Where Income Is Highest

Metropolitan Area	Average Annual Earnings	Number Employed
Worcester, MA-CT	$91,790	110
Rochester, MN	$88,810	120
Baltimore-Towson, MD	$73,480	370
New York–Northern New Jersey–Long Island, NY-NJ-PA	$72,810	1,770
Hartford–West Hartford–East Hartford, CT	$72,450	220

Demonstrate and teach patient care in classroom and clinical units to nursing students. Includes both teachers primarily engaged in teaching and those who do a combination of both teaching and research. Initiate, facilitate, and moderate classroom discussions. Prepare and deliver lectures to undergraduate or graduate students on topics such as pharmacology, mental health nursing, and community health-care practices. Keep abreast of developments in their field by reading current literature, talking with colleagues, and participating in professional conferences. Prepare course materials such as syllabi, homework assignments, and handouts. Supervise students' laboratory and clinical work. Evaluate and grade students' classwork, laboratory and clinic work, assignments, and papers. Collaborate with colleagues to address teaching and research issues. Plan, evaluate, and revise curricula, course content, and course materials and methods of instruction. Assess clinical education needs and patient and client teaching needs, utilizing a variety of methods. Compile, administer, and grade examinations or assign this work to others. Advise students on academic and vocational curricula and on career issues. Maintain student attendance records, grades, and other required records. Maintain regularly scheduled office hours to advise and assist students. Supervise undergraduate or graduate teaching, internship, and research work. Conduct research in a particular field of knowledge and publish findings in professional journals, books, and/or electronic media. Participate in student recruitment, registration, and placement activities. Serve on academic or administrative committees that deal with institutional policies, departmental matters, and academic issues. Coordinate training programs with area universities, clinics, hospitals, health agencies, and/or vocational schools. Compile bibliographies of specialized materials for outside reading assignments. Select and obtain materials and supplies such as textbooks and laboratory equipment. Participate in campus and community events. Write grant proposals to procure external research funding. Act as advisers to student organizations.

Other Considerations for Income: Earnings for college faculty vary according to rank and type of institution, geographic area, and field. According to a 2006–2007 survey by the American Association of University Professors, salaries for full-time faculty averaged $73,207. By rank, the average was $98,974 for professors, $69,911 for associate professors, $58,662 for assistant professors, $42,609 for instructors, and $48,289 for lecturers. Faculty in 4-year institutions earn higher salaries, on average, than do those in 2-year schools. Many faculty members have significant earnings in addition to their base salary from consulting, teaching additional courses, research, writing for publication, or other employment. In addition, many college and university faculty enjoy unique benefits, including access to campus facilities, tuition waivers for dependents, housing and travel allowances, and paid leave for sabbaticals. Part-time faculty and instructors usually have fewer benefits than full-time faculty.

Personality Type: Social-Investigative. **Career Clusters:** 05 Education and Training; 08 Health Science. **Career Pathways:** 05.3 Teaching/Training; 08.1 Therapeutic Services. **Skills:** Science; Instructing; Writing; Social Perceptiveness; Reading Comprehension; Learning Strategies; Service Orientation; Critical Thinking.

Education and Training Program: Pre-Nursing Studies. **Related Knowledge/Courses:** Therapy and Counseling; Sociology and Anthropology; Biology; Medicine and Dentistry; Philosophy and Theology; Psychology.

Obstetricians and Gynecologists

- ❋ Annual Earnings: $166,400+
- ❋ Beginning Wage: $95,350
- ❋ Earnings Growth Potential: Cannot be calculated
- ❋ Growth: 14.2%
- ❋ Annual Job Openings: 38,027
- ❋ Self-Employed: 14.7%
- ❋ Part-Time: 8.1%
- ❋ Job Security: Most secure
- ❋ Education/Training Required: First professional degree

The Department of Labor reports this information for the occupation Physicians and Surgeons. The job openings listed here are shared with other specializations within that occupation, including Allergists and Immunologists; Anesthesiologists; Dermatologists; Family and General Practitioners; Hospitalists; Internists, General; Neurologists; Nuclear Medicine Physicians; Ophthalmologists; Pathologists; Pediatricians, General; Physical Medicine and Rehabilitation Physicians; Preventive Medicine Physicians; Psychiatrists; Radiologists; Sports Medicine Physicians; Surgeons; and Urologists.

Industries in Which Income Is Highest

Industry	Average Annual Earnings	Number Employed
Ambulatory Health Care Services	$166,400+	16,700
Hospitals	$166,400+	2,540

Metropolitan Areas Where Income Is Highest

Metropolitan Area	Average Annual Earnings	Number Employed
New York–Northern New Jersey–Long Island, NY-NJ-PA	$166,400+	1,150
Los Angeles–Long Beach–Santa Ana, CA	$166,400+	830
Washington-Arlington-Alexandria, DC-VA-MD-WV	$166,400+	680
Houston–Sugar Land–Baytown, TX	$166,400+	590
Dallas–Fort Worth–Arlington, TX	$166,400+	540

Diagnose, treat, and help prevent diseases of women, especially those affecting the reproductive system and the process of childbirth. Care for and treat women during prenatal, natal, and post-natal periods. Explain procedures and discuss test results or prescribed treatments with patients. Treat diseases of female organs. Monitor patients' condition and progress and re-evaluate treatments as necessary. Perform cesarean sections or other surgical procedures as needed to preserve patients' health and deliver babies safely. Prescribe or administer therapy, medication, and other specialized medical care to treat or prevent illness, disease, or injury. Analyze records, reports, test results, or examination information to diagnose medical condition of patient. Collect, record, and maintain patient information, such as medical histories, reports, and examination results. Advise patients and community members concerning diet, activity, hygiene, and disease prevention.

Refer patient to medical specialist or other practitioner when necessary. Consult with, or provide consulting services to, other physicians. Direct and coordinate activities of nurses, students, assistants, specialists, therapists, and other medical staff. Plan, implement, or administer health programs in hospitals, businesses, or communities for prevention and treatment of injuries or illnesses. Prepare government and organizational reports on birth, death, and disease statistics; workforce evaluations; or the medical status of individuals. Conduct research to develop or test medications, treatments, or procedures to prevent or control disease or injury.

Other Considerations for Income: Earnings of physicians and surgeons are among the highest of any occupation; Obstetricians and Gynecologists are in the middle range of earners among medical specialists. The Medical Group Management Association's Physician Compensation and Production Survey of 2005 reported earnings of $203,270 for Obstetricians and Gynecologists with less than two years in their specialty and $247,348 for those with more than one year in their specialty. These figures cover salary, bonus and incentive payments, research stipends, honoraria, and distribution of profits. Self-employed physicians—those who own or are part owners of their medical practice—generally have higher median incomes than salaried physicians, but their must provide for their own health insurance and retirement.

Personality Type: Investigative-Social-Realistic. **Career Cluster:** 08 Health Science. **Career Pathway:** 08.1 Therapeutic Services. **Skills:** Science; Judgment and Decision Making; Reading Comprehension; Complex Problem Solving; Active Learning; Social Perceptiveness; Critical Thinking; Active Listening.

Education and Training Program: Medicine (MD). **Related Knowledge/Courses:** Medicine and Dentistry; Therapy and Counseling; Biology; Psychology; Sociology and Anthropology; Chemistry.

Occupational Health and Safety Specialists

❋ Annual Earnings: $62,250
❋ Beginning Wage: $35,870
❋ Earnings Growth Potential: High (42.4%)
❋ Growth: 8.1%
❋ Annual Job Openings: 3,440
❋ Self-Employed: 2.4%
❋ Part-Time: 8.0%
❋ Job Security: More secure than most
❋ Education/Training Required: Bachelor's degree

Industries in Which Income Is Highest

Industry	Average Annual Earnings	Number Employed
Utilities	$72,040	1,160
Waste Management and Remediation Services	$71,570	1,070
Management of Companies and Enterprises	$67,950	1,450
Transportation Equipment Manufacturing	$67,110	1,190
Chemical Manufacturing	$64,430	1,630

Metropolitan Areas Where Income Is Highest

Metropolitan Area	Average Annual Earnings	Number Employed
Knoxville, TN	$94,610	170
San Francisco–Oakland–Fremont, CA	$80,590	740
Washington-Arlington-Alexandria, DC-VA-MD-WV	$78,150	1,100
Anchorage, AK	$77,130	180
Bakersfield, CA	$76,370	90

Review, evaluate, and analyze work environments and design programs and procedures to control, eliminate, and prevent diseases or injuries caused by chemical, physical, and biological agents or ergonomic factors. Order suspension of activities that pose threats to workers' health and safety. Recommend measures to help protect workers from potentially hazardous work methods, pro-cesses, or materials. Investigate accidents to identify causes and to determine how such accidents might be prevented in the future. Investigate the adequacy of ventilation, exhaust equipment, lighting, and other conditions that could affect employee health, comfort, or performance. Develop and maintain hygiene programs such as noise surveys, continuous atmosphere monitoring, ventilation surveys, and asbestos management plans. Inspect and evaluate workplace environments, equipment, and practices in order to ensure compliance with safety standards and government regulations. Collaborate with engineers and physicians to institute control and remedial measures for hazardous and potentially hazardous conditions or equipment. Conduct safety training and education programs and demonstrate the use of safety equipment. Provide new-employee health and safety orientations and develop materials for these presentations. Collect samples of dust, gases, vapors, and other potentially toxic materials for analysis. Investigate health-related complaints and inspect facilities to ensure that they comply with public health legislation and regulations. Coordinate "right-to-know" programs regarding hazardous chemicals and other substances. Maintain and update emergency response plans and procedures. Develop and maintain medical monitoring programs for employees. Inspect specified areas to ensure the presence of fire prevention equipment, safety equipment, and first-aid supplies. Conduct audits at hazardous waste sites or industrial sites and participate in hazardous waste site investigations. Collect samples of hazardous materials or arrange for sample collection. Maintain inventories of hazardous materials and hazardous wastes, using waste tracking systems, to ensure that materials are handled properly.

Other Considerations for Income: Most Occupational Health and Safety Specialists work in large private firms or for federal, state, and local governments, most of which generally offer benefits more generous than those offered by smaller firms.

Personality Type: Investigative-Conventional. **Career Clusters:** 08 Health Science; 13 Manufacturing. **Career Pathways:** 08.3 Health Informatics; 13.4 Quality Assurance. **Skills:** Science; Management of Financial Resources; Technology Design; Persuasion; Systems Analysis; Management of Material Resources; Operations Analysis; Systems Evaluation.

Education and Training Programs: Environmental Health; Industrial Safety Technology/Technician; Occupational Health and Industrial Hygiene; Occupational Safety and Health Technology/Technician; Quality Control and Safety Technologies/Technicians, Other. **Related Knowledge/Courses:** Chemistry; Biology; Physics; Engineering and Technology; Public Safety and Security; Building and Construction.

Occupational Therapist Assistants

- ❁ Annual Earnings: $48,230
- ❁ Beginning Wage: $31,150
- ❁ Earnings Growth Potential: Medium (35.4%)
- ❁ Growth: 25.4%
- ❁ Annual Job Openings: 2,634
- ❁ Self-Employed: 3.5%
- ❁ Part-Time: 17.8%
- ❁ Job Security: Most secure
- ❁ Education/Training Required: Associate degree

Industries in Which Income Is Highest

Industry	Average Annual Earnings	Number Employed
Ambulatory Health Care Services	$50,640	9,510
Nursing and Residential Care Facilities	$50,060	5,370
Hospitals	$45,840	6,660
Educational Services	$41,420	1,900

Metropolitan Areas Where Income Is Highest

Metropolitan Area	Average Annual Earnings	Number Employed
Lynchburg, VA	$63,350	70
San Diego–Carlsbad–San Marcos, CA	$62,130	190
Houston–Sugar Land–Baytown, TX	$61,270	410
Jacksonville, FL	$59,890	80
San Antonio, TX	$59,630	210

Assist occupational therapists in providing occupational therapy treatments and procedures. May, in accordance with state laws, assist in development of treatment plans, carry out routine functions, direct activity programs, and document the progress of treatments. Generally requires formal training. Observe and record patients' progress, attitudes, and behavior and maintain this information in client records. Maintain and promote a positive attitude toward clients and their treatment programs. Monitor patients' performance in therapy activities, providing encouragement. Select therapy activities to fit patients' needs and capabilities. Instruct, or assist in instructing, patients and families in home programs, basic living skills, and the care and use of adaptive equipment. Evaluate the daily living skills and capacities of physically, developmentally, or emotionally disabled clients. Aid patients in dressing and grooming themselves. Implement, or assist occupational therapists with implementing, treatment plans designed to help clients function independently. Report to supervisors, verbally or in writing, on patients' progress, attitudes, and behavior. Alter treatment programs to obtain better results if treatment is not having the intended effect. Work under the direction of occupational therapists to plan, implement, and administer educational, vocational, and recreational programs that restore and enhance performance in individuals with functional impairments. Design, fabricate, and repair assistive devices and make adaptive changes to equipment and environments. Assemble, clean, and maintain equipment and materials for patient use. Teach patients how to deal constructively with their emotions. Perform clerical duties such as scheduling appointments, collecting data, and documenting health insurance billings. Transport patients to and from the occupational therapy work area. Demonstrate therapy techniques such as manual and creative arts or games. Order any needed educational or treatment supplies. Assist educational specialists or clinical psychologists in administering situational or diagnostic tests to measure client's abilities or progress.

Other Considerations for Income: No additional information.

Personality Type: Social-Realistic. **Career Cluster:** 08 Health Science. **Career Pathway:** 08.1 Therapeutic Services. **Skills:** Social Perceptiveness; Operations Analysis; Equipment Selection; Writing; Service Orientation; Persuasion; Monitoring; Time Management.

Education and Training Program: Occupational Therapist Assistant Training. **Related Knowledge/Courses:** Therapy and Counseling; Psychology; Sociology and Anthropology; Philosophy and Theology; Medicine and Dentistry; Biology.

Occupational Therapists

❀ Annual Earnings: $66,780
❀ Beginning Wage: $42,820
❀ Earnings Growth Potential: Medium (35.9%)
❀ Growth: 23.1%
❀ Annual Job Openings: 8,338
❀ Self-Employed: 8.6%
❀ Part-Time: 29.8%
❀ Job Security: Most secure
❀ Education/Training Required: Master's degree

Industries in Which Income Is Highest

Industry	Average Annual Earnings	Number Employed
Administrative and Support Services	$76,890	1,480
Nursing and Residential Care Facilities	$71,350	10,670
Ambulatory Health Care Services	$69,870	29,860
Hospitals	$67,790	28,540
Educational Services	$60,150	13,090

Metropolitan Areas Where Income Is Highest

Metropolitan Area	Average Annual Earnings	Number Employed
Naples–Marco Island, FL	$96,120	80
Valdosta, GA	$89,280	70
Las Vegas–Paradise, NV	$88,090	430
Chico, CA	$86,610	70
San Francisco–Oakland–Fremont, CA	$85,770	950

Assess, plan, organize, and participate in rehabilitative programs that help restore vocational, homemaking, and daily living skills, as well as general independence, to disabled persons. Plan, organize, and conduct occupational therapy programs in hospital, institutional, or community settings to help rehabilitate those impaired because of illness, injury, or psychological or developmental problems. Test and evaluate patients' physical and mental abilities and analyze medical data to determine realistic rehabilitation goals for patients. Select activities that will help individuals learn work and life-management skills within limits of their mental and physical capabili-

ties. Evaluate patients' progress and prepare reports that detail progress. Complete and maintain necessary records. Train caregivers to provide for the needs of patients during and after therapies. Recommend changes in patients' work or living environments, consistent with their needs and capabilities. Develop and participate in health promotion programs, group activities, or discussions to promote client health, facilitate social adjustment, alleviate stress, and prevent physical or mental disability. Consult with rehabilitation team to select activity programs and coordinate occupational therapy with other therapeutic activities. Plan and implement programs and social activities to help patients learn work and school skills and adjust to handicaps. Design and create, or requisition, special supplies and equipment such as splints, braces and computer-aided adaptive equipment. Conduct research in occupational therapy. Provide training and supervision in therapy techniques and objectives for students and nurses and other medical staff. Help clients improve decision making, abstract reasoning, memory, sequencing, coordination, and perceptual skills, using computer programs. Advise on health risks in the workplace and on health-related transition to retirement. Lay out materials such as puzzles, scissors, and eating utensils for use in therapy, and clean and repair these tools after therapy sessions. Provide patients with assistance in locating and holding jobs.

Other Considerations for Income: No additional information.

Personality Type: Social-Investigative. **Career Cluster:** 08 Health Science. **Career Pathway:** 08.1 Therapeutic Services. **Skills:** Service Orientation; Systems Evaluation; Management of Personnel Resources; Systems Analysis; Negotiation.

Education and Training Program: Occupational Therapy/Therapist. **Related Knowledge/Courses:** Therapy and Counseling; Psychology; Sociology and Anthropology; Medicine and Dentistry; Biology; Education and Training.

Operations Research Analysts

* Annual Earnings: $69,000
* Beginning Wage: $40,000
* Earnings Growth Potential: High (42.0%)
* Growth: 10.6%
* Annual Job Openings: 5,727
* Self-Employed: 0.2%
* Part-Time: 5.6%
* Job Security: More secure than most
* Education/Training Required: Master's degree

Industries in Which Income Is Highest

Industry	Average Annual Earnings	Number Employed
Merchant Wholesalers, Durable Goods	$78,950	1,060
Professional, Scientific, and Technical Services	$77,930	14,380
Data Processing, Hosting and Related Services	$76,070	2,260
Computer and Electronic Product Manufacturing	$73,720	1,660
Management of Companies and Enterprises	$71,470	4,160

Metropolitan Areas Where Income Is Highest

Metropolitan Area	Average Annual Earnings	Number Employed
Spartanburg, SC	$109,000	80
Washington-Arlington-Alexandria, DC-VA-MD-WV	$96,330	5,300
Ann Arbor, MI	$94,540	90
Colorado Springs, CO	$93,340	200
Las Cruces, NM	$93,240	100

Formulate and apply mathematical modeling and other optimizing methods, using a computer to develop and interpret information that assists management with decision making, policy formulation, or other managerial functions. Formulate mathematical or simulation models of problems, relating constants and variables, restrictions, alternatives, and conflicting objectives and their numerical parameters. Collaborate with others in the organization to ensure successful implementation of chosen problem solutions. Analyze information obtained from management in order to conceptualize and define operational problems. Perform validation and testing of models to ensure adequacy; reformulate models as necessary. Collaborate with senior managers and decision-makers to identify and solve a variety of problems and to clarify management objectives. Define data requirements; then gather and validate information, applying judgment and statistical tests. Study and analyze information about alternative courses of action in order to determine which plan will offer the best outcomes. Prepare management reports defining and evaluating problems and recommending solutions. Break systems into their component parts, assign numerical values to each component, and examine the mathematical relationships between them. Specify manipulative or computational methods to be applied to models. Observe the current system in operation and gather and analyze information about each of the parts of component problems, using a variety of sources. Design, conduct, and evaluate experimental operational models in cases where models cannot be developed from existing data. Develop and apply time and cost networks in order to plan, control, and review large projects. Develop business methods and procedures, including accounting systems, file systems, office systems, logistics systems, and production schedules.

Other Considerations for Income: Employer-sponsored training is often another part of an analyst's compensation. Some analysts attend advanced university classes on these subjects at their employer's expense.

Personality Type: Investigative-Conventional-Enterprising. **Career Clusters:** 04 Business, Management, and Administration; 15 Science, Technology, Engineering, and Mathematics. **Career Pathways:** 04.1 Management; 04.4 Business Analysis; 15.1 Engineering and Technology; 15.3 Science and Mathematics. **Skills:** Programming; Systems Analysis; Operations Analysis; Mathematics; Science; Systems Evaluation; Complex Problem Solving; Judgment and Decision Making.

Education and Training Programs: Management Science; Management Sciences and Quantitative Methods, Other; Operations Research. **Related Knowledge/Courses:** Mathematics; Engineering and Technology; Computers and Electronics; Production and Processing; Economics and Accounting; Administration and Management.

Ophthalmologists

- ❀ Annual Earnings: $166,400+
- ❀ Beginning Wage: $49,710
- ❀ Earnings Growth Potential: Cannot be calculated
- ❀ Growth: 14.2%
- ❀ Annual Job Openings: 38,027
- ❀ Self-Employed: 14.7%
- ❀ Part-Time: 8.1%
- ❀ Job Security: No data available
- ❀ Education/Training Required: First professional degree

The Department of Labor reports this information for the occupation Physicians and Surgeons. The job openings listed here are shared with other specializations within that occupation, including Allergists and Immunologists; Anesthesiologists; Dermatologists; Family and General Practitioners; Hospitalists; Internists, General; Neurologists; Nuclear Medicine Physicians; Obstetricians and Gynecologists; Pathologists; Pediatricians, General; Physical Medicine and Rehabilitation Physicians; Preventive Medicine Physicians; Psychiatrists; Radiologists; Sports Medicine Physicians; Surgeons; and Urologists.

Industries in Which Income Is Highest

Industry	Average Annual Earnings	Number Employed
Ambulatory Health Care Services	$166,400+	147,400
Administrative and Support Services	$166,400+	1,310
Federal, State, and Local Government	$162,300	28,180
Professional, Scientific, and Technical Services	$107,470	1,210
Hospitals	$72,130	72,490

Metropolitan Areas Where Income Is Highest

Metropolitan Area	Average Annual Earnings	Number Employed
Los Angeles–Long Beach–Santa Ana, CA	$166,400+	8,810
Boston-Cambridge-Quincy, MA-NH	$166,400+	6,380
Dallas–Fort Worth–Arlington, TX	$166,400+	4,950
Tampa–St. Petersburg–Clearwater, FL	$166,400+	3,810
Portland-Vancouver-Beaverton, OR-WA	$166,400+	3,180

Diagnose, treat, and help prevent diseases and injuries of the eyes and related structures. No task data available.

Other Considerations for Income: Earnings of physicians and surgeons are among the highest of any occupation. Separate earnings figures for Ophthalmologists are not available.

Personality Type: Investigative-Social-Realistic. **Career Cluster:** 08 Health Science. **Career Pathway:** 08.1 Therapeutic Services. **Skills:** No data available.

Education and Training Program: Ophthalmology Residency Program. **Related Knowledge/Courses:** No data available.

Optometrists

- ❀ Annual Earnings: $96,320
- ❀ Beginning Wage: $46,860
- ❀ Earnings Growth Potential: Very high (51.3%)
- ❀ Growth: 11.3%
- ❀ Annual Job Openings: 1,789
- ❀ Self-Employed: 25.5%
- ❀ Part-Time: 20.8%
- ❀ Job Security: Most secure
- ❀ Education/Training Required: First professional degree

Industries in Which Income Is Highest

Industry	Average Annual Earnings	Number Employed
Health and Personal Care Stores	$100,960	2,590
Ambulatory Health Care Services	$95,960	21,820

Metropolitan Areas Where Income Is Highest

Metropolitan Area	Average Annual Earnings	Number Employed
Orlando-Kissimmee, FL	$158,770	100
New Orleans–Metairie–Kenner, LA	$132,240	90
Memphis, TN-MS-AR	$120,270	90
Jacksonville, FL	$117,600	110
Akron, OH	$117,600	60

Diagnose, manage, and treat conditions and diseases of the human eye and visual system. Examine eyes and visual systems, diagnose problems or impairments, prescribe corrective lenses, and provide treatment. May prescribe therapeutic drugs to treat specific eye conditions. Examine eyes, using observation, instruments, and pharmaceutical agents, to determine visual acuity and perception, focus, and coordination and to diagnose diseases and other abnormalities such as glaucoma or color blindness. Prescribe medications to treat eye diseases if state laws permit. Analyze test results and develop treatment plans. Prescribe, supply, fit, and adjust eyeglasses, contact lenses, and other vision aids. Educate and counsel patients on contact lens care, visual hygiene, lighting arrangements, and safety factors. Remove foreign bodies from eyes. Consult with and refer patients to ophthalmologist or other health care practitioners if additional medical treatment is determined necessary. Provide patients undergoing eye surgeries such as cataract and laser vision correction, with pre- and post-operative care. Prescribe therapeutic procedures to correct or conserve vision. Provide vision therapy and low vision rehabilitation.

Other Considerations for Income: Self-employed optometrists, including those working in partnerships, must provide their own benefits. Optometrists employed by others typically enjoy paid vacation, sick leave, and pension contributions.

Personality Type: Investigative-Social-Realistic. **Career Cluster:** 08 Health Science. **Career Pathway:** 08.1 Therapeutic Services. **Skills:** Reading Comprehension; Quality Control Analysis; Systems Analysis; Systems Evaluation; Judgment and Decision Making; Service Orientation; Operation and Control.

Education and Training Program: Optometry (OD). **Related Knowledge/Courses:** Medicine and Dentistry; Biology; Therapy and Counseling; Physics; Sales and Marketing; Economics and Accounting.

Oral and Maxillofacial Surgeons

❋ Annual Earnings: $166,400+
❋ Beginning Wage: $94,650
❋ Earnings Growth Potential: Cannot be calculated
❋ Growth: 9.1%
❋ Annual Job Openings: 400
❋ Self-Employed: 30.6%
❋ Part-Time: 25.9%
❋ Job Security: Less secure than most
❋ Education/Training Required: First professional degree

Industries in Which Income Is Highest

Industry	Average Annual Earnings	Number Employed
Ambulatory Health Care Services	$166,400+	4,640
Hospitals	$165,820	70

Metropolitan Areas Where Income Is Highest

Metropolitan Area	Average Annual Earnings	Number Employed
New York–Northern New Jersey–Long Island, NY-NJ-PA	$166,400+	520
San Jose–Sunnyvale–Santa Clara, CA	$166,400+	200
Boston-Cambridge-Quincy, MA-NH	$166,400+	190
Minneapolis–St. Paul–Bloomington, MN-WI	$166,400+	110
Virginia Beach–Norfolk–Newport News, VA-NC	$166,400+	80

Perform surgery on mouth, jaws, and related head and neck structure to execute difficult and multiple extractions of teeth, to remove tumors and other abnormal growths, to correct abnormal jaw relations by mandibular or maxillary revision, to prepare mouth for insertion of dental prosthesis, or to treat fractured jaws. Administer general and local anesthetics. Remove impacted, damaged, and non-restorable teeth. Evaluate the position of the wisdom teeth in order to determine whether problems exist currently or might occur in the future. Collaborate with other professionals such as restorative dentists and orthodontists in order to plan treatment. Perform surgery to prepare the mouth for dental implants and to aid in the regeneration of deficient bone and gum tissues. Remove tumors and other abnormal growths of the oral and facial regions, using surgical instruments. Treat infections of the oral cavity, salivary glands, jaws, and neck. Treat problems affecting the oral mucosa such as mouth ulcers and infections. Provide emergency treatment of facial injuries, including facial lacerations, intra-oral lacerations, and fractured facial bones. Perform surgery on the mouth and jaws in order to treat conditions such as cleft lip and palate and jaw growth problems. Restore form and function by moving skin, bone, nerves, and other tissues from other parts of the body in order to reconstruct the jaws and face. Perform minor cosmetic procedures such as chin and cheekbone enhancements and minor facial rejuvenation procedures including the use of Botox and laser technology. Treat snoring problems, using laser surgery.

Other Considerations for Income: Self-employed dentists in private practice tend to earn more than do salaried dentists. Dentists who are salaried often receive benefits paid by their employer, with health insurance and malpractice insurance being among the most common. However, like other business owners, self-employed dentists must provide their own health insurance, life insurance, retirement plans, and other benefits.

Personality Type: Realistic-Social-Investigative. **Career Cluster:** 08 Health Science. **Career Pathway:** 08.1 Therapeutic Services. **Skills:** Science; Management of Financial Resources; Equipment Selection; Service Orientation; Complex Problem Solving; Management of Personnel Resources; Active Learning; Reading Comprehension.

Education and Training Programs: Oral and Maxillofacial Surgery Residency Program; Oral/Maxillofacial Surgery (Cert., MS, PhD). **Related Knowledge/Courses:** Medicine and Dentistry; Biology; Therapy and Counseling; Chemistry; Psychology; Personnel and Human Resources.

Orthodontists

- ❋ Annual Earnings: $166,400+
- ❋ Beginning Wage: $100,980
- ❋ Earnings Growth Potential: Cannot be calculated
- ❋ Growth: 9.2%
- ❋ Annual Job Openings: 479
- ❋ Self-Employed: 43.3%
- ❋ Part-Time: 25.9%
- ❋ Job Security: Less secure than most
- ❋ Education/Training Required: First professional degree

Industries in Which Income Is Highest

Industry	Average Annual Earnings	Number Employed
Ambulatory Health Care Services	$166,400+	5,450

Metropolitan Areas Where Income Is Highest

Metropolitan Area	Average Annual Earnings	Number Employed
New York–Northern New Jersey–Long Island, NY-NJ-PA	$166,400+	300
Washington-Arlington-Alexandria, DC-VA-MD-WV	$166,400+	170
Chicago-Naperville-Joliet, IL-IN-WI	$166,400+	160
Boston-Cambridge-Quincy, MA-NH	$166,400+	100
Dallas–Fort Worth–Arlington, TX	$166,400+	90

Examine, diagnose, and treat dental malocclusions and oral cavity anomalies. Design and fabricate appliances to realign teeth and jaws to produce and maintain normal function and to improve appearance. Fit dental appliances in patients' mouths to alter the position and relationship of teeth and jaws and to realign teeth. Study diagnostic records such as medical/dental histories, plaster models of the teeth, photos of a patient's face and teeth, and X-rays to develop patient treatment plans. Diagnose teeth and jaw or other dental-facial abnormalities. Examine patients to assess abnormalities of jaw development, tooth position, and other dental-facial structures. Prepare diagnostic and treatment records. Adjust dental appliances periodically to produce and maintain normal function. Provide patients with proposed treatment plans and cost estimates. Instruct dental officers and technical assistants in orthodontic procedures and techniques. Coordinate orthodontic services with other dental and medical services. Design and fabricate appliances, such as space maintainers, retainers, and labial and lingual arch wires.

Other Considerations for Income: Self-employed dentists in private practice tend to earn more than do salaried dentists. Dentists who are salaried often receive benefits paid by their employer, with health insurance and malpractice insurance being among the most common. However, like other business owners, self-employed dentists must provide their own health insurance, life insurance, retirement plans, and other benefits.

Personality Type: Investigative-Realistic-Social. **Career Cluster:** 08 Health Science. **Career Pathway:** 08.1 Therapeutic Services. **Skills:** Management of Financial Resources; Equipment Selection; Management of Personnel Resources; Management of Material Resources; Technology Design; Judgment and Decision Making; Operations Analysis; Service Orientation.

Education and Training Programs: Orthodontics Specialty; Orthodontics/Orthodontology. **Related Knowledge/Courses:** Medicine and Dentistry; Biology; Sales and Marketing; Economics and Accounting; Personnel and Human Resources; Customer and Personal Service.

Orthotists and Prosthetists

* Annual Earnings: $62,590
* Beginning Wage: $33,430
* Earnings Growth Potential: High (46.6%)
* Growth: 11.8%
* Annual Job Openings: 295
* Self-Employed: 6.5%
* Part-Time: 15.4%
* Job Security: More secure than most
* Education/Training Required: Bachelor's degree

Industries in Which Income Is Highest

Industry	Average Annual Earnings	Number Employed
Health and Personal Care Stores	$70,400	1,140
Miscellaneous Manufacturing	$67,590	2,080
Federal, State, and Local Government	$65,410	470
Hospitals	$49,790	580
Ambulatory Health Care Services	$48,890	880

Metropolitan Areas Where Income Is Highest

Metropolitan Area	Average Annual Earnings	Number Employed
Jacksonville, FL	$94,070	40
Greenville, SC	$86,680	40
Miami–Fort Lauderdale–Miami Beach, FL	$82,260	50
Columbus, OH	$78,290	50
Minneapolis–St. Paul–Bloomington, MN-WI	$72,820	60

Assist patients with disabling conditions of limbs and spine or with partial or total absence of limb by fitting and preparing orthopedic braces or prostheses. Examine, interview, and measure patients in order to determine their appliance needs and to identify factors that could affect appliance fit. Fit, test, and evaluate devices on patients and make adjustments for proper fit, function, and comfort. Instruct patients in the use and care of orthoses and prostheses. Design orthopedic and prosthetic devices based on physicians' prescriptions and examination and measurement of patients. Maintain patients' records. Make and modify plaster casts of areas that will be fitted with prostheses or orthoses for use in the device construction process. Select materials and components to be used, based on device design. Confer with physicians to formulate specifications and prescriptions for orthopedic or prosthetic devices. Repair, rebuild, and modify prosthetic and orthopedic appliances. Construct and fabricate appliances or supervise others who are constructing the appliances. Train and supervise orthopedic and prosthetic assistants and technicians and other support staff. Update skills and knowledge by attending conferences and seminars. Show and explain orthopedic and prosthetic appliances to health-care workers. Research new ways to construct and use orthopedic and prosthetic devices. Publish research findings and present them at conferences and seminars.

Other Considerations for Income: No additional information.

Personality Type: Social-Realistic-Investigative. **Career Cluster:** 08 Health Science. **Career Pathway:** 08.3 Health Informatics. **Skills:** Technology Design; Management of Financial Resources; Management of Material Resources; Operations Analysis; Service Orientation; Equipment Selection; Science; Management of Personnel Resources.

Education and Training Programs: Assistive/Augmentative Technology and Rehabilitation Engineering; Orthotist/Prosthetist. **Related Knowledge/Courses:** Engineering and Technology; Medicine and Dentistry; Therapy and Counseling; Design; Psychology; Production and Processing.

Park Naturalists

- ❀ Annual Earnings: $58,720
- ❀ Beginning Wage: $35,190
- ❀ Earnings Growth Potential: High (40.1%)
- ❀ Growth: 5.3%
- ❀ Annual Job Openings: 1,161
- ❀ Self-Employed: 3.9%
- ❀ Part-Time: 4.9%
- ❀ Job Security: More secure than most
- ❀ Education/Training Required: Bachelor's degree

The Department of Labor reports this information for the occupation Conservation Scientists. The job openings listed here are shared with other specializations within that occupation, including Range Managers; and Soil and Water Conservationists.

Industries in Which Income Is Highest

Industry	Average Annual Earnings	Number Employed
Federal, State, and Local Government	$60,060	12,560
Religious, Grantmaking, Civic, Professional, and Similar Organizations	$52,530	1,490

Metropolitan Areas Where Income Is Highest

Metropolitan Area	Average Annual Earnings	Number Employed
Anchorage, AK	$79,740	100
Washington-Arlington-Alexandria, DC-VA-MD-WV	$78,220	400
San Jose–Sunnyvale–Santa Clara, CA	$74,550	70
Miami–Fort Lauderdale–Miami Beach, FL	$74,450	60
Los Angeles–Long Beach–Santa Ana, CA	$74,240	100

Plan, develop, and conduct programs to inform public of historical, natural, and scientific features of national, state, or local park. Provide visitor services by explaining regulations; answering visitor requests, needs, and complaints; and providing information about the park and surrounding areas. Conduct field trips to point out scientific, historic, and natural features of parks, forests, historic sites, or other attractions. Prepare and present illustrated lectures and interpretive talks about park features. Perform emergency duties to protect human life, government property, and natural features of park. Confer with park staff to determine subjects and schedules for park programs. Assist with operations of general facilities, such as visitor centers. Plan, organize, and direct activities of seasonal staff members. Perform routine maintenance on park structures. Prepare brochures and write newspaper articles. Construct historical, scientific, and nature visitor-center displays. Research stories regarding the area's natural history or environment. Interview specialists in desired fields to obtain and develop data for park information programs. Compile and maintain official park photographic and information files. Take photographs and motion pictures for use in lectures and publications and to develop displays. Survey park to determine forest conditions and distribution and abundance of fauna and flora. Plan and develop audiovisual devices for public programs.

Other Considerations for Income: In private industry, starting salaries for students with a bachelor's degree were comparable with starting salaries in the federal government, but starting salaries in state and local governments were usually lower. Conservation scientists and foresters who work for federal, state, and local governments and large private firms generally receive more generous benefits than do those working for smaller firms. Governments usually have good pension, health, and leave plans.

Personality Type: Social-Realistic-Artistic. **Career Cluster:** 01 Agriculture, Food and Natural Resource. **Career**

Pathway: 01.5 Natural Resources Systems. **Skills:** Management of Personnel Resources; Management of Financial Resources; Science; Service Orientation; Writing; Management of Material Resources; Reading Comprehension; Persuasion.

Education and Training Programs: Forest Management/Forest Resources Management; Forest Sciences and Biology; Forestry, General; Forestry, Other; Land Use Planning and Management/Development; Natural Resources and Conservation, Other; Natural Resources Management and Policy; Natural Resources Management and Policy, Other; Natural Resources/Conservation, General; Water, Wetlands, and Marine Resources Management; Wildlife, Fish and Wildlands Science and Management. **Related Knowledge/Courses:** Biology; History and Archeology; Geography; Sociology and Anthropology; Communications and Media; Customer and Personal Service.

Pathologists

- ❋ Annual Earnings: $166,400+
- ❋ Beginning Wage: $49,710
- ❋ Earnings Growth Potential: Cannot be calculated
- ❋ Growth: 14.2%
- ❋ Annual Job Openings: 38,027
- ❋ Self-Employed: 14.7%
- ❋ Part-Time: 8.1%
- ❋ Job Security: No data available
- ❋ Education/Training Required: First professional degree

The Department of Labor reports this information for the occupation Physicians and Surgeons. The job openings listed here are shared with other specializations within that occupation, including Allergists and Immunologists; Anesthesiologists; Dermatologists; Family and General Practitioners; Hospitalists; Internists, General; Neurologists; Nuclear Medicine Physicians; Obstetricians and Gynecologists; Ophthalmologists; Pediatricians, General; Physical Medicine and Rehabilitation Physicians; Preventive Medicine Physicians; Psychiatrists; Radiologists; Sports Medicine Physicians; Surgeons; and Urologists.

Industries in Which Income Is Highest

Industry	Average Annual Earnings	Number Employed
Ambulatory Health Care Services	$166,400+	147,400
Administrative and Support Services	$166,400+	1,310
Federal, State, and Local Government	$162,300	28,180
Professional, Scientific, and Technical Services	$107,470	1,210
Hospitals	$72,130	72,490

Metropolitan Areas Where Income Is Highest

Metropolitan Area	Average Annual Earnings	Number Employed
Los Angeles–Long Beach–Santa Ana, CA	$166,400+	8,810
Boston-Cambridge-Quincy, MA-NH	$166,400+	6,380
Dallas–Fort Worth–Arlington, TX	$166,400+	4,950
Tampa–St. Petersburg–Clearwater, FL	$166,400+	3,810
Portland-Vancouver-Beaverton, OR-WA	$166,400+	3,180

Diagnose presence and stage of diseases, using laboratory techniques and patient specimens. Study the nature, cause, and development of diseases. May perform autopsies. No task data available.

Other Considerations for Income: Earnings of physicians and surgeons are among the highest of any occupation. Separate earnings figures for Pathologists are not available.

Personality Type: Investigative-Realistic. **Career Cluster:** 08 Health Science. **Career Pathway:** 08.2 Diagnostics Services. **Skills:** No data available.

Education and Training Program: Pathology Residency Program. **Related Knowledge/Courses:** No data available.

Pediatricians, General

✸ Annual Earnings: $146,040
✸ Beginning Wage: $79,930
✸ Earnings Growth Potential: High (45.3%)
✸ Growth: 14.2%
✸ Annual Job Openings: 38,027
✸ Self-Employed: 14.7%
✸ Part-Time: 8.1%
✸ Job Security: Most secure
✸ Education/Training Required: First professional degree

The Department of Labor reports this information for the occupation Physicians and Surgeons. The job openings listed here are shared with other specializations within that occupation, including Allergists and Immunologists; Anesthesiologists; Dermatologists; Family and General Practitioners; Hospitalists; Internists, General; Neurologists; Nuclear Medicine Physicians; Obstetricians and Gynecologists; Ophthalmologists; Pathologists; Physical Medicine and Rehabilitation Physicians; Preventive Medicine Physicians; Psychiatrists; Radiologists; Sports Medicine Physicians; Surgeons; and Urologists.

Industries in Which Income Is Highest

Industry	Average Annual Earnings	Number Employed
Hospitals	$147,180	3,990
Ambulatory Health Care Services	$147,020	23,730
Educational Services	$113,630	1,250

Metropolitan Areas Where Income Is Highest

Metropolitan Area	Average Annual Earnings	Number Employed
Portland-Vancouver-Beaverton, OR-WA	$166,400+	260
Louisville–Jefferson County, KY-IN	$166,400+	200
San Antonio, TX	$166,400+	190
Austin–Round Rock, TX	$166,400+	170
El Paso, TX	$166,400+	130

Diagnose, treat, and help prevent children's diseases and injuries. Examine patients or order, perform, and interpret diagnostic tests to obtain information on medi-

cal condition and determine diagnosis. Examine children regularly to assess their growth and development. Prescribe or administer treatment, therapy, medication, vaccination, and other specialized medical care to treat or prevent illness, disease, or injury in infants and children. Collect, record, and maintain patient information, such as medical history, reports, and examination results. Advise patients, parents or guardians, and community members concerning diet, activity, hygiene, and disease prevention. Treat children who have minor illnesses, acute and chronic health problems, and growth and development concerns. Explain procedures and discuss test results or prescribed treatments with patients and parents or guardians. Monitor patients' condition and progress and re-evaluate treatments as necessary. Plan and execute medical care programs to aid in the mental and physical growth and development of children and adolescents. Refer patient to medical specialist or other practitioner when necessary. Direct and coordinate activities of nurses, students, assistants, specialists, therapists, and other medical staff. Provide consulting services to other physicians. Plan, implement, or administer health programs or standards in hospital, business, or community for information, prevention, or treatment of injury or illness. Operate on patients to remove, repair, or improve functioning of diseased or injured body parts and systems. Conduct research to study anatomy and develop or test medications, treatments, or procedures to prevent or control disease or injury. Prepare reports for government or management of birth, death, and disease statistics; workforce evaluations; or medical status of individuals.

Other Considerations for Income: Earnings of physicians and surgeons are among the highest of any occupation, but Pediatricians are among the lowest-paid physicians. The Medical Group Management Association's Physician Compensation and Production Survey of 2005 reported earnings of $132,953 for Pediatricians with less than two years in their specialty and $161,331 for those with more than one year in their specialty. These figures cover salary, bonus and incentive payments, research stipends, honoraria, and distribution of profits. Self-employed physicians—those who own or are part owners of their medical practice—generally have higher median incomes than salaried physicians, but their must provide for their own health insurance and retirement.

Personality Type: Investigative-Social. **Career Cluster:** 08 Health Science. **Career Pathway:** 08.1 Therapeutic Services. **Skills:** Science; Social Perceptiveness; Active Learning; Reading Comprehension; Critical Thinking;

Persuasion; Management of Financial Resources; Monitoring.

Education and Training Program: Medicine (MD). **Related Knowledge/Courses:** Medicine and Dentistry; Therapy and Counseling; Biology; Psychology; Chemistry; Sociology and Anthropology.

Personal Financial Advisors

✻ Annual Earnings: $69,050
✻ Beginning Wage: $34,390
✻ Earnings Growth Potential: Very high (50.2%)
✻ Growth: 41.0%
✻ Annual Job Openings: 17,114
✻ Self-Employed: 30.9%
✻ Part-Time: 7.7%
✻ Job Security: Least secure
✻ Education/Training Required: Bachelor's degree

Industries in Which Income Is Highest

Industry	Average Annual Earnings	Number Employed
Securities, Commodity Contracts, and Other Financial Investments and Related Activities	$78,360	89,270
Professional, Scientific, and Technical Services	$64,420	6,900
Insurance Carriers and Related Activities	$63,360	6,770
Management of Companies and Enterprises	$62,810	3,250
Credit Intermediation and Related Activities	$61,130	31,050

Metropolitan Areas Where Income Is Highest

Metropolitan Area	Average Annual Earnings	Number Employed
Worcester, MA-CT	$137,290	170
El Paso, TX	$118,180	60
New York–Northern New Jersey–Long Island, NY-NJ-PA	$112,900	24,320
Macon, GA	$112,520	100
Trenton-Ewing, NJ	$110,440	350

Advise clients on financial plans, using knowledge of tax and investment strategies, securities, insurance, pension plans, and real estate. Duties include assessing clients' assets, liabilities, cash flows, insurance coverages, tax statuses, and financial objectives to establish investment strategies. Prepare and interpret for clients information such as investment performance reports, financial document summaries, and income projections. Recommend strategies clients can use to achieve their financial goals and objectives, including specific recommendations in such areas as cash management, insurance coverage, and investment planning. Build and maintain client bases, keeping current client plans up-to-date and recruiting new clients on an ongoing basis. Devise debt liquidation plans that include payoff priorities and timelines. Implement financial planning recommendations, or refer clients to someone who can assist them with plan implementation. Interview clients to determine their current incomes, expenses, insurance coverages, tax statuses, financial objectives, risk tolerances, and other information needed to develop financial plans. Monitor financial market trends to ensure that plans are effective, and to identify any necessary updates. Explain and document for clients the types of services that are to be provided, and the responsibilities to be taken by personal financial advisors. Explain to individuals and groups the details of financial assistance available to college and university students, such as loans, grants, and scholarships. Guide clients in the gathering of information such as bank account records, income tax returns, life and disability insurance records, pension plan information, and wills. Analyze financial information obtained from clients to determine strategies for meeting clients' financial objectives. Meet with clients' other advisors, including attorneys, accountants, trust officers, and investment bankers, to fully understand clients' financial goals and circumstances. Answer clients' questions about the purposes and details of financial plans and strategies. Open accounts for clients, and disburse funds from account to creditors as agents for clients. Authorize release of financial aid funds to students.

Other Considerations for Income: Personal financial advisors who work for financial services firms are generally paid a salary plus bonus. Advisors who work for financial investment or planning firms or who are self-employed either charge hourly fees for their services or opt to earn their money through fees on stock and insurance purchases. Advisors generally receive commissions for financial products they sell in addition to charging a fee. Those who manage a client's assets may charge a percentage of those assets. Earnings of self-employed workers are not included in the medians given here.

Personality Type: Enterprising-Conventional-Social. **Career Cluster:** 06 Finance. **Career Pathway:** 06.1 Financial and Investment Planning. **Skills:** Management of Financial Resources; Persuasion; Mathematics; Speaking; Complex Problem Solving; Active Listening; Judgment and Decision Making; Service Orientation.

Education and Training Programs: Finance, General; Financial Planning and Services. **Related Knowledge/Courses:** Economics and Accounting; Sales and Marketing; Law and Government; Customer and Personal Service; Mathematics; Computers and Electronics.

Petroleum Engineers

❀ Annual Earnings: $108,020
❀ Beginning Wage: $57,820
❀ Earnings Growth Potential: High (46.5%)
❀ Growth: 5.2%
❀ Annual Job Openings: 1,016
❀ Self-Employed: 9.2%
❀ Part-Time: 2.9%
❀ Job Security: More secure than most
❀ Education/Training Required: Bachelor's degree

Industries in Which Income Is Highest

Industry	Average Annual Earnings	Number Employed
Oil and Gas Extraction	$119,960	8,130
Petroleum and Coal Products Manufacturing	$109,900	1,680
Management of Companies and Enterprises	$108,380	1,410
Professional, Scientific, and Technical Services	$107,860	3,580
Support Activities for Mining	$90,860	3,710

Metropolitan Areas Where Income Is Highest

Metropolitan Area	Average Annual Earnings	Number Employed
Anchorage, AK	$165,070	590
Denver-Aurora, CO	$146,570	700
San Francisco–Oakland–Fremont, CA	$131,000	300
Houston–Sugar Land–Baytown, TX	$128,050	6,790
Midland, TX	$121,870	430

Devise methods to improve oil and gas production and determine the need for new or modified tool designs. Oversee drilling and offer technical advice to achieve economical and satisfactory progress. Assess costs and estimate the production capabilities and economic value of oil and gas wells to evaluate the economic viability of potential drilling sites. Monitor production rates and plan rework processes to improve production. Analyze data to recommend placement of wells and supplementary processes to enhance production. Specify and supervise well modification and stimulation programs to maximize oil and gas recovery. Direct and monitor the completion and evaluation of wells, well testing, or well surveys. Assist engineering and other personnel to solve operating problems. Develop plans for oil and gas field drilling and for product recovery and treatment. Maintain records of drilling and production operations. Confer with scientific, engineering, and technical personnel to resolve design, research, and testing problems. Write technical reports for engineering and management personnel. Evaluate findings to develop, design, or test equipment or processes. Assign work to staff to obtain maximum utilization of personnel. Interpret drilling and testing information for personnel. Design and implement environmental controls on oil and gas operations. Coordinate the installation, maintenance, and operation of mining and oilfield equipment. Supervise the removal of drilling equipment, the removal of any waste, and the safe return of land to structural stability when wells or pockets are exhausted. Inspect oil and gas wells to determine that installations are completed. Simulate reservoir performance for different recovery techniques, using computer models. Take samples to assess the amount and quality of oil, the depth at which resources lie, and the equipment needed to properly extract them. Coordinate activities of workers engaged in research, planning, and development. Design or modify mining and oilfield machinery and tools, applying engineering principles. Test machinery and equipment to ensure that it is safe and conforms to performance specifications.

Other Considerations for Income: As a group, engineers earn some of the highest average starting salaries among those holding bachelor's degrees. Petroleum Engineers are among the best-paid of the various kinds of engineers. Separate earnings figures for Petroleum Engineers with various degrees are not available.

Personality Type: Investigative-Realistic-Conventional. **Career Cluster:** 15 Science, Technology, Engineering, and Mathematics. **Career Pathway:** 15.1 Engineering and Technology. **Skills:** Management of Financial Resources; Science; Operations Analysis; Troubleshooting; Mathematics; Technology Design; Judgment and Decision Making; Operation Monitoring.

Education and Training Program: Petroleum Engineering. **Related Knowledge/Courses:** Engineering and Technology; Physics; Geography; Chemistry; Design; Economics and Accounting.

Petroleum Pump System Operators, Refinery Operators, and Gaugers

❋ Annual Earnings: $55,010
❋ Beginning Wage: $34,650
❋ Earnings Growth Potential: Medium (37.0%)
❋ Growth: –13.4%
❋ Annual Job Openings: 4,477
❋ Self-Employed: 0.1%
❋ Part-Time: 0.6%
❋ Job Security: Least secure
❋ Education/Training Required: Long-term on-the-job training

Industries in Which Income Is Highest

Industry	Average Annual Earnings	Number Employed
Petroleum and Coal Products Manufacturing	$57,490	22,590
Pipeline Transportation	$56,000	4,930
Oil and Gas Extraction	$54,640	9,100
Merchant Wholesalers, Nondurable Goods	$50,810	1,280

Metropolitan Areas Where Income Is Highest

Metropolitan Area	Average Annual Earnings	Number Employed
San Francisco–Oakland–Fremont, CA	$68,570	2,070
Toledo, OH	$65,970	600
Beaumont–Port Arthur, TX	$64,890	1,930
Los Angeles–Long Beach–Santa Ana, CA	$62,700	1,620
Bakersfield, CA	$62,180	1,200

Control the operation of petroleum-refining or -processing units. May specialize in controlling manifold and pumping systems, gauging or testing oil in storage tanks, or regulating the flow of oil into pipelines. Monitor process indicators, instruments, gauges, and meters in order to detect and report any possible problems. Control or operate manifold and pumping systems to circulate liquids through a petroleum refinery. Operate control panels to coordinate and regulate process variables such as temperature and pressure and to direct product flow rate according to process schedules. Lower thermometers into tanks to obtain temperature readings. Perform tests to check the qualities and grades of products, such as assessing levels of bottom sediment, water, and foreign materials in oil samples, using centrifugal testers. Inspect pipelines, tightening connections and lubricating valves as necessary. Calculate test result values, using standard formulas. Coordinate shutdowns and major projects. Conduct general housekeeping of units, including wiping up oil spills and performing general cleaning duties. Clean interiors of processing units by circulating chemicals and solvents within units. Clamp seals around valves to secure tanks. Verify that incoming and outgoing products are moving through the correct meters and that meters are working properly. Synchronize activities with other pumphouses to ensure a continuous flow of products and a minimum of contamination between products. Start pumps and open valves or use automated equipment to regulate the flow of oil in pipelines and into and out of tanks. Maintain and repair equipment or report malfunctioning equipment to supervisors so that repairs can be scheduled. Plan movement of products through lines to processing, storage, and shipping units, utilizing knowledge of system interconnections and capacities. Read and analyze specifications, schedules, logs, test results, and laboratory recommendations to determine how to set equipment controls to produce the required qualities and quantities of products. Read automatic gauges at specified intervals to determine the flow rate of oil into or from tanks and the amount of oil in tanks.

Other Considerations for Income: No additional information.

Personality Type: Realistic-Conventional. **Career Cluster:** 13 Manufacturing. **Career Pathway:** 13.1 Production. **Skills:** Operation Monitoring; Operation and Control; Science; Troubleshooting; Repairing; Equipment Maintenance; Quality Control Analysis; Installation.

Education and Training Program: Mechanic and Repair Technologies/Technicians, Other. **Related Knowledge/Courses:** Mechanical; Chemistry; Engineering and Technology; Public Safety and Security; Production and Processing; Education and Training.

Pharmacists

- ❀ Annual Earnings: $106,410
- ❀ Beginning Wage: $77,390
- ❀ Earnings Growth Potential: Low (27.3%)
- ❀ Growth: 21.7%
- ❀ Annual Job Openings: 16,358
- ❀ Self-Employed: 0.5%
- ❀ Part-Time: 18.1%
- ❀ Job Security: Most secure
- ❀ Education/Training Required: First professional degree

Industries in Which Income Is Highest

Industry	Average Annual Earnings	Number Employed
General Merchandise Stores	$112,460	29,240
Management of Companies and Enterprises	$111,450	1,610
Insurance Carriers and Related Activities	$108,390	1,290
Administrative and Support Services	$108,340	5,220
Food and Beverage Stores	$107,420	21,690

Metropolitan Areas Where Income Is Highest

Metropolitan Area	Average Annual Earnings	Number Employed
Yuba City, CA	$129,860	70
Santa Barbara–Santa Maria, CA	$128,640	190
Modesto, CA	$127,390	330
Santa Cruz–Watsonville, CA	$126,090	160
Chico, CA	$125,360	120

Compound and dispense medications, following prescriptions issued by physicians, dentists, or other authorized medical practitioners. Review prescriptions to assure accuracy, to ascertain the needed ingredients, and to evaluate their suitability. Provide information and advice regarding drug interactions, side effects, dosage, and proper medication storage. Analyze prescribing trends to monitor patient compliance and to prevent excessive usage or harmful interactions. Order and purchase pharmaceutical supplies, medical supplies, and drugs, maintaining stock and storing and handling it properly. Maintain records such as pharmacy files; patient profiles; charge system files; inventories; control records for radioactive nuclei; and registries of poisons, narcotics, and controlled drugs. Provide specialized services to help patients manage conditions such as diabetes, asthma, smoking cessation, or high blood pressure. Advise customers on the selection of medication brands, medical equipment, and health-care supplies. Collaborate with other health-care professionals to plan, monitor, review, and evaluate the quality and effectiveness of drugs and drug regimens, providing advice on drug applications and characteristics. Compound and dispense medications as prescribed by doctors and dentists by calculating, weighing, measuring, and mixing ingredients or oversee these activities. Offer health promotion and prevention activities—for example, training people to use devices such as blood-pressure or diabetes monitors. Refer patients to other health professionals and agencies when appropriate. Prepare sterile solutions and infusions for use in surgical procedures, emergency rooms, or patients' homes. Plan, implement, and maintain procedures for mixing, packaging, and labeling pharmaceuticals according to policy and legal requirements to ensure quality, security, and proper disposal. Assay radiopharmaceuticals, verify rates of disintegration, and calculate the volume required to produce the desired results to ensure proper dosages.

Other Considerations for Income: According to a 2006 survey by Drug Topics Magazine, full-time pharmacists earned an average of $102,336, while part-time pharmacists earned an average of $55,589.

Personality Type: Investigative-Conventional-Social. **Career Cluster:** 08 Health Science. **Career Pathways:** 08.1 Therapeutic Services; 08.5 Biotechnology Research and Development. **Skills:** Science; Reading Comprehension; Social Perceptiveness; Active Listening; Instructing; Mathematics; Speaking; Critical Thinking.

Education and Training Programs: Clinical, Hospital, and Managed Care Pharmacy (MS, PhD); Industrial and Physical Pharmacy and Cosmetic Sciences (MS, PhD); Medicinal and Pharmaceutical Chemistry (MS, PhD); Natural Products Chemistry and Pharmacognosy (MS, PhD); Pharmaceutics and Drug Design (MS, PhD); Pharmacoeconomics/Pharmaceutical Economics (MS, PhD); Pharmacy (PharmD [USA], PharmD or BS/BPharm [Canada]); Pharmacy Administration and Pharmacy Policy and Regulatory Affairs (MS, PhD); others. **Related Knowledge/Courses:** Biology; Medicine and Dentistry; Chemistry; Therapy and Counseling; Psychology; Clerical.

Philosophy and Religion Teachers, Postsecondary

- ❁ Annual Earnings: $59,540
- ❁ Beginning Wage: $33,430
- ❁ Earnings Growth Potential: High (43.9%)
- ❁ Growth: 22.9%
- ❁ Annual Job Openings: 3,120
- ❁ Self-Employed: 0.4%
- ❁ Part-Time: 27.8%
- ❁ Job Security: Most secure
- ❁ Education/Training Required: Doctoral degree

Industries in Which Income Is Highest

Industry	Average Annual Earnings	Number Employed
Educational Services	$59,850	18,000

Metropolitan Areas Where Income Is Highest

Metropolitan Area	Average Annual Earnings	Number Employed
Durham, NC	$81,330	110
Houston–Sugar Land–Baytown, TX	$79,840	220
San Diego–Carlsbad–San Marcos, CA	$77,010	120
San Jose–Sunnyvale–Santa Clara, CA	$76,740	70
Riverside–San Bernardino–Ontario, CA	$75,900	120

Teach courses in philosophy, religion, and theology. Evaluate and grade students' classwork, assignments, and papers. Initiate, facilitate, and moderate classroom discussions. Prepare and deliver lectures to undergraduate and graduate students on topics such as ethics, logic, and contemporary religious thought. Prepare course materials such as syllabi, homework assignments, and handouts. Compile, administer, and grade examinations or assign this work to others. Keep abreast of developments in their field by reading current literature, talking with colleagues, and participating in professional conferences. Maintain student attendance records, grades, and other required records. Plan, evaluate, and revise curricula, course content, and course materials and methods of instruction.

Maintain regularly scheduled office hours to advise and assist students. Select and obtain materials and supplies such as textbooks. Advise students on academic and vocational curricula and on career issues. Conduct research in a particular field of knowledge and publish findings in professional journals, books, or electronic media. Perform administrative duties such as serving as department head. Serve on academic or administrative committees that deal with institutional policies, departmental matters, and academic issues. Collaborate with colleagues to address teaching and research issues. Participate in campus and community events. Participate in student recruitment, registration, and placement activities. Compile bibliographies of specialized materials for outside reading assignments. Supervise undergraduate and graduate teaching, internship, and research work. Act as advisers to student organizations. Write grant proposals to procure external research funding. Provide professional consulting services to government or industry.

Other Considerations for Income: Earnings for college faculty vary according to rank and type of institution, geographic area, and field. According to a 2006–2007 survey by the American Association of University Professors, salaries for full-time faculty averaged $73,207. By rank, the average was $98,974 for professors, $69,911 for associate professors, $58,662 for assistant professors, $42,609 for instructors, and $48,289 for lecturers. Faculty in 4-year institutions earn higher salaries, on average, than do those in 2-year schools. Many faculty members have significant earnings in addition to their base salary from consulting, teaching additional courses, research, writing for publication, or other employment. In addition, many college and university faculty enjoy unique benefits, including access to campus facilities, tuition waivers for dependents, housing and travel allowances, and paid leave for sabbaticals. Part-time faculty and instructors usually have fewer benefits than full-time faculty.

Personality Type: Social-Artistic-Investigative. **Career Clusters:** 05 Education and Training; 10 Human Service. **Career Pathways:** 05.3 Teaching/Training; 10.2 Counseling and Mental Health Services. **Skills:** Writing; Instructing; Reading Comprehension; Critical Thinking; Speaking; Learning Strategies; Social Perceptiveness; Persuasion.

Education and Training Programs: Bible/Biblical Studies; Buddhist Studies; Christian Studies; Divinity/Ministry (BD, MDiv.); Ethics; Hindu Studies; Humanities/Humanistic Studies; Missions/Missionary Studies and Missiology; Pastoral Counseling and Specialized Ministries, Other; Pastoral Studies/Counseling; Philosophy; Philosophy and Religious Studies, Other; Philosophy, Other; Pre-Theology/Pre-Ministerial Studies; Rabbinical Studies (M.H.L./Rav); Religion/Religious Studies; Religious Education; Religious/Sacred Music; others. **Related Knowledge/Courses:** Philosophy and Theology; History and Archeology; Sociology and Anthropology; Foreign Language; English Language; Education and Training.

Physical Medicine and Rehabilitation Physicians

- ❋ Annual Earnings: $166,400+
- ❋ Beginning Wage: $49,710
- ❋ Earnings Growth Potential: Cannot be calculated
- ❋ Growth: 14.2%
- ❋ Annual Job Openings: 38,027
- ❋ Self-Employed: 14.7%
- ❋ Part-Time: 8.1%
- ❋ Job Security: No data available
- ❋ Education/Training Required: First professional degree

The Department of Labor reports this information for the occupation Physicians and Surgeons. The job openings listed here are shared with other specializations within that occupation, including Allergists and Immunologists; Anesthesiologists; Dermatologists; Family and General Practitioners; Hospitalists; Internists, General; Neurologists; Nuclear Medicine Physicians; Obstetricians and Gynecologists; Ophthalmologists; Pathologists; Pediatricians, General; Preventive Medicine Physicians; Psychiatrists; Radiologists; Sports Medicine Physicians; Surgeons; and Urologists.

Industries in Which Income Is Highest

Industry	Average Annual Earnings	Number Employed
Ambulatory Health Care Services	$166,400+	147,400
Administrative and Support Services	$166,400+	1,310
Federal, State, and Local Government	$162,300	28,180
Professional, Scientific, and Technical Services	$107,470	1,210
Hospitals	$72,130	72,490

Metropolitan Areas Where Income Is Highest

Metropolitan Area	Average Annual Earnings	Number Employed
Los Angeles–Long Beach–Santa Ana, CA	$166,400+	8,810
Boston-Cambridge-Quincy, MA-NH	$166,400+	6,380
Dallas–Fort Worth–Arlington, TX	$166,400+	4,950
Tampa–St. Petersburg–Clearwater, FL	$166,400+	3,810
Portland-Vancouver-Beaverton, OR-WA	$166,400+	3,180

Diagnose and treat disorders requiring physiotherapy to provide physical, mental, and occupational rehabilitation. No task data available.

Other Considerations for Income: Earnings of physicians and surgeons are among the highest of any occupation. Separate earnings figures for Physical Medicine and Rehabilitation Physicians are not available.

Personality Type: Investigative-Social-Realistic. **Career Cluster:** 08 Health Science. **Career Pathway:** 08.1 Therapeutic Services. **Skills:** No data available.

Education and Training Program: Physical Medicine and Rehabilitation Residency Program. **Related Knowledge/Courses:** No data available.

Physical Therapists

- ❋ Annual Earnings: $72,790
- ❋ Beginning Wage: $50,350
- ❋ Earnings Growth Potential: Low (30.8%)
- ❋ Growth: 27.1%
- ❋ Annual Job Openings: 12,072
- ❋ Self-Employed: 8.4%
- ❋ Part-Time: 22.7%
- ❋ Job Security: Most secure
- ❋ Education/Training Required: Master's degree

Industries in Which Income Is Highest

Industry	Average Annual Earnings	Number Employed
Nursing and Residential Care Facilities	$76,370	12,310
Administrative and Support Services	$74,370	2,750
Social Assistance	$73,500	1,990
Hospitals	$73,000	53,410
Ambulatory Health Care Services	$72,850	85,180

Metropolitan Areas Where Income Is Highest

Metropolitan Area	Average Annual Earnings	Number Employed
Laredo, TX	$95,920	70
Wichita Falls, TX	$93,960	100
Alexandria, LA	$93,630	80
Longview, TX	$91,550	60
Danville, VA	$88,120	70

Assess, plan, organize, and participate in rehabilitative programs that improve mobility, relieve pain, increase strength, and decrease or prevent deformity of patients suffering from disease or injury. Perform and document initial exams, evaluating data to identify problems and determine diagnoses prior to interventions. Plan, prepare, and carry out individually designed programs of physical treatment to maintain, improve, or restore physical functioning; alleviate pain; and prevent physical dysfunction in patients. Record prognoses, treatments, responses, and progresses in patients' charts or enter information into computers. Identify and document goals, anticipated progresses, and plans for reevaluation. Evaluate effects of treatments at various stages and adjust treatments to achieve maximum benefits. Administer manual exercises, massages, or traction to help relieve pain, increase patient strength, or decrease or prevent deformity or crippling. Test and measure patients' strength, motor development and function, sensory perception, functional capacity, and respiratory and circulatory efficiency and record data. Instruct patients and families in treatment procedures to be continued at home. Confer with patients, medical practitioners, and appropriate others to plan, implement, and assess intervention programs. Review physicians' referrals and patients' medical records to help determine diagnoses and physical therapy treatments required. Obtain patients' informed consent to proposed interventions. Discharge patients from physical therapy when goals or projected outcomes have been attained and provide for appropriate follow-up care or referrals. Provide information to patients about proposed interventions, material risks, and expected benefits and any reasonable alternatives. Inform patients when diagnoses reveal findings outside the scope of physical therapy to treat and refer to appropriate practitioners. Direct, supervise, assess, and communicate with supportive personnel. Provide educational information about physical therapy and physical therapists, injury prevention, ergonomics, and ways to promote health. Refer clients to community resources and services.

Other Considerations for Income: No additional information.

Personality Type: Social-Investigative-Realistic. **Career Cluster:** 08 Health Science. **Career Pathway:** 08.3 Health Informatics. **Skills:** Systems Evaluation; Systems Analysis; Management of Personnel Resources; Service Orientation; Persuasion.

Education and Training Programs: Kinesiotherapy/ Kinesiotherapist; Physical Therapy/Therapist. **Related Knowledge/Courses:** Therapy and Counseling; Medicine and Dentistry; Psychology; Education and Training; Biology; Customer and Personal Service.

Physician Assistants

- ❋ Annual Earnings: $81,230
- ❋ Beginning Wage: $51,360
- ❋ Earnings Growth Potential: Medium (36.8%)
- ❋ Growth: 27.0%
- ❋ Annual Job Openings: 7,147
- ❋ Self-Employed: 1.8%
- ❋ Part-Time: 15.6%
- ❋ Job Security: Most secure
- ❋ Education/Training Required: Master's degree

Industries in Which Income Is Highest

Industry	Average Annual Earnings	Number Employed
Hospitals	$84,850	17,660
Ambulatory Health Care Services	$80,400	47,450
Federal, State, and Local Government	$78,660	3,060
Educational Services	$74,220	1,970

Metropolitan Areas Where Income Is Highest

Metropolitan Area	Average Annual Earnings	Number Employed
Sacramento–Arden-Arcade–Roseville, CA	$109,300	640
Anchorage, AK	$107,380	120
San Jose–Sunnyvale–Santa Clara, CA	$102,890	240
Chattanooga, TN-GA	$102,550	120
Bremerton-Silverdale, WA	$96,690	60

Under the supervision of physicians, provide healthcare services typically performed by a physician. Conduct complete physicals, provide treatment, and counsel patients. May, in some cases, prescribe medication. Must graduate from an accredited educational program for physician assistants. Examine patients to obtain information about their physical conditions. Obtain, compile, and record patient medical data, including health history, progress notes, and results of physical examinations. Interpret diagnostic test results for deviations from normal. Make tentative diagnoses and decisions about management and treatment of patients. Prescribe therapy or medication with physician approval. Administer or order diagnostic tests, such as X-ray, electrocardiogram, and laboratory tests. Instruct and counsel patients about prescribed therapeutic regimens, normal growth and development, family planning, emotional problems of daily living, and health maintenance. Perform therapeutic procedures such as injections, immunizations, suturing and wound care, and infection management. Provide physicians with assistance during surgery or complicated medical procedures. Visit and observe patients on hospital rounds or house calls, updating charts, ordering therapy, and reporting back to physicians. Supervise and coordinate activities of technicians and technical assistants. Order medical and laboratory supplies and equipment.

Other Considerations for Income: Income varies by specialty, practice setting, geographical location, and years of experience. Employers often pay for their employees' liability insurance, registration fees with the Drug Enforcement Administration, state licensing fees, and credentialing fees.

Personality Type: Social-Investigative-Realistic. **Career Cluster:** 08 Health Science. **Career Pathway:** 08.2 Diagnostics Services. **Skills:** Systems Evaluation; Judgment and Decision Making; Service Orientation; Systems Analysis; Social Perceptiveness; Reading Comprehension; Persuasion; Negotiation.

Education and Training Program: Physician Assistant Training. **Related Knowledge/Courses:** Medicine and Dentistry; Biology; Therapy and Counseling; Psychology; Chemistry; Sociology and Anthropology.

Physicians and Surgeons

See *Allergists and Immunologists; Anesthesiologists; Dermatologists; Family and General Practitioners; Hospitalists; Internists, General; Neurologists; Nuclear Medicine Physicians; Obstetricians and Gynecologists; Ophthalmologists; Pathologists; Pediatricians, General; Physical Medicine and Rehabilitation Physicians; Preventive Medicine Physicians; Psychiatrists; Radiologists; Sports Medicine Physicians; Surgeons; and Urologists, described separately.*

Physicists

❀ Annual Earnings: $102,890
❀ Beginning Wage: $57,160
❀ Earnings Growth Potential: High (44.4%)
❀ Growth: 6.8%
❀ Annual Job Openings: 1,302
❀ Self-Employed: 0.8%
❀ Part-Time: 5.2%
❀ Job Security: More secure than most
❀ Education/Training Required: Doctoral degree

Industries in Which Income Is Highest

Industry	Average Annual Earnings	Number Employed
Federal, State, and Local Government	$104,320	3,350
Professional, Scientific, and Technical Services	$103,350	7,550
Educational Services	$77,450	1,430

Metropolitan Areas Where Income Is Highest

Metropolitan Area	Average Annual Earnings	Number Employed
San Jose–Sunnyvale–Santa Clara, CA	$132,140	90
Washington-Arlington-Alexandria, DC-VA-MD-WV	$120,990	1,340
Milwaukee–Waukesha–West Allis, WI	$117,810	60
San Francisco–Oakland–Fremont, CA	$111,200	650
Detroit-Warren-Livonia, MI	$111,030	60

Conduct research into phases of physical phenomena, develop theories and laws on basis of observation and experiments, and devise methods to apply laws and theories to industry and other fields. Perform complex calculations as part of the analysis and evaluation of data, using computers. Describe and express observations and conclusions in mathematical terms. Analyze data from research conducted to detect and measure physical phenomena. Report experimental results by writing papers for scientific journals or by presenting information at scientific conferences. Design computer simulations to model physical data so that it can be better understood. Collaborate with other scientists in the design, development, and testing of experimental, industrial, or medical equipment, instrumentation, and procedures. Direct testing and monitoring of contamination of radioactive equipment and recording of personnel and plant area radiation exposure data. Observe the structure and properties of matter and the transformation and propagation of energy, using equipment such as masers, lasers, and telescopes, in order to explore and identify the basic principles governing these phenomena. Develop theories and laws on the basis of observation and experiments and apply these theories and laws to problems in areas such as nuclear energy, optics, and aerospace technology. Teach physics to students. Develop manufacturing, assembly, and fabrication processes of lasers, masers, and infrared and other light-emitting and light-sensitive devices. Conduct application evaluations and analyze results in order to determine commercial, industrial, scientific, medical, military, or other uses for electro-optical devices. Develop standards of permissible concentrations of radioisotopes in liquids and gases. Conduct research pertaining to potential environmental impacts of atomic energy–related industrial development in order to determine licensing qualifications. Advise authorities of procedures to be followed in radiation incidents or hazards and assist in civil defense planning.

P

Other Considerations for Income: According to a 2007 National Association of Colleges and Employers survey, the average annual starting salary offer to physics doctoral degree candidates was $52,469.

Personality Type: Investigative-Realistic. **Career Cluster:** 15 Science, Technology, Engineering, and Mathematics. **Career Pathway:** 15.3 Science and Mathematics. **Skills:** Programming; Science; Mathematics; Complex Problem Solving; Management of Financial Resources; Systems Analysis; Writing; Critical Thinking.

Education and Training Programs: Acoustics; Astrophysics; Atomic/Molecular Physics; Condensed Matter and Materials Physics; Elementary Particle Physics; Health/Medical Physics; Nuclear Physics; Optics/Optical Sciences; Physics, General; Physics, Other; Plasma and High-Temperature Physics; Theoretical and Mathematical Physics. **Related Knowledge/Courses:** Physics; Mathematics; Engineering and Technology; Computers and Electronics; English Language; Telecommunications.

Physics Teachers, Postsecondary

❋ Annual Earnings: $74,390
❋ Beginning Wage: $42,300
❋ Earnings Growth Potential: High (43.1%)
❋ Growth: 22.9%
❋ Annual Job Openings: 2,155
❋ Self-Employed: 0.4%
❋ Part-Time: 27.8%
❋ Job Security: Most secure
❋ Education/Training Required: Doctoral degree

Industries in Which Income Is Highest

Industry	Average Annual Earnings	Number Employed
Educational Services	$74,240	12,270

Metropolitan Areas Where Income Is Highest

Metropolitan Area	Average Annual Earnings	Number Employed
Raleigh-Cary, NC	$106,650	100
San Diego–Carlsbad–San Marcos, CA	$103,580	270
Rochester, NY	$102,370	170
Sacramento–Arden-Arcade–Roseville, CA	$99,980	100
Baltimore-Towson, MD	$96,260	120

Teach courses pertaining to the laws of matter and energy. Includes both teachers primarily engaged in teaching and those who do a combination of both teaching and research. Evaluate and grade students' classwork, laboratory work, assignments, and papers. Prepare and deliver lectures to undergraduate and/or graduate students on topics such as quantum mechanics, particle physics, and optics. Compile, administer, and grade examinations or assign this work to others. Maintain student attendance records, grades, and other required records. Supervise students' laboratory work. Prepare course materials such as syllabi, homework assignments, and handouts. Maintain regularly scheduled office hours to advise and assist students. Supervise undergraduate and/or graduate teaching, internship, and research work. Keep abreast of developments in their field by reading current literature, talking with colleagues, and participating in professional conferences. Plan, evaluate, and revise curricula, course content, and course materials and methods of instruction. Initiate, facilitate, and moderate classroom discussions. Conduct research in a particular field of knowledge and publish findings in professional journals, books, and/or electronic media. Advise students on academic and vocational curricula and on career issues. Select and obtain materials and supplies such as textbooks and laboratory equipment. Collaborate with colleagues to address teaching and research issues. Participate in student recruitment, registration, and placement activities. Serve on academic or administrative committees that deal with institutional policies, departmental matters, and academic issues. Write grant proposals to procure external research funding. Perform administrative duties such as serving as department head. Act as advisers to student organizations. Provide professional consulting services to government and/or industry. Compile bibliographies of specialized materials for outside reading assignments. Participate in campus and community events.

Other Considerations for Income: Earnings for college faculty vary according to rank and type of institution, geographic area, and field. According to a 2006–2007 survey by the American Association of University Professors, salaries for full-time faculty averaged $73,207. By rank, the average was $98,974 for professors, $69,911 for associate professors, $58,662 for assistant professors, $42,609 for instructors, and $48,289 for lecturers. Faculty in 4-year institutions earn higher salaries, on average, than do those in 2-year schools. Many faculty members have significant earnings in addition to their base salary from consulting, teaching additional courses, research, writing for publication, or other employment. In addition, many college and university faculty enjoy unique benefits, including access to campus facilities, tuition waivers for dependents, housing and travel allowances, and paid leave for sabbaticals. Part-time faculty and instructors usually have fewer benefits than full-time faculty.

Personality Type: Social-Investigative. **Career Clusters:** 05 Education and Training; 15 Science, Technology, Engineering, and Mathematics. **Career Pathway:** 05.3 Teaching/Training; 15.3 Science and Mathematics. **Skills:** Science; Programming; Mathematics; Instructing; Writing; Reading Comprehension; Learning Strategies; Critical Thinking.

Education and Training Programs: Acoustics; Atomic/Molecular Physics; Condensed Matter and Materials Physics; Elementary Particle Physics; Nuclear Physics; Optics/Optical Sciences; Physics, General; Physics, Other; Plasma and High-Temperature Physics; Theoretical and Mathematical Physics. **Related Knowledge/Courses:** Physics; Mathematics; Chemistry; Engineering and Technology; Education and Training; Computers and Electronics.

Pilots, Ship

❋ Annual Earnings: $61,960
❋ Beginning Wage: $29,330
❋ Earnings Growth Potential: Very high (52.7%)
❋ Growth: 17.9%
❋ Annual Job Openings: 2,665
❋ Self-Employed: 6.8%
❋ Part-Time: 4.8%
❋ Job Security: Least secure
❋ Education/Training Required: Work experience in a related occupation

The Department of Labor reports this information for the occupation Captains, Mates, and Pilots of Water Vessels. The job openings listed here are shared with other specializations within that occupation, including Mates—Ship, Boat, and Barge; and Ship and Boat Captains.

Industries in Which Income Is Highest

Industry	Average Annual Earnings	Number Employed
Support Activities for Transportation	$67,910	9,510
Water Transportation	$67,040	11,640
Federal, State, and Local Government	$55,620	2,180
Scenic and Sightseeing Transportation	$38,380	3,660

Metropolitan Areas Where Income Is Highest

Metropolitan Area	Average Annual Earnings	Number Employed
Detroit-Warren-Livonia, MI	$137,730	60
Memphis, TN-MS-AR	$89,540	190
Houston–Sugar Land–Baytown, TX	$79,320	1,530
Baton Rouge, LA	$78,360	480
Houma–Bayou Cane–Thibodaux, LA	$75,570	3,350

Command ships to steer them into and out of harbors, estuaries, straits, and sounds and on rivers, lakes, and bays. Must be licensed by U.S. Coast Guard with limitations indicating class and tonnage of vessels for which licenses are valid and routes and waters that may be piloted. Maintain and repair boats and equipment. Give directions to crew members who are steering ships. Make nautical maps. Set ships' courses to avoid reefs, outlying shoals, and other hazards, using navigational aids such as lighthouses and buoys. Report to appropriate authorities any violations of federal or state pilotage laws. Relieve crew members on tugs and launches. Provide assistance to vessels approaching or leaving seacoasts, navigating harbors, and docking and undocking. Provide assistance in maritime rescue operations. Prevent ships under their navigational control from engaging in unsafe operations. Operate amphibious craft during troop landings. Maintain ships' logs. Learn to operate new technology systems and procedures, through the use of instruction, simulators, and models. Advise ships' masters on harbor rules and customs procedures. Steer ships into and out of berths or signal tugboat captains to berth and unberth ships. Serve as vessels' docking masters upon arrival at a port and when at a berth. Operate ship-to-shore radios to exchange information needed for ship operations. Consult maps, charts, weather reports, and navigation equipment to determine and direct ship movements. Direct courses and speeds of ships, based on specialized knowledge of local winds, weather, water depths, tides, currents, and hazards. Oversee cargo storage on or below decks.

Other Considerations for Income: No additional information.

Personality Type: Realistic-Conventional-Investigative. **Career Cluster:** 16 Transportation, Distribution, and Logistics. **Career Pathway:** 16.1 Transportation Operations. **Skills:** Operation and Control; Operation Monitoring; Judgment and Decision Making; Management of Personnel Resources; Troubleshooting; Equipment Maintenance; Negotiation; Coordination.

Education and Training Programs: Commercial Fishing; Marine Science/Merchant Marine Officer; Marine Transportation, Other. **Related Knowledge/Courses:** Transportation; Geography; Public Safety and Security; Telecommunications; Mechanical; Law and Government.

Podiatrists

- ❇ Annual Earnings: $113,560
- ❇ Beginning Wage: $47,940
- ❇ Earnings Growth Potential: Very high (57.8%)
- ❇ Growth: 9.5%
- ❇ Annual Job Openings: 648
- ❇ Self-Employed: 23.9%
- ❇ Part-Time: 23.6%
- ❇ Job Security: Most secure
- ❇ Education/Training Required: First professional degree

Industries in Which Income Is Highest

Industry	Average Annual Earnings	Number Employed
Educational Services	$116,550	120
Ambulatory Health Care Services	$116,210	8,370
Federal, State, and Local Government	$104,960	630
Hospitals	$75,480	520

Metropolitan Areas Where Income Is Highest

Metropolitan Area	Average Annual Earnings	Number Employed
Detroit-Warren-Livonia, MI	$166,400+	200
Atlanta–Sandy Springs–Marietta, GA	$166,400+	110
Milwaukee–Waukesha–West Allis, WI	$166,400+	50
Minneapolis–St. Paul–Bloomington, MN-WI	$161,870	80
Kansas City, MO-KS	$154,540	70

Diagnose and treat diseases and deformities of the human foot. Treat bone, muscle, and joint disorders affecting the feet. Diagnose diseases and deformities of the foot, using medical histories, physical examinations, X-rays, and laboratory test results. Prescribe medications, corrective devices, physical therapy, or surgery. Treat conditions such as corns, calluses, ingrown nails, tumors, shortened tendons, bunions, cysts, and abscesses by surgical methods. Advise patients about treatments and foot care techniques necessary for prevention of future problems. Refer patients to physicians when symptoms indicative of systemic disorders, such as arthritis or diabetes, are observed in feet and legs. Correct deformities by means of plaster casts and strapping. Make and fit prosthetic appliances. Perform administrative duties such as hiring employees, ordering supplies, and keeping records. Educate the public about the benefits of foot care through techniques such as speaking engagements, advertising, and other forums. Treat deformities, using mechanical methods, such as whirlpool or paraffin baths, and electrical methods, such as shortwave and low-voltage currents.

Other Considerations for Income: Podiatrists enjoy very high earnings, and those in partnerships tended to earn higher net incomes than those in solo practice. A salaried podiatrist typically receives heath insurance and retirement benefits from their employer, whereas self-employed chiropractors must provide for their own health insurance and retirement. Also, solo practitioners must absorb the costs of running their own offices.

Personality Type: Investigative-Social-Realistic. **Career Cluster:** 08 Health Science. **Career Pathway:** 08.1 Therapeutic Services. **Skills:** Science; Active Listening; Complex Problem Solving; Management of Financial Resources; Reading Comprehension; Equipment Selection; Active Learning; Judgment and Decision Making.

Education and Training Program: Podiatric Medicine/Podiatry (DPM). **Related Knowledge/Courses:** Medicine and Dentistry; Biology; Therapy and Counseling; Sales and Marketing; Chemistry; Economics and Accounting.

Poets, Lyricists, and Creative Writers

❋ Annual Earnings: $53,070
❋ Beginning Wage: $28,020
❋ Earnings Growth Potential: High (47.2%)
❋ Growth: 12.8%
❋ Annual Job Openings: 24,023
❋ Self-Employed: 65.9%
❋ Part-Time: 21.8%
❋ Job Security: More secure than most
❋ Education/Training Required: Bachelor's degree

The Department of Labor reports this information for the occupation Writers and Authors. The job openings listed here are shared with other specializations within that occupation, including Copy Writers.

Industries in Which Income Is Highest

Industry	Average Annual Earnings	Number Employed
Motion Picture and Sound Recording Industries	$69,400	2,500
Federal, State, and Local Government	$65,970	1,850
Professional, Scientific, and Technical Services	$60,130	11,050
Performing Arts, Spectator Sports, and Related Industries	$59,720	2,690
Management of Companies and Enterprises	$53,600	1,190

Metropolitan Areas Where Income Is Highest

Metropolitan Area	Average Annual Earnings	Number Employed
San Diego–Carlsbad–San Marcos, CA	$78,930	510
Los Angeles–Long Beach–Santa Ana, CA	$75,530	4,040
Washington-Arlington-Alexandria, DC-VA-MD-WV	$70,740	2,700
San Jose–Sunnyvale–Santa Clara, CA	$66,490	260
New York–Northern New Jersey–Long Island, NY-NJ-PA	$65,580	6,110

Create original written works, such as scripts, essays, prose, poetry, or song lyrics, for publication or performance. Revise written material to meet personal standards and to satisfy needs of clients, publishers, directors, or producers. Choose subject matter and suitable form to express personal feelings and experiences or ideas or to narrate stories or events. Plan project arrangements or outlines and organize material accordingly. Prepare works in appropriate format for publication and send them to publishers or producers. Follow appropriate procedures to get copyrights for completed work. Write fiction or nonfiction prose such as short stories, novels, biographies, articles, descriptive or critical analyses, and essays. Develop factors such as themes, plots, characterizations, psychological analyses, historical environments, action, and dialogue to create material. Confer with clients, editors, publishers, or producers to discuss changes or revisions to written material. Conduct research to obtain factual information and authentic detail, using sources such as newspaper accounts, diaries, and interviews. Write narrative, dramatic, lyric, or other types of poetry for publication. Attend book launches and publicity events or conduct public readings. Write words to fit musical compositions, including lyrics for operas, musical plays, and choral works. Adapt text to accommodate musical requirements of composers and singers. Teach writing classes. Write humorous material for publication or for performances such as comedy routines, gags, and comedy shows. Collaborate with other writers on specific projects.

Other Considerations for Income: Writers who are not on the staff of publishers usually have very uneven earnings and do not get fringe benefits. Their earnings may depend partly on their success at self-promotion, which can boost sales of existing works (and thus royalties) and can contribute to a reputation that will help interest publishers in future manuscripts.

Personality Type: Artistic-Investigative. **Career Cluster:** 03 Arts, Audio/Video Technology, and Communications. **Career Pathway:** 03.4 Performing Arts. **Skills:** Writing; Social Perceptiveness; Management of Financial Resources; Persuasion; Active Listening; Reading Comprehension; Speaking; Critical Thinking.

Education and Training Programs: Broadcast Journalism; Business/Corporate Communications; Communication, Journalism, and Related Programs, Other; Family and Consumer Sciences/Human Sciences Communication; Journalism; Mass Communication/Media Studies; Playwriting and Screenwriting; Speech Communication and Rhetoric. **Related Knowledge/Courses:** Fine Arts; Communications and Media; Philosophy and Theology; Sociology and Anthropology; Sales and Marketing; History and Archeology.

Police and Sheriff's Patrol Officers

See *Police Patrol Officers* and *Sheriffs and Deputy Sheriffs*, *described separately.*

Police Detectives

- ❀ Annual Earnings: $60,910
- ❀ Beginning Wage: $36,500
- ❀ Earnings Growth Potential: High (40.1%)
- ❀ Growth: 17.3%
- ❀ Annual Job Openings: 14,746
- ❀ Self-Employed: 0.3%
- ❀ Part-Time: 2.2%
- ❀ Job Security: Most secure
- ❀ Education/Training Required: Work experience in a related occupation

The Department of Labor reports this information for the occupation Detectives and Criminal Investigators. The job openings listed here are shared with other specializations within that occupation, including Criminal Investigators and Special Agents; Immigration and Customs Inspectors; Intelligence Analysts; and Police Identification and Records Officers.

Industries in Which Income Is Highest

Industry	Average Annual Earnings	Number Employed
Federal, State, and Local Government	$60,780	103,680

Metropolitan Areas Where Income Is Highest

Metropolitan Area	Average Annual Earnings	Number Employed
San Jose–Sunnyvale–Santa Clara, CA	$92,430	310
Washington-Arlington-Alexandria, DC-VA-MD-WV	$88,440	4,590
Springfield, MA-CT	$82,690	60
Brunswick, GA	$80,960	350
New Haven, CT	$79,550	200

Conduct investigations to prevent crimes or solve criminal cases. Provide testimony as witnesses in court. Secure deceased bodies and obtain evidence from them, preventing bystanders from tampering with bodies prior to medical examiners' arrival. Examine crime scenes to obtain clues and evidence such as loose hairs, fibers, clothing, or weapons. Obtain evidence from suspects. Record progress of investigations, maintain informational files on suspects, and submit reports to commanding officers or magistrates to authorize warrants. Check victims for signs of life such as breathing and pulse. Prepare charges or responses to charges, or information for court cases, according to formalized procedures. Obtain facts or statements from complainants, witnesses, and accused persons and record interviews, using recording devices. Prepare and serve search and arrest warrants. Note, mark, and photograph locations of objects found such as footprints, tire tracks, bullets, and bloodstains, and take measurements of each scene. Question individuals or observe persons and establishments to confirm information given to patrol officers. Preserve, process, and analyze items of evidence obtained from crime scenes and suspects, placing them in proper containers and destroying evidence no longer needed. Secure persons at scenes, keeping witnesses from conversing or leaving scenes before investigators arrive. Take photographs from all angles of relevant parts of crime scenes, including entrance and exit routes and streets and intersections. Analyze completed police reports to determine what additional information and investigative work is needed. Obtain summary of incidents from officers in charge at crime scenes, taking care to avoid disturbing evidence. Provide information to lab personnel concerning the source of each item of evidence and tests to be performed. Examine records and governmental agency files to find identifying data about suspects. Block or rope off scenes and check perimeters to ensure that scenes are completely secured.

Other Considerations for Income: Total earnings for local, state, and special police and detectives frequently exceed the stated salary because of payments for overtime, which can be significant. In addition to the common benefits—paid vacation, sick leave, and medical and life insurance—most police and sheriffs' departments provide officers with special allowances for uniforms. Because police officers usually are covered by liberal pension plans, many retire at half pay after 25 or 30 years of service.

Personality Type: Enterprising-Investigative. **Career Cluster:** 12 Law, Public Safety, Corrections, and Security. **Career Pathway:** 12.4 Law Enforcement Services. **Skills:** Negotiation; Systems Analysis; Operation Monitoring; Systems Evaluation; Operation and Control.

Education and Training Programs: Criminal Justice/ Police Science; Criminalistics and Criminal Science. **Related Knowledge/Courses:** Public Safety and Security; Law and Government; Psychology; Therapy and Counseling; Customer and Personal Service; Philosophy and Theology.

Police Identification and Records Officers

- ❋ Annual Earnings: $60,910
- ❋ Beginning Wage: $36,500
- ❋ Earnings Growth Potential: High (40.1%)
- ❋ Growth: 17.3%
- ❋ Annual Job Openings: 14,746
- ❋ Self-Employed: 0.3%
- ❋ Part-Time: 2.2%
- ❋ Job Security: Most secure
- ❋ Education/Training Required: Work experience in a related occupation

The Department of Labor reports this information for the occupation Detectives and Criminal Investigators. The job openings listed here are shared with other specializations within that occupation, including Criminal Investigators and Special

Agents; Immigration and Customs Inspectors; Intelligence Analysts; and Police Detectives.

Industries in Which Income Is Highest

Industry	Average Annual Earnings	Number Employed
Federal, State, and Local Government	$60,780	103,680

Metropolitan Areas Where Income Is Highest

Metropolitan Area	Average Annual Earnings	Number Employed
San Jose–Sunnyvale–Santa Clara, CA	$92,430	310
Washington-Arlington-Alexandria, DC-VA-MD-WV	$88,440	4,590
Springfield, MA-CT	$82,690	60
Brunswick, GA	$80,960	350
New Haven, CT	$79,550	200

Collect evidence at crime scene, classify and identify fingerprints, and photograph evidence for use in criminal and civil cases. Photograph crime or accident scenes for evidence records. Analyze and process evidence at crime scenes and in the laboratory, wearing protective equipment and using powders and chemicals. Look for trace evidence, such as fingerprints, hairs, fibers, or shoe impressions, using alternative light sources when necessary. Dust selected areas of crime scene and lift latent fingerprints, adhering to proper preservation procedures. Testify in court and present evidence. Package, store, and retrieve evidence. Serve as technical advisor and coordinate with other law enforcement workers to exchange information on crime scene collection activities. Perform emergency work during off-hours. Submit evidence to supervisors. Process film and prints from crime or accident scenes. Identify, classify, and file fingerprints, using systems such as the Henry Classification system.

Other Considerations for Income: Total earnings for local, state, and special police and detectives frequently exceed the stated salary because of payments for overtime, which can be significant. In addition to the common benefits—paid vacation, sick leave, and medical and life insurance—most police and sheriffs' departments provide officers with special allowances for uniforms. Because police officers usually are covered by liberal pension plans, many retire at half pay after 25 or 30 years of service.

Personality Type: Conventional-Realistic-Investigative. **Career Cluster:** 12 Law, Public Safety, Corrections, and Security. **Career Pathway:** 12.4 Law Enforcement Services. **Skills:** Persuasion; Judgment and Decision Making; Negotiation; Service Orientation; Social Perceptiveness; Critical Thinking; Speaking; Science.

Education and Training Programs: Criminal Justice/Police Science; Criminalistics and Criminal Science. **Related Knowledge/Courses:** Law and Government; Public Safety and Security; Telecommunications; Customer and Personal Service; Psychology; Computers and Electronics.

Police Patrol Officers

❋ Annual Earnings: $51,410

❋ Beginning Wage: $30,070

❋ Earnings Growth Potential: High (41.5%)

❋ Growth: 10.8%

❋ Annual Job Openings: 37,842

❋ Self-Employed: 0.0%

❋ Part-Time: 1.1%

❋ Job Security: Most secure

❋ Education/Training Required: Long-term on-the-job training

The Department of Labor reports this information for the occupation Police and Sheriff's Patrol Officers. The job openings listed here are shared with other specializations within that occupation, including Sheriffs and Deputy Sheriffs.

Industries in Which Income Is Highest

Industry	Average Annual Earnings	Number Employed
Federal, State, and Local Government	$51,630	618,590
Educational Services	$43,350	13,560

Metropolitan Areas Where Income Is Highest

Metropolitan Area	Average Annual Earnings	Number Employed
San Jose–Sunnyvale–Santa Clara, CA	$91,670	2,330
Santa Rosa–Petaluma, CA	$78,000	680
Los Angeles–Long Beach–Santa Ana, CA	$77,800	24,360
Santa Cruz–Watsonville, CA	$77,730	350
Vallejo-Fairfield, CA	$77,100	910

Patrol assigned areas to enforce laws and ordinances, regulate traffic, control crowds, prevent crime, and arrest violators. Provide for public safety by maintaining order, responding to emergencies, protecting people and property, enforcing motor vehicle and criminal laws, and promoting good community relations. Monitor, note, report, and investigate suspicious persons and situations, safety hazards, and unusual or illegal activity in patrol area. Record facts to prepare reports that document incidents and activities. Identify, pursue, and arrest suspects and perpetrators of criminal acts. Patrol specific areas on foot, horseback, or motorized conveyance, responding promptly to calls for assistance. Review facts of incidents to determine whether criminal acts or statute violations were involved. Investigate traffic accidents and other accidents to determine causes and to determine whether crimes have been committed. Render aid to accident victims and other persons requiring first aid for physical injuries. Testify in court to present evidence or act as witness in traffic and criminal cases. Photograph or draw diagrams of crime or accident scenes and interview principals and eyewitnesses. Relay complaint and emergency-request information to appropriate agency dispatchers. Evaluate complaint and emergency-request information to determine response requirements. Process prisoners and prepare and maintain records of prisoner bookings and prisoner statuses during booking and pre-trial processes. Monitor traffic to ensure motorists observe traffic regulations and exhibit safe driving procedures. Issue citations or warnings to violators of motor vehicle ordinances. Direct traffic flow and reroute traffic during emergencies. Inform citizens of community services and recommend options to facilitate longer-term problem resolution. Provide road information to assist motorists. Inspect public establishments to ensure compliance with rules and regulations. Act as official escorts at times, such as when leading funeral processions or firefighters.

Other Considerations for Income: Total earnings for local, state, and special police and detectives frequently exceed the stated salary because of payments for overtime, which can be significant. In addition to the common benefits—paid vacation, sick leave, and medical and life insurance—most police and sheriffs' departments provide officers with special allowances for uniforms. Because police officers usually are covered by liberal pension plans, many retire at half pay after 25 or 30 years of service.

Personality Type: Realistic-Enterprising-Conventional. **Career Cluster:** 12 Law, Public Safety, Corrections, and Security. **Career Pathway:** 12.4 Law Enforcement Services. **Skills:** Negotiation; Persuasion; Service Orientation.

Education and Training Programs: Criminal Justice/Police Science; Criminalistics and Criminal Science. **Related Knowledge/Courses:** Psychology; Public Safety and Security; Law and Government; Customer and Personal Service; Therapy and Counseling; Sociology and Anthropology.

Political Science Teachers, Postsecondary

❋ Annual Earnings: $67,200
❋ Beginning Wage: $36,910
❋ Earnings Growth Potential: High (45.1%)
❋ Growth: 22.9%
❋ Annual Job Openings: 2,435
❋ Self-Employed: 0.4%
❋ Part-Time: 27.8%
❋ Job Security: Most secure
❋ Education/Training Required: Doctoral degree

Industries in Which Income Is Highest

Industry	Average Annual Earnings	Number Employed
Educational Services	$67,210	14,330

Metropolitan Areas Where Income Is Highest

Metropolitan Area	Average Annual Earnings	Number Employed
Philadelphia-Camden-Wilmington, PA-NJ-DE-MD	$93,390	370
Pittsburgh, PA	$88,890	130
Providence–Fall River–Warwick, RI-MA	$86,400	120
Los Angeles–Long Beach–Santa Ana, CA	$85,560	320
Boston-Cambridge-Quincy, MA-NH	$82,920	390

Teach courses in political science, international affairs, and international relations. Initiate, facilitate, and moderate classroom discussions. Prepare and deliver lectures to undergraduate or graduate students on topics such as classical political thought, international relations, and democracy and citizenship. Evaluate and grade students' classwork, assignments, and papers. Compile, administer, and grade examinations or assign this work to others. Prepare course materials such as syllabi, homework assignments, and handouts. Keep abreast of developments in their field by reading current literature, talking with colleagues, and participating in professional conferences. Plan, evaluate, and revise curricula, course content, and course materials and methods of instruction. Maintain student attendance records, grades, and other required records. Maintain regularly scheduled office hours in order to advise and assist students. Advise students on academic and vocational curricula and on career issues. Select and obtain materials and supplies such as textbooks. Conduct research in a particular field of knowledge and publish findings in professional journals, books, and electronic media. Supervise undergraduate and graduate teaching, internship, and research work. Collaborate with colleagues to address teaching and research issues. Serve on academic or administrative committees that deal with institutional policies, departmental matters, and academic issues. Participate in student recruitment, registration, and placement activities. Participate in campus and community events. Compile bibliographies of specialized materials for outside reading assignments. Act as advisers to student organizations. Perform administrative duties such as serving as department head. Write grant proposals to procure external research funding. Provide professional consulting services to government and industry.

Other Considerations for Income: Earnings for college faculty vary according to rank and type of institution, geographic area, and field. According to a 2006–2007 survey by the American Association of University Professors, salaries for full-time faculty averaged $73,207. By rank, the average was $98,974 for professors, $69,911 for associate professors, $58,662 for assistant professors, $42,609 for instructors, and $48,289 for lecturers. Faculty in 4-year institutions earn higher salaries, on average, than do those in 2-year schools. Many faculty members have significant earnings in addition to their base salary from consulting, teaching additional courses, research, writing for publication, or other employment. In addition, many college and university faculty enjoy unique benefits, including access to campus facilities, tuition waivers for dependents, housing and travel allowances, and paid leave for sabbaticals. Part-time faculty and instructors usually have fewer benefits than full-time faculty.

Personality Type: Social-Enterprising-Artistic. **Career Clusters:** 05 Education and Training; 07 Government and Public Administration; 15 Science, Technology, Engineering, and Mathematics. **Career Pathways:** 05.3 Teaching/Training; 07.1 Governance; 07.4 Planning; 15.3 Science and Mathematics. **Skills:** Writing; Instructing; Reading Comprehension; Learning Strategies; Persuasion; Critical Thinking; Speaking; Active Learning.

Education and Training Programs: American Government and Politics (United States); Humanities/Humanistic Studies; International Relations and Affairs; Political Science and Government, General; Political Science and Government, Other; Social Science Teacher Education. **Related Knowledge/Courses:** History and Archeology; Philosophy and Theology; Sociology and Anthropology; Geography; Law and Government; English Language.

Political Scientists

- ❋ Annual Earnings: $104,130
- ❋ Beginning Wage: $47,220
- ❋ Earnings Growth Potential: Very high (54.7%)
- ❋ Growth: 5.3%
- ❋ Annual Job Openings: 318
- ❋ Self-Employed: 7.5%
- ❋ Part-Time: 20.1%
- ❋ Job Security: Most secure
- ❋ Education/Training Required: Master's degree

Industries in Which Income Is Highest

Industry	Average Annual Earnings	Number Employed
Federal, State, and Local Government	$109,630	2,550
Professional, Scientific, and Technical Services	$74,030	490
Educational Services	$48,190	240

Metropolitan Areas Where Income Is Highest

Metropolitan Area	Average Annual Earnings	Number Employed
Washington-Arlington-Alexandria, DC-VA-MD-WV	$111,410	2,620
Los Angeles–Long Beach–Santa Ana, CA	$82,180	50
New York–Northern New Jersey–Long Island, NY-NJ-PA	$73,930	100
Milwaukee–Waukesha–West Allis, WI	$67,230	90
Seattle-Tacoma-Bellevue, WA	$66,030	90

Study the origin, development, and operation of political systems. Research a wide range of subjects, such as relations between the United States and foreign countries, the beliefs and institutions of foreign nations, or the politics of small towns or a major metropolis. Teach political science. Disseminate research results through academic publications, written reports, or public presentations. Identify issues for research and analysis. Develop and test theories, using information from interviews, newspapers, periodicals, case law, historical papers, polls, and/or statistical sources. Maintain current knowledge of government policy decisions. Collect, analyze, and interpret data such as election results and public opinion surveys; report on findings, recommendations, and conclusions. Interpret and analyze policies; public issues; legislation; and the operations of governments, businesses, and organizations. Evaluate programs and policies and make related recommendations to institutions and organizations. Write drafts of legislative proposals and prepare speeches, correspondence, and policy papers for governmental use. Forecast political, economic, and social trends. Consult with and advise government officials, civic bodies, research agencies, the media, political parties, and others concerned with political issues. Provide media commentary and/or criticism related to public policy and political issues and events.

Other Considerations for Income: In the federal government, social scientists with a bachelor's degree and no experience often started at a yearly salary of $28,862 or $35,572 in 2007, depending on their college records. Those with a master's degree could start at $43,731, and those with a Ph.D. degree could begin at $52,912, while some individuals with experience and an advanced degree could start at $63,417. Beginning salaries were higher in selected areas of the country where the prevailing local pay level was higher.

Personality Type: Investigative-Artistic-Social. **Career Clusters:** 07 Government and Public Administration; 15 Science, Technology, Engineering, and Mathematics. **Career Pathways:** 07.1 Governance; 15.3 Science and Mathematics. **Skills:** Writing; Reading Comprehension; Critical Thinking; Speaking; Active Learning; Instructing; Complex Problem Solving; Persuasion.

Education and Training Programs: American Government and Politics (United States); Canadian Government and Politics; International Relations and Affairs; International/Global Studies; Political Science and Government, General; Political Science and Government, Other. **Related Knowledge/Courses:** History and Archeology; Law and Government; Philosophy and Theology; Sociology and Anthropology; Foreign Language; Geography.

Postal Service Clerks

- ❋ Annual Earnings: $55,920
- ❋ Beginning Wage: $44,970
- ❋ Earnings Growth Potential: Very low (19.6%)
- ❋ Growth: 1.2%
- ❋ Annual Job Openings: 3,703
- ❋ Self-Employed: 0.0%
- ❋ Part-Time: 4.2%
- ❋ Job Security: Most secure
- ❋ Education/Training Required: Short-term on-the-job training

Industries in Which Income Is Highest

Industry	Average Annual Earnings	Number Employed
Postal Service	$55,970	77,800

Metropolitan Areas Where Income Is Highest

Metropolitan Area	Average Annual Earnings	Number Employed
Trenton-Ewing, NJ	$57,570	90
Macon, GA	$57,360	60
Jacksonville, FL	$57,300	290
San Antonio, TX	$57,290	320
Dayton, OH	$57,270	220

Perform any combination of tasks in a post office, such as receiving letters and parcels; selling postage and revenue stamps, postal cards, and stamped envelopes; filling out and selling money orders; placing mail in pigeonholes of mail rack or in bags according to state, address, or other scheme; and examining mail for correct postage. Keep money drawers in order and record and balance daily transactions. Weigh letters and parcels; compute mailing costs based on type, weight, and destination; and affix correct postage. Obtain signatures from recipients of registered or special delivery mail. Register, certify, and insure letters and parcels. Sell and collect payment for products such as stamps, prepaid mail envelopes, and money orders. Check mail to ensure correct postage and ensure that packages and letters are in proper condition for mailing. Answer questions regarding mail regulations and procedures, postage rates, and post office boxes. Complete forms regarding changes of address, theft or loss of mail, or special services such as registered or priority mail. Provide assistance to the public in complying with federal regulations of Postal Service and other federal agencies. Sort incoming and outgoing mail according to type and destination by hand or by operating electronic mail-sorting and scanning devices. Cash money orders. Rent post office boxes to customers. Put undelivered parcels away, retrieve them when customers come to claim them, and complete any related documentation. Provide customers with assistance in filing claims for mail theft or lost or damaged mail. Respond to complaints regarding mail theft, delivery problems, and lost or damaged mail, filling out forms and making appropriate referrals for investigation. Receive letters and parcels and place mail into bags. Feed mail into postage-canceling devices or hand-stamp mail to cancel postage. Transport mail from one workstation to another. Set postage meters and calibrate them to ensure correct operation. Post announcements or government information on public bulletin boards.

Other Considerations for Income: Postal Service workers enjoy a variety of employer-provided benefits similar to those enjoyed by federal government workers. The American Postal Workers Union, the National Association of Letter Carriers, the National Postal Mail Handlers Union, and the National Rural Letter Carriers Association together represent most of these workers.

Personality Type: Conventional-Realistic. **Career Cluster:** 04 Business, Management, and Administration. **Career Pathway:** 04.6 Administrative and Information Support. **Skills:** None met the criteria.

Education and Training Program: General Office Occupations and Clerical Services. **Related Knowledge/Courses:** Sales and Marketing; Transportation; Clerical; Public Safety and Security.

Postal Service Mail Carriers

* Annual Earnings: $50,290
* Beginning Wage: $36,180
* Earnings Growth Potential: Low (28.1%)
* Growth: 1.0%
* Annual Job Openings: 16,710
* Self-Employed: 0.0%
* Part-Time: 7.1%
* Job Security: Most secure
* Education/Training Required: Short-term on-the-job training

Industries in Which Income Is Highest

Industry	Average Annual Earnings	Number Employed
Postal Service	$50,290	354,570

Metropolitan Areas Where Income Is Highest

Metropolitan Area	Average Annual Earnings	Number Employed
Honolulu, HI	$54,560	880
New Haven, CT	$54,190	790
Pittsfield, MA	$53,900	110
Laredo, TX	$53,680	120
Dubuque, IA	$53,580	130

Sort mail for delivery. Deliver mail on established routes by vehicle or on foot. Obtain signed receipts for registered, certified, and insured mail; collect associated charges; and complete any necessary paperwork. Sort mail for delivery, arranging it in delivery sequence. Deliver mail to residences and business establishments along specified routes by walking and/or driving, using a combination of satchels, carts, cars, and small trucks. Return to the post office with mail collected from homes, businesses, and public mailboxes. Turn in money and receipts collected along mail routes. Sign for cash-on-delivery and registered mail before leaving post offices. Record address changes and redirect mail for those addresses. Hold mail for customers who are away from delivery locations. Bundle mail in preparation for delivery or transportation to relay boxes. Leave notices telling patrons where to collect mail that could not be delivered. Meet schedules for the collection and return of mail. Return incorrectly addressed mail to senders. Maintain accurate records of deliveries. Answer customers' questions about postal services and regulations. Provide customers with change of address cards and other forms. Report any unusual circumstances concerning mail delivery, including the condition of street letter boxes. Register, certify, and insure parcels and letters. Travel to post offices to pick up the mail for routes and/or pick up mail from postal relay boxes. Enter change of address orders into computers that process forwarding address stickers. Complete forms that notify publishers of address changes. Sell stamps and money orders.

Other Considerations for Income: Rural mail carriers are reimbursed for mileage put on their own vehicles while delivering mail. Postal Service workers enjoy a variety of employer-provided benefits similar to those enjoyed by federal government workers. The American Postal Workers Union, the National Association of Letter Carriers, the National Postal Mail Handlers Union, and the National Rural Letter Carriers Association together represent most of these workers.

Personality Type: Conventional-Realistic. **Career Cluster:** 04 Business, Management, and Administration. **Career Pathway:** 04.6 Administrative and Information Support. **Skills:** None met the criteria.

Education and Training Program: General Office Occupations and Clerical Services. **Related Knowledge/ Courses:** Transportation; Public Safety and Security.

Postal Service Mail Sorters, Processors, and Processing Machine Operators

* Annual Earnings: $50,600
* Beginning Wage: $27,160
* Earnings Growth Potential: High (46.3%)
* Growth: –8.4%
* Annual Job Openings: 6,855
* Self-Employed: 0.0%
* Part-Time: 3.8%
* Job Security: Most secure
* Education/Training Required: Short-term on-the-job training

Industries in Which Income Is Highest

Industry	Average Annual Earnings	Number Employed
Postal Service	$50,610	185,610

Metropolitan Areas Where Income Is Highest

Metropolitan Area	Average Annual Earnings	Number Employed
Ann Arbor, MI	$56,320	70
Port St. Lucie–Fort Pierce, FL	$55,470	60
La Crosse, WI-MN	$55,260	60
Bowling Green, KY	$54,810	90
Saginaw–Saginaw Township North, MI	$54,770	240

Prepare incoming and outgoing mail for distribution. Examine, sort, and route mail by state, type of mail, or other scheme. Load, operate, and occasionally adjust and repair mail-processing, -sorting, and -canceling machinery. Keep records of shipments, pouches, and sacks and perform other duties related to mail handling within the postal service. Must complete a competitive exam. Direct items according to established routing schemes, using computer-controlled keyboards or voice recognition equipment. Bundle, label, and route sorted mail to designated areas depending on destinations and according to established procedures and deadlines. Serve the public at counters or windows, such as by selling stamps and weighing parcels. Supervise other mail sorters. Train new workers. Distribute incoming mail into the correct boxes or pigeonholes. Operate various types of equipment, such as computer scanning equipment, addressographs, mimeographs, optical character readers, and bar-code sorters. Search directories to find correct addresses for redirected mail. Clear jams in sorting equipment. Open and label mail containers. Check items to ensure that addresses are legible and correct, that sufficient postage has been paid or the appropriate documentation is attached, and that items are in a suitable condition for processing. Rewrap soiled or broken parcels. Weigh articles to determine required postage. Move containers of mail, using equipment such as forklifts and automated "trains." Sort odd-sized mail by hand, sort mail that other workers have been unable to sort, and segregate items requiring special handling. Accept and check containers of mail from large-volume mailers, couriers, and contractors. Load and unload mail trucks, sometimes lifting containers of mail onto equipment that transports items to sorting stations. Cancel letter or parcel post stamps by hand. Dump sacks of mail onto conveyors for culling and sorting.

Other Considerations for Income: Postal Service workers enjoy a variety of employer-provided benefits similar to those enjoyed by federal government workers. The American Postal Workers Union, the National Association of Letter Carriers, the National Postal Mail Handlers Union, and the National Rural Letter Carriers Association together represent most of these workers.

Personality Type: Conventional-Realistic. **Career Cluster:** 04 Business, Management, and Administration. **Career Pathway:** 04.6 Administrative and Information Support. **Skills:** None met the criteria.

Education and Training Program: General Office Occupations and Clerical Services. **Related Knowledge/ Course:** Biology.

Postmasters and Mail Superintendents

❋ Annual Earnings: $59,310
❋ Beginning Wage: $38,770
❋ Earnings Growth Potential: Low (34.6%)
❋ Growth: –0.8%
❋ Annual Job Openings: 1,627
❋ Self-Employed: 0.0%
❋ Part-Time: 3.2%
❋ Job Security: Most secure
❋ Education/Training Required: Work experience in a related occupation

Industries in Which Income Is Highest

Industry	Average Annual Earnings	Number Employed
Postal Service	$59,310	26,400

Metropolitan Areas Where Income Is Highest

Metropolitan Area	Average Annual Earnings	Number Employed
Los Angeles–Long Beach–Santa Ana, CA	$86,040	120
Detroit-Warren-Livonia, MI	$75,290	100
San Francisco–Oakland–Fremont, CA	$73,700	80
New York–Northern New Jersey–Long Island, NY-NJ-PA	$73,690	580
Seattle-Tacoma-Bellevue, WA	$73,380	70

Direct and coordinate operational, administrative, management, and supportive services of a U.S. post office or coordinate activities of workers engaged in postal and related work in assigned post office. Organize and supervise activities such as the processing of incoming and outgoing mail. Direct and coordinate operational, management, and supportive services of one or a number of postal facilities. Resolve customer complaints. Hire and train employees and evaluate their performance. Prepare employee work schedules. Negotiate labor disputes. Prepare and submit detailed and summary reports of post office activities to designated supervisors. Collect rents for post office boxes. Issue and cash money orders. Inform the public of available services and of postal laws and regulations. Select and train postmasters and managers of associate postal units. Confer with suppliers to obtain bids for proposed purchases and to requisition supplies; disburse funds according to federal regulations.

Other Considerations for Income: Postal Service workers enjoy a variety of employer-provided benefits similar to those enjoyed by federal government workers. The American Postal Workers Union, the National Association of Letter Carriers, the National Postal Mail Handlers Union, and the National Rural Letter Carriers Association together represent most of these workers.

Personality Type: Enterprising-Conventional-Social. **Career Cluster:** 07 Government and Public Administration. **Career Pathway:** 07.1 Governance. **Skills:** Negotiation; Persuasion; Monitoring; Service Orientation; Management of Financial Resources; Management of Personnel Resources; Active Listening; Coordination.

Education and Training Program: Public Administration. **Related Knowledge/Courses:** Production and Processing; Public Safety and Security; Personnel and Human Resources; Clerical; Economics and Accounting; Psychology.

Power Plant Operators

❋ Annual Earnings: $58,470
❋ Beginning Wage: $38,020
❋ Earnings Growth Potential: Medium (35.0%)
❋ Growth: 2.7%
❋ Annual Job Openings: 1,796
❋ Self-Employed: 0.0%
❋ Part-Time: 0.6%
❋ Job Security: Most secure
❋ Education/Training Required: Long-term on-the-job training

Industries in Which Income Is Highest

Industry	Average Annual Earnings	Number Employed
Utilities	$59,570	25,290
Federal, State, and Local Government	$52,580	5,590

Metropolitan Areas Where Income Is Highest

Metropolitan Area	Average Annual Earnings	Number Employed
Wenatchee, WA	$90,800	70
Fresno, CA	$76,320	190
San Diego–Carlsbad–San Marcos, CA	$75,620	100
Oxnard–Thousand Oaks–Ventura, CA	$75,150	80
San Jose–Sunnyvale–Santa Clara, CA	$73,780	170

Control, operate, or maintain machinery to generate electric power. Includes auxiliary equipment operators. Operate or control power-generating equipment, including boilers, turbines, generators, and reactors, using control boards or semi-automatic equipment. Monitor and inspect power plant equipment and indicators to detect evidence of operating problems. Adjust controls to generate specified electrical power or to regulate the flow of power between generating stations and substations. Regulate equipment operations and conditions such as water levels based on data from recording and indicating instruments or from computers. Take readings from charts, meters, and gauges at established intervals and take corrective steps as necessary. Inspect records and logbook entries and communicate with other plant personnel to assess equipment operating status. Start or stop generators, auxiliary pumping equipment, turbines, and other power plant equipment and connect or disconnect equipment from circuits. Control and maintain auxiliary equipment, such as pumps, fans, compressors, condensers, feedwater heaters, filters, and chlorinators, to supply water, fuel, lubricants, air, and auxiliary power. Clean, lubricate, and maintain equipment such as generators, turbines, pumps, and compressors in order to prevent equipment failure or deterioration. Communicate with systems operators to regulate and coordinate transmission loads and frequencies and line voltages. Record and compile operational data, completing and maintaining forms, logs, and reports. Open and close valves and switches in sequence upon signals from other workers in order to start or shut down auxiliary units. Collect oil, water, and electrolyte samples for laboratory analysis. Make adjustments or minor repairs, such as tightening leaking gland and pipe joints; report any needs for major repairs. Control generator output to match the phase, frequency, and voltage of electricity supplied to panels.

Other Considerations for Income: No additional information.

Personality Type: Realistic-Conventional. **Career Cluster:** 13 Manufacturing. **Career Pathway:** 13.1 Production. **Skills:** Operation Monitoring; Equipment Maintenance; Operation and Control; Technology Design; Systems Evaluation; Science; Equipment Selection; Coordination.

Education and Training Programs: No related CIP programs; this job is learned through long-term on-the-job training. **Related Knowledge/Courses:** Physics; Mechanical; Chemistry; Engineering and Technology; Public Safety and Security; Computers and Electronics.

Preventive Medicine Physicians

* Annual Earnings: $166,400+
* Beginning Wage: $49,710
* Earnings Growth Potential: Cannot be calculated
* Growth: 14.2%
* Annual Job Openings: 38,027
* Self-Employed: 14.7%
* Part-Time: 8.1%
* Job Security: No data available
* Education/Training Required: First professional degree

The Department of Labor reports this information for the occupation Physicians and Surgeons. The job openings listed here are shared with other specializations within that occupation, including Allergists and Immunologists; Anesthesiologists; Dermatologists; Family and General Practitioners; Hospitalists; Internists, General; Neurologists; Nuclear Medicine Physicians; Obstetricians and Gynecologists; Ophthalmologists; Pathologists; Pediatricians, General; Physical Medicine and Rehabilitation Physicians; Psychiatrists; Radiologists; Sports Medicine Physicians; Surgeons; and Urologists.

Industries in Which Income Is Highest

Industry	Average Annual Earnings	Number Employed
Ambulatory Health Care Services	$166,400+	147,400
Administrative and Support Services	$166,400+	1,310
Federal, State, and Local Government	$162,300	28,180
Professional, Scientific, and Technical Services	$107,470	1,210
Hospitals	$72,130	72,490

Metropolitan Areas Where Income Is Highest

Metropolitan Area	Average Annual Earnings	Number Employed
Los Angeles–Long Beach–Santa Ana, CA	$166,400+	8,810
Boston-Cambridge-Quincy, MA-NH	$166,400+	6,380
Dallas–Fort Worth–Arlington, TX	$166,400+	4,950
Tampa–St. Petersburg–Clearwater, FL	$166,400+	3,810
Portland-Vancouver-Beaverton, OR-WA	$166,400+	3,180

Apply knowledge of general preventive medicine and public health issues to promote health care to groups or individuals and aid in the prevention or reduction of risk of disease, injury, disability, or death. May practice population-based medicine or diagnose and treat patients in the context of clinical health promotion and disease prevention. No task data available.

Other Considerations for Income: Earnings of physicians and surgeons are among the highest of any occupation. Separate earnings figures for Preventive Medicine Physicians are not available.

Personality Type: Social-Investigative-Realistic. **Career Cluster:** 08 Health Science. **Career Pathway:** 08.1 Therapeutic Services. **Skills:** No data available.

Education and Training Program: Medicine (MD). **Related Knowledge/Courses:** No data available.

Producers

- ❀ Annual Earnings: $64,430
- ❀ Beginning Wage: $30,250
- ❀ Earnings Growth Potential: Very high (53.0%)
- ❀ Growth: 11.1%
- ❀ Annual Job Openings: 8,992
- ❀ Self-Employed: 29.5%
- ❀ Part-Time: 9.0%
- ❀ Job Security: More secure than most
- ❀ Education/Training Required: Work experience plus degree

The Department of Labor reports this information for the occupation Producers and Directors. The job openings listed here are shared with other specializations within that occupation, including Directors—Stage, Motion Pictures, Television, and Radio; Program Directors; Talent Directors; and Technical Directors/Managers.

Industries in Which Income Is Highest

Industry	Average Annual Earnings	Number Employed
Professional, Scientific, and Technical Services	$87,270	6,370
Motion Picture and Sound Recording Industries	$85,900	24,890
Publishing Industries (Except Internet)	$68,350	1,170
Federal, State, and Local Government	$62,950	1,860
Broadcasting (Except Internet)	$58,340	27,400

Metropolitan Areas Where Income Is Highest

Metropolitan Area	Average Annual Earnings	Number Employed
Oxnard–Thousand Oaks–Ventura, CA	$104,940	190
Los Angeles–Long Beach–Santa Ana, CA	$103,490	15,150
New York–Northern New Jersey–Long Island, NY-NJ-PA	$97,940	13,430
San Francisco–Oakland–Fremont, CA	$79,300	1,500
Washington-Arlington-Alexandria, DC-VA-MD-WV	$74,730	2,620

Plan and coordinate various aspects of radio, television, stage, or motion picture production, such as selecting script; coordinating writing, directing, and editing; and arranging financing. Coordinate the activities of writers, directors, managers, and other personnel throughout the production process. Monitor post-production processes to ensure accurate completion of all details. Perform management activities such as budgeting, scheduling, planning, and marketing. Determine production size, content, and budget, establishing details such as production schedules and management policies. Compose and edit scripts or provide screenwriters with story outlines from which scripts can be written. Conduct meetings with staff to discuss production progress and to ensure production objectives are attained. Resolve personnel problems that arise during the production process by acting as liaisons between dissenting parties when necessary. Produce shows for special occasions, such as holidays or testimonials. Edit and write news stories from information collected by reporters. Write and submit proposals to bid on contracts for projects. Hire directors, principal cast members, and key production staff members. Arrange financing for productions. Select plays, scripts, books, or ideas to be produced. Review film, recordings, or rehearsals to ensure conformance to production and broadcast standards. Perform administrative duties such as preparing operational reports, distributing rehearsal call sheets and script copies, and arranging for rehearsal quarters. Obtain and distribute costumes, props, music, and studio equipment needed to complete productions. Negotiate contracts with artistic personnel, often in accordance with collective bargaining agreements. Maintain knowledge of minimum wages and working conditions established by unions or associations of actors and technicians. Plan and coordinate the production of musical recordings, selecting music and directing performers. Negotiate with parties, including independent producers and the distributors and broadcasters who will be handling completed productions.

Other Considerations for Income: The most successful producers and directors may have extraordinarily high earnings but for others, because earnings may be erratic, many supplement their income by holding jobs in other fields. Stage producers seldom get a set fee; instead, they get a percentage of a show's earnings or ticket sales.

Personality Type: Enterprising-Artistic. **Career Cluster:** 03 Arts, Audio/Video Technology, and Communications. **Career Pathways:** 03.4 Performing Arts; 03.5 Journalism and Broadcasting. **Skills:** Writing; Monitoring; Management of Financial Resources; Management of Personnel Resources; Negotiation; Coordination; Equipment Selection; Speaking.

Education and Training Programs: Cinematography and Film/Video Production; Directing and Theatrical Production; Drama and Dramatics/Theatre Arts, General; Dramatic/Theatre Arts and Stagecraft, Other; Film/Cinema/Video Studies; Radio and Television. **Related Knowledge/Courses:** Communications and Media; Fine Arts; Clerical; Sales and Marketing; Telecommunications; English Language.

Producers and Directors

See *Directors—Stage, Motion Pictures, Television, and Radio; Producers; Program Directors; Talent Directors; and Technical Directors/Managers,* described separately.

Product Safety Engineers

- ❀ Annual Earnings: $72,490
- ❀ Beginning Wage: $43,540
- ❀ Earnings Growth Potential: Medium (39.9%)
- ❀ Growth: 9.6%
- ❀ Annual Job Openings: 1,105
- ❀ Self-Employed: 1.1%
- ❀ Part-Time: 2.0%
- ❀ Job Security: More secure than most
- ❀ Education/Training Required: Bachelor's degree

The Department of Labor reports this information for the occupation Health and Safety Engineers, Except Mining Safety Engineers and Inspectors. The job openings listed here are shared with other specializations within that occupation, including Fire-Prevention and Protection Engineers; and Industrial Safety and Health Engineers.

Industries in Which Income Is Highest

Industry	Average Annual Earnings	Number Employed
Federal, State, and Local Government	$79,770	3,870
Professional, Scientific, and Technical Services	$77,660	4,000
Chemical Manufacturing	$75,550	2,360
Waste Management and Remediation Services	$72,380	1,210
Heavy and Civil Engineering Construction	$65,140	1,860

Metropolitan Areas Where Income Is Highest

Metropolitan Area	Average Annual Earnings	Number Employed
San Jose–Sunnyvale–Santa Clara, CA	$94,140	160
Kennewick-Richland-Pasco, WA	$90,170	120
Chicago-Naperville-Joliet, IL-IN-WI	$88,820	1,140
Knoxville, TN	$88,170	90
Huntsville, AL	$86,540	100

Develop and conduct tests to evaluate product safety levels and recommend measures to reduce or eliminate hazards. Report accident investigation findings. Conduct

P

research to evaluate safety levels for products. Evaluate potential health hazards or damage that could occur from product misuse. Investigate causes of accidents, injuries, or illnesses related to product usage in order to develop solutions to minimize or prevent recurrence. Recommend procedures for detection, prevention, and elimination of physical, chemical, or other product hazards. Participate in preparation of product usage and precautionary label instructions.

Other Considerations for Income: As a group, engineers earn some of the highest average starting salaries among those holding bachelor's degrees. Separate earnings figures for Product Safety Engineers are not available, but they are probably similar to those for Health and Safety Engineers, who are among the lowest-paid of the various kinds of engineers.

Personality Type: Investigative-Realistic-Conventional. **Career Cluster:** 15 Science, Technology, Engineering, and Mathematics. **Career Pathway:** 15.1 Engineering and Technology. **Skills:** Science; Systems Analysis; Technology Design; Operations Analysis; Quality Control Analysis; Mathematics; Systems Evaluation; Persuasion.

Education and Training Program: Environmental/Environmental Health Engineering. **Related Knowledge/Courses:** Engineering and Technology; Design; Physics; Mechanical; Chemistry; Public Safety and Security.

Program Directors

- ❋ Annual Earnings: $64,430
- ❋ Beginning Wage: $30,250
- ❋ Earnings Growth Potential: Very high (53.0%)
- ❋ Growth: 11.1%
- ❋ Annual Job Openings: 8,992
- ❋ Self-Employed: 29.5%
- ❋ Part-Time: 9.0%
- ❋ Job Security: More secure than most
- ❋ Education/Training Required: Work experience plus degree

The Department of Labor reports this information for the occupation Producers and Directors. The job openings listed here are shared with other specializations within that occupation, including Directors—Stage, Motion Pictures, Television, and Radio; Producers; Talent Directors; and Technical Directors/Managers.

Industries in Which Income Is Highest

Industry	Average Annual Earnings	Number Employed
Professional, Scientific, and Technical Services	$87,270	6,370
Motion Picture and Sound Recording Industries	$85,900	24,890
Publishing Industries (Except Internet)	$68,350	1,170
Federal, State, and Local Government	$62,950	1,860
Broadcasting (Except Internet)	$58,340	27,400

Metropolitan Areas Where Income Is Highest

Metropolitan Area	Average Annual Earnings	Number Employed
Oxnard–Thousand Oaks–Ventura, CA	$104,940	190
Los Angeles–Long Beach–Santa Ana, CA	$103,490	15,150
New York–Northern New Jersey–Long Island, NY-NJ-PA	$97,940	13,430
San Francisco–Oakland–Fremont, CA	$79,300	1,500
Washington-Arlington-Alexandria, DC-VA-MD-WV	$74,730	2,620

Direct and coordinate activities of personnel engaged in preparation of radio or television station program schedules and programs such as sports or news. Plan and schedule programming and event coverage based on broadcast length; time availability; and other factors such as community needs, ratings data, and viewer demographics. Monitor and review programming to ensure that schedules are met, guidelines are adhered to, and performances are of adequate quality. Direct and coordinate activities of personnel engaged in broadcast news, sports, or programming. Check completed program logs for accuracy and conformance with FCC rules and regulations and resolve program log inaccuracies. Establish work schedules and assign work to staff members. Coordinate activities between departments such as news and programming. Perform personnel duties such as hiring staff and evaluating work performance. Evaluate new and existing programming for suitability and to assess the need for changes, using information such as audience surveys and feedback. Develop budgets for programming and broadcasting activities and monitor expenditures to ensure that they remain within budgetary limits. Confer with directors and production staff to discuss issues such as production and casting problems, budgets, policies, and news coverage. Select, acquire, and maintain programs, music, films, and other needed materials and obtain legal clearances for their use as necessary. Monitor network transmissions for advisories concerning daily program schedules, program content, special feeds, or program changes. Develop promotions for current programs and specials. Prepare copy and edit tape so that material is ready for broadcasting. Develop ideas for programs and features that a station could produce. Participate in the planning and execution of fundraising activities. Review information about programs and schedules to ensure accuracy and provide such information to local media outlets as necessary. Read news, read or record public service and promotional announcements, and otherwise participate as a member of an on-air shift as required.

Other Considerations for Income: The most successful producers and directors may have extraordinarily high earnings but for others, because earnings may be erratic, many supplement their income by holding jobs in other fields.

Personality Type: Enterprising-Conventional-Artistic. **Career Cluster:** 03 Arts, Audio/Video Technology, and Communications. **Career Pathways:** 03.4 Performing Arts; 03.5 Journalism and Broadcasting. **Skills:** Operations Analysis; Management of Financial Resources; Management of Personnel Resources; Coordination; Writing; Time Management; Equipment Selection; Monitoring.

Education and Training Programs: Cinematography and Film/Video Production; Directing and Theatrical Production; Drama and Dramatics/Theatre Arts, General; Dramatic/Theatre Arts and Stagecraft, Other; Film/Cinema/Video Studies; Radio and Television. **Related Knowledge/Courses:** Telecommunications; Communications and Media; Computers and Electronics; Clerical; Personnel and Human Resources; Engineering and Technology.

Prosthodontists

❋ Annual Earnings: $166,400+
❋ Beginning Wage: $72,710
❋ Earnings Growth Potential: Cannot be calculated
❋ Growth: 10.7%
❋ Annual Job Openings: 54
❋ Self-Employed: 51.3%
❋ Part-Time: 25.9%
❋ Job Security: Less secure than most
❋ Education/Training Required: First professional degree

Industries in Which Income Is Highest

Industry	Average Annual Earnings	Number Employed
Ambulatory Health Care Services	$166,400+	340

Metropolitan Areas Where Income Is Highest

Metropolitan Area	Average Annual Earnings	Number Employed

Insufficient data available

Construct oral prostheses to replace missing teeth and other oral structures to correct natural and acquired deformation of mouth and jaws; to restore and maintain oral function, such as chewing and speaking; and to improve appearance. Replace missing teeth and associated oral structures with permanent fixtures, such as crowns and bridges, or removable fixtures, such as dentures. Fit prostheses to patients, making any necessary adjustments and modifications. Design and fabricate dental prostheses or supervise dental technicians and laboratory bench workers who construct the devices. Measure and take impressions of patients' jaws and teeth to determine the shape and size of dental prostheses, using face bows, dental articulators, recording devices, and other materials. Collaborate with general dentists, specialists, and other health professionals to develop solutions to dental and oral health concerns. Repair, reline, and/or rebase dentures. Restore function and aesthetics to traumatic injury victims

P

or to individuals with diseases or birth defects. Use bonding technology on the surface of the teeth to change tooth shape or to close gaps. Treat facial pain and jaw joint problems. Place veneers onto teeth to conceal defects. Bleach discolored teeth to brighten and whiten them.

Other Considerations for Income: Self-employed dentists in private practice tend to earn more than do salaried dentists. Dentists who are salaried often receive benefits paid by their employer, with health insurance and malpractice insurance being among the most common. However, like other business owners, self-employed dentists must provide their own health insurance, life insurance, retirement plans, and other benefits.

Personality Type: Investigative-Realistic. **Career Cluster:** 08 Health Science. **Career Pathway:** 08.1 Therapeutic Services. **Skills:** Science; Management of Financial Resources; Social Perceptiveness; Equipment Selection; Reading Comprehension; Active Learning; Complex Problem Solving; Technology Design.

Education and Training Programs: Prosthodontics Specialty; Prosthodontics/Prosthodontology (Cert., MS, PhD). **Related Knowledge/Courses:** Medicine and Dentistry; Biology; Chemistry; Psychology; Engineering and Technology; Sales and Marketing.

Psychiatrists

- ❋ Annual Earnings: $154,200
- ❋ Beginning Wage: $60,120
- ❋ Earnings Growth Potential: Very high (61.0%)
- ❋ Growth: 14.2%
- ❋ Annual Job Openings: 38,027
- ❋ Self-Employed: 14.7%
- ❋ Part-Time: 8.1%
- ❋ Job Security: Most secure
- ❋ Education/Training Required: First professional degree

The Department of Labor reports this information for the occupation Physicians and Surgeons. The job openings listed here are shared with other specializations within that occupation, including Allergists and Immunologists; Anesthesiologists; Dermatologists; Family and General Practitioners; Hospitalists; Internists, General; Neurologists; Nuclear Medicine Physicians; Obstetricians and Gynecologists; Ophthalmologists; Pathologists; Pediatricians, General; Physical Medicine and Rehabilitation Physicians; Preventive Medicine Physicians; Radiologists; Sports Medicine Physicians; Surgeons; and Urologists.

Industries in Which Income Is Highest

Industry	Average Annual Earnings	Number Employed
Federal, State, and Local Government	$158,560	2,590
Hospitals	$154,320	7,320
Ambulatory Health Care Services	$154,140	9,700

Metropolitan Areas Where Income Is Highest

Metropolitan Area	Average Annual Earnings	Number Employed
Boston-Cambridge-Quincy, MA-NH	$166,400+	720
San Francisco–Oakland–Fremont, CA	$166,400+	500
Seattle-Tacoma-Bellevue, WA	$166,400+	370
Riverside–San Bernardino–Ontario, CA	$166,400+	270
Hartford–West Hartford–East Hartford, CT	$166,400+	260

Diagnose, treat, and help prevent disorders of the mind. Prescribe, direct, and administer psychotherapeutic treatments or medications to treat mental, emotional, or behavioral disorders. Analyze and evaluate patient data and test findings to diagnose nature and extent of mental disorders. Collaborate with physicians, psychologists, social workers, psychiatric nurses, or other professionals to discuss treatment plans and progress. Gather and maintain patient information and records, including social and medical histories obtained from patients, relatives, and other professionals. Design individualized care plans, using a variety of treatments. Counsel outpatients and other patients during office visits. Examine or conduct laboratory or diagnostic tests on patients to provide information on general physical conditions and mental disorders. Advise and inform guardians, relatives, and significant others of patients' conditions and treatments. Teach, take continuing education classes, attend conferences and seminars, and conduct research and publish findings to increase understanding of mental, emotional, and behavioral states and disorders. Review and evaluate treatment procedures and outcomes of other psychiatrists and medical professionals. Prepare and submit case reports and summaries to government and mental health agencies.

Serve on committees to promote and maintain community mental health services and delivery systems.

Other Considerations for Income: Earnings of physicians and surgeons are among the highest of any occupation; Psychiatrists are in the middle range of earners among medical specialists. The Medical Group Management Association's Physician Compensation and Production Survey of 2005 reported earnings of $173,922 for Psychiatrists with less than two years in their specialty and $180,000 for those with more than one year in their specialty. These figures cover salary, bonus and incentive payments, research stipends, honoraria, and distribution of profits. Self-employed physicians—those who own or are part owners of their medical practice—generally have higher median incomes than salaried physicians, but their must provide for their own health insurance and retirement.

Personality Type: Investigative-Social-Artistic. **Career Cluster:** 08 Health Science. **Career Pathway:** 08.1 Therapeutic Services. **Skills:** Social Perceptiveness; Negotiation; Systems Analysis; Persuasion; Systems Evaluation; Service Orientation; Judgment and Decision Making; Complex Problem Solving.

Education and Training Program: Medicine (MD). **Related Knowledge/Courses:** Therapy and Counseling; Medicine and Dentistry; Psychology; Biology; Sociology and Anthropology; Philosophy and Theology.

Psychology Teachers, Postsecondary

- ❋ Annual Earnings: $63,630
- ❋ Beginning Wage: $35,040
- ❋ Earnings Growth Potential: High (44.9%)
- ❋ Growth: 22.9%
- ❋ Annual Job Openings: 5,261
- ❋ Self-Employed: 0.4%
- ❋ Part-Time: 27.8%
- ❋ Job Security: Most secure
- ❋ Education/Training Required: Doctoral degree

Industries in Which Income Is Highest

Industry	Average Annual Earnings	Number Employed
Educational Services	$63,630	31,400

Metropolitan Areas Where Income Is Highest

Metropolitan Area	Average Annual Earnings	Number Employed
Fort Collins–Loveland, CO	$85,180	60
San Diego–Carlsbad–San Marcos, CA	$81,320	460
Columbus, OH	$80,950	170
New York–Northern New Jersey–Long Island, NY-NJ-PA	$77,720	2,020
San Francisco–Oakland–Fremont, CA	$76,750	430

Teach courses in psychology, such as child, clinical, and developmental psychology, and psychological counseling. Prepare and deliver lectures to undergraduate and/or graduate students on topics such as abnormal psychology, cognitive processes, and work motivation. Evaluate and grade students' classwork, laboratory work, assignments, and papers. Initiate, facilitate, and moderate classroom discussions. Compile, administer, and grade examinations or assign this work to others. Keep abreast of developments in their field by reading current literature, talking with colleagues, and participating in professional conferences. Prepare course materials such as syllabi, homework assignments, and handouts. Plan, evaluate, and revise curricula, course content, and course materials and methods of instruction. Maintain student attendance records, grades, and other required records. Supervise undergraduate and/or graduate teaching, internship, and research work. Maintain regularly scheduled office hours to advise and assist students. Conduct research in a particular field of knowledge and publish findings in professional journals, books, and electronic media. Advise students on academic and vocational curricula and on career issues. Select and obtain materials and supplies such as textbooks. Collaborate with colleagues to address teaching and research issues. Serve on academic or administrative committees that deal with institutional policies, departmental matters, and academic issues. Compile bibliographies of specialized materials for outside reading assignments. Participate in student recruitment, registration, and placement activities. Supervise students' laboratory work. Perform administrative duties such as serving as department head. Act as advisers to student organizations. Write grant proposals to procure external research funding. Participate in campus and community events. Provide professional consulting services to government and industry.

Other Considerations for Income: Earnings for college faculty vary according to rank and type of institution, geographic area, and field. According to a 2006–2007 survey by the American Association of University Professors, salaries for full-time faculty averaged $73,207. By rank, the average was $98,974 for professors, $69,911 for associate professors, $58,662 for assistant professors, $42,609 for instructors, and $48,289 for lecturers. Faculty in 4-year institutions earn higher salaries, on average, than do those in 2-year schools. Many faculty members have significant earnings in addition to their base salary from consulting, teaching additional courses, research, writing for publication, or other employment. In addition, many college and university faculty enjoy unique benefits, including access to campus facilities, tuition waivers for dependents, housing and travel allowances, and paid leave for sabbaticals. Part-time faculty and instructors usually have fewer benefits than full-time faculty.

Personality Type: Social-Investigative-Artistic. **Career Clusters:** 05 Education and Training; 08 Health Science; 10 Human Service. **Career Pathways:** 05.3 Teaching/Training; 08.1 Therapeutic Services; 10.2 Counseling and Mental Health Services. **Skills:** Science; Learning Strategies; Instructing; Social Perceptiveness; Writing; Reading Comprehension; Critical Thinking; Active Learning.

Education and Training Programs: Humanities/Humanistic Studies; Marriage and Family Therapy/Counseling; Psychology Teacher Education; Psychology, General; Psychology, Other; Social Science Teacher Education. **Related Knowledge/Courses:** Therapy and Counseling; Psychology; Sociology and Anthropology; Philosophy and Theology; Education and Training; English Language.

Public Relations Managers

- ❀ Annual Earnings: $89,430
- ❀ Beginning Wage: $46,870
- ❀ Earnings Growth Potential: High (47.6%)
- ❀ Growth: 16.9%
- ❀ Annual Job Openings: 5,781
- ❀ Self-Employed: 1.7%
- ❀ Part-Time: 5.4%
- ❀ Job Security: Least secure
- ❀ Education/Training Required: Work experience plus degree

Industries in Which Income Is Highest

Industry	Average Annual Earnings	Number Employed
Securities, Commodity Contracts, and Other Financial Investments and Related Activities	$115,800	1,910
Professional, Scientific, and Technical Services	$109,920	8,280
Management of Companies and Enterprises	$101,130	4,970
Credit Intermediation and Related Activities	$97,560	3,050
Insurance Carriers and Related Activities	$92,260	1,340

Metropolitan Areas Where Income Is Highest

Metropolitan Area	Average Annual Earnings	Number Employed
San Jose–Sunnyvale–Santa Clara, CA	$141,600	460
Washington-Arlington-Alexandria, DC-VA-MD-WV	$128,140	2,750
Trenton-Ewing, NJ	$124,480	170
New York–Northern New Jersey–Long Island, NY-NJ-PA	$121,060	7,140
Sacramento–Arden-Arcade–Roseville, CA	$120,370	380

Plan and direct public relations programs designed to create and maintain a favorable public image for employer or client or, if engaged in fundraising, plan and direct activities to solicit and maintain funds for

special projects and nonprofit organizations. Identify main client groups and audiences and determine the best way to communicate publicity information to them. Write interesting and effective press releases, prepare information for media kits, and develop and maintain company Internet or intranet Web pages. Develop and maintain the company's corporate image and identity, which includes the use of logos and signage. Manage communications budgets. Manage special events such as sponsorship of races, parties introducing new products, or other activities the firm supports to gain public attention through the media without advertising directly. Draft speeches for company executives and arrange interviews and other forms of contact for them. Assign, supervise, and review the activities of public relations staff. Evaluate advertising and promotion programs for compatibility with public relations efforts. Establish and maintain effective working relationships with local and municipal government officials and media representatives. Confer with labor relations managers to develop internal communications that keep employees informed of company activities. Direct activities of external agencies, establishments, and departments that develop and implement communication strategies and information programs. Formulate policies and procedures related to public information programs, working with public relations executives. Respond to requests for information about employers' activities or status. Establish goals for soliciting funds, develop policies for collection and safeguarding of contributions, and coordinate disbursement of funds. Facilitate consumer relations or the relationship between parts of the company such as the managers and employees or different branch offices. Maintain company archives. Manage in-house communication courses. Produce films and other video products, regulate their distribution, and operate film library. Observe and report on social, economic, and political trends that might affect employers.

Other Considerations for Income: Salary levels vary substantially, depending upon the level of managerial responsibility, length of service, education, size of firm, location, and industry. For example, manufacturing firms usually pay these managers higher salaries than nonmanufacturing firms. Many managers earn bonuses equal to 10 percent or more of their salaries.

Personality Type: Enterprising-Artistic. **Career Cluster:** 04 Business, Management, and Administration. **Career Pathway:** 04.1 Management. **Skills:** Management of Financial Resources; Monitoring; Social Perceptiveness; Writing; Service Orientation; Operations Analysis; Speaking; Persuasion.

Education and Training Program: Public Relations/Image Management. **Related Knowledge/Courses:** Sales and Marketing; Communications and Media; Customer and Personal Service; Personnel and Human Resources; English Language; Administration and Management.

Public Relations Specialists

- ❀ Annual Earnings: $51,280
- ❀ Beginning Wage: $30,140
- ❀ Earnings Growth Potential: High (41.2%)
- ❀ Growth: 17.6%
- ❀ Annual Job Openings: 51,216
- ❀ Self-Employed: 4.9%
- ❀ Part-Time: 13.9%
- ❀ Job Security: Most secure
- ❀ Education/Training Required: Bachelor's degree

Industries in Which Income Is Highest

Industry	Average Annual Earnings	Number Employed
Computer and Electronic Product Manufacturing	$68,390	1,570
Telecommunications	$63,920	1,690
Utilities	$63,400	1,670
Securities, Commodity Contracts, and Other Financial Investments and Related Activities	$57,710	2,180
Professional, Scientific, and Technical Services	$56,730	57,150

Metropolitan Areas Where Income Is Highest

Metropolitan Area	Average Annual Earnings	Number Employed
San Jose–Sunnyvale–Santa Clara, CA	$86,550	2,030
Washington-Arlington-Alexandria, DC-VA-MD-WV	$79,590	16,410
Oxnard–Thousand Oaks–Ventura, CA	$71,560	380
Sacramento–Arden-Arcade–Roseville, CA	$67,320	2,210
Lewiston-Auburn, ME	$64,560	60

P

Engage in promoting or creating goodwill for individuals, groups, or organizations by writing or selecting favorable publicity material and releasing it through various communications media. May prepare and arrange displays and make speeches. Prepare or edit organizational publications for internal and external audiences, including employee newsletters and stockholders' reports. Respond to requests for information from the media or designate another appropriate spokesperson or information source. Establish and maintain cooperative relationships with representatives of community, consumer, employee, and public interest groups. Plan and direct development and communication of informational programs to maintain favorable public and stockholder perceptions of an organization's accomplishments and agenda. Confer with production and support personnel to produce or coordinate production of advertisements and promotions. Arrange public appearances, lectures, contests, or exhibits for clients to increase product and service awareness and to promote goodwill. Study the objectives, promotional policies, and needs of organizations to develop public relations strategies that will influence public opinion or promote ideas, products, and services. Consult with advertising agencies or staff to arrange promotional campaigns in all types of media for products, organizations, or individuals. Confer with other managers to identify trends and key group interests and concerns or to provide advice on business decisions. Coach client representatives in effective communication with the public and with employees. Prepare and deliver speeches to further public relations objectives. Purchase advertising space and time as required to promote client's product or agenda. Plan and conduct market and public opinion research to test products or determine potential for product success, communicating results to client or management.

Other Considerations for Income: No additional information.

Personality Type: Enterprising-Artistic-Social. **Career Clusters:** 03 Arts, Audio/Video Technology, and Communications; 04 Business, Management, and Administration. **Career Pathways:** 03.5 Journalism and Broadcasting; 04.1 Management. **Skills:** Service Orientation; Management of Financial Resources; Persuasion; Writing; Negotiation; Social Perceptiveness; Judgment and Decision Making; Monitoring.

Education and Training Programs: Family and Consumer Sciences/Human Sciences Communication; Health Communication; Political Communication; Public Relations/Image Management; Speech Communication and Rhetoric. **Related Knowledge/Courses:** Communications and Media; Sales and Marketing; English Language; Geography; Computers and Electronics; Customer and Personal Service.

Purchasing Agents and Buyers, Farm Products

- ❀ Annual Earnings: $49,670
- ❀ Beginning Wage: $28,990
- ❀ Earnings Growth Potential: High (41.6%)
- ❀ Growth: –8.6%
- ❀ Annual Job Openings: 1,618
- ❀ Self-Employed: 5.1%
- ❀ Part-Time: 3.8%
- ❀ Job Security: More secure than most
- ❀ Education/Training Required: Long-term on-the-job training

Industries in Which Income Is Highest

Industry	Average Annual Earnings	Number Employed
Food Manufacturing	$51,290	1,660
Merchant Wholesalers, Nondurable Goods	$50,590	5,010

Metropolitan Areas Where Income Is Highest

Metropolitan Area	Average Annual Earnings	Number Employed
New York–Northern New Jersey–Long Island, NY-NJ-PA	$84,630	530
Kansas City, MO-KS	$81,450	160
San Francisco–Oakland–Fremont, CA	$66,390	170
Washington-Arlington-Alexandria, DC-VA-MD-WV	$61,650	110
Springfield, MA-CT	$61,580	70

Purchase farm products for further processing or resale. Advise farm groups and growers on land preparation and livestock care techniques that will maximize the quantity and quality of production. Arrange for processing or resale of purchased products. Arrange for transportation and/or storage of purchased products. Examine and test crops and products to estimate their value, determine their grade, and locate any evidence of disease or insect damage. Maintain records of business transactions and product inventories, reporting data to companies or government agencies as necessary. Negotiate contracts with farmers for the production or purchase of farm products. Review orders to determine product types and quantities required to meet demand. Estimate land production possibilities, surveying property and studying factors such as crop rotation history, soil fertility, and irrigation facilities. Sell supplies such as seed, feed, fertilizers, and insecticides, arranging for loans or financing as necessary. Coordinate and direct activities of workers engaged in cutting, transporting, storing, or milling products and in maintaining records. Purchase farm products such as milk, grains, and Christmas trees for further processing or for resale. Calculate applicable government grain quotas.

Other Considerations for Income: Purchasing managers, buyers, and purchasing agents receive the same benefits package as other workers, including vacations, sick leave, life and health insurance, and pension plans.

Personality Type: Enterprising-Conventional-Realistic. **Career Cluster:** 01 Agriculture, Food and Natural Resource. **Career Pathway:** 01.1 Food Products and Processing Systems. **Skills:** Management of Financial Resources; Operations Analysis; Negotiation; Quality Control Analysis; Judgment and Decision Making; Management of Material Resources; Systems Analysis; Coordination.

Education and Training Program: Agricultural/Farm Supplies Retailing and Wholesaling. **Related Knowledge/Courses:** Food Production; Economics and Accounting; Production and Processing; Sales and Marketing; Geography; Transportation.

Purchasing Agents, Except Wholesale, Retail, and Farm Products

* Annual Earnings: $53,940
* Beginning Wage: $33,650
* Earnings Growth Potential: Medium (37.6%)
* Growth: 0.1%
* Annual Job Openings: 22,349
* Self-Employed: 1.6%
* Part-Time: 3.8%
* Job Security: More secure than most
* Education/Training Required: Long-term on-the-job training

Industries in Which Income Is Highest

Industry	Average Annual Earnings	Number Employed
Federal, State, and Local Government	$64,730	44,090
Telecommunications	$64,390	4,480
Oil and Gas Extraction	$64,360	1,120
Publishing Industries (Except Internet)	$62,870	1,490
Utilities	$61,700	3,450

Metropolitan Areas Where Income Is Highest

Metropolitan Area	Average Annual Earnings	Number Employed
Washington-Arlington-Alexandria, DC-VA-MD-WV	$72,190	10,740
Huntsville, AL	$71,620	1,820
Albany, GA	$71,090	110
Kokomo, IN	$70,610	70
Warner Robins, GA	$70,480	360

Purchase machinery, equipment, tools, parts, supplies, or services necessary for the operation of an establishment. Purchase raw or semi-finished materials for manufacturing. Purchase the highest-quality merchandise at the lowest possible price and in correct amounts. Prepare purchase orders, solicit bid proposals, and review requisitions for goods and services. Research and evaluate suppliers based on price, quality, selection, service, support, availability, reliability, production and distribution capabilities, and the supplier's reputation and history. Analyze price proposals, financial reports, and other data and information to determine reasonable prices. Monitor and follow applicable laws and regulations. Negotiate, or renegotiate, and administer contracts with suppliers, vendors, and other representatives. Monitor shipments to ensure that goods come in on time and trace shipments and follow up on undelivered goods in the event of problems. Confer with staff, users, and vendors to discuss defective or unacceptable goods or services and determine corrective action. Evaluate and monitor contract performance to ensure compliance with contractual obligations and to determine need for changes. Maintain and review computerized or manual records of items purchased, costs, delivery, product performance, and inventories. Review catalogs, industry periodicals, directories, trade journals, and Internet sites and consult with other department personnel to locate necessary goods and services. Study sales records and inventory levels of current stock to develop strategic purchasing programs that facilitate employee access to supplies. Interview vendors and visit suppliers' plants and distribution centers to examine and learn about products, services, and prices. Arrange the payment of duty and freight charges. Hire, train, and/or supervise purchasing clerks, buyers, and expediters. Write and review product specifications, maintaining a working technical knowledge of the goods or services to be purchased. Monitor changes affecting supply and demand, tracking market conditions, price trends, or futures markets.

Other Considerations for Income: Purchasing managers, buyers, and purchasing agents receive the same benefits package as other workers, including vacations, sick leave, life and health insurance, and pension plans.

Personality Type: Conventional-Enterprising. **Career Cluster:** 14 Marketing, Sales, and Service. **Career Pathway:** 14.3 Buying and Merchandising. **Skills:** Operations Analysis; Management of Material Resources; Management of Financial Resources; Writing; Mathematics; Speaking; Management of Personnel Resources; Judgment and Decision Making.

Education and Training Programs: Insurance; Merchandising and Buying Operations; Sales, Distribution, and Marketing Operations, General. **Related Knowledge/Courses:** Clerical; Economics and Accounting; Production and Processing; Administration and Management; Computers and Electronics; Communications and Media.

Purchasing Managers

* ❋ Annual Earnings: $89,160
* ❋ Beginning Wage: $51,490
* ❋ Earnings Growth Potential: High (42.2%)
* ❋ Growth: 3.4%
* ❋ Annual Job Openings: 7,243
* ❋ Self-Employed: 2.7%
* ❋ Part-Time: 1.9%
* ❋ Job Security: More secure than most
* ❋ Education/Training Required: Work experience plus degree

Industries in Which Income Is Highest

Industry	Average Annual Earnings	Number Employed
Management of Companies and Enterprises	$103,910	9,040
Professional, Scientific, and Technical Services	$103,370	3,980
Computer and Electronic Product Manufacturing	$98,350	4,930
Federal, State, and Local Government	$96,170	5,870
Chemical Manufacturing	$94,120	1,910

Metropolitan Areas Where Income Is Highest

Metropolitan Area	Average Annual Earnings	Number Employed
Washington-Arlington-Alexandria, DC-VA-MD-WV	$115,230	2,870
Austin–Round Rock, TX	$113,800	280
Trenton-Ewing, NJ	$113,490	60
Kennewick-Richland-Pasco, WA	$111,940	70
Boulder, CO	$111,430	80

Plan, direct, or coordinate the activities of buyers, purchasing officers, and related workers involved in purchasing materials, products, and services. Maintain records of goods ordered and received. Locate vendors of materials, equipment, or supplies and interview them to determine product availability and terms of sales. Prepare and process requisitions and purchase orders for supplies and equipment. Control purchasing department budgets.

Interview and hire staff and oversee staff training. Review purchase order claims and contracts for conformance to company policy. Analyze market and delivery systems to assess present and future material availability. Develop and implement purchasing and contract management instructions, policies, and procedures. Participate in the development of specifications for equipment, products, or substitute materials. Resolve vendor or contractor grievances and claims against suppliers. Represent companies in negotiating contracts and formulating policies with suppliers. Review, evaluate, and approve specifications for issuing and awarding bids. Direct and coordinate activities of personnel engaged in buying, selling, and distributing materials, equipment, machinery, and supplies. Prepare bid awards requiring board approval. Prepare reports regarding market conditions and merchandise costs. Administer online purchasing systems. Arrange for disposal of surplus materials.

Other Considerations for Income: Purchasing managers, buyers, and purchasing agents receive the same benefits package as other workers, including vacations, sick leave, life and health insurance, and pension plans.

Personality Type: Enterprising-Conventional. **Career Cluster:** 04 Business, Management, and Administration. **Career Pathway:** 04.1 Management. **Skills:** Management of Material Resources; Management of Financial Resources; Negotiation; Operations Analysis; Systems Evaluation; Mathematics; Operation Monitoring; Operation and Control.

Education and Training Program: Purchasing, Procurement/Acquisitions and Contracts Management. **Related Knowledge/Courses:** Production and Processing; Economics and Accounting; Transportation; Administration and Management; Personnel and Human Resources; Sales and Marketing.

Quality Control Systems Managers

- ❀ Annual Earnings: $83,290
- ❀ Beginning Wage: $50,330
- ❀ Earnings Growth Potential: Medium (39.6%)
- ❀ Growth: –5.9%
- ❀ Annual Job Openings: 14,889
- ❀ Self-Employed: 2.0%
- ❀ Part-Time: 1.6%
- ❀ Job Security: No data available
- ❀ Education/Training Required: Bachelor's degree

The Department of Labor reports this information for the occupation Industrial Production Managers. The job openings listed here are shared with other specializations within that occupation, including Biofuels Production Managers; Biomass Production Managers; Geothermal Production Managers; Hydroelectric Production Managers; and Methane/Landfill Gas Collection System Operators.

Industries in Which Income Is Highest

Industry	Average Annual Earnings	Number Employed
Oil and Gas Extraction	$104,890	1,590
Professional, Scientific, and Technical Services	$103,550	3,450
Petroleum and Coal Products Manufacturing	$103,100	1,220
Utilities	$101,110	1,740
Management of Companies and Enterprises	$99,660	6,180

Metropolitan Areas Where Income Is Highest

Metropolitan Area	Average Annual Earnings	Number Employed
Austin–Round Rock, TX	$112,900	690
Cedar Rapids, IA	$110,680	530
Leominster-Fitchburg-Gardner, MA	$107,340	70
Saginaw–Saginaw Township North, MI	$106,880	140
Ann Arbor, MI	$104,600	320

Plan, direct, or coordinate quality assurance programs. Formulate quality control policies and control quality of laboratory and production efforts. No task data available.

Other Considerations for Income: No additional information.

Personality Type: Enterprising-Conventional-Realistic. **Career Cluster:** 04 Business, Management, and Administration. **Career Pathway:** 04.1 Management. **Skills:** No data available.

Education and Training Programs: Business Administration and Management, General; Business/Commerce, General; Operations Management and Supervision. **Related Knowledge/Courses:** No data available.

Radiation Therapists

❁ Annual Earnings: $72,910
❁ Beginning Wage: $47,910
❁ Earnings Growth Potential: Low (34.3%)
❁ Growth: 24.8%
❁ Annual Job Openings: 1,461
❁ Self-Employed: 0.0%
❁ Part-Time: 10.3%
❁ Job Security: Most secure
❁ Education/Training Required: Associate degree

Industries in Which Income Is Highest

Industry	Average Annual Earnings	Number Employed
Ambulatory Health Care Services	$73,530	3,550
Hospitals	$71,840	10,360

Metropolitan Areas Where Income Is Highest

Metropolitan Area	Average Annual Earnings	Number Employed
San Jose–Sunnyvale–Santa Clara, CA	$95,760	90
Los Angeles–Long Beach–Santa Ana, CA	$90,920	540
Seattle-Tacoma-Bellevue, WA	$89,710	210
New York–Northern New Jersey– Long Island, NY-NJ-PA	$87,900	910
San Francisco–Oakland–Fremont, CA	$87,320	260

Provide radiation therapy to patients as prescribed by radiologists according to established practices and standards. Position patients for treatment with accuracy according to prescription. Administer prescribed doses of radiation to specific body parts, using radiation therapy equipment according to established practices and standards. Check radiation therapy equipment to ensure proper operation. Review prescriptions, diagnoses, patient charts, and identification. Follow principles of radiation protection for patients, radiation therapists, and others. Maintain records, reports, and files as required, including such information as radiation dosages, equipment settings, and patients' reactions. Conduct most treatment sessions independently, in accordance with long-term treatment plans and under general direction of patients' physicians. Enter data into computers and set controls to operate and adjust equipment and regulate dosages. Observe and reassure patients during treatments and report unusual reactions to physicians or turn equipment off if unexpected adverse reactions occur. Calculate actual treatment dosages delivered during each session. Check for side effects such as skin irritation, nausea, and hair loss to assess patients' reaction to treatment. Prepare and construct equipment such as immobilization, treatment, and protection devices. Educate, prepare, and reassure patients and their families by answering questions, providing physical assistance, and reinforcing physicians' advice regarding treatment reactions and post-treatment care. Provide assistance to other health care personnel during dosimetry procedures and tumor localization. Help physicians, radiation oncologists, and clinical physicists to prepare physical and technical aspects of radiation treatment plans, using information about patient conditions and anatomies. Photograph treated areas of patients and process film. Act as liaisons with medical physicists and supportive care personnel. Train and supervise student or subordinate radiotherapy technologists. Implement appropriate follow-up care plans.

R

Other Considerations for Income: Some employers of Radiation Therapists also reimburse their employees for the cost of continuing education.

Personality Type: Social-Realistic-Conventional. **Career Cluster:** 08 Health Science. **Career Pathway:** 08.2 Diagnostics Services. **Skills:** Operation Monitoring; Operation and Control; Quality Control Analysis; Systems Analysis; Equipment Maintenance.

Education and Training Program: Medical Radiologic Technology/Science—Radiation Therapist. **Related Knowledge/Courses:** Medicine and Dentistry; Biology; Physics; Psychology; Philosophy and Theology; Therapy and Counseling.

Radio Frequency Identification Device Specialists

* Annual Earnings: $86,370
* Beginning Wage: $55,330
* Earnings Growth Potential: Medium (35.9%)
* Growth: 3.7%
* Annual Job Openings: 5,699
* Self-Employed: 2.2%
* Part-Time: 2.0%
* Job Security: No data available
* Education/Training Required: Bachelor's degree

The Department of Labor reports this information for the occupation Electronics Engineers, Except Computer. The job openings listed here are shared with other specializations within that occupation.

Industries in Which Income Is Highest

Industry	Average Annual Earnings	Number Employed
Federal, State, and Local Government	$94,670	17,330
Transportation Equipment Manufacturing	$92,510	4,780
Professional, Scientific, and Technical Services	$89,350	26,300
Computer and Electronic Product Manufacturing	$88,590	35,720
Management of Companies and Enterprises	$85,980	4,200

Metropolitan Areas Where Income Is Highest

Metropolitan Area	Average Annual Earnings	Number Employed
Tucson, AZ	$111,210	900
Durham, NC	$106,990	530
Utica-Rome, NY	$106,730	230
San Jose–Sunnyvale–Santa Clara, CA	$105,950	7,290
Trenton-Ewing, NJ	$104,960	230

Design and implement radio frequency identification device (RFID) systems used to track shipments or goods. No task data available.

Other Considerations for Income: As a group, engineers earn some of the highest average starting salaries among those holding bachelor's degrees. Separate earnings figures for Radio Frequency Identification Device Specialists are not available, but they are probably similar to those for Electronics Engineers, who are paid in the middle range among the various kinds of engineers. According to a 2007 survey by the National Association of Colleges and Employers, average starting salaries for Electrical/Electronics and Communications Engineers were $55,292 with a bachelor's, $66,309 with a master's, and $75,982 with a Ph.D.

Personality Type: Realistic-Investigative-Conventional. **Career Cluster:** 15 Science, Technology, Engineering, and Mathematics. **Career Pathway:** 15.1 Engineering and Technology. **Skills:** No data available.

Education and Training Program: Electrical and Electronics Engineering. **Related Knowledge/Courses:** No data available.

Radiologic Technicians

* Annual Earnings: $52,210
* Beginning Wage: $35,100
* Earnings Growth Potential: Low (32.8%)
* Growth: 15.1%
* Annual Job Openings: 12,836
* Self-Employed: 1.1%
* Part-Time: 17.3%
* Job Security: Most secure
* Education/Training Required: Associate degree

The Department of Labor reports this information for the occupation Radiologic Technologists and Technicians. The job openings listed here are shared with other specializations within that occupation, including Radiologic Technologists.

Industries in Which Income Is Highest

Industry	Average Annual Earnings	Number Employed
Administrative and Support Services	$58,300	2,570
Professional, Scientific, and Technical Services	$56,390	1,240
Educational Services	$56,210	1,420
Hospitals	$52,930	128,060
Federal, State, and Local Government	$52,530	4,620

Metropolitan Areas Where Income Is Highest

Metropolitan Area	Average Annual Earnings	Number Employed
San Jose–Sunnyvale–Santa Clara, CA	$77,630	680
Lake Havasu City–Kingman, AZ	$72,390	110
Stockton, CA	$70,720	330
Modesto, CA	$69,330	190
Barnstable Town, MA	$68,630	240

Maintain and use equipment and supplies necessary to demonstrate portions of the human body on X-ray film or fluoroscopic screen for diagnostic purposes. Use beam-restrictive devices and patient-shielding techniques to minimize radiation exposure to patient and staff. Position X-ray equipment and adjust controls to set exposure factors, such as time and distance. Position patient on examining table and set up and adjust equipment to obtain optimum view of specific body area as requested by physician. Determine patients' X-ray needs by reading requests or instructions from physicians. Make exposures necessary for the requested procedures, rejecting and repeating work that does not meet established standards. Process exposed radiographs, using film processors or computer-generated methods. Explain procedures to patients to reduce anxieties and obtain cooperation. Perform procedures such as linear tomography; mammography; sonograms; joint and cyst aspirations; routine contrast studies; routine fluoroscopy; and examinations of the head, trunk, and extremities under supervision of physician. Prepare and set up X-ray room for patient. Assure that sterile supplies, contrast materials, catheters, and other required equipment are present and in working order, requisitioning materials as necessary. Maintain records of patients examined, examinations performed, views taken, and technical factors used. Provide assistance to physicians or other technologists in the performance of more complex procedures. Monitor equipment operation and report malfunctioning equipment to supervisor. Provide students and other technologists with suggestions of additional views, alternate positioning, or improved techniques to ensure the images produced are of the highest quality. Coordinate work of other technicians or technologists when procedures require more than one person. Assist with on-the-job training of new employees and students and provide input to supervisors regarding training performance. Maintain a current file of examination protocols. Operate mobile X-ray equipment in operating room, in emergency room, or at patient's bedside.

Other Considerations for Income: No additional information.

Personality Type: Realistic-Conventional-Social. **Career Cluster:** 08 Health Science. **Career Pathways:** 08.1 Therapeutic Services; 08.2 Diagnostics Services. **Skills:** Science; Operation Monitoring; Equipment Selection; Operation and Control; Service Orientation; Active Listening; Writing; Negotiation.

Education and Training Programs: Allied Health Diagnostic, Intervention, and Treatment Professions, Other; Medical Radiologic Technology/Science—Radiation Therapist; Radiologic Technology/Science—Radiographer. **Related Knowledge/Courses:** Medicine and Dentistry; Physics; Psychology; Biology; Chemistry; Customer and Personal Service.

Radiologic Technologists

* Annual Earnings: $52,210
* Beginning Wage: $35,100
* Earnings Growth Potential: Low (32.8%)
* Growth: 15.1%
* Annual Job Openings: 12,836
* Self-Employed: 1.1%
* Part-Time: 17.3%
* Job Security: Most secure
* Education/Training Required: Associate degree

The Department of Labor reports this information for the occupation Radiologic Technologists and Technicians. The job openings listed here are shared with other specializations within that occupation, including Radiologic Technicians.

Industries in Which Income Is Highest

Industry	Average Annual Earnings	Number Employed
Administrative and Support Services	$58,300	2,570
Professional, Scientific, and Technical Services	$56,390	1,240
Educational Services	$56,210	1,420
Hospitals	$52,930	128,060
Federal, State, and Local Government	$52,530	4,620

Metropolitan Areas Where Income Is Highest

Metropolitan Area	Average Annual Earnings	Number Employed
San Jose–Sunnyvale–Santa Clara, CA	$77,630	680
Lake Havasu City–Kingman, AZ	$72,390	110
Stockton, CA	$70,720	330
Modesto, CA	$69,330	190
Barnstable Town, MA	$68,630	240

Take X-rays and Computerized Axial Tomography (CAT or CT) scans or administer nonradioactive materials into patient's bloodstream for diagnostic purposes. Includes technologists who specialize in other modalities such as computed tomography, ultrasound, and magnetic resonance. Use radiation safety measures and protection devices to comply with government regulations and to ensure safety of patients and staff. Review and evaluate developed X-rays, videotape, or computer-generated information to determine if images are satisfactory for diagnostic purposes. Position imaging equipment and adjust controls to set exposure times and distances, according to specification of examinations. Explain procedures and observe patients to ensure safety and comfort during scans. Key commands and data into computers to document and specify scan sequences, adjust transmitters and receivers, or photograph certain images. Operate or oversee operation of radiologic and magnetic imaging equipment to produce images of the body for diagnostic purposes. Position and immobilize patients on examining tables. Record, process, and maintain patient data and treatment records, and prepare reports. Take thorough and accurate patient medical histories. Remove and process film. Set up examination rooms, ensuring that all necessary equipment is ready. Monitor patients' conditions and reactions, reporting abnormal signs to physicians. Coordinate work with clerical personnel or other technologists. Provide assistance in dressing or changing seriously ill, injured, or disabled patients. Demonstrate new equipment, procedures, and techniques to staff and provide technical assistance. Collaborate with other medical team members such as physicians and nurses to conduct angiography or special vascular procedures. Prepare and administer oral or injected contrast media to patients. Monitor video displays of areas being scanned and adjust density or contrast to improve picture quality. Operate fluoroscope to aid physicians to view and guide wires or catheters through blood vessels to areas of interest. Assign duties to radiologic staffs to maintain patient flows and achieve production goals. Perform scheduled maintenance and minor emergency repairs on radiographic equipment.

Other Considerations for Income: No additional information.

Personality Type: Realistic-Social. **Career Cluster:** 08 Health Science. **Career Pathways:** 08.1 Therapeutic Services; 08.2 Diagnostics Services. **Skills:** Operation Monitoring; Operation and Control.

Education and Training Programs: Allied Health Diagnostic, Intervention, and Treatment Professions, Other; Medical Radiologic Technology/Science—Radiation Therapist; Radiologic Technology/Science—Radiographer. **Related Knowledge/Courses:** Medicine and Dentistry; Physics; Customer and Personal Service; Biology; Psychology; Chemistry.

Radiologic Technologists and Technicians

See *Radiologic Technicians* and *Radiologic Technologists,* described separately.

Radiologists

* Annual Earnings: $166,400+
* Beginning Wage: $49,710
* Earnings Growth Potential: Cannot be calculated
* Growth: 14.2%
* Annual Job Openings: 38,027
* Self-Employed: 14.7%
* Part-Time: 8.1%
* Job Security: No data available
* Education/Training Required: First professional degree

The Department of Labor reports this information for the occupation Physicians and Surgeons. The job openings listed here are shared with other specializations within that occupation, including Allergists and Immunologists; Anesthesiologists; Dermatologists; Family and General Practitioners; Hospitalists; Internists, General; Neurologists; Nuclear Medicine Physicians; Obstetricians and Gynecologists; Ophthalmologists; Pathologists; Pediatricians, General; Physical Medicine and Rehabilitation Physicians; Preventive Medicine Physicians; Psychiatrists; Sports Medicine Physicians; Surgeons; and Urologists.

Industries in Which Income Is Highest

Industry	Average Annual Earnings	Number Employed
Ambulatory Health Care Services	$166,400+	147,400
Administrative and Support Services	$166,400+	1,310
Federal, State, and Local Government	$162,300	28,180
Professional, Scientific, and Technical Services	$107,470	1,210
Hospitals	$72,130	72,490

Metropolitan Areas Where Income Is Highest

Metropolitan Area	Average Annual Earnings	Number Employed
Los Angeles–Long Beach–Santa Ana, CA	$166,400+	8,810
Boston-Cambridge-Quincy, MA-NH	$166,400+	6,380
Dallas–Fort Worth–Arlington, TX	$166,400+	4,950
Tampa–St. Petersburg–Clearwater, FL	$166,400+	3,810
Portland-Vancouver-Beaverton, OR-WA	$166,400+	3,180

Examine and diagnose disorders and diseases, using X-rays and radioactive materials. May treat patients. No task data available.

Other Considerations for Income: Earnings of physicians and surgeons are among the highest of any occupation. Separate earnings figures for Radiologists are not available.

Personality Type: Investigative-Realistic-Social. **Career Cluster:** 08 Health Science. **Career Pathway:** 08.2 Diagnostics Services. **Skills:** No data available.

Education and Training Programs: Diagnostic Radiology Residency Program; Radiologic Physics Residency Program. **Related Knowledge/Courses:** No data available.

Railroad Conductors and Yardmasters

* Annual Earnings: $52,830
* Beginning Wage: $32,620
* Earnings Growth Potential: Medium (38.3%)
* Growth: 9.1%
* Annual Job Openings: 3,235
* Self-Employed: 0.0%
* Part-Time: 0.3%
* Job Security: Less secure than most
* Education/Training Required: Moderate-term on-the-job training

Industries in Which Income Is Highest

Industry	Average Annual Earnings	Number Employed
Rail Transportation	$51,810	35,500

Metropolitan Areas Where Income Is Highest

Metropolitan Area	Average Annual Earnings	Number Employed

Insufficient data available

Conductors coordinate activities of train crew on passenger or freight train. Coordinate activities of switch-engine crew within yard of railroad, industrial plant, or similar location. Yardmasters coordinate activities of workers engaged in railroad traffic operations, such as the makeup or breakup of trains; yard switching; and review train schedules and switching orders. Signal engineers to begin train runs, stop trains, or change speed, using telecommunications equipment or hand signals. Receive information regarding train or rail problems from dispatchers or from electronic monitoring devices. Direct and instruct workers engaged in yard activities, such as switching tracks, coupling and uncoupling cars, and routing inbound and outbound traffic. Keep records of the contents and destination of each train car and make sure that cars are added or removed at proper points on routes. Operate controls to activate track switches and traffic signals. Instruct workers to set warning signals in front and at rear of trains during emergency stops. Direct engineers to move cars to fit planned train configurations, combining or separating cars to make up or break up trains. Receive instructions from dispatchers regarding trains' routes, timetables, and cargoes. Review schedules, switching orders, way bills, and shipping records to obtain cargo loading and unloading information and to plan work. Confer with engineers regarding train routes, timetables, and cargoes and to discuss alternative routes when there are rail defects or obstructions. Arrange for the removal of defective cars from trains at stations or stops. Inspect each car periodically during runs. Observe yard traffic to determine tracks available to accommodate inbound and outbound traffic. Document and prepare reports of accidents, unscheduled stops, or delays. Confirm routes and destination information for freight cars. Supervise and coordinate crew activities to transport freight and passengers and to provide boarding, porter, maid, and meal services to passengers. Supervise workers in the inspection and maintenance of mechanical equipment to ensure efficient and safe train operation. Record departure and arrival times, messages, tickets and revenue collected, and passenger accommodations and destinations.

Other Considerations for Income: Most railroad transportation workers are paid according to miles traveled or hours worked, whichever leads to higher earnings. Factors such as seniority, job assignments, and location impact potential earnings. Seventy-four percent of railroad transportation workers are members of unions compared to 12 percent for all occupations. Many different railroad unions represent various crafts on the railroads. Among the largest of the railroad employee unions are the United Transportation Union and the Brotherhood of Locomotive Engineers and Trainmen.

Personality Type: Enterprising-Realistic-Conventional. **Career Cluster:** 16 Transportation, Distribution, and Logistics. **Career Pathway:** 16.1 Transportation Operations. **Skills:** Operation and Control; Operation Monitoring; Coordination; Equipment Maintenance; Troubleshooting; Instructing.

Education and Training Program: Truck and Bus Driver/Commercial Vehicle Operator and Instructor. **Related Knowledge/Courses:** Transportation; Public Safety and Security; Mechanical.

Range Managers

- Annual Earnings: $58,720
- Beginning Wage: $35,190
- Earnings Growth Potential: High (40.1%)
- Growth: 5.3%
- Annual Job Openings: 1,161
- Self-Employed: 3.9%
- Part-Time: 4.9%
- Job Security: More secure than most
- Education/Training Required: Bachelor's degree

The Department of Labor reports this information for the occupation Conservation Scientists. The job openings listed here are shared with other specializations within that occupation, including Park Naturalists; and Soil and Water Conservationists.

Industries in Which Income Is Highest

Industry	Average Annual Earnings	Number Employed
Federal, State, and Local Government	$60,060	12,560
Religious, Grantmaking, Civic, Professional, and Similar Organizations	$52,530	1,490

Metropolitan Areas Where Income Is Highest

Metropolitan Area	Average Annual Earnings	Number Employed
Anchorage, AK	$79,740	100
Washington-Arlington-Alexandria, DC-VA-MD-WV	$78,220	400
San Jose–Sunnyvale–Santa Clara, CA	$74,550	70
Miami–Fort Lauderdale–Miami Beach, FL	$74,450	60
Los Angeles–Long Beach–Santa Ana, CA	$74,240	100

Research or study range land management practices to provide sustained production of forage, livestock, and wildlife. Regulate grazing and help ranchers plan and organize grazing systems to manage, improve, and protect rangelands and maximize their use. Measure and assess vegetation resources for biological assessment companies, environmental impact statements, and rangeland monitoring programs. Maintain soil stability and vegetation for non-grazing uses, such as wildlife habitats and outdoor recreation. Mediate agreements among rangeland users and preservationists as to appropriate land use and management. Study rangeland management practices and research range problems to provide sustained production of forage, livestock, and wildlife. Manage forage resources through fire, herbicide use, or revegetation to maintain a sustainable yield from the land. Offer advice to rangeland users on water management, forage production methods, and control of brush. Plan and direct construction and maintenance of range improvements such as fencing, corrals, stock-watering reservoirs, and soil-erosion control structures. Tailor conservation plans to landowners' goals, such as livestock support, wildlife, or recreation. Develop technical standards and specifications used to manage, protect, and improve the natural resources of rangelands and related grazing lands. Study grazing patterns to determine number and kind of livestock that can be most profitably grazed and to determine the best grazing seasons. Plan and implement revegetation of disturbed sites. Study

forage plants and their growth requirements to determine varieties best suited to particular range. Develop methods for protecting range from fire and rodent damage and for controlling poisonous plants. Manage private livestock operations. Develop new and improved instruments and techniques for activities such as range reseeding.

Other Considerations for Income: In private industry, starting salaries for students with a bachelor's degree were comparable with starting salaries in the federal government, but starting salaries in state and local governments were usually lower. Conservation scientists and foresters who work for federal, state, and local governments and large private firms generally receive more generous benefits than do those working for smaller firms. Governments usually have good pension, health, and leave plans.

Personality Type: Realistic-Investigative-Enterprising. **Career Cluster:** 01 Agriculture, Food and Natural Resource. **Career Pathway:** 01.5 Natural Resources Systems. **Skills:** Negotiation; Science; Management of Financial Resources; Coordination; Persuasion; Writing; Systems Evaluation; Complex Problem Solving.

Education and Training Programs: Forest Management/Forest Resources Management; Forest Sciences and Biology; Forestry, General; Forestry, Other; Land Use Planning and Management/Development; Natural Resources and Conservation, Other; Natural Resources Management and Policy; Natural Resources Management and Policy, Other; Natural Resources/Conservation, General; Water, Wetlands, and Marine Resources Management; Wildlife, Fish and Wildlands Science and Management. **Related Knowledge/Courses:** Biology; Geography; Food Production; History and Archeology; Law and Government; Engineering and Technology.

Real Estate Brokers

❋ Annual Earnings: $57,500
❋ Beginning Wage: $25,470
❋ Earnings Growth Potential: Very high (55.7%)
❋ Growth: 11.1%
❋ Annual Job Openings: 18,689
❋ Self-Employed: 63.5%
❋ Part-Time: 15.5%
❋ Job Security: Less secure than most
❋ Education/Training Required: Work experience in a related occupation

Industries in Which Income Is Highest

Industry	Average Annual Earnings	Number Employed
Real Estate	$57,450	45,740
Credit Intermediation and Related Activities	$56,720	1,020

Metropolitan Areas Where Income Is Highest

Metropolitan Area	Average Annual Earnings	Number Employed
Bellingham, WA	$166,400+	60
San Francisco–Oakland–Fremont, CA	$113,660	760
Atlanta–Sandy Springs–Marietta, GA	$108,190	710
Minneapolis–St. Paul–Bloomington, MN-WI	$105,950	210
Grand Rapids–Wyoming, MI	$97,960	120

Operate real estate office or work for commercial real estate firm, overseeing real estate transactions. Other duties usually include selling real estate or renting properties and arranging loans. Sell, for a fee, real estate owned by others. Obtain agreements from property owners to place properties for sale with real estate firms. Monitor fulfillment of purchase contract terms to ensure that they are handled in a timely manner. Compare a property with similar properties that have recently sold to determine its competitive market price. Act as an intermediary in negotiations between buyers and sellers over property prices and settlement details and during the closing of sales. Generate lists of properties for sale, their locations and descriptions, and available financing options, using computers. Maintain knowledge of real estate law; local economies; fair housing laws; and types of available mortgages, financing options, and government programs. Check work completed by loan officers, attorneys, and other professionals to ensure that it is performed properly. Arrange for financing of property purchases. Appraise property values, assessing income potential when relevant. Maintain awareness of current income tax regulations, local zoning, building and tax laws, and growth possibilities of the area where a property is located. Manage and operate real estate offices, handling associated business details. Supervise agents who handle real estate transactions. Rent properties or manage rental properties. Arrange for title searches of properties being sold. Give buyers virtual tours of properties in which they are interested, using computers. Review property details to ensure that environmental regulations are met. Develop, sell, or lease property used for industry or manufacturing. Maintain working knowledge of various factors that determine a farm's capacity to produce, including agricultural variables and proximity to market centers and transportation facilities.

Other Considerations for Income: Commissions on sales are the main source of earnings of real estate agents and brokers. The rate of commission varies according to whatever the agent and broker agree on, the type of property, and its value. The percentage paid on the sale of farm and commercial properties or unimproved land is typically higher than the percentage paid for selling a home. Commissions may be divided among several agents and brokers. The broker or agent who obtains a listing usually shares the commission with the broker or agent who sells the property and with the firms that employ each of them.

Personality Type: Enterprising-Conventional. **Career Cluster:** 14 Marketing, Sales, and Service. **Career Pathway:** 14.2 Professional Sales and Marketing. **Skills:** Management of Financial Resources; Negotiation; Mathematics; Judgment and Decision Making; Active Listening; Persuasion; Service Orientation; Complex Problem Solving.

Education and Training Program: Real Estate. **Related Knowledge/Courses:** Sales and Marketing; Law and Government; Building and Construction; Customer and Personal Service; Personnel and Human Resources; Economics and Accounting.

Recreation and Fitness Studies Teachers, Postsecondary

- ❋ Annual Earnings: $55,140
- ❋ Beginning Wage: $28,840
- ❋ Earnings Growth Potential: High (47.7%)
- ❋ Growth: 22.9%
- ❋ Annual Job Openings: 3,010
- ❋ Self-Employed: 0.4%
- ❋ Part-Time: 27.8%
- ❋ Job Security: Most secure
- ❋ Education/Training Required: Doctoral degree

Industries in Which Income Is Highest

Industry	Average Annual Earnings	Number Employed
Educational Services	$55,430	17,000

Metropolitan Areas Where Income Is Highest

Metropolitan Area	Average Annual Earnings	Number Employed
San Diego–Carlsbad–San Marcos, CA	$86,120	330
Los Angeles–Long Beach–Santa Ana, CA	$83,910	880
Sacramento–Arden-Arcade–Roseville, CA	$81,140	130
San Francisco–Oakland–Fremont, CA	$80,900	430
Riverside–San Bernardino–Ontario, CA	$72,750	170

Teach courses pertaining to recreation, leisure, and fitness studies, including exercise physiology and facilities management. Evaluate and grade students' classwork, assignments, and papers. Maintain student attendance records, grades, and other required records. Prepare and deliver lectures to undergraduate and graduate students on topics such as anatomy, therapeutic recreation, and conditioning theory. Prepare course materials such as syllabi, homework assignments, and handouts. Maintain regularly scheduled office hours to advise and assist students. Compile, administer, and grade examinations or assign this work to others. Plan, evaluate, and revise curricula, course content, and course materials and methods of instruction. Initiate, facilitate, and moderate classroom discussions. Keep abreast of developments in their field by reading current literature, talking with colleagues, and participating in professional conferences. Advise students on academic and vocational curricula and on career issues. Participate in student recruitment, registration, and placement activities. Collaborate with colleagues to address teaching and research issues. Select and obtain materials and supplies such as textbooks. Participate in campus and community events. Serve on academic or administrative committees that deal with institutional policies, departmental matters, and academic issues. Compile bibliographies of specialized materials for outside reading assignments. Supervise undergraduate or graduate teaching, internship, and research work. Perform administrative duties such as serving as department heads. Prepare students to act as sports coaches. Conduct research in a particular field of knowledge and publish findings in professional journals, books, or electronic media. Act as advisers to student organizations. Write grant proposals to procure external research funding. Provide professional consulting services to government or industry.

Other Considerations for Income: Earnings for college faculty vary according to rank and type of institution, geographic area, and field. According to a 2006–2007 survey by the American Association of University Professors, salaries for full-time faculty averaged $73,207. By rank, the average was $98,974 for professors, $69,911 for associate professors, $58,662 for assistant professors, $42,609 for instructors, and $48,289 for lecturers. Faculty in 4-year institutions earn higher salaries, on average, than do those in 2-year schools. Many faculty members have significant earnings in addition to their base salary from consulting, teaching additional courses, research, writing for publication, or other employment. In addition, many college and university faculty enjoy unique benefits, including access to campus facilities, tuition waivers for dependents, housing and travel allowances, and paid leave for sabbaticals. Part-time faculty and instructors usually have fewer benefits than full-time faculty.

Personality Type: Social. **Career Clusters:** 01 Agriculture, Food and Natural Resource; 05 Education and Training. **Career Pathways:** 01.5 Natural Resources Systems; 05.1 Administration and Administrative Support; 05.3 Teaching/Training. **Skills:** Instructing; Learning Strategies; Science; Social Perceptiveness; Persuasion; Time Management; Management of Financial Resources; Writing.

Education and Training Programs: Health and Physical Education, General; Parks, Recreation and Leisure Studies; Sport and Fitness Administration/Management. **Related Knowledge/Courses:** Education and Training; Philosophy and Theology; Therapy and Counseling; Psychology; Medicine and Dentistry; Sociology and Anthropology.

Registered Nurses

- ❋ Annual Earnings: $62,450
- ❋ Beginning Wage: $43,410
- ❋ Earnings Growth Potential: Low (30.5%)
- ❋ Growth: 23.5%
- ❋ Annual Job Openings: 233,499
- ❋ Self-Employed: 0.8%
- ❋ Part-Time: 21.8%
- ❋ Job Security: Most secure
- ❋ Education/Training Required: Associate degree

Industries in Which Income Is Highest

Industry	Average Annual Earnings	Number Employed
Administrative and Support Services	$67,720	98,770
Religious, Grantmaking, Civic, Professional, and Similar Organizations	$64,540	2,030
Federal, State, and Local Government	$64,340	144,990
Merchant Wholesalers, Nondurable Goods	$64,150	1,010
Hospitals	$63,890	1,535,440

Metropolitan Areas Where Income Is Highest

Metropolitan Area	Average Annual Earnings	Number Employed
San Jose–Sunnyvale–Santa Clara, CA	$109,110	14,590
San Francisco–Oakland–Fremont, CA	$97,590	32,780
Modesto, CA	$91,910	3,040
Vallejo-Fairfield, CA	$88,500	3,010
Napa, CA	$88,030	1,430

Assess patient health problems and needs, develop and implement nursing care plans, and maintain medical records. Administer nursing care to ill, injured, convalescent, or disabled patients. Monitor, record, and report symptoms and changes in patients' conditions. Maintain accurate, detailed reports and records. Record patients' medical information and vital signs. Order, interpret, and evaluate diagnostic tests to identify and assess patients' conditions. Modify patient treatment plans as indicated by patients' responses and conditions. Direct and supervise less skilled nursing or health-care personnel or supervise particular units. Consult and coordinate with health-care team members to assess, plan, implement, and evaluate patient care plans. Monitor all aspects of patient care, including diet and physical activity. Instruct individuals, families, and other groups on topics such as health education, disease prevention, and childbirth and develop health improvement programs. Prepare patients for, and assist with, examinations and treatments. Assess the needs of individuals, families, or communities, including assessment of individuals' home or work environments to identify potential health or safety problems. Provide health care, first aid, immunizations, and assistance in convalescence and rehabilitation in locations such as schools, hospitals, and industry. Prepare rooms, sterile instruments, equipment, and supplies and ensure that stock of supplies is maintained. Inform physicians of patients' conditions during anesthesia. Administer local, inhalation, intravenous, and other anesthetics. Perform physical examinations, make tentative diagnoses, and treat patients en route to hospitals or at disaster site triage centers. Observe nurses and visit patients to ensure proper nursing care. Conduct specified laboratory tests. Direct and coordinate infection control programs, advising and consulting with specified personnel about necessary precautions. Prescribe or recommend drugs; medical devices; or other forms of treatment such as physical therapy, inhalation therapy, or related therapeutic procedures.

Other Considerations for Income: Many employers offer flexible work schedules, child care, educational benefits, and bonuses.

Personality Type: Social-Investigative-Conventional. **Career Cluster:** 08 Health Science. **Career Pathway:** 08.1 Therapeutic Services. **Skills:** Social Perceptiveness; Systems Analysis; Quality Control Analysis; Systems Evaluation; Management of Personnel Resources; Operation Monitoring; Service Orientation; Judgment and Decision Making.

Education and Training Programs: Adult Health Nurse/Nursing; Clinical Nurse Specialist Training; Critical Care Nursing; Family Practice Nurse/Nursing; Maternal/Child Health and Neonatal Nurse/Nursing; Nurse Anesthetist Training; Nurse Midwife/Nursing Midwifery; Nursing Science; Occupational and Environmental Health Nursing; Pediatric Nurse/Nursing; Perioperative/Operating Room and Surgical Nurse/Nursing; Psychiatric/Mental Health Nurse/Nursing; Public Health/Community Nurse/Nursing; Registered Nursing/Registered Nurse Training. **Related Knowledge/Courses:** Medicine and

Dentistry; Psychology; Therapy and Counseling; Biology; Philosophy and Theology; Sociology and Anthropology.

Regulatory Affairs Specialists

❋ Annual Earnings: $48,890
❋ Beginning Wage: $29,490
❋ Earnings Growth Potential: Medium (39.7%)
❋ Growth: 4.9%
❋ Annual Job Openings: 15,841
❋ Self-Employed: 0.4%
❋ Part-Time: 5.0%
❋ Job Security: No data available
❋ Education/Training Required: Work experience in a related occupation

The Department of Labor reports this information for the occupation Compliance Officers, Except Agriculture, Construction, Health and Safety, and Transportation. The job openings listed here are shared with other specializations within that occupation, including Coroners; Environmental Compliance Inspectors; Equal Opportunity Representatives and Officers; Government Property Inspectors and Investigators; and Licensing Examiners and Inspectors.

Industries in Which Income Is Highest

Industry	Average Annual Earnings	Number Employed
Postal Service	$77,500	1,970
Utilities	$74,890	1,880
Securities, Commodity Contracts, and Other Financial Investments and Related Activities	$70,720	6,480
Telecommunications	$64,400	2,560
Chemical Manufacturing	$61,920	3,910

Metropolitan Areas Where Income Is Highest

Metropolitan Area	Average Annual Earnings	Number Employed
Brunswick, GA	$83,080	500
Bridgeport-Stamford-Norwalk, CT	$73,120	640
Warner Robins, GA	$69,670	80
San Francisco–Oakland–Fremont, CA	$67,520	4,370
Hartford–West Hartford–East Hartford, CT	$67,460	1,420

Coordinate and document internal regulatory processes, such as internal audits, inspections, license renewals, or registrations. May compile and prepare materials for submission to regulatory agencies. No task data available.

Other Considerations for Income: No additional information.

Personality Type: Conventional-Enterprising. **Career Cluster:** 12 Law, Public Safety, Corrections, and Security. **Career Pathway:** 12.6 Inspection Services. **Skills:** No data available.

Education and Training Program: Business Administration and Management, General. **Related Knowledge/Courses:** Biology; Law and Government; Medicine and Dentistry; Clerical; English Language; Chemistry.

Respiratory Therapists

❋ Annual Earnings: $52,200
❋ Beginning Wage: $37,920
❋ Earnings Growth Potential: Low (27.4%)
❋ Growth: 22.6%
❋ Annual Job Openings: 5,563
❋ Self-Employed: 1.1%
❋ Part-Time: 15.0%
❋ Job Security: Most secure
❋ Education/Training Required: Associate degree

Industries in Which Income Is Highest

Industry	Average Annual Earnings	Number Employed
Administrative and Support Services	$61,100	3,570
Ambulatory Health Care Services	$53,810	5,920
Hospitals	$52,090	84,110
Nursing and Residential Care Facilities	$51,900	3,550
Health and Personal Care Stores	$48,960	1,270

Metropolitan Areas Where Income Is Highest

Metropolitan Area	Average Annual Earnings	Number Employed
Salinas, CA	$81,740	70
San Jose–Sunnyvale–Santa Clara, CA	$79,530	590
Poughkeepsie-Newburgh-Middletown, NY	$70,020	190
Santa Rosa–Petaluma, CA	$69,850	120
San Francisco–Oakland–Fremont, CA	$69,750	1,070

Assess, treat, and care for patients with breathing disorders. Assume primary responsibility for all respiratory care modalities, including the supervision of respiratory therapy technicians. Initiate and conduct therapeutic procedures; maintain patient records; and select, assemble, check, and operate equipment. Set up and operate devices such as mechanical ventilators, therapeutic gas administration apparatus, environmental control systems, and aerosol generators, following specified parameters of treatment. Provide emergency care, including artificial respiration, external cardiac massage, and assistance with cardiopulmonary resuscitation. Determine requirements for treatment, such as type, method, and duration of therapy; precautions to be taken; and medication and dosages, compatible with physicians' orders. Monitor patient's physiological responses to therapy, such as vital signs, arterial blood gases, and blood chemistry changes, and consult with physician if adverse reactions occur. Read prescription, measure arterial blood gases, and review patient information to assess patient condition. Work as part of a team of physicians, nurses, and other health-care professionals to manage patient care. Enforce safety rules and ensure careful adherence to physicians' orders. Maintain charts that contain patients' pertinent identification and therapy information. Inspect, clean, test, and maintain respiratory therapy equipment to ensure equipment is functioning safely and efficiently, ordering repairs when necessary. Educate patients and their families about their conditions and teach appropriate disease management techniques, such as breathing exercises and the use of medications and respiratory equipment. Explain treatment procedures to patients to gain cooperation and allay fears. Relay blood analysis results to a physician. Perform pulmonary function and adjust equipment to obtain optimum results in therapy. Perform bronchopulmonary drainage and assist or instruct patients in performance of breathing exercises. Demonstrate respiratory care procedures to trainees and other health-care personnel. Teach, train, supervise, and utilize the assistance of students, respiratory therapy technicians, and assistants. Make emergency visits to resolve equipment problems.

Other Considerations for Income: No additional information.

Personality Type: Social-Investigative-Realistic. **Career Cluster:** 08 Health Science. **Career Pathway:** 08.1 Therapeutic Services. **Skills:** Science; Mathematics; Operation Monitoring; Reading Comprehension; Active Learning; Troubleshooting; Instructing; Service Orientation.

Education and Training Program: Respiratory Care Therapy/Therapist. **Related Knowledge/Courses:** Medicine and Dentistry; Biology; Customer and Personal Service; Therapy and Counseling; Psychology; Chemistry.

Rotary Drill Operators, Oil and Gas

* Annual Earnings: $49,800
* Beginning Wage: $30,510
* Earnings Growth Potential: Medium (38.7%)
* Growth: –5.4%
* Annual Job Openings: 2,145
* Self-Employed: 2.5%
* Part-Time: 0.7%
* Job Security: Less secure than most
* Education/Training Required: Moderate-term on-the-job training

Industries in Which Income Is Highest

Industry	Average Annual Earnings	Number Employed
Support Activities for Mining	$50,400	23,450
Oil and Gas Extraction	$45,780	1,990

Metropolitan Areas Where Income Is Highest

Metropolitan Area	Average Annual Earnings	Number Employed
Shreveport–Bossier City, LA	$67,400	280
Casper, WY	$64,720	220
Los Angeles–Long Beach–Santa Ana, CA	$59,980	70
Oxnard–Thousand Oaks–Ventura, CA	$59,310	210
Oklahoma City, OK	$56,330	1,710

Set up or operate a variety of drills to remove petroleum products from the earth and to find and remove core samples for testing during oil and gas exploration. Train crews and introduce procedures to make drill work more safe and effective. Observe pressure gauge and move throttles and levers to control the speed of rotary tables and to regulate pressure of tools at bottoms of boreholes. Count sections of drill rod to determine depths of boreholes. Push levers and brake pedals to control gasoline, diesel, electric, or steam draw works that lower and raise drill pipes and casings in and out of wells. Connect sections of drill pipe, using hand tools and powered wrenches and tongs. Maintain records of footage drilled, location and nature of strata penetrated, materials and tools used, services rendered, and time required. Maintain and adjust machinery to ensure proper performance. Start and examine operation of slush pumps to ensure circulation and consistency of drilling fluid or mud in well. Locate and recover lost or broken bits, casings, and drill pipes from wells, using special tools. Weigh clay and mix with water and chemicals to make drilling mud. Direct rig crews in drilling and other activities, such as setting up rigs and completing or servicing wells. Monitor progress of drilling operations and select and change drill bits according to the nature of strata, using hand tools. Repair or replace defective parts of machinery, such as rotary drill rigs, water trucks, air compressors, and pumps, using hand tools. Clean and oil pulleys, blocks, and cables. Bolt together pump and engine parts and connect tanks and flow lines. Remove core samples during drilling to determine the nature of the strata being drilled. Cap wells with packers or turn valves to regulate outflow of oil from wells. Line drilled holes with pipes and install all necessary hardware to prepare new wells. Position and prepare truck-mounted derricks at drilling areas that are specified on field maps. Plug observation wells and restore sites. Lower and explode charges in boreholes to start flow of oil from wells.

Other Considerations for Income: No additional information.

Personality Type: Realistic-Enterprising-Conventional. **Career Cluster:** 01 Agriculture, Food, and Natural Resource. **Career Pathway:** 01.5 Natural Resources Systems. **Skills:** Repairing; Equipment Maintenance; Operation Monitoring; Operation and Control; Installation; Operations Analysis; Troubleshooting; Systems Analysis.

Education and Training Program: Well Drilling/Driller. **Related Knowledge/Courses:** Mechanical; Chemistry; Personnel and Human Resources; Transportation; Physics; Mathematics.

Sales Agents, Financial Services

* Annual Earnings: $68,680
* Beginning Wage: $30,900
* Earnings Growth Potential: Very high (55.0%)
* Growth: 24.8%
* Annual Job Openings: 47,750
* Self-Employed: 17.7%
* Part-Time: 6.9%
* Job Security: Least secure
* Education/Training Required: Bachelor's degree

The Department of Labor reports this information for the occupation Securities, Commodities, and Financial Services Sales Agents. The job openings listed here are shared with other specializations within that occupation, including Sales Agents, Securities and Commodities; and Securities and Commodities Traders.

Industries in Which Income Is Highest

Industry	Average Annual Earnings	Number Employed
Securities, Commodity Contracts, and Other Financial Investments and Related Activities	$87,180	158,690
Management of Companies and Enterprises	$81,940	7,460
Administrative and Support Services	$68,510	1,670
Funds, Trusts, and Other Financial Vehicles	$61,110	2,490
Insurance Carriers and Related Activities	$59,920	9,520

Metropolitan Areas Where Income Is Highest

Metropolitan Area	Average Annual Earnings	Number Employed
Bridgeport-Stamford-Norwalk, CT	$165,330	5,300
San Francisco–Oakland–Fremont, CA	$112,720	7,650
Cape Coral–Fort Myers, FL	$112,610	490
Longview, TX	$107,990	70
Memphis, TN-MS-AR	$104,950	1,230

Sell financial services such as loan, tax, and securities counseling to customers of financial institutions and business establishments. Determine customers' financial services needs and prepare proposals to sell services that address these needs. Contact prospective customers to present information and explain available services. Sell services and equipment, such as trusts, investments, and check processing services. Prepare forms or agreements to complete sales. Develop prospects from current commercial customers, referral leads, and sales and trade meetings. Review business trends in order to advise customers regarding expected fluctuations. Make presentations on financial services to groups to attract new clients. Evaluate costs and revenue of agreements to determine continued profitability.

Other Considerations for Income: Because this is a sales occupation, many workers are paid a commission based on the amount of stocks, bonds, mutual funds, insurance, and other products they sell. Earnings from commissions are likely to be high when there is much buying and selling, and low when there is a slump in market activity. Most firms provide sales agents with a steady income by paying a draw against commission—a minimum salary based on

commissions they can be expected to earn. Trainee brokers usually are paid a salary until they develop a client base. The salary gradually decreases in favor of commissions as the broker gains clients. Investment bankers in corporate finance and mergers and acquisitions are generally paid a base salary with the opportunity to earn a substantial bonus. At the higher levels, bonuses far exceed base salary. This arrangement works similarly to commissions but gives banks greater flexibility to reward members of the team who were more effective. Since investment bankers in sales and trading departments generally work alone, they generally work on commissions. Benefits in the securities industry are generally very good. They normally include health care, retirement, and life insurance. Securities firms may also give discounts to employees on financial services that they sell to customers. Other benefits may include paid lunches with clients, paid dinners for employees who work late, and often extensive travel opportunities.

Personality Type: Enterprising-Conventional. **Career Cluster:** 06 Finance. **Career Pathway:** 06.1 Financial and Investment Planning. **Skills:** Persuasion; Management of Financial Resources; Service Orientation; Negotiation; Operations Analysis; Speaking; Monitoring; Judgment and Decision Making.

Education and Training Programs: Business and Personal/Financial Services Marketing Operations; Financial Planning and Services; Investments and Securities. **Related Knowledge/Courses:** Sales and Marketing; Economics and Accounting; Customer and Personal Service; Law and Government; Mathematics; Personnel and Human Resources.

Sales Agents, Securities and Commodities

- ❋ Annual Earnings: $68,680
- ❋ Beginning Wage: $30,900
- ❋ Earnings Growth Potential: Very high (55.0%)
- ❋ Growth: 24.8%
- ❋ Annual Job Openings: 47,750
- ❋ Self-Employed: 17.7%
- ❋ Part-Time: 6.9%
- ❋ Job Security: Least secure
- ❋ Education/Training Required: Bachelor's degree

The Department of Labor reports this information for the occupation Securities, Commodities, and Financial Services Sales Agents. The job openings listed here are shared with other specializations within that occupation, including Sales Agents, Financial Services; and Securities and Commodities Traders.

Industries in Which Income Is Highest

Industry	Average Annual Earnings	Number Employed
Securities, Commodity Contracts, and Other Financial Investments and Related Activities	$87,180	158,690
Management of Companies and Enterprises	$81,940	7,460
Administrative and Support Services	$68,510	1,670
Funds, Trusts, and Other Financial Vehicles	$61,110	2,490
Insurance Carriers and Related Activities	$59,920	9,520

Metropolitan Areas Where Income Is Highest

Metropolitan Area	Average Annual Earnings	Number Employed
Bridgeport-Stamford-Norwalk, CT	$165,330	5,300
San Francisco–Oakland–Fremont, CA	$112,720	7,650
Cape Coral–Fort Myers, FL	$112,610	490
Longview, TX	$107,990	70
Memphis, TN-MS-AR	$104,950	1,230

Buy and sell securities in investment and trading firms and develop and implement financial plans for individuals, businesses, and organizations. Complete sales order tickets and submit for processing of client requested transactions. Interview clients to determine clients' assets, liabilities, cash flow, insurance coverage, tax status, and financial objectives. Record transactions accurately and keep clients informed about transactions. Develop financial plans based on analysis of clients' financial status and discuss financial options with clients. Review all securities transactions to ensure accuracy of information and ensure that trades conform to regulations of governing agencies. Offer advice on the purchase or sale of particular securities. Relay buy or sell orders to securities exchanges or to firm trading departments. Identify potential clients, using advertising campaigns, mailing lists, and personal contacts.

Review financial periodicals, stock and bond reports, business publications, and other material to identify potential investments for clients and to keep abreast of trends affecting market conditions. Contact prospective customers to determine customer needs, present information, and explain available services. Prepare documents needed to implement plans selected by clients. Analyze market conditions to determine optimum times to execute securities transactions. Explain stock market terms and trading practices to clients. Inform and advise concerned parties regarding fluctuations and securities transactions affecting plans or accounts. Calculate costs for billings and commissions purposes. Supply the latest price quotes on any security, as well as information on the activities and financial positions of the corporations issuing these securities. Prepare financial reports to monitor client or corporate finances. Read corporate reports and calculate ratios to determine best prospects for profit on stock purchases and to monitor client accounts.

Other Considerations for Income: Because this is a sales occupation, many workers are paid a commission based on the amount of stocks, bonds, mutual funds, insurance, and other products they sell. Earnings from commissions are likely to be high when there is much buying and selling, and low when there is a slump in market activity. Most firms provide sales agents with a steady income by paying a draw against commission—a minimum salary based on commissions they can be expected to earn. Trainee brokers usually are paid a salary until they develop a client base. The salary gradually decreases in favor of commissions as the broker gains clients. Investment bankers in corporate finance and mergers and acquisitions are generally paid a base salary with the opportunity to earn a substantial bonus. At the higher levels, bonuses far exceed base salary. This arrangement works similarly to commissions but gives banks greater flexibility to reward members of the team who were more effective. Since investment bankers in sales and trading departments generally work alone, they generally work on commissions. Benefits in the securities industry are generally very good. They normally include health care, retirement, and life insurance. Securities firms may also give discounts to employees on financial services that they sell to customers. Other benefits may include paid lunches with clients, paid dinners for employees who work late, and often extensive travel opportunities.

Personality Type: Enterprising-Conventional. **Career Cluster:** 06 Finance. **Career Pathway:** 06.1 Financial and Investment Planning. **Skills:** Management of Financial Resources; Persuasion; Social Perceptiveness; Negotiation;

Judgment and Decision Making; Service Orientation; Speaking; Time Management.

Education and Training Programs: Business and Personal/Financial Services Marketing Operations; Financial Planning and Services; Investments and Securities. **Related Knowledge/Courses:** Economics and Accounting; Customer and Personal Service; Sales and Marketing; Clerical; Law and Government; Mathematics.

Sales Engineers

- ❋ Annual Earnings: $83,100
- ❋ Beginning Wage: $49,640
- ❋ Earnings Growth Potential: High (40.3%)
- ❋ Growth: 8.5%
- ❋ Annual Job Openings: 7,371
- ❋ Self-Employed: 0.0%
- ❋ Part-Time: 2.0%
- ❋ Job Security: Least secure
- ❋ Education/Training Required: Bachelor's degree

Industries in Which Income Is Highest

Industry	Average Annual Earnings	Number Employed
Publishing Industries (Except Internet)	$101,440	1,680
Professional, Scientific, and Technical Services	$93,690	17,930
Telecommunications	$90,270	5,890
Wholesale Electronic Markets and Agents and Brokers	$84,340	7,050
Computer and Electronic Product Manufacturing	$83,100	8,140

Metropolitan Areas Where Income Is Highest

Metropolitan Area	Average Annual Earnings	Number Employed
Santa Rosa–Petaluma, CA	$107,550	180
San Jose–Sunnyvale–Santa Clara, CA	$107,190	6,960
Oxnard–Thousand Oaks–Ventura, CA	$101,840	480
Durham, NC	$101,730	210
San Francisco–Oakland–Fremont, CA	$98,350	4,050

Sell business goods or services, the selling of which requires a technical background equivalent to a baccalaureate degree in engineering. Plan and modify product configurations to meet customer needs. Confer with customers and engineers to assess equipment needs and to determine system requirements. Collaborate with sales teams to understand customer requirements, to promote the sale of company products, and to provide sales support. Secure and renew orders and arrange delivery. Develop, present, or respond to proposals for specific customer requirements, including request for proposal responses and industry-specific solutions. Sell products requiring extensive technical expertise and support for installation and use, such as material handling equipment, numerical-control machinery, and computer systems. Diagnose problems with installed equipment. Prepare and deliver technical presentations that explain products or services to customers and prospective customers. Recommend improved materials or machinery to customers, documenting how such changes will lower costs or increase production. Provide technical and non-technical support and services to clients or other staff members regarding the use, operation, and maintenance of equipment. Research and identify potential customers for products or services. Visit prospective buyers at commercial, industrial, or other establishments to show samples or catalogs and to inform them about product pricing, availability, and advantages. Create sales or service contracts for products or services. Arrange for demonstrations or trial installations of equipment. Keep informed on industry news and trends; products; services; competitors; relevant information about legacy, existing, and emerging technologies; and the latest product-line developments. Attend company training seminars to become familiar with product lines. Provide information needed for the development of custom-made machinery. Develop sales plans to introduce products in new markets. Write technical documentation for products. Identify resale opportunities and support them to achieve sales plans.

Other Considerations for Income: Compensation varies significantly by the type of firm and the product sold. Most employers offer a combination of salary and commission payments or a salary plus a bonus. Those working in independent sales companies may solely earn commissions. Commissions usually are based on the amount of sales, whereas bonuses may depend on individual performance, on the performance of all workers in the group or district, or on the company's performance. Earnings from commissions and bonuses may vary greatly from year to year, depending on sales ability, the demand for the company's products or services, and the overall economy. In addition to their earnings, sales engineers who work for manufacturers usually are reimbursed for expenses such as transportation, meals, hotels, and customer entertainment. In addition to typical benefits, sales engineers may get personal use of a company car and frequent-flyer mileage. Some companies offer incentives such as free vacation trips or gifts for outstanding performance. Sales engineers who work in independent firms may have higher but less stable earnings and, often, relatively few benefits. Most independent sales engineers do not earn any income while on vacation.

Personality Type: Enterprising-Realistic-Investigative. **Career Cluster:** 14 Marketing, Sales, and Service. **Career Pathway:** 14.2 Professional Sales and Marketing. **Skills:** Operations Analysis; Science; Systems Evaluation; Technology Design; Programming; Installation; Equipment Selection; Mathematics.

Education and Training Program: Selling Skills and Sales Operations. **Related Knowledge/Courses:** Sales and Marketing; Engineering and Technology; Design; Physics; Computers and Electronics; Customer and Personal Service.

Sales Managers

※ Annual Earnings: $97,260
※ Beginning Wage: $47,010
※ Earnings Growth Potential: Very high (51.7%)
※ Growth: 10.2%
※ Annual Job Openings: 36,392
※ Self-Employed: 2.2%
※ Part-Time: 4.1%
※ Job Security: Least secure
※ Education/Training Required: Work experience plus degree

Industries in Which Income Is Highest

Industry	Average Annual Earnings	Number Employed
Securities, Commodity Contracts, and Other Financial Investments and Related Activities	$146,730	5,070
Motion Picture and Sound Recording Industries	$137,530	1,150
Other Information Services	$133,340	1,240
Professional, Scientific, and Technical Services	$124,470	22,300
Computer and Electronic Product Manufacturing	$118,330	6,890

Metropolitan Areas Where Income Is Highest

Metropolitan Area	Average Annual Earnings	Number Employed
New York–Northern New Jersey–Long Island, NY-NJ-PA	$138,210	22,830
San Jose–Sunnyvale–Santa Clara, CA	$131,600	5,000
New Bedford, MA	$130,010	110
Ocala, FL	$128,350	150
Bellingham, WA	$125,300	110

Direct the actual distribution or movement of products or services to customers. Coordinate sales distribution by establishing sales territories, quotas, and goals and establish training programs for sales representatives. Analyze sales statistics gathered by staff to determine sales potential and inventory requirements and monitor customer preferences. Resolve customer complaints regarding sales and service. Oversee regional and local sales managers and their staffs. Plan and direct staffing, training, and performance evaluations to develop and control sales and service programs. Determine price schedules and discount rates. Review operational records and reports to project sales and determine profitability. Monitor customer preferences to determine focus of sales efforts. Prepare budgets and approve budget expenditures. Confer or consult with department heads to plan advertising services and to secure information on equipment and customer specifications. Direct and coordinate activities involving sales of manufactured products, services, commodities, real estate, or other subjects of sale. Confer with potential customers regarding equipment needs and advise customers on types of equipment to purchase. Direct foreign sales and service outlets of an organization. Advise dealers and distributors on policies and operating procedures to ensure functional effectiveness of businesses. Visit franchised dealers to stimulate interest in establishment or expansion of leasing programs. Direct clerical staff to keep records of export correspondence, bid requests, and credit collections and to maintain current information on tariffs, licenses, and restrictions. Direct, coordinate, and review activities in sales and service accounting and recordkeeping and in receiving and shipping operations. Assess marketing potential of new and existing store locations, considering statistics and expenditures. Represent company at trade association meetings to promote products.

Other Considerations for Income: Salary levels vary substantially, depending upon the level of managerial responsibility, length of service, education, size of firm, location, and industry. For example, manufacturing firms usually pay these managers higher salaries than nonmanufacturing firms. For sales managers, the size of their sales territory is another important determinant of salary. Many managers earn bonuses equal to 10 percent or more of their salaries.

Personality Type: Enterprising-Conventional. **Career Clusters:** 04 Business, Management, and Administration; 10 Human Service; 14 Marketing, Sales, and Service. **Career Pathways:** 04.1 Management; 10.5 Consumer Services Career; 14.1 Management and Entrepreneurship; 14.4 Marketing Communications and Promotion. **Skills:** Management of Financial Resources; Management of Personnel Resources; Systems Evaluation; Systems Analysis; Persuasion; Negotiation; Monitoring; Management of Material Resources.

Education and Training Programs: Business Administration and Management, General; Business/Commerce, General; Consumer Merchandising/Retailing Management; Marketing, Other; Marketing/Marketing Management, General. **Related Knowledge/Courses:** Sales and Marketing; Personnel and Human Resources; Economics and Accounting; Administration and Management; Customer and Personal Service; Psychology.

Sales Representatives, Wholesale and Manufacturing, Except Technical and Scientific Products

- ❀ Annual Earnings: $51,330
- ❀ Beginning Wage: $26,950
- ❀ Earnings Growth Potential: High (47.5%)
- ❀ Growth: 8.4%
- ❀ Annual Job Openings: 156,215
- ❀ Self-Employed: 4.0%
- ❀ Part-Time: 6.7%
- ❀ Job Security: Least secure
- ❀ Education/Training Required: Work experience in a related occupation

Industries in Which Income Is Highest

Industry	Average Annual Earnings	Number Employed
Petroleum and Coal Products Manufacturing	$65,750	1,530
Paper Manufacturing	$65,240	9,690
Textile Mills	$65,110	2,220
Computer and Electronic Product Manufacturing	$62,760	10,730
Utilities	$62,340	2,260

Metropolitan Areas Where Income Is Highest

Metropolitan Area	Average Annual Earnings	Number Employed
Danbury, CT	$91,020	980
Napa, CA	$76,630	720
Corvallis, OR	$70,370	70
Santa Rosa–Petaluma, CA	$68,050	2,240
Salinas, CA	$67,840	1,200

Sell goods for wholesalers or manufacturers to businesses or groups of individuals. Work requires substantial knowledge of items sold. Answer customers' questions about products, prices, availability, product uses, and credit terms. Recommend products to customers based on customers' needs and interests. Contact regular and prospective customers to demonstrate products, explain product features, and solicit orders. Estimate or quote prices, credit or contract terms, warranties, and delivery dates. Consult with clients after sales or contract signings to resolve problems and to provide ongoing support. Prepare drawings, estimates, and bids that meet specific customer needs. Provide customers with product samples and catalogs. Identify prospective customers by using business directories, following leads from existing clients, participating in organizations and clubs, and attending trade shows and conferences. Arrange and direct delivery and installation of products and equipment. Monitor market conditions; product innovations; and competitors' products, prices, and sales. Negotiate details of contracts and payments and prepare sales contracts and order forms. Perform administrative duties, such as preparing sales budgets and reports, keeping sales records, and filing expense account reports. Obtain credit information about prospective customers. Forward orders to manufacturers. Check stock levels and reorder merchandise as necessary. Plan, assemble, and stock product displays in retail stores or make recommendations to retailers regarding product displays, promotional programs, and advertising. Negotiate with retail merchants to improve product exposure such as shelf positioning and advertising. Train customers' employees to operate and maintain new equipment. Buy products from manufacturers or brokerage firms and distribute them to wholesale and retail clients.

Other Considerations for Income: Compensation methods for those representatives working for an independent sales company vary significantly by the type of firm and the product sold. Most employers use a combination of salary and commissions or salary plus bonus. Commissions usually are based on the amount of sales, whereas bonuses may depend on individual performance, on the performance of all sales workers in the group or district, or on the company's performance. Unlike those working directly for a manufacturer or wholesaler, sales representatives working for an independent sales company usually are not reimbursed for expenses. Depending on the type of product or products they are selling, their experience in the field, and the number of clients they have, they can earn significantly more or less than those working in direct sales for a manufacturer or wholesaler. In addition to their earnings, sales representatives working directly for a manufacturer or wholesaler usually are reimbursed for expenses such as transportation costs, meals, hotels, and entertaining customers. They often receive benefits such as health and life insurance, pension plans, vacation and sick leave, personal use of a company car, and frequent flyer mileage.

Some companies offer incentives such as free vacation trips or gifts for outstanding sales workers.

Personality Type: Conventional-Enterprising. **Career Cluster:** 14 Marketing, Sales, and Service. **Career Pathway:** 14.2 Professional Sales and Marketing; 14.3 Buying and Merchandising. **Skills:** Negotiation; Persuasion; Service Orientation; Management of Financial Resources; Operations Analysis; Time Management; Speaking; Installation.

Education and Training Programs: Apparel and Accessories Marketing Operations; Business, Management, Marketing, and Related Support Services, Other; Fashion Merchandising; General Merchandising, Sales, and Related Marketing Operations, Other; Insurance; Sales, Distribution, and Marketing Operations, General; Special Products Marketing Operations; Specialized Merchandising, Sales, and Marketing Operations, Other. **Related Knowledge/Courses:** Sales and Marketing; Economics and Accounting; Customer and Personal Service; Transportation; Mathematics; Administration and Management.

Sales Representatives, Wholesale and Manufacturing, Technical and Scientific Products

* Annual Earnings: $70,200
* Beginning Wage: $34,980
* Earnings Growth Potential: Very high (50.2%)
* Growth: 12.4%
* Annual Job Openings: 43,469
* Self-Employed: 4.2%
* Part-Time: 6.7%
* Job Security: Least secure
* Education/Training Required: Work experience in a related occupation

Industries in Which Income Is Highest

Industry	Average Annual Earnings	Number Employed
Data Processing, Hosting and Related Services	$79,480	3,120
Management of Companies and Enterprises	$77,860	8,090
Professional, Scientific, and Technical Services	$77,800	42,710
Wholesale Electronic Markets and Agents and Brokers	$77,190	58,690
Telecommunications	$75,240	12,050

Metropolitan Areas Where Income Is Highest

Metropolitan Area	Average Annual Earnings	Number Employed
Wenatchee, WA	$106,560	60
Ogden-Clearfield, UT	$101,580	390
Sacramento–Arden-Arcade–Roseville, CA	$97,970	2,340
Barnstable Town, MA	$96,930	340
San Jose–Sunnyvale–Santa Clara, CA	$95,310	7,780

Sell goods for wholesalers or manufacturers where technical or scientific knowledge is required in such areas as biology, engineering, chemistry, and electronics that is normally obtained from at least two years of postsecondary education. Contact new and existing customers to discuss their needs and to explain how these needs could be met by specific products and services. Answer customers' questions about products, prices, availability, product uses, and credit terms. Quote prices, credit terms, and other bid specifications. Emphasize product features based on analyses of customers' needs and on technical knowledge of product capabilities and limitations. Negotiate prices and terms of sales and service agreements. Maintain customer records, using automated systems. Identify prospective customers by using business directories, following leads from existing clients, participating in organizations and clubs, and attending trade shows and conferences. Prepare sales contracts for orders obtained and submit orders for processing. Select the correct products or assist customers in making product selections based on customers' needs, product specifications, and applicable regulations. Collaborate with colleagues to exchange information such as selling strategies and marketing information. Prepare sales presentations and proposals that explain product specifications and applications. Provide customers with ongoing technical support. Demonstrate and explain the operation and use of products. Inform customers of estimated delivery schedules, service contracts, warranties, or other information pertaining to purchased products. Attend sales and trade meetings and read related publications in order to obtain information about market conditions, business trends, and industry developments. Visit establishments to evaluate needs and to promote product or service sales. Complete expense reports, sales reports, and other paperwork. Initiate sales campaigns and follow marketing plan guidelines in order to meet sales and production expectations. Recommend ways for customers to alter product usage in order to improve production. Complete product and development training as required.

Other Considerations for Income: Compensation methods for those representatives working for an independent sales company vary significantly by the type of firm and the product sold. Most employers use a combination of salary and commissions or salary plus bonus. Commissions usually are based on the amount of sales, whereas bonuses may depend on individual performance, on the performance of all sales workers in the group or district, or on the company's performance. Unlike those working directly for a manufacturer or wholesaler, sales representatives working for an independent sales company usually are not reimbursed for expenses. Depending on the type of product or products they are selling, their experience in the field, and the number of clients they have, they can earn significantly more or less than those working in direct sales for a manufacturer or wholesaler. In addition to their earnings, sales representatives working directly for a manufacturer or wholesaler usually are reimbursed for expenses such as transportation costs, meals, hotels, and entertaining customers. They often receive benefits such as health and life insurance, pension plans, vacation and sick leave, personal use of a company car, and frequent flyer mileage. Some companies offer incentives such as free vacation trips or gifts for outstanding sales workers.

Personality Type: Enterprising-Conventional. **Career Cluster:** 14 Marketing, Sales, and Service. **Career Pathway:** 14.2 Professional Sales and Marketing. **Skills:** Persuasion; Negotiation; Science; Management of Financial Resources; Service Orientation; Coordination; Operations Analysis; Social Perceptiveness.

Education and Training Programs: Business, Management, Marketing, and Related Support Services, Other;

Selling Skills and Sales Operations. **Related Knowledge/Courses:** Sales and Marketing; Customer and Personal Service; Production and Processing; Administration and Management; Computers and Electronics; Transportation.

School Psychologists

* ❁ Annual Earnings: $64,140
* ❁ Beginning Wage: $37,900
* ❁ Earnings Growth Potential: High (40.9%)
* ❁ Growth: 15.8%
* ❁ Annual Job Openings: 8,309
* ❁ Self-Employed: 34.2%
* ❁ Part-Time: 24.0%
* ❁ Job Security: Most secure
* ❁ Education/Training Required: Doctoral degree

The Department of Labor reports this information for the occupation Clinical, Counseling, and School Psychologists. The job openings listed here are shared with other specializations within that occupation, including Clinical Psychologists; and Counseling Psychologists.

Industries in Which Income Is Highest

Industry	Average Annual Earnings	Number Employed
Administrative and Support Services	$72,400	1,140
Hospitals	$70,240	9,210
Professional, Scientific, and Technical Services	$70,010	1,020
Ambulatory Health Care Services	$65,810	19,180
Educational Services	$64,410	46,390

Metropolitan Areas Where Income Is Highest

Metropolitan Area	Average Annual Earnings	Number Employed
Vallejo-Fairfield, CA	$92,560	210
Dayton, OH	$91,750	210
Visalia-Porterville, CA	$90,930	80
Trenton-Ewing, NJ	$89,310	270
Stockton, CA	$87,780	130

Investigate processes of learning and teaching and develop psychological principles and techniques applicable to educational problems. Compile and interpret students' test results, along with information from teachers and parents, to diagnose conditions and to help assess eligibility for special services. Report any pertinent information to the proper authorities in cases of child endangerment, neglect, or abuse. Assess an individual child's needs, limitations, and potential, using observation, review of school records, and consultation with parents and school personnel. Select, administer, and score psychological tests. Provide consultation to parents, teachers, administrators, and others on topics such as learning styles and behavior modification techniques. Promote an understanding of child development and its relationship to learning and behavior. Collaborate with other educational professionals to develop teaching strategies and school programs. Counsel children and families to help solve conflicts and problems in learning and adjustment. Develop individualized educational plans in collaboration with teachers and other staff members. Maintain student records, including special education reports, confidential records, records of services provided, and behavioral data. Serve as a resource to help families and schools deal with crises, such as separation and loss. Attend workshops, seminars, or professional meetings to remain informed of new developments in school psychology. Design classes and programs to meet the needs of special students. Refer students and their families to appropriate community agencies for medical, vocational, or social services. Initiate and direct efforts to foster tolerance, understanding, and appreciation of diversity in school communities. Collect and analyze data to evaluate the effectiveness of academic programs and other services, such as behavioral management systems. Provide educational programs on topics such as classroom management, teaching strategies, or parenting skills.

Other Considerations for Income: No additional information.

Personality Type: Investigative-Social. **Career Clusters:** 08 Health Science; 10 Human Service. **Career Pathways:** 08.1 Therapeutic Services; 10.2 Counseling and Mental Health Services. **Skills:** Social Perceptiveness; Negotiation; Learning Strategies; Persuasion; Writing; Active Listening; Service Orientation; Active Learning.

Education and Training Programs: Psychoanalysis and Psychotherapy; Psychology, General. **Related Knowledge/Courses:** Therapy and Counseling; Psychology; Sociology and Anthropology; Philosophy and Theology; Education and Training; Medicine and Dentistry.

Secondary School Teachers, Except Special and Vocational Education

※ Annual Earnings: $51,180
※ Beginning Wage: $34,280
※ Earnings Growth Potential: Low (33.0%)
※ Growth: 5.6%
※ Annual Job Openings: 93,166
※ Self-Employed: 0.0%
※ Part-Time: 7.8%
※ Job Security: Most secure
※ Education/Training Required: Bachelor's degree

Industries in Which Income Is Highest

Industry	Average Annual Earnings	Number Employed
Educational Services	$51,230	1,081,960
Federal, State, and Local Government	$44,280	2,720
Administrative and Support Services	$43,540	4,020

Metropolitan Areas Where Income Is Highest

Metropolitan Area	Average Annual Earnings	Number Employed
Yuba City, CA	$77,130	430
Napa, CA	$74,590	440
Chicago-Naperville-Joliet, IL-IN-WI	$72,680	41,840
Bridgeport-Stamford-Norwalk, CT	$71,590	4,190
Modesto, CA	$70,510	2,270

Instruct students in secondary public or private schools in one or more subjects at the secondary level, such as English, mathematics, or social studies. May be designated according to subject matter specialty, such as typing instructors, commercial teachers, or English teachers. Establish and enforce rules for behavior and procedures for maintaining order among the students for whom they are responsible. Instruct through lectures, discussions, and demonstrations in one or more subjects such as English, mathematics, or social studies. Establish clear objectives for all lessons, units, and projects and communicate those objectives to students. Prepare, administer, and grade tests and assignments to evaluate students' progress. Prepare materials and classrooms for class activities. Adapt teaching methods and instructional materials to meet students' varying needs and interests. Assign and grade classwork and homework. Maintain accurate and complete student records as required by laws, district policies, and administrative regulations. Enforce all administration policies and rules governing students. Observe and evaluate students' performance, behavior, social development, and physical health. Plan and conduct activities for a balanced program of instruction, demonstration, and work time that provides students with opportunities to observe, question, and investigate. Prepare students for later grades by encouraging them to explore learning opportunities and to persevere with challenging tasks. Guide and counsel students with adjustment and/or academic problems or special academic interests. Instruct and monitor students in the use and care of equipment and materials to prevent injuries and damage. Prepare for assigned classes and show written evidence of preparation upon request of immediate supervisors. Meet with parents and guardians to discuss their children's progress and to determine their priorities for their children and their resource needs. Confer with parents or guardians, other teachers, counselors, and administrators in order to resolve students' behavioral and academic problems. Use computers, audiovisual aids, and other equipment and materials to supplement presentations.

Other Considerations for Income: Teachers can boost their earnings in a number of ways. In some schools, teachers receive extra pay for coaching sports and working with students in extracurricular activities. Getting a master's degree or national certification often results in a raise in pay, as does acting as a mentor. Some teachers earn extra income during the summer by teaching summer school or performing other jobs in the school system. Although private school teachers generally earn less than public school teachers, they may be given other benefits, such as free or subsidized housing.

Personality Type: Social-Artistic-Enterprising. **Career Cluster:** 05 Education and Training. **Career Pathway:** 05.3 Teaching/Training. **Skills:** Learning Strategies; Social Perceptiveness; Persuasion; Monitoring; Instructing; Time Management; Negotiation; Service Orientation.

Education and Training Programs: Agricultural Teacher Education; Art Teacher Education; Biology Teacher Education; Business Teacher Education; Chemistry Teacher Education; Computer Teacher Education; Drama and Dance Teacher Education; Driver and Safety Teacher Education; English/Language Arts Teacher Education; Family and Consumer Sciences/Home Economics Teacher Education; Foreign Language Teacher Education; French Language Teacher Education; Geography Teacher Education; German Language Teacher Education; others. **Related Knowledge/Courses:** History and Archeology; Philosophy and Theology; Sociology and Anthropology; Education and Training; Geography; Therapy and Counseling.

Securities and Commodities Traders

- ❋ Annual Earnings: $68,680
- ❋ Beginning Wage: $30,900
- ❋ Earnings Growth Potential: Very high (55.0%)
- ❋ Growth: 24.8%
- ❋ Annual Job Openings: 47,750
- ❋ Self-Employed: 17.7%
- ❋ Part-Time: 6.9%
- ❋ Job Security: No data available
- ❋ Education/Training Required: Bachelor's degree

The Department of Labor reports this information for the occupation Securities, Commodities, and Financial Services Sales Agents. The job openings listed here are shared with other specializations within that occupation, including Sales Agents, Financial Services; and Sales Agents, Securities and Commodities.

Industries in Which Income Is Highest

Industry	Average Annual Earnings	Number Employed
Securities, Commodity Contracts, and Other Financial Investments and Related Activities	$87,180	158,690
Management of Companies and Enterprises	$81,940	7,460
Administrative and Support Services	$68,510	1,670
Funds, Trusts, and Other Financial Vehicles	$61,110	2,490
Insurance Carriers and Related Activities	$59,920	9,520

Metropolitan Areas Where Income Is Highest

Metropolitan Area	Average Annual Earnings	Number Employed
Bridgeport-Stamford-Norwalk, CT	$165,330	5,300
San Francisco–Oakland–Fremont, CA	$112,720	7,650
Cape Coral–Fort Myers, FL	$112,610	490
Longview, TX	$107,990	70
Memphis, TN-MS-AR	$104,950	1,230

Buy and sell securities and commodities to transfer debt, capital, or risk. Establish and negotiate unit prices and terms of sale. No task data available.

Other Considerations for Income: Benefits in the securities industry are generally very good. They normally include health care, retirement, and life insurance. Securities firms may also give discounts to employees on financial services that they sell to customers. Other benefits may include paid lunches with clients, paid dinners for employees who work late, and often extensive travel opportunities.

Personality Type: Enterprising-Conventional. **Career Cluster:** 06 Finance. **Career Pathway:** 06.1 Financial and Investment Planning. **Skills:** No data available.

Education and Training Programs: Business and Personal/Financial Services Marketing Operations; Financial Planning and Services; Investments and Securities. **Related Knowledge/Courses:** No data available.

Securities, Commodities, and Financial Services Sales Agents

See *Sales Agents, Financial Services; Sales Agents, Securities and Commodities; and Securities and Commodities Traders, described separately.*

Sheriffs and Deputy Sheriffs

- ❈ Annual Earnings: $51,410
- ❈ Beginning Wage: $30,070
- ❈ Earnings Growth Potential: High (41.5%)
- ❈ Growth: 10.8%
- ❈ Annual Job Openings: 37,842
- ❈ Self-Employed: 0.0%
- ❈ Part-Time: 1.1%
- ❈ Job Security: Most secure
- ❈ Education/Training Required: Long-term on-the-job training

The Department of Labor reports this information for the occupation Police and Sheriff's Patrol Officers. The job openings listed here are shared with other specializations within that occupation, including Police Patrol Officers.

Industries in Which Income Is Highest

Industry	Average Annual Earnings	Number Employed
Federal, State, and Local Government	$51,630	618,590
Educational Services	$43,350	13,560

Metropolitan Areas Where Income Is Highest

Metropolitan Area	Average Annual Earnings	Number Employed
San Jose–Sunnyvale–Santa Clara, CA	$91,670	2,330
Santa Rosa–Petaluma, CA	$78,000	680
Los Angeles–Long Beach–Santa Ana, CA	$77,800	24,360
Santa Cruz–Watsonville, CA	$77,730	350
Vallejo-Fairfield, CA	$77,100	910

Enforce law and order in rural or unincorporated districts or serve legal processes of courts. May patrol courthouse, guard court or grand jury, or escort defendants. Drive vehicles or patrol specific areas to detect law violators, issue citations, and make arrests. Investigate illegal or suspicious activities. Verify that the proper legal charges have been made against law offenders. Execute arrest warrants, locating and taking persons into custody. Record daily activities and submit logs and other related reports and paperwork to appropriate authorities. Patrol and guard courthouses, grand jury rooms, or assigned areas to provide security, enforce laws, maintain order, and arrest violators. Notify patrol units to take violators into custody or to provide needed assistance or medical aid. Place people in protective custody. Serve statements of claims, subpoenas, summonses, jury summonses, orders to pay alimony, and other court orders. Take control of accident scenes to maintain traffic flow, to assist accident victims, and to investigate causes. Question individuals entering secured areas to determine their business, directing and rerouting individuals as necessary. Transport or escort prisoners and defendants en route to courtrooms, prisons or jails, attorneys' offices, or medical facilities. Locate and confiscate real or personal property, as directed by court order. Manage jail operations and tend to jail inmates.

Other Considerations for Income: Total earnings for local, state, and special police and detectives frequently exceed the stated salary because of payments for overtime, which can be significant. In addition to the common benefits—paid vacation, sick leave, and medical and life insurance—most police and sheriffs' departments provide officers with special allowances for uniforms. Because police officers usually are covered by liberal pension plans, many retire at half-pay after 25 or 30 years of service.

Personality Type: Enterprising-Realistic-Social. **Career Cluster:** 12 Law, Public Safety, Corrections, and Security. **Career Pathways:** 12.3 Security and Protective Services; 12.4 Law Enforcement Services. **Skills:** Negotiation; Persuasion; Social Perceptiveness; Service Orientation; Equipment Selection; Complex Problem Solving; Judgment and Decision Making; Coordination.

Education and Training Programs: Criminal Justice/ Police Science; Criminalistics and Criminal Science. **Related Knowledge/Courses:** Public Safety and Security; Law and Government; Telecommunications; Psychology; Therapy and Counseling; Philosophy and Theology.

Ship and Boat Captains

❋ Annual Earnings: $61,960
❋ Beginning Wage: $29,330
❋ Earnings Growth Potential: Very high (52.7%)
❋ Growth: 17.9%
❋ Annual Job Openings: 2,665
❋ Self-Employed: 6.8%
❋ Part-Time: 4.8%
❋ Job Security: Least secure
❋ Education/Training Required: Work experience in a related occupation

The Department of Labor reports this information for the occupation Captains, Mates, and Pilots of Water Vessels. The job openings listed here are shared with other specializations within that occupation, including Mates—Ship, Boat, and Barge; and Pilots, Ship.

Industries in Which Income Is Highest

Industry	Average Annual Earnings	Number Employed
Support Activities for Transportation	$67,910	9,510
Water Transportation	$67,040	11,640
Federal, State, and Local Government	$55,620	2,180
Scenic and Sightseeing Transportation	$38,380	3,660

Metropolitan Areas Where Income Is Highest

Metropolitan Area	Average Annual Earnings	Number Employed
Detroit-Warren-Livonia, MI	$137,730	60
Memphis, TN-MS-AR	$89,540	190
Houston–Sugar Land–Baytown, TX	$79,320	1,530
Baton Rouge, LA	$78,360	480
Houma–Bayou Cane–Thibodaux, LA	$75,570	3,350

Command vessels in oceans, bays, lakes, rivers, and coastal waters. Assign watches and living quarters to crew members. Sort logs, form log booms, and salvage lost logs. Perform various marine duties such as checking for oil spills or other pollutants around ports and harbors, and patrolling beaches. Contact buyers to sell cargo such as fish. Tow and maneuver barges, or signal for tugboats to tow barges to destinations. Signal passing vessels, using whistles, flashing lights, flags, and radios. Resolve questions or problems with customs officials. Read gauges to verify sufficient levels of hydraulic fluid, air pressure, and oxygen. Purchase supplies and equipment. Measure depths of water, using depth-measuring equipment. Maintain boats and equipment on board, such as engines, winches, navigational systems, fire extinguishers, and life preservers. Collect fares from customers, or signal ferryboat helpers to collect fares. Arrange for ships to be fueled, restocked with supplies, and/or repaired. Signal crew members or deckhands to rig tow lines, open or close gates and ramps, and pull guard chains across entries. Maintain records of daily activities, personnel reports, ship positions and movements, ports of call, weather and sea conditions, pollution control efforts, and/or cargo and passenger statuses. Inspect vessels to ensure efficient and safe operation of vessels and equipment, and conformance to regulations. Direct and coordinate crew members or workers performing activities such as loading and unloading cargo, steering vessels, operating engines, and operating, maintaining, and repairing ship equipment. Compute positions, set courses, and determine speeds by using charts, area plotting sheets, compasses, sextants, and knowledge of local conditions. Calculate sightings of land, using electronic sounding devices, and following contour lines on charts. Monitor the loading and discharging of cargo or passengers. Interview and hire crew members.

Other Considerations for Income: Since companies provide food and housing at sea and it is difficult to spend money while working, the workers are able to save a large portion of their pay. Annual pay for captains of larger vessels, such as container ships, oil tankers, or passenger ships may exceed $100,000, but only after many years of experience. Similarly, earnings of captains of tugboats are dependent on the port and the nature of the cargo.

Personality Type: Enterprising-Realistic. **Career Cluster:** 16 Transportation, Distribution, and Logistics. **Career Pathway:** 16.1 Transportation Operations. **Skills:** Operation and Control; Operation Monitoring; Equipment Maintenance; Judgment and Decision Making; Troubleshooting; Management of Personnel Resources; Repairing; Management of Material Resources.

Education and Training Programs: Commercial Fishing; Marine Science/Merchant Marine Officer; Marine Transportation, Other. **Related Knowledge/Courses:** Transportation; Public Safety and Security; Geography; Telecommunications; Psychology; Mechanical.

Ship Engineers

* Annual Earnings: $60,690
* Beginning Wage: $34,420
* Earnings Growth Potential: High (43.3%)
* Growth: 14.1%
* Annual Job Openings: 1,102
* Self-Employed: 0.0%
* Part-Time: 5.7%
* Job Security: Less secure than most
* Education/Training Required: Work experience in a related occupation

Industries in Which Income Is Highest

Industry	Average Annual Earnings	Number Employed
Water Transportation	$64,070	5,750
Support Activities for Transportation	$59,420	2,630
Federal, State, and Local Government	$54,530	1,470

Metropolitan Areas Where Income Is Highest

Metropolitan Area	Average Annual Earnings	Number Employed
Baltimore-Towson, MD	$125,600	100
Seattle-Tacoma-Bellevue, WA	$70,720	820
New York–Northern New Jersey–Long Island, NY-NJ-PA	$66,530	730
Philadelphia-Camden-Wilmington, PA-NJ-DE-MD	$65,070	210
Boston-Cambridge-Quincy, MA-NH	$63,040	110

Supervise and coordinate activities of crew engaged in operating and maintaining engines; boilers; deck machinery; and electrical, sanitary, and refrigeration equipment aboard ship. Record orders for changes in ship speed and direction, and note gauge readings and test data, such as revolutions per minute and voltage output, in engineering logs and bellbooks. Install engine controls, propeller shafts, and propellers. Perform and participate in emergency drills as required. Fabricate engine replacement parts such as valves, stay rods, and bolts, using metalworking machinery. Operate and maintain off-loading liquid pumps and valves. Maintain and repair engines, electric motors, pumps, winches and other mechanical and electrical equipment, or assist other crew members with maintenance and repair duties. Maintain electrical power, heating, ventilation, refrigeration, water, and sewerage. Monitor and test operations of engines and other equipment so that malfunctions and their causes can be identified. Monitor engine, machinery, and equipment indicators when vessels are underway, and report abnormalities to appropriate shipboard staff. Start engines to propel ships, and regulate engines and power transmissions to control speeds of ships, according to directions from captains or bridge computers. Order and receive engine rooms' stores such as oil and spare parts; maintain inventories and record usage of supplies. Act as liaisons between ships' captains and shore personnel to ensure that schedules and budgets are maintained and that ships are operated safely and efficiently. Clean engine parts, and keep engine rooms clean. Supervise the activities of marine engine technicians engaged in the maintenance and repair of mechanical and electrical marine vessels, and inspect their work to ensure that it is performed properly. Maintain complete records of engineering department activities, including machine operations. Perform general marine vessel maintenance and repair work such as repairing leaks, finishing interiors, refueling, and maintaining decks.

Other Considerations for Income: Because companies provide food and housing at sea and it is difficult to spend money while working, the workers are able to save a large portion of their pay. The rate of unionization for marine transportation workers is about 16 percent, higher than the average for all occupations. Unionization rates vary by region. In unionized areas, merchant marine officers and seamen, both veterans and beginners, are hired for voyages through union hiring halls or directly by shipping companies. Hiring halls rank the candidates by the length of time the person has been out of work and fill open slots accordingly. Most major seaports have hiring halls.

Personality Type: Realistic-Conventional-Enterprising. **Career Cluster:** 16 Transportation, Distribution, and Logistics. **Career Pathway:** 16.1 Transportation Operations. **Skills:** Repairing; Installation; Equipment Maintenance; Operation Monitoring; Operation and Control; Troubleshooting; Systems Analysis; Science.

Education and Training Program: Marine Maintenance/Fitter and Ship Repair Technology/Technician. **Related Knowledge/Courses:** Mechanical; Engineering and Technology; Building and Construction; Transportation; Chemistry; Public Safety and Security.

Social and Community Service Managers

* ❀ Annual Earnings: $55,980
* ❀ Beginning Wage: $33,310
* ❀ Earnings Growth Potential: High (40.5%)
* ❀ Growth: 24.7%
* ❀ Annual Job Openings: 23,788
* ❀ Self-Employed: 5.9%
* ❀ Part-Time: 11.6%
* ❀ Job Security: More secure than most
* ❀ Education/Training Required: Bachelor's degree

Industries in Which Income Is Highest

Industry	Average Annual Earnings	Number Employed
Hospitals	$68,850	3,990
Federal, State, and Local Government	$62,690	28,370
Ambulatory Health Care Services	$60,420	4,190
Management of Companies and Enterprises	$60,110	3,070
Educational Services	$59,300	3,890

Metropolitan Areas Where Income Is Highest

Metropolitan Area	Average Annual Earnings	Number Employed
Bradenton-Sarasota-Venice, FL	$92,330	100
Orlando-Kissimmee, FL	$89,560	120
Olympia, WA	$86,180	120
Trenton-Ewing, NJ	$83,460	380
Chico, CA	$83,210	70

Plan, organize, or coordinate the activities of a social service program or community outreach organization. Oversee the program or organization's budget and policies regarding participant involvement, program requirements, and benefits. Work may involve directing social workers, counselors, or probation officers. Establish and maintain relationships with other agencies and organizations in community to meet community needs and to ensure that services are not duplicated. Prepare and maintain records and reports, such as budgets, personnel records, or training manuals. Direct activities of professional and technical staff members and volunteers. Evaluate the work of staff and volunteers to ensure that programs are of appropriate quality and that resources are used effectively. Establish and oversee administrative procedures to meet objectives set by boards of directors or senior management. Participate in the determination of organizational policies regarding such issues as participant eligibility, program requirements, and program benefits. Research and analyze member or community needs to determine program directions and goals. Speak to community groups to explain and interpret agency purposes, programs, and policies. Recruit, interview, and hire or sign up volunteers and staff. Represent organizations in relations with governmental and media institutions. Plan and administer budgets for programs, equipment, and support services. Analyze proposed legislation, regulations, or rule changes to determine how agency services could be impacted. Act as consultants to agency staff and other community programs regarding the interpretation of program-related federal, state, and county regulations and policies. Implement and evaluate staff training programs. Direct fundraising activities and the preparation of public relations materials.

Other Considerations for Income: No additional information.

Personality Type: Enterprising-Social. **Career Clusters:** 04 Business, Management, and Administration; 07 Government and Public Administration; 10 Human Service. **Career Pathways:** 04.1 Management; 07.1 Governance; 07.7 Public Management and Administration; 10.3 Family and Community Services. **Skills:** Social Perceptiveness; Management of Personnel Resources; Service Orientation; Systems Evaluation; Negotiation; Persuasion; Monitoring; Writing.

Education and Training Programs: Business Administration and Management, General; Business, Management, Marketing, and Related Support Services, Other; Business/Commerce, General; Community Organization and Advocacy; Entrepreneurship/Entrepreneurial Studies; Human Services, General; Non-Profit/Public/Organizational Management; Public Administration. **Related Knowledge/Courses:** Therapy and Counseling; Psychology; Sociology and Anthropology; Philosophy and Theology; Personnel and Human Resources; Customer and Personal Service.

Social Work Teachers, Postsecondary

❀ Annual Earnings: $59,140
❀ Beginning Wage: $33,570
❀ Earnings Growth Potential: High (43.2%)
❀ Growth: 22.9%
❀ Annual Job Openings: 1,292
❀ Self-Employed: 0.4%
❀ Part-Time: 27.8%
❀ Job Security: Most secure
❀ Education/Training Required: Doctoral degree

Industries in Which Income Is Highest

Industry	Average Annual Earnings	Number Employed
Educational Services	$59,130	7,930

Metropolitan Areas Where Income Is Highest

Metropolitan Area	Average Annual Earnings	Number Employed
Los Angeles–Long Beach–Santa Ana, CA	$98,850	80
Columbus, OH	$77,470	130
Philadelphia-Camden-Wilmington, PA-NJ-DE-MD	$72,780	220
Baltimore-Towson, MD	$69,480	110
Washington-Arlington-Alexandria, DC-VA-MD-WV	$69,110	480

Teach courses in social work. Initiate, facilitate, and moderate classroom discussions. Evaluate and grade students' classwork, assignments, and papers. Prepare and deliver lectures to undergraduate or graduate students on topics such as family behavior, child and adolescent mental health, and social intervention evaluation. Keep abreast of developments in their field by reading current literature, talking with colleagues, and participating in professional conferences. Supervise students' laboratory work and fieldwork. Conduct research in a particular field of knowledge and publish findings in professional journals, books, or electronic media. Prepare course materials such as syllabi, homework assignments, and handouts. Maintain regularly scheduled office hours to advise and assist students. Supervise undergraduate or graduate teaching, internship, and research work. Plan, evaluate, and revise curricula, course content, and course materials and methods of instruction. Collaborate with colleagues and with community agencies to address teaching and research issues. Compile, administer, and grade examinations or assign this work to others. Advise students on academic and vocational curricula and on career issues. Maintain student attendance records, grades, and other required records. Write grant proposals to procure external research funding. Serve on academic or administrative committees that deal with institutional policies, departmental matters, and academic issues. Perform administrative duties such as serving as department head. Compile bibliographies of specialized materials for outside reading assignments. Select and obtain materials and supplies such as textbooks and laboratory equipment. Participate in student recruitment, registration, and placement activities. Participate in campus and community events. Provide professional consulting services to government and industry. Act as advisers to student organizations.

Other Considerations for Income: Earnings for college faculty vary according to rank and type of institution, geographic area, and field. According to a 2006–2007 survey by the American Association of University Professors, salaries for full-time faculty averaged $73,207. By rank, the average was $98,974 for professors, $69,911 for associate professors, $58,662 for assistant professors, $42,609 for instructors, and $48,289 for lecturers. Faculty in 4-year institutions earn higher salaries, on average, than do those in 2-year schools. Many faculty members have significant earnings in addition to their base salary from consulting, teaching additional courses, research, writing for publication, or other employment. In addition, many college and university faculty enjoy unique benefits, including access to campus facilities, tuition waivers for dependents, housing and travel allowances, and paid leave for sabbaticals. Part-time faculty and instructors usually have fewer benefits than full-time faculty.

Personality Type: Social-Investigative. **Career Clusters:** 05 Education and Training; 10 Human Service. **Career Pathways:** 05.3 Teaching/Training; 10.2 Counseling and Mental Health Services; 10.3 Family and Community Services. **Skills:** Social Perceptiveness; Service Orientation; Instructing; Learning Strategies; Writing; Complex Problem Solving; Critical Thinking; Negotiation.

Education and Training Programs: Clinical/Medical Social Work; Social Work; Teacher Education and Professional Development, Specific Subject Areas, Other. **Related Knowledge/Courses:** Therapy and Counseling; Sociology and Anthropology; Psychology; Philosophy and Theology; Education and Training; English Language.

Sociologists

- ❀ Annual Earnings: $68,570
- ❀ Beginning Wage: $40,720
- ❀ Earnings Growth Potential: High (40.6%)
- ❀ Growth: 10.0%
- ❀ Annual Job Openings: 403
- ❀ Self-Employed: 0.0%
- ❀ Part-Time: 24.0%
- ❀ Job Security: Most secure
- ❀ Education/Training Required: Master's degree

Industries in Which Income Is Highest

Industry	Average Annual Earnings	Number Employed
Religious, Grantmaking, Civic, Professional, and Similar Organizations	$89,090	400
Professional, Scientific, and Technical Services	$73,070	2,120
Educational Services	$61,430	1,420
Federal, State, and Local Government	$58,420	400

Metropolitan Areas Where Income Is Highest

Metropolitan Area	Average Annual Earnings	Number Employed
Washington-Arlington-Alexandria, DC-VA-MD-WV	$84,400	760
San Francisco–Oakland–Fremont, CA	$75,820	370
Los Angeles–Long Beach–Santa Ana, CA	$68,120	150
Boston-Cambridge-Quincy, MA-NH	$62,920	200
Philadelphia-Camden-Wilmington, PA-NJ-DE-MD	$62,030	160

Study human society and social behavior by examining the groups and social institutions that people form, as well as various social, religious, political, and business organizations. May study the behavior and interaction of groups, trace their origin and growth, and analyze the influence of group activities on individual members. Analyze and interpret data in order to increase the understanding of human social behavior. Prepare publications and reports containing research findings. Plan and conduct research to develop and test theories about societal issues such as crime, group relations, poverty, and aging. Collect data about the attitudes, values, and behaviors of people in groups, using observation, interviews, and review of documents. Develop, implement, and evaluate methods of data collection, such as questionnaires or interviews. Teach sociology. Direct work of statistical clerks, statisticians, and others who compile and evaluate research data. Consult with and advise individuals such as administrators, social workers, and legislators regarding social issues and policies, as well as the implications of research findings. Collaborate with research workers in other disciplines. Develop approaches to the solution of groups' problems based on research findings in sociology and related disciplines. Observe group interactions and role affiliations to collect data, identify problems, evaluate progress, and determine the need for additional change. Develop problem intervention procedures, utilizing techniques such as interviews, consultations, role-playing, and participant observation of group interactions.

Other Considerations for Income: No additional information.

Personality Type: Investigative-Artistic-Social. **Career Clusters:** 10 Human Service; 15 Science, Technology, Engineering, and Mathematics. **Career Pathways:** 10.3 Family and Community Services; 15.3 Science and Mathematics. **Skills:** Science; Writing; Management of Financial Resources; Reading Comprehension; Critical Thinking; Complex Problem Solving; Mathematics; Active Learning.

Education and Training Programs: Criminology; Demography and Population Studies; Sociology; Urban Studies/Affairs. **Related Knowledge/Courses:** Sociology and Anthropology; Philosophy and Theology; History and Archeology; Psychology; English Language; Mathematics.

Sociology Teachers, Postsecondary

❀ Annual Earnings: $61,280
❀ Beginning Wage: $32,710
❀ Earnings Growth Potential: High (46.6%)
❀ Growth: 22.9%
❀ Annual Job Openings: 2,774
❀ Self-Employed: 0.4%
❀ Part-Time: 27.8%
❀ Job Security: Most secure
❀ Education/Training Required: Doctoral degree

Industries in Which Income Is Highest

Industry	Average Annual Earnings	Number Employed
Educational Services	$61,270	16,430

Metropolitan Areas Where Income Is Highest

Metropolitan Area	Average Annual Earnings	Number Employed
San Francisco–Oakland–Fremont, CA	$100,970	250
Los Angeles–Long Beach–Santa Ana, CA	$89,370	440
Riverside–San Bernardino–Ontario, CA	$88,670	100
Milwaukee–Waukesha–West Allis, WI	$86,460	150
Lubbock, TX	$80,910	70

Teach courses in sociology. Evaluate and grade students' classwork, assignments, and papers. Prepare and deliver lectures to undergraduate and graduate students on topics such as race and ethnic relations, measurement and data collection, and workplace social relations. Initiate, facilitate, and moderate classroom discussions. Prepare course materials such as syllabi, homework assignments, and handouts. Compile, administer, and grade examinations or assign this work to others. Keep abreast of developments in their field by reading current literature, talking with colleagues, and participating in professional conferences. Maintain student attendance records, grades, and other required records. Maintain regularly scheduled office hours in order to advise and assist students. Plan, evaluate, and revise curricula, course content, and course materials and methods of instruction. Advise students on academic and vocational curricula and on career issues. Collaborate with colleagues to address teaching and research issues. Conduct research in a particular field of knowledge and publish findings in professional journals, books, or electronic media. Select and obtain materials and supplies such as textbooks and laboratory equipment. Supervise undergraduate and graduate teaching, internship, and research work. Serve on academic or administrative committees that deal with institutional policies, departmental matters, and academic issues. Participate in student recruitment, registration, and placement activities. Perform administrative duties such as serving as department head. Supervise students' laboratory work and fieldwork. Write grant proposals to procure external research funding. Act as advisers to student organizations. Compile bibliographies of specialized materials for outside reading assignments. Participate in campus and community events. Provide professional consulting services to government and industry.

Other Considerations for Income: Earnings for college faculty vary according to rank and type of institution, geographic area, and field. According to a 2006–2007 survey by the American Association of University Professors, salaries for full-time faculty averaged $73,207. By rank, the average was $98,974 for professors, $69,911 for associate professors, $58,662 for assistant professors, $42,609 for instructors, and $48,289 for lecturers. Faculty in 4-year institutions earn higher salaries, on average, than do those in 2-year schools. Many faculty members have significant earnings in addition to their base salary from consulting, teaching additional courses, research, writing for publication, or other employment. In addition, many college and university faculty enjoy unique benefits, including access to campus facilities, tuition waivers for dependents, housing and travel allowances, and paid leave for sabbaticals. Part-time faculty and instructors usually have fewer benefits than full-time faculty.

Personality Type: Social-Investigative-Artistic. **Career Clusters:** 05 Education and Training; 15 Science, Technology, Engineering, and Mathematics. **Career Pathways:** 05.3 Teaching/Training; 15.3 Science and Mathematics. **Skills:** Science; Instructing; Writing; Learning Strategies; Social Perceptiveness; Critical Thinking; Speaking; Reading Comprehension.

Education and Training Programs: Humanities/Humanistic Studies; Social Science Teacher Education; Sociology. **Related Knowledge/Courses:** Sociology and Anthropology; Philosophy and Theology; History and Archeology; Education and Training; English Language; Geography.

Software Quality Assurance Engineers and Testers

* Annual Earnings: $75,150
* Beginning Wage: $40,660
* Earnings Growth Potential: High (45.9%)
* Growth: 15.1%
* Annual Job Openings: 14,374
* Self-Employed: 6.6%
* Part-Time: 5.6%
* Job Security: More secure than most
* Education/Training Required: Associate degree

The Department of Labor reports this information for the occupation Computer Specialists, All Other. The job openings listed here are shared with other specializations within that occupation, including Business Intelligence Analysts; Computer Systems Engineers/Architects; Data Warehousing Specialists; Database Architects; Document Management Specialists; Electronic Commerce Specialists; Geographic Information Systems Technicians; Geospatial Information Scientists and Technologists; Information Technology Project Managers; Network Designers; Video Game Designers; Web Administrators; and Web Developers.

Industries in Which Income Is Highest

Industry	Average Annual Earnings	Number Employed
Petroleum and Coal Products Manufacturing	$97,090	1,070
Transportation Equipment Manufacturing	$82,770	3,010
Oil and Gas Extraction	$81,350	1,710
Federal, State, and Local Government	$80,670	71,650
Management of Companies and Enterprises	$78,200	14,820

Metropolitan Areas Where Income Is Highest

Metropolitan Area	Average Annual Earnings	Number Employed
Washington-Arlington-Alexandria, DC-VA-MD-WV	$97,170	19,470
Atlantic City, NJ	$96,600	510
Pascagoula, MS	$95,430	60
San Jose–Sunnyvale–Santa Clara, CA	$92,710	3,580
Baltimore-Towson, MD	$89,730	5,650

Develop and execute software test plans in order to identify software problems and their causes. Design test plans, scenarios, scripts, or procedures. Test system modifications to prepare for implementation. Document software defects, using a bug tracking system, and report defects to software developers. Develop testing programs that address areas such as database impacts, software scenarios, regression testing, negative testing, error or bug retests, or usability. Identify, analyze, and document problems with program function, output, online screens, or content. Monitor bug resolution efforts and track successes. Create or maintain databases of known test defects. Plan test schedules or strategies in accordance with project scope or delivery dates. Participate in product design reviews to provide input on functional requirements, product designs, schedules, or potential problems. Review software documentation to ensure technical accuracy, compliance, or completeness or to mitigate risks. Document test procedures to ensure replicability and compliance with standards. Develop or specify standards, methods, or procedures to determine product quality or release readiness. Update automated test scripts to ensure currency. Investigate customer problems referred by technical support. Install, maintain, or use software testing programs. Provide feedback and recommendations to developers on software usability and functionality. Monitor program performance to ensure efficient and problem-free operations. Install and configure recreations of software production environments to allow testing of software performance. Collaborate with field staff or customers to evaluate or diagnose problems and recommend possible solutions. Conduct software compatibility tests with programs, hardware, operating systems, or network environments. Identify program deviance from standards and suggest modifications to ensure compliance. Design or develop automated testing tools. Coordinate user or third-party testing.

Other Considerations for Income: No additional information.

Personality Type: Investigative-Conventional-Realistic. **Career Cluster:** 11 Information Technology. **Career Pathway:** 11.4 Programming and Software Development. **Skills:** Quality Control Analysis; Programming; Systems Analysis; Systems Evaluation; Troubleshooting; Technology Design; Operations Analysis; Writing.

Education and Training Programs: Computer and Information Sciences and Support Services, Other; Computer and Information Sciences, General; Computer Engineering Technologies/Technicians, Other; Computer Engineering, General; Computer Science; Computer Software Engineering; Computer Systems Networking and Telecommunications; E-Commerce/Electronic Commerce; Information Science/Studies; Information Technology; System, Networking, and LAN/WAN Management/Manager; Web Page, Digital/Multimedia and Information Resources Design; others. **Related Knowledge/Courses:** Computers and Electronics; Engineering and Technology; Design; English Language; Mathematics; Clerical.

Soil and Plant Scientists

- ❊ Annual Earnings: $58,390
- ❊ Beginning Wage: $34,260
- ❊ Earnings Growth Potential: High (41.3%)
- ❊ Growth: 8.4%
- ❊ Annual Job Openings: 850
- ❊ Self-Employed: 19.5%
- ❊ Part-Time: 11.4%
- ❊ Job Security: Most secure
- ❊ Education/Training Required: Bachelor's degree

Industries in Which Income Is Highest

Industry	Average Annual Earnings	Number Employed
Federal, State, and Local Government	$62,890	2,780
Professional, Scientific, and Technical Services	$62,360	3,180
Merchant Wholesalers, Nondurable Goods	$56,870	1,810
Educational Services	$46,850	1,580

Metropolitan Areas Where Income Is Highest

Metropolitan Area	Average Annual Earnings	Number Employed
Washington-Arlington-Alexandria, DC-VA-MD-WV	$87,830	380
San Francisco–Oakland–Fremont, CA	$86,520	370
Sacramento–Arden-Arcade–Roseville, CA	$77,710	170
Atlanta Sandy Springs–Marietta, GA	$70,740	80
Raleigh-Cary, NC	$70,270	80

Conduct research in breeding, physiology, production, yield, and management of crops and agricultural plants, their growth in soils, and control of pests or study the chemical, physical, biological, and mineralogical composition of soils as they relate to plant or crop growth. May classify and map soils and investigate effects of alternative practices on soil and crop productivity. Communicate research and project results to other professionals and the public or teach related courses, seminars or workshops. Provide information and recommendations to farmers and other landowners regarding ways in which they can best use land, promote plant growth, and avoid or correct problems such as erosion. Investigate responses of soils to specific management practices to determine the use capabilities of soils and the effects of alternative practices on soil productivity. Develop methods of conserving and managing soil that can be applied by farmers and forestry companies. Conduct experiments to develop new or improved varieties of field crops, focusing on characteristics such as yield, quality, disease resistance, nutritional value, or adaptation to specific soils or climates. Investigate soil problems and poor water quality to determine sources and effects. Study soil characteristics to classify soils on the basis of factors such as geographic location, landscape position, and soil properties. Develop improved measurement techniques, soil conservation methods, soil sampling devices, and related technology. Conduct experiments investigating how soil forms and changes and how it interacts with land-based ecosystems and living organisms. Identify degraded or contaminated soils and develop plans to improve their chemical, biological, and physical characteristics. Survey undisturbed and disturbed lands for classification, inventory, mapping, environmental impact assessments, environmental protection planning, and conservation and reclamation planning. Plan and supervise land conservation and reclamation programs for industrial development projects and waste management programs for composting and farming. Perform chemical analyses of the microorganism content of soils to determine microbial reactions and chemical mineralogical relationships to plant growth.

Other Considerations for Income: No additional information.

Personality Type: Investigative-Realistic. **Career Cluster:** 01 Agriculture, Food and Natural Resource. **Career Pathway:** 01.2 Plant Systems. **Skills:** Science; Management of Financial Resources; Writing; Management of Material Resources; Reading Comprehension; Management of Personnel Resources; Mathematics; Time Management.

Education and Training Programs: Agricultural and Horticultural Plant Breeding; Agriculture, General; Horticultural Science; Plant Protection and Integrated Pest Management; Plant Sciences, General; Plant Sciences, Other; Range Science and Management; Soil Chemistry and Physics; Soil Microbiology; Soil Science and Agronomy, General. **Related Knowledge/Courses:** Biology; Food Production; Geography; Chemistry; Physics; Communications and Media.

Soil and Water Conservationists

- ❀ Annual Earnings: $58,720
- ❀ Beginning Wage: $35,190
- ❀ Earnings Growth Potential: High (40.1%)
- ❀ Growth: 5.3%
- ❀ Annual Job Openings: 1,161
- ❀ Self-Employed: 3.9%
- ❀ Part-Time: 4.9%
- ❀ Job Security: More secure than most
- ❀ Education/Training Required: Bachelor's degree

The Department of Labor reports this information for the occupation Conservation Scientists. The job openings listed here are shared with other specializations within that occupation, including Park Naturalists; and Range Managers.

Industries in Which Income Is Highest

Industry	Average Annual Earnings	Number Employed
Federal, State, and Local Government	$60,060	12,560
Religious, Grantmaking, Civic, Professional, and Similar Organizations	$52,530	1,490

Metropolitan Areas Where Income Is Highest

Metropolitan Area	Average Annual Earnings	Number Employed
Anchorage, AK	$79,740	100
Washington-Arlington-Alexandria, DC-VA-MD-WV	$78,220	400
San Jose–Sunnyvale–Santa Clara, CA	$74,550	70
Miami–Fort Lauderdale–Miami Beach, FL	$74,450	60
Los Angeles–Long Beach–Santa Ana, CA	$74,240	100

Plan and develop coordinated practices for soil erosion control, soil and water conservation, and sound land use. Develop and maintain working relationships with local government staff and board members. Advise land users such as farmers and ranchers on conservation plans, problems, and alternative solutions and provide technical and planning assistance. Apply principles of specialized fields of science, such as agronomy, soil science, forestry, or agriculture, to achieve conservation objectives. Plan soil management and conservation practices, such as crop rotation, reforestation, permanent vegetation, contour plowing, or terracing, to maintain soil and conserve water. Visit areas affected by erosion problems to seek sources and solutions. Monitor projects during and after construction to ensure projects conform to design specifications. Compute design specifications for implementation of conservation practices, using survey and field information technical guides, engineering manuals, and calculator. Revisit land users to view implemented land use practices and plans. Coordinate and implement technical, financial, and administrative assistance programs for local government units to ensure efficient program implementation and timely responses to requests for assistance. Analyze results of investigations to determine measures needed to maintain or restore proper soil management. Participate on work teams to plan, develop, and implement water and land management programs and policies. Develop, conduct, and/or participate in surveys, studies, and investigations of various land uses, gathering information for use in developing corrective action plans. Survey property to mark locations and measurements, using surveying instruments. Compute cost estimates of different conservation practices based on needs of land users, maintenance requirements, and life expectancy of practices. Provide information, knowledge, expertise, and training to government agencies at all levels to solve water and soil management problems and to assure coordination of resource protection activities.

Other Considerations for Income: In private industry, starting salaries for students with a bachelor's degree were comparable with starting salaries in the federal government, but starting salaries in state and local governments were usually lower. Conservation scientists and foresters who work for federal, state, and local governments and large private firms generally receive more generous benefits than do those working for smaller firms. Governments usually have good pension, health, and leave plans.

Personality Type: Investigative-Realistic-Enterprising. **Career Cluster:** 01 Agriculture, Food and Natural Resource. **Career Pathway:** 01.5 Natural Resources Systems. **Skills:** Operations Analysis; Persuasion; Science; Quality Control Analysis; Installation; Equipment Selection; Judgment and Decision Making; Mathematics.

Education and Training Programs: Forest Management/Forest Resources Management; Forest Sciences and Biology; Forestry, General; Forestry, Other; Land Use Planning and Management/Development; Natural Resources and Conservation, Other; Natural Resources Management and Policy; Natural Resources Management and Policy, Other; Natural Resources/Conservation, General; Water, Wetlands, and Marine Resources Management; Wildlife, Fish and Wildlands Science and Management. **Related Knowledge/Courses:** Geography; Biology; Engineering and Technology; Design; History and Archeology; Food Production.

Solar Energy Installation Managers

- ✹ Annual Earnings: $58,140
- ✹ Beginning Wage: $35,790
- ✹ Earnings Growth Potential: Medium (38.4%)
- ✹ Growth: 9.1%
- ✹ Annual Job Openings: 82,923
- ✹ Self-Employed: 24.4%
- ✹ Part-Time: 3.0%
- ✹ Job Security: No data available
- ✹ Education/Training Required: Work experience in a related occupation

The Department of Labor reports this information for the occupation First-Line Supervisors/Managers of Construction Trades and Extraction Workers. The job openings listed here are shared with other specializations within that occupation.

Industries in Which Income Is Highest

Industry	Average Annual Earnings	Number Employed
Utilities	$68,240	3,830
Mining (Except Oil and Gas)	$66,950	8,510
Oil and Gas Extraction	$65,680	3,400
Professional, Scientific, and Technical Services	$65,320	4,770
Support Activities for Mining	$63,280	15,450

Metropolitan Areas Where Income Is Highest

Metropolitan Area	Average Annual Earnings	Number Employed
San Francisco–Oakland–Fremont, CA	$84,020	8,600
Anchorage, AK	$83,780	540
San Jose–Sunnyvale–Santa Clara, CA	$79,870	3,150
Chicago-Naperville-Joliet, IL-IN-WI	$78,490	10,610
Vallejo-Fairfield, CA	$77,460	580

Direct work crews installing residential or commercial solar photovoltaic or thermal systems. No task data available.

Other Considerations for Income: No additional information.

Personality Type: No data available. **Career Cluster:** 02 Architecture and Construction. **Career Pathway:** 02.2 Construction. **Skills:** No data available.

Education and Training Programs: Building/Construction Site Management/Manager; Carpentry/Carpenter; Construction Trades, Other; Electrician; Roofer. **Related Knowledge/Courses:** No data available.

Solar Sales Representatives and Assessors

❋ Annual Earnings: $70,200
❋ Beginning Wage: $34,980
❋ Earnings Growth Potential: Very high (50.2%)
❋ Growth: 12.4%
❋ Annual Job Openings: 43,469
❋ Self-Employed: 4.2%
❋ Part-Time: 6.7%
❋ Job Security: No data available
❋ Education/Training Required: Work experience in a related occupation

The Department of Labor reports this information for the occupation Sales Representatives, Wholesale and Manufacturing, Technical and Scientific Products. The job openings listed here are shared with other specializations within that occupation.

Industries in Which Income Is Highest

Industry	Average Annual Earnings	Number Employed
Data Processing, Hosting and Related Services	$79,480	3,120
Management of Companies and Enterprises	$77,860	8,090
Professional, Scientific, and Technical Services	$77,800	42,710
Wholesale Electronic Markets and Agents and Brokers	$77,190	58,690
Telecommunications	$75,240	12,050

Metropolitan Areas Where Income Is Highest

Metropolitan Area	Average Annual Earnings	Number Employed
Wenatchee, WA	$106,560	60
Ogden-Clearfield, UT	$101,580	390
Sacramento–Arden-Arcade–Roseville, CA	$97,970	2,340
Barnstable Town, MA	$96,930	340
San Jose–Sunnyvale–Santa Clara, CA	$95,310	7,780

Contact new or existing customers to determine their solar equipment needs, suggest systems or equipment, or estimate costs. No task data available.

Other Considerations for Income: Most employers use a combination of salary and commissions or salary plus bonus. Commissions usually are based on the amount of sales, whereas bonuses may depend on individual performance, on the performance of all sales workers in the group or district, or on the company's performance. Unlike those working directly for a manufacturer or wholesaler, sales representatives working for an independent sales company usually are not reimbursed for expenses. Depending on the type of product or products they are selling, their experience in the field, and the number of clients they have, they can earn significantly more or less than those working in direct sales for a manufacturer or wholesaler. In addition to their earnings, sales representatives working directly for a manufacturer or wholesaler usually are reimbursed for expenses such as transportation costs, meals, hotels, and entertaining customers. They often receive benefits such as health and life insurance, pension plans, vacation and sick leave, personal use of a company car, and frequent flyer mileage. Some companies offer incentives such as free vacation trips or gifts for outstanding sales workers.

Personality Type: No data available. **Career Cluster:** 14 Marketing, Sales, and Service. **Career Pathway:** 14.2 Professional Sales and Marketing. **Skills:** No data available.

Education and Training Programs: Business, Management, Marketing, and Related Support Services, Other; Selling Skills and Sales Operations. **Related Knowledge/Courses:** No data available.

Special Education Teachers, Middle School

❀ Annual Earnings: $50,810
❀ Beginning Wage: $35,180
❀ Earnings Growth Potential: Low (30.8%)
❀ Growth: 15.8%
❀ Annual Job Openings: 8,846
❀ Self-Employed: 0.3%
❀ Part-Time: 9.6%
❀ Job Security: Most secure
❀ Education/Training Required: Bachelor's degree

Industries in Which Income Is Highest

Industry	Average Annual Earnings	Number Employed
Educational Services	$50,810	99,580

Metropolitan Areas Where Income Is Highest

Metropolitan Area	Average Annual Earnings	Number Employed
Modesto, CA	$73,580	80
Bridgeport-Stamford-Norwalk, CT	$71,210	390
Norwich–New London, CT-RI	$67,720	140
San Diego–Carlsbad–San Marcos, CA	$67,680	470
Kingston, NY	$67,400	80

Teach middle school subjects to educationally and physically handicapped students. Includes teachers who specialize and work with audibly and visually handicapped students and those who teach basic academic and life processes skills to the mentally impaired. Establish and enforce rules for behavior and policies and procedures to maintain order among students. Maintain accurate and complete student records and prepare reports on children and activities as required by laws, district policies, and administrative regulations. Prepare materials and classrooms for class activities. Confer with parents, administrators, testing specialists, social workers, and professionals to develop individual educational plans designed to promote students' educational, physical, and social development. Develop and implement strategies to meet the needs of students with a variety of handicapping conditions. Teach socially acceptable behavior, employing techniques such as behavior modification and positive reinforcement. Modify the general education curriculum for special-needs students based upon a variety of instructional techniques and instructional technology. Employ special educational strategies and techniques during instruction to improve the development of sensory- and perceptual-motor skills, language, cognition, and memory. Confer with parents or guardians, other teachers, counselors, and administrators to resolve students' behavioral and academic problems. Instruct through lectures, discussions, and demonstrations in one or more subjects such as English, mathematics, or social studies. Coordinate placement of students with special needs into mainstream classes. Meet with parents and guardians to discuss their children's progress and to determine their priorities for their children and their resource needs. Guide and counsel students with adjustment or academic problems or special academic interests. Prepare, administer, and grade tests and assignments to evaluate students' progress. Observe and evaluate students' performance, behavior, social development, and physical health. Establish clear objectives for all lessons, units, and projects and communicate those objectives to students.

Other Considerations for Income: Teachers can boost their earnings in a number of ways. In some schools, teachers receive extra pay for coaching sports and working with students in extracurricular activities. Getting a master's degree or national certification often results in a raise in pay, as does acting as a mentor. Some teachers earn extra income during the summer by teaching summer school or performing other jobs in the school system. Although private school teachers generally earn less than public school teachers, they may be given other benefits, such as free or subsidized housing.

Personality Type: Social-Artistic. **Career Cluster:** 05 Education and Training. **Career Pathway:** 05.3 Teaching/Training. **Skills:** Learning Strategies; Social Perceptiveness; Instructing; Monitoring; Persuasion; Writing; Negotiation; Time Management.

Education and Training Program: Special Education and Teaching, General. **Related Knowledge/Courses:** Geography; History and Archeology; Psychology; Therapy and Counseling; Sociology and Anthropology; Education and Training.

Special Education Teachers, Preschool, Kindergarten, and Elementary School

* ❋ Annual Earnings: $50,020
* ❋ Beginning Wage: $33,770
* ❋ Earnings Growth Potential: Low (32.5%)
* ❋ Growth: 19.6%
* ❋ Annual Job Openings: 20,049
* ❋ Self-Employed: 0.3%
* ❋ Part-Time: 9.6%
* ❋ Job Security: More secure than most
* ❋ Education/Training Required: Bachelor's degree

Industries in Which Income Is Highest

Industry	Average Annual Earnings	Number Employed
Educational Services	$50,520	211,840
Federal, State, and Local Government	$49,220	1,890
Ambulatory Health Care Services	$46,360	1,470
Nursing and Residential Care Facilities	$40,090	1,080
Social Assistance	$37,720	9,420

Metropolitan Areas Where Income Is Highest

Metropolitan Area	Average Annual Earnings	Number Employed
Visalia-Porterville, CA	$82,720	220
Ann Arbor, MI	$70,860	160
New Haven, CT	$70,510	480
Norwich–New London, CT-RI	$69,050	380
Washington-Arlington-Alexandria, DC-VA-MD-WV	$68,050	5,290

Teach elementary and preschool school subjects to educationally and physically handicapped students. Includes teachers who specialize and work with audibly and visually handicapped students and those who teach basic academic and life processes skills to the mentally impaired. Instruct students in academic subjects, using a variety of techniques such as phonetics, multisensory learning, and repetition to reinforce learning and to meet students' varying needs and interests. Employ special educational strategies and techniques during instruction to improve the development of sensory- and perceptual-motor skills, language, cognition, and memory. Teach socially acceptable behavior, employing techniques such as behavior modification and positive reinforcement. Modify the general education curriculum for special-needs students based upon a variety of instructional techniques and technologies. Meet with parents and guardians to discuss their children's progress and to determine their priorities for their children and their resource needs. Plan and conduct activities for a balanced program of instruction, demonstration, and work time that provides students with opportunities to observe, question, and investigate. Establish and enforce rules for behavior and policies and procedures to maintain order among the students for whom they are responsible. Confer with parents, administrators, testing specialists, social workers, and professionals to develop individual educational plans designed to promote students' educational, physical, and social development. Maintain accurate and complete student records and prepare reports on children and activities as required by laws, district policies, and administrative regulations. Establish clear objectives for all lessons, units, and projects and communicate those objectives to students. Develop and implement strategies to meet the needs of students with a variety of handicapping conditions. Prepare classrooms for class activities and provide a variety of materials and resources for children to explore, manipulate, and use, both in learning activities and imaginative play. Confer with parents or guardians, teachers, counselors, and administrators to resolve students' behavioral and academic problems.

Other Considerations for Income: Teachers can boost their earnings in a number of ways. In some schools, teachers receive extra pay for coaching sports and working with students in extracurricular activities. Getting a master's degree or national certification often results in a raise in pay, as does acting as a mentor. Some teachers earn extra income during the summer by teaching summer school or performing other jobs in the school system. Although private school teachers generally earn less than public school teachers, they may be given other benefits, such as free or subsidized housing.

Personality Type: Social-Artistic. **Career Cluster:** 05 Education and Training. **Career Pathway:** 05.3 Teaching/Training. **Skills:** Learning Strategies; Instructing; Social Perceptiveness; Monitoring; Negotiation; Time Management; Coordination; Writing.

Education and Training Programs: Education/Teaching of Individuals with Autism; Education/Teaching of Individuals with Emotional Disturbances; Education/Teaching of Individuals with Hearing Impairments Including Deafness; Education/Teaching of Individuals with Mental Retardation; Education/Teaching of Individuals with Multiple Disabilities; Education/Teaching of Individuals with Orthopedic and Other Physical Health Impairments; Education/Teaching of Individuals with Specific Learning Disabilities; others. **Related Knowledge/Courses:** Psychology; History and Archeology; Therapy and Counseling; Geography; Philosophy and Theology; Sociology and Anthropology.

Special Education Teachers, Secondary School

- ❀ Annual Earnings: $51,340
- ❀ Beginning Wage: $35,150
- ❀ Earnings Growth Potential: Low (31.5%)
- ❀ Growth: 8.5%
- ❀ Annual Job Openings: 10,601
- ❀ Self-Employed: 0.3%
- ❀ Part-Time: 9.6%
- ❀ Job Security: Most secure
- ❀ Education/Training Required: Bachelor's degree

Industries in Which Income Is Highest

Industry	Average Annual Earnings	Number Employed
Federal, State, and Local Government	$53,080	1,400
Educational Services	$51,480	142,910

Metropolitan Areas Where Income Is Highest

Metropolitan Area	Average Annual Earnings	Number Employed
Bridgeport-Stamford-Norwalk, CT	$74,920	820
Washington-Arlington-Alexandria, DC-VA-MD-WV	$73,240	3,870
Modesto, CA	$72,620	320
San Diego–Carlsbad–San Marcos, CA	$71,790	810
Visalia-Porterville, CA	$71,770	120

Teach secondary school subjects to educationally and physically handicapped students. Includes teachers who specialize and work with audibly and visually handicapped students and those who teach basic academic and life processes skills to the mentally impaired. Maintain accurate and complete student records and prepare reports on children and activities as required by laws, district policies, and administrative regulations. Prepare materials and classrooms for class activities. Teach socially acceptable behavior, employing techniques such as behavior modification and positive reinforcement. Establish and enforce rules for behavior and policies and procedures to maintain order among students. Confer with parents, administrators, testing specialists, social workers, and professionals to develop individual educational plans designed to promote students' educational, physical, and social development. Instruct through lectures, discussions, and demonstrations in one or more subjects such as English, mathematics, or social studies. Employ special educational strategies and techniques during instruction to improve the development of sensory- and perceptual-motor skills, language, cognition, and memory. Plan and conduct activities for a balanced program of instruction, demonstration, and work time that provides students with opportunities to observe, question, and investigate. Prepare students for later grades by encouraging them to explore learning opportunities and to persevere with challenging tasks. Teach personal development skills such as goal setting, independence, and self-advocacy. Establish clear objectives for all lessons, units, and projects and communicate those objectives to students. Develop and implement strategies to meet the needs of students with a variety of handicapping conditions. Modify the general education curriculum for special-needs students based upon a variety of instructional techniques and technologies. Meet with other professionals to discuss individual students' needs and progress. Confer with parents or guardians, other teachers, counselors, and administrators to resolve students' behavioral and academic problems.

Other Considerations for Income: Teachers can boost their earnings in a number of ways. In some schools, teachers receive extra pay for coaching sports and working with students in extracurricular activities. Getting a master's degree or national certification often results in a raise in pay, as does acting as a mentor. Some teachers earn extra income during the summer by teaching summer school or performing other jobs in the school system. Although private school teachers generally earn less than public school teachers, they may be given other benefits, such as free or subsidized housing.

Personality Type: Social-Investigative. **Career Cluster:** 05 Education and Training. **Career Pathway:** 05.3 Teaching/Training. **Skills:** Learning Strategies; Social Perceptiveness; Negotiation; Instructing; Persuasion; Service Orientation; Time Management; Writing.

Education and Training Program: Special Education and Teaching, General. **Related Knowledge/Courses:** Therapy and Counseling; History and Archeology; Geography; Psychology; Philosophy and Theology; Sociology and Anthropology.

Speech-Language Pathologists

* Annual Earnings: $62,930
* Beginning Wage: $41,240
* Earnings Growth Potential: Low (34.5%)
* Growth: 10.6%
* Annual Job Openings: 11,160
* Self-Employed: 8.8%
* Part-Time: 24.6%
* Job Security: Most secure
* Education/Training Required: Master's degree

Industries in Which Income Is Highest

Industry	Average Annual Earnings	Number Employed
Nursing and Residential Care Facilities	$78,030	5,220
Ambulatory Health Care Services	$69,110	21,600
Hospitals	$68,250	14,990
Federal, State, and Local Government	$66,130	3,780
Social Assistance	$63,150	3,240

Metropolitan Areas Where Income Is Highest

Metropolitan Area	Average Annual Earnings	Number Employed
San Diego–Carlsbad–San Marcos, CA	$86,390	820
Salinas, CA	$86,310	100
Waterbury, CT	$83,390	70
Santa Barbara–Santa Maria, CA	$82,710	120
Stockton, CA	$81,780	150

Assess and treat persons with speech, language, voice, and fluency disorders. May select alternative communication systems and teach their use. May perform research related to speech and language problems. Monitor patients' progress and adjust treatments accordingly. Evaluate hearing and speech/language test results and medical or background information to diagnose and plan treatment for speech, language, fluency, voice, and swallowing disorders. Administer hearing or speech and language evaluations, tests, or examinations to patients to collect information on type and degree of impairments, using written and oral tests and special instruments. Record information on the initial evaluation, treatment, progress, and discharge of clients. Develop and implement treatment plans for problems such as stuttering, delayed language, swallowing disorders, and inappropriate pitch or harsh voice problems based on own assessments and recommendations of physicians, psychologists, or social workers. Develop individual or group programs in schools to deal with speech or language problems. Instruct clients in techniques for more effective communication, including sign language, lip reading, and voice improvement. Teach clients to control or strengthen tongue, jaw, face muscles, and breathing mechanisms. Develop speech exercise programs to reduce disabilities. Consult with and advise educators or medical staff on speech or hearing topics, such as communication strategies or speech and language stimulation. Instruct patients and family members in strategies to cope with or avoid communication-related misunderstandings. Design, develop, and employ alternative diagnostic or communication devices and strategies. Conduct lessons and direct educational or therapeutic games to assist teachers dealing with speech problems. Refer clients to additional medical or educational services if needed. Participate in conferences or training or publish research results to share knowledge of new hearing or speech disorder treatment methods or technologies. Communicate with non-speaking students, using sign language or computer technology.

Other Considerations for Income: Some employers reimburse Speech-Language Pathologists for their required continuing education credits.

Personality Type: Social-Investigative-Artistic. **Career Cluster:** 08 Health Science. **Career Pathway:** 08.1 Therapeutic Services. **Skills:** Learning Strategies; Instructing; Social Perceptiveness; Speaking; Monitoring; Service Orientation; Reading Comprehension; Active Learning.

Education and Training Programs: Audiology/Audiologist and Speech-Language Pathology/Pathologist; Communication Disorders Sciences and Services, Other; Communication Disorders, General; Communication Sciences and Disorders, General; Speech-Language Pathology/Pathologist. **Related Knowledge/Courses:** Therapy and Counseling; English Language; Psychology; Sociology and Anthropology; Education and Training; Medicine and Dentistry.

Sports Medicine Physicians

※ Annual Earnings: $166,400+
※ Beginning Wage: $49,710
※ Earnings Growth Potential: Cannot be calculated
※ Growth: 14.2%
※ Annual Job Openings: 38,027
※ Self-Employed: 14.7%
※ Part-Time: 8.1%
※ Job Security: No data available
※ Education/Training Required: First professional degree

The Department of Labor reports this information for the occupation Physicians and Surgeons. The job openings listed here are shared with other specializations within that occupation, including Allergists and Immunologists; Anesthesiologists; Dermatologists; Family and General Practitioners; Hospitalists; Internists, General; Neurologists; Nuclear Medicine Physicians; Obstetricians and Gynecologists; Ophthalmologists; Pathologists; Pediatricians, General; Physical Medicine and Rehabilitation Physicians; Preventive Medicine Physicians; Psychiatrists; Radiologists; Surgeons; and Urologists.

Industries in Which Income Is Highest

Industry	Average Annual Earnings	Number Employed
Ambulatory Health Care Services	$166,400+	147,400
Administrative and Support Services	$166,400+	1,310
Federal, State, and Local Government	$162,300	28,180
Professional, Scientific, and Technical Services	$107,470	1,210
Hospitals	$72,130	72,490

Metropolitan Areas Where Income Is Highest

Metropolitan Area	Average Annual Earnings	Number Employed
Los Angeles–Long Beach–Santa Ana, CA	$166,400+	8,810
Boston-Cambridge-Quincy, MA-NH	$166,400+	6,380
Dallas–Fort Worth–Arlington, TX	$166,400+	4,950
Tampa–St. Petersburg–Clearwater, FL	$166,400+	3,810
Portland-Vancouver-Beaverton, OR-WA	$166,400+	3,180

Diagnose, treat, and help prevent injuries that occur during sporting events, athletic training, and physical activities. No task data available.

Other Considerations for Income: Earnings of physicians and surgeons are among the highest of any occupation. Separate earnings figures for Sports Medicine Physicians are not available.

Personality Type: Investigative-Social-Realistic. **Career Cluster:** 08 Health Science. **Career Pathway:** 08.1 Therapeutic Services. **Skills:** No data available.

Education and Training Program: Orthopedic Sports Medicine Residency Program. **Related Knowledge/ Courses:** No data available.

Stationary Engineers and Boiler Operators

❀ Annual Earnings: $49,790
❀ Beginning Wage: $30,630
❀ Earnings Growth Potential: Medium (38.5%)
❀ Growth: 3.4%
❀ Annual Job Openings: 1,892
❀ Self-Employed: 0.0%
❀ Part-Time: 2.6%
❀ Job Security: Most secure
❀ Education/Training Required: Long-term on-the-job training

Industries in Which Income Is Highest

Industry	Average Annual Earnings	Number Employed
Utilities	$56,570	3,090
Federal, State, and Local Government	$53,300	8,460
Real Estate	$52,580	1,950
Hospitals	$49,860	5,770
Paper Manufacturing	$48,360	2,830

Metropolitan Areas Where Income Is Highest

Metropolitan Area	Average Annual Earnings	Number Employed
Springfield, IL	$74,480	90
Peoria, IL	$73,770	100
San Jose–Sunnyvale–Santa Clara, CA	$70,930	80
Chicago-Naperville-Joliet, IL-IN-WI	$67,880	1,450
Kennewick-Richland-Pasco, WA	$62,030	100

Operate or maintain stationary engines, boilers, or other mechanical equipment to provide utilities for buildings or industrial processes. Operate equipment such as steam engines, generators, motors, turbines, and steam boilers. Operate or tend stationary engines; boilers; and auxiliary equipment such as pumps, compressors and air-conditioning equipment to supply and maintain steam or heat for buildings, marine vessels, or pneumatic tools. Observe and interpret readings on gauges, meters, and charts registering various aspects of boiler operation to ensure that boilers are operating properly. Test boiler water quality or arrange for testing and take any necessary corrective action, such as adding chemicals to prevent corrosion and harmful deposits. Activate valves to maintain required amounts of water in boilers, to adjust supplies of combustion air, and to control the flow of fuel into burners. Monitor boiler water, chemical, and fuel levels and make adjustments to maintain required levels. Fire coal furnaces by hand or with stokers and gas- or oil-fed boilers, using automatic gas feeds or oil pumps. Monitor and inspect equipment, computer terminals, switches, valves, gauges, alarms, safety devices, and meters to detect leaks or malfunctions and to ensure that equipment is operating efficiently and safely. Analyze problems and take appropriate action to ensure continuous and reliable operation of equipment and systems. Maintain daily logs of operation, maintenance, and safety activities, including test results, instrument readings, and details of equipment malfunctions and maintenance work. Adjust controls or valves on equipment to provide power and to regulate and set operations of system or industrial processes. Switch from automatic controls to manual controls and isolate equipment mechanically and electrically to allow for safe inspection and repair work. Clean and lubricate boilers and auxiliary equipment and make minor adjustments as needed, using hand tools. Check the air quality of ventilation systems and make adjustments to ensure compliance with mandated safety codes.

Other Considerations for Income: No additional information.

Personality Type: Realistic-Investigative-Conventional. **Career Cluster:** 13 Manufacturing. **Career Pathway:** 13.3 Maintenance, Installation, and Repair. **Skills:** Repairing; Equipment Maintenance; Operation Monitoring; Installation; Operation and Control; Systems Analysis; Operations Analysis; Troubleshooting.

Education and Training Program: Building/Property Maintenance. **Related Knowledge/Courses:** Mechanical; Building and Construction; Chemistry; Physics; Engineering and Technology; Design.

Statisticians

* Annual Earnings: $72,610
* Beginning Wage: $39,740
* Earnings Growth Potential: High (45.3%)
* Growth: 8.5%
* Annual Job Openings: 3,433
* Self-Employed: 6.0%
* Part-Time: 13.1%
* Job Security: Most secure
* Education/Training Required: Master's degree

Industries in Which Income Is Highest

Industry	Average Annual Earnings	Number Employed
Chemical Manufacturing	$89,980	1,340
Professional, Scientific, and Technical Services	$80,610	4,720
Federal, State, and Local Government	$75,430	6,120
Insurance Carriers and Related Activities	$63,020	2,000
Educational Services	$58,280	1,860

Metropolitan Areas Where Income Is Highest

Metropolitan Area	Average Annual Earnings	Number Employed
Oxnard–Thousand Oaks–Ventura, CA	$92,430	190
San Jose–Sunnyvale–Santa Clara, CA	$92,090	240
Washington-Arlington-Alexandria, DC-VA-MD-WV	$91,950	3,500
San Francisco–Oakland–Fremont, CA	$89,340	540
Chicago-Naperville-Joliet, IL-IN-WI	$86,600	480

Engage in the development of mathematical theory or apply statistical theory and methods to collect, organize, interpret, and summarize numerical data to provide usable information. May specialize in fields such as bio-statistics, agricultural statistics, business statistics, economic statistics, or other fields. Report results of statistical analyses, including information in the form of graphs, charts, and tables. Process large amounts of data for statistical modeling and graphic analysis, using computers. Identify relationships and trends in data, as well as any factors that could affect the results of research. Analyze and interpret statistical data in order to identify significant differences in relationships among sources of information. Prepare data for processing by organizing information, checking for any inaccuracies, and adjusting and weighting the raw data. Evaluate the statistical methods and procedures used to obtain data in order to ensure validity, applicability, efficiency, and accuracy. Evaluate sources of information in order to determine any limitations in terms of reliability or usability. Plan data collection methods for specific projects and determine the types and sizes of sample groups to be used. Design research projects that apply valid scientific techniques and utilize information obtained from baselines or historical data in order to structure uncompromised and efficient analyses. Develop an understanding of fields to which statistical methods are to be applied in order to determine whether methods and results are appropriate. Supervise and provide instructions for workers collecting and tabulating data. Apply sampling techniques or utilize complete enumeration bases in order to determine and define groups to be surveyed. Adapt statistical methods in order to solve specific problems in many fields, such as economics, biology, and engineering. Develop and test experimental designs, sampling techniques, and analytical methods. Examine theories, such as those of probability and inference, in order to discover mathematical bases for new or improved methods of obtaining and evaluating numerical data.

Other Considerations for Income: Some employers offer tuition reimbursement.

Personality Type: Conventional-Investigative. **Career Clusters:** 04 Business, Management, and Administration; 15 Science, Technology, Engineering, and Mathematics. **Career Pathways:** 04.2 Business Financial Management and Accounting; 15.3 Science and Mathematics. **Skills:** Programming; Science; Mathematics; Writing; Active Learning; Negotiation; Complex Problem Solving; Operations Analysis.

Education and Training Programs: Applied Mathematics, General; Biostatistics; Business Statistics; Mathematical Statistics and Probability; Mathematics, General; Statistics, General; Statistics, Other. **Related Knowledge/Courses:** Mathematics; Computers and Electronics; English Language; Law and Government; Education and Training.

Storage and Distribution Managers

❀ Annual Earnings: $79,000
❀ Beginning Wage: $45,320
❀ Earnings Growth Potential: High (42.6%)
❀ Growth: 8.3%
❀ Annual Job Openings: 6,994
❀ Self-Employed: 2.6%
❀ Part-Time: 2.3%
❀ Job Security: More secure than most
❀ Education/Training Required: Work experience in a related occupation

The Department of Labor reports this information for the occupation Transportation, Storage, and Distribution Managers. The job openings listed here are shared with other specializations within that occupation, including Transportation Managers.

Industries in Which Income Is Highest

Industry	Average Annual Earnings	Number Employed
Management of Companies and Enterprises	$93,550	5,620
Computer and Electronic Product Manufacturing	$93,480	1,120
Professional, Scientific, and Technical Services	$89,890	1,870
Couriers and Messengers	$89,380	3,240
Federal, State, and Local Government	$87,570	12,700

Metropolitan Areas Where Income Is Highest

Metropolitan Area	Average Annual Earnings	Number Employed
Olympia, WA	$106,850	60
Niles–Benton Harbor, MI	$99,710	100
Miami–Fort Lauderdale–Miami Beach, FL	$99,050	1,340
Deltona–Daytona Beach–Ormond Beach, FL	$97,400	70
Rochester, NY	$95,940	190

Plan, direct, and coordinate the storage and distribution operations within organizations or the activities of organizations that are engaged in storing and distributing materials and products. Prepare and manage departmental budgets. Supervise the activities of workers engaged in receiving, storing, testing, and shipping products or materials. Interview, select, and train warehouse and supervisory personnel. Plan, develop, and implement warehouse safety and security programs and activities. Prepare or direct preparation of correspondence; reports; and operations, maintenance, and safety manuals. Issue shipping instructions and provide routing information to ensure that delivery times and locations are coordinated. Review invoices, work orders, consumption reports, and demand forecasts to estimate peak delivery periods and to issue work assignments. Confer with department heads to coordinate warehouse activities such as production, sales, records control, and purchasing. Inspect physical conditions of warehouses, vehicle fleets, and equipment and order testing, maintenance, repair, or replacement as necessary. Schedule and monitor air or surface pickup, delivery, or distribution of products or materials. Respond to customers' or shippers' questions and complaints regarding storage and distribution services. Develop and document standard and emergency operating procedures for receiving, handling, storing, shipping, or salvaging products or materials. Develop and implement plans for facility modification or expansion such as equipment purchase or changes in space allocation or structural design. Track and trace goods while they are en route to their destinations, expediting orders when necessary. Negotiate with carriers, warehouse operators, and insurance company representatives for services and preferential rates. Arrange for necessary shipping documentation and contact customs officials to effect release of shipments. Evaluate freight costs and the inventory costs associated with transit times to ensure that costs are appropriate. Advise sales and billing departments of transportation charges for customers' accounts.

Other Considerations for Income: No additional information.

Personality Type: Enterprising-Conventional. **Career Clusters:** 04 Business, Management, and Administration; 07 Government and Public Administration; 16 Transportation, Distribution, and Logistics. **Career Pathways:** 04.1 Management; 07.1 Governance; 16.1 Transportation Operations; 16.2 Logistics, Planning, and Management Services. **Skills:** Management of Financial Resources; Management of Personnel Resources; Management of Material Resources; Systems Analysis; Systems Evaluation; Negotiation.

Education and Training Programs: Aeronautics/Aviation/Aerospace Science and Technology, General; Aviation/Airway Management and Operations; Business Administration and Management, General; Business/Commerce, General; Logistics, Materials, and Supply Chain Management; Public Administration; Transportation/Mobility Management. **Related Knowledge/Courses:** Transportation; Personnel and Human Resources; Production and Processing; Administration and Management; Economics and Accounting; Psychology.

Subway and Streetcar Operators

- ❈ Annual Earnings: $53,220
- ❈ Beginning Wage: $33,140
- ❈ Earnings Growth Potential: Medium (37.7%)
- ❈ Growth: 12.1%
- ❈ Annual Job Openings: 587
- ❈ Self-Employed: 0.0%
- ❈ Part-Time: 0.9%
- ❈ Job Security: Less secure than most
- ❈ Education/Training Required: Moderate-term on-the-job training

Industries in Which Income Is Highest

Industry	Average Annual Earnings	Number Employed
Federal, State, and Local Government	$53,430	7,160
Transit and Ground Passenger Transportation	$52,350	150
Scenic and Sightseeing Transportation	$19,280	50

Metropolitan Areas Where Income Is Highest

Metropolitan Area	Average Annual Earnings	Number Employed

Insufficient data available

Operate subway or elevated suburban train with no separate locomotive or electric-powered streetcar to transport passengers. May handle fares. Operate controls to open and close transit vehicle doors. Drive and control rail-guided public transportation such as subways; elevated trains; and electric-powered streetcars, trams, or trolleys in order to transport passengers. Monitor lights indicating obstructions or other trains ahead and watch for car and truck traffic at crossings to stay alert to potential hazards. Direct emergency evacuation procedures. Regulate vehicle speed and the time spent at each stop in order to maintain schedules. Report delays, mechanical problems, and emergencies to supervisors or dispatchers, using radios. Make announcements to passengers, such as notifications of upcoming stops or schedule delays. Complete reports, including shift summaries and incident or accident reports. Greet passengers; provide information; and answer questions concerning fares, schedules, transfers, and routings. Attend meetings on driver and passenger safety in order to learn ways in which job performance might be affected. Collect fares from passengers and issue change and transfers. Record transactions and coin receptor readings in order to verify the amount of money collected.

Other Considerations for Income: Most railroad transportation workers are paid according to miles traveled or hours worked, whichever leads to higher earnings. Factors such as seniority, job assignments, and location impact potential earnings. Seventy-four percent of railroad transportation workers are members of unions compared to 12 percent for all occupations. Many subway operators are members of the Amalgamated Transit Union, while others belong to the Transport Workers Union of North America.

Personality Type: Realistic-Conventional. **Career Cluster:** 16 Transportation, Distribution, and Logistics. **Career Pathway:** 16.1 Transportation Operations. **Skills:** Operation and Control; Operation Monitoring; Troubleshooting; Active Listening; Service Orientation.

Education and Training Program: Truck and Bus Driver/Commercial Vehicle Operator and Instructor. **Related Knowledge/Courses:** Transportation; Public Safety and Security; Customer and Personal Service; Telecommunications; Mechanical; Communications and Media.

Surgeons

* Annual Earnings: $166,400+
* Beginning Wage: $117,060
* Earnings Growth Potential: Cannot be calculated
* Growth: 14.2%
* Annual Job Openings: 38,027
* Self-Employed: 14.7%
* Part-Time: 8.1%
* Job Security: Most secure
* Education/Training Required: First professional degree

The Department of Labor reports this information for the occupation Physicians and Surgeons. The job openings listed here are shared with other specializations within that occupation, including Allergists and Immunologists; Anesthesiologists; Dermatologists; Family and General Practitioners; Hospitalists; Internists, General; Neurologists; Nuclear Medicine Physicians; Obstetricians and Gynecologists; Ophthalmologists; Pathologists; Pediatricians, General; Physical Medicine and Rehabilitation Physicians; Preventive Medicine Physicians; Psychiatrists; Radiologists; Sports Medicine Physicians; and Urologists.

Industries in Which Income Is Highest

Industry	Average Annual Earnings	Number Employed
Ambulatory Health Care Services	$166,400+	39,190
Hospitals	$166,400+	6,100
Educational Services	$166,400+	1,440

Metropolitan Areas Where Income Is Highest

Metropolitan Area	Average Annual Earnings	Number Employed
New York–Northern New Jersey–Long Island, NY-NJ-PA	$166,400+	2,370
Chicago-Naperville-Joliet, IL-IN-WI	$166,400+	2,150
Los Angeles–Long Beach–Santa Ana, CA	$166,400+	1,730
Philadelphia-Camden-Wilmington, PA-NJ-DE-MD	$166,400+	1,590
Boston-Cambridge-Quincy, MA-NH	$166,400+	1,540

Treat diseases, injuries, and deformities by invasive methods, such as manual manipulation, or by using instruments and appliances. Analyze patient's medical history, medication allergies, physical condition, and examination results to verify operation's necessity and to determine best procedure. Operate on patients to correct deformities, repair injuries, prevent and treat diseases, or improve or restore patients' functions. Follow established surgical techniques during the operation. Prescribe preoperative and postoperative treatments and procedures, such as sedatives, diets, antibiotics, and preparation and treatment of the patient's operative area. Examine patient to provide information on medical condition and surgical risk. Diagnose bodily disorders and orthopedic conditions and provide treatments, such as medicines and surgeries, in clinics, hospital wards, and operating rooms. Direct and coordinate activities of nurses, assistants, specialists, residents, and other medical staff. Provide consultation and surgical assistance to other physicians and surgeons. Refer patient to medical specialist or other practitioners when necessary. Examine instruments, equipment, and operating room to ensure sterility. Prepare case histories. Manage surgery services, including planning, scheduling and coordination, determination of procedures, and procurement of supplies and equipment. Conduct research to develop and test surgical techniques that can improve operating procedures and outcomes.

Other Considerations for Income: Earnings of physicians and surgeons are among the highest of any occupation, and Surgeons are among the best-paid medical specialists. The Medical Group Management Association's Physician Compensation and Production Survey of 2005 reported earnings of $228,839 for Surgeons with less than two years in their specialty and $282,504 for those with more than one year in their specialty. These figures cover salary, bonus and incentive payments, research stipends, honoraria, and distribution of profits. Self-employed physicians—those who own or are part owners of their medical practice—generally have higher median incomes than salaried physicians, but their must provide for their own health insurance and retirement.

Personality Type: Investigative-Realistic-Social. **Career Cluster:** 08 Health Science. **Career Pathway:** 08.1 Therapeutic Services. **Skills:** Science; Reading Comprehension; Judgment and Decision Making; Complex Problem Solving; Management of Financial Resources; Critical Thinking; Equipment Selection; Technology Design.

Education and Training Program: Medicine (MD). **Related Knowledge/Courses:** Medicine and Dentistry;

Biology; Therapy and Counseling; Psychology; Chemistry; Customer and Personal Service.

Surveyors

- ❉ Annual Earnings: $52,980
- ❉ Beginning Wage: $29,600
- ❉ Earnings Growth Potential: High (44.1%)
- ❉ Growth: 23.7%
- ❉ Annual Job Openings: 14,305
- ❉ Self-Employed: 3.7%
- ❉ Part-Time: 4.6%
- ❉ Job Security: Less secure than most
- ❉ Education/Training Required: Bachelor's degree

Industries in Which Income Is Highest

Industry	Average Annual Earnings	Number Employed
Federal, State, and Local Government	$61,320	5,460
Construction of Buildings	$55,000	1,130
Professional, Scientific, and Technical Services	$52,030	44,470
Heavy and Civil Engineering Construction	$51,480	2,280

Metropolitan Areas Where Income Is Highest

Metropolitan Area	Average Annual Earnings	Number Employed
Santa Barbara–Santa Maria, CA	$97,710	90
Yuba City, CA	$82,070	90
Anchorage, AK	$80,620	350
Los Angeles–Long Beach–Santa Ana, CA	$76,720	2,030
Stockton, CA	$76,200	80

Make exact measurements and determine property boundaries. Provide data relevant to the shape, contour, gravitation, location, elevation, or dimension of land or land features on or near Earth's surface for engineering, mapmaking, mining, land evaluation, construction, and other purposes. Verify the accuracy of survey data including measurements and calculations conducted at survey sites. Calculate heights, depths, relative positions, property lines, and other characteristics of terrain. Search legal records, survey records, and land titles to obtain information about property boundaries in areas to be surveyed. Prepare and maintain sketches, maps, reports, and legal descriptions of surveys to describe, certify, and assume liability for work performed. Direct or conduct surveys to establish legal boundaries for properties, based on legal deeds and titles. Prepare or supervise preparation of all data, charts, plots, maps, records, and documents related to surveys. Write descriptions of property boundary surveys for use in deeds, leases, or other legal documents. Compute geodetic measurements and interpret survey data to determine positions, shapes, and elevations of geomorphic and topographic features. Determine longitudes and latitudes of important features and boundaries in survey areas using theodolites, transits, levels, and satellite-based global positioning systems (GPS). Record the results of surveys including the shape, contour, location, elevation, and dimensions of land or land features. Coordinate findings with the work of engineering and architectural personnel, clients, and others concerned with projects. Establish fixed points for use in making maps, using geodetic and engineering instruments. Train assistants and helpers, and direct their work in such activities as performing surveys or drafting maps. Plan and conduct ground surveys designed to establish baselines, elevations, and other geodetic measurements. Adjust surveying instruments to maintain their accuracy. Analyze survey objectives and specifications to prepare survey proposals or to direct others in survey proposal preparation. Develop criteria for survey methods and procedures.

Other Considerations for Income: No additional information.

Personality Type: Realistic-Conventional-Investigative. **Career Cluster:** 02 Architecture and Construction. **Career Pathway:** 02.1 Design/Pre-Construction. **Skills:** Management of Personnel Resources; Operation Monitoring; Quality Control Analysis; Systems Evaluation; Systems Analysis; Mathematics; Operation and Control.

Education and Training Program: Surveying Technology/Surveying. **Related Knowledge/Courses:** Geography; Design; Building and Construction; History and Archeology; Engineering and Technology; Mathematics.

Talent Directors

- ❀ Annual Earnings: $64,430
- ❀ Beginning Wage: $30,250
- ❀ Earnings Growth Potential: Very high (53.0%)
- ❀ Growth: 11.1%
- ❀ Annual Job Openings: 8,992
- ❀ Self-Employed: 29.5%
- ❀ Part-Time: 9.0%
- ❀ Job Security: More secure than most
- ❀ Education/Training Required: Long-term on-the-job training

The Department of Labor reports this information for the occupation Producers and Directors. The job openings listed here are shared with other specializations within that occupation, including Directors—Stage, Motion Pictures, Television, and Radio; Producers; Program Directors; and Technical Directors/Managers.

Industries in Which Income Is Highest

Industry	Average Annual Earnings	Number Employed
Professional, Scientific, and Technical Services	$87,270	6,370
Motion Picture and Sound Recording Industries	$85,900	24,890
Publishing Industries (Except Internet)	$68,350	1,170
Federal, State, and Local Government	$62,950	1,860
Broadcasting (Except Internet)	$58,340	27,400

Metropolitan Areas Where Income Is Highest

Metropolitan Area	Average Annual Earnings	Number Employed
Oxnard–Thousand Oaks–Ventura, CA	$104,940	190
Los Angeles–Long Beach–Santa Ana, CA	$103,490	15,150
New York–Northern New Jersey–Long Island, NY-NJ-PA	$97,940	13,430
San Francisco–Oakland–Fremont, CA	$79,300	1,500
Washington-Arlington-Alexandria, DC-VA-MD-WV	$74,730	2,620

Audition and interview performers to select most appropriate talent for parts in stage, television, radio, or motion picture productions. Review performer information such as photos, resumes, voice tapes, videos, and union membership in order to decide whom to audition for parts. Read scripts and confer with producers in order to determine the types and numbers of performers required for a given production. Select performers for roles or submit lists of suitable performers to producers or directors for final selection. Audition and interview performers in order to match their attributes to specific roles or to increase the pool of available acting talent. Maintain talent files that include information such as performers' specialties, past performances, and availability. Prepare actors for auditions by providing scripts and information about roles and casting requirements. Serve as liaisons between directors, actors, and agents. Attend or view productions in order to maintain knowledge of available actors. Negotiate contract agreements with performers, with agents, or between performers and agents or production companies. Contact agents and actors in order to provide notification of audition and performance opportunities and to set up audition times. Hire and supervise workers who help locate people with specified attributes and talents. Arrange for and/or design screen tests or auditions for prospective performers. Locate performers or extras for crowd and background scenes and stand-ins or photo doubles for actors by direct contact or through agents.

Other Considerations for Income: The most successful producers and directors may have extraordinarily high earnings but for others, because earnings may be erratic, many supplement their income by holding jobs in other fields.

Personality Type: Enterprising-Artistic. **Career Cluster:** 03 Arts, Audio/Video Technology, and Communications. **Career Pathways:** 03.4 Performing Arts; 03.5 Journalism and Broadcasting. **Skills:** Management of Financial Resources; Management of Personnel Resources; Persuasion; Social Perceptiveness; Negotiation; Judgment and Decision Making; Time Management; Management of Material Resources.

Education and Training Programs: Cinematography and Film/Video Production; Directing and Theatrical Production; Drama and Dramatics/Theatre Arts, General; Dramatic/Theatre Arts and Stagecraft, Other; Film/Cinema/Video Studies; Radio and Television. **Related Knowledge/Courses:** Fine Arts; Communications and Media; Clerical; Computers and Electronics; Sales and Marketing; Telecommunications.

Tax Examiners, Collectors, and Revenue Agents

❋ Annual Earnings: $48,100
❋ Beginning Wage: $28,390
❋ Earnings Growth Potential: High (41.0%)
❋ Growth: 2.1%
❋ Annual Job Openings: 4,465
❋ Self-Employed: 0.0%
❋ Part-Time: 3.9%
❋ Job Security: Most secure
❋ Education/Training Required: Bachelor's degree

Industries in Which Income Is Highest

Industry	Average Annual Earnings	Number Employed
Federal, State, and Local Government	$48,100	66,030

Metropolitan Areas Where Income Is Highest

Metropolitan Area	Average Annual Earnings	Number Employed
Bridgeport-Stamford-Norwalk, CT	$82,200	200
New Haven, CT	$75,710	120
Milwaukee–Waukesha–West Allis, WI	$72,840	210
Grand Rapids–Wyoming, MI	$72,780	80
Hartford–West Hartford–East Hartford, CT	$72,750	670

Determine tax liability or collect taxes from individuals or business firms according to prescribed laws and regulations. Collect taxes from individuals or businesses according to prescribed laws and regulations. Maintain knowledge of tax code changes and of accounting procedures and theory to properly evaluate financial information. Maintain records for each case, including contacts, telephone numbers, and actions taken. Confer with taxpayers or their representatives to discuss the issues, laws, and regulations involved in returns and to resolve problems with returns. Contact taxpayers by mail or telephone to address discrepancies and to request supporting documentation. Send notices to taxpayers when accounts are delinquent. Notify taxpayers of any overpayment or underpayment and either issue a refund or request further payment. Conduct independent field audits and investigations of income tax returns to verify information or to amend tax liabilities. Review filed tax returns to determine whether claimed tax credits and deductions are allowed by law. Review selected tax returns to determine the nature and extent of audits to be performed on them. Enter tax return information into computers for processing. Examine accounting systems and records to determine whether accounting methods used were appropriate and in compliance with statutory provisions. Process individual and corporate income tax returns and sales and excise tax returns. Impose payment deadlines on delinquent taxpayers and monitor payments to ensure that deadlines are met. Check tax forms to verify that names and taxpayer identification numbers are correct, that computations have been performed correctly, or that amounts match those on supporting documentation. Examine and analyze tax assets and liabilities to determine resolution of delinquent tax problems. Recommend criminal prosecutions or civil penalties. Determine appropriate methods of debt settlement, such as offers of compromise, wage garnishment, or seizure and sale of property.

Other Considerations for Income: IRS employees receive family, vacation, and sick leave. Full-time permanent IRS employees are offered tax deferred retirement savings and investment plans with employer matching contributions, health insurance, and life insurance.

Personality Type: Conventional-Enterprising. **Career Cluster:** 07 Government and Public Administration. **Career Pathway:** 07.5 Revenue and Taxation. **Skills:** Service Orientation; Mathematics; Speaking; Active Learning; Complex Problem Solving; Instructing; Operations Analysis; Active Listening.

Education and Training Programs: Accounting; Taxation. **Related Knowledge/Courses:** Law and Government; Customer and Personal Service; Economics and Accounting; Computers and Electronics; Clerical; Mathematics.

T

Technical Directors/Managers

- ❋ Annual Earnings: $64,430
- ❋ Beginning Wage: $30,250
- ❋ Earnings Growth Potential: Very high (53.0%)
- ❋ Growth: 11.1%
- ❋ Annual Job Openings: 8,992
- ❋ Self-Employed: 29.5%
- ❋ Part-Time: 9.0%
- ❋ Job Security: More secure than most
- ❋ Education/Training Required: Long-term on-the-job training

The Department of Labor reports this information for the occupation Producers and Directors. The job openings listed here are shared with other specializations within that occupation, including Directors—Stage, Motion Pictures, Television, and Radio; Producers; Program Directors; and Talent Directors.

Industries in Which Income Is Highest

Industry	Average Annual Earnings	Number Employed
Professional, Scientific, and Technical Services	$87,270	6,370
Motion Picture and Sound Recording Industries	$85,900	24,890
Publishing Industries (Except Internet)	$68,350	1,170
Federal, State, and Local Government	$62,950	1,860
Broadcasting (Except Internet)	$58,340	27,400

Metropolitan Areas Where Income Is Highest

Metropolitan Area	Average Annual Earnings	Number Employed
Oxnard–Thousand Oaks–Ventura, CA	$104,940	190
Los Angeles–Long Beach–Santa Ana, CA	$103,490	15,150
New York–Northern New Jersey–Long Island, NY-NJ-PA	$97,940	13,430
San Francisco–Oakland–Fremont, CA	$79,300	1,500
Washington-Arlington-Alexandria, DC-VA-MD-WV	$74,730	2,620

Coordinate activities of technical departments, such as taping, editing, engineering, and maintenance, to produce radio or television programs. Direct technical aspects of newscasts and other productions, checking and switching between video sources and taking responsibility for the on-air product, including camera shots and graphics. Test equipment to ensure proper operation. Monitor broadcasts to ensure that programs conform to station or network policies and regulations. Observe pictures through monitors and direct camera and video staff concerning shading and composition. Act as liaisons between engineering and production departments. Supervise and assign duties to workers engaged in technical control and production of radio and television programs. Schedule use of studio and editing facilities for producers and engineering and maintenance staff. Confer with operations directors to formulate and maintain fair and attainable technical policies for programs. Operate equipment to produce programs or broadcast live programs from remote locations. Train workers in use of equipment such as switchers, cameras, monitors, microphones, and lights. Switch between video sources in a studio or on multi-camera remotes, using equipment such as switchers, video slide projectors, and video effects generators. Set up and execute video transitions and special effects such as fades, dissolves, cuts, keys, and supers, using computers to manipulate pictures as necessary. Collaborate with promotions directors to produce on-air station promotions. Discuss filter options, lens choices, and the visual effects of objects being filmed with photography directors and video operators. Follow instructions from production managers and directors during productions, such as commands for camera cuts, effects, graphics, and takes.

Other Considerations for Income: The most successful producers and directors may have extraordinarily high earnings but for others, because earnings may be erratic, many supplement their income by holding jobs in other fields.

Personality Type: Enterprising-Realistic-Conventional. **Career Cluster:** 03 Arts, Audio/Video Technology, and Communications. **Career Pathways:** 03.1 Audio and Video Technology and Film; 03.4 Performing Arts; 03.5 Journalism and Broadcasting. **Skills:** Operation and Control; Operation Monitoring; Monitoring; Systems Analysis; Equipment Selection; Installation; Troubleshooting; Time Management.

Education and Training Programs: Cinematography and Film/Video Production; Directing and Theatrical Production; Drama and Dramatics/Theatre Arts, General; Dramatic/Theatre Arts and Stagecraft, Other; Film/Cinema/Video Studies; Radio and Television. **Related**

Knowledge/Courses: Communications and Media; Telecommunications; Computers and Electronics; Philosophy and Theology; Engineering and Technology; Sales and Marketing.

Technical Writers

❀ Annual Earnings: $61,620
❀ Beginning Wage: $36,500
❀ Earnings Growth Potential: High (40.8%)
❀ Growth: 19.5%
❀ Annual Job Openings: 7,498
❀ Self-Employed: 6.0%
❀ Part-Time: 6.5%
❀ Job Security: More secure than most
❀ Education/Training Required: Bachelor's degree

Industries in Which Income Is Highest

Industry	Average Annual Earnings	Number Employed
Computer and Electronic Product Manufacturing	$66,600	4,030
Federal, State, and Local Government	$65,360	1,330
Transportation Equipment Manufacturing	$63,850	1,910
Publishing Industries (Except Internet)	$63,440	5,140
Professional, Scientific, and Technical Services	$62,510	18,520

Metropolitan Areas Where Income Is Highest

Metropolitan Area	Average Annual Earnings	Number Employed
San Jose–Sunnyvale–Santa Clara, CA	$91,170	1,350
Boston-Cambridge-Quincy, MA-NH	$81,380	2,270
San Francisco–Oakland–Fremont, CA	$80,940	1,160
Oxnard–Thousand Oaks–Ventura, CA	$80,730	230
Seattle-Tacoma-Bellevue, WA	$78,610	1,350

Write technical materials, such as equipment manuals, appendices, or operating and maintenance instructions. May assist in layout work. Organize material and complete writing assignment according to set standards regarding order, clarity, conciseness, style, and terminology. Maintain records and files of work and revisions. Edit, standardize, or make changes to material prepared by other writers or establishment personnel. Confer with customer representatives, vendors, plant executives, or publisher to establish technical specifications and to determine subject material to be developed for publication. Review published materials and recommend revisions or changes in scope, format, content, and methods of reproduction and binding. Select photographs, drawings, sketches, diagrams, and charts to illustrate material. Study drawings, specifications, mockups, and product samples to integrate and delineate technology, operating procedure, and production sequence and detail. Interview production and engineering personnel and read journals and other material to become familiar with product technologies and production methods. Observe production, developmental, and experimental activities to determine operating procedure and detail. Arrange for typing, duplication, and distribution of material. Assist in laying out material for publication. Analyze developments in specific field to determine need for revisions in previously published materials and development of new material. Review manufacturer's and trade catalogs, drawings, and other data relative to operation, maintenance, and service of equipment. Draw sketches to illustrate specified materials or assembly sequence.

Other Considerations for Income: According to the Society for Technical Communication, the median annual salary for entry-level technical writers was $40,400 in 2005. The median annual salary for midlevel nonsupervisory technical writers was $52,140, and for senior nonsupervisory technical writers, $69,000.

Personality Type: Artistic-Investigative-Conventional. **Career Clusters:** 03 Arts, Audio/Video Technology, and Communications; 04 Business, Management, and Administration. **Career Pathways:** 03.5 Journalism and Broadcasting; 04.5 Marketing. **Skills:** Writing; Technology Design; Quality Control Analysis; Active Listening; Operations Analysis; Reading Comprehension; Coordination; Active Learning.

Education and Training Programs: Business/Corporate Communications; Speech Communication and Rhetoric. **Related Knowledge/Courses:** Communications and Media; Clerical; English Language; Computers and Electronics; Education and Training; Engineering and Technology.

Telecommunications Equipment Installers and Repairers, Except Line Installers

❋ Annual Earnings: $55,600
❋ Beginning Wage: $31,330
❋ Earnings Growth Potential: High (43.7%)
❋ Growth: 2.5%
❋ Annual Job Openings: 13,541
❋ Self-Employed: 4.1%
❋ Part-Time: 3.1%
❋ Job Security: More secure than most
❋ Education/Training Required: Postsecondary vocational training

Industries in Which Income Is Highest

Industry	Average Annual Earnings	Number Employed
Management of Companies and Enterprises	$57,990	2,900
Telecommunications	$57,400	134,040
Broadcasting (Except Internet)	$55,010	6,470
Professional, Scientific, and Technical Services	$54,350	5,280
Federal, State, and Local Government	$52,740	3,070

Metropolitan Areas Where Income Is Highest

Metropolitan Area	Average Annual Earnings	Number Employed
Albany-Schenectady-Troy, NY	$72,740	630
Binghamton, NY	$70,510	80
Fairbanks, AK	$67,550	90
New York–Northern New Jersey–Long Island, NY-NJ-PA	$65,170	13,770
Cheyenne, WY	$64,030	80

Set up, rearrange, or remove switching and dialing equipment used in central offices. Service or repair telephones and other communication equipment on customers' properties. May install equipment in new locations or install wiring and telephone jacks in buildings under construction. Note differences in wire and cable colors so that work can be performed correctly. Test circuits and components of malfunctioning telecommunications equipment to isolate sources of malfunctions, using test meters, circuit diagrams, polarity probes, and other hand tools. Test repaired, newly installed, or updated equipment to ensure that it functions properly and conforms to specifications, using test equipment and observation. Drive crew trucks to and from work areas. Inspect equipment on a regular basis to ensure proper functioning. Repair or replace faulty equipment such as defective and damaged telephones, wires, switching system components, and associated equipment. Remove and remake connections to change circuit layouts, following work orders or diagrams. Demonstrate equipment to customers, explain how it is to be used, and respond to any inquiries or complaints. Analyze test readings, computer printouts, and trouble reports to determine equipment repair needs and required repair methods. Adjust or modify equipment to enhance equipment performance or to respond to customer requests. Remove loose wires and other debris after work is completed. Request support from technical service centers when on-site procedures fail to solve installation or maintenance problems. Communicate with bases, using telephones or two-way radios, to receive instructions or technical advice or to report equipment status. Assemble and install communication equipment such as data and telephone communication lines, wiring, switching equipment, wiring frames, power apparatus, computer systems, and networks. Collaborate with other workers to locate and correct malfunctions. Review manufacturers' instructions, manuals, technical specifications, building permits, and ordinances to determine communication equipment requirements and procedures. Test connections to ensure that power supplies are adequate and that communications links function.

Other Considerations for Income: Telecommunications equipment installers and repairers employed by large telecommunications companies who also belong to unions often have very good benefits, including health, dental, vision, and life insurance. They also usually have good retirement and leave policies. Those working for small independent companies and contractors may get fewer benefits.

Personality Type: Realistic-Investigative-Conventional. **Career Cluster:** 03 Arts, Audio/Video Technology, and Communications. **Career Pathway:** 03.6 Telecommunications. **Skills:** Installation; Repairing; Troubleshooting; Technology Design; Equipment Selection; Systems Analysis; Quality Control Analysis; Equipment Maintenance.

Education and Training Program: Communications Systems Installation and Repair Technology. **Related Knowledge/Courses:** Telecommunications; Mechanical; Computers and Electronics; Engineering and Technology; Design; Public Safety and Security.

Telecommunications Line Installers and Repairers

- ❈ Annual Earnings: $48,090
- ❈ Beginning Wage: $25,790
- ❈ Earnings Growth Potential: High (46.4%)
- ❈ Growth: 4.6%
- ❈ Annual Job Openings: 14,719
- ❈ Self-Employed: 3.3%
- ❈ Part-Time: 1.9%
- ❈ Job Security: More secure than most
- ❈ Education/Training Required: Long-term on-the-job training

Industries in Which Income Is Highest

Industry	Average Annual Earnings	Number Employed
Telecommunications	$55,220	98,210
Professional, Scientific, and Technical Services	$50,080	4,520
Broadcasting (Except Internet)	$39,880	11,140
Specialty Trade Contractors	$37,710	29,230
Heavy and Civil Engineering Construction	$34,590	16,720

Metropolitan Areas Where Income Is Highest

Metropolitan Area	Average Annual Earnings	Number Employed
Glens Falls, NY	$75,040	140
Anchorage, AK	$65,660	250
New York–Northern New Jersey–Long Island, NY-NJ-PA	$64,950	17,130
Buffalo–Niagara Falls, NY	$64,450	360
Albany-Schenectady-Troy, NY	$61,720	620

String and repair telephone and television cable, including fiber optics and other equipment for transmitting messages or television programming. Travel to customers' premises to install, maintain, and repair audio and visual electronic reception equipment and accessories. Inspect and test lines and cables, recording and analyzing test results to assess transmission characteristics and locate faults and malfunctions. Splice cables, using hand tools, epoxy, or mechanical equipment. Measure signal strength at utility poles, using electronic test equipment. Set up service for customers, installing, connecting, testing, and adjusting equipment. Place insulation over conductors and seal splices with moisture-proof covering. Access specific areas to string lines and install terminal boxes, auxiliary equipment, and appliances, using bucket trucks or by climbing poles and ladders or entering tunnels, trenches, or crawl spaces. String cables between structures and lines from poles, towers, or trenches and pull lines to proper tension. Install equipment such as amplifiers and repeaters to maintain the strength of communications transmissions. Lay underground cable directly in trenches or string it through conduits running through trenches. Pull up cable by hand from large reels mounted on trucks; then pull lines through ducts by hand or with winches. Clean and maintain tools and test equipment. Explain cable service to subscribers after installation and collect any installation fees that are due. Compute impedance of wires from poles to houses to determine additional resistance needed for reducing signals to desired levels. Use a variety of construction equipment to complete installations, including digger derricks, trenchers, and cable plows. Dig trenches for underground wires and cables. Dig holes for power poles, using power augers or shovels; set poles in place with cranes; and hoist poles upright, using winches. Fill and tamp holes, using cement, earth, and tamping devices. Participate in the construction and removal of telecommunication towers and associated support structures.

Other Considerations for Income: Earnings for line installers and repairers are higher than those in most other occupations that do not require postsecondary education. Many line installers and repairers belong to unions, principally the Communications Workers of America, the International Brotherhood of Electrical Workers, and the Utility Workers Union of America. For these workers, union contracts set wage rates, wage increases, and the time needed to advance from one job level to the next. Good health, education, and vacation benefits are common in the occupation.

Personality Type: Realistic-Enterprising. **Career Cluster:** 13 Manufacturing. **Career Pathway:** 13.3 Maintenance,

Installation and Repair. **Skills:** Installation; Troubleshooting; Repairing; Equipment Maintenance; Programming; Technology Design; Quality Control Analysis; Equipment Selection.

Education and Training Program: Communications Systems Installation and Repair Technology. **Related Knowledge/Courses:** Telecommunications; Engineering and Technology; Building and Construction; Customer and Personal Service; Design; Transportation.

Telecommunications Specialists

* Annual Earnings: $71,100
* Beginning Wage: $41,660
* Earnings Growth Potential: High (41.4%)
* Growth: 53.4%
* Annual Job Openings: 35,086
* Self-Employed: 17.5%
* Part-Time: 8.6%
* Job Security: No data available
* Education/Training Required: Bachelor's degree

The Department of Labor reports this information for the occupation Network Systems and Data Communications Analysts. The job openings listed here are shared with other specializations within that occupation.

Industries in Which Income Is Highest

Industry	Average Annual Earnings	Number Employed
Securities, Commodity Contracts, and Other Financial Investments and Related Activities	$83,780	4,540
Transportation Equipment Manufacturing	$81,960	1,260
Computer and Electronic Product Manufacturing	$78,230	4,590
Utilities	$76,970	1,460
Telecommunications	$75,870	30,630

Metropolitan Areas Where Income Is Highest

Metropolitan Area	Average Annual Earnings	Number Employed
San Jose–Sunnyvale–Santa Clara, CA	$95,390	3,480
Seattle-Tacoma-Bellevue, WA	$83,240	5,890
New York–Northern New Jersey–Long Island, NY-NJ-PA	$82,810	21,360
Washington-Arlington-Alexandria, DC-VA-MD-WV	$82,750	16,110
San Francisco–Oakland–Fremont, CA	$82,530	6,020

Design or configure voice and data communications systems, supervise installation, and arrange for post-installation service and maintenance. No task data available.

Other Considerations for Income: Telecommunications Specialists are paid less well than most other computer specialists.

Personality Type: No data available. **Career Cluster:** 11 Information Technology. **Career Pathway:** 11.4 Programming and Software Development. **Skills:** No data available.

Education and Training Programs: Computer and Information Sciences, General; Computer and Information Systems Security/Information Assurance; Computer Systems Analysis/Analyst; Computer Systems Networking and Telecommunications; Information Technology. **Related Knowledge/Courses:** No data available.

Training and Development Managers

* Annual Earnings: $87,700
* Beginning Wage: $48,280
* Earnings Growth Potential: High (44.9%)
* Growth: 15.6%
* Annual Job Openings: 3,759
* Self-Employed: 1.6%
* Part-Time: 2.7%
* Job Security: More secure than most
* Education/Training Required: Work experience plus degree

Industries in Which Income Is Highest

Industry	Average Annual Earnings	Number Employed
Professional, Scientific, and Technical Services	$97,680	2,630
Management of Companies and Enterprises	$93,140	4,930
Insurance Carriers and Related Activities	$91,950	1,830
Hospitals	$86,370	1,540
Credit Intermediation and Related Activities	$85,240	1,990

Metropolitan Areas Where Income Is Highest

Metropolitan Area	Average Annual Earnings	Number Employed
Durham, NC	$120,140	160
New York–Northern New Jersey–Long Island, NY-NJ-PA	$119,730	3,140
Worcester, MA-CT	$115,540	70
San Jose–Sunnyvale–Santa Clara, CA	$112,400	240
San Francisco–Oakland–Fremont, CA	$111,800	500

Plan, direct, or coordinate the training and development activities and staff of organizations. Prepare training budgets for departments or organizations. Evaluate instructor performances and the effectiveness of training programs, providing recommendations for improvements. Analyze training needs to develop new training programs or modify and improve existing programs. Conduct or arrange for ongoing technical training and personal development classes for staff members. Plan, develop, and provide training and staff development programs, using knowledge of the effectiveness of methods such as classroom training, demonstrations, on-the-job training, meetings, conferences, and workshops. Conduct orientation sessions and arrange on-the-job training for new hires. Confer with management and conduct surveys to identify training needs based on projected production processes, changes, and other factors. Train instructors and supervisors in techniques and skills for training and dealing with employees. Develop and organize training manuals, multimedia visual aids, and other educational materials. Develop testing and evaluation procedures. Review and evaluate training and apprenticeship programs for compliance with government standards. Coordinate established

courses with technical and professional courses provided by community schools and designate training procedures.

Other Considerations for Income: Training and Development Managers are in the middle range of earners among human resource managers. According to a July 2007 salary survey conducted by the National Association of Colleges and Employers, bachelor's degree candidates majoring in human resources, including labor and industrial relations, received starting offers averaging $41,680 a year.

Personality Type: Enterprising-Social. **Career Cluster:** 04 Business, Management, and Administration. **Career Pathway:** 04.3 Human Resources. **Skills:** Management of Financial Resources; Management of Personnel Resources; Systems Evaluation; Systems Analysis; Learning Strategies; Persuasion; Speaking; Management of Material Resources.

Education and Training Programs: Human Resources Development; Human Resources Management/Personnel Administration, General. **Related Knowledge/Courses:** Education and Training; Personnel and Human Resources; Sociology and Anthropology; Sales and Marketing; Therapy and Counseling; English Language.

Training and Development Specialists

- ❀ Annual Earnings: $51,450
- ❀ Beginning Wage: $29,470
- ❀ Earnings Growth Potential: High (42.7%)
- ❀ Growth: 18.3%
- ❀ Annual Job Openings: 35,862
- ❀ Self-Employed: 2.3%
- ❀ Part-Time: 7.6%
- ❀ Job Security: More secure than most
- ❀ Education/Training Required: Work experience plus degree

Industries in Which Income Is Highest

Industry	Average Annual Earnings	Number Employed
Utilities	$74,400	3,130
Computer and Electronic Product Manufacturing	$63,630	3,000
Publishing Industries (Except Internet)	$61,920	2,640
Transportation Equipment Manufacturing	$60,740	1,840
Telecommunications	$60,060	4,700

Metropolitan Areas Where Income Is Highest

Metropolitan Area	Average Annual Earnings	Number Employed
San Luis Obispo–Paso Robles, CA	$87,570	100
Kennewick-Richland-Pasco, WA	$75,500	130
San Francisco–Oakland–Fremont, CA	$72,930	2,950
Champaign-Urbana, IL	$71,680	160
San Jose–Sunnyvale–Santa Clara, CA	$71,420	1,410

Conduct training and development programs for employees. Monitor, evaluate, and record training activities and program effectiveness. Offer specific training programs to help workers maintain or improve job skills. Assess training needs through surveys; interviews with employees; focus groups; or consultation with managers, instructors, or customer representatives. Develop alternative training methods if expected improvements are not seen. Organize and develop, or obtain, training procedure manuals and guides and course materials such as handouts and visual materials. Present information, using a variety of instructional techniques and formats such as role playing, simulations, team exercises, group discussions, videos, and lectures. Evaluate training materials prepared by instructors, such as outlines, text, and handouts. Design, plan, organize, and direct orientation and training for employees or customers of industrial or commercial establishments. Monitor training costs to ensure budget is not exceeded and prepare budget reports to justify expenditures. Select and assign instructors to conduct training. Schedule classes based on availability of classrooms, equipment, and instructors. Keep up with developments in their individual areas of expertise by reading current journals, books, and magazine articles. Supervise instructors, evaluate instructor performances, and refer instructors to classes for skill development. Coordinate recruitment and placement of training program participants. Attend meetings and seminars to obtain information for use in training programs or to inform management of training program statuses. Negotiate contracts with clients, including desired training outcomes, fees, and expenses. Devise programs to develop executive potential among employees in lower-level positions. Screen, hire, and assign workers to positions based on qualifications.

Other Considerations for Income: Training and Development Specialists are in the middle range of earners among human resource specialists. According to a July 2007 salary survey conducted by the National Association of Colleges and Employers, bachelor's degree candidates majoring in human resources, including labor and industrial relations, received starting offers averaging $41,680 a year.

Personality Type: Social-Artistic-Conventional. **Career Cluster:** 04 Business, Management, and Administration. **Career Pathway:** 04.3 Human Resources. **Skills:** Systems Evaluation; Systems Analysis; Learning Strategies; Management of Personnel Resources; Writing; Negotiation; Instructing.

Education and Training Programs: Human Resources Management/Personnel Administration, General; Organizational Behavior Studies. **Related Knowledge/Courses:** Education and Training; Sociology and Anthropology; Sales and Marketing; Clerical; Personnel and Human Resources; Psychology.

Transportation Engineers

* Annual Earnings: $74,600
* Beginning Wage: $48,140
* Earnings Growth Potential: Medium (35.5%)
* Growth: 18.0%
* Annual Job Openings: 15,979
* Self-Employed: 4.9%
* Part-Time: 3.2%
* Job Security: No data available
* Education/Training Required: Bachelor's degree

The Department of Labor reports this information for the occupation Civil Engineers. The job openings listed here are shared with other specializations within that occupation, including Water/Wastewater Engineers.

Industries in Which Income Is Highest

Industry	Average Annual Earnings	Number Employed
Management of Companies and Enterprises	$82,150	1,870
Utilities	$76,300	2,210
Real Estate	$75,430	1,060
Federal, State, and Local Government	$75,010	70,850
Professional, Scientific, and Technical Services	$74,680	140,330

Metropolitan Areas Where Income Is Highest

Metropolitan Area	Average Annual Earnings	Number Employed
Baton Rouge, LA	$96,260	1,370
San Jose–Sunnyvale–Santa Clara, CA	$93,020	1,560
Houston–Sugar Land–Baytown, TX	$92,640	13,920
Oxnard–Thousand Oaks–Ventura, CA	$91,210	720
Santa Rosa–Petaluma, CA	$90,820	280

Develop plans for surface transportation projects according to established engineering standards and state or federal construction policy. Prepare plans, estimates, or specifications to design transportation facilities. Plan alterations and modifications of existing streets, highways, or freeways to improve traffic flow. No task data available.

Other Considerations for Income: As a group, engineers earn some of the highest average starting salaries among those holding bachelor's degrees. Separate earnings figures for Transportation Engineers are not available, but they are probably similar to those for Civil Engineers, who are among the lower-paid of the various kinds of engineers. According to a 2007 survey by the National Association of Colleges and Employers, the average starting salary for Civil Engineers with a bachelor's were $48,509 with a bachelor's, $48,280 with a master's, and $62,275 with a Ph.D.

Personality Type: Realistic-Investigative. **Career Cluster:** 15 Science, Technology, Engineering, and Mathematics. **Career Pathway:** 15.1 Engineering and Technology. **Skills:** No data available.

Education and Training Programs: Civil Engineering, General; Civil Engineering, Other; Transportation and Highway Engineering; Water Resources Engineering. **Related Knowledge/Courses:** No data available.

Transportation Inspectors

See *Aviation Inspectors; Freight and Cargo Inspectors; and Transportation Vehicle, Equipment and Systems Inspectors, Except Aviation, described separately.*

Transportation Managers

* Annual Earnings: $79,000
* Beginning Wage: $45,320
* Earnings Growth Potential: High (42.6%)
* Growth: 8.3%
* Annual Job Openings: 6,994
* Self-Employed: 2.6%
* Part-Time: 2.3%
* Job Security: More secure than most
* Education/Training Required: Work experience in a related occupation

The Department of Labor reports this information for the occupation Transportation, Storage, and Distribution Managers. The job openings listed here are shared with other specializations within that occupation, including Storage and Distribution Managers.

Industries in Which Income Is Highest

Industry	Average Annual Earnings	Number Employed
Management of Companies and Enterprises	$93,550	5,620
Computer and Electronic Product Manufacturing	$93,480	1,120
Professional, Scientific, and Technical Services	$89,890	1,870
Couriers and Messengers	$89,380	3,240
Federal, State, and Local Government	$87,570	12,700

Metropolitan Areas Where Income Is Highest

Metropolitan Area	Average Annual Earnings	Number Employed
Olympia, WA	$106,850	60
Niles–Benton Harbor, MI	$99,710	100
Miami–Fort Lauderdale–Miami Beach, FL	$99,050	1,340
Deltona–Daytona Beach–Ormond Beach, FL	$97,400	70
Rochester, NY	$95,940	190

Plan, direct, and coordinate the transportation operations within an organization or the activities of organizations that provide transportation services. Direct activities related to dispatching, routing, and tracking transportation vehicles such as aircraft and railroad cars. Plan, organize, and manage the work of subordinate staff to ensure that the work is accomplished in a manner consistent with organizational requirements. Direct investigations to verify and resolve customer or shipper complaints. Serve as contact persons for all workers within assigned territories. Implement schedule and policy changes. Collaborate with other managers and staff members to formulate and implement policies, procedures, goals, and objectives. Monitor operations to ensure that staff members comply with administrative policies and procedures, safety rules, union contracts, and government regulations. Promote safe work activities by conducting safety audits, attending company safety meetings, and meeting with individual staff members. Develop criteria, application instructions, procedural manuals, and contracts for federal and state public transportation programs. Monitor spending to ensure that expenses are consistent with approved budgets. Direct and coordinate, through subordinates, activities of operations department to obtain use of equipment, facilities, and human resources. Direct activities of staff performing repairs and maintenance to equipment, vehicles, and facilities. Conduct investigations in cooperation with government agencies to determine causes of transportation accidents and to improve safety procedures. Analyze expenditures and other financial information to develop plans, policies, and budgets for increasing profits and improving services. Negotiate and authorize contracts with equipment and materials suppliers and monitor contract fulfillment. Supervise workers assigning tariff classifications and preparing billing. Set operations policies and standards, including determination of safety procedures for the handling of dangerous goods.

Other Considerations for Income: No additional information.

Personality Type: Enterprising-Conventional. **Career Cluster:** 04 Business, Management, and Administration; 16 Transportation, Distribution, and Logistics. **Career Pathway:** 04.1 Management; 16.1 Transportation Operations; 16.2 Logistics, Planning, and Management Services. **Skills:** Negotiation; Time Management; Coordination; Management of Financial Resources; Mathematics; Monitoring; Management of Material Resources; Writing.

Education and Training Programs: Aeronautics/Aviation/Aerospace Science and Technology, General; Aviation/Airway Management and Operations; Business Administration and Management, General; Business/Commerce, General; Logistics, Materials, and Supply Chain Management; Public Administration; Transportation/Mobility Management. **Related Knowledge/Courses:** Transportation; Geography; Production and Processing; Personnel and Human Resources; Administration and Management; Economics and Accounting.

Transportation Vehicle, Equipment, and Systems Inspectors, Except Aviation

❋ Annual Earnings: $55,250
❋ Beginning Wage: $27,560
❋ Earnings Growth Potential: Very high (50.1%)
❋ Growth: 16.4%
❋ Annual Job Openings: 2,122
❋ Self-Employed: 5.9%
❋ Part-Time: 3.7%
❋ Job Security: More secure than most
❋ Education/Training Required: Work experience in a related occupation

The Department of Labor reports this information for the occupation Transportation Inspectors. The job openings listed here are shared with other specializations within that occupation, including Aviation Inspectors; and Freight and Cargo Inspectors.

Industries in Which Income Is Highest

Industry	Average Annual Earnings	Number Employed
Federal, State, and Local Government	$62,100	11,310
Air Transportation	$59,340	1,380
Rail Transportation	$52,220	3,920
Support Activities for Transportation	$41,720	2,830
Truck Transportation	$39,650	1,170

Metropolitan Areas Where Income Is Highest

Metropolitan Area	Average Annual Earnings	Number Employed
Milwaukee–Waukesha–West Allis, WI	$92,180	60
Minneapolis–St. Paul–Bloomington, MN-WI	$89,530	170
Denver-Aurora, CO	$89,370	180
Washington-Arlington-Alexandria, DC-VA-MD-WV	$88,780	440
Oklahoma City, OK	$87,430	190

Inspect and monitor transportation equipment, vehicles, or systems to ensure compliance with regulations and safety standards. Conduct vehicle or transportation equipment tests, using diagnostic equipment. Investigate and make recommendations on carrier requests for waiver of federal standards. Prepare reports on investigations or inspections and actions taken. Issue notices and recommend corrective actions when infractions or problems are found. Investigate incidents or violations such as delays, accidents, and equipment failures. Investigate complaints regarding safety violations. Inspect repairs to transportation vehicles and equipment to ensure that repair work was performed properly. Examine transportation vehicles, equipment, or systems to detect damage, wear, or malfunction. Inspect vehicles and other equipment for evidence of abuse, damage, or mechanical malfunction. Examine carrier operating rules, employee qualification guidelines, and carrier training and testing programs for compliance with regulations or safety standards. Inspect vehicles or equipment to ensure compliance with rules, standards, or regulations.

Other Considerations for Income: No additional information.

Personality Type: Realistic-Conventional-Investigative. **Career Cluster:** 16 Transportation, Distribution, and Logistics. **Career Pathway:** 16.1 Transportation Operations. **Skills:** Repairing; Equipment Maintenance; Troubleshooting; Installation; Quality Control Analysis; Systems Analysis; Operation Monitoring; Systems Evaluation.

Education and Training Programs: No related CIP programs; this job is learned through work experience in a related occupation. **Related Knowledge/Courses:** Mechanical; Transportation; Public Safety and Security; Engineering and Technology; Administration and Management; Physics.

Transportation, Storage, and Distribution Managers

See *Storage and Distribution Managers and Transportation Managers, described separately.*

Treasurers and Controllers

* Annual Earnings: $99,330
* Beginning Wage: $53,860
* Earnings Growth Potential: High (45.8%)
* Growth: 12.6%
* Annual Job Openings: 57,589
* Self-Employed: 4.6%
* Part-Time: 4.2%
* Job Security: Less secure than most
* Education/Training Required: Work experience plus degree

The Department of Labor reports this information for the occupation Financial Managers. The job openings listed here are shared with other specializations within that occupation, including Financial Managers, Branch or Department.

Industries in Which Income Is Highest

Industry	Average Annual Earnings	Number Employed
Securities, Commodity Contracts, and Other Financial Investments and Related Activities	$138,090	39,480
Motion Picture and Sound Recording Industries	$129,160	1,730
Publishing Industries (Except Internet)	$118,510	5,260
Telecommunications	$115,570	3,140
Management of Companies and Enterprises	$115,520	46,420

Metropolitan Areas Where Income Is Highest

Metropolitan Area	Average Annual Earnings	Number Employed
San Jose–Sunnyvale–Santa Clara, CA	$135,000	5,540
New York–Northern New Jersey–Long Island, NY-NJ-PA	$134,500	62,030
San Francisco–Oakland–Fremont, CA	$125,600	13,220
Boulder, CO	$122,720	300
Bridgeport-Stamford-Norwalk, CT	$115,410	4,700

Direct financial activities, such as planning, procurement, and investments, for all or part of an organization. Prepare and file annual tax returns or prepare financial information so that outside accountants can complete tax returns. Prepare or direct preparation of financial statements, business activity reports, financial position forecasts, annual budgets, and/or reports required by regulatory agencies. Supervise employees performing financial reporting, accounting, billing, collections, payroll, and budgeting duties. Delegate authority for the receipt, disbursement, banking, protection, and custody of funds, securities, and financial instruments. Maintain current knowledge of organizational policies and procedures, federal and state policies and directives, and current accounting standards. Conduct or coordinate audits of company accounts and financial transactions to ensure compliance with state and federal requirements and statutes. Receive and record requests for disbursements; authorize disbursements in accordance with policies and procedures. Monitor financial activities and details such as reserve levels to ensure that all legal and regulatory requirements are met. Monitor and evaluate the performance

of accounting and other financial staff; recommend and implement personnel actions such as promotions and dismissals. Develop and maintain relationships with banking, insurance, and non-organizational accounting personnel in order to facilitate financial activities. Coordinate and direct the financial planning, budgeting, procurement, or investment activities of all or part of an organization. Develop internal control policies, guidelines, and procedures for activities such as budget administration, cash and credit management, and accounting. Analyze the financial details of past, present, and expected operations in order to identify development opportunities and areas where improvement is needed. Advise management on short-term and long-term financial objectives, policies, and actions.

Other Considerations for Income: Large organizations often pay more than small ones, and salary levels also can depend on the type of industry and location. Many financial managers in both public and private industry receive additional compensation in the form of bonuses, which, like salaries, vary substantially by size of firm. Deferred compensation in the form of stock options is becoming more common, especially for senior-level executives.

Personality Type: Conventional-Enterprising. **Career Clusters:** 04 Business, Management, and Administration; 06 Finance. **Career Pathways:** 04.2 Business, Financial Management, and Accounting; 06.1 Financial and Investment Planning. **Skills:** Management of Financial Resources; Management of Material Resources; Judgment and Decision Making; Management of Personnel Resources; Mathematics; Negotiation; Time Management; Operations Analysis.

Education and Training Programs: Accounting and Business/Management; Accounting and Finance; Credit Management; Finance and Financial Management Services, Other; Finance, General; International Finance; Public Finance. **Related Knowledge/Courses:** Economics and Accounting; Administration and Management; Personnel and Human Resources; Law and Government; Mathematics; English Language.

Urban and Regional Planners

- ❋ Annual Earnings: $59,810
- ❋ Beginning Wage: $37,960
- ❋ Earnings Growth Potential: Medium (36.5%)
- ❋ Growth: 14.5%
- ❋ Annual Job Openings: 1,967
- ❋ Self-Employed: 0.2%
- ❋ Part-Time: 6.0%
- ❋ Job Security: More secure than most
- ❋ Education/Training Required: Master's degree

Industries in Which Income Is Highest

Industry	Average Annual Earnings	Number Employed
Professional, Scientific, and Technical Services	$63,300	7,610
Federal, State, and Local Government	$58,970	29,020

Metropolitan Areas Where Income Is Highest

Metropolitan Area	Average Annual Earnings	Number Employed
San Jose–Sunnyvale–Santa Clara, CA	$84,320	250
San Francisco–Oakland–Fremont, CA	$81,800	810
Salinas, CA	$78,290	90
Hartford–West Hartford–East Hartford, CT	$75,640	150
Las Vegas–Paradise, NV	$74,500	170

Develop comprehensive plans and programs for use of land and physical facilities of local jurisdictions such as towns, cities, counties, and metropolitan areas. Design, promote, and administer government plans and policies affecting land use, zoning, public utilities, community facilities, housing, and transportation. Hold public meetings and confer with government, social scientists, lawyers, developers, the public, and special interest groups to formulate and develop land use or community plans. Recommend approval, denial, or conditional approval of proposals. Determine the effects of regulatory limitations on projects. Assess the feasibility of proposals and identify necessary changes. Create, prepare, or requisition graphic and narrative reports on land use data, including land area maps overlaid with geographic variables such as population density. Conduct field investigations, surveys, impact studies, or other research to compile and analyze data on economic, social, regulatory, and physical factors affecting land use. Advise planning officials on project feasibility, cost-effectiveness, regulatory conformance, and possible alternatives. Discuss with planning officials the purpose of land use projects such as transportation, conservation, residential, commercial, industrial, and community use. Keep informed about economic and legal issues involved in zoning codes, building codes, and environmental regulations. Mediate community disputes and assist in developing alternative plans and recommendations for programs or projects. Coordinate work with economic consultants and architects during the formulation of plans and the design of large pieces of infrastructure. Review and evaluate environmental impact reports pertaining to private and public planning projects and programs. Supervise and coordinate the work of urban planning technicians and technologists. Investigate property availability.

Other Considerations for Income: No additional information.

Personality Type: Investigative-Enterprising-Artistic. **Career Cluster:** 07 Government and Public Administration. **Career Pathway:** 07.4 Planning. **Skills:** Complex Problem Solving; Persuasion; Writing; Coordination; Judgment and Decision Making; Service Orientation; Speaking; Social Perceptiveness.

Education and Training Program: City/Urban, Community and Regional Planning. **Related Knowledge/Courses:** Geography; History and Archeology; Transportation; Design; Law and Government; Sociology and Anthropology.

Urologists

- ❋ Annual Earnings: $166,400+
- ❋ Beginning Wage: $49,710
- ❋ Earnings Growth Potential: Cannot be calculated
- ❋ Growth: 14.2%
- ❋ Annual Job Openings: 38,027
- ❋ Self-Employed: 14.7%
- ❋ Part-Time: 8.1%
- ❋ Job Security: No data available
- ❋ Education/Training Required: First professional degree

The Department of Labor reports this information for the occupation Physicians and Surgeons. The job openings listed here are shared with other specializations within that occupation, including Allergists and Immunologists; Anesthesiologists; Dermatologists; Family and General Practitioners; Hospitalists; Internists, General; Neurologists; Nuclear Medicine Physicians; Obstetricians and Gynecologists; Ophthalmologists; Pathologists; Pediatricians, General; Physical Medicine and Rehabilitation Physicians; Preventive Medicine Physicians; Psychiatrists; Radiologists; Sports Medicine Physicians; and Surgeons.

Industries in Which Income Is Highest

Industry	Average Annual Earnings	Number Employed
Ambulatory Health Care Services	$166,400+	147,400
Administrative and Support Services	$166,400+	1,310
Federal, State, and Local Government	$162,300	28,180
Professional, Scientific, and Technical Services	$107,470	1,210
Hospitals	$72,130	72,490

Metropolitan Areas Where Income Is Highest

Metropolitan Area	Average Annual Earnings	Number Employed
Los Angeles–Long Beach–Santa Ana, CA	$166,400+	8,810
Boston-Cambridge-Quincy, MA-NH	$166,400+	6,380
Dallas–Fort Worth–Arlington, TX	$166,400+	4,950
Tampa–St. Petersburg–Clearwater, FL	$166,400+	3,810
Portland-Vancouver-Beaverton, OR-WA	$166,400+	3,180

Diagnose, treat, and help prevent benign and malignant medical and surgical disorders of the genitourinary system and the renal glands. No task data available.

Other Considerations for Income: Earnings of physicians and surgeons are among the highest of any occupation. Separate earnings figures for Urologists are not available, but they probably earn roughly the same as Obstetricians and Gynecologists, who are in the middle range of earners among medical specialists. The Medical Group Management Association's Physician Compensation and Production Survey of 2005 reported earnings of

$203,270 for Obstetricians and Gynecologists with less than two years in their specialty and $247,348 for those with more than one year in their specialty. These figures cover salary, bonus and incentive payments, research stipends, honoraria, and distribution of profits. Self-employed physicians—those who own or are part owners of their medical practice—generally have higher median incomes than salaried physicians, but their must provide for their own health insurance and retirement.

Personality Type: Investigative-Social-Realistic. **Career Cluster:** 08 Health Science. **Career Pathway:** 08.1 Therapeutic Services. **Skills:** No data available.

Education and Training Program: Urology Residency Program. **Related Knowledge/Courses:** No data available.

Veterinarians

* Annual Earnings: $79,050
* Beginning Wage: $46,610
* Earnings Growth Potential: High (41.0%)
* Growth: 35.0%
* Annual Job Openings: 5,301
* Self-Employed: 17.1%
* Part-Time: 13.4%
* Job Security: Most secure
* Education/Training Required: First professional degree

Industries in Which Income Is Highest

Industry	Average Annual Earnings	Number Employed
Professional, Scientific, and Technical Services	$79,320	49,080
Federal, State, and Local Government	$76,750	1,990

Metropolitan Areas Where Income Is Highest

Metropolitan Area	Average Annual Earnings	Number Employed
Bridgeport-Stamford-Norwalk, CT	$123,760	190
Cape Coral–Fort Myers, FL	$114,770	100
Santa Barbara–Santa Maria, CA	$113,980	70
San Jose–Sunnyvale–Santa Clara, CA	$109,560	220
Sacramento–Arden-Arcade–Roseville, CA	$106,890	470

Diagnose and treat diseases and dysfunctions of animals. May engage in a particular function, such as research and development, consultation, administration, technical writing, sale or production of commercial products, or rendering of technical services to commercial firms or other organizations. Includes veterinarians who inspect livestock. Examine animals to detect and determine the nature of diseases or injuries. Treat sick or injured animals by prescribing medication, setting bones, dressing wounds, or performing surgery. Inoculate animals against various diseases such as rabies and distemper. Collect body tissue, feces, blood, urine, or other body fluids for examination and analysis. Operate diagnostic equipment such as radiographic and ultrasound equipment and interpret the resulting images. Advise animal owners regarding sanitary measures, feeding, and general care necessary to promote health of animals. Educate the public about diseases that can be spread from animals to humans. Train and supervise workers who handle and care for animals. Provide care to a wide range of animals or specialize in a particular species, such as horses or exotic birds. Euthanize animals. Establish and conduct quarantine and testing procedures that prevent the spread of diseases to other animals or to humans and that comply with applicable government regulations. Conduct postmortem studies and analyses to determine the causes of animals' deaths. Perform administrative duties such as scheduling appointments, accepting payments from clients, and maintaining business records. Drive mobile clinic vans to farms so that health problems can be treated or prevented. Direct the overall operations of animal hospitals, clinics, or mobile services to farms. Specialize in a particular type of treatment such as dentistry, pathology, nutrition, surgery, microbiology, or internal medicine. Inspect and test horses, sheep, poultry, and other animals to detect the presence of communicable diseases. Research diseases to which animals could be susceptible. Plan and execute animal nutrition and reproduction programs. Inspect animal housing facilities to determine their cleanliness and adequacy. Determine the effects of drug therapies, antibiotics, or new surgical techniques by testing them on animals.

Other Considerations for Income: According to a survey by the American Veterinary Medical Association, average starting salaries of veterinary medical college graduates in 2006 varied from around $40,000 to around $60,000, with equine vets earning the least and vets working exclusively with large animals earning the most.

Personality Type: Investigative-Realistic. **Career Cluster:** 01 Agriculture, Food, and Natural Resource; 08 Health Science. **Career Pathway:** 01.3 Animal Systems; 08.1 Therapeutic Services. **Skills:** Science; Management of Financial Resources; Reading Comprehension; Judgment and Decision Making; Complex Problem Solving; Management of Personnel Resources; Equipment Selection; Management of Material Resources.

Education and Training Programs: Comparative and Laboratory Animal Medicine (Cert., MS, PhD); Laboratory Animal Medicine; Large Animal/Food Animal and Equine Surgery and Medicine (Cert., MS, PhD); Small/Companion Animal Surgery and Medicine (Cert., MS, PhD); Theriogenology; Veterinary Anatomy (Cert., MS, PhD); Veterinary Anesthesiology; Veterinary Biomedical and Clinical Sciences, Other (Cert., MS, PhD); Veterinary Dentistry; Veterinary Dermatology; Veterinary Emergency and Critical Care Medicine; others. **Related Knowledge/Courses:** Medicine and Dentistry; Biology; Chemistry; Therapy and Counseling; Sales and Marketing; Personnel and Human Resources.

Video Game Designers

❋ Annual Earnings: $75,150
❋ Beginning Wage: $40,660
❋ Earnings Growth Potential: High (45.9%)
❋ Growth: 15.1%
❋ Annual Job Openings: 14,374
❋ Self-Employed: 6.6%
❋ Part-Time: 5.6%
❋ Job Security: No data available
❋ Education/Training Required: Associate degree

The Department of Labor reports this information for the occupation Computer Specialists, All Other. The job openings listed here are shared with other specializations within that occupation, including Business Intelligence Analysts; Computer Systems Engineers/Architects; Data Warehousing Specialists; Database Architects; Document Management Specialists; Electronic Commerce Specialists; Geographic Information Systems Technicians; Geospatial Information Scientists and Technologists; Information Technology Project Managers; Network Designers; Software Quality Assurance Engineers and Testers; Web Administrators; and Web Developers.

Industries in Which Income Is Highest

Industry	Average Annual Earnings	Number Employed
Petroleum and Coal Products Manufacturing	$97,090	1,070
Transportation Equipment Manufacturing	$82,770	3,010
Oil and Gas Extraction	$81,350	1,710
Federal, State, and Local Government	$80,670	71,650
Management of Companies and Enterprises	$78,200	14,820

Metropolitan Areas Where Income Is Highest

Metropolitan Area	Average Annual Earnings	Number Employed
Washington-Arlington-Alexandria, DC-VA-MD-WV	$97,170	19,470
Atlantic City, NJ	$96,600	510
Pascagoula, MS	$95,430	60
San Jose–Sunnyvale–Santa Clara, CA	$92,710	3,580
Baltimore-Towson, MD	$89,730	5,650

Design core features of video games. Specify innovative game and role-play mechanics, storylines, and character biographies. Create and maintain design documentation. Guide and collaborate with production staff to produce games as designed. No task data available.

Other Considerations for Income: Very experienced Video Game Designers may work on a project-by-project basis and be able to negotiate compensation for each project.

Personality Type: No data available. **Career Cluster:** 11 Information Technology. **Career Pathway:** 11.4 Programming and Software Development. **Skills:** No data available.

Education and Training Programs: Computer and Information Sciences and Support Services, Other; Computer and Information Sciences, General; Computer Engineering Technologies/Technicians, Other; Computer Engineering, General; Computer Science; Computer Software Engineering; Computer Systems Networking and Telecommunications; E-Commerce/Electronic Commerce; Information Science/Studies; Information Technology; System, Networking, and LAN/WAN Management/Manager; Web Page, Digital/Multimedia and Information Resources Design; others. **Related Knowledge/Courses:** No data available.

Vocational Education Teachers, Secondary School

※ Annual Earnings: $51,580
※ Beginning Wage: $34,980
※ Earnings Growth Potential: Low (32.2%)
※ Growth: –4.6%
※ Annual Job Openings: 7,639
※ Self-Employed: 0.0%
※ Part-Time: 7.8%
※ Job Security: Most secure
※ Education/Training Required: Work experience plus degree

Industries in Which Income Is Highest

Industry	Average Annual Earnings	Number Employed
Educational Services	$51,660	97,620
Federal, State, and Local Government	$48,100	1,880

Metropolitan Areas Where Income Is Highest

Metropolitan Area	Average Annual Earnings	Number Employed
Visalia-Porterville, CA	$75,140	130
New Haven, CT	$73,930	180
New York–Northern New Jersey–Long Island, NY-NJ-PA	$72,050	4,300
Stockton, CA	$70,440	240
Hartford–West Hartford–East Hartford, CT	$69,600	630

Teach or instruct vocational or occupational subjects at the secondary school level. Prepare materials and classroom for class activities. Maintain accurate and complete student records as required by law, district policy, and administrative regulations. Instruct students individually and in groups, using various teaching methods such as lectures, discussions, and demonstrations. Observe and evaluate students' performance, behavior, social development, and physical health. Establish and enforce rules for behavior and procedures for maintaining order among the students for whom they are responsible. Instruct and monitor students the in use and care of equipment and materials to prevent injury and damage. Plan and conduct activities for a balanced program of instruction, demonstration, and work time that provides students with opportunities to observe, question, and investigate. Prepare, administer, and grade tests and assignments to evaluate students' progress. Enforce all administration policies and rules governing students. Assign and grade classwork and homework. Instruct students in the knowledge and skills required in a specific occupation or occupational field, using a systematic plan of lectures; discussions; audiovisual presentations; and laboratory, shop, and field studies. Establish clear objectives for all lessons, units, and projects and communicate those objectives to students. Use computers, audiovisual aids, and other equipment and materials to supplement presentations. Plan and supervise work-experience programs in businesses, industrial shops, and school laboratories. Prepare students for later grades by encouraging them to explore learning opportunities and to persevere with challenging tasks. Confer with parents or guardians, other teachers, counselors, and administrators in order to resolve students' behavioral and academic problems. Guide and counsel students with adjustment or academic problems or special academic interests.

Other Considerations for Income: Teachers can boost their earnings in a number of ways. In some schools, teachers receive extra pay for coaching sports and working with students in extracurricular activities. Getting a master's degree or national certification often results in a raise in pay, as does acting as a mentor. Some teachers earn extra income during the summer by teaching summer school or performing other jobs in the school system. Although private school teachers generally earn less than public school teachers, they may be given other benefits, such as free or subsidized housing.

Personality Type: Social. **Career Cluster:** 05 Education and Training. **Career Pathway:** 05.3 Teaching/Training. **Skills:** Management of Financial Resources; Learning Strategies; Management of Material Resources; Social Perceptiveness; Instructing; Persuasion; Monitoring; Management of Personnel Resources.

Education and Training Program: Technology Teacher Education/Industrial Arts Teacher Education. **Related Knowledge/Courses:** Education and Training; Therapy and Counseling; Sociology and Anthropology; Psychology; Mechanical; Design.

Water Resource Specialists

- ❋ Annual Earnings: $112,800
- ❋ Beginning Wage: $65,960
- ❋ Earnings Growth Potential: High (41.5%)
- ❋ Growth: 11.4%
- ❋ Annual Job Openings: 3,661
- ❋ Self-Employed: 0.6%
- ❋ Part-Time: 4.4%
- ❋ Job Security: No data available
- ❋ Education/Training Required: Work experience plus degree

The Department of Labor reports this information for the occupation Natural Sciences Managers. The job openings listed here are shared with other specializations within that occupation, including Clinical Research Coordinators.

Industries in Which Income Is Highest

Industry	Average Annual Earnings	Number Employed
Chemical Manufacturing	$139,610	5,660
Management of Companies and Enterprises	$136,560	2,160
Professional, Scientific, and Technical Services	$125,560	16,240
Federal, State, and Local Government	$95,610	12,760
Educational Services	$91,920	1,990

Metropolitan Areas Where Income Is Highest

Metropolitan Area	Average Annual Earnings	Number Employed
San Jose–Sunnyvale–Santa Clara, CA	$166,400+	860
Philadelphia-Camden-Wilmington, PA-NJ-DE-MD	$162,090	1,740
New York–Northern New Jersey–Long Island, NY-NJ-PA	$149,910	3,540
San Francisco–Oakland–Fremont, CA	$149,110	2,250
San Diego–Carlsbad–San Marcos, CA	$141,210	1,300

Design or implement programs and strategies related to water resource issues, such as supply, quality, and regulatory compliance issues. No task data available.

Other Considerations for Income: No additional information.

Personality Type: No data available. **Career Cluster:** 15 Science, Technology, Engineering, and Mathematics. **Career Pathway:** 15.3 Science and Mathematics. **Skills:** No data available.

Education and Training Programs: Geology/Earth Science, General; Geochemistry; Geological and Earth Sciences/Geosciences, Other; Hydrology and Water Resources Science; Oceanography, Chemical and Physical. **Related Knowledge/Courses:** No data available.

Water/Wastewater Engineers

❋ Annual Earnings: $74,600
❋ Beginning Wage: $48,140
❋ Earnings Growth Potential: Medium (35.5%)
❋ Growth: 18.0%
❋ Annual Job Openings: 15,979
❋ Self-Employed: 4.9%
❋ Part-Time: 3.2%
❋ Job Security: No data available
❋ Education/Training Required: Bachelor's degree

The Department of Labor reports this information for the occupation Civil Engineers. The job openings listed here are shared with other specializations within that occupation, including Transportation Engineers.

Industries in Which Income Is Highest

Industry	Average Annual Earnings	Number Employed
Management of Companies and Enterprises	$82,150	1,870
Utilities	$76,300	2,210
Real Estate	$75,430	1,060
Federal, State, and Local Government	$75,010	70,850
Professional, Scientific, and Technical Services	$74,680	140,330

Metropolitan Areas Where Income Is Highest

Metropolitan Area	Average Annual Earnings	Number Employed
Baton Rouge, LA	$96,260	1,370
San Jose–Sunnyvale–Santa Clara, CA	$93,020	1,560
Houston–Sugar Land–Baytown, TX	$92,640	13,920
Oxnard–Thousand Oaks–Ventura, CA	$91,210	720
Santa Rosa–Petaluma, CA	$90,820	280

Design or oversee projects involving provision of fresh water, disposal of wastewater and sewage, or prevention of flood-related damage. Prepare environmental documentation for water resources, regulatory program compliance, data management and analysis, and

fieldwork. **Perform hydraulic modeling and pipeline design.** No task data available.

Other Considerations for Income: As a group, engineers earn some of the highest average starting salaries among those holding bachelor's degrees. Separate earnings figures for Water/Wastewater Engineers are not available, but they are probably similar to those for Civil Engineers, who are among the lower-paid of the various kinds of engineers. According to a 2007 survey by the National Association of Colleges and Employers, the average starting salary for Civil Engineers with a bachelor's were $48,509 with a bachelor's, $48,280 with a master's, and $62,275 with a Ph.D.

Personality Type: No data available. **Career Cluster:** 15 Science, Technology, Engineering, and Mathematics. **Career Pathway:** 15.1 Engineering and Technology. **Skills:** No data available.

Education and Training Programs: Civil Engineering, General; Civil Engineering, Other; Transportation and Highway Engineering; Water Resources Engineering. **Related Knowledge/Courses:** No data available.

Web Administrators

- ❈ Annual Earnings: $75,150
- ❈ Beginning Wage: $40,660
- ❈ Earnings Growth Potential: High (45.9%)
- ❈ Growth: 15.1%
- ❈ Annual Job Openings: 14,374
- ❈ Self-Employed: 6.6%
- ❈ Part-Time: 5.6%
- ❈ Job Security: More secure than most
- ❈ Education/Training Required: Bachelor's degree

The Department of Labor reports this information for the occupation Computer Specialists, All Other. The job openings listed here are shared with other specializations within that occupation, including Business Intelligence Analysts; Computer Systems Engineers/Architects; Data Warehousing Specialists; Database Architects; Document Management Specialists; Electronic Commerce Specialists; Geographic Information Systems Technicians; Geospatial Information Scientists and Technologists; Information Technology Project Managers; Network Designers; Software Quality Assurance Engineers and Testers; Video Game Designers; and Web Developers.

Industries in Which Income Is Highest

Industry	Average Annual Earnings	Number Employed
Petroleum and Coal Products Manufacturing	$97,090	1,070
Transportation Equipment Manufacturing	$82,770	3,010
Oil and Gas Extraction	$81,350	1,710
Federal, State, and Local Government	$80,670	71,650
Management of Companies and Enterprises	$78,200	14,820

Metropolitan Areas Where Income Is Highest

Metropolitan Area	Average Annual Earnings	Number Employed
Washington-Arlington-Alexandria, DC-VA-MD-WV	$97,170	19,470
Atlantic City, NJ	$96,600	510
Pascagoula, MS	$95,430	60
San Jose–Sunnyvale–Santa Clara, CA	$92,710	3,580
Baltimore-Towson, MD	$89,730	5,650

Manage Web environment design, deployment, development, and maintenance activities. Perform testing and quality assurance of Web sites and Web applications. Back up or modify applications and related data to provide for disaster recovery. Determine sources of Web page or server problems, and take action to correct such problems. Review or update Web page content or links in a timely manner, using appropriate tools. Monitor systems for intrusions or denial of service attacks, and report security breaches to appropriate personnel. Implement Web site security measures, such as firewalls or message encryption. Administer Internet/intranet infrastructure, including components such as Web, file transfer protocol (FTP), news, and mail servers. Collaborate with development teams to discuss, analyze, or resolve usability issues. Test backup or recovery plans regularly and resolve any problems. Monitor Web developments through continuing education, reading, or participation in professional conferences, workshops, or groups. Implement updates, upgrades, and patches in a timely manner to limit loss of service. Identify or document backup or recovery plans. Collaborate with Web developers to create and operate internal and external Web sites, or to manage projects, such as e-marketing campaigns. Install or configure Web server software or hardware to ensure that directory structure is well-defined, logical, secure, and that files are named properly. Gather, analyze, or document user feedback to locate or resolve sources of problems. Develop Web site performance metrics. Identify or address interoperability requirements. Document installation or configuration procedures to allow maintenance and repetition. Identify, standardize, and communicate levels of access and security. Track, compile, and analyze Web site usage data. Test issues such as system integration, performance, and system security on a regular schedule or after any major program modifications. Recommend Web site improvements, and develop budgets to support recommendations. Inform Web site users of problems, problem resolutions, or application changes and updates.

Other Considerations for Income: Web Administrators are paid less well than most other computer specialists.

Personality Type: Conventional-Enterprising-Investigative. **Career Cluster:** 11 Information Technology. **Career Pathway:** 11.4 Programming and Software Development. **Skills:** Programming; Systems Evaluation; Systems Analysis; Troubleshooting; Operations Analysis; Technology Design; Installation; Equipment Selection.

Education and Training Programs: Computer and Information Sciences and Support Services, Other; Computer and Information Sciences, General; Computer Engineering Technologies/Technicians, Other; Computer Engineering, General; Computer Science; Computer Software Engineering; Computer Systems Networking and Telecommunications; E-Commerce/Electronic Commerce; Information Science/Studies; Information Technology; System, Networking, and LAN/WAN Management/Manager; Web Page, Digital/Multimedia and Information Resources Design; others. **Related Knowledge/Courses:** Computers and Electronics; Telecommunications; Design; Communications and Media; Sales and Marketing; Clerical.

Web Developers

* Annual Earnings: $75,150
* Beginning Wage: $40,660
* Earnings Growth Potential: High (45.9%)
* Growth: 15.1%
* Annual Job Openings: 14,374
* Self-Employed: 6.6%
* Part-Time: 5.6%
* Job Security: More secure than most
* Education/Training Required: Bachelor's degree

The Department of Labor reports this information for the occupation Computer Specialists, All Other. The job openings listed here are shared with other specializations within that occupation, including Business Intelligence Analysts; Computer Systems Engineers/Architects; Data Warehousing Specialists; Database Architects; Document Management Specialists; Electronic Commerce Specialists; Geographic Information Systems Technicians; Geospatial Information Scientists and Technologists; Information Technology Project Managers; Network Designers; Software Quality Assurance Engineers and Testers; Video Game Designers; and Web Administrators.

Industries in Which Income Is Highest

Industry	Average Annual Earnings	Number Employed
Petroleum and Coal Products Manufacturing	$97,090	1,070
Transportation Equipment Manufacturing	$82,770	3,010
Oil and Gas Extraction	$81,350	1,710
Federal, State, and Local Government	$80,670	71,650
Management of Companies and Enterprises	$78,200	14,820

Metropolitan Areas Where Income Is Highest

Metropolitan Area	Average Annual Earnings	Number Employed
Washington-Arlington-Alexandria, DC-VA-MD-WV	$97,170	19,470
Atlantic City, NJ	$96,600	510
Pascagoula, MS	$95,430	60
San Jose–Sunnyvale–Santa Clara, CA	$92,710	3,580
Baltimore-Towson, MD	$89,730	5,650

Develop and design Web applications and Web sites. Create and specify architectural and technical parameters. Direct Web site content creation, enhancement, and maintenance. Design, build, or maintain Web sites, using authoring or scripting languages, content creation tools, management tools, and digital media. Perform or direct Web site updates. Write, design, or edit Web page content or direct others producing content. Confer with management or development teams to prioritize needs, resolve conflicts, develop content criteria, or choose solutions. Back up files from Web sites to local directories for instant recovery in case of problems. Identify problems uncovered by testing or customer feedback and correct problems or refer problems to appropriate personnel for correction. Evaluate code to ensure that it is valid; is properly structured; meets industry standards; and is compatible with browsers, devices, or operating systems. Maintain understanding of current Web technologies or programming practices through continuing education; reading; or participation in professional conferences, workshops, or groups. Analyze user needs to determine technical requirements. Develop or validate test routines and schedules to ensure that test cases mimic external interfaces and address all browser and device types. Develop databases that support Web applications and Web sites. Renew domain name registrations. Collaborate with management or users to develop e-commerce strategies and to integrate these strategies with Web sites. Write supporting code for Web applications or Web sites. Communicate with network personnel or Web site hosting agencies to address hardware or software issues affecting Web sites. Design and implement Web site security measures such as firewalls or message encryption. Perform Web site tests according to planned schedules or after any Web site or product revisions. Select programming languages, design tools, or applications. Incorporate technical considerations into Web site design plans, such as budgets, equipment, performance requirements, or legal issues, including accessibility and privacy.

Other Considerations for Income: Web Developers are paid in the middle range of earnings, compared to those of other computer specialists.

Personality Type: Conventional-Investigative-Realistic. **Career Cluster:** 11 Information Technology. **Career Pathway:** 11.4 Programming and Software Development. **Skills:** Programming; Troubleshooting; Operations Analysis; Technology Design; Systems Evaluation; Quality Control Analysis; Systems Analysis; Complex Problem Solving.

Education and Training Programs: Computer and Information Sciences and Support Services, Other; Computer and Information Sciences, General; Computer Engineering Technologies/Technicians, Other; Computer Engineering, General; Computer Science; Computer Software Engineering; Computer Systems Networking and Telecommunications; E-Commerce/Electronic Commerce; Information Science/Studies; Information Technology; System, Networking, and LAN/WAN Management/Manager; Web Page, Digital/Multimedia and Information Resources Design; others. **Related Knowledge/Courses:** Computers and Electronics; Design; Sales and Marketing; Communications and Media; Telecommunications; Clerical.

Wholesale and Retail Buyers, Except Farm Products

- ❋ Annual Earnings: $48,710
- ❋ Beginning Wage: $28,710
- ❋ Earnings Growth Potential: High (41.1%)
- ❋ Growth: –0.1%
- ❋ Annual Job Openings: 19,847
- ❋ Self-Employed: 12.0%
- ❋ Part-Time: 15.6%
- ❋ Job Security: More secure than most
- ❋ Education/Training Required: Long-term on-the-job training

Industries in Which Income Is Highest

Industry	Average Annual Earnings	Number Employed
Computer and Electronic Product Manufacturing	$69,030	1,830
Management of Companies and Enterprises	$56,400	18,550
Motor Vehicle and Parts Dealers	$56,080	6,590
Wholesale Electronic Markets and Agents and Brokers	$53,650	9,030
Warehousing and Storage	$52,350	1,190

Metropolitan Areas Where Income Is Highest

Metropolitan Area	Average Annual Earnings	Number Employed
Austin–Round Rock, TX	$65,430	1,060
Spartanburg, SC	$64,710	80
Baton Rouge, LA	$64,180	390
Savannah, GA	$62,310	80
Tampa–St. Petersburg–Clearwater, FL	$61,870	690

Buy merchandise or commodities, other than farm products, for resale to consumers at the wholesale or retail level, including both durable and nondurable goods. Analyze past buying trends, sales records, price, and quality of merchandise to determine value and yield. Select, order, and authorize payment for merchandise according to contractual agreements. May conduct meetings with sales personnel and introduce new products. Examine, select, order, and purchase at the most favorable price merchandise consistent with quality, quantity, specification requirements, and other factors. Negotiate prices, discount terms, and transportation arrangements for merchandise. Analyze and monitor sales records, trends, and economic conditions to anticipate consumer buying patterns and determine what the company will sell and how much inventory is needed. Interview and work closely with vendors to obtain and develop desired products. Authorize payment of invoices or return of merchandise. Inspect merchandise or products to determine value or yield. Set or recommend markup rates, markdown rates, and selling prices for merchandise. Confer with sales and purchasing personnel to obtain information about customer needs and preferences. Consult with store or merchandise managers about budget and goods to be purchased. Conduct staff meetings with sales personnel to introduce new merchandise. Manage the department for which they buy. Use computers to organize and locate inventory and operate spreadsheet and word-processing software. Provide clerks with information to print on price tags, such as price, markups or markdowns, manufacturer number, season code, and style number. Train and supervise sales and clerical staff. Determine which products should be featured in advertising, the advertising medium to be used, and when the ads should be run. Monitor competitors' sales activities by following their advertisements in newspapers and other media.

Other Considerations for Income: Purchasing managers, buyers, and purchasing agents receive the same benefits package as other workers, including vacations, sick leave, life and health insurance, and pension plans. In addition to receiving standard benefits, retail buyers often earn cash bonuses based on their performance and may receive discounts on merchandise bought from their employer.

Personality Type: Enterprising-Conventional. **Career Cluster:** 14 Marketing, Sales, and Service. **Career Pathways:** 14.2 Professional Sales and Marketing; 14.3 Buying and Merchandising. **Skills:** Management of Financial Resources; Management of Material Resources; Operations Analysis; Quality Control Analysis; Negotiation; Service Orientation; Equipment Selection; Management of Personnel Resources.

Education and Training Programs: Apparel and Accessories Marketing Operations; Apparel and Textile Marketing Management; Fashion Merchandising; Insurance; Merchandising and Buying Operations; Sales, Distribution, and Marketing Operations, General. **Related Knowledge/Courses:** Production and Processing; Sales and Marketing; Economics and Accounting; Administration and Management; Building and Construction; Customer and Personal Service.

Writers and Authors

See *Copy Writers and Poets, Lyricists and Creative Writers,* described separately.

Zoologists and Wildlife Biologists

❋ Annual Earnings: $55,290
❋ Beginning Wage: $33,550
❋ Earnings Growth Potential: Medium (39.3%)
❋ Growth: 8.7%
❋ Annual Job Openings: 1,444
❋ Self-Employed: 2.6%
❋ Part-Time: 7.3%
❋ Job Security: More secure than most
❋ Education/Training Required: Bachelor's degree

Industries in Which Income Is Highest

Industry	Average Annual Earnings	Number Employed
Professional, Scientific, and Technical Services	$57,550	3,590
Federal, State, and Local Government	$56,460	11,690

Metropolitan Areas Where Income Is Highest

Metropolitan Area	Average Annual Earnings	Number Employed
Washington-Arlington-Alexandria, DC-VA-MD-WV	$99,950	320
Barnstable Town, MA	$84,720	100
Raleigh-Cary, NC	$73,260	100
Wenatchee, WA	$66,890	70
New York–Northern New Jersey–Long Island, NY-NJ-PA	$64,820	190

Study the origins, behavior, diseases, genetics, and life processes of animals and wildlife. May specialize in wildlife research and management, including the collection and analysis of biological data to determine the environmental effects of present and potential use of land and water areas. Study animals in their natural habitats, assessing effects of environment and industry on animals, interpreting findings, and recommending alternative operating conditions for industry. Inventory or estimate plant and wildlife populations. Analyze characteristics of animals to identify and classify them. Make recommendations on management systems and planning for wildlife populations and habitat, consulting with stakeholders and the public at large to explore options. Disseminate information by writing reports and scientific papers or journal articles and by making presentations and giving talks for schools, clubs, interest groups, and park interpretive programs. Study characteristics of animals such as origin, interrelationships, classification, life histories and diseases, development, genetics, and distribution. Perform administrative duties such as fundraising, public relations, budgeting, and supervision of zoo staff. Organize and conduct experimental studies with live animals in controlled or natural surroundings. Oversee the care and distribution of zoo animals, working with curators and zoo directors to determine the best way to contain animals, maintain their habitats, and manage facilities. Coordinate preventive programs to control the outbreak of wildlife diseases. Prepare collections of preserved specimens or microscopic slides for species identification and study of development or disease. Raise specimens for study and observation or for use in experiments. Collect and dissect animal specimens and examine specimens under microscope.

Other Considerations for Income: According to the National Association of Colleges and Employers, beginning salary offers in 2007 averaged $34,953 a year for bachelor's degree recipients in biological and life sciences.

Personality Type: Investigative-Realistic. **Career Clusters:** 01 Agriculture, Food and Natural Resource; 15 Science, Technology, Engineering, and Mathematics. **Career Pathways:** 01.5 Natural Resources Systems; 15.3 Science and Mathematics. **Skills:** Science; Management of Financial Resources; Writing; Coordination; Operations Analysis; Persuasion; Judgment and Decision Making; Reading Comprehension.

Education and Training Programs: Animal Behavior and Ethology; Animal Physiology; Cell/Cellular Biology and Anatomical Sciences, Other; Ecology; Entomology; Wildlife Biology; Wildlife, Fish and Wildlands Science and Management; Zoology/Animal Biology; Zoology/Animal Biology, Other. **Related Knowledge/Courses:** Biology; Geography; Law and Government; English Language; Administration and Management; Computers and Electronics.

APPENDIX A

Definitions of Skills and Knowledge/ Courses Referenced in This Book

Definitions of Skills	
Skill Name	Definition
Active Learning	Working with new material or information to grasp its implications.
Active Listening	Listening to what other people are saying and asking questions as appropriate.
Complex Problem Solving	Identifying complex problems, reviewing the options, and implementing solutions.
Coordination	Adjusting actions in relation to others' actions.
Critical Thinking	Using logic and analysis to identify the strengths and weaknesses of different approaches.
Equipment Maintenance	Performing routine maintenance and determining when and what kind of maintenance is needed.
Equipment Selection	Determining the kind of tools and equipment needed to do a job.
Installation	Installing equipment, machines, wiring, or programs to meet specifications.
Instructing	Teaching others how to do something.
Judgment and Decision Making	Weighing the relative costs and benefits of a potential action.
Learning Strategies	Using multiple approaches when learning or teaching new things.
Management of Financial Resources	Determining how money will be spent to get the work done and accounting for these expenditures.
Management of Material Resources	Obtaining and seeing to the appropriate use of equipment, facilities, and materials needed to do certain work.

Definitions of Skills

Skill Name	Definition
Management of Personnel Resources	Motivating, developing, and directing people as they work; identifying the best people for the job.
Mathematics	Using mathematics to solve problems.
Monitoring	Assessing how well one is doing when learning or doing something.
Negotiation	Bringing others together and trying to reconcile differences.
Operation and Control	Controlling operations of equipment or systems.
Operation Monitoring	Watching gauges, dials, or other indicators to make sure a machine is working properly.
Operations Analysis	Analyzing needs and product requirements to create a design.
Persuasion	Persuading others to approach things differently.
Programming	Writing computer programs for various purposes.
Quality Control Analysis	Evaluating the quality or performance of products, services, or processes.
Reading Comprehension	Understanding written sentences and paragraphs in work-related documents.
Repairing	Repairing machines or systems, using the needed tools.
Science	Using scientific methods to solve problems.
Service Orientation	Actively looking for ways to help people.
Social Perceptiveness	Being aware of others' reactions and understanding why they react the way they do.
Speaking	Talking to others to effectively convey information.
Systems Analysis	Determining how a system should work and how changes will affect outcomes.
Systems Evaluation	Looking at many indicators of system performance and taking into account their accuracy.
Technology Design	Generating or adapting equipment and technology to serve user needs.
Time Management	Managing one's own time and the time of others.
Troubleshooting	Determining what is causing an operating error and deciding what to do about it.
Writing	Communicating effectively with others in writing as indicated by the needs of the audience.

Definitions of Knowledge/Courses

Knowledge/Course Name	Definition
Administration and Management	Knowledge of principles and processes involved in business and organizational planning, coordination, and execution. This includes strategic planning, resource allocation, manpower modeling, leadership techniques, and production methods.
Biology	Knowledge of plant and animal living tissue, cells, organisms, and entities, including their functions, interdependencies, and interactions with each other and the environment.
Building and Construction	Knowledge of materials, methods, and the appropriate tools to construct objects, structures, and buildings.
Chemistry	Knowledge of the composition, structure, and properties of substances and of the chemical processes and transformations that they undergo. This includes uses of chemicals and their interactions, danger signs, production techniques, and disposal methods.
Clerical Studies	Knowledge of administrative and clerical procedures and systems such as word-processing systems, filing and records management systems, stenography and transcription, forms, design principles, and other office procedures and terminology.
Communications and Media	Knowledge of media production, communication, and dissemination techniques and methods, including alternative ways to inform and entertain via written, oral, and visual media.
Computers and Electronics	Knowledge of electric circuit boards, processors, chips, and computer hardware and software, including applications and programming.
Customer and Personal Service	Knowledge of principles and processes for providing customer and personal services, including needs assessment techniques, quality service standards, alternative delivery systems, and customer satisfaction evaluation techniques.
Design	Knowledge of design techniques, principles, tools, and instruments involved in the production and use of precision technical plans, blueprints, drawings, and models.
Economics and Accounting	Knowledge of economic and accounting principles and practices, the financial markets, banking, and the analysis and reporting of financial data.
Education and Training	Knowledge of instructional methods and training techniques, including curriculum design principles, learning theory, group and individual teaching techniques, design of individual development plans, and test design principles.
Engineering and Technology	Knowledge of equipment, tools, and mechanical devices and their uses to produce motion, light, power, technology, and other applications.

Definitions of Knowledge/Courses

Knowledge/Course Name	Definition
English Language	Knowledge of the structure and content of the English language, including the meaning and spelling of words, rules of composition, and grammar.
Fine Arts	Knowledge of theory and techniques required to produce, compose, and perform works of music, dance, visual arts, drama, and sculpture.
Food Production	Knowledge of techniques and equipment for the planting, growing, and harvesting of food for consumption, including crop rotation methods, animal husbandry, and food storage/handling techniques.
Foreign Language	Knowledge of the structure and content of a foreign (non-English) language, including the meaning and spelling of words, rules of composition and grammar, and pronunciation.
Geography	Knowledge of various methods for describing the location and distribution of land, sea, and air masses, including their physical locations, relationships, and characteristics.
History and Archeology	Knowledge of past historical events and their causes, indicators, and impact on particular civilizations and cultures.
Law and Government	Knowledge of laws, legal codes, court procedures, precedents, government regulations, executive orders, agency rules, and the democratic political process.
Mathematics	Knowledge of numbers and their operations and interrelationships, including arithmetic, algebra, geometry, calculus, and statistics and their applications.
Mechanical Devices	Knowledge of machines and tools, including their designs, uses, benefits, repair, and maintenance.
Medicine and Dentistry	Knowledge of the information and techniques needed to diagnose and treat injuries, diseases, and deformities. This includes symptoms, treatment alternatives, drug properties and interactions, and preventive health-care measures.
Personnel and Human Resources	Knowledge of policies and practices involved in personnel/human resource functions. This includes recruitment, selection, training, and promotion regulations and procedures; compensation and benefits packages; labor relations and negotiation strategies; and personnel information systems.
Philosophy and Theology	Knowledge of different philosophical systems and religions, including their basic principles, values, ethics, ways of thinking, customs, and practices and their impact on human culture.
Physics	Knowledge and prediction of physical principles, laws, and applications, including air, water, material dynamics, light, atomic principles, heat, electric theory, earth formations, and meteorological and related natural phenomena.

(continued)

(continued)

Definitions of Knowledge/Courses

Knowledge/Course Name	Definition
Production and Processing	Knowledge of inputs, outputs, raw materials, waste, quality control, costs, and techniques for maximizing the manufacture and distribution of goods.
Psychology	Knowledge of human behavior and performance, mental processes, psychological research methods, and the assessment and treatment of behavioral and affective disorders.
Public Safety and Security	Knowledge of weaponry; public safety; security operations, rules, regulations, precautions, and prevention; and the protection of people, data, and property.
Sales and Marketing	Knowledge of principles and methods involved in showing, promoting, and selling products or services. This includes marketing strategies and tactics, product demonstration and sales techniques, and sales control systems.
Sociology and Anthropology	Knowledge of group behavior and dynamics; societal trends and influences; and cultures and their history, migrations, ethnicity, and origins.
Telecommunications	Knowledge of transmission, broadcasting, switching, control, and operation of telecommunications systems.
Therapy and Counseling	Knowledge of information and techniques needed to rehabilitate physical and mental ailments and to provide career guidance, including alternative treatments, rehabilitation equipment and its proper use, and methods to evaluate treatment effects.
Transportation	Knowledge of principles and methods for moving people or goods by air, rail, sea, or road, including their relative costs, advantages, and limitations.

APPENDIX B

The Skill-Income Connection

It's no secret that employers value certain skills more than others. As part of the research for this book, we wondered whether high-paying occupations are associated with certain skills more than with others. So we employed a statistical procedure called *correlation* that shows how well one variable can predict another. In this case, we wanted to see how well the presence of a skill can predict income. We used skills ratings from the O*NET database and income figures from the Bureau of Labor Statistics.

Our analysis produced the following list of skills. Every skill on this list has at least a reasonably high correlation (better than 0.5) with income—which means that jobs that demand a high level of this skill tend to have a high level of income. The skills are ordered by the amount of correlation, which means that the skills nearest the beginning are the best predictors of high income. We also thought it would be handy for you to see which jobs in this book demand a high level of each skill, so we have listed the jobs that include each skill among its top three skills.

Keep in mind that most jobs demand a *combination* of skills, and one way to command higher pay is to have a special combination of skills that is scarce among other people with the same job title. For example, you may be the one chemist in your lab who is an excellent writer or the one sales representative in your company who has enough programming skill to advise the technology staff about how to improve sales-tracking software.

Skills Linked to High Occupational Earnings

Skill	Jobs That Demand a High Level of This Skill
Complex Problem Solving	Architects, Except Landscape and Naval; Clinical Psychologists; Internists, General; Podiatrists; Urban and Regional Planners
Judgment and Decision Making	Administrative Law Judges, Adjudicators, and Hearing Officers; Atmospheric and Space Scientists; Chief Executives; Claims Examiners, Property and Casualty Insurance; Compensation, Benefits, and Job Analysis Specialists; Directors—Stage, Motion Pictures, Television, and Radio; Emergency Management Specialists;

(continued)

(continued)

Skills Linked to High Occupational Earnings

Skill	Jobs That Demand a High Level of This Skill
	Financial Analysts; Industrial-Organizational Psychologists; Insurance Adjusters, Examiners, and Investigators; Internists, General; Judges, Magistrate Judges, and Magistrates; Licensing Examiners and Inspectors; Medical Scientists, Except Epidemiologists; Obstetricians and Gynecologists; Physician Assistants; Pilots, Ship; Police Identification and Records Officers; Surgeons; Treasurers and Controllers
Reading Comprehension	Administrative Law Judges, Adjudicators, and Hearing Officers; Coroners; Court Reporters; Dental Hygienists; Editors; Environmental Science Teachers, Postsecondary; Epidemiologists; Family and General Practitioners; Historians; Obstetricians and Gynecologists; Optometrists; Pharmacists; Philosophy and Religion Teachers, Postsecondary; Political Science Teachers, Postsecondary; Political Scientists; Surgeons; Veterinarians
Critical Thinking	Anthropology and Archeology Teachers, Postsecondary; Area, Ethnic, and Cultural Studies Teachers, Postsecondary; Criminal Justice and Law Enforcement Teachers, Postsecondary; Law Teachers, Postsecondary; Political Scientists
Active Learning	Dental Hygienists; Electrical Drafters; Natural Sciences Managers; Pediatricians, General
Active Listening	Administrative Law Judges, Adjudicators, and Hearing Officers; Arbitrators, Mediators, and Conciliators; Counseling Psychologists; Court Reporters; Editors; Podiatrists
Writing	Agricultural Sciences Teachers, Postsecondary; Anthropologists; Anthropology and Archeology Teachers, Postsecondary; Archeologists; Area, Ethnic, and Cultural Studies Teachers, Postsecondary; Biochemists and Biophysicists; Biological Science Teachers, Postsecondary; Broadcast News Analysts; Business Teachers, Postsecondary; Claims Examiners, Property and Casualty Insurance; Communications Teachers, Postsecondary; Credit Analysts; Criminal Justice and Law Enforcement Teachers, Postsecondary; Dietitians and Nutritionists; Economics Teachers, Postsecondary; Editors; Education Teachers, Postsecondary; English Language and Literature Teachers, Postsecondary; Environmental Compliance Inspectors; Environmental Science Teachers, Postsecondary; Foreign Language and Literature Teachers, Postsecondary; Forestry and Conservation Science Teachers, Postsecondary; Geographers; Geography Teachers, Postsecondary; Health Specialties Teachers, Postsecondary; Historians; History Teachers, Postsecondary; Home Economics Teachers, Postsecondary; Insurance Underwriters; Law Teachers, Postsecondary; Lawyers; Library Science Teachers, Postsecondary; Market Research Analysts; Nursing Instructors and Teachers, Postsecondary; Philosophy and Religion Teachers, Postsecondary;

Skills Linked to High Occupational Earnings

Skill	Jobs That Demand a High Level of This Skill
	Poets, Lyricists and Creative Writers; Political Science Teachers, Postsecondary; Political Scientists; Producers; Sociologists; Sociology Teachers, Postsecondary; Soil and Plant Scientists; Technical Writers; Urban and Regional Planners; Zoologists and Wildlife Biologists
Speaking	Art, Drama, and Music Teachers, Postsecondary; Broadcast News Analysts; Credit Analysts; Economics Teachers, Postsecondary; Insurance Underwriters; Licensing Examiners and Inspectors; Tax Examiners, Collectors, and Revenue Agents
Monitoring	Elementary School Teachers, Except Special Education; Financial Examiners; Instructional Coordinators; Middle School Teachers, Except Special and Vocational Education; Postmasters and Mail Superintendents; Producers; Public Relations Managers; Technical Directors/Managers
Persuasion	Advertising and Promotions Managers; Agents and Business Managers of Artists, Performers, and Athletes; Arbitrators, Mediators, and Conciliators; Claims Examiners, Property and Casualty Insurance; Communications Teachers, Postsecondary; Copy Writers; Counseling Psychologists; Economists; Equal Opportunity Representatives and Officers; Fire Inspectors; First-Line Supervisors/Managers of Non-Retail Sales Workers; First-Line Supervisors/Managers of Police and Detectives; Fish and Game Wardens; Immigration and Customs Inspectors; Insurance Adjusters, Examiners, and Investigators; Insurance Appraisers, Auto Damage; Judges, Magistrate Judges, and Magistrates; Lawyers; Loan Officers; Market Research Analysts; Personal Financial Advisors; Police Identification and Records Officers; Police Patrol Officers; Postmasters and Mail Superintendents; Public Relations Specialists; Sales Agents, Financial Services; Sales Agents, Securities and Commodities; Sales Representatives, Wholesale and Manufacturing, Except Technical and Scientific Products; Sales Representatives, Wholesale and Manufacturing, Technical and Scientific Products; Secondary School Teachers, Except Special and Vocational Education; Sheriffs and Deputy Sheriffs; Soil and Water Conservationists; Talent Directors; Urban and Regional Planners
Negotiation	Agents and Business Managers of Artists, Performers, and Athletes; Arbitrators, Mediators, and Conciliators; Criminal Investigators and Special Agents; Crop and Livestock Managers; Education Administrators, Elementary and Secondary School; Educational, Vocational, and School Counselors; Environmental Compliance Inspectors; Equal Opportunity Representatives and Officers; First-Line Supervisors/Managers of Correctional Officers; First-Line Supervisors/Managers of Non-Retail Sales Workers; Insurance Adjusters, Examiners, and Investigators; Insurance Appraisers, Auto Damage; Judges, Magistrate Judges, and Magistrates; Lawyers; Market Research Analysts; Police Detectives; Police Identification

(continued)

(continued)

Skills Linked to High Occupational Earnings

Skill	Jobs That Demand a High Level of This Skill
	and Records Officers; Police Patrol Officers; Postmasters and Mail Superintendents; Psychiatrists; Purchasing Agents and Buyers, Farm Products; Purchasing Managers; Range Managers; Real Estate Brokers; Sales Representatives, Wholesale and Manufacturing, Except Technical and Scientific Products; Sales Representatives, Wholesale and Manufacturing, Technical and Scientific Products; School Psychologists; Sheriffs and Deputy Sheriffs; Special Education Teachers, Secondary School; Transportation Managers
Coordination	Air Traffic Controllers; Art Directors; Landscape Architects; Railroad Conductors and Yardmasters; Transportation Managers
Time Management	Broadcast News Analysts; Directors—Stage, Motion Pictures, Television, and Radio; Multi-Media Artists and Animators; Transportation Managers
Management of Personnel Resources	Administrative Services Managers; Auditors; Construction Managers; Directors—Stage, Motion Pictures, Television, and Radio; Education Administrators, Elementary and Secondary School; Education Administrators, Postsecondary; Financial Managers, Branch or Department; Fire Investigators; First-Line Supervisors/Managers of Correctional Officers; First-Line Supervisors/Managers of Non-Retail Sales Workers; First-Line Supervisors/Managers of Police and Detectives; First-Line Supervisors/Managers of Production and Operating Workers; First-Line Supervisors/Managers of Transportation and Material-Moving Machine and Vehicle Operators; Funeral Directors; Gaming Managers; General and Operations Managers; Industrial Production Managers; Medical and Health Services Managers; Municipal Fire Fighting and Prevention Supervisors; Occupational Therapists; Orthodontists; Park Naturalists; Physical Therapists; Program Directors; Sales Managers; Social and Community Service Managers; Storage and Distribution Managers; Surveyors; Talent Directors; Training and Development Managers

Index

D

E

M